Handbook of
Advertising
Management

Handbook of Advertising Management

Roger Barton *Editor*

MCGRAW-HILL BOOK COMPANY

**New York   St. Louis   San Francisco   Dusseldorf   London
Mexico   Panama   Sydney   Toronto**

HANDBOOK OF ADVERTISING MANAGEMENT

07-03966-6

6789BPBP798

56,298

To Daniel Starch

Preface

This is a book written primarily for corporate advertising managers. In planning it the question naturally arose: "How much should the corporate advertising manager know about advertising, and what should be the nature of his knowledge?"

This question pertains not only to those who now bear the title, but also to others, such as product and brand managers, who may at some time assume widening responsibilities in advertising. It is also of interest to those in advertising agencies who work with advertising managers and even to any person preparing for an advertising career.

It seems obvious that the advertising manager should seek to know principles rather than details; he is a manager rather than a technician. With respect to copy, for instance, he need not know how to write an advertisement, but he should be able to distinguish between good and bad copy and to recognize excellence readily. The same observation applies to his knowledge of advertising research or media planning.

One of his broadest responsibilities is an understanding of the social and economic significance of the advertising his company produces. A company cannot disregard the effect that its advertising may have upon the taste and manners of its audience.

An acquaintance with the principles of efficient organization will be of major concern. These include the proper place of advertising in the corporate structure and the appropriate organization and functions of the advertising department. The manager and his associates will have to coordinate their efforts with those in other functions, such as sales, so this also will be an area of his concern. He has to exercise the skills of personnel management with his own people, and here effective principles are known and can be vastly rewarding if followed. The manager should have a clear understanding of the structure and functions of advertising agencies, not only those of his own agency or agencies, but also those of agencies in general.

Since advertising is a part of marketing, he should strive to understand how advertising works, whether, for instance, he is always able to convert a favorable attitude toward his brand into increased sales. Consumer behavior is a complicated subject, but he must be aware of its major principles, for therein lies the basis for much of the strategy of his business.

The manager should obviously have stated goals for both marketing and advertising, and this implies knowing how to develop a marketing or advertising plan and to avoid needless detail in such documents. Every manager must know how to determine the appropriation he requires for advertising and how to budget and control expenditures.

In the large area of copy, the manager must have some acquaintance with the principles of copy strategy, and assure himself that it implements his advertising plan. He should appreciate how this strategy is executed in the different forms of print and broadcast advertising and in the out-of-home media such as outdoor, transit, and point-of-purchase.

With respect to media, the manager will need to know the principles of planning and to understand the natures of the different media and the purposes of advertising to which each is best suited.   He knows that he should evaluate the results of his advertising, and although he may not be able always to determine its sales effectiveness, he does know that he can measure copy and media effectiveness.   He will want to have some familiarity with the uses of the computer in advertising and marketing.

There are special kinds of advertising with which he may desire to be familiar in varying degrees, such as public relations and sales promotion.   Other large special areas of interest are advertising to business and to the farm market and international advertising.

It is vital that the manager be aware of some of the legal pitfalls in his advertising activity, at least to the extent that he realizes when he should consult his legal counsel.   Finally, he should know precisely the language of advertising.   Valuable effort has been wasted at times when a manager meant one thing in his use of a term and his agency thought he meant something else.

This appears to be a large area of knowledge, and it is, because the responsibility of the corporate advertising manager is a large one.   But it is one not impossible to achieve if he seeks always to find the principles in what are frequently vastly detailed operations.   This Handbook attempts to present these principles.

In the editing of this book I have had valuable help from the staffs of the Association of National Advertisers and the American Association of Advertising Agencies, chiefly in recommendations of persons highly qualified to write the chapters.   I am indebted for suggestions regarding the structure of the book to Kenneth Laird, then chairman of the board of Tatham-Laird & Kudner and chairman of the American Advertising Federation, and to Carroll Swan, then editor of *Media-scope* magazine and co-author of "Management of the Advertising Function."   I am grateful to M. Joseph Dooher, editor of Industrial and Business Books, McGraw-Hill Book Company, who has been a helpful and understanding friend in this enterprise, and to my wife, who encouraged me in periods of disappointment and read the interminable proofs.   Finally, I thank the able men who somehow in their busy days completed chapters that often entailed prodigious amounts of work.

Roger Barton

Contents

The Contributors

PETER W. ALLPORT is president of the Association of National Advertisers, an organization which represents some 500 corporations that use advertising to market products or services on a national or regional basis.

He has been with the ANA since 1945, after service in the copy department at Erwin, Wasey, and has been president of the association since 1960. Mr. Allport has been chairman of the Advertising Advisory Committee to the Department of Commerce, and is currently a director of the Advertising Council, the Advertising Research Foundation, and the Brand Names Foundation. He was graduated from Brown University in 1941 and served as a lieutenant in the Navy in World War II.

JULES BACKMAN, economist, educator, and author, is research professor in economics at New York University, where he took his

D.C.S. in 1935. His latest book is "Advertising and Competition."

Dr. Backman has rendered much in public service: with the Securities and Exchange Commission, OPA, President's Cost of Living Committee, New York Joint Legislative Committee on Rents, New York Milk Shed Price Committee, economic advisor in Steel Wage Cases, member of the Governor's Committee on Milk Marketing.

He has written many books, of which some of the latest are "Inflation and Price Indexes," "Studies in Chemical Economics," "The Economics of the Electrical Machinery Industry," "Pricing: Policies and Practices," "Wage Determination." Between 1943 and 1948 he was an editorial writer for the New York *Times*.

Dr. Backman has won many awards: New York University Meritorious Service Award, Madden Award, Man of the Year 1961 Award of New York University Alumni. He is an honorary fellow of American Statistical Association, member of the American Economics Association and of the Society of Business Advertising Professors (president, 1955). He was president of New York University Alumni Federation from 1954 to 1956.

WARREN A. BAHR is executive vice president and director of media planning and relations at Young & Rubicam. He was vice president and associate media director from 1960 to 1961 and vice president of the Television-Radio Department from 1961 to 1962.

Mr. Bahr received a bachelor's degree in arts from Gettysburg College in 1948 and a law degree from the University of Virginia Law School in 1950. He served in the Army from 1942 to 1945, receiving the Bronze Star Medal and two Purple Hearts.

CECIL E. BARGER, vice president of Sander Allen Advertising, Inc., Chicago, has had more than twenty years of experience in farm advertising. Previously he was vice president of Compton Advertising, and account executive on agricultural products for the Upjohn Company and the Quaker Oats Company. At Aubrey, Finlay, Marley & Hodgson he was account executive on International Harvester tractors and farm equipment and creative director on all farm accounts. For three years he was assistant editor of *Missouri Ruralist* and *Kansas Farmer*. He received a B.S. degree in agricultural journalism from the University of Missouri in 1938 and now owns and operates a farm in Missouri that raises Angus cattle.

ROGER BARTON, editor of "The Handbook of Advertising Management," has edited four magazines in advertising: *Media/scope, Advertising Agency, Advertising & Selling,* and *American Printer.* He has held executive positions with Daniel Starch and Staff and Alfred Politz Research, Inc., and was president and chairman of Barton and Goold, a New York advertising agency. He has been associated with the Newark *Evening News* in editorial capacities since 1927, and still writes a weekly nature column.

Mr. Barton has written "Advertising Agency Operations and Management," "Media in Advertising," and "How to Watch Birds." He edited "Advertising Handbook" in 1950. For eighteen years he lectured in advertising at the Columbia University Graduate School of Business. He served for six years in World War II, a lieutenant colonel in Military Intelligence, and received the Legion of Merit. Mr. Barton holds degrees from Harvard College and Columbia University.

DONALD BRIGHT BUCKLEY is partner with Bernard Kahn in Kahn/Buckley Associates, a firm that works with advertisers and agencies in the creative aspects of advertising.

Prior to the founding of this firm in 1968, Mr. Buckley was creative director for Foote, Cone & Belding in New York and associate creative director at Grey Advertising. Before his service in the Navy in World War II, he was a copy writer with Van Sant, Dugdale in Baltimore; Stockton, West, Burkhart in Cincinnati; and Batten, Barton, Durstine & Osborn and also Warwick & Legler in New York.

DANIEL E. CALLANAN is vice president and general manager of Mutual Transit Sales, a Metromedia company that is the national sales organization for the transit advertising business. Prior to joining Metromedia, he was divisional sales manager of *Sales Management* magazine. He joined Bill Brothers Publications in 1952, and served as associate publisher of both *Yankee Grocer* and *Grocer-Graphic.* A graduate of Boston College, Mr. Callanan served in the Marines in World War II.

GEORGE EMERSON COLE has been vice president and creative director of the Institute of Outdoor Advertising since 1966. Previously he was creative supervisor at several New York advertising agencies and project engineer with General Electric Company. He was graduated from Cornell University with degrees in mechanical engineering and business administration.

CHARLES R. CORCORAN, vice president of The Equitable Life Assurance Society of the United States, began with the company in 1946 and has served in the area of communications. He has had responsibility for publications, press relations, public relations, advertising, film production, and graphic services. Mr. Corcoran has held executive offices in the Life Advertisers Association, and was president from 1968 to 1969, of the New York Chapter of the Public Relations Society of America. He also serves as governor of the Human Resources Center, Long Island, New York, as trustee of Loretto Heights College, Denver, and on advisory committees for Fordham University and Hofstra University.

JOHN HENDERSON CRICHTON is president of the American Association of Advertising Agencies. He joined the association in January, 1962, and became its president the following May. Previously he had served on the editorial staff of *Advertising Age* for twenty-one years, becoming editor in 1958. Mr. Crichton was graduated in 1940 from the University of Missouri with a degree in journalism. He served in the Navy for three years in World War II.

CORNELIUS DuBOIS is a research consultant with a background of thirteen years with Foote, Cone & Belding (ending as chairman of the research committee), two with Geyer Advertising, four with Cornelius DuBois and Company, and more than ten years as research director for Time, Inc., a period interrupted by government service.

Mr. DuBois has been president of the Market Research Council, New York Chapter of the American Marketing Association, and the Copy Research Council. He was graduated from Harvard College.

EDWIN W. EBEL was with General Foods Corporation from 1948 to 1966, serving as vice president, advertising services, during the last fourteen years. Before that he had been associated with Pedlar & Ryan; Tracy Locke Dawson; the *American Weekly;* and Calkins & Holden.

Mr. Ebel was chairman of the Association of National Advertisers from 1955 to 1956, and chairman of the board of directors of the Advertising Council in the same two years. He is a lifetime director of the latter organization. He has served also as director and member of the executive committee of the Advertising Federation of America and director of the American Institute of Food Distribution. He is a founder member of the American Marketing Association and an honorary life member of the International Radio and Television Society. Since 1965 Mr. Ebel has been a director of the Academy of Television Arts and Sciences Foundation. In World War II he served in the Army as a major, and received the Legion of Merit.

WILLIAM H. EWEN is director of corporate advertising, Borden, Inc., and chairman of the Association of National Advertisers. He has been with Borden since 1936, serving as assistant vice president in the foods company division from 1960 to 1961, and as director of corporate advertising since 1962. He was chairman of the board of the Audit Bureau of Circulations in 1965, and has been a member of the board of directors of the National Better Business Bureau and Advertising Research Foundation. His hobby is steamboats, and he was president of the Steamship Historical Society from 1946 to 1950.

PAUL E. J. GERHOLD was elected president of the Advertising Research Foundation in 1968. He had had a long association with the ARF, being chairman of the board from 1966 to 1967. Before joining the ARF he was director of research development and planning, J. Walter Thompson Company. Previously he had been manager of research at Dancer-Fitzgerald-Sample and vice president in charge of media and research and vice chairman of the Plans Board at Foote, Cone & Belding. Earlier he had been research supervisor with Lord & Thomas in Chicago.

Mr. Gerhold has been president of both the Market Research Council and the Copy Research Council. He took his B.S. and M.B.A. degrees at Northwestern University, and in World War II served as a captain in the Army Quartermaster Corps.

BUDD GORE is vice president of the National Retail Merchants Association, manager of its Sales Promotion Division, and publisher of *Stores* magazine. In retailing he has held the posts of advertising manager of Marshall Field & Co., Chicago, and sales promotion manager of the Halle Bros. Co., Cleveland; the H. & S. Pogue Co., Cincinnati; and L. S. Ayres & Co., Indianapolis. He has been sales promotion manager, retail advertising manager, advertising manager, and assistant to the general manager of the Chicago *Daily News* and assistant to the executive editor of the Chicago *Sun-Times.*

Mr. Gore attended the Aeronautical University and the University of Chicago.   In World War II he was chief administrative officer of the Manhattan Project's Metallurgical Laboratory at the University of Chicago and chief warden of the Chicago Civil Defense Corps.

ROBERT M. GRAY retired in 1967 as advertising and sales promotion manager of Humble Oil & Refining Company.   He now teaches advertising on a part-time basis at the University of Texas.

Mr. Gray joined Esso Standard Oil Company in 1934, and was in charge of field advertising from 1936 to 1942.   He then served for two years as assistant advertising and sales promotion manager for Esso Standard, and was named manager in 1944.   After the merger of Esso Standard with Humble, he became manager of Humble's advertising and sales promotion in 1961.

Mr. Gray has served as chairman and director of the American Advertising Federation; vice president and director of the Traffic Audit Bureau; director and honorary lifetime director of the Advertising Council; vice president and director of the Audit Bureau of Circulations; chairman of the Advertising Subcommittee, American Petroleum Institute; member of the Advertising Committee, International Chamber of Commerce; founding director of the Advertising Educational Foundation; and president and director of the Advertising Club of New York.

ALLAN GREENBERG is vice president and director of research, Doyle Dane Bernbach, Inc.   Prior to this position he worked in a variety of research capacities with a manufacturer, a television research organization, and another advertising agency.   He has written extensively on research methodology, communications, advertising measurement, and product testing for the *Journal of Marketing, Public Opinion Quarterly, Journal of Marketing Research,* and *Journal of Advertising Research.*

He is a member of the American Association for Public Opinion Research, American Sociological Association, the Copy Research Council, the Travel Research Association, and is on the Research Committee of the AAAA.   He is also a vice chairman of the Technical Committee of the Advertising Research Foundation and a director of the New York Chapter of American Marketing Association.

WHIT HOBBS, who joined Benton & Bowles in 1963, is a senior vice president of the agency in charge of its new-product development group. He and his associates work with clients on the development and launching of new products, primarily in the food area. In 1965 an experimental group headed by Mr. Hobbs was formed to handle workshop experimentation, special creative assignments, long-range creative planning, and development of new creative talent. It was called HPW, the letters representing the names of the three men who ran it.

A graduate of Harvard, Mr. Hobbs has taught creative workshops at New York University, City College of New York, and Columbia University. Before joining Benton & Bowles, he was associated with Batten, Barton, Durstine & Osborn for twenty years.

RICHARD P. JONES, vice president and director of media, joined J. Walter Thompson Company in 1955 after six years with Leo Burnett Company in Chicago. A native of Mississippi, his early experience was in the cotton business after graduation from the Woodberry Forest School. He began his advertising career with D'Arcy Advertising in St. Louis in 1941.

After five years in the Navy in World War II, Mr. Jones returned to D'Arcy for three years. He moved to Leo Burnett in 1949, where he served as an account representative and media group supervisor. He was named vice president and manager of media at J. Walter Thompson in 1958, and became director of media in 1960. Mr. Jones has served as chairman of the board of the Traffic Audit Bureau; president of the Media Directors Council; chairman of the Magazine and Newspaper Committees of the AAAA. He is a member of the board of governors, International Radio and Television Society.

DONALD M. LEWIS, JR., manager, Advertising and Customer Services, Consumer Products Division, Eastman Kodak Company, joined the company in 1936. He was employed in New York City as assistant to the manager of the New York Display Department until May, 1941, when he entered military service. He returned in 1945 as assistant manager of the New York Display Department, and served till 1949, when he transferred to Kodak headquarters in Rochester as display manager in the Advertising Department.

Mr. Lewis was named manager of advertising promotion in 1958 and the following year assistant director of sales promotion. He was appointed manager, Advertising and Customer Services, Consumer Products Division, in December, 1964. He attended Hamilton College, the Rochester Institute of Technology Art School, and the American School of Design.

MALCOLM A. McNIVEN is vice president, Marketing Research Department, Coca-Cola USA. Previously he was manager of advertising research, E. I. du Pont de Nemours & Company. Other positions he has held were supervisor, Industrial Testing Service, Pennsylvania State University; instructor of psychology, University of Maryland Overseas Program, and research fellow, Instructional Film Research Program, Pennsylvania State University. In 1966 he was adjunct professor at Wharton School, University of Pennsylvania, giving a course in consumer behavior, and has been a guest lecturer at numerous other universities.

Dr. McNiven took his doctorate in experimental psychology at Pennsylvania State University in 1955, and his bachelor's and master's degrees in experimental psychology at Denison University and Ohio University. He is a fellow in the American Psychological Association and a director of the Advertising Research Foundation.

WILLIAM A. MARSTELLER is chairman of the board of Marsteller Inc., which he founded in 1951. He was president until 1960. The divisions of his firm include Marsteller Research, marketing counsel; Burson-Marsteller Associates, public relations; and Marsteller International, with overseas service offices in 111 cities here and abroad.

Born in Champaign, Ill., he took his B.S. at the University of Illinois and served as reporter on Chicago and downstate Illinois newspapers. After four years with Massachusetts Mutual Life Insurance Company, ultimately as supervisor of young salesmen, he joined Edward Valves, Inc., and its parent company, Rockwell Manufacturing Company, in 1941, advancing through various positions to vice president of marketing in 1950. Mr. Marsteller has long been active in the AAAA, variously as chairman of the Central

Council, director for two different terms, and secretary-treasurer. He was president of the Association of Industrial Advertisers from 1947 to 1949.

GORDON E. MIRACLE is associate professor, Department of Advertising, Michigan State University. He taught previously at the Universities of Michigan and Wisconsin. Dr. Miracle is the author of "Management of International Advertising" and numerous articles, cases, book reviews, and professional papers dealing with international advertising. He has served in faculty and administrative capacities for various conferences, seminars, and executive development programs.

Dr. Miracle maintains memberships and active participation in both educational and professional associations, including the American Economic Association, American Marketing Association, Association for Education in International Business, and the World Trade Club of Detroit. He has served as a consultant or researcher to numerous business and professional organizations.

FRANK NOETTLING is the founder and president of Frank Noettling Associates, Inc., personnel consultants to management. Previously he was personnel vice president of Benton & Bowles and personnel manager at McCann-Erickson. A graduate of Northwestern University with a bachelor of science degree in psychology, his early experience was as an industrial psychologist with R. R. Donnelley & Sons Company.

EDWARD PAPAZIAN is a vice president and media director of Batten, Barton, Durstine & Osborn and manager of its Media Department. He has held this position since 1969, previously having been associate media director responsible for all media analysis and computer applications, as the agency's Linear Programing Model for media selection. He supervised media plans for accounts like Gillette, Lever Brothers, Pillsbury, Scott Paper, and administered the agency's network and spot buying groups.

Mr. Papazian was graduated from Columbia College with a liberal arts degree in 1953 and from the Columbia Graduate School of Business with a master of science degree in business and marketing.

ARTHUR S. PEARSON is director of market planning and research, Bristol-Myers Company, where he was formerly director of
market planning and director of market research, Bristol-Myers
Products Division. Previously he was research director of the
Grocery Products Division of Ralston Purina Company in St. Louis
and manager of research, Jell-O Division, General Foods Corporation. Mr. Pearson started his research career with the Bureau of
the Census in Washington, and also did productivity research with
the U.S. Department of Labor.

He is a graduate of Columbia College and has done graduate
work in statistics at George Washington University and the U.S. De-
partment of Agriculture Graduate School. He is a member of the
Advertising Research Foundation's Technical Committee, the Market
Research Council, the National Industrial Conference Board's
Council of Market Research Directors, and chairman of the Plan-
ning and Evaluation Committee of the Association of National
Advertisers.

CHARLES RAMOND is founder and president of Marketing
Control, Inc., in New York, and co-founder and board chairman
of Marketing Control Ltd. in London. Dr. Ramond also serves
as adjunct professor of business at Columbia University, consultant
to the Advertising Research Foundation, and editor of its *Journal
of Advertising Research,* which he founded in 1960 during his six
years as ARF technical director. He went to ARF from Du Pont
where, as first manager of its advertising research section, he began
its efforts to develop sales measures of advertising effectiveness.

He is a captain in the U.S. Army Reserve, and in 1966 went to
Viet Nam, where he spent three months directing research designed
to increase Viet Cong defection. He studied experimental psychology at Iowa State University, and received a Ph.D. in 1953. His
publications include a privately issued textbook, "The Limits of
Science in Marketing," articles in psychological and trade journals,
and chapters in business handbooks.

PAUL M. ROTH is vice president and director, media, radio and
TV programing, Kenyon & Eckhardt, Inc. Since joining the agency
in 1962 his responsibilities have included television, media, research, and marketing. He was elected a vice president in 1965, assumed responsibility for media operations in all Kenyon & Eck-

hardt offices, and in 1967 was elected to the board of directors. Previously he had been with Benton & Bowles.

Mr. Roth attended Allegheny College, from which he was graduated Phi Beta Kappa. He received his M.B.A. from the Harvard Graduate School of Business Administration in 1956. He is the author of "How to Plan Media: A Guide for Marketing and Advertising Personnel," 1968.

ARTHUR F. RUDY has been employed by Armstrong Cork Company since 1941, and is presently manager of Production, Control and Office Services, Advertising and Promotion Department. He holds a B.S. degree from Franklin and Marshall College, and an M.A. degree from the University of Pennsylvania. He has written for professional publications.

HOWARD STUMPF is president of Point-of-Purchase Advertising Institute, a position he has held since 1966. Prior to that he was manager of the H&H Display Division of West Virginia Pulp & Paper Company, being in charge of that company's nationwide display operations. His duties included bringing together autonomous regional operating units into one national sales and production organization. While in West Virginia, Mr. Stumpf served POPAI as chairman of the board and treasurer and general chairman of POPAI's 1961 Symposium and Exhibit.

Before joining West Virginia Pulp & Paper, he was merchandising manager of Wilson Plastics, now a division of Foster Grant, Inc. He earlier served as a field salesman for the Industrial Division of Armstrong Cork Company.

WILLIAM D. TYLER is a creative consultant for some of America's best-known advertisers, media, and agencies. He started in advertising as a brand manager for Borden, became a copy writer at Young & Rubicam, then copy chief at Doherty, Clifford, Steers & Shenfield and then at Dancer-Fitzgerald-Sample.

In his tenure with the Leo Burnett Company, Mr. Tyler created many noted campaigns, organized the Copy Department, and served as copy chief and finally as head of the Plans Board. As executive vice president at Benton & Bowles, where he headed Creative Services, he was credited with having raised the agency's creative reputation from tenth to fourth among large New York agencies. For years Mr. Tyler has written a column for *Advertising Age,* where he picks the ten best advertisements of the month.

SAM B. VITT is senior vice president and executive director of the Media-program Department at Ted Bates & Company. He joined Bates in 1964 from Doherty, Clifford, Steers & Shenfield, where he was vice president in charge of the Media-programing Department. Before that he held media posts at two major agencies and television responsibilities at CBS-TV Network.

Mr. Vitt is a contributing editor to *Media-scope* magazine, and previously wrote a monthly column for *Madison Avenue.* He is active in the work of the AAAA, the International Radio and Television Society, and other industry groups, and has received awards for his contributions, most recently the Station Representatives Association's Gold Key for advertising leadership. His career has included service as advertising director of a banking law journal and production of a record album for a Broadway musical show.

HARRY B. WALSH is creative director of the Direct Response Division of Ogilvy & Mather, where he handles direct-mail and mail-order advertising for such clients as Shell Oil, Nationwide Insurance, American Express, Mercedes-Benz, General Foods, and Lever Brothers.

He started his advertising career in the conventional agency field. In 1962 he set up his own mail-order company, which he later sold to Breck's of Boston. Subsequently he worked as an account executive at Vos & Reichberg, as a consultant to a Connecticut mail-order publishing company, and as a writer and account executive at Wunderman, Ricotta & Kline. He is a graduate of Bowdoin College and a former Air Force fighter pilot.

GILBERT H. WEIL, who has his law offices in New York City, has the title of general counsel for both the Association of National Advertisers and the Advertising Research Foundation. He was born, bred, and educated in New York City, attending undergraduate and law school at New York University.

Mr. Weil's law practice is mostly commercial, with major emphasis in the marketing, advertising, and distributional areas. He wrote "Legal Rules of the Road to Honest Advertising," published by the ANA, and has taught advertising law. He was in the Navy in World War II.

JOSEPH B. WILKINSON retired in 1967, having been vice president of McCann-Erickson and manager of its Houston office. He was also a consultant to that agency. In 1929 he and two others formed the Franke-Wilkinson-Schiwetz agency, which eventually became Wilkinson, Schiwetz & Tips before its merger with McCann-Erickson in 1954. At the latter agency, Mr. Wilkinson handled bank, cotton, food, gasoline, industrial, and real estate advertising.

Educated at the U.S. Naval Academy (two years) and at Vanderbilt University, he received his bachelor's degree from the latter institution in 1922. There followed four years of teaching at preparatory schools in Tennessee and work for a firm of highway contractors. He went to Houston in 1928 as associate editor of Acco Press, a farmers' house organ. Mr. Wilkinson was on active duty with the Army for five years in World War II, and is now a colonel, AUS retired.

ROBERT J. WILLIAMS has been manager of Consumer Products Marketing Research, The Dow Chemical Company, since 1965. His main assignment has been to organize a marketing research and information system for the company's expanding consumer products business.

From 1961 to 1965 he was director of marketing intelligence, Edward Dalton Company, a division of Mead Johnson Company. For four years previous to this, Dr. Williams was vice president of Alfred Politz Research, Inc., and between 1949 and 1957 he was a member of the faculty of the Department of Psychology, Columbia University, as associate professor. From 1953 to 1957 he was head of the Psychology Department in the Columbia School of General Studies. Dr. Williams took his doctorate in experimental psychology at Columbia in 1952.

M. E. ZIEGENHAGEN is director of advertising and public relations for The Babcock & Wilcox Company, a position he has held since he joined the organization in 1960. He is responsible at the corporate level for directing and coordinating advertising and public relations, and serves all divisions and subsidiaries in these functions.

After he received his B.S. degree in mechanical engineering from the University of North Dakota in 1937, he joined General Electric Company, eventually receiving assignments in advertising and public relations at the plants in Pittsfield, Massachusetts, and Schenectady,

New York.   Between 1942 and 1945 he served in the Navy as an engineering officer aboard a destroyer in the South Pacific.

Returning to GE after the war, Mr. Ziegenhagen continued his career in advertising and public relations.   In 1952 he became manager of advertising and sales promotion for Worthington Corporation, where he served until he joined Babcock & Wilcox.   He is a former member of the board of directors of the Association of National Advertisers, and served as chairman of its Advertising Management Committee.   He currently heads the advertising and marketing organization program for the ANA.

Handbook of
Advertising
Management

PART ONE
Advertising in Our Society

CHAPTER ONE

Advertising in Our Society

PETER W. ALLPORT   *President, Association of National Advertisers*

Why should a practical handbook on advertising management open with a discussion of such a subject as "Advertising in Our Society"? The answer in blunt terms is relatively easy.   There is no other choice.   Consideration of advertising in relation to society is a penalty of success and size.   It stems from being an $18 billion operation; from having largely replaced the retail sales clerk as the source of product information; from being the principal support of our media of communications; from advertising's position as a major vehicle for corporate growth and diversification; from, in short, becoming virtually indispensable to our economy and society.

This, in our history, is not a new phenomenon.   Advertising has now caught up with the other chief components of our economic structure.

Prior to the turn of the century, as manufacturing emerged from cottage industry to mass production, it, too, was called upon to see itself in relation to mankind's hopes and aspirations. Child labor was out. Safety and decent working conditions were in. Today a guaranteed annual wage is an approaching reality. Somewhat later, the financial community made its adjustment. Absconding bankers, watered stock, and a rigged market became intolerable in a society which needed a reliable and a large-scale financial apparatus, and when most persons looked to their paycheck and passbook for survival, rather than to the output of the family farm.

Today, marketing and its visible, articulate, and pervasive partner, advertising, have joined production and finance as indispensable ingredients of economic survival and growth. As a consequence, the spotlight of social responsibility is now on marketing. While society will tolerate frailty in that which is unimportant to it, it must demand excellence—and will impose it if necessary—from that which is indispensable. Accordingly, to survive as a free institution and free business function, advertising and advertising personnel must think of themselves in relation to society.

But how? Perhaps the first rule for advertising management if advertising is to operate relatively freely is the admonition, "See yourself as others see you." Just seeing may not always be enough. Understanding and corresponding action may also be required. Furthermore, "seeing yourself," for both advertising and its critics, can be a baffling and frustrating experience. Often the other's understanding and definitions are at variance with yours. Accordingly, this chapter summarizes some views of advertising as its critics see it, as well as the contrasting outlook of the advertising community. It will also touch on some of the procedures and activities of the advertising community which help it keep its house in order. The purpose is to help in the execution in that relatively new, but vital, aspect of the management of the advertising function—know your critics and act accordingly—so that someone else's idea of excellence will not be imposed.

THE ADVERTISING INDUSTRY MYTH

Advertising more often than not—with pride in the advertising community, with chagrin among its critics—is described as an $18 billion industry. Perhaps this concept of advertising's monolithic nature and of its relatively great size is the most important contribution to misunderstanding.

How Advertising Funds Are Spent

What, in contrast, are the facts? It is true, of course, that currently $18 billion is committed annually to some form of advertising activity. The amount is growing. In 1947 it was about $4.3 billion. Projections for 1975 (if projections for the GNP are accurate and if advertising expenditures stay at about 2.3 per cent of GNP) are $27.7 billion. What is this vast sum spent for? The following figures for 1968 (the most recent year for which all the data are in) document advertising's multiplicity of uses.

In 1968 the biggest single commitment of advertising dollars—some $5.3 billion—went into newspapers. The great bulk of this was retail advertising—informative, factual advertisements aimed at helping the housewife know where merchandise was available and at what price. Well over another $1 billion of this expenditure was for personal and other classified advertising. The smallest amount —$990 million—was for national advertising.

The second largest advertising expenditure in 1968 was for television—$3.2 billion. In contrast to newspapers, national advertising was the dominant element in television. Here too, local advertising was important—over $500 million spent.

Direct mail ranked third in 1968, with approximately $2.6 billion. An exact breakdown of direct-mail expenditures is not available, but a high proportion of it certainly was devoted to charity, educational, and other fund drives. Much of direct mail is also committed to sampling and couponing. Many millions, in any event, have little to do with the myth of a single, monolithic, persuasive force.

General magazines followed direct mail in 1968. Advertisers, primarily national advertisers selling consumer products, invested approximately $1.3 billion in the medium.

Radio and business publications were in fifth and sixth places with just over $1 billion spent for radio and $714 million in business publications. In radio again, a portion, perhaps as much as a half, was spent by retail advertisers—telling where to buy and at what price. Business-publication advertising is, of course, aimed at an entirely different audience. In terms of purpose, it is more akin to retail than to national advertising in its effort to give the sophisticated industrial purchasing agent facts about where to buy.

No Monolithic Industry

To recapitulate: while advertising is an $18 billion investment, this does not suggest a monolithic industry aimed at a single purpose. To the contrary:

1. Most advertising represents the efforts of hundreds of thousands of retailers, large and small, to let consumers know what merchandise they have to sell and at what price.

2. A large slice of advertising is committed for classified advertising—jobs wanted or available, houses for rent, lost and found, as well as Yellow Page listings and the like.

3. In any year, many millions are for charities, churches, and public service. In 1968, the Advertising Council, the advertising community's organized public service vehicle, reported that more than $350 million was contributed for public service messages alone.

4. Well over $1 billion represents business or professional advertising—technical messages to the professional buyer.

5. Finally, a very sizable but by no means dominant segment of total advertising is spent by many thousands of firms to draw attention to the consumer benefits they have built into their products and services. The scope of these advertisements extends from automobiles to chewing gum, from soup to bikinis, from proprietary medicines to household furnishings. In 1968, the rough total for national advertising was considerably under $11 billion. The sum is large. But it is far short of the $18 billion worth of monolithic persuasive power which is too frequently ascribed (or claimed) for advertising.

Advertising Is an Activity

No, advertising is not a multibillion-dollar power which threatens to dominate our society. Nor is it a definable industry by any accepted standard of the term. To the contrary, advertising is an activity. It is an activity engaged in by any number of individuals or concerns when it is useful for their needs: by hundreds of thousands of local retailers, service and entertainment businesses; professional people and the like; by our schools, churches, and charitable organizations; and also by manufacturers, insurance companies and banks.

Further, advertising is not only an activity or resource available to millions of individuals, it is an activity in whose execution many—across a variety of industry lines—participate. Magazine and newspaper publishers are among them. So are television and radio broadcasters. Advertisers whose industry classifications range across the full spectrum of our economy are involved. Printers, typographers, engravers, electrotypers, photographers, film producers, as well as actors, models, and commercial artists make their professional skills available through advertising. Each has an involvement and a degree of interest in advertising.

Accordingly, advertising is not a classifiable industry, and it is certainly not monolithic. The only industry involved is the advertising agency business, which employs approximately 35,000 professionals. Advertising agencies are vitally important for the effective execution of many, particularly national, advertising and marketing programs. In relation to the diffuse and diversified total, "Madison Avenue" is small indeed. The $18 billion monolith is no more than a myth which has for too long distorted both the defense and the criticism of advertising. Unfortunately, it is a myth which advertising people have helped to perpetuate. While it exists, it will make understanding between advertising and its critics more difficult.

THE ADVERTISING POINT OF VIEW

While advertising is not an industry, and is certainly not a massive, single-minded force, those in advertising—the advertising community—do have a point of view. It is a good one. The common view of the advertising community rests on three convictions:

1. Free competitive enterprise built on profit and reinvestment will provide the greatest good for the greatest number.

2. Free consumer choice is essential to both competitive enterprise and to human gratification.

3. Free consumer choice will not exist in the sense of being acted upon unless both information and a degree of stimulation are present.

These convictions—with a degree of question concerning the third—are not unique to advertising. They are widely shared in our society. When these convictions are accepted, it then becomes axiomatic that our economic system will not work without advertising and that our human gratifications will deteriorate unless the economic structure is operating successfully.   When they are not, the basic premises on which advertising rests are subject to question.

Shared Convictions

Along with these fundamental convictions, the advertising community shares some professional understandings which help form its point of view.   These understandings may not be so widely shared in society as a whole as are the fundamental free-enterprise convictions. However, they are virtually self-evident to the business and advertising communities.   Perhaps much of the difficulty advertising and its critics have in seeing eye to eye stems from these professional understandings.

Specifically, the advertising community understands:

1. *That growth for a business enterprise is essential.*   With rising populations and technological change, standing still amounts to regression.

2. *That growth demands change.*   Neither the economy nor the individual company can grow unless the thinking habits, living habits, and buying habits change.   There must be upward mobility.

3. *That change—upward mobility—does not occur automatically or even easily.*   It is easier to live as our fathers did.   Habits must be broken if change and growth are to occur.

With this professional understanding, the breaking of habits, of traditions, of things as they are or were, becomes a virtue.   The businessman and the members of the advertising community read such books as Vance Packard's "The Waste Makers," and perhaps agree with some of his statements.   But their response is, "What's the shouting about?   If change is not induced, growth will be impossible.   A little dissatisfaction with one's status quo is good, and it is part of advertising's role—notably of national advertising—to stimulate such dissatisfaction."   However, many do not share advertising's common understanding.   To the contrary, they see change as disruptive, and they blame advertising for it.

The advertising community's point of view is also formed by shared technical knowledge.   At two points, as a technician, the advertising man can run afoul of his critics.   These points are

"Sell the sizzle, not the steak."

"Repeat and repeat and repeat . . ."

On the whole, advertising's critics accept the need for product information: "An informed consumer is fundamental to the classic model of a free economy." These critics more often than not do not accept the advertising view that to be effective, information must be made palatable, and that it can never be fully absorbed. These and other questions of technique can separate further the views of the advertising community and its critics.

Advertising's Limitations

The advertising community's point of view also stems from a shared acceptance of certain limitations. For society as a whole, on the other hand, which has not been brought up with them, they often represent grounds for skepticism, criticism, or downright anger.

High among these limitations are the following:

1. *Advertising has relatively little capacity to select its audience.* To be sure, an advertisement in *Motor Boating* will reach only the boat-enthusiast audience. But a cosmetic ad in *The New Yorker* will be seen (and largely turned off) by thousands of males, while the women tune out the shaving cream commercial on prime-time television. For the most part, the limited audience selectivity imposes no more than a moment of boredom on the nonaudience for that particular ad. Boredom, however, can change to annoyance and even anger when, for instance, children are exposed to so-called adult ads; or liquor, tobacco, and the like are seen by abstainers; or the poor see advertising for products or services beyond their reach.

2. *Advertising's capabilities are limited.* No one, at any time, has faced his typewriter and deliberately tried to write a dull, stupid, or insipid ad. But "Hamlet" is a better play than "Coriolanus," and sometimes even the best copy writer or art director has a bad day. Many thousands of consumer-oriented ads or commercials are prepared each year. By definition, one-half of these will fall below the quality mean. For the advertising community this is regrettable, but it is an unavoidable occurrence. For the critic, it means he may be exposed to a great deal which is, by comparison, substandard.

3. *Advertising budgets are not unlimited* Many ads or commercials are provocative and exciting the first time, and a few subsequent times they are seen. But at the twentieth or twenty-fifth time, they are obnoxious. For the advertising community there are the need to repeat and the inability to finance additional waves of ads and commercials. Even the tolerant critic must shrug in despair at times, re-

membering always that it is his time, interest, and goodwill which are being solicited.

4. *Television is murder.* All advertising's technical limitations —along with many of its greatest strenghts—peak in the television medium.   It reaches a greater audience than any, with less capacity for selectivity than any; the high quality of a good commercial makes the duds even drabber, and the cost of an added wave of commercials is staggering.   Television's limitations are facts which the advertising community has no choice but to accept with regret.   But television viewing is the national pastime.   The critics look at it saying that there may be an explanation, but there is no excuse.

5. *The inevitable profit motive.* Finally, in the evolution of its point of view, the advertising community tends to think parochially. The operations and individual profits of a single company or even brand must dominate thinking and actions.

In the United States—perhaps less so elsewhere—this single-mindedness is viewed as desirable.   Advertising, after all, is an activity engaged in as one of several alternatives to maximize sales and profits.   Any thought process which does not keep that at the forefront would make little sense in the business and advertising community.   Similarly, it is a point of view which is in tune with our American social and economic tradition.   Our tradition glorifies individual initiative and competition, while it condemns cooperation and mutual understandings among competitors.   Hence, the view of the advertising community, and of business generally, is to outdo your competitor.   The limit is that which is declared illegal by law.   Advertising would consider any other course to be bad business.

Many of advertising's severest critics, however, have not been trained in the tradition of competition.   To the contrary, many of them, particularly those in the learned professions, see cooperation and group action as virtues rather than faults.   In relation to advertising, their instinctive reaction is, "Why not get together and agree to prohibit this, or do that?"   They forget that advertising is subject to our antitrust laws and tradition, and that what would be gained through the possible elimination of some of advertising's annoyance factors would be too great a loss to our economy in initiative and competition.

Summary   It is apparent that the advertising community has a point of view which in several important respects may differ from that of large segments of the general public.   Advertising thinking starts with the premise that change is essential and that a little dissatisfaction is desirable.   The advertising community is also convinced that change does not come about automatically.   In this it departs from the view of many of its critics, although not from the thinking of psychologists and sociologists who have studied the question.   Advertising persons are also tolerant—their critics say too tolerant—of technical, mechanical, and financial limitations.   Advertising views them as essential.   Advertising's critics claim they are not immutable facts, but problems which advertising should resolve.

Finally, those in advertising think and act in relation to the sales and profits of their individual companies rather than as a professional body.   This point of view has great merit.   But once again, it represents a different standpoint from that of many of its critics, and adds to the difficulty of seeing eye to eye.

ADDITIONAL IMPAIRMENTS TO UNDERSTANDING

Up to this point, I have outlined briefly some of the points of view and self-evident truths held and understood by those in business and advertising which may not be understood or be acceptable to the nonbusiness-oriented person.   The summary suggests that there are almost inevitable points of conflict or disagreement.   Based on these alone, it will be difficult if not impossible for advertising to achieve universal popularity, just as it is impossible for all teachers to be beloved by their students, or all employers to command the unwavering loyalty of their employees.   Advertising, after all, encourages people to act and to change.   But the moments in history are rare during which most people welcomed an admonition to do more or different things from what they were already doing.

However, in addition to the inevitable areas of disagreement between the advertising community and the public generally, there are other charges against advertising advanced by special segments of society.   These too contribute to the problem of seeing eye to eye, and should be understood and counteracted by the practicing advertising man if advertising is to continue to have sufficient freedom to perform its economic function efficiently and productively.

Without assigning weights or degrees of significance to the individual points, here are some of the principal and persistent concerns about advertising raised by segments of our society.

"Advertising Encourages Unsound or False Values"   Advertising, some claim, encourages a materialistic, even hedonistic, outlook.   The Puritan tradition is far from dead in the United States.   Many who adhere to it feel that advertising encourages self-indulgence and other vices.   They are particularly concerned about advertising's effect on children and young people.

"Advertising Controls Our Media of Communications"   The charge is often advanced that advertisers use their economic power to control our news media.   Despite the great weight of evidence to the contrary, it is assumed that the editorial function is subservient to the medium's sales department.

A similar charge is also frequently made in relation to television programing.   In this instance many claim that insufficient quality and diversity exist in television because advertisers will participate only in programs with mass audience appeal.   Little recognition is given to the many outstanding programs aired, or to the problems simply of generating the quantities of quality fare desired.

"Advertising Raises Prices"   No one wants to pay more than is necessary, and many see advertising as an extra expense added to the cost of products and services.   Too few, unfortunately, recognize that the alternatives to advertising would be even costlier.

"Advertising—the Whipping Boy"   In some instances advertising is criticized not for itself but because of the product or service which it is promoting.   Prohibitionists, for instance, will urge the elimination of alcoholic beverage advertising; those who oppose self-medication are critical of proprietary drug advertising; those who find some current motion pictures offensive object to the ads for those movies.

In a somewhat similar vein, advertising is criticized because some people dislike the medium which is used or some of the medium's practices.   Outdoor advertising is frequently a case in point.   Television programing sometimes arouses irritations which backlash against advertising.

"Even Truthful Advertising Can Be Wrong or Deceptive"   Many will concede that most advertising is truthful in a legal sense but will nevertheless charge it with being misleading.   The criticism appears to be aimed at the techniques of advertising.   They believe they would prefer a stolid and detailed description of the product in contrast to the excitement which a good copy writer tries to inject into each ad.   Any emotional appeal, in contrast to a rational appeal, is misleading in the eyes of these critics.

"Advertising Is Anticompetitive"   Some see a danger to open competition in large-scale advertising.   These critics are frequently economists who are fearful that the power of the purse held by a large advertiser will permit him to monopolize a market.   Recent studies, notably Dr. Jules Backman's "Advertising and Competition," provide grounds for reassuring these critics.   Nevertheless, the fear persists and is one more charge directed against advertising.

THE SIGNIFICANCE OF AREAS OF MISUNDERSTANDING

So much for the criticisms.   What does it all add up to?   What meaning do these areas of misunderstanding have to the advertiser?   And what, if anything, can the individual advertising man or woman do to minimize the criticism of advertising or guard against its consequences?

To recapitulate briefly, we have seen that advertising in our society performs a virtually essential economic function.   In performing this function, however, advertising in the United States also tends to articulate latent consumer desires and press for upward economic and social mobility.   Advertising, in effect, is pushing us a little bit. While we may accept intellectually the need for advertising, we may also somewhat resent it.   Additionally, virtually all members of society are in daily contact with advertising.   This alone leaves the impression of great size and influence, and to this image has been added the myth of an $18 billion industry.   We have also noted that the practical requirements of advertising, along with some of its inevitable limitations, provide grounds for misunderstanding.   Similarly, segments of the population may have qualms about certain aspects of advertising.   In some instances these qualms relate to deeply held moral standards or intellectual beliefs. Finally, we have noted that the advertising community thinks of advertising as a private activity. Its function is to maximize the sales and profits of the individual firm. To some extent our day-by-day attitude is that, if legal, what we say and do in advertising is strictly the advertiser's own business.

Herein may be the crux of the question, because advertising, no more and perhaps a good deal less than finance or manufacturing, can be considered private. To the contrary, it is designed to influence consumer action, and therefore by definition must have a public impact. Further, in our society the public holds the final sovereignty. It may encourage some forms of social or economic activity, tolerate others, discourage some, and even prohibit a few.

Advertising today is probably reasonably close to the top of the public-interest scale; it is largely encouraged and certainly tolerated. But advertising is also intrusive, somewhat pushy, and rarely totally lovable. To stay at the levels of encouragement or toleration it, more than most aspects of business, must mind its manners. When derelictions in advertising occur, they stand out clearly and sharply, and they impinge directly and personally on great numbers of consumers. Advertising's values and virtues, however, are often less clear and certainly less personal. With such a balance, there will always be the possibility that the sovereign public could change its mind and discourage or even prohibit some aspects of advertising.

To keep this from happening is an essential, perhaps the first, responsibility of advertising management. The key is the simple admonition to "see yourself as others see you" and to act accordingly. But obviously, this is more easily said than done. Accordingly, the remainder of this chapter will discuss briefly some of the self-regulatory techniques and philosophies that may help in this important area of management responsibility.

SELF-REGULATION IN ADVERTISING

Since the early years of this century when people in advertising initially acted to meet their collective interests and needs through the formation of the Advertising Federation of America, there has been a conscious recognition that advertising and society were intertwined, and programs or projects to help resolve issues and conflicts have

been developed. Then, as today, these programs could be categorized roughly as those involving group action and those which relate
solely to the individual advertiser, agency, or medium. As current
practice in both the group-action area and in what the individual
company can do represents the means through which advertising
management can execute its social function, a brief discussion of both
follows.

ACTION BY THE ADVERTISING COMMUNITY

In the early days of organized advertising—through the 1920s—the
principal thrust of the activities of such organizations as the Advertising Federation of America (now American Advertising Federation),
the American Association of Advertising Agencies, and the Association of National Advertisers, as well as the then existing media associations, was to protect the reputable businesses from the disreputa-
ble. To this end the Better Business Bureau structure was organized. Similarly, within the advertising community itself, the Audit
Bureau of Circulations was established.

The Advertising Federation of America, with the support of
others, was, in fact, a leading stimulus to legislation under President
Wilson, which resulted in the formation of the Federal Trade Commission. The objective was to get advertising's own house in order
by prohibiting the flagrant abuser the privilege of doing business,
and to set minimum standards to which any reputable businessman
could subscribe. The aim, in short, was to make competition among
business organizations viable through the establishment of minimum
ground rules. This limited objective was appropriate to the times
and completely laudable. It would, however, be insufficient today
when our concern must include not only the needs of competition but
also the impact of advertising on society as a whole.

Accordingly, let us review briefly some representative current advertising community programs and their objectives.

The many programs designed to help advertising's self-regulatory
process are well described in a booklet published by the Department
of Commerce entitled "Self-regulation in Advertising." This report
was prepared jointly by most of the leading media and advertising
associations, and is available from them as well as from the U.S Government Printing Office.

With the availability of "Self-regulation in Advertising," it is probably unnecessary to describe all the codes and operations which exist.   However, a word about two of them may be in order.   These —the Code of the National Association of Broadcasters and the Interchange of the American Association of Advertising Agencies and the Association of National Advertisers—are illustrative of self-regulation generally and are specific examples of two different approaches to the self-regulatory process.

The NAB Code

The NAB Code to which most television and radio broadcasters subscribe has a long history which need not be detailed here.   Suffice it to say that it has these characteristics:

1. A governing body composed of practicing broadcasters whose word is final and who may impose their rulings on all subscribing broadcasters or users of the medium

2. A detailed, lengthy, and codified set of rules which constitute the code itself, and which may encompass virtually all aspects of broadcasting operations

3. A full-time administrator who interprets the code on a day-by-day basis and whose findings are binding on subscribers and advertisers unless an appeal is sustained by the governing body

It must be obvious that the NAB concept of self-regulation visualizes a powerful, even authoritarian, structure.   The code, for example, can prevent individual broadcasters from accepting commercials for certain product classifications, from running certain specific commercials or programs which the administrator believes to be in violation of the code, and empowers the administrator to require the withdrawal or modification of programs or commercials as he sees fit.

The NAB Code has teeth: it can keep a commercial, as far as subscribing stations are concerned, off the air.   It has been pointed out from time to time that it has broader powers than are vested in any single government agency, and in fact, that the granting of such powers of censorship to a government agency would be strongly resisted and might well be unconstitutional.   This, of course, imposes a great burden on the NAB to wield its power responsibly.   Advertisers and agencies, for example, frequently point out that as far as they are concerned, the NAB Code is not self-regulation but is regulation by the medium rather than by the government.   A code with teeth calls for procedures equivalent to the due process one has before the Federal Trade Commission or the courts. This is rarely if ever achieved in a self-regulatory process.

The AAAA-ANA Interchange

The Interchange in philosophy and concept is quite different from the NAB Code. The Interchange does not have power but relies on persuasion—and a rather soft-sell at that.

The characteristics of the Interchange are as follows:

1. Its scope and authority are limited. The Interchange is restricted to good taste in advertising and is barred from considering questions of truth or falsity, as the sponsoring organizations recognize that they do not have the facilities to test an advertising claim, and that truth and falsity are the province of the Federal Trade Commission and the courts.

2. The Interchange hands down an opinion rather than a finding. The members of the Interchange (twenty individuals drawn equally from the AAAA and ANA) vote individually on any complaint they receive. This vote as "our judgment" is then relayed to the advertiser and agency which placed the ad involved.

3. The Interchange works in secret. No one other than the members of the Interchange, and the advertiser or agency which placed the advertisement about which a complaint is received, is told of the group's opinion.

4. Remedial action is voluntary. If a majority in the Interchange believe that an ad or commercial is in bad taste, it states the reasons to the advertiser and agency concerned, suggests that the ad be modified, and requests the courtesy of a reply.

The Interchange has rarely been unsuccessful when it has suggested that an ad or commercial be modified or withdrawn. This speaks well for the statesmanship of the advertising community, because such action is purely voluntary. In essence the concept of the Interchange is service in helping advertisers and agencies to evaluate their advertising, in contrast to regulation or dictation.

As indicated, many other self-regulatory procedures exist within the advertising community. The characteristics of most of them fall somewhere between the NAB Code and the Interchange, although few if any have the power which is vested in the NAB. Quite obviously, self-regulation of this nature has great merit, and deserves the support of everyone in advertising.   At the same time, too much should not be expected of it.   Organized self-regulation with power requires agreement among competitors to refrain from certain actions or to adopt others.   Such agreements are risky, and should be entered into only with caution and an understanding of the possible consequences.   On occasion advertising may be better advised to rely on an impartial and disinterested arbiter—even if this is the government—rather than on agreement among competitors.

SELF-REGULATION BY THE INDIVIDUAL COMPANY

Very frequently when the term *self-regulation* is used, the assumption is that it pertains only to a program sponsored by a professional group, an industry-wide organization, or the like.   Such a definition, however, is incorrect.   True self-regulation is that which the individual, or the individual company, applies to itself; the standard of conduct which it demands of itself; and the procedure it adopts to ensure the maintenance of those standards.   The purist, in fact, would say that self-regulation cannot be delegated.

As this is true, and because group action in this area can rarely have definitive power, individual self-regulation is by far the more important to advertising in relation to society.   Assurance that adequate standards and procedures exist is therefore also a prime responsibility of an executive working in the field of advertising, whether it be for an advertiser, agency, or advertising medium.

In this connection, change may well be in the wind.   For example, it has long been the practice of responsible advertisers to have a set of standards to which they expected their advertising to adhere.   Most of these codes or standards were generalized statements.   They stipulated that the company's advertising would be truthful, in good taste, and that it would be designed to enhance the public standing of the company.

Such statements reflected good intent.   But recently questions have arisen as to whether or not they serve as adequate guidelines or as an adequate checklist to the harried copy writer, or to the equally harried line executive who must approve copy, when their problem is to come up with ads that will beat the competitor's latest high-powered promotion.

In short, such generalizations present a problem.   It is a problem of omission rather than commission.   But it is also a problem which some companies are tackling directly.

Example of One Major Advertiser

As an example of change, one major advertiser recently reviewed its standards and procedures.   Intention was to give life to its advertising code; to make a living document that is relevant to the specific problems and issues of the day, and which could serve as guidelines throughout its advertising and marketing organization.

First step was to assign responsibility.   A task force from marketing, the agency, and the public relations group was asked to draft the guidelines.   Significantly, however, they were also given the job of reviewing and amending them periodically.   Issues change.   The company wants to make sure that its code is current as well as specific.

Management also asked that the advertising approval form used by the company contain a column related to the guidelines and requiring an initial from all those responsible for creative approval, signifying that the storyboard or layout had been judged in reference to the guidelines.

Guidelines   The current guidelines themselves obviously contain much which is pertinent only to the company or industry.   The following, however, more or less paraphrased, is included in the more broadly based sections:

1. Does the advertisement contain information which will be useful to the consumer?   At a minimum, does it contain an element which can be positively identified as a consumer service?
2. Has the use of minority groups as models or actors been considered?
3. Does the ad in any way conflict with our national social aspirations?   Current areas of concern which call for particular attention are:
   a. Excessive violence
   b. Representations which violate rules of safety
   c. Representations which violate standards for keeping America beautiful
   d. Racial or religious biases of any kind
4. Would you be pleased to have this ad or commercial seen by *your* children?

5. Does the ad in any way conflict with any claim or statement we make, or are required to make, in our packaging or labeling?

6. Will the ad or commercial be appropriate to any medium, program, or time slot in which it is likely to appear?

It is probable that even better standards and better procedures than those adopted by the company referred to here will be developed.   Nevertheless, they represent the best current practice, and are a great improvement over the generalizations or platitudes of the old-fashioned codes.   Every advertisement, because it stimulates action, tries to get us to do something, will never be popular with all people all of the time.   However, advertising and society should be able to live together without excessive conflict if advertisers, agencies, and media adopt and abide by standards which are both sound and relevant to the society they serve.

CHAPTER TWO

Advertising in
the National Economy

JULES BACKMAN *Research Professor in Economics, New York University*

RELATIVE IMPORTANCE OF ADVERTISING

The total output of goods and services in the American economy was about $850 billion in 1968. This enormous volume was produced and handled by more than 75 million persons and by millions of enterprises. Production is only one part of economic activity. Goods must be moved from the primary producer to the final consumer. This involves warehousing, transportation, retailing, and other marketing activities. As a result, marketing has become a vital part of the process by which it is decided what to produce, how much to produce, and at what price goods should be sold. Advertising is part of this broad marketing process.

The criticism most frequently made of marketing is that it absorbs too large a part of total costs. One study indicated that in 1954 and 1958, marketing accounted for slightly more than 45 per cent of the total cost of producing and distributing goods.[1] Business concerns constantly check the effectiveness of alternative means of marketing. Advertising is selected to do the job when businessmen believe it to be the most effective method to reach their objectives.

The importance of advertising in our economy can be measured in three ways: (1) total *dollar* advertising expenditures, (2) real advertising expenditures which eliminate the price factor, and (3) relative importance of advertising expenditures as compared with comprehensive measures of the national economy, such as gross national product and personal consumption expenditures.

Dollar Advertising Expenditures

During the post-World War II period, total dollar expenditures for advertising increased from $3.4 billion in 1946 to almost $17 billion in 1967. This was a significant expansion in terms of dollars. Despite the emergence of television, all the important media shared to a greater or lesser degree in this expansion as is shown below:

	1946	1967	Increase
	(In Millions of Dollars)		
Newspapers.	1,158	4,900	3,742
Magazines.	427	1,281	854
Radio.	455	1,027	572
Television.	0	2,923	2,923
Direct mail.	334	2,478	2,144

Although the introduction and expansion of television advertising has dominated much of the public discussion, the total dollar volume of newspaper advertising increased more than did television advertising. It is also interesting to note that the increase in expenditures for direct mail was not far behind that in television advertising. This result will not appear to be too surprising in light of the volume of such items in one's daily mail. In connection with these comparisons it must also be kept in mind that total advertising expenditures in 1946, while greater than in the prewar period, were held down because of the shortage of consumer goods.

The changes in dollar totals alone since 1946 do nót tell the full

[1] Reavis Cox, Charles S. Goodman, and Thomas C. Fichandler, "Distribution in a High-level Economy," Prentice-Hall, Inc., Englewood Cliffs, N.J., 1965, p. 158.

story. The first two postwar decades were characterized by price inflation and by marked economic growth. The real significance of these dollar totals must be evaluated against the sharp rise in advertising costs and the expansion in the economy.

Real Advertising Expenditures

Advertising rates have risen as part of the general price inflation since World War II. A special index of advertising costs for eight media [2] rose by 48.1 per cent between 1946 and 1966. Although total media advertising expenditures increased by 396 per cent in that period, when the price factor is removed, the rise was 235 per cent. Both of these rates of increase are relatively large. Nevertheless, it is clear that the postwar price inflation has acted to increase the magnitude of the rise in advertising expenditures.

Relative Importance of Advertising Expenditures

The United States economy has experienced a tremendous expansion whether measured in dollars or in real terms. Thus, gross national product (GNP) increased from about $100 billion in 1940 to $209 billion in 1946 and $790 billion in 1967. Personal consumption expenditures (PCE) increased from $71 billion to $143 billion and then to $492 billion.

Advertising expenditures were equal to about 2.25 per cent of GNP before World War II and then declined to 1.61 per cent in 1946; the average was 2.24 per cent in 1966 and 2.13 per cent in 1967. Comparisons with GNP may be somewhat misleading because the share accounted for by government increased from 14.7 per cent in 1939 to 22.6 per cent in 1967. As a result, relationships with total GNP currently tend to understate the importance of advertising. Nevertheless, the large dollar rise in advertising expenditures has about paralleled the rise in GNP.

A more meaningful comparison is with PCE. Prior to World War II, advertising expenditures averaged about 3 per cent of PCE. The ratio hit a high of 3.7 per cent in 1956 and then declined to 3.4 per cent in 1967. These data suggest a much more modest relative increase in the importance of advertising than implied by the dollar figures alone.

[2] Jules Backman, "Advertising and Competition," New York University Press, 1967, appendix B.

The enormous growth in the economy has been accompanied by a somewhat larger rise in advertising. Although cause-and-effect relationships are difficult to disentangle, it seems far more probable that the rise in economic activity has caused the rise in advertising than the reverse. The total demand for all consumer goods is most significantly influenced by total disposable personal income as is shown by the fact that total retail sales are closely correlated to broad changes in such incomes.

Potential markets have expanded as incomes and living standards have risen and as consumers have been able to purchase products they previously could not afford. In the United States incomes expanded very sharply after the depressed 1930s. Per capita disposable income rose from $537 in 1939 to $2,744 in 1967. Part of this gain was eroded by price inflation. Nevertheless, after eliminating the inflation factor, real per capita disposable income in 1958 dollars doubled —from $1,190 in 1939 to $2,401 in 1967.

As incomes rose, an increasing proportion and a much larger number of dollars were available to buy products other than food, clothing, and shelter. Thus, for example, food accounted for 33.5 per cent of the average worker's budget in 1934 to 1936 but only 22.9 per cent in December 1966. According to the National Industrial Conference Board, discretionary spending power increased from $69 billion in 1946 to $233 billion in 1967. Much more spending power became available to seek out the many options consumers have when they can afford to buy more than the necessities of life. The result was an enormous opportunity for advertising which increased markedly.

Advertising and the Business Cycle

The trends during the course of the business cycle also underline the fact that advertising is a result of rather than the cause of the levels of economic activity. When the level of economic activity grows less rapidly or turns down, company executives press to curtail advertising expenditures. Thus, *The Wall Street Journal* (July 25, 1967) reported: "The sluggishness of the U.S. economy is being felt with particular impact on Madison Avenue as companies pare their advertising outlays to conserve working capital."

Thomas Dillon, president of Batten, Barton, Durstine & Osborn, was quoted as stating: "The lag reflects cost-cutting efforts by companies hit hard by the sales and profit squeeze." Similarly, Samuel B. Vitt, senior vice president of Ted Bates & Company, noted: "When the business outlook is bright, an advertiser will boost outlays based on pure optimism, but when the economy slows up, it takes a lot more than a predicted upturn to bring ad spending back to its former levels."

The tendency to cut advertising expenditures during periods when economic activity records small changes or declines is reflected in the national totals. Thus, total advertising expenditures fell sharply in the 1938 recession. In 1958, when gross national product in dollar terms increased only modestly ($441 billion in 1957 to $447 billion in 1958), total expenditures in eight media declined ($6,137 million in 1957 to $6,031 million in 1958).

These data do not reflect the full decline in the physical volume of advertising, because the cost of advertising increased by 3.5 per cent in 1958. When the price factor is eliminated, the physical volume of advertising in the eight media fell from $6,307 million in 1957 to $5,990 million in 1959 or by 5.0 per cent. During the same year, gross national product adjusted for price changes fell by 1.2 per cent. Again in 1961 when gross national product recorded only a small rise, both money and real advertising expenditures were cut back.[3]

These data show clearly that advertising expenditures reflect the trends in economic activity during the business cycle. However, they do not tell the full story. Over longer periods, the total level of economic activity has been significantly influenced by the large number of new and improved products. Advertising plays a role in the development of markets for such products, thus contributing to economic growth.

ADVERTISING AND ECONOMIC GROWTH

Since World War II, economic growth has become a key objective of national economic policy throughout the world. Fiscal and monetary policies have been tailored to provide an environment favorable to economic growth. The expanding investment in research and development has yielded dividends in terms of rising productivity and a flow of new products which has contributed significantly to in-

[3] For basic data see Backman, *op. cit.*, pp. 201, 202.

creased economic output, greater investment opportunities, more numerous and more productive job opportunities, and rising levels of living.   The population explosion initially expanded the physical volume of goods and services required and by the 1960s was providing significant increments to the labor force.   These have been important forces contributing to economic growth.

Expansion of Markets

Advertising has made its contribution to economic growth by helping to expand markets, particularly for new products.   Thus, a company is encouraged to invest in research and development (R&D) because it believes that through advertising it can inform the public quickly about the availability of new products.   One observer has described the process as follows:

> . . . advertising, by acquainting the consumer with the values of new products, widens the market for these products, pushes forward their acceptance by the consumer and encourages the investment and entrepreneurship necessary for innovation. Advertising, in short, holds out the promise of a greater and speedier return than would occur without such methods thus stimulating investment, growth, and diversity.[4]

The explosive growth in spending for industrial research and development in the post-World War II period is shown in Table 1.

TABLE 1   Research and Development Expenditures, Selected Years, 1946–1968, in Millions of Dollars

	Financed by industry	Financed by government	Total
1946	NA	NA	1,050
1951	NA	NA	2,150
1955	2,460	2,180	4,640
1960	4,430	6,080	10,510
1965	6,440	7,760	14,200
1966	7,100	8,300	15,400
1967	7,750	8,850	16,600
1968 (est.)	8,200	9,100	17,300

NA—not available.

SOURCE: National Science Foundation.

[4] David M. Blank, Some Comments on the Role of Advertising in the American Economy: A Plea for Revaluation, in L. George Smith (ed.), "Reflections on Prog-

Flow of New Products   One result has been a steady flow of new products (e.g., color television, diet drinks, electric toothbrushes, Corfam, miracle drugs, instant tea), new processes (e.g., stay press, spray cans), and changes in old products (e.g., color phones, detergents, filter cigarettes, deodorants).   If such products are to move in volume from the laboratory to the marketplace, potential customers must learn about them.   Advertising plays the key role in this informational process.   Without it the profit incentive to engage in research and development for consumer goods could be significantly impaired.

Among the most intensively advertised products have been toilet preparations (14.7 per cent of sales), cleaning and polishing preparations (12.6 per cent), and drugs (9.4 per cent).   These have been industries in which large numbers of new products have become available.

The increases in relative importance of these highly advertised products as a percentage of total personal consumption expenditures in real terms between 1947 and 1966 was as follows:

Toilet articles and preparations from 0.68 per cent to 1.12 per cent

Cleaning, polishing, and household supplies from 0.87 per cent to 1.05 per cent

Drug preparations and sundries from 0.82 per cent to 1.24 per cent

For many companies, new products account for an expanding proportion of their sales.   Thus, for General Foods "in the fiscal year ending April 1 [1968] half of the company's record capital expenditures of $80 million were invested in facilities to produce new products. . . . Significantly, 46 per cent of the nearly three-quarters of a billion dollar increase in General Foods' net sales in the last 10 years came from new products introduced in that period."

Similarly, it has been reported that "the success of Colgate-

ress in Marketing," Northern Illinois University, 1964 Educators Conference, American Marketing Association, Chicago, 1964, p. 15.   See also Neil H. Borden, The Role of Advertising in Various Stages of Corporate and Economic Growth, in Peter D. Bennett (ed.), "Marketing and Economic Development," Pennsylvania State University, 1965 Fall Conference, American Marketing Association, Chicago, 1965; and Neil H. Borden, "The Economic Effects of Advertising," Richard D. Irwin, Inc., Chicago, 1942, chap. 24.

Palmolive Company's new products program, initiated in 1961, is best exemplified by the fact that more than 40 per cent of the billion dollar sales in 1967, came from products that did not exist in 1960." [5]

The pattern has been similar for other companies which are large advertisers. It is the composite expansion in all these companies which is reflected in national growth rates. While there have been increases in the volume of old-line products, it has been the expansion in new products and processes which has contributed the yeast for economic growth.

However, it must be kept in mind that we have a very complex and dynamic economy. It is not always possible to determine fully cause-and-effect relationships. Advertising has facilitated the acceptance of new products and hence has been an integral part of the growth process. But its contribution should not be exaggerated.

INFORMATIONAL ROLE OF ADVERTISING

Advertising plays a major informational role in our economy because (1) products are available in such wide varieties, (2) new and improved products are offered in such great numbers, and (3) existing products must be called to the attention of new consumers who are added to the market as a result of the expansion in incomes, the population explosion, and changes in tastes and styles.

Need for Product Information Grows

As our economy has grown more complex, there has been an increasing need for information concerning the wide variety of products available. In the relatively small communities of several centuries ago, the basic necessities of life were the main purchases made. In Wagner's *Die Meistersinger* everyone in the community knew that Hans Sachs was the shoemaker. And they also knew the butcher, the baker, and the candlestick maker. The meager information required about products and their availability was known to all. Advertising was not necessary. This is·still probably substantially true in the subsistence economies of Africa and Asia.

Instead of goods being produced by craftsmen living and working

---

[5] Ted Sanchagrin, The New Excitement in New Products and New Packages, *Marketing/ Communications*, May, 1968, p. 82.

within a limited area, they are now manufactured in plants which may be located all around the globe. Products may be made by small local companies or by industrial giants or by foreign companies with unpronounceable names. The consumer is faced with a dizzying number of choices—if he knows the products are available. Advertising is one of the instrumentalities in bridging the gap between production and awareness by the consumer. It tells him about the existence of the product, its uses, often where to buy it, and sometimes its price.

Of course, consumers accumulate a considerable amount of information from their neighbors and as a result of individual experimentation. Thus, as Wroe Alderson has pointed out: "Information provided by advertising is only one incremental addition to what the consumer already knows but it may be enough to establish the identity of the product which will satisfy his need." [6]

New Customers Each Year As the population increases, large numbers of new potential customers are added each year. The total population in the United States increased from 131 million in 1939 to 152 million in 1950 and more than 200 million in 1968. Continuous large-scale advertising provides reminders to old customers and provides the information required to obtain some part of the patronage of new customers. Periodically, new fads develop (e.g., Nehru jackets for men in 1968) and these must be advertised. The consumer has a wide variety of products and brands from which to choose. Improvements in products may be small [7] in the short run but they can result in significant changes over time. Thus, for example, the miracle fibers made possible the development of wash-and-wear clothing which performs the same functions as the cotton and wool products it has replaced but involves entirely different upkeep problems and standards of comfort. Just imagine the traveler of the 1920s taking a two-week trip to Europe with only two shirts, two pairs of socks, etc.!

[6] Wroe Alderson, A New Approach to Advertising Theory, in Parker Holmes, Ralph Brownlee, and Robert Bartels (eds.), "Readings in Marketing," Charles E. Merrill Books, Inc., Columbus, Ohio, 1963, p. 373.

[7] It must be recognized that some product changes have been criticized as being trivial and intended to provide a new "talking point" for purposes of advertising rather than yielding any significant benefits to the customer (e.g., tailfins for automobiles).

Information a Valuable Resource   Professor George J. Stigler has concluded that "information is a valuable resource," that advertising is "the obvious method of identifying buyers and sellers" which "reduces drastically the cost of search," and that "it is clearly an immensely powerful instrument for the elimination of ignorance. . . ." [8]

Often this information is required to create interest in and demand for a product.   It has been suggested that:

> . . . to a significant degree General Foods and the U.S. food market created each other.   Before a new product appears, customers are rarely conscious of wanting it.   There was no spontaneous demand for ready-to-eat cereals; frozen foods required a sustained marketing effort stretching over many years; instant coffee had been around for decades, supplying a market that did not amount to a tenth of its present level. General Foods' corporate skill consists largely in knowing enough about American tastes to foresee what products will be accepted.[9]

Adequacy of Information

Does advertising provide enough information or the right kind of information?   Many critics charge that the information required about products in a modern, complex society is not met adequately by advertising because it often is emotional in its appeal.   By its nature advertising emphasizes—and sometimes overemphasizes—the positive. It may be aggressively persuasive.   The potential customer can learn only what is "good" about a product, not what is "bad."

Government as Information Source

To provide balance, it has been proposed that the federal government make available comprehensive information about many products.   Thus, Donald F. Turner, then in charge of the Antitrust Division, proposed:

> . . . that Government policies be directed toward neutral vehicles of information which tend to deal directly with the uncertainty.   We all know that such consumer research organizations as Consumer Reports

---

[8] George J. Stigler, The Economics of Information, *The Journal of Political Economy*, June, 1961, pp. 213, 216, 220.   See also S. A. Ozga, Imperfect Markets through Lack of Knowledge, *Quarterly Journal of Economics*, February, 1960, pp. 29, 33–34; and Wroe Alderson, "Dynamic Market Behavior," Richard D. Irwin, Inc., Homewood, Ill., 1965, pp. 128–131.

[9] General Foods Is Five Billion Particulars, *Fortune*, March, 1964, p. 117.

tend to promote informed consumer judgment, and we can reasonably surmise that reports of that kind, if generally circulated, would significantly limit the ability of advertising to enhance degrees of monopoly power, to say nothing of enabling consumers to spend their dollars more fruitfully. . . . One prospective solution, would be governmental efforts in this direction, either direct government evaluation and publication, or financial support for private organizations of this type.[10]

Similar proposals have been made for the drug industry, which spends substantial sums on promotion and advertising. The industry's sales force—known as *detail men*—calls on physicians in their offices and tells them about new drugs. Materials must be supplied describing any harmful side effects of drugs. Nevertheless, critics have complained that doctors do not get the full story. One proposal is the publication of a drug compendium which would list all drugs approved by the Federal Food and Drug Administration. This compendium, which would be updated quarterly, would contain complete descriptions of the drugs including information about possible side effects and established dosages.

The availability of additional information should be helpful to many consumers. The extent to which such information will be used, however, is not clear. Thus, for example, for many years, comprehensive information has been published by Consumers Union in its monthly reports. Circulation of its publication (*Consumer Reports*) exceeds one million. However, circulation figures alone probably understate its influence. The emphasis in these reports is upon the functional usefulness of different products. Frequently, they have pointed out that little, if any, relationship exists between quality and price.[11] However, consumers are interested in more than the functioning of a product. They want a refrigerator which not only preserves food but fits into the decor of a kitchen, has revolving shelves, has special compartments, etc.

It is important to keep this experience in mind because *Consumer*

[10] Donald F. Turner, "Advertising and Competition," an address before the Briefing Conference on Federal Controls of Advertising and Promotion sponsored by the Federal Bar Association, Washington, June 2, 1966.

[11] According to Consumers Union their ". . . product ratings are usually based on estimated overall quality without regard to price. Best Buy Ratings are accorded to products that are not only rated high in overall quality but also priced relatively low." *Consumer Reports*, March, 1968, p. 115.

Reports go much further in advancing conclusions about the relative merits of competing products than could be done in government compilations or compendiums. And yet, although they have undoubtedly influenced many consumers in their purchases of some items, they appear to have had only a minor effect upon overall consumer buying habits and patterns.

How Much Advertising Is Informational?

Advertising is criticized as being excessively persuasive rather than informative. Certainly, this is true for some advertising. Although it is difficult to determine what part of total advertising expenditures is primarily informative, some "guesstimates" can be made from the available data. In 1967 total expenditures for media advertising aggregated $13.5 billion distributed as follows: [12]

Classified advertising was $1.3 billion

Other local newspaper advertising, largely retail, was $2.7 billion

Local radio and local television advertising was $1.2 billion

Spot radio and spot television advertising was $1.2 billion

National advertising on network television, network radio, magazines, and newspapers was $3.8 billion

Business paper advertising was $712 million

Direct mail was $2.5 billion

Classified advertising and local advertising are overwhelmingly informational in nature, as is much of the direct mail. Certainly some national advertising also performs this function, since a significant part is for the promotion of new products for which the informational role is vital. These figures suggest that substantially less than half of total advertising is of the type that has been attacked as being excessively persuasive or wasteful.[13]

Social Cost of Advertising

The social cost of advertising is considerably less than suggested by expenditures data alone. Thus, in 1967 over $10 billion was spent for advertising in newspapers, magazines, radio, and television; another $745 million was spent on farm and business publications.

[12] This total excludes a miscellaneous category of $3.3 billion.

[13] For the United Kingdom, the "disputed proportion" of advertising expenditures has been estimated at about 30 per cent of the total. Walter Taplin, "Advertising: A New Approach," Little, Brown and Company, Boston, 1963, p. 126.

Without such expenditures, these sources of news and entertainment would have had to charge higher subscription rates or to be subsidized by the government or some combination of both.

Despite some criticism of the power of advertisers, we are likely to have a more independent press when it is financed through advertising than when it is subsidized or completely controlled by the government, as the experience in many other countries unfortunately has demonstrated.

ADVERTISING IN THE MARKETING PROCESS

Advertising is only one selling tool.   It is part of a broad marketing process which includes personal selling, product planning, pricing, varying channels of distribution, promotions, packaging, games, display materials, and technical services.   Food stores have used the inducement of stamp plans, prize contests, free samples, and price-off coupons.   Gasoline stations have offered various types of games which have been featured in their advertising.

Advertising as a Marketing Alternative

Advertising cannot be considered in a vacuum.   Generally it is a question of alternatives.   If advertising is not used, some other type of sales effort will be made.   A company must determine the total amount to be spent on marketing and the relationship among each of the instruments available.

Often marketing techniques are complementary rather than substitutable.   The availability of a variety of approaches to the marketing problem allows for a certain amount of substitution among them. The combination selected usually is at the option of the company, although competitive pressures may result in greater emphasis upon some of the alternatives available.

Advertising Ratios for Product Groups   Although total advertising expenditures average about 3.4 per cent of personal consumption expenditures, the ratios for specific groups of products vary widely from this average as a result of diverse marketing strategies.   Thus, for toilet preparations, soft drinks, soaps and detergents, gums, and candies advertising outlays often exceed 10 per cent of sales.   On the other hand, for clothing, motor vehicles, and sugar the ratios are less than 1 per cent.   For tobacco, beer, and drugs the advertising as a percentage of sales averages between 5 per cent and 10 per cent. Clearly, advertising does not play the same role for all products. Highly advertised items tend to be brand-name products which, with some exceptions, sell for less than $1 per unit, are subject to frequent repeat purchases,[14] and are available from many retail establishments.

Proliferation of Brands

For these highly advertised products new brands proliferate as companies seek to obtain larger market shares.   Advertising tends to be more intensive for new brands and for new products in order to achieve this objective.   An A. C. Nielsen study has shown that for fourteen brands of new cold cereals introduced from 1957 to August 1, 1961, advertising in major media accounted for 47 per cent of sales the first year, 22 per cent the second year, and 21 per cent the third year.[15]

Within an industry, the mix also may vary widely as companies follow different marketing strategies.   For example, although the cosmetics industry has been estimated to spend about 15 per cent of its sales on advertising, Avon has spent only 2.7 per cent on advertising because it sells on a house-to-house basis.[16] Yet it has been a highly successful company.

Role of Advertising

The role given to advertising also varies among products within a company as executives determine which marketing mix will be most effective for each product or group of products.   Some interesting data showing these variations were made available by Canadian companies in response to a legislative inquiry.[17]

GENERAL FOODS LIMITED: For the year ending March 31, 1966 the relative importance of advertising as a percentage of sales was less than 1

[14] According to Procter & Gamble Company "the typical consumer" buys soap or detergent fifty times a year, toothpaste eleven times and coffee twenty-two times. "Annual Report for the Year Ended June 30, 1966," p. 6.

[15] "Studies of Organization and Competition in Grocery Manufacturing," Technical Study no. 6, National Commission on Food Marketing, Washington, June, 1966, p. 152.

[16] Penelope Orth, Cosmetics: The Brand Is Everything, *Printers' Ink*, Nov. 1, 1963, p. 30.

[17] Special Joint Committee of the Senate and House of Commons on Consumer Credit (Prices), Ottawa, 1966.

per cent for Walter Baker chocolate, orange juice, and frozen vegetables and 17 per cent or higher for dessert toppings (18.4 per cent) and cereals (17.0 per cent).   For other products, the ratios were between these extremes—packaged desserts (10.4 per cent) and dry dog foods (7.2 per cent).   (p. 1242)

COLGATE-PALMOLIVE LIMITED: In the 10 months ending October 1966, advertising accounted for less than 5 per cent of sales for Encore liquid detergent (4.3 per cent) and Ajax floor and wall cleaner (4.0 per cent).   At the other extreme, the ratio was 42.7 per cent for Ajax detergent and 31.7 per cent for Ajax liquid cleaners.   However, for Fab detergent the ratio was 8.9 per cent and Ajax cleaner 13.5 per cent. (p. 1655)

PROCTER AND GAMBLE COMPANY OF CANADA LIMITED: In the year ending June 30, 1966, the advertising-sales ratio was 20.7 per cent for toiletries, 11.3 per cent for packaged detergents, and 8.2 per cent for cake mixes. (p. 1740)

LEVER BROTHERS LIMITED: In 1966, 15.6 per cent was spent for regular Dove soap, 11.6 per cent for Lux bath soap, 8.4 per cent for regular All and 4.8 per cent for Breeze giant. (p. 2138)

A study in Great Britain reported the following ratios were used by Unilever Ltd. for advertising and sales promotion: [18]

Advertising and Promotion
as Per Cent of Recommended Retail Price

Detergents	16
Fruit squash	9
Ice cream	6
Margarine	6
Frozen foods	4

It is evident from these data that the marketing strategy varies widely among products as management decides—rightly or wrongly—that advertising can be more or less effective.

Discount Houses   Expenditures for advertising often are substituted for other types of selling effort.   This substitution has been readily apparent in the history of the discount house.   These stores have featured well-advertised brands which were presold and, hence, virtually eliminated the need for floor stocks and reduced the need for space and for many salesmen.

[18] Economists Advisory Group, "The Economics of Advertising," London, July 7, 1967, p. 14.

The *Harvard Business Review* conducted an extensive survey of advertising in 1962 and reported:

> What would happen if advertising expenditures were eliminated? Would other selling expenses take their place? *Definitely yes,* reply businessmen. Over 85 per cent believe that other selling expenses would take advertising's place if advertising were eliminated, with only 10 per cent disagreeing. This finding holds generally true irrespective of management level, industry, or function.[19]

Advertising is undertaken where it is the most effective and most economical way to appeal to customers. It is a relatively low-cost method of communicating with all potential customers, and this explains its widespread adoption by many companies.

ADVERTISING AND COMPETITION [20]

Competition long has been viewed as a key force in the American economy. Thus, questions raised concerning the impact of advertising on competition are important. Is advertising competitive or anticompetitive? Does it provide evidence of competition or does it inhibit competition?

The businessman has no difficulty identifying what he considers to be competition. He experiences the competitive impact of a new product or of one which is packaged more attractively or of one which is advertised more intensively and with greater imagination. He experiences the effects when a new competitor enters the market or when an existing competitor undertakes to expand its share of the market. Against this background, he is understandably puzzled when he is told that these everyday experiences are not really competition because there are only a few firms in his market or because he differentiates his product in order to gain a market identity and the hoped-for loyalty of some customers or because he advertises intensively.

[19] Stephen A. Greyser, Businessmen Re Advertising: Yes, But . . . , *Harvard Business Review*, May-June, 1962, p. 30.

[20] The material in this section has been largely adapted from Backman, *op. cit.*, pp. 1–4, 155–157.

Competition a Pervasive Fact

Competition is a pervasive fact of economic life even though it is difficult, or sometimes impossible, to measure its exact extent.   The essence of competition is rivalry.   Competition results in pressures to improve products and to find more economical ways to produce and to distribute them.   The firm that fails to respond to competitive pressures loses out to its more imaginative or more efficient rivals. The consumer benefits by the availability of new and better products to satisfy his ever-expanding desires.

Although the intensely competitive nature of advertising is a matter of common observation, it is claimed that advertising is so successful that monopolistic advantages accrue to the large advertisers.[21] The claimed anticompetitive effects of advertising may be summarized as follows:

1.   The large company has the power of the large purse, which enables it to spend substantial sums on advertising, particularly to implement varying degrees of product differentiation which enables a company to preempt part of a market.

2.   Advertising thus creates a barrier to new firms entering an industry or a product market.

3.   The result is high economic concentration.

4.   Because of their protected position and because of product differentiation these firms can charge monopolistic prices which are too high.   Moreover, they must recover the cost of the advertising by charging higher prices.

5.   High prices in turn result in excessively large profits.

Cause and Effect

How strong or inevitable is this chain of cause and effect?   Do the results flow as described?   Actually, the chain is broken at several points.

1.   It is true that large companies have financial as well as nonfinancial advantages as compared with smaller companies.   Nevertheless, financial power usually has not acted as an effective

---

[21] Henry C. Simons, "Economic Policy for a Free Society," University of Chicago Press, 1948, p. 95; and Turner, *op. cit.*   One of the most severe indictments of advertising is contained in The Labour Party, "Report of a Commission of Enquiry into Advertising" (Reith Report), London, 1966, 205 pp.

barrier to entry.   Other large companies also have the "power of the purse."   Smaller companies have available local and regional advertising media at much lower costs than national media.   This has been important because so many markets are local in nature.

National brands must meet the competition of other national brands, private brands, local or regional brands, substitute products, and products sold solely on a price basis.   The dynamic, competitive nature of these markets is underlined by the marked changes in brand shares, the successes achieved by many new national brands and private brands against so-called entrenched brands, and the inability of well-known and financially strong companies successfully to establish new brands at will.   These developments indicate that the degree of market power, which supposedly accompanies product differentiation identified by brand names and implemented by large-scale advertising, is much weaker than claimed and is usually outweighed by competitive pressures.

2.   There has been no relationship between the extent of economic concentration and the intensity of advertising as measured by advertising-sales ratios.   In most industries, the composition of the Big Fours has changed over time as smaller companies have grown in size and have taken the competitive measure of their larger rivals. Smaller companies often have been especially alert to the opportunities created when new products have been developed.   The Big Fours have not been exclusive clubs.   New entrants to the market have successfully breached the citadel.   The top as reflected in the Big Four has proved to be slippery in all but a few markets.

3.   No relationship is found between advertising-sales ratios and changes in prices during the post-World War II period.   Cost-price-volume relationships are very complex and change over the life cycle of a product.   Prices are determined by many factors other than costs.   Even where costs play a role, an expenditure as large as 5 to 15 per cent of total costs for advertising would not be the determinant of prices.   Moreover, advertising costs are not net.   If they were eliminated, other marketing costs would be incurred and in many instances the selling job would be done less efficiently or at a higher cost.

Companies which allegedly have developed strong market power for their brands through heavy advertising and thus allegedly have been insulated from price competition generally have been unable to exploit the postwar price inflation by above-average price hikes. Rather, the companies with the greatest intensity of advertising often recorded less than average increases or even decreases in prices.

4. Companies with relatively high advertising-sales ratios tend to have somewhat higher profit rates than less intensive advertisers. These higher profits appear to reflect the larger volume resulting from successful advertising rather than the exercise of market power to charge high monopolistic prices. The investment in advertising appears to yield a modest return in light of the risks of failure assumed.

The alleged flow of control from the "power of the purse" to "excessive profits," therefore, is not supported by the available evidence. The barrier to entry supposedly created by large financial requirements is weak. The relationship between advertising intensity and high economic concentration is nonexistent. There appears to be no link between advertising intensity and price increases. Intensive advertisers appear to have only moderately higher profit rates than other companies. The record shows clearly that advertising is highly competitive, not anticompetitive.

BIBLIOGRAPHY

BACKMAN, JULES: "Advertising and Competition," New York University Press, 1967.

────: Is Advertising Wasteful? *Journal of Marketing*, January, 1968.

BLANK, DAVID M.: Some Comments on the Role of Advertising in the American Economy: A Plea for Revaluation, in L. George Smith (ed.), "Reflections On Progress in Marketing," 1964 Educators Conference, American Marketing Association, Chicago, 1964.

BORDEN, NEIL H.: The Role of Advertising in Various Stages of Corporate and Economic Growth, in Peter D. Bennett (ed.), "Marketing and Economic Development," 1965 Fall Conference, American Marketing Association, Chicago, 1965.

CONSUMER CREDIT (PRICES): Proceedings of the Special Joint Committee of the Senate and House of Commons, 26 vols., Ottawa, 1966.

ECONOMISTS ADVISORY GROUP: "The Economics of Advertising," London, July 7, 1967.

FERGUSON, JAMES M.: "Advertising and Liquor," Center Research Report no. 1, Center for Research in Government Policy and Business, University of Rochester, College of Business Administration, Rochester, N.Y., 1967.

FIRESTONE, O. J.: "The Economic Implications of Advertising," Methuen Publications, Toronto, 1967.

FREY, ALBERT W.: "Advertising," 3d ed., The Ronald Press Company, New York, 1961.

KLEPPNER, OTTO: "Advertising Procedure," 5th ed., Prentice-Hall, Inc., Englewood Cliffs, N.J., 1966.

MACHLUP, FRITZ: "The Production and Distribution of Knowledge in the United States," Princeton University Press, Princeton, N.J., 1962.

SANDAGE, C. H., and VERNON FRYBURGER: "Advertising Theory and Practice," 6th ed., Richard D. Irwin, Inc., Homewood, Ill., 1963.

STIGLER, GEORGE J.: The Economics of Information, *The Journal of Political Economy,* June, 1961.

TAPLIN, WALTER: "Advertising: A New Approach," Little, Brown and Company, Boston, 1963.

TURNER, DONALD F.: "Advertising and Competition," an Address before the Briefing Conference on Federal Controls of Advertising and Promotion sponsored by the Federal Bar Association, Washington, June 2, 1966.

PART TWO
Organization

CHAPTER THREE

Advertising in
the Corporate Structure*

ROBERT M. GRAY *formerly Advertising and Sales Promotion Manager, Humble Oil & Refining Company*

JOSEPH B. WILKINSON *formerly Vice President, McCann-Erickson, Inc.*

ORGANIZATION A PERPLEXING PROBLEM

As corporations have developed into today's giant structures, managements have been taxed to organize them for efficient operation. Where to place the advertising function is as difficult to answer for the organizational chart makers as any question they are asked. There are no simple formulas. Since a supervisor or manager can exercise control over only a limited number of persons, decentralization appears to be the best solution in many instances. But decentralization raises almost as many questions as it answers. For one example, should the decentralization be complete or only partial?

* The authors would like to express their deep appreciation to those managers and their assistants who took time from busy schedules to complete and return the questionnaires sent them.

There are many others, and the answers most often are obtained empirically.

In the Marketing Mix?

Many of the chart makers regard advertising's place to be in the marketing mix, and forthwith make it a subfunction of marketing.   But to many marketers, advertising is the principal ingredient in the mix. To make marketing a subfunction of advertising is patently a little ridiculous.   On the other hand, if the success or failure of a marketing operation depends on advertising, it may be also a little ridiculous to make advertising a subfunction of marketing.   This dilemma is made more painful by the fact that forcing the mass consumption of mass-produced goods depends ever more heavily on advertising, and there are first-rate marketing men, trained to an engineering-financial solution to most problems, who simply do not understand how to use the personal skills and talents upon which much of the best advertising is based, even when advertising solves their marketing problems brilliantly.

Acquisitions, diversifications, and mergers further complicate both the general problem of corporate organization and the specific problem of where to place the advertising function to give it maximum utility.   When one company acquires another, the usual practice is to let the acquired company run itself for the time being.   This is decentralization to the nth degree.   Usually a sort of hybrid vigor is generated, but sooner or later this will fade, and the purchasing company will be forced to examine its loose-knit organization.   Mergers sometimes unite two different marketing philosophies.   The marketing policies that immediately follow are consequently compromises.

Nature of Advertising

The nature of advertising poses another problem for management. Advertising people are not members of a profession in the sense that physicians are, but their work sets them apart from other employees, so that in some corporations advertising is a sort of enclave within the business, like the medical department.   It is, therefore, easy to place it in any of several places on the organizational chart. In some of these, it can be so surrounded that the skills and talents it protects have no egress to the business, and advertising's contribution to the success of the company is consequently less than it could be. In others, there is no enclave and the special qualifications that advertising brings to the solution of the company's problems are diluted. The goal is to give advertising a living room in which it can flourish, as in the enclave, and at the same time place it close enough to the objectives and the problems of marketing to prevent its effort from becoming tangential. It is a delicate matter.

It is the more so because of the characteristics of advertising personnel. Their devotion to their vocation not infrequently is beyond all reason. Many of them have abilities and training, even native skills, that would enable them to function well—and perhaps more to their personal profit—in other corporate careers. But they prefer advertising, responding to its peculiar challenge to their wits, and they render to advertising a loyalty and a faith that must be seen to be believed. If too much autonomy is given to such persons, advertising has a tendency to hoe its own row, or to assume too much importance in the marketing mix; if too little, the advertising ingredient loses its piquancy, and its contribution is flat and stale.

Public Relations Advertising

Earlier it was noted that advertising's position in marketing is increasingly important. Now, as corporations grow and change, managements have begun to recognize what advertising can accomplish for them in the field of public relations. Not all use advertising in this role as adroitly as they might, but those who understand that a business giant has a certain duty to explain itself to investors and customers have used advertising quite effectively to do this, with candid presentations that win the confidence of investors and the goodwill of the public. Much of the advertising budgeted for this purpose is dictated by departments of public relations. On the face of it, this appears to be reasonable, for many of the desired objectives are the same. But the techniques of public relations vary widely from those of advertising, and men trained to them can so dampen the advertising that supports public relations as to curtail its effectiveness, sometimes seriously.

Advertising's Job in Public Relations

Advertising's job is not much different from the work it does for marketing, though it pushes ideas, ideals, and information instead of

soap or automobiles or gasolines.   When this advertising carries a
message for customers as well as for investors and governments, its
purpose must in part derive from a company's marketing objectives as
well as those of public relations.   This opens a new debate on the
place of advertising in the corporate structure and suggests that companies which find such advertising profitable should not subordinate
it to either public relations or marketing.   Wherever the advertising
function is placed by a company—whether it is given more or less
autonomy, or made subordinate to public relations or marketing—
its position there has been or may well be affected by the number and
the quality of the services rendered by advertising agencies.

Control by Brand Managers

One of the reasons for the currently fashionable control of advertising
in some companies by brand or market managers in marketing is the
thought that the advertising agency can supply all the needed advertising skills and talents and will present advertising's case as elo-
quently as would company administrators of the advertising function.

This is true.   But, first, both the agency and the product manager,
individually and together, lack the perspective of a company advertising man.   Second, in an intensely competitive market the advertising effort should have everything and anything both company and
agency can supply.   Finally, it must be remembered that the agency
is a separate profit-making entity, that agency account managers are
here today and gone tomorrow, that brand managers are often reas-
signed or lured away by other companies.   Company advertising
personnel are interested primarily in the company's profits, and their
continuity of service is relatively much longer than that of agency
people or brand managers.

The inevitable conclusion is that the assignment of the advertising
function within the corporate structure is a complex question, a
problem not easily solved, and that many solutions raise almost as
many questions as they answer.

200 CORPORATIONS SURVEYED

In an effort to learn how the country's major companies have solved
the complexities of finding a place for the advertising function in

their organizations, the authors of this chapter mailed detailed questionnaires to the 200 largest corporations in the United States as listed by *Fortune* magazine.   More than half completed the questionnaires and returned them.   This number is too small to make tabulations without an oversize probability of error, but the respondents were different enough in their fields and in their operations to provide an excellent cross section of advertising organizations.

PRACTICES OF A FEW BIG COMPANIES

To a few big companies (call them Group A) there is no problem. These companies are not really marketers in the sense that they do not sell to a mass of consumers.   Their sales run into many millions of dollars, but these are sales of raw materials, heavy equipment (much of it built to customers' specifications), and products like airplanes that sell for very high prices to very few corporate and governmental customers.

Advertising a Part of Public Relations

Such companies usually regard advertising as a part of their public relations activities.   In some cases, the advertising manager reports directly to the manager of public relations.   In a few others, both advertising and public relations report to a layer of management called *communications,* which might also have control over employee communications.   In the latter instance, the director of communications frequently is a vice president.   On an organizational chart, the advertising function is an activity of corporate headquarters and reports through one channel or another to the company's principal management.   Thus, advertising can occupy a fairly high place on the corporate totem pole in the sense that the advertising manager has contacts with the highest-ranking officers of the company and makes his presentations to the principal executive officer, to whom he is sometimes directly responsible.

How Important Is Advertising?

But however rarefied the atmosphere in which the advertising manager lives, only one of the respondent companies in this group considered advertising very necessary to its operations.   Another at the opposite end of the scale ranked advertising as not at all important to the company. The others thought advertising to be either moderately or considerably important. Considering the opinion overlap between *moderately* and *considerably,* it appears that advertising is considered useful by about half of the respondent companies, but not much more than an accessory of the public relations program by the other half.

Sales Participation Minor

An executive concerned with sales participates in the setting of advertising objectives in less than a third of the companies in Group A. The principal executive officer sets the objectives in slightly more than a third of the companies, and the advertising manager sets his own objectives in the rest. All the companies make their budgets to conform to the cost of the task advertising is expected to do. This means, of course, that budgets follow some traditional pattern influenced by special advertising opportunities (like the opportunity to sponsor one or more appropriate television special programs) or the lack of them, and by business conditions.

Principal Agency Contact

The principal agency contact in most of the Group A companies is the advertising manager, but in a few the agency reports to the public relations manager. In half the companies the advertising manager approves his own preliminary advertising plans, and in half these instances he also gives final approval to the advertising as it appears. Final approval is more often with the company's principal executive officer.

COMPANIES WITH DECENTRALIZED CONTROL

All the other respondents were marketing companies. Some of them considered that the advertising function had been decentralized in their operations; the others, that control of advertising was centralized. The companies with decentralized control were placed in Group B for analysis (49 companies), and those with centralized control into Group C.

Group B included about half of all the respondent corporations, but 40 per cent had in fact centralized some part of their advertising, and often a large portion. Much of the decentralization resulted from acquisitions, mergers, and diversifications. One company which recently embarked on a program of diversification both within the company and through acquisitions regards its advertising as decentralized, but the truth is that it operates a centralized, functional advertising department for all the products it originally marketed, and has not yet disturbed the organization of advertising within its acquisitions. Contact between the parent company and the acquisitions is only on the level of executive management.

Another very large company marketing a variety of products handles the advertising of mass consumer products on a decentralized basis, with separate advertising departments within divisions, but handles advertising for its industrial products through a centralized department so functional that it employs agencies in only one or two instances. In this company, the central advertising department exercises a gentle control over the advertising departments of the divisions. Managers are appointed on the advice of the company advertising manager, and presumably he also can suggest their removal; the company manager is consulted on the selection of advertising agencies, and he reviews budgets.

A third company is so completely decentralized that it has no headquarters advertising staff.

How Advertising Management Reports

Since advertising must be an essential ingredient of the marketing mix in the Group B companies, and their advertising expenditures are in the multimillion-dollar class, it would be imagined that the roll of their company officers would include a number of vice presidents, advertising. But this is currently true in only five of the companies, approximately one-eighth of the total. In the others, advertising management reports to marketing management or executive management, and since these are all marketing companies, it can be assumed that in most instances executive and marketing management mean the same thing.

In approximately a third of these companies, headquarters advertising exercises no control over the advertising plans and budgets of company subdivisions, except as these may come to light in overall plans submitted to executive management for approval. There is even less control over creative work, media selection, and the measurement of advertising effectiveness.   Only three companies stated that they maintain tight control over all phases of the advertising of their divisions and subsidiaries.

Control of Budgets

In one company in seven of the Group B companies, headquarters controls the advertising budgets of divisions and subsidiaries completely, and control is split with the subordinate staff in a few more. Final approval of advertising plans is held by company headquarters in 20 per cent of the companies, and exercised jointly with the divisions and subsidiaries in a few more.   In these companies— those with some control over budgets and plans—headquarters usually has a veto power over the plans of subordinate echelons, but this is never used frequently; it is used occasionally, however, by 80 per cent of the headquarters staffs that have it, and it is hardly ever used by a few.

Buying of Media   In about half of the companies in which the headquarters advertising staff has more than nominal direct authority over the advertising of company subdivisions (which is about 25 per cent of the total respondents in Group B), headquarters makes bulk purchases of media.   This is always done in consultation with the agencies involved, but subordinate intracompany advertising staffs are not often consulted.

Nine of the forty-nine companies have highly organized headquarters advertising departments with subsections for the supervision and appraisal of the work of subordinate staffs in the fields of planning, budgeting, creative execution, and media selection.   In the same nine companies, the headquarters staff measures the effectiveness of the advertising done by company subdivisions.

In other companies, any control that exists is just enough to assure that the advertising of divisions and subsidiaries conforms with company policies and that the work of one division is passed on to the others for information.

Selection of Agencies

In only a third of the companies does the headquarters staff participate in the selection of advertising agencies.   In half of these instances (in one-sixth of all the companies in Group B) headquarters actually makes the selection; in the other half agency appointment is a joint undertaking of headquarters and the subordinate staff involved.   The remaining two-thirds of all the companies in Group B leave divisions and subsidiaries free to choose their agencies without interference.

Eight Group B companies give advertising professional status by promoting advertising men, with the line of promotion terminating at the top in headquarters, and advertising personnel are sometimes transferred to advertising posts in other divisions or subsidiaries. This occurs frequently in only one of the respondent companies, occasionally in 21, and infrequently in 12.   In most of the decentralized companies, unless advertising men can find promotion and compensation elsewhere in the division or subsidiary, promotion ends when a man becomes advertising manager on a subordinate staff. This suggests that advertising jobs in companies so organized are little more than training for other positions in marketing.

Chance of Being an Officer

Though only five of the headquarters advertising managers in the Group B companies are company officers, more than twice that number of advertising managers have attained executive status at one time or another, including, of course, the current five.   There have been fourteen vice presidents appointed from a succession of advertising managers, five advertising men have been elected to boards of directors, two have become board chairmen, three have been company presidents, and three have become executive vice presidents.   None has been named a treasurer.   It is likely that those who attained the highest ranks in the business hierarchy—the executive vice presidents, the presidents, the chairmen—were the same persons. Promotions to executive positions were considered unusual in 5 of the companies but not so in 9.   It follows, therefore, that in the 49 Group B companies, advertising managers have about one chance in three of becoming officers of their companies, and these are good odds.

COMPANIES WITH CENTRALIZED CONTROL

The third group of respondent companies—call it Group C—consisted of 38 marketing companies in which the advertising function is centralized.   By coincidence the same number of companies as in Group B, 5, have advertising managers who also are officers of their companies.   Most of the advertising managers of Group C companies report to marketing managements.   But in 6 of the companies they report to executive management, which, again, may be primarily concerned with marketing, and in 7 to the principal executive officer, the 7 including, of course, the 5 advertising managers who also are company officers.

Brand Managers

Most of the companies in this group utilize the brand- or market-manager type of operation.   These marketing persons have much to do with the advertising for the products they manage, and in some companies so much that the advertising function actually is decentralized to their control, whatever its position on an organizational chart.   For example, the determination of an advertising budget is generally considered to be a decision of first importance in the marketing of a product; in 4 of the Group C companies, this is altogether a brand manager's responsibility; it is 75 per cent his responsibility in 7 companies; and in the rest he has an equal voice with the advertising men.   Brand managers are less active in the selection of media; they have responsibility for this advertising function in only 3 companies, and as much as a 50 per cent say-so in only 12.   Their control of the creative aspect of advertising is 100 per cent in 2 companies, and 50 per cent in 13.   In 26 of the companies, the advertising department is the principal agency contact, in 11 it is the brand managers, and in 1, a rather special case, the company's creative director. The brand manager has nothing whatever to do with advertising in only 4 of the Group C companies.

In 20 of the companies, about half, advertising management sponsors advertising to the next level of management for approval.   In 4 companies this is the responsibility of the brand managers.   In 8 companies it is the joint responsibility of the advertising department and the brand managers.   And in 1 company, this chore is assumed by marketing management.

The advertising department has a veto power over the advertising proposals of brand managers in 17 of the companies; in 4 it does not. Where the power exists, it is frequently exercised in 2 companies, occasionally in 10, and hardly ever in 5.

Planning and Buying Media

Sixteen of the Group C companies make bulk purchases of media. This is generally done in consultation with the advertising agencies involved. Purchases are discussed before they are made with brand managers frequently in 6 companies and occasionally in 6 more. Executive management of 5 companies generally interests itself in bulk media purchases and occasionally in another 5.

The centralized advertising departments have special sections for advertising planning in 12 companies, for media selection and evaluation in 14, and for the control of budgets in 17.

In working with their agencies, 4 of the Group C companies do all the planning within their own advertising departments, 75 per cent of it in 12 companies, 50 per cent in 12. Planning is almost exclusively an agency function in 3 of the companies. Every company in the group does some of its creative work: all of it in 3 companies; 75 per cent in 1; 50 per cent in 10; 25 per cent in 9; and less than 25 per cent in only 10. One company selects its own media; 75 per cent of this work is done by 5 companies, 50 per cent by 14, 25 per cent by 8, and less than 25 per cent by 5. Twenty-six companies assume the entire responsibility of making advertising budgets; six permit a 25 per cent participation by their agencies; and in one case, the company turns over most of the budgeting responsibility to its agencies.

Promotion Opportunities

Advertising managers of this group of companies become company officers more frequently than those of the Group B companies. At one time or another, four advertising managers in Group C have been elected to boards of directors, four have become board chairmen, two have been made presidents, two have been executive vice presidents, and eighteen have been vice presidents. Even one treasurer has come from an advertising department. Some of these offices were held by the same person, but promotions to officers have been made in 21 of the 38 respondent companies; in 7 cases, the promotions were considered unusual, in 14 they were not.

Degrees of Centralization

In considering the Group B and Group C companies, a decision to place a company in one group or the other, or both, was made to simplify examination of the questionnaires. The fact is, however, that only about half the respondent companies can claim to be either completely centralized or completely decentralized insofar as the advertising function is concerned. There are roughly three degrees of shading between centralization and decentralization.

First, there is a group of companies that have decentralized their advertising to divisions and subsidiaries to a point where advertising in company headquarters is either nonexistent, a service department of minor importance, or a staff section only. In a number of these companies, advertising within the divisions and subsidiaries is highly centralized.

Second, there are corporations which have decentralized their advertising to divisions and subsidiaries which have further decentralized the advertising function to the control of brand and market managers.

And third, there are companies that hold the advertising function centralized for major products, and decentralize it for others, and the reverse.

ARGUMENTS FOR DECENTRALIZATION

Perhaps the best argument for complete decentralization of the advertising function is that the size of modern corporations makes it impractical to organize in any other fashion. Certainly 100 per cent decentralization seats the function firmly on the back of a division or subsidiary. It follows that the subdivisions must have a free hand to use advertising as much or as little as they please. As long as a division meets the corporate objectives, it can, within certain broad limitations, run its business the way it wants to. If its management is shrewd, able, and experienced, the division or subsidiary will make its goals, of which profit is the chief one, and few questions are asked in higher echelons of the company.

Only one company among those studied goes all the way in the decentralization of its advertising. This company has no advertising function on the corporate-headquarters level. Each division and subsidiary has its own advertising manager, who presumably makes or breaks his business career within the company subdivision he serves; and his professional status in advertising is measured by the importance of the division or subsidiary to overall company operations and its competitive position in its marketing area.

Military Concept   Another company described its operations in military terms. *Tactical* advertising is decentralized to the operating divisions. The corporate advertising authority has a dual responsibility to evaluate divisional performance and to originate and direct *strategic* corporate advertising including communications regarding new-product development.

A third company is divided into twelve autonomous operating divisions by type of market, each headed by a vice president or general manager responsible for profits in his area. It is, therefore, his decision whether or not he requires an advertising staff. Some divisions are further divided into type-of-market departments. One major division has ten subdivisions. Four have advertising departments and the other six sell to a relatively small number of customers and do no advertising. Another division with several departments has a centralized advertising department servicing the entire division. In the corporation, there is a total of eight advertising managers, each empowered to select his own agencies with the approval of his division chief. At the parent-company level, one man coordinates advertising staff activities, which were not specified, and approves all advertising to assure that it conforms with company policy. He reports to the president of the company.

A Vice President, Advertising   In a fourth company, the advertising manager in the headquarters is a vice president. He is responsible for staff advertising activities within the company and for overall company advertising policies. He is active, for example, in the transfer of advertising personnel from one subdivision of the company to another, and presumably in their promotion to bigger and better jobs. He exercises a degree of control over all advertising plans, creative materials, media selection, and the measurement of advertising effectiveness, but more over budgets. Since he is an officer of the company, it would be assumed that his control in these matters is more than nominal, and the assumption is confirmed by the fact that advertising of the company, whatever the division or subsidiary that produces it, has a family resemblance that quickly identifies it to an observer with average experience in the advertising trade. It should be added that most of this company's advertising has been very successful.

No Headquarters Advertising Staff

Management of the company with no headquarters advertising staff appears to have delegated a substantial amount of its authority without diminishing its responsibility.   There is too much money spent on advertising these days and too many normal risks of failure to make this sort of organization wise.   A management informed by a competent headquarters advertising staff might be able to prevent an advertising fiasco in one of the subdivisions, and to save the company some millions of dollars in lost sales, ineffective advertising expense, and the time required to get the subdivision back on the right track.

Weaknesses in Staff Organization   There are, of course, weaknesses in any staff organization.   The staff man usually has direct authority only to advise and suggest, and his contributions to corporate operations most often depend on his personal strengths and weaknesses. In the case of an advertising staff man, this is doubly true, because the persons whom he advises are not always able to judge his competence as an advertising professional.   But they will react to his personality, just as all men are affected by the people with whom they associate.   Any authority exercised by an advertising staff man derives from the backing he gets from management.   If his personality is strong, he is likely to get such backing and consequently to influence the advertising of the company's subdivisions.   If it is not, the company is running the same risks as one with no headquarters advertising staff at all.

The last company cited as an example of decentralized advertising management seems to have solved the problems posed by decentralization better than most.   To use another military analogy, the principal advertising executive of the company functions not as a general staff officer but more as the chief of a special staff section, with direct authority to assign specially trained personnel to subordinate formations, move them about for maximum usefulness, and to supervise their professional operations.

ORGANIZATION WHERE ADVERTISING IS RELATIVELY UNIMPORTANT

Most of the companies in Group A have centralized the advertising function.   Indeed, advertising is so relatively unimportant to their operations, there is no reason why they should not.

Oil companies also centralize the control of their advertising for the most part.   The products they sell are related and usually sold by one-brand dealers.   There certainly would be no advantage to them in frittering away their advertising budgets by decentralizing geographically.   Gasoline buyers are a fairly homogeneous lot in the mobile United States and respond to the same advertising appeal in both Maine and California; and the cost of national advertising to oil companies with national distribution is less than the cost of the same effort in local and regional media.

Other companies manufacturing and marketing related products also centralize their advertising.   One of these companies has carried centralization of the advertising function to such an extreme that its advertising department does practically all the work that usually would be performed by an advertising agency.   Apparently this company's agencies do little more than make media recommendations and supply about half the creative work on a few product lines.

Another considers that its advertising is centralized because the title of advertising manager is in the organizational chart of company headquarters.   Administratively, the advertising manager reports to the director of communications.   But divisional marketing vice presidents select their own agencies, and product managers are the principal agency contacts.   In this instance, however, the centralized advertising department has been able to achieve a considerable influence among the divisions and the product managers through services that are valuable in determining creative approaches and selecting media, and in packaging, printing, and product design. This service is extensively patronized by the divisions that market consumer products, so that in the end, the advertising manager's control of advertising, exercised through service, advice, and moral persuasion, justifies a "centralized" classification for the advertising function.

The Era of Centralization

There was a time when practically all advertising was centralized in corporate headquarters organizations.   That may be one reason why it has become so often decentralized in modern corporate operations; centralization is old-fashioned.   The example of centralized governmental bureaucracies certainly is enough to frighten any corporate management into decentralizing.   Fashions, however, have a tendency to be adopted, in the world of business as in the realm of women's clothing, without enough thought being given to whether or not they are appropriate.   Following the fashionable trend, certain corporate functions are sometimes needlessly decentralized, and among these is advertising.   A company's medical service, its legal service, its purchasing, its research and development functions will be kept in the corporate headquarters while advertising, also a professional service, is decentralized.

Some Advantages of Centralization

A centralized advertising function enables a company to bring its maximum potential of advertising skill and talent to bear on advertising problems anywhere in the company.   While there are advertising specialists, most good advertising men are generalists in their field and able to adapt to good advantage a technique developed in the marketing of, say, soap to top off a successful marketing plan for any other consumer product.   Centralization, of course, is not always possible.   For instance, a diversified company with an autonomous operation on the West Coast and another on the East—not unusual in this day of conglomerates—might find it impossible to serve both operations with a single advertising department in its corporate headquarters.

Practically, it has been the experience of many companies that decentralization of advertising should be resisted until it no longer can be deferred.

Centralization is a simpler form of organization, it brings the pulling power of a team to the load of work and responsibility, and it comes closer to assuring that each element enters the marketing mix in a proper proportion.

**COMPROMISES BETWEEN
CENTRALIZATION AND
DECENTRALIZATION**

Many corporate advertising organizations are, of course, compromises between centralization and decentralization.   Some of them seem to work quite well.   Others depend on people and are therefore far from being foolproof.

One of the commonest compromises is based on the Army Corps type of organization of World War II.   Veterans of that war will recall that a corps was a tactical, not an administrative, unit. Divisions were attached to it or detached as the tactical mission of the corps required the presence of more or fewer troops. Administration was contained within the divisions, and the corps staff was concerned only with a division's ability to function as a combat unit. The supply section of the corps staff, for example, did not bother with the actual supply of the troops, but only made sure they had been supplied to an extent that would enable them to function efficiently. It was a critic of the performance of the supply sections of the divisions and a liaison on supply matters between division commanders and the corps commander.

This worked well for the military. It is doubtful that it works as well in business, and for three reasons: first, the critical role of the advertising manager at company headquarters may be resented by subordinate echelons of the business; second, the advertising manager often does not report directly to his "general," the principal executive officer of the business; and third, unless the advertising manager has been promoted to his job after service in a company subdivision, managers of the subdivisions are not likely to feel that he understands their problems well enough to assist in the solution of them.

In this type of organization, the advertising in the subdivisions may be highly centralized. If this is true, it can be assumed that subdivisional advertising is in the hands of experienced managers in the confidence of the marketing management of the subdivision. Practically, there is not much an advertising manager in headquarters can do to assist or direct them; they do not need assistance, and they would balk at direction. Thus the only function remaining to headquarters advertising is not as staff, but as a centralized organization, just like those in the subdivisions, for handling such advertising as cannot be assigned to a subdivision of the company. How important this function is depends on the policies of the company.

Decentralization to Company Subdivisions

A second compromise involves the decentralization of advertising to company subdivisions which further decentralize to brand or market managers. Doubtless there is something a headquarters advertising manager can do in the way of advice on advertising, both to company management and managers of the subdivisions, provided he is an exceptional individual. In this instance management of the company's advertising is so diffused that there is no real management, and the company's advertising agencies become its advertising managers. This is not an uncommon situation, especially in smaller companies with the brand-manager type of marketing organization.

Centralized Control for Major Products

A third common compromise is centralized control for major products, decentralized control for others, and vice versa. In the first instance, this compromise often works quite well, for the centralized control of advertising for major products sets standards and policies for the decentralized advertising so that it has the effect of controlling it, too. The upshot is that for all practical purposes the company's advertising function is centralized. In the second instance, the grouping of products of less importance to be advertised under the control of a centralized advertising organization generally is undertaken because the volume of advertising of each product is so small that separate advertising organizations cannot be justified. The result is an operation similar to complete decentralization of the advertising function.

Effect of Acquisitions

Another compromise is almost universal when a company with centralized advertising control seeks acquisitions. The acquisition continues to operate as a separate entity, and advertising management consequently must be labeled decentralized. This usually is a temporary situation unless the parent organization is a conglomerate. If it is temporary, the parent company may find it profitable to make it so for the shortest possible time; an important step in the development of a company by acquisition is the planning of the organizational structure of the resultant corporation, and this includes, of course, the placement of the advertising function in its operations. Otherwise, there is much and costly duplication of overhead and effort.

Situation among Conglomerates Conglomerates are another matter. These behemoths of business are put together to hedge the risks inherent in operating within a single field of business, or to increase the profitability of surplus capital, or both. In any case, the subsidiaries within the conglomerate are so diverse in their operations and differ so widely in their marketing objectives that there really is not much reason to centralize the advertising function, and advertising's place in the corporate structure should be separately considered for each subsidiary company in the conglomerate.

BRAND MANAGERS AND ADVERTISING MANAGERS

The November 18, 1968, issue of *Advertising Age* reported the results of a study by *Grocery Manufacturer* on the place of brand managers in the marketing of products sold through supermarkets. *Advertising Age's* lead paragraph read: "Product managers are displacing the advertising director at many companies selling through supermarkets." This was based on *Grocery Manufacturer's* report, which was quoted:

> Numerous product managers mentioned that their company no longer had an ad director in the traditional sense. . . .
> The role of the company advertising department or advertising director is mentioned in relatively few instances. Those product managers discussing it are most often with large companies which maintain a corporate advertising service group, mainly concerned with coordinating media buys.

Why Brand Managers in Advertising?

To assign the advertising function to brand managers is a neat and appealing method of settling it within the corporate structure. It eliminates advertising overhead, which pleases the company controller; it eliminates any possibility of friction between marketing and advertising men, which pleases the general management; it adds stature and dignity to the brand manager's company status, which pleases him; and it enables the advertising agency to have a larger finger in the company's advertising, which certainly should please the agency. From an organizational point of view, it presumably makes one man responsible for all aspects of a product's success or failure, though in practice the brand manager has more responsibility than authority so that he rarely has to assume the entire blame for a failure.

The *Grocery Manufacturer* study indicates that the brand-manager system is here to stay, that most marketing managements in the field of foods and home products would not be without it.

Should Brand Managers Direct Advertising?

In the face of such approval of the system, its merit to marketers is beyond question, and the authors of this chapter certainly have no quarrel with it. But they do question the *uniform desirability* of placing the responsibility for advertising in the brand manager's hands.

Brand managers are of necessity generalists of marketing. They are trained to the management of functions and not to the execution of operations within functions. The brand manager, for instance, may suggest, may even demand, changes in the product he manages, but he certainly makes no attempt to direct any specific operation of its manufacture. He calls on functional departments for details of that part of his marketing plan which deals with the specifics of shipping and warehousing. He relies on a sales force to place his product on supermarket shelves and keep it there. He manages.

Lack of Qualifications When, however, it comes to the advertising of his product, he is expected to assume the specific functions of a professional advertising man. This is quite a burden. He rarely has the advertising talent, training, and experience to know first-rate advertising, to sense the strengths and weaknesses of an advertising plan, creative work, a media plan. He does—or should—know how much he can afford to spend on advertising, but not how to budget the expenditure for maximum returns. Usually he is a young man —the *Grocery Manufacturer* study revealed that 57.7 per cent of brand managers are under thirty-five, and about one brand manager in five is under thirty—and in the habit of young men, he either seeks formula solutions to advertising problems to hide his lack of advertising knowledge, or attempts to display his brilliant freedom from the hidebound with bizarre experiments.

Overly Dependent upon Agencies He is almost invariably prone to place too much dependence on the advertising agency with which he works. It is a tribute to the sense of responsibility of most agencies that the brand-manager system has worked as well as it has, for, as pointed out earlier, the agency as a profit-making business is a separate entity from its clients. Agencies have picked up the pieces for literally hundreds of brand managers, have coddled and trained them, and "taught them the way to promotion and pay." But an agency will be inclined to give advertising as much importance as possible in the marketing mix, and this may be too much. To put the shoe on another foot, a cost squeeze on the brand manager may cause him arbitrarily to reduce advertising to a point where it is unable to perform its function; the agency is not within the company, and if it protests too vigorously, some brand managers have the power to end its plaints by changing agencies. The client generally is the loser.

Need for Professional Scrutiny of Advertising When the advertising function is an operation independent from brand management but cooperative with it, approval of advertising plans and materials is generally through advertising channels to the final approving authority in the company. The process gives advertising professional scrutiny until it reaches a single, final authorization, where, it is hoped, professional advertising people can defend their work from personal opinions and the whims of marketing and general management executives. But when approval goes through marketing channels from the brand manager, it must pass through the hands of nonprofessionals who, even when they profess to be completely objective, find it difficult to resist their own advertising likes and dislikes, the feelings of their wives, and even the opinions of their teen-age children. "My wife, I think, is an average housewife" and "my kids are pretty typical" introduce many an advertising criticism. It all starts with the brand manager himself, when his agency first submits its work. Advertising, its planning and execution, when presented by nonprofessionals in the field, is that part of the marketing plan most vulnerable to executive whim.

For these reasons, and no doubt there are others—as, for instance, that advertising supervised by brand managers tends to be imitative, lacking in originality, slavishly fashionable and without style—it would seem that the American business genius would be able to devise an organization that would permit advertising to be as functional as, say, manufacturing. It is believed this could be done in such a way that it would not impair but improve the marketing process.

ADVERTISING AND SALES PROMOTION

There is a growing tendency to separate sales promotion from advertising in company organizations. At times, the separation is so extreme that the two functions almost operate at cross purposes. Each manager goes his way, advertising according to his plan, and sales promotion according to another plan or expediently, as sales may require an injection of promotional activity for revitalization. This sad situation can be expected two years out of three when advertising is centralized, either companywide or within a subdivision, and sales promotion is decentralized, either geographically or to brand managers.

Centralization Recommended

Since the authors of this chapter are both advertising men, it may be suggested that they are biased in favor of combining advertising and sales promotion as a single function. The accusation may be on the mark. On the other hand, both of the authors have had experience in situations in which advertising and sales promotion worked in double harness, and in others in which each was treated as a separate function under different managers. This experience has spanned a good many years, and it indicates very strongly that on an empirical basis most companies will find it profitable to organize advertising and sales promotion as a single activity under a single head.

An exception would be the various kinds of price cutting practiced in the name of sales promotion, especially in supermarkets. But should these be considered promotional? Especially when so many of them are put into effect to resist some form of competitive action, or to adjust a price to maintain a market position, or to shore up a sales slide that might have been caused by too little advertising and genuine sales promotion. Granted that some sort of flexibility in pricing a product is necessary, shouldn't this be provided for in the pricing section of the marketing plan, and provision made for it in the revenue the product is expected to produce? Price adjustment is too continuous and universal to be called promotion.

Case against Combining Advertising and Sales Promotion The different forms of price cutting excepted, the case for combining sales promotion with advertising in the organization of the latter function is a strong one. Nevertheless, there are those who oppose it. One argument they use is that sales promotion serves the special needs of the sales force, with which the advertising department may not be closely connected on a working basis. This actually is no argument at all. Advertising also serves the sales force and packaging and company prestige and the marketing manager's friendliness with the presidents of supermarket chains. And if the advertising people in a company cannot work closely enough with a sales force to understand its needs, the situation is remedied easily enough through the expenditure of reasonable sums for travel expense.

Sales Promotional Materials Specialized A second argument frequently advanced is that sales promotion materials are so specialized their production should be separately handled from the production of advertising materials. Not so, at least not in the experience of the authors. In fact, when men purchase and supervise the production of materials for both advertising and sales promotion, what they learn from one group of suppliers helps them in prodding the other to better service.

Different Theaters of Operation? A third invalid argument is that advertising and sales promotion function in different theaters of operation, but against a common target. They are in fact mutually supporting and operate in a single theater. The armed services long since recognized that all the forces operating in a single theater against a common target should have one commander, and the same principle should apply in marketing.

The argument for combining the two functions is simple and forthright. Advertising and sales promotion generally have the same objectives and frequently use the same appeals. When they are combined, the production of materials for each is better coordinated and occasionally more economical. The one frequently supplements the other, and the more frequently it does, the more effective each becomes. Under one leadership, company organization is simplified, and the competition for expense dollars is eliminated.

RELATIONSHIP BETWEEN CLIENTS AND AGENCIES

Earlier it was stated that advertising's place in a corporate structure could be influenced by the service rendered by advertising agencies to the company.   It is pertinent, therefore, to examine the relationship that exists between agencies and their clients.

What can an agency do?   The answer to that question is that most agencies have the capability of rendering almost any service an advertiser may desire, and that a good many go beyond advertising into the field of marketing.   The extension of these agency services in the fairly recent past has been in part the result of the intense competition among agencies for business and the demands placed on them by their clients.   The supplanting of sales managers by marketing managers is also a fairly recent development in business history.

The agencies, which by and large have a considerable number of bright and alert individuals on their staffs, were quick to accept the marketing gospel, to become missionaries to those of their clients who were a little mystified by the burgeoning new techniques.   This brought the better missionaries more business, not only from new clients but from those whom the agencies already served.   Laggard agencies were forced to expand their services, the number of marketing missionaries multiplied, and the competition for converts increased.   When the change-over to modern marketing practices was complete, advertising expenditures had risen to formidable figures, and agency commissions supported so many activities other than advertising that average agency profits as a percentage of billing began a slide that only lately has been stopped.

Emphasis on Marketing

In their desire to become forces in marketing, some agencies neglected their original purpose, the creation of effective advertising for the mass media, and placed their reliance on massive repetition of a single idea, often one that was not very imaginative to start with. Advertisers, however, sought out so-called marketing agencies, and these so dazzled them with statistical material that consideration of advertising was often concentrated on research, media, and market studies.   This was and is valuable in advertising to a mass market.

Importance of Effective Advertising

Then someone remembered that imaginative, creative advertising messages have an effect on consumer purchases.   Bright, some of them brilliant, writers of advertising, advertising artists, and producers of radio and television commercials within the agencies began to concentrate on that aspect of advertising.   The success of this approach, neglected for some years, was immediate, and the agencies that practiced it most competently began to take business away from competitors with reputations for marketing expertise.   The "creative" agency became the rage.

So, again, a well-rounded agency can render almost any service a marketer reasonably may ask for.   Its equipment to do this is what has made the brand- or market-manager type of marketing operation possible, and the agency service rendered to this type of operation contributes to the elimination of advertising directors mentioned in the study by *Grocery Manufacturer*.

Desirable Scope of Agency Services

In companies in which advertising is still considered as a function of the business, as well as in those which one day may convince themselves it should be, agency service probably should be less comprehensive.   Its practical management of advertising for the brand manager, for example, automatically would be eliminated, and much of the marketing work the agency does no longer would be necessary. Agencies bring to a functional advertising organization the creation of effective advertising, a large order in itself, an ability to make sound recommendations on the selection of media, experience in the scheduling of advertising, cost studies to support an advertising manager's budget requests, and an objective point of view to the consideration of advertising plans and their execution, to say nothing of the extensive record keeping required by a large advertising expenditure. Most managers utilize these agency offerings in their evaluations of corporate advertising objectives, in the making of the advertising plan, and in its implementation.   All this covers a lot of ground.   If the agency's talents are wisely handled by the advertising manager, he receives at least a dollar in service for every dollar of commissions collected by the agency, and sometimes a little more.

Need for Confidence

In the more successful advertiser-agency relationships, the advertiser gives the agency the same confidence it gives to its attorneys.   The advertiser must, within reasonable limits, make the agency privy to its company and marketing objectives.   He should make available to the agency those internal studies that may affect the advertising.   He should provide the agency with an insight into other company functions which affect products and their advertising—research and development, product service, liaison with manufacturing, marketing, the field force, and so on.   He should bring the agency into the planning of his advertising.   And he should have the agency represented when the plan and its implementation are presented to the final authority for approval—some advertisers expect their agencies to participate in such presentations.

Final Responsibility with Advertiser   The agency, however, must remember that final responsibility always is the advertiser's.   It is the advertiser's loss if the advertising is ineffective, and it is the right and the duty of the advertising manager to reject plans and production that in his professional judgment will not be profitable to his company.   Unless the agency is incredibly stupid or the advertising manager is unthinkably capricious, differences of opinion should take place in the early stages of planning, where it is, of course, appropriate to discuss opposing points of view.   These usually are reconciled, but if they cannot be, the agency should resign the account or the advertiser should discharge the agency.   Many of the differences that arise between advertiser and agency result from conflicts between the personalities assigned by each to administer its responsibilities in the association between the two.   Here again, the agency must remember that the advertiser is its employer, and if the agency man working on the account is *persona non grata* to the advertiser, his agency should change him at once.

Compensation of Agencies   It is not within the province of this chapter to discuss the compensation of advertising agencies.   Most advertisers concede that the workman is worthy of his hire, and most agencies are content with a reasonable profit.   Some advertisers contend that the commission system of agency compensation rewards agencies too generously.   Some agencies counter that the commission system is the most practical form of compensation, but it actually pays the agency less than it should.   In some cases each probably is right.

ORGANIZATION FOR SPECIFIC NEEDS

It should go without saying that the advertising function of any given company should be organized to meet its specific needs.   Some companies do it one way, some another.

It may be helpful, however, to review the more usual methods of organizing the advertising function.   Assume that advertising is a function in the cases considered, that all advertising authority has not been delegated to brand managers, and that the advertising people on the payroll give an honest day's work for their inflated dollar.

Organization by Functions

Some companies organize their advertising departments by functions. At the head is an executive manager, an advertising professional whose previous experience in advertising has entitled him to be considered a generalist.   Most of these managers are better in one phase of advertising than another, because it either interests them most or their previous service has involved some specialization in it.   But all of them have been in advertising long enough to have a general knowledge of the trade that is good enough and broad enough to enable them to accept or reject suggestions and advice, and to make decisions affecting all phases of their companies' advertising.   Depending principally on the size of the company, the manager may have an assistant, and if it is at all possible, this man should be in training to become his successor when the manager retires.

U nder the manager, there are six sections, each headed by a specialist hopefully on his way to becoming a generalist.   If advertising is the main sustainer of the company's profit, sections may include any number of subordinate members.   In other companies, the section's head may be its only member.   In still others, one man may head two or more sections.

Importance of Planning   The most important of the sections is planning.   This section maintains close liaison with marketing and attempts to match marketing's forward planning with its own.   Once a plan is approved, the section must be prepared to make prompt changes in it to meet exigencies or take advantage of opportunities. Its forward planning, of course, is under almost continuous review. The section works closely with other sections of the advertising department, leans on them for information and for the preparation of specific portions of the overall advertising plan and the changes in it.   Rather frequently an advertising manager, or his assistant, or both head the planning section in addition to their executive duties.

Section on Budgets   A second section is devoted to budgets.   It is well to have this section headed either by an advertising man who has a talent for accounting or by an accountant who has a talent for advertising. This section assists the planning section in the preparation of advertising plans, assembles the current budget, and keeps up-to-date and accurate estimates of expenditures against the various items of the budget. The section should be prepared to assemble and supply quick and accurate advertising costs to marketers, to maintain liaison with the agencies regarding their expenditures and commitments, and ideally, to supply the manager of the department with a daily or weekly budget status report. It should be in close touch with whatever phase of the company's accounting process is concerned with advertising in the overall company bookkeeping. Because this section of necessity would be concerned with proofs of publication and such, and because its personnel are better trained in the handling of tedious details than most others in advertising, this section probably should be in charge of the advertising archives of the company.

Creative Work A third section specializes in creative work. Most company advertising depends heavily on agencies in this phase of its operations, but agencies cannot produce first-rate creative advertising out of blue sky. This section in the company's advertising department accordingly supplies the agencies with all the information to be found in manufacturing, marketing, research and development, field sales, or any other service that might supply the material to ignite an advertising fire. The head of the section probably will have ideas of his own that he would like to have the agencies implement. The right man at the head of this section can be a source of inspiration to agency creative departments. At the same time, he is required to be the archcritic of their creative work. Preliminary creative plans are submitted to him. He works closely with them in the development of the plans, suggests changes or commends the preparation as the plan advances, reviews the final effort for flaws, and accepts it for further approval. The head of the creative section of the company's advertising department has its most interesting job.

Media Evaluation and Selection Media evaluation and selection is the fourth section. In some companies this section matches planning in importance, for there are advertising economies that can be effected through the purchase of television time, magazine pages, newspaper lines, and the like in bulk, and then apportionment of the purchases to various subsidiaries of the company, divisions, or products. The head of the section must be, therefore, an authority on media, as skilled in its use, and as knowledgeable of the strengths, weaknesses, and costs of different media as the media specialists in his company's advertising agencies. He should be a shrewd negotiator and should have a wide circle of business friends among the different media. The position of section head graduates a good many men to better jobs as advertising managers.

Measurements of Effectiveness The fifth section is devoted to the measurement of advertising effectiveness. A good many companies eliminate this section from their advertising departments and give its responsibilities to marketing research. Others maintain the section headed by a man who usually depends on company research facilities, independent research organizations, and the research departments of the advertising agencies for the performance of needed research. When research results are in the hands of the section head, he should be equipped to interpret them to the advertising manager, to other section heads, and to marketing and other company executives. In the course of his work, he can be of material value to the department through the pretesting of creative work, by determining, to some extent at least, whether a marketing failure was due to advertising or other causes, by tests of the effectiveness of different media, and so on. If he is a first-rate man for the job, his line of promotion probably should be through one or another of the company's research facilities and not in the advertising department, but not always. This is one reason why the section is not always present in advertising departments. In such cases, however, marketing research generally assigns a man especially to advertising research, and this man works so closely with advertising as to make him, in effect, a section head.

Sales Promotion Section Finally, there is the sales promotion section. This section does the planning for sales promotion activities, supervises the creative work involved, attends to the distribution of materials—in short, renders an overall promotional service. Its planning is integrated with the advertising plan, and so is its budget; and its creative work generally, but not always, is based on the creative development of the advertising. The section head works closely with the marketers, and through them with field sales.

Organization by Projects, Products, Markets, Media

Other forms of advertising department organization are by projects, products, markets, and media.   In the first instance, the section heads are project managers, and each combines such advertising functions as are necessary within his section.   Though one section may handle several different projects, this type of organization seems to be a little cumbersome, and it must surely give rise to duplication of manpower, as project managers tend to build small advertising departments of their own within the advertising department, a symptom of developing bureaucracy.   There is no reason why the advertising for any company project or product cannot be handled through the functional sections first described.

Organization by media, however, works quite well in companies that principally market related products through outlets that are more or less controlled.   Usually the media are broadly defined as electronic, print, or outdoor, and the section heads are generalists in those fields.   Planning becomes a joint undertaking, with the chief responsibility for it in the hands of the department manager.   His staff also includes the persons who manage the budget, some of whose responsibilities in a functional organization are assumed by the media section.   In this case, sales promotion usually is treated as a single medium, and so are the different media addressed to industrial consumers.

When a Functional Organization Is Desirable

When the advertising function of a company is centralized, a functional organization of the single advertising department obviously is desirable.   This also applies to the centralized advertising departments of decentralized divisions and subsidiaries.   But in the latter case, a somewhat simpler organization is indicated for the headquarters advertising department.   The best which turned up in the study of large corporations is the one that resembles the military's special staff sections, previously described.

When a company's marketing department utilizes the brand- or market-manager type of marketing organization, the functionally organized advertising department must work closely with the different brand managers.   This can be done in any of several ways.   One is to establish assistant advertising managers to handle the advertising of one or more products. All these assistants utilize the functional sections of the advertising departments as need arises. The assistants work as closely with the brand managers as their chief does with marketing management.

CENTRALIZED OPERATION RECOMMENDED

All evidence leads to one conclusion: Except when a company is a conglomerate, advertising best serves it when maintained as a centralized, functional operation. If this is done, most of the problems connected with the placement of advertising in the corporate structure tend to solve themselves.

Advertising must be centralized in fact as well as on organizational charts. Some companies consider their advertising centralized simply because their advertising departments are shown on organizational charts as separate boxes reporting directly to marketing or executive management, when actually the advertising is decentralized to the control of brand or market managers. In spite of the praise heaped on this system of marketing organization in the *Grocery Manufacturer* survey, the same study revealed that brand-manager control of advertising was a weakness. In such companies, centralization of advertising control in the hands of a functional advertising department will enhance the efficiency and economy of the company's advertising effort.

Improved Efficiency from Centralization

Companies that have decentralized their advertising to divisions and subsidiaries as they have decentralized their other operations will have the same experience of improved efficiency if they recover control of advertising to a centralized advertising management. Under decentralized management, it is a common experience that advertising performance among subordinate echelons of the company is spotty; with a return to centralized control of advertising, the quality of the advertising tends to become uniform at the highest existing level.

A centralized, functional advertising organization adapts more readily to the changing needs of the company. It quickly assimilates the advertising organizations of acquisitions, and insofar as advertising is concerned, it shortens the period of adjustment when two or more companies merge their operations. A centralized, functional advertising department will enable a company to arrive at a more rational, mutually profitable relationship with its advertising agencies if for no other reason than because professionals work more productively together.

This chapter has avoided a presentation of organizational charts, and it is not appropriate to present one here. There is no really fixed way to represent in one chart a centralized, functional advertising organization that will meet the needs of the thousands of corporations that find advertising a profitable endeavor.

Two Simple Rules   There are, however, two simple rules to follow:

1. Advertising management in the top echelon of company management must have both responsibility and authority.

2. Professional advertising people must handle all the company's advertising at all levels and look to advertising management in the top echelon for recognition and promotion.

If a company's advertising organization meets those two criteria, it *is* centralized and it *is* functional.

CHAPTER FOUR

Structure and Functions of the Advertising Department

M. E. ZIEGENHAGEN *Director of Advertising and Public Relations, The Babcock & Wilcox Company*

Where should we position advertising in our company and how should we organize it?

This question is being asked by a growing number of chief executive officers and top marketing men today, and the reason is clear. They are experiencing advertising problems and inefficiencies that no longer respond to conventional treatment: hiring a hot new agency or injecting new faces in the advertising department lends hope for a time, but when the dust has settled the same old problems and the same inefficiencies are often there, framed against a background of rising marketing costs.

A Liggett & Myers marketing executive, speaking to an audience of advertising and marketing executives a few years ago, asked, "Would you believe that the marketing problems which many companies are now experiencing might stem not from people but from *the way that management has the people working?*"

In the light of studies made since then, his insight looks increasingly sound. In particular, we find compelling evidence that the primary problems of advertising are rooted in the basic plan by which companies handle the work of advertising.

"The plan for handling the work" is, of course, one of the simplest definitions of organization. But advertising organization—the plan for handling the work of advertising—is anything but simple today. Advertising work is no longer a sideline specialty handled mainly by the advertising department and the agency. As advertising has grown in importance it has received a growing work input from sales, product, and brand managers; from marketing heads, from general managers and top management, and from many others in engineering, manufacturing, and finance who often play a part in the approval and budgeting of advertising.

Getting this growing band of persons—including some who have little feeling for advertising—to team together on the delicate job of turning out consistently effective advertisements or commercials is a challenge that relatively few companies meet. Surprisingly, the challenge has evoked relatively little organized thought and effort, despite signs that growing organization problems are canceling much of the nation's growing investment of advertising dollars and advertising creativity.

FOCUS OF THE PROBLEM: THE LARGE, MULTIDIVISION COMPANY

Large multidivision companies have the lion's share of knotty advertising organization problems today and the most to gain by applying the principles and practices covered in this chapter.

At the same time, other companies, including smaller, nondivisionalized firms, will find that most of the problems discussed here apply equally well to them, and that the problems which are not yet acute will become so as their companies grow, acquire more divisions, decentralize, or possibly merge with a multidivision company. In short, these other companies have much to gain by anticipating and avoiding serious problems around the bend.

The studies on which this chapter is based [1] emphasize that the big

[1] Including the continuing Advertising/Marketing Organization Study conducted by the Association of National Advertisers, which involves a sample base of 250 companies manufacturing industrial products (35 per cent); consumer durable

opportunities for improving marketing communications are not concentrated in the consumer-product companies in which advertising is obviously such a big factor in corporate success.   Instead, the opportunities are widespread.   Most large multidivision industrial-product companies—especially those that have products and markets that are reasonably kindred—can usually benefit just as much as the company selling toothpaste, toasters, or biscuits.   They can do so because they are usually able to implement more of the principles and practices that follow in this chapter and extend them to a much broader range of marketing and corporate communications.

**Root of the Problem: Marketing
Fragmentation**

The chief executive can often trace his most serious advertising problems to a series of vital, and successful, operating decisions which he or his predecessors made in the preceding decade or so: decisions to add products and grow, to acquire, diversify, divisionalize, decentralize, and then continue diversifying.

In this process, he necessarily transferred much of the direct responsibility for line marketing (and with it, advertising) from headquarters to his division heads.   As their individual operations grew, they usually were forced to delegate much of it to marketing managers who, in turn, delegated part of it to product or brand managers.

For companies with a swelling list of products and markets, this fragmentation of the overall marketing effort has usually given it increased vitality, flexibility, and effectiveness.   Clearly, more managers are needed at lower levels to get the company to grasp the many marketing programs and the increasing complexity of modern marketing.

But what about the advertising sector of marketing?   The record indicates that, to date, it has not proved nearly so adaptable to decentralization and fragmentation as have other marketing functions. Where line marketing has matured, it is true that advertising, along with other marketing functions, has received better marketing direc-

---

goods (15 per cent); consumer softgoods (6 per cent); consumer packaged goods (28 per cent); services (11 per cent); and others (5 per cent).

Other major conclusions are based in part on a penetrating study made for ANA by Booz, Allen & Hamilton, Inc.   This involved interviews with 190 executives of 73 advertisers, 16 agencies, and 15 other organizations.   See ANA's book, "Management and Advertising Problems."

tion, better decisions on what marketing objectives to pursue, what products to promote to what market, and what to spend on each program.   More often than not, this important gain in *direction* has been largely offset by losses in the follow-through stages of advertising *execution,* that is, in the delicate and increasingly complex process of determining *how to say it.*

The problem plainly hinges on the difficulty of transferring responsibility for the creative execution of advertising from a few individuals to many.   Because of this difficulty, relatively few companies have found a way to fragment their advertising activity and still retain for top management a businesslike control of its quality and effectiveness.

The Main Symptom: Spotty Advertising

In the multidivision company (and, most obviously, the conglomerate) the dominant symptom of advertising organization problems is the spotty quality of advertising done for the various divisions and subsidiaries.

This is emphasized today by the fact that some of it is top-notch, usually better than anything done in the past.   Most of it, however, has to be labeled run-of-the-mill, a trail of wasted opportunities to the professionals who turn out the top programs.   A part of it is usually so mediocre that even the unhappy agency that turned it out will privately agree that it is probably wasteful.

Thus, when the marketing-minded chief executive officer and his associates go to the conference room for that periodic review of company-wide advertising, they witness a growing quality-control problem that would set off no end of alarms on the production line.   Frequently, it sets off an explosion in the conference room too.   Too often, nothing comes of it because the responsibility for advertising effectiveness is so widely diffused that top management, and even top marketing management, has lost control of it.

In companies that are marketing leaders, the chief executive is weary of being told he needs advertising; he knows it.   He is wary of those who continually tell him, with a commissionable glint in the eye, that he needs more of it; he knows that *better* advertising could obviate the need for more.   He stands ready, however, to welcome and reward the rare marketing man, advertising manager, agency head, or management consultant who can tell him what he needs to do to get strong, professional advertising for *all* his divisions, to support *all* his major marketing opportunities.

Conventional Advertising Wisdom No Longer Holds

What, he asks, does it take to upgrade the bottom 80 per cent of that advertising and boost the return on the large investment it represents?

Quick answers and conventional wisdom no longer help him very much. Advertising, he is reminded, is a "people business." A creative-people business. If he wants top-notch advertising right across the board, he must have top-notch creative people in all his agencies and, it is hoped, in his headquarters and division advertising staffs. To the degree that he fails to procure the needed creative personnel, his company-wide advertising display on the conference-room wall will contain large patches of mediocrity.

Why, he asks, do those same advertising people who made such a big splash for another division, or another company, create scarcely a ripple when they take on some of his divisions that most need help in advertising and marketing? Indeed, why do some of them with the best records even decline at times to tackle some of his toughest problems?

If he will follow through on these questions, the chances are that he will head directly into the subject of advertising organization, into the way that management has the advertising personnel, the product and brand managers, and all the others working on the process of planning and creating his advertising programs.

GUIDELINES FOR EFFECTIVENESS

He will find, too, that there are ways in which he can provide a relatively small group of creative persons with the leverage needed to improve that bottom 80 per cent of his division advertising.

The eleven guide rules that follow are those that others have used most effectively to do that.

1. Put Your Advertising Organization Plan in Writing This is the first decision to make. Doing so permits you to get the plan endorsed by the chief executive officer and distributed by him to all those who play a key role in funding, planning, approving, and creating advertising.

Without this step, and without continuing top-level interest and support, the record shows that the best advertising organization plan is soon pulled out of shape, and the work of the best advertising personnel is watered down.

Decide, too, right at the start, that your company advertising plan will go beyond the general objectives, the organization charts, and the all-purpose position guides that so often pass for a plan. To work, your plan must face the sensitive questions of basic responsibility that today are usually swept under the rug with the explanation that it is better to "play it loose" and leave these things to "collaboration." The collaborators are very apt to produce unhappy compromises if you do not make it clear who sets the marketing direction the advertising is to follow, who is responsible for executing the advertising and approving it and who has the last word in the hiring of a new advertising agency.

The remaining guide rules that follow are intended to help you write this plan. They deal with basic factors in the order in which most companies will want to consider them.

2. Nail Down the Major Advertising Objectives These objectives must provide a clear written understanding of what you are organizing to do. This most obvious of needs is the most overlooked.

Naturally, these objectives will often be framed at lower levels, but in their final approved form, they should reflect the considered advertising needs of the company as seen by the chief executive officer. Then, they are most apt to provide not only for the needs of the individual operating divisions, but also for company front advertising or marketing programs he considers vital, and for coordination of advertising with other company communications programs.

For example, the president of one integrated, multidivision company with a wide range of kindred products and markets established this relatively ambitious priority of needs:

a. Provide highly effective skills for improving the advertising programs of all divisions.

b. Integrate advertising fully with the marketing of individual products of the divisions.

c. Establish effective cross-division or company-wide advertising programs to support marketing programs in which a group of related products from various divisions are promoted as a group to common markets.

d. Coordinate product advertising of the divisions with other related communication programs (such as corporate advertising and public relations programs) whenever this will increase the combined impact and lower the overall cost of these programs.

Why, some ask, is it necessary to formalize objectives such as *a* and *b?* Surely, everyone in a multidivision company would agree and work for them. The reason for emphasizing them is painfully clear to anyone who, over the years, has grappled with the realities of providing *both* of these requirements. One finds these two "obvious" needs to be largely in conflict if he adopts one of the more common methods of positioning and organizing advertising in a multidivision company. For this reason, much of the advertising of multidivision companies is apt to be weak on either marketing integration or on creative technique, or both. For this reason, keeping both of these basic objectives up front and center, on paper, provides a healthy stimulus to innovate and to adapt the advertising organization in ways that will fill both needs in good measure. It is even more important to do so when other objectives such as *c* and *d* are added.

3. Position and Structure the Advertising Department To Achieve Top-management Objectives When should the product advertising activity be centralized in a multidivision company? When should it be decentralized? How can you strike the balance that best fills your specific needs?

Usually, the man who organizes the overall marketing operation has a quick and simple answer: Advertising, an integral part of marketing, should be centralized or decentralized to the same degree and in much the same way as marketing. How else, he reasons, can we hold the operating divisions in a multidivision company responsible for overall results and for profit?

This quick answer sounds logical and is usually adopted because it is the simplest way to decide the matter in a decentralized multidivision company. Nevertheless, it should be questioned by the executive who is intent on increasing the effectiveness of his overall advertising investment. By investing some extra thought and effort, a knowledgeable task group can usually come up with a better solution.

A good first step for the task group is to fill out a table like the one shown in Figure 1.   If its members have an intimate grasp of the sensitive advertising process and of the marketing operation in an operating division, they will be able to evaluate the relative advantages of centralization and decentralization *in terms of the company's specific marketing and advertising needs.*[2]

Centralize—or decentralize?

Company Needs	Importance (BASIS: 10)	Centralize	Decentralize
▪ Provide effective advertising skills	10	9	5
▪ Integrate advertising with marketing of individual products	10	4	8
▪ Initiate multi-division advertising to common markets	6	8	4
▪ Coordinate advertising with other communications (as PR)	5	8	5

Figure 1 Chart for evaluating centralization versus decentralization in terms of the campaign's specific marketing and advertising needs.   Same method is useful for determining positioning of advertising function in headquarters or division organization, and how it should be structured.

The needs at the left of the chart, you will note, are those of the integrated multidivision company mentioned above.   The "scores" for centralization and decentralization, in the two right-hand columns, were agreed on by a task force in the same company at the start of its study of the advertising organization.

[2] Because there are so many degrees of advertising decentralization, it is helpful to agree on fairly precise definitions such as these:
A centralized advertising activity is located at or directed by corporate head-

In arriving at the scores, the task force was influenced by past experience in their own companies and in other companies it studied. This told them that a centralized advertising department has a clear advantage in providing effective advertising skills, in handling multidivision or corporate advertising, and in coordinating advertising with other communications programs such as public relations. It also told them, however, that it usually had difficulty in integrating advertising programs with individual division marketing programs as effectively as a decentralized advertising organization.

Filling out this chart will seldom point out any sure answers, but it can reveal the major problems and opportunities. In this case, it showed the task force that they were unlikely to fill their basic advertising needs if they followed any of the conventional patterns for centralizing or decentralizing the advertising function. This, in turn, caused them to break trail later on in developing a sound blend of centralization and decentralization, one that in actual experience is now scoring high on all four of the advertising objectives set forth by the chief executive officer. They did this by implementing a number of the basic principles and practices discussed later in this chapter.

OTHER ALTERNATIVES. After determining the degree of centralization or decentralization needed, we must decide where the advertising function can best be positioned in the headquarters or division organization, and how it should be structured.

Although there is no end of possible variations of the most common methods illustrated in Figures 2 to 7, a task force having a good feeling for both advertising and overall marketing can narrow the alternatives quickly and logically by following the same basic discipline described above, that is, by matching the various alternatives against

---

quarters, reporting to a corporate sales or marketing head or to others in top management. In operation, it gets the necessary product, market, and budget information (the "what") from the divisions it serves, and then controls the execution of the various programs (the "how") by (1) providing the needed information and guidance to the advertising agency and other services; and (2) then reviewing and approving the completed work before getting division approval.

A decentralized advertising activity has individual units located in each major division, usually reporting to a division head or to a division marketing or sales head. The division advertising, sales, and marketing people control both the "what" and the "how" of the advertising job, getting only advice and counsel, plus miscellaneous services from a central advertising function.

the company's established advertising objectives. In this chapter, we can include only a few of the most helpful insights:

a. Don't be unduly influenced by what other companies do. To date, few have given their advertising organization the study it deserves, so copying even the leaders in your field can put you far be-

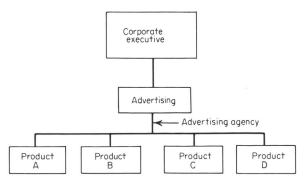

Figure 2 Centralized advertising department organized by product or market.

hind where you would be if you wisely organized to fill *your* specific needs.

b. Frequently, you can best fill your needs by combining the advantages of two alternative methods, and taking specific steps to

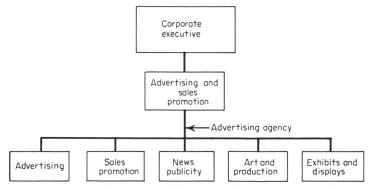

Figure 3 Centralized advertising and sales promotion, department organized by advertising subfunction.

overcome the inherent disadvantages of each.   The guide rules that follow will help you do this.

c. When the marketing organization is organized by product or by market, the product advertising activity should usually be structured in the same way to integrate best the advertising and marketing effort.   However, when the marketing organization is structured by function (sales, service, product planning), it does not follow that advertising should be organized by advertising subfunction (Figure 3).

d. Organization by advertising subfunction is most feasible in companies marketing basic materials or services which do not require the advertising men to acquire deep knowledge of a wide range of products and complex applications.   Frequently, supporting functional units attached to a product- or market-type organization (Figure 4) provide the best balance.   In general, going to a basic product-

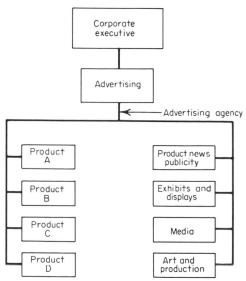

Figure 4   Centralized advertising department organized by product, with supporting functional units.

or market-type advertising organization offers these advantages over a functional organization:

1. It minimizes the functional fences between advertising subfunctions and simplifies development of unified programs.

2. It helps develop marketing-minded advertising men who talk the language of the product and marketing managers, work with them more effectively, and become better prepared for higher marketing responsibilities within the company.

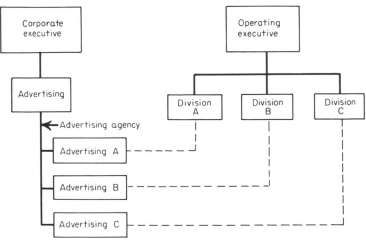

Figure 5 Centralized advertising department with responsibility for advertising *execution* (the "how"), serving line divisions with responsibility for providing marketing *direction* for advertising (the "what").

4. Make Sure That Advertising Gets Sound Marketing Direction It is helpful when everyone concerned with advertising thinks of the direction setting ("what") and the execution ("how") parts of advertising as the first and second halves of a single process. This is a healthy reminder that a poor job on the direction-setting first half of the process assures poor advertising results regardless of the dollars, zeal, and creativity poured into the creation of the advertising program.

This helps to flag the unfortunate fact that, at all levels in the company, attention is apt to be focused primarily on the more exciting, ever-changing second half, the final execution. Too little thought and effort go into the fact-getting and painful decision making that must often precede it. Consequently, the advertising, even though bright, creative, and provocative, often runs like a loose pulley on a shaft.

Although many marketing heads are well aware of this, it is safe to say that providing sound, clear-cut marketing direction is seldom done well unless a marketing-minded top management insists on firm practices for doing the job thoroughly.

The written marketing plan—approved and supported by division management and in line with corporate-level plans—is far and away the most effective management tool for giving sound direction to advertising and to all other marketing functions as well.

Written marketing plans capable of doing this are still relatively uncommon, as any candid survey of advertising and marketing men will quickly reveal. This is true despite all the emphasis on modern marketing since the early 1950s, and despite broad agreement that a sound written marketing plan is the key to its implementation.

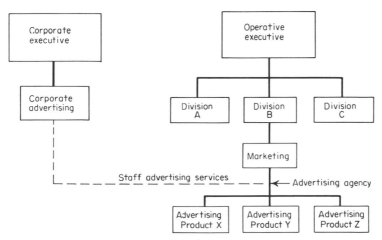

Figure 6 Decentralized advertising department organized by product, with corporate advertising unit providing media services and staff counsel.

Actually, many of these companies have in the past made an earnest effort to initiate written marketing plans for all major programs, only to have the effort bog down. The trouble, it seems, is that they tried to go too far in a single leap. Their people were not ready for the fact-getting and planning disciplines that are required. The plans were bulky but inadequate, division management did not use them as a plan of action, and the whole effort was, in many cases, talked into disrepute.

With this in mind, the following method is suggested for the many companies who desire but still do not have adequate written marketing plans, and whose advertising (along with other marketing functions) still suffers for lack of unified direction. Many companies have used this method to develop written marketing plans in a logical transition.

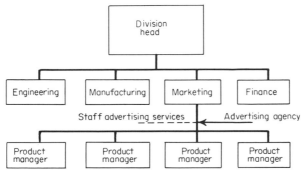

Figure 7 Fully decentralized advertising department in which responsibility for both direction and execution of advertising is delegated to marketing head and to individual product managers.

a. Move first to a plan that provides sound marketing direction for product advertising. A *real* marketing plan—like *real* marketing itself—has two main parts:

1. *An analysis of the problem* that provides a basis of fact for major conclusions and marketing objectives.

2. *A plan of action* that calls for integrated teamwork of *all* functions involved. It tells who is in charge, who does what and when to achieve the established marketing objectives.

The follow-through plan of action is, of course, the payoff part of modern marketing and of corporate-level planning as well. It is also the point at which marketing planning and corporate-level plans often stumble. The great majority of organizations that meet difficulty or defeat in trying to go all the way in one step may well consider a preliminary step that takes them well past the midway point. This is to prepare what some companies call a *marketing audit* for advertising and sales promotion alone. The first part includes, necessarily, the same analysis of the problem needed for a complete marketing plan.   The plan of action, however, is limited *initially* to the plan of action for advertising and sales promotion.

   b. Upgrade the marketing audit into a real marketing plan. This marketing audit will provide sound marketing direction for advertising.   It will also give all the operating people who are exposed to it some feeling of what a full marketing plan could do for them.   The first part of the marketing audit—the analysis of the overall marketing problem, basic conclusions, and resulting marketing objectives—is naturally useful for the other marketing functions, and adds some degree of marketing coordination.

   However, its inadequacy as a real marketing plan stands out. Missing is the follow-through plan of action for functions other than advertising.   Why do all that work for advertising alone?   Why not include *our* plan of action too?   At this point, a marketing-minded management can fan this dissatisfaction into positive action that adds the plan of action for all major functions, plus clear-cut management responsibility for carrying out the entire plan.

   Why should management use the *advertising* plan in this way to spearhead full marketing planning?   Actual experience offers two reasons:

   1. In many companies, the annual advertising plan is usually the best (or only) annual written plan in the area of marketing.   Advertising men, by necessity, are familiar with planning techniques.

   2. The discipline of planning to communicate publicly with customers and prospects creates an ideal climate and a sharp needle for digging up available marketing facts and initiating marketing research to get what is not then available.

   For this reason, a team of marketing-minded advertising and line marketing people can usually do the best job of annually updating the first part of a marketing plan, that is, analyzing the overall marketing problem, arriving at conclusions, and setting objectives. What's more, this job, very costly if done separately, gets done at little cost as a natural by-product of the advertising process.   It provides, each year, a stimulus for division management to add the follow-through plan of action for all functions and create a real marketing plan.

   5. Organize to Attract, Encourage, and Protect Creativity To do this, we return again to one of the most practical organizing concepts of advertising, the allocation of advertising responsibility into the direction-setting "what" of the product or marketing manager and the functional or creative "how" of the advertising man.

While most top executives and marketing managers readily support the *concept* of dividing advertising responsibility in this way, few of them ever do what it takes to go from the concept to the actual *practice* of it. Firming the responsibility at the "what"-"how" line, they fear, will introduce human problems and further diffuse advertising responsibility. Even the advertising men often hesitate to push for it, apparently feeling that the marketing trend of the past decade—in which many of them have lost control of the "how"—has gone too far to arrest, and that, despite the spotty advertising, they are no longer in a position to bell the cat.

For these reasons, the understanding and personal support of the chief executive is usually essential to implement this sound principle of advertising organization. And he, along with his marketing people, has a compelling reason to do so: all signs indicate that those companies that have really taken the step have almost always been able to upgrade the quality of their advertising throughout their various divisions and to boost the return on their advertising investment. In implementing the concept, he can draw on a sound rationale and on specific practices that leading companies have used successfully.

THE RATIONALE. Men who excel in making the hard "what" decisions in marketing and in other functions of a business usually come from a different mold than those who excel in making the "how" or creative decisions in advertising. The record throughout industry indicates that relatively few can make both types of decisions without turning in a mediocre performance in one area or the other.

How about the product or brand managers who are making an important contribution in many consumer-product companies? To an increasing degree, they and their marketing managers work directly with the advertising agency and give the final stamp of approval to both the "what" and the "how" of their advertising. Do they not disprove the above rationale, and perhaps point the way for the successful integration of advertising within the line marketing organization throughout all industry?

Would that they did and could! For then the advertising organization problems of the multidivision company would be far simpler. But we must note that the product manager's direction of advertising "how" is, increasingly, being questioned. And we must also note that the product or brand managers who wear both "what" and the "how" hats successfully are usually in companies that a management consultant is apt to classify as "advertising companies" insofar as advertising is a prime factor in their marketing success. Consequently, advertising is the major part of the job—the part in which they have the most clear-cut responsibility and authority. Indeed, some of those who wear both hats successfully are marketing-minded former advertising men recruited from the company advertising department or the agency—men who have a good feeling for advertising quality themselves and who know how to give adequate rein to a capable creative agency. Their other marketing duties are mainly as a coordinator of functions over which others exercise line responsibility. As product managers, they are primarily advertising men, and they are as much the exception as the product manager in a science-oriented company selling complex equipment for space exploration, who is apt to be 95 per cent engineer.

The great bulk of product managers through industry have heavy responsibilities other than advertising, with experience and aptitudes to match. The growing problems of advertising organization in multidivision companies attest to the fact that they cannot successfully wear both the "what" and the "how" hats of advertising.

THE SUCCESSFUL PRACTICES. Following are the insights and practices that characterize the thinking of companies that have successfully implemented (or reestablished) the "what" and "how" division of labor between product managers and advertising men:

a. Management takes positive steps to make sure that the product manager and the advertising man both share a clear understanding of their "what" and "how" responsibilities. The "what" and "how" line is drawn at different points in different companies, but it is drawn clearly and in writing, as in this excerpt from the advertising plan of one company:

> The product manager is responsible for providing sound marketing direction for advertising programs. He develops the marketing plan for management approval. He decides *what* products are to be promoted to *what* markets within the framework of corporate-level plans; *what* the marketing objectives are, and *what* communication goals will

best help to realize them. With management approval, he decides *what* will be spent to help attain the communication goals.

The advertising manager is responsible for the functional decisions which determine *how* the communications goals are to be achieved. Typically, he decides on the creative strategy and the advertising techniques to be used. He decides on the specific advertising media to be used. After consulting with division marketing management, he decides on the agency that is to do the creative work for him.

b. The advertising–product manager relationship thrives on a healthy exchange of *ideas* and *counsel* that flow freely to and fro across that "what" and "how" line of responsibility. Product managers and others develop and express strong opinions on the creative aspects of their advertising. Advertising men do the same for the marketing goals and marketing strategy of product managers. Both frequently sell ideas that take root and succeed far outside their area of authority. But both know that they are free to reject advice that falls in their specific areas of responsibility.

c. In practice, the "what" and "how" organizing concept works to develop superior strength in both areas. Strong, creative advertising men are attracted to the advertising department and to the agency. At the same time, top-management insistence on superior performance in the "what" area of marketing develops marketing men who provide better direction not only for advertising but also for other marketing functions.

6. Use the Advertising Agency for All the Work It Can Do Best—without Relinquishing Self-sufficiency in Providing Marketing Direction An ANA study conducted by Booz, Allen & Hamilton shows that the agency services used by leading United States marketers extend across this entire range:

1. Advertising only

2. Advertising and selected services in areas such as sales promotion and marketing research

3. Advertising and other selected services plus marketing counsel in areas such as product and marketing planning

4. Advertising and other selected services, plus important marketing contributions that make the agency a marketing partner and sometimes enable it to exercise marketing leadership

What are the guidelines to follow in seeking the right level of agency services?

SELECTING THE RIGHT AGENCY.   As the ANA study points out, nearly every leading marketer agrees that agencies can create better advertisements than marketers can.   The advertising agency, they say, can provide creative skills and specialized services that a company cannot match economically.   In truth, many companies could not match the agency contribution at any price, because they cannot maintain the objectivity provided by a strong, creative agency that is not *too* dependent on the client.   Objectivity, the lifeblood of good communications is very hard to maintain within most company hierarchies, and this is the main reason why the advertising agency is such a durable institution.   A prime organizing principle in most leading marketing organizations is to preserve and use this objectivity of the outside agency in the creation of advertising and in other areas of marketing in which the agency has competence.

In what other areas, beyond advertising, should you expect your agency to contribute?

Prudence dictates that a company remain self-sufficient in those marketing functions, such as marketing planning, that are vital to its survival.   But many alert companies with strong agencies do not hesitate to draw on the agency for help even in marketing planning when this will speed the day when the company is more self-sufficient in that area.   As they develop new products and diversify, these companies frequently find themselves with a product or market with which they are relatively unfamiliar.   Short-term outside help in marketing planning, from an agency or marketing consultant that knows the market, is then needed to get the product off the ground and also to speed the day when the company has adequate in-house marketing leadership.

7. Reduce the Advertising Approval Line to the Minimum—Preferably to an Advertising Approval Point   Top management does not normally consider the process of approval of advertising to be a part of the advertising "organization."   Yet, organization is "the plan for doing the work"—*all* the work.   The advertising approval process is a critically important part of the work of advertising, one in which needed improvements must be supported by top management.

The approval of print advertisement or commercial is usually a drawn-out process involving eight or nine persons, frequently a dozen or more.   Moreover, it is usually carried out in a way that saps much of the potential effectiveness of the advertising submitted.   This is a needless waste which many alert companies are taking steps to eliminate.

The steps they take to do this usually take them from the first toward the third of the three methods described below.

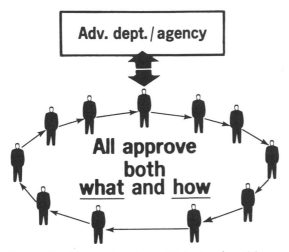

Figure 8   Conventional, inefficient advertising approval line in which approvers judge both "what" and "how."

Method 1
1. Long approval line
2. Approvers judge both
"what" and "how"

This, unfortunately, is by far the most common method.   The advertisement goes for approval to a long line of individuals.   Because they have received no clear guidelines on the contribution they are expected to make, the changes they request cover the "how" (creative execution) as well as the "what" (marketing direction).   Changes are numerous, and many are harmful.

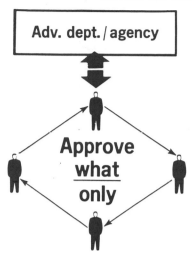

Figure 9 Simplified approval process in which the approval line is shortened and approvers make suggestions on all aspects of advertising, but are directed to make changes only on matters affecting marketing direction, content, and accuracy.

Method 2
1. Short approval line
2. Approvers concentrate on the "what" factors (marketing direction)

Here, management has initiated two important changes which simplify the approval process and eliminate much of the harmful effect of method 1:

a. They have limited the approval line to relatively few persons who are most directly concerned with advertising and are most able to direct it.

b. They have taken pains to set up a clear guideline, based on that handy organizing principle involving the "what" and "how" responsibilities for advertising. The marketing men and general management people in the approval line, while encouraged to make suggestions on all aspects of the advertisement, are directed to make changes only on matters involving marketing direction, content, and accuracy. As a result, suggestions involving creative strategy and techniques are referred back to the advertising people.

When this method is used, the approval line contributes far more than it takes away from the advertising. More (but not all) good advertising comes through the approval line intact.

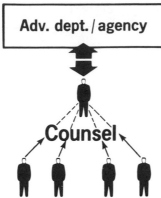

One point contact in marketing approves <u>what</u>

Figure 10 Ideal approval process using an approval *point* rather than a line. One man approves advertising after getting counsel on advertising "what" from those he feels can contribute.

Method 3
1. Approval *point* replaces
the approval line.
2. Approvers concentrate
on the "what" (marketing
direction)

Here, management makes another advance by pinpointing further the direct responsibility for the "what" and the "how" of the advertising under review.

It does this by establishing a one-point contact for all advertising approvals in each area—a man known to have a good grasp of the overall marketing situation and a good grasp of advertising as well.

One company which employs this method most successfully describes the role of the one-point approval contact in this way:

> He approves all advertising and sales promotion for his marketing area, drawing on (1) his own good grasp of the products, markets, and organization, and also on (2) expert counsel which he solicits from as many as he feels necessary.
>
> He weighs all requests and suggestions carefully, but does not seek to

get the exact wording and layout approved by all who provide counsel.   Instead, he makes sure that they agree the advertising is in accord with the established marketing and advertising strategy.   He asks them to check the basic content and accuracy of the advertising, and to check special matters in areas such as sales and distributor policy.   He then has the knowledge, the self-reliance, and the authority to settle on the final version in collaboration with the advertising people.

Thus, he is held directly responsible for providing sound marketing direction for the advertising while the advertising manager is directly responsible for communicating the sales message effectively.

AUTHORITY IN A SINGLE INDIVIDUAL.   Most advertising and marketing men have apparently accepted long advertising approval lines as inevitable.   While applauding the principles behind methods 2 and 3, they feel that those who try to implement them are dreaming. However, actual experience shows they can be implemented and work splendidly—provided top management is interested enough to support the governing principles and the advertising people are firm enough in applying them.

In his excellent series entitled "The Management of the Marketing Function," marketing consultant Clarence Eldredge endorses this general thinking, and adds a vital point when he states that "nothing would make a greater contribution to advertising creativity than to scrap the multi-approval process and delegate to a single individual the authority to approve advertising, *provided* always [and this he underscores] that the basic advertising and marketing strategy has been formally approved by the marketing director and general manager."

Eldredge reminds us that there is a precondition for effective, streamlined approval methods: firm, clear marketing direction. Long approval lines and continuing revisions of advertising programs usually reflect indecision on basic marketing and advertising strategies that should have been settled long before.   Short, effective approval lines, or one-man approval points, are a blessing available to heads-up marketing groups who think through their marketing and advertising strategies, put them on paper, and make them known in advance to those who would otherwise be in a long approval line.

8. Combine the Advertising and Sales Promotion Functions whenever They Require the Same Basic Skills and Source Material   Should advertising and sales promotion be combined or should they be separate functions in your company? The answer depends on what the term "sales promotion" means to you. However, there is a good guide rule that can be used by any company: Combine the two functions whenever the actual preparation of advertising and sales promotion material requires the same basic skills and source material.

In some packaged-goods companies, for example, sales promotion consists mainly of "promotions" such as off-label deals that are little more than price reductions; give-away promotions or contests that offer special inducements to consumers, the trade, or dealer organizations. The skills and information needed to stage such promotions often have little in common with those needed for creating or directing advertising, and so the advertising and sales promotion functions may logically be separated as shown in Figure 11. They may even

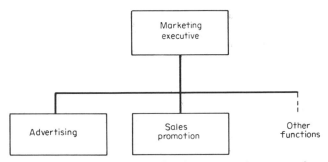

Figure 11 Advertising and sales promotion are often separate, reporting to a marketing executive, when the two functions require different skills and source material.

report upward through different marketing executives and compete furiously for the same budget dollars.

In most companies, however, the term "sales promotion" is a catchall referring to a broad range of sales-support activities other than space and broadcast advertising. In some cases, as in consumer-durable companies and in those marketing industrial parts and equipment, much of the sales promotion may be directed to the trade, sales force, or dealer organization. When this deals mainly with the same product-market information, and draws on the same communications skills as does the advertising, the sales promotion function may logically be positioned directly alongside the advertising function as shown in Figure 12, supervised by a manager who directs and coordinates both.

In many industrial companies that sell direct, and in many consumer-product companies as well, nearly all advertising and sales

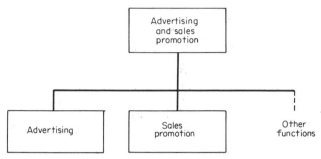

Figure 12 Advertising and sales promotion are often separate, but coordinated closely by a manager of advertising and sales promotion, when the sales promotion is directed mainly to the trade, sales force, or dealer organization.

promotion communications focus on consumer benefits of their products and services and draw on the identical skills and source information. In these companies, a tight integration of advertising and sales promotion is obviously best, and there is no better way to achieve it than to combine these related efforts at the supervisory level as shown in Figure 13.

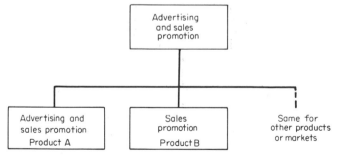

Figure 13 Advertising and sales promotion are one integrated function in many industrial and consumer-product, companies in which these functions draw on identical skills and source material.

There are many companies in which advertising and sales promotion clearly draw on the same skills and source material, but are nevertheless separated, sometimes in apparent competition.   In these cases, marketing management will wisely review the original reason for separating the two functions.   More often than not, they will find that a former advertising and sales promotion manager, and his agency, became too enamored of the space or broadcast advertising programs and neglected the sales literature and related promotion materials needed to make the advertising pay off.   Consequently, sales promotion was broken out solely to get the difficult, time-consuming work of sales promotion done.   When this is the case, management has much to gain by combining the two functions again, under a manager who sees the big advantage and economy of coordinating them and who can *manage* to do so.

9. Encourage the Advertising and Sales Promotion Department to Provide Related Marketing Services whenever Practicable   A growing number of companies are combining the advertising and sales promotion function with other specialized marketing services that are closely related.   The additional services usually begin with assistance in marketing research and extend naturally to include teamwork in marketing-planning activities and other areas.   In some cases, they include marketing-training programs to help the operating units achieve more effective marketing teamwork.   Frequently, the broadened activity takes on the title of "marketing services" or "marketing communications."

Companies seeking to get this over-and-above contribution from their advertising activity may benefit from these observations drawn from successful marketing services groups of this type:

a. The first requirement is that the advertising department head and his division contact personnel be marketing-minded advertising men, with a good feeling for effective advertising and a grasp of modern marketing and the disciplines that make it effective.   Men of this type will invariably begin collaborating closely with their product managers on marketing research, marketing planning, and other related activities that have to be done before an effective advertising program can be initiated.

b. This good teamwork accelerates when management takes the step recommended under guide rule 4, above.   A firm management requirement for written marketing audits or marketing plans, together with an offer of assistance from advertising and other marketing support groups, speeds the process of getting advertising and sales promotion men working closely with the line marketing people who most need help in fact-finding and marketing planning. This assistance should, of course, be provided as a catalyst rather than as a permanent service, to encourage the line marketing group to become wholly self-sufficient in this area.

c. The fact-getting and planning resulting from this teamwork directly benefits all areas of the operation. It is done, furthermore, at very low cost. In the area of marketing research, for example, little additional administrative costs are incurred, because the personal contacts, the close collaboration, and the research that is often required to define the basic needs are done as a normal part of the advertising and sales promotion job; getting the research work done requires relatively little additional time, because it can usually be done most objectively and economically by outside research personnel.

d. The former advertising department becomes increasingly aware of the realities of the marketing situation, and the marketing organization provides increasingly good direction not only for advertising but also for other marketing functions. Rapport between advertising and marketing men improves, and advertising recommendations, including budget proposals, gain in credibility.

e. The broad challenge offered by a marketing services activity of this kind increases the company's ability to attract and develop able, marketing-minded advertising men. It broadens their experience and capabilities, and it also helps to hold those who rise to top positions. There, they are no longer dead-ended in a specialized advertising job, with no place to go except other companies and agencies. Instead, they frequently move into line-marketing activities where their combination of marketing and communications skills prove valuable.

10. Coordinate Advertising and Sales Promotion with the Public Relations Activity The advertising and the public relations departments are organizationally separate in some companies. They are also separated, and relatively out of touch, in many other companies where both logic and experience indicate they should be working together very closely, under a director of public relations and advertising.

One way management can help decide how closely to coordinate the two functions is to ask these two questions:

a. To what degree do the communications objectives of your advertising and your public relations programs overlap? In many companies, a thoughtful effort to determine the communication goals for all major public relations and advertising audiences will reveal that some goals are common to many of them. A *primary* goal, for example, might be to show all public relations and advertising audiences that the company is competent, reliable, diverse, growing, progressive, and profitable. The *secondary* communication audiences such as employees and the financial community will, of course, vary widely and call for disseminating distinctly different information. Achieving the primary goal may be very important, and require the same basic communication skills for all audiences. When this is the case, a close organizational tie between advertising and public relations is suggested. To determine how close the tie should be, it is well to ask the second question:

b. How valuable to your public relations programs is specific news and information on your company's products and markets? The value of such information may be relatively small in a company marketing, let us say, only salt or a basic industrial material that meets common industry specifications and has no readily apparent product advantages. The same is doubtless true for many packaged-goods products.

Many other products and services have very interesting and distinctive features and advantages. News concerning them can be used effectively throughout all the company's public relations programs to help achieve the primary communication goals. This may be true for products running from heavy capital goods equipment through office machines, small appliances, softwear, and drugs. In all these the advertising and public relations functions are frequently combined.

Answers to these two questions will often suggest a close coordination of advertising and public relations when, in fact, they are separate and striving hard to remain independent and self-sufficient. In this case, as in the case of separate advertising and sales promotion functions, a study will often show that the company does not need separate, specialized functions but, instead, a director who is interested in both functions and able to manage them.

CORPORATE ADVERTISING. Corporate-level advertising, like public relations, may be focused on any one or a combination of different audiences.   In deciding where to position it, we must go back to basic communication objectives.   Where these overlap substantially for the corporate advertising and for product advertising, and where both draw on the same basic skills and source material, the corporate advertising can regularly be handled most effectively and economically by the advertising department.   In other cases, the corporate advertising may be focused solely on the financial community or some other special audience, and contain little or no product or market information; it may be that it can be handled best by a public relations group that is in close touch with the chief executive and his top financial and legal aides.

PRODUCT NEWS PUBLICITY.   Positioning the product news publicity function very often presents a Hobson's choice.

The case for positioning it with the public relations activity is usually strong.   Having within the company a single contact for all product and corporate news can be a decided convenience for the news media.   It also makes possible a valuable degree of control and coordination within the company.   When the company's products are unique, with a strong potential for making news in the general press and broadcast media, positioning the product and corporate news relations group in the public relations department offers clear benefits to the corporate-level news activity.

In the same company, however, we may also find compelling reasons for making the product news activity an integral part of the product advertising and sales promotion group.

One reason for this is that a vital part of the public relations activity is usually done for and under the watchful eye of top management. This work, understandably, has an urgency and priority that frequently cause the trade-magazine level of product releases and signed-article activity to get lost in the shuffle.   Meanwhile, the product advertising department, with no responsibility for product news relations, is not motivated even to plan for optimum use of it in their programing and budgeting.   As a result, they use more costly media for goals they could achieve at much less cost in the news columns.

Where product news coverage can carry an important part of the marketing communications load, it seems wise to position the product news activity with product advertising, making that activity clearly responsible for transmitting to the public relations group the 10 per cent or so of product news that may have potential for coverage in the general news media.

11. Make Advertising Organization Changes in a Transition Rather than a Revolution   Most of the changes required in an advertising organization can be foreseen, often years in advance.   This is particularly true of changes that are required to adapt to a major restructuring of the corporate organization, and those that are needed to help increase the effectiveness of advertising and marketing.

Communications functions can be severely disrupted by organization upheavals, and management has much to gain by planning ahead so that advertising and marketing personnel can collaborate on a reasonable transition.   Important changes in advertising organization can often lead to related changes in the company organization structure.   The big advantage is that it can avoid changes that overshoot the mark and cause the quality of advertising to deteriorate, as has so often been the case during the decentralizing and marketing revolutions.

DECENTRALIZATION

Let us consider, for example, the medium-sized company that has so far maintained a centralized, functional corporate organization structure and a highly centralized advertising department.   The company is growing and diversifying, and it is only a matter of time before it is divisionalized and decentralized.   What should be done with the central advertising department, and when?

The time to start is now, and the first step is the preparation of a written organization plan for advertising as proposed in guide rule 1, above.   Let us assume here that the advertising objectives of the chief executive officer indicate an organization in which the marketing direction of advertising (the "what") is fully decentralized and the functional planning and execution (the "how") is to remain centralized.   Then, several logical steps to be considered can be drawn from the other guide rules above:

1. If the central department is organized with heavy emphasis on advertising subfunctions or media (advertising, sales promotion, exhibits and displays, art and production), a good first move is to reorganize the advertising activity as soon as possible around the com-

pany's principal products and markets. The goal is to anticipate and match as closely as possible the divisional setup to come.

2. Candidates for the divisional contact positions should be selected, and special efforts made to orient them to marketing and to the products and markets of the operations they are to serve. If their former experience has been confined to one or a few functions of advertising, or in an agency, they should be trained to become "promotional general managers," able to plan and produce a businesslike combination of many promotional tools to match the communication needs of a specific product and market area. To permit this, it is usually necessary to transfer to the agency the bulk of the functional creative work involved in the actual preparation of advertising, so that the time and effort spent administering those functions can be channeled elsewhere.

3. If not done previously, responsibility and authority for the marketing direction or "what" of advertising should be transferred to the marketing units served. This should be completed, or well under way, before actual organization in divisions.

4. When decentralization actually takes place, a copy of the written organization plan for advertising should be issued to all the division heads and managers concerned, along with other information on new operating procedures. This will avoid a great deal of jockeying, discourage the sprouting of many small advertising empires, and pave the way for a smooth, effective transfer of advertising authority to the operating units. At this time, too, management should emphasize that the central advertising activity is to be held responsible for *executing* all advertising to standards that meet or beat those of competition, so that the remaining line responsibility for directing advertising (as defined in guide rule 5) gives them adequate control of that function.

5. At the same time, management should stress the divisions' responsibilities for providing sound marketing direction for advertising. The written organization plan for advertising should call for marketing audits to direct advertising effort if adequate marketing plans are not available. By monitoring these efforts, management will exert a constructive force for close advertising and marketing teamwork, because the line marketing people and marketing-minded advertising men will usually collaborate to get the job done. This collaboration is further strengthened when the central advertising

and sales promotion group is encouraged to provide related marketing services, as covered in guide rule 9. This teamwork on the direction-setting phase of advertising and marketing usually does wonders to pave the way for agreement on the functional or creative phase of advertising to come.

6. Plans should be set in advance for performing at the division that part of the advertising job that can be performed best and most economically there. This is especially true for operating divisions remote from headquarters. Then, an advertising and sales promotion man at the division can best (a) provide source material; (b) serve as a one-point contact for approval of advertising; and (c) plan and prepare that part of the sales promotion program that goes "to or through the salesman and distributor," that is, promotion material that is prepared in limited quantities for individual customers or to small audiences.

Special precautions should be taken to keep the division advertising personnel cooperating, rather than competing, with those in the central group.

Some companies achieve this while carrying out an effective training program at the same time. To perform the in-division work, they assign their strongest, most promising young men, who are hired by and remain on the payroll of the central advertising department. After two to four years on the division sales promotion job, they are expected to advance, either into a more responsible position in the central advertising department or in division marketing activities on the division payroll. In either case, the climate for good advertising and marketing teamwork is improved. This system helps avoid the situation that regularly weakens the advertising effort of most multi-division companies, that of having a mediocre performer dead-ended in the division advertising manager job.

Where division advertising personnel are on the division payroll and report to division marketing, their functional responsibility to the central group should be made clear in the written organization plan for advertising and in the "what" and "how" division of responsibility. This functional responsibility can be further strengthened in many constructive ways: (a) a basic advertising training course given to all headquarters and division personnel, to implant the same basic principles of advertising effectiveness; (b) regular annual seminars to iron out common problems, review future plans, and strengthen the bonds of cooperation; (c) a planned rotation program that puts strong advertising men in the division positions and brings the best of them back to the central department with field experience that increases the value of their services to the divisions.

Steps like these, when planned well in advance and implemented on time, permit a decentralizing multidivision company to move smoothly and quickly to a sound balance between advertising centralization and decentralization.

When such a transition is not carried out, the functionally oriented central advertising function will be found lacking and will be pulled apart by the centrifugal forces of decentralization. Then, the spotty advertising quality and other problems begin to appear, and before many years management is wondering if there is not a need for some recentralization.

RECENTRALIZATION OF ADVERTISING

Companies that find they have overshot the mark in decentralizing both the "what" and the "how" of advertising face a problem that is many times more difficult than carrying out a measured decentralization program.

The hard fact, of course, is that this usually requires asking the divisions to relinquish much of their "how" responsibility for advertising—something that line marketing managers have often learned to enjoy and that provides security for division advertising people and their individual agencies.

Some companies seek to effect a cure with strong headquarters staff assistance that provides expert advice and counsel and periodic monitoring of the division advertising programs by staff experts and top management. While this can help, it usually reveals that the decisions line marketing people make in the "how" area of advertising are often subjective and that it is very difficult for them and their division advertising people to accept even the most expert advice from staff or agency experts. To date, even the best results achieved through the staff advice-and-counsel route appear to be unconvincing.

What, then, is the best way to "bite the bullet" and recentralize the "how" responsibility?

Experience suggests that this requires direct top-management support for two steps that are carried out not as a transition but as directly and promptly as possible:

1. Issuance by top management of the new written plan for advertising organization, with the "how" responsibilities centralized.

2. Concurrently, announcement of a carefully planned headquarters advertising unit made up of the strongest men available from within and without the company. Regardless of their strengths, they will have rough sledding for several years. However, if the advertising organization plan is sound and enforced, they will inevitably upgrade advertising quality to a degree that brings a reassuring response from the marketplace and increasing support from both top and divisional management.

CHAPTER FIVE

Coordination of Advertising with Sales and Other Functions

WILLIAM H. EWEN *Director of Corporate Advertising, Borden, Inc., Chairman, Association of National Advertisers*

Prior to the recognition of marketing as a process involving almost all the functions of a company, advertising was often looked upon as a thing apart. Its relationship to sales was nominal. In many organizations it was viewed principally as a tool of top management, to be turned on or off at will—or at whim. Sales and advertising departments often found themselves in conflict, competing for funds and cooperating only when absolutely necessary.

In those times a company was likely to be manufacturing oriented. It was the job of the advertising department to advertise, and of the sales department to sell whatever the company made. Advertising seldom became involved with other departments on a regular basis. Occasionally a request might come in from the plant manager in Oshkosh for an ad to be placed in the annual dinner program of the local Elks Club, but this was rare. Generally, the attitude of people in the various departments could be expressed as, "I'll do my job. You do yours, and let's not interfere with each other." While this type of situation may still exist to some degree in companies lacking marketing sophistication, it is largely a relic of the past. Today, understanding of the marketing process and its proper functioning within the company's physical structure is vital to corporate survival. In fact, marketing might be compared to the circulatory system of the human body, with the various organs performing their special jobs to keep the blood moving and healthy. In marketing, as in the human system, each separate function is dependent upon the others, and all are interconnected. Marketing resembles the bloodstream in that it is a circular process, sending goods out and returning profits.

In discussing advertising's relationships with other marketing functions, we have to keep in mind the fact that hardly any two companies are exactly alike in their organizational structures or in their operating policies, even if they are in the same line of business. There are wide variations, for example, between companies marketing small-price, high-turnover consumer items, and those manufacturing and selling high-cost industrial machines.

LIST OF MARKETING ACTIVITIES

Let us look at the list of marketing activities which follows, then review advertising's practical relationships with each of them. The items on the list are typical of a consumer-products company, and not all would be found on a similar tally for an industrial manufacturer.

Advertising, obviously, would be more directly related to some of these activities than to others. For example, sales and sales promotion are functions close to advertising in purpose, method, and result. Pricing and per-unit profit estimating are related mainly for determining budgets. Here is the list:

1. Marketing research
   a. Testing of concepts
   b. Product-market testing
   c. Testing of alternatives
   d. Determining customer characteristics
   e. Analyzing markets

2. Research and development
   a. Determining feasibility of new product
   b. Developing formula, specifications, etc.
   c. Determining ingredient costs
   d. Improving product
   e. Improving costs through formula changes
3. Packaging
   a. Determining package form, sizes, etc.
   b. Determining packaging feasibility
   c. Determining package costs
   d. Handling of labeling and package decoration
4. Engineering
   a. Designing manufacturing facility
   b. Improving manufacturing facility
   c. Determining plant construction costs
   d. Determining plant improvement costs
5. Manufacturing
   a. Determining plant capacity
   b. Producing of goods
   c. Packaging of goods
   d. Improving procedures to increase capacity, lower costs, etc.
6. Quality control
   a. Checking of product output regularly to make sure standards are being met
   b. Checking of plant housekeeping, checking the handling of raw materials, and the handling and storing of finished products
7. Purchasing
   a. Determining best sources of raw materials
   b. Purchasing of raw materials
   c. Purchasing of packaging materials
   d. Purchasing of plant equipment
   e. Purchasing of vehicles
   f. Purchasing of supplies for plant and office use
8. Sales
   a. Making personal calls on customers and prospects
   b. Generating orders for product
   c. Reporting on product movement or problems
   d. Obtaining special displays, features, etc.
   e. Explaining product, pricing and profit, deals, advertising and promotional support to trade
   f. Working with brokers, wholesalers, distributors, vendors, etc.
   g. Demonstrating new products to trade

     h. Gaining new accounts

     i. Allocating sales time to products in "push periods"

     j. Checking on trade or consumer complaints

     k. Checking and reporting on competitive activity or special market situations

     l. Checking product availability in stores

     m. Upgrading product location in store, increasing shelf stock on display, checking of pricing

9. Distribution

     a. Handling warehousing of product until sold

     b. Setting up physical distribution system in accordance with needs

     c. Maintaining vehicle fleets where company-owned

10. Sales promotion

     a. Developing special promotions and producing merchandising materials for these

     b. Developing and producing standard merchandising aids for continuing use

     c. Preparing trade and consumer letters, brochures, and other informative materials

     d. Locating suitable self-liquidating premiums, dealer premiums, developing contests, etc.

11. Public relations

     a. Generating news features about the business, its people, and its products

     b. Handling press inquiries and interviews

     c. Preparing statements and releases

     d. Helping counter unfavorable publicity

     e. Preparing and distributing communications to special-interest groups such as stockholders, suppliers, financial community, government, etc.

     f. Handling regular product publicity

12. Marketing analysis

     a. Determining pricing and estimating per-unit profit

     b. Estimating pay-out period on new products

     c. Estimating investment needed in given period

     d. Analyzing sales results, reporting variance from objectives

     e. Helping set sales and profit objectives

     f. Analyzing and reporting on competitive activity

13. Customer services

     a. Answering customer inquiries

     b. Adjusting customer complaints

     c. Handling distribution of special materials offered to consumers

14. Employee relations
    a. Hiring of required qualified personnel
    b. Handling of union negotiations
    c. Maintaining of employee records
    d. Handling of employee benefits
    e. Adjusting employee complaints
    f. Acting as transmission agency in informing employees on company activities
15. Legal services
    a. Drafting and monitoring of all legal documents of company including contracts
    b. Advising management in any actions involving outsiders, including acquisitions
    c. Conducting of legal action where necessary
    d. Reviewing all product and advertising statements for compliance with legal requirements
    e. Safeguarding patents and trademarks
16. Financial (controller, accounting)
    a. Establishing of accounting procedures
    b. Controlling income and expenditures
    c. Maintaining financial records, budgets, etc.
    d. Controlling customer accounts, billing

Obviously, this list is not all-inclusive. However, it does cover the major operating functions that relate to marketing. Advertising was not included because its connections with the other activities will be explored fully on the following pages.

ADVERTISING'S RELATIONSHIP TO MARKETING ACTIVITIES

Advertising and Marketing Research

Practically every company that shows growth is dependent on new products and new uses for existing products. New-product concepts are not the exclusive right of any function or department. An idea may come from any part of the business, and many organizations encourage their employees to "Think up," as the late Alex Osborn put it.

Once an idea is submitted, and not rejected for some obvious reason, it begins the long journey toward product introduction. A first step is to test the basic concept among consumers. If they like the product idea, and indicate they would buy such an item, the project moves into the first phases of development.   Often the comments of consumers at this embryo stage help direct the marketing team in modifying the product to make it even more acceptable.   The research report and verbatim playbacks provide a bank of valuable data for later use in developing advertising strategy and copy.

Advertising people should be fully informed on the plans and results of such testing, and they should be given copies of the report for study.   Sometimes, advertising people may be able to suggest a slightly different line of questioning that will make the research more informative.

If and when the new product reaches the point of market testing, marketing research can weigh the effectiveness of the advertising strategy along with other factors contributing to success or the lack of it.

In the testing of concepts on new uses for present products, the circumstances are much the same as for new products.   Here, too, advertising and marketing research should work together.

Marketing research also can help determine precisely the characteristics of customers for a given product.   This is essential information for advertising.

In a typical company, marketing research compiles and makes available a great deal of basic market information.   This can be tremendously helpful to advertising people and to their agencies in pinpointing market areas, customers, and the media that will reach them most efficiently.

Research and Development and Advertising

Again, thinking in terms of a new product, R&D will attempt to create physically the product in the image evolving from concept testing.   Here is the first real test of practicality.   Can the product be made at all?   Can it be made as described, or can modifications be made without destroying the basic idea?   Are ingredients readily available?   What will the cost of the finished product be?   Can R&D add some exotic touch that will make the product even more appealing than it would be as originally conceived?

All these questions, and the results of research and development work, are of vital interest to advertising.   Now the physical characteristics of the product come to the fore: the choice ingredients; the special properties; the flavor, if it is a food.   Here is another gold mine for fact-hungry advertising copy writers.   It has been said time and again that research people and advertising people do not talk the same language.   This is nonsense.   Assuming that there are no personality clashes, a joint discussion of product development work often sparks valuable ideas on both sides.

Later, when the product actually is ready to be advertised, R&D personnel can provide counsel on the accuracy of copy claims.   They should be consulted.

Packaging Development and Advertising

Most products have to be packaged to be sold, and in today's marketing the package is no longer just a container.   It is the payoff, where at long last the product comes face to face with the consumer.   If she likes what she sees, she may buy.   If the package has no appeal, the prospect is likely to leave it on the shelf.

Today's packages are, in effect, three-dimensional advertisements at the point of purchase.   They must combine artistry, ingenious construction, adequate product protection, and a whole raft of printed information about what is inside.   Requirements of the marketplace have virtually turned this function into a profession, with talented designers and skilled engineers available for counseling.

Many large companies maintain packaging departments.   Others depend on outside designers or on package-manufacturing companies for professional help and service.   In whatever way this activity is handled, there must be coordination with advertising.   It has come to be standard procedure at this point in time to feature the product package in all visual media—print, television, and outdoor boards.   Consideration must be given, therefore, as to how the package will look when it appears on a magazine page or in a television commercial—often in small size.   Advertising people should work with packaging people in the development stages to make sure that the product puts its best foot forward in media as well as on store shelves.

Because of their background and experience, many advertising people, both company and agency, can contribute to better package decor.   All too often they are left out when this subject is being discussed.

Engineering and Advertising

Admittedly, there are not many occasions when these two functions are brought together. This is unfortunate, since both involve highly creative thinking and planning. Time spent by an advertising man studying the efficient layout of a new plant, or watching the operation of an ingenious production line, can bring a new dimension to his own thinking. The work of the engineers often can be the subject of a corporate business or trade advertisement. With industrial products the engineering department is usually the prime source of advertising ideas.

It is advisable for advertising and engineering to maintain at least some liaison. The benefits can be well worth the effort.

Manufacturing and Advertising

Manufacturing can assist advertising by providing copy points on care and handling of the product in the making. If there are special steps taken to assure a superior result, so much the better, especially if the competitor's process is less thorough. Advertising should allow manufacturing to see how it will portray the product in pictures and in words so that there will be no discrepancies between what the consumer sees on television and what she sees when she opens the package. If the bowl of soup in the ad shows six carrots, the can on the shelf should not contain less. Company reputations have been damaged, and sales have been badly hurt by products that were not "as advertised."

The cooperation between advertising and manufacturing, therefore, can provide both a creative stimulus and a safeguard against "false and misleading" advertising.

Quality Control and Advertising

Most companies marketing consumer items maintain regular checks of quality. Depending on the type of product, this can range from a fully equipped, well-staffed laboratory to a simple mechanical testing facility. The thoroughness with which this unit does its job is of great importance to advertising, because it assures that products measure up to what is said about them. As in the case of manufacturing, regular contacts by advertising people with quality control can prevent serious consumer complaints.

On the positive side, quality control also can be a valuable source of copy ideas. The number of checks that are made regularly, what they are, and who makes them are all useful points.

Purchasing and Advertising

Purchasing is usually thought of by advertising people in terms of obtaining audiovisual equipment for presentations or some such activity. This is shortsighted. Like other functions discussed so far, purchasing can often provide a sound basis for advertising claims. This department is usually charged with responsibility for buying product ingredients and raw materials. Purchasing men are often skilled in tracking down the best supplies obtainable, and this effort can have an important effect on product quality. The "Lucky Strike—Fine Tobacco" campaign was a good example of the teaming of purchasing and advertising.

Advertising people should know what is going on in purchasing that is special; and they should be prepared to utilize the information.

Sales and Advertising

This is the big one! These two fields of activity are interrelated at so many points and are so mutually interdependent that one could hardly exist without the other. Advertising can create a favorable climate for selling, but it cannot actually make a sale. The salesman by personal calls, word of mouth, and demonstrations cannot generate alone the large volume required to market a consumer product successfully. Without elaboration here are some important areas where sales and advertising should be closely coordinated:

1. Definition of current market areas of opportunity
2. Definition of areas of future sales expansion
3. Selection of individual market media that will best serve to implement the marketing plan, provide most useful consumer impact, and assist the trade
4. Establishment of product "push" periods and appropriate dates for advertising support
5. Assurance that warehouses and retail stores will be adequately stocked when advertising appears
6. Preparation, well in advance, of salesmen's kits to inform the trade of product promotional plans, to help generate orders, to gain

store displays and features, and to promote other retail sales activities

7. Development of appropriate merchandising and point-of-purchase materials; assurance that these will be delivered in time and will be used

8. Report back to advertising on success of campaigns in sales areas; reports on competitive advertising activity

These are just a few of the activities vital to both sales and advertising, and where a cooperative effort is essential.

The lines of communication between the two functions must be open continuously to prevent serious malfunctioning of the marketing plans.

In a company where sales to the trade are handled through wholesalers, brokers, or distributors, it is the responsibility of the sales department to brief these intermediaries fully on marketing and advertising plans, and to get them to follow through with the promotional effort as completely as they would if they were part of the company's sales force.

To facilitate coordination, the specific responsibilities of sales and advertising should be clearly spelled out, then followed.

Distribution and Advertising

The distribution function, although extremely important, is largely a mechanical one. Advertising's contacts with it are seldom direct. The responsibility for having the right products in the right quantities in the right places at the right time is usually a matter for sales and distribution working together.

However, distribution people should be informed of advertising and promotional activities so that they can be prepared to take emergency steps more intelligently if an unforeseen problem arises.

In instances where a company owns its own vehicles, advertising should not overlook the possibility of using these traveling billboards to extend the reach of messages.

Sales Promotion and Advertising

Of all functions discussed so far, sales promotion comes closest to being a part of advertising. Sales promotion may work out the details for a contest, a storewide promotion, a sweepstakes, a self-liquidating premium promotion; and any one of these could be featured in advertising.

Sales promotion also is charged with responsibility for developing effective point-of-purchase materials, catalogs, dealer aids, and other important tools for the sales force.   All these should tie in with advertising by using the same themes, pictures, and basic copy points. The duplicate use of expensive art usually can save a great deal of money.

In some companies sales promotion is a part of advertising.   In others it is part of sales.   In those instances where store promotion work is the dominant activity, sales promotion may operate independently.

It hardly needs to be said that this function must be closely coordinated with advertising on a constant basis.   To allow the two to follow separate courses is a dissipation of effort and a waste of money.

Public Relations and Advertising

Historically, these two functions have been closely connected, particularly with regard to publicity.   In many companies advertising and public relations are in a single department.   In some they report to the same management executive.

Both operations, essentially, aim for the same target—the public. Advertising does its work through paid-for time and space media. Public relations, often using the same media, accomplishes its objectives through news releases, editorial features, and press conferences.   Public relations usually encompasses a great deal more than just publicity, but this is the part of its work that is closest to advertising.   Therefore, we shall stay within this area in discussing coordination.

Advertising ideas can sometimes start with interesting facts uncovered by public relations.   News stories, conversely, may originate from development of advertising.   Such publicity, if based on reasonably broad interests, may be used by major media.   Also to be kept in mind are such workaday things as informing the retailers of your promotional activities through short breezy releases offered to the trade press.

In a sense, each of the two functions can be considered an extension of the other, keeping in mind that rules of editorial ethics must be observed carefully in contacts with the press.   Good editorial people connected with the public press can smell a promotional activity a mile away, and usually will reject releases that appear to be self-seeking. Advertising people without experience in press contacts should rely on their skilled public relations associates to work the other side of the street.

As a general rule, where public relations and advertising are separate functions within a company, representatives of both groups should schedule frequent, regular meetings to report activities under way and to combine efforts wherever possible. Such meetings can be very fruitful.

Marketing Analysis and Advertising

Marketing analysis is at the same time one of the least glamorous but most vital functions in a successful marketing operation. A company must develop plans on the basis of all available pertinent information including recent past performance. Usually, the work in this area is done by brand managers or marketing managers, using data from a number of sources. Out of this come the long-term and short-term marketing plans, sales and profit forecasts, reports on past results, and other information required by top management as well as others within the company.

Out of marketing analyses come the answers to such questions as, "How much *should* we spend for advertising this year on this product?" and "How much *can* we spend, realistically?"

Advertising, obviously, is closely tied to marketing analysis, and in those companies where advertising budget requests are not initiated by advertising people, there should be a good liaison between this group and the people responsible for the analysis and recommendations.

Legal Services and Advertising

Most large business organizations maintain law departments, and increasingly these are becoming involved with matters of advertising and promotion. The day when the friendly company lawyer was looked upon by advertising people as someone to be tolerated, and whose advice could be taken with a grain of salt, is past. Government scrutiny of advertising claims at all levels, from municipal to federal, makes law department guidance essential. In fact, in many companies today, the law department checks and approves *all* advertising. While this may sometimes seem like a nuisance to advertising persons, it need not be if good liaison is established.

Law departments are usually responsible for protection of symbols, trademarks, and copyrights, and since these are used regularly in advertising, the law department's rules should always be observed.

There are many other subjects involving advertising where the lawyer's counsel should be sought. These include such matters as use of competitors' names in advertisements, rules for contests and sweepstakes, special state regulations affecting promotions, and so on.

While it is always possible that the law department can extricate a company from a messy situation due to unwise or illegal advertising, it is much better to stay out of trouble by maintaining good liaison between advertising and the law department and by checking all claims and promotional activities before they have reached the point of no revision.

Customer Services and Advertising

Every company dealing with the public can expect to hear from customers and prospects. Sometimes these communications take the form of angry letters or phone calls. Occasionally they are complimentary. Frequently they are requests for special information, booklets, locations of sales outlets, and so on.

It is in a company's best interests, of course, to handle all such contacts promptly, courteously, and factually. Most organizations have one or more staff personnel assigned directly to this function. In a multidivision company it is often best to have each division handle the communications relating to its own products or service.

It is a good idea for advertising people to keep in touch with customer services regularly for several reasons. First, many customer inquiries or complaints have to do with advertised products or services. Even if the contacts do not involve the advertising itself, it is helpful to know how consumers are reacting to products and what they are saying.

A considerable amount of advertising, especially in the retail field, includes direct sales offers. Where these are short-term, the orders and inquiries may be handled by customer services personnel. In the case of widely advertised premiums, cash refunds, etc., it is usually necessary to contract with a well-staffed mail-order house to handle the returns. In either case advertising should be posted on developments at least on a weekly basis.

Good examples of the interdependence of advertising and customer relations may be found in the industrial-products companies. A great deal of their advertising is designed to stimulate inquiries that can be followed up by sales calls.   The proper handling of these in the early stages is extremely important.

Employee Relations and Advertising

It cannot be argued with any logic that employees should be kept in the dark about company activities.   Among other things, advertising is a category on which they should be informed and be able to speak about intelligently with family friends and outside associates.   For example, if a company plans to use a major television show, employees generally should be given the facts.   This can be done through regular channels such as flash bulletins for posting on departmental boards, house magazines, and individual pocket schedules.

The importance of employee enthusiasm in talking up company advertising activities should not be underestimated.

Financial Functions and Advertising

Last, but certainly far from least in importance, is advertising liaison with financial people in the organization.   Formulation of budget procedures, record keeping, paying of bills, getting approval of appropriations are all areas where the money functions play a key role.

Advertising persons should be sure that they take the time to discuss procedures and practices thoroughly with financial personnel, preferably before standards are set.   If this is not done, it is likely that the financial people will make the decisions, possibly with unhappy results for advertising.

It is always well for advertising to inform the controller's office, the accounting department, and the disbursements section on what is being done at any given time, and why.   Some understanding of advertising's objectives and its ways of operating, by financial people, can help smooth the way in the day-to-day contacts between the two functions.

The foregoing discussion of advertising's interrelationships with other functions and departments does not cover every situation, of course.   It is designed especially to serve as a guide, and to provide a base on which each advertising practitioner using this handbook can write his own plan of action.

Editor's note: The reader is invited to refer to other chapters in this book where contributors have treated in detail some of the subjects that are merely outlined in this chapter.

CHAPTER SIX

Management of Advertising Personnel

FRANK NOETTLING *President, Frank Noettling Associates, Inc.*

A growing company will always have growing needs. In an advertising operation, the biggest asset inevitably is people. The most important raw material is the information provided to those people, and the sole justification for its existence is communication created and executed *by* those people. Thus, here, perhaps more than in any other industry, we feel the constant pressure to provide a steady flow of manpower and to devise a professional means of motivating and utilizing it, once employed. The challenge becomes one of developing management skills to such a degree that a manager will inspire his men to build a profitable and intellectually sound organization.

Three Critical Areas

So, should that organization be unsettled by a personnel shake-up, causing unproductive gaps in the organization chart or lapses in personal career advancement, morale at all levels is bound to be jeopardized.   A close look at a low-morale, unproductive organization is certain to uncover a management group that has taken an inadequate approach to personnel management.   It has failed or faltered in some or all of these areas:

1. Determining, in advance, the personnel requirements of its company
2. Developing sources to provide such personnel
3. Devising the best means of using that personnel, once obtained

Stated simply, from the company's standpoint, it is a question of "Who'll we need, where'll we find him, and what'll we do with him after we have him?"   Unless management devotes sufficient effort in facing and answering these questions, the corporation becomes an unprofitable slave to itself.   Management is forced into wholly defensive, catch-up-if-possible moves that leave no time for positive, creative leadership.

At first consideration, the idea of a long-range, broad-perspective approach to management of advertising personnel may be resisted by those responsible for the job.   There is a tendency, perhaps, to view advertising as a particularly strange type of activity, and advertising persons as even stranger, and to assume that a logical approach to either is impractical.   The manager who feels this way will generally attempt to solve problems rather than maximize opportunities, and do so on an ad hoc basis.   He will think in terms of "one man, one job," and seldom relate either that man or his job to the overall organization and its future.

Such a manager overlooks certain fundamentals of personnel management, fundamentals which I believe should be clearly understood before anything can be gained from a detailed consideration of the three-part problem outlined above.

Essential Need for Logic   To begin with, the very fact that advertising is an unusual type of activity, at times appearing to defy all logic, makes it all the more essential to apply logic whenever possible.   If it is true that this business is more volatile than most, then any effort that *can* be made toward stability *should* be made.   The effect will not be to deprive the advertising operation of its dynamism, its excitement and thrust, but to provide a sounder basis from which the creative forces can operate.   The most gifted genius in the world still needs a climate calm enough to function in; constant personnel upheavals—and the threat of them—are far from conducive to productivity in any field, and particularly one which depends heavily on the sensitivity of its people.

What Is an "Advertising Man"?   In the second place, the manager who believes he needs an "advertising man" to fill an advertising job is apt to be disappointed.   I have never known an "advertising man."   I have known creative persons and perceptive persons, articulate and persuasive persons, single-minded and strong-minded, impressive and expressive; but no single, precise configuration of traits or aptitudes is alone required for success in advertising.   Stated another, more portentous way, no particular combination of skills or experiences guarantees that a certain man will succeed in the job. Accordingly, capable persons may well be passed over while the search goes on for that mythical creature, "a born ad man."

There is a further danger in the tendency of some managers to think in terms of "advertising men." They may be confusing *means* with *ends*.   It is possible to become so immersed in the day-to-day activities, pressures, and problems of the advertising business that advertising becomes an end in itself.   Consequently, a manager is apt to hire a man who shows promise of being able to produce (or somehow contribute to the production of) finished advertising, and fire him when he does not.   The same manager is apt to be totally unconcerned with the effectiveness of the advertising as reflected by consumer acceptance of the product.   In short, such a manager loses sight of the fact that the whole purpose of advertising (at least the kind an advertiser is justified in paying for) is to serve a marketing objective.

To prevent falling into the same trap, it is practical to equate advertising and marketing personnel for the remainder of this discussion.

No Ad Hoc Decisions   A final fundamental that anyone responsible for personnel management must come to grips with is that, in actuality, there can be no such thing as an ad hoc personnel decision.   It is impossible to divorce a single hiring or firing act from the overall context in which it is done.   Unless the man and his job are utterly insignificant, his coming or going is bound to have some effect on the company's present and future; and if they *are* insignificant, the personnel manager should not be wasting time on the decision.   Personnel *moves* must not be confused with personnel *management*, and regrettably, too many managers become so immersed in their daily problems that they lose sight of their objectives. True management involves a great deal more than a series of one-time problems, the resolving of which contributes little to the company's overall effectiveness.

Accordingly, each single hiring, promoting, demoting, or firing decision should be made in a bigger context than the immediate needs of the job requirements. Ad hoc personnel decisions can be among the most costly moves a company makes. Every time a new man has to be slotted in a job, the cost to his organization goes up. A dollars-and-cents evaluation of this drain may be difficult to make, but the move is costly. Perhaps there are strained relationships with other workers during the break-in period; perhaps there is an impedance of the work flow; perhaps work is left undone by those who have to neglect responsibilities while they either try to fill the gap left by the previous man or try to help the new man get his bearings; perhaps the work turned out suffers in quality as well as quantity.

There is no way to predict how these costs may snowball. Something resembling a formula could be expressed, however, on this subject. *The smaller the perspective from which a personnel decision is made, the greater the chances that it will prove costly.* This does not mean that every personnel decision should be needlessly labored over and delayed as the job goes unfilled, the work piles up, and the problems mount; some moves cannot afford to be put off. Nor do I advocate waiting "till all the facts are in"; all the facts will *never* be in, at least not in time for a decision maker of average longevity to capitalize on them. What counts is not the *length of time* taken to reach a decision, but the *breadth of view* applied. Breadth of view is at the heart of the threefold approach referred to earlier.

Successful Management of Personnel

This approach will bear restating now, so that we can proceed to amplify and illustrate it.

Successful management of personnel requires:

1. Determining, in advance, the personnel requirements of the company (or department)
2. Developing sources to provide such personnel
3. Devising the best means of using that personnel, once obtained

In actual practice, the efforts devoted to each of the three types of activity outlined will, of course, overlap. Those who are responsible for personnel will not be able to follow a chronological plan, spending one month, say, on determining the personnel to be needed, the next on developing sources, and so on, but will more often have to be concerned with all three areas concurrently. Nevertheless, it is highly important to perceive the personnel management responsibility as divided *distinctly* into these three areas of responsibility and to act accordingly. This is to make sure that one aspect of the personnel management job does not get short-changed because all the attention is given to another. For example, the necessity to develop sources of personnel (which has a way of becoming synonymous with "looking for the right people") can become so important, especially under the pressure of filling open jobs, that planning for the future —in terms of determining in advance the personnel requirements of the company—may be neglected. On the other hand, there is a temptation to relax once the "right man" has been found for a given job, with the result that devising the best means of using that man *in* the job, and thereafter, is given insufficient attention.

The manager of personnel needs to remind himself periodically that he is doing a thorough, successful job *only* if he is giving sufficient attention and effort to each of the three areas named, regardless of any time sequence he may follow in doing so.

DETERMINING PERSONNEL REQUIREMENTS

Let us concentrate now on the first area: *determining, in advance, the personnel requirements of the company.* The most productive way of dealing with this area is to divide personnel needs into quantitative characteristics and qualitative characteristics.

Quantitative Characteristics

The quantitative considerations are fairly self-explanatory. Each department estimates the *number* of persons it will need at given points in the future, say one, two, and five years from now. Of course, even such straightforward numerical estimating should be done on as scientific a basis as possible. The department head who merely muses, "We're busy now and use five people, we'll probably be busier next year so we should need seven or eight" is hardly much help. For him, and his peers, a list should be provided of factors that may well have a bearing on the number of people to be needed in future operations. The object is to promote accurate estimations. Such a list should include:

1. Rate of change in number of people in department over past (one, two, or five years) *directly resulting* from increase or decrease of work load

2. Rate of change in number of projects handled over similar period

3. Normal rate of turnover of personnel

It will be perceived that factors 1 and 3 are quite different; but it is surprising how often quantitative estimates of future personnel needs fail to make the distinction. Those charged with overall responsibility for company personnel have a big stake in recognizing the difference. To illustrate, the *total* number of men in a department may have remained absolutely constant over the past five years. That of itself would indicate no change in size of work load during that time. But suppose the department consisted of twenty persons, and every year four of them had left. To the personnel manager—growth or no growth in productivity—that would mean staffing a whole new department every five years.

Rate of Change

The picture provided by factor 1 will give some fairly realistic idea of how many would have to be added for each additional increment of work assignment made to that department. The ratios may vary considerably. For example, historically a 25 per cent increase in work load may have necessitated a 25 per cent increase in personnel; but a 50 per cent increase in work load may have necessitated a 100 per cent increase in personnel. What the *actual* increase in work load is apt to be is determined by a simple projection of factor 2. Here again, we are looking to the past to give us some inkling of the future, but in the context of an advertising and marketing operation, this is sometimes the only source of guidance available for such a projection.

In any event, by having some idea of the rate of increase in the work load of a department, and having some idea of what percentage increase of personnel will be necessary to handle the work, we can arrive at a more accurate projection. When the rate of turnover has been superimposed on this projection, and the process repeated for each department, the manager of personnel has a rather good picture of his quantitative manpower requirements.

New Business and Automation Certain other factors should be considered that may be beyond the scope of the department head. These include *the prospect of developing new business* (information which the department head may not be privy to) and *the possibilities of automation performing certain jobs in the future.* While it is rare that a quantitative value can be assigned to these factors in terms of exact difference they will make in numbers of persons needed, a reasoned consideration of them can provide more accurate work-force projections.

Qualitative Characteristics of Personnel

The second factor in predetermining personnel requirements is an estimation of the *qualitative* characteristics needed. Here is where the job of planning ahead is apt to get bogged down.

Most department heads can be specific enough when it comes to thinking in terms of *numbers* of persons needed; but when it comes to *qualifications,* they tend to lapse into generalizations. "Intelligent," "resourceful," "creative" are qualities they will invariably list as essential. A personnel manager could produce a thousand people with these qualifications and still not have one man who is right for the particular advertising or marketing job. When you realize that not only does the advertising and marketing field differ from most others, but each company active in that field will differ from every other, it is easy to see that a better focus on necessary traits and talents than the usual "intelligent, resourceful, creative" specification is needed.

Thinking in Specific Terms The personnel manager must stimulate the appropriate department head to think in more detailed, specific terms. I have yet to see the printed form that can encourage this kind of contribution from respondents. Simply allowing space for "remarks" on the form will produce little beyond the expected "intelligent, resourceful, creative" comment. A long list of qualifications —to be checked off, or ranked in order of importance—is somewhat better, only because more adjectives are thrust upon the department head for consideration.

As in most situations, the person-to-person confrontation is best. An open-end discussion will generally produce a more tangible profile of what is to be sought in personnel for the company. To get the most out of such a discussion, however, the personnel manager should not rely on, nor expect, the other party to the discussion to take the lead. Instead, the manager should be prepared to draw out the desired information and opinions.

The one most important thing to do, accordingly, is to steer the discussion away from the abstract. Asking the other person merely to tick off qualifications gives him no tangible frame of reference; a better approach is to name some actual individual known to him—perhaps someone already working in his department, perhaps an outsider—and to determine what *that* person has that either fills the bill or disqualifies him, in the eyes of the department head, for a given job. Another way to get at the same information is to name several actual persons, then state the hypothetical problem: "If you had to hire from among those I have named for this particular job, who would be your choice—and *why?*" Needless to say, the "why" is the big part of the question. ˙ As the other person develops his notions in terms of *actual persons,* he will generally expand sufficiently to provide a good overall picture of what qualities he feels are necessary in the man for that job. Another advantage of this whole exercise is that it forces the department head himself to come to grips with what is needed in his people. He, as well as you, will arrive at a clearer picture of qualitative requirements.

The Forward-looking Approach A stumbling block to many discussions of personnel qualifications is the tendency of human beings to look backward instead of forward. Your interviewee may be inclined to think of a job in terms of the man who held it previously. "If we could find another guy like Joe, we'd be all set," he will assure you. Now there is nothing wrong with using Joe as a point of departure, as an actual individual whose qualifications can stimulate the discussion. But too often Joe's characteristics will be cited as ideal simply because the department head has no difficulty imagining Joe in the job (although he may have when Joe first started). The trick then is to get him to imagine *other* people in the job. In fact, this is a crucial part of the challenge of the entire personnel job: to get management to conceive of other people in specific jobs. If it cannot, the organization is apt to stagnate.

To encourage a forward-looking approach, it may be better to hypothesize a job, to invent one that does not presently exist in the company, but is similar to those that do; then to ask the interviewee to select job candidates from among named people and give reasons for his choice.

Value of Opinions   Since people generally like to be asked their opinions, the discussion will be more productive for you if the other party is led to feel that he is being interviewed for his *feelings* as well as the facts he can provide.   A question might be stated this way: "If you were sending a boy to college, knowing he'd have to take over this job eventually, what sort of courses would you have him take?" You'll obtain a lot more from his response than you would from a form asking him to list "educational requirements."   Similar questions can be posed with regard to business experience, job training, and the like.   If you notice that the interviewee is getting a little emotional as he discusses what "the present crop of trainees doesn't have" or uses the occasion to get anything else off his chest, that is not the time to shut him off.   You will probably find out more about the problems, the ins and outs of his department and its operations, from this part of the discussion than from all the rest.

Effect in Personnel Requirements of Rate of Change in Number of Products

With both the quantitative and the qualitative requirements estimated, you have come a long way in completing the first big part of the personnel management responsibility: determining, in advance, the personnel requirements of your company.   But there is another aspect to the task, which if overlooked can make the best-laid personnel plans of today look inadequate tomorrow.   It deserves some consideration now before we move on to the second major responsibility of personnel management.

It is no longer surprising to pick up a business publication or an annual report and read that "50 per cent of the corporation's sales last year were in products that did not exist ten years ago."   The percentage figures may vary, but the story is basically the same in company after company.   This has tremendous significance in terms of personnel requirements.

As your company adds new products, new operations, and new markets, it will almost certainly have to create jobs to service them. Not too far into the future, you may be able to look back and say, "50 per cent of our activity is in jobs that didn't exist five years ago."

Therefore, any personnel projections made today purely on a *historical* basis could prove to be practically worthless—unless allowance is made for growth, not just in existing activities, but from new activities coming into being.

Need for Flexibility in a Personnel Program   In this context of change, a successful personnel policy requires a certain amount of opportunism. Flexibility should be built into the long-range plan, first by remembering that it is a *plan* and not an irrevocable commitment. If a man were to walk into some companies today with a brand-new, tremendously profitable idea that would require the addition of twenty new people to the organization, he would get turned away— not because his idea was suspect, but because the company decision makers on matters of personnel were not prepared to add twenty people.

Some flexibility can be achieved by the application of a little more imagination. Many of the new products marketed in the past ten years could not have been totally unforeseen. They were logical extensions of existing product forms. And by looking around us— with an open mind—we should be able to foresee new areas of activity in our own organizations. These may not necessarily require the addition of personnel, but they will certainly mean that different skills, aptitudes, and backgrounds will be required.

SOURCES TO PROVIDE PERSONNEL

We move on now to the next major area of personnel management responsibility: *developing sources to provide the necessary personnel.* These sources are usually thought of as either *internal* or *external* to the organization.

This is an obvious dichotomy, of course, but one which often involves questions of basic company policy, and frequently very strong feelings. Accordingly, before developing means of tapping personnel sources, it is essential to consider the rationales offered for each of these two different approaches.

Promotion from Within

In organizations which rely on internal sources, the policy is usually expressed as one of "promote from within." Some companies live by this policy, and the argument generally offered in support of it, whether explicit in policy statements or implicit in management attitudes, is that it produces a healthy effect on the morale of company personnel.   The idea is that nothing is so demoralizing to a man as being passed over in favor of one from another organization, and that nothing is so reassuring as being elevated to a higher level.

This rationale has much to be said for it, including the fact that it is subscribed to by some corporations with whose financial success I am not about to argue.   Then again, such success may indicate only that the "promote from within" approach is *usually* better.   In any event, it is not always wise to adhere to it slavishly.

Dangers of Automatic Promotion   While it is always good for a company to let its people know that merit will be rewarded, anything that tends to make the rewarding process *automatic*—or seem so—is likely to work against the company's best interests.   While insecurity is bad from the worker's standpoint, too much security is bad from the company's.   It may discourage competitiveness, a determination to make one's best effort, a strong desire to excel.   In the advertising and marketing fields, whatever diminishes these traits and motivations is especially hard to justify.

One more reservation about the wisdom of a promote-from-within policy has to be registered.   In Biblical language, "a prophet is not without honor, save in his own country."   When a man is promoted to Chief, after having been an Indian for quite a spell, are the other Indians going to accept readily any innovations, any visionary approaches he brings to the job, or are they going to have him so firmly fixed in their minds as the guy who did what he was told that they will never wholeheartedly be able to follow his lead?

The "Look-outside" Approach

On the other hand, the organization that persists in passing over its own people and bringing in newcomers for all key positions indicates a lack of confidence in (1) its own people, and (2) its own ability to develop people, which is worse.

The rationale offered for the "look-outside" approach is that an infusion of new blood is healthy and even necessary.   This may indeed be true—at least in specific situations.   But if it once becomes obvious to the rank and file that such transfusions are going to take place only when the job to be filled is a *key* one, they are going to lose their incentive.   Any worker worth his salt in the advertising and marketing field who knows it is futile to aspire to a higher position in the organization, or who knows that his promotion will be more or less automatic, is sapped of his drive to get ahead.

Best Approach: A Hedge

Between the two extremes—relying on internal sources exclusively, or external exclusively—the best approach is a hedge, a little of each.   And perhaps the majority of companies, if they have a definite policy at all, have one that fits this description.   Thus their attitude is that it is usually better to promote from within *if* the promotable material is available; if not, they will turn to outside sources.   This allows the man who is charged with the hiring or promoting decision to obtain whoever seems to him the best man available for the job.

This is certainly a freedom to be desired.   But as we have determined, there is no such thing as a single personnel decision.   Even though one candidate may appear to possess exactly the skills required for an open job, there may be serious ramifications in offering it to him.   It is these ramifications which may outweigh the feasibility of filling that job with a "heavyweight," ramifications which encourage companies to adhere to personnel promotion polices.

In any event, whether a company pursues a rigid policy of "promote from within," or is willing to bring in outsiders to fill key spots, either approach answers only the problem of input to the top—an important part of the personnel man's responsibility, but still only a part.

Need to Systematize

Input of personnel at lower levels may not be so heady a business for the personnel manager, but without satisfactory provisions for this activity, a company will either wind up with all Chiefs and no Indians, or be filled with lower echelon people who are not promotable. The challenge in this area is difficult enough, without the added complication of an unsystematic approach.   The need to systematize the task requires careful scrutiny by the personnel manager.

"Personnel Circuitry"   To begin with, it is important that the personnel man become familiar with what I call the "personnel circuitry" of his company.   It may take a few weekends of poring over personnel files, but the result is worth the effort.   The idea is to form a clear mental diagram that traces the path typically taken by workers entering each department.   Do they typically come in at the "bottom" (meaning without actual previous experience) or from the "side" (meaning from a comparable rank in either another company or another department in this company)?   Do they typically make lateral moves (to comparable ranks in the same or other departments) before moving up, or do they proceed straight up?   Do they usually complete the circuit of their career within the given department? And so on.

Personnel Self-sufficiency   With enough of this kind of analysis, the personnel man can then take the next important step—that of formulating an accurate idea of the *personnel self-sufficiency* of his company.   At this point he should be able to sit back and, thinking of his company as a wasting-assets corporation with people as its only asset, determine how long it would be able to support itself until those assets had to be replenished or had depreciated to zero.   This is not merely an academic exercise; it is often surprising what sources of personnel can be turned up this way—and what you can learn about the operations of the whole enterprise, too.

To illustrate: Let us say that employees starting in Department A must have some background in market research, and that such people are ten times harder to find than suitable people for Department B, who can start in right after college.   But let us also say that because of the exposure that the workers in Department B get to market research, they generally can qualify for starting positions in Department A.   There is in this situation, then, an element of company self-sufficiency—in that B can generate a certain amount of personnel for A.   Conditions in the marketplace for talent actually make it economically more feasible, and sounder from an all-around business standpoint, to overstaff Department B somewhat, bringing in all its people at the bottom (and at a lower dollar figure) and gradually identifying some of them for moves into Department A, rather than bringing in *any* outsiders for A.

Variation of Self-sufficiency Exercise   A variation of the self-sufficiency exercise is to suppose that suddenly all channels of personnel input from the "side" are cut off and that the only source of new personnel is from the bottom.   Imagine that your company is unable to hire anyone from another company with job experience in the function he would perform for your organization, and that you must rely on people just starting in the business and at the lowest echelons.   Assuming an adequate supply of such people, how long would it take to move them up the ladder—so that higher jobs would not have to either go unfilled as their occupants retire or resign, or be filled with frustrated people who should be moving up but cannot because no one is immediately available to handle their jobs? Even an approximate answer will give you some idea of the pressure on the personnel department in terms of what sort of demands it may have to supply.   Note that this is a different question from the matter of the quantitative estimating discussed earlier, as required of department heads.   In their case, the question is primarily one of estimating the number of people they will require at precise points in time; but they cannot be expected to know the rate of personnel *flow* through the entire company, nor what percentage of that flow can be provided for by bringing in people new to the business, and what cannot.   This kind of analysis is the responsibility of personnel management.

When You Look Outside   In any event, the purpose of these various exercises in corporate introspection is to enable you to be more realistic when you look outside—to campuses, personnel agencies, even competitors—for personnel input.   Knowing approximately the volume of personnel input required by your company, and the levels —bottom of the ladder, middle echelon, or top—at which that input can or must be made, you will know in turn whether it makes sense to put your major effort in campus recruitment; to concentrate on specific campuses; to develop a special kind of training program; to build personnel "bridges" to certain types of companies where impending cutbacks or mergers may open up a potential supply of good material; to rely on agents and advertising to pull in likely candidates, and so on.

Campus Recruitment   On the subject of these efforts, a few things should be said.   First, regarding the campus program: Today's level of sophistication and education makes it more important than ever that college recruitment be done on a professional basis.   This does not mean giving your presentation such a high Madison Avenue sheen that the sober student looking for a business connection where he will be taken seriously will be frightened off.   It simply means making adequate preparations so that the people worth hiring develop sufficient respect for your organization that they aspire to employment there.

Employment Agencies Regarding the use of employment agencies: All too often a flurry of résumés is generated, most of which are a waste of the company's, the agent's, and the candidate's time.   When this happens, it is frequently because the job, its requirements, and the necessary qualifications for filling it are poorly, if at all, defined to the agency.   If it is part of your plan to use such agencies—and they can often be a good source of material—give them the benefit of your best possible guidance.   The time that is saved may be your own.

Personnel Shopping List In the preceding sections, we have taken steps toward creating what will be, in effect, a "shopping list" for the personnel department.   On the basis of the determinations and con- siderations built into such a list, the department can do its shopping for the people needed in present and future advertising and market- ing activities.   But like many shopping housewives, some managers of personnel have perhaps become too conditioned to the supermar- ket approach, to looking for each "item" on their list in the appro- priately designated section.   In short, they may have developed a more or less restricted outlook about where certain types of people are to be found for certain types of jobs.

What Kind of Experience? This tendency may not be so strong as it was once, as personnel professionals have moved from an emphasis on experience to an emphasis on aptitudes.   Even so, I suspect there are many managers who still feel strongly that "if you want somebody who can do that job, get somebody who *has* done it."   Thus they look for copy writers among copy writers, product managers among product managers, and so forth—a practice that may be foreclosing areas of vast personnel potential.

The trend today throughout business and industry—as com- panies merge, as different disciplines join forces in complex projects, as electronic communications and programed teaching make all types of knowledge readily accessible—is to a cross-pollination of skills and abilities.   Even the man who calls himself a "specialist" now is often possessed of such a wide array of talents and knowledge that he would have been classified as a minor Leonardo da Vinci not too long ago.   The interweaving of disciplines and technology and informa- tion so prevalent today is bound to open up new sources of qualified personnel.   At this juncture, I cannot offer proof that a good orni- thologist will make a good ad manager, or even an outstanding psychologist a fair marketing man.   But I can offer the reminder that "gold is where you find it"—and it may well be in the best interests of personnel seekers to do their panning in some previously unworked stream.

BEST MEANS OF USING PERSONNEL

Let us move on to the third major responsibility in the managing of advertising and marketing personnel: *devising the best means of using that personnel, once obtained.*

Certain aspects of this responsibility involve problems and considerations that are peculiar to the handling of advertising or marketing people, and some are aspects that apply to the handling of personnel generally.   We shall take them in that order.

Problems Peculiar to Advertising Personnel   As suggested earlier, there is perhaps a tendency to feel that anything resembling a logical approach to dealing with people in this field is impractical—because of the very nature of the field and the people in it.   This sort of work requires more than the usual share of creativity, and creative people are supposed to be unpredictable, unfathomable, and even unmanageable when expected to function in a business context.

That they may be unpredictable and sometimes unfathomable, I will concede; but unmanageable, no.   If we differ on this, it may be because we have different ideas of what "manageable" means.

Excess of Management   I have known managers—sometimes thoroughly professional, highly efficient ones—whose big mistake in this field was an *excess* of management.   They insisted on calling staff meetings, holding conferences, and threshing out things that did not need threshing out.   They persisted in "managing" what did not require managing—and the result was resistance from their people, rather than cooperation.   The fewer management exercises forced on the creative staff, the better.   I do not advocate letting them go their wild, undisciplined ways, but do advocate enabling them to do as much of their creative work as possible *before* insisting on harnessing it.

Now, of course, if the so-called creative person happens to be one of those who professes to scorn commercialization—and therefore management—of his genius, that is another matter.   In such a case, it will be a good idea to find out if his professions are genuine, and if he really feels the way he says, you had better evaluate realistically his contribution to the business and decide accordingly whether he should be allowed to continue—before he poisons the whole atmosphere for his fellow workers.

Three Phases of Management's Job

But assuming that the creative people in question are not of this type, and management is not oppressive, the conflict of goals—their's and management's—can still be a potential source of problems. It is my thesis that if management will conceive its job here in three distinct phases and act accordingly, many of the problems can be avoided.

The "Clear-guidance Phase" First is the "clear-guidance phase." Letting creative people alone long enough to be creative is wise, but not at the outset of a project. Too often, management presents merely a vague inkling of what is expected, then waits to see what the creative group will come up with, hoping that somebody's hunch in the creative group will clear up what management itself is fuzzy about. Such quasi-assignments frequently begin with "See if you can come up with a couple of ideas for . . . ," and the outcome is left to chance. The creative people then go back to their offices and try to out-guess management. When they come back with concepts— often fully executed, unfortunately—the concepts are more often than not way off target. Result: The one who made the assignment is not satisfied (and may erroneously question the qualifications of his creative people), the creative people are disgruntled because their work is rejected, and valuable time is lost.

The better way, and this puts the initial burden where it should be, on the manager, is to give creative people the clearest possible guidance at the outset. Such guidance will generally be more successful if it is primarily addressed to *objectives*—to spelling out end results required of whatever creative approach is eventually accepted, rather than telling the doers how to go about doing their work.

At times, of course, it will be necessary to make assignments of an exploratory nature—for example, where creative people are asked to submit ideas and approaches so that management can then determine the initial feasibility of a project. In such a case, the fact that the work is to serve an exploratory purpose should be explained, as should any other relevant information that will help to guide those who have to do the creating.

The "Let-alone Phase"   Next is the "let-alone phase." This should be the easiest, but for managers with a tendency to overmanage, it is the most difficult.   If they do not *see* something happening, they conclude that nothing *is* happening.   The one given the assignment is called in to make a progress report, which not only interrupts his progress, but forces him to reveal partly worked out ideas—showing them in their worst possible light.   How many creative cakes have fallen as a result of this insistence on opening the oven too soon, it would be impossible to calculate.

If the nature of the project is such as to dictate the feasibility of checkpoints along the way, so that the worker cannot proceed too far in the wrong direction, then establish these checkpoints at the time the assignment is made. ' Let the man know that something must be seen in two weeks and again in four weeks, and so on, right from the start. He will not only be able to function better in the interim, but time and effort will not be wasted on "eyewash"—the tangible but meaningless material that some workers feel compelled to create, just to satisfy management that results are forthcoming, while the actual work is being produced free from surveillance.

The "Review Phase"   The last phase is the "review phase," in which the creative work passes in review before management.   No one can tell the decision makers what they should like; the considerations they bring to bear on their determination to approve or disapprove are matters for their own judgment.   But one thing is essential: the same objectives, the same ground rules that were spelled out to the creative people when the assignment was made, should be in force when the material is reviewed.

I know of cases where creative material was reviewed not only with the original objectives disregarded, but by a group completely different from that which first made the assignment.   Result: The group quickly decided that the work presented to it was all wrong (and began to question qualifications of the creative people *and* those who had made the assignment), the creative people were disgusted (questioning in their minds both groups), and valuable time was lost.

Who Should Review   Whenever possible, those who *make* the assignment should be the first to review the work done to *fill* that assignment.   If they are not satisfied, using the objectives communicated to the workers as a measuring device, the work should be revised accordingly, before any presentation is made to a higher level.   Violation of this procedure is one of the surest ways to convince creative people that management either is not fair in its approach to the decision-making process, or is unqualified to judge the merits of a piece of creative work. At that point, they will indeed begin to behave in a way that makes management suspect they are "unmanageable."

In sum, then, give them clear guidance, let them alone while they follow it, then review in accord with the objectives set forth when the assignment was made. Incidentally, application of this threefold procedure to "creative" people does not mean merely to artists or copy writers, but to anyone in the entire marketing activity from whom any kind of effort that can be designated as creative is required. My experience has been that the results will more than justify the self-discipline required of management in applying this procedure.

Placing and Moving People

In general, devising the best means of using personnel is a matter of *placing* people properly to begin with and of *moving* them properly thereafter. Getting them into the right slots to begin with is challenge enough in itself, but for personnel management, the task does not end there. No successful organization can continue to be successful with frozen personnel assets. Both the people themselves and the company's best interests require that provision be made for a certain amount of dynamism within the structure. Men want to move up, a fact that is at once a problem and an opportunity. It is a problem because moving up requires a suitable position they can move up to, and causes a chain reaction of moves; it is an opportunity because it provides an inducement that can be used to encourage the individual's best effort.

From the personnel manager's standpoint, the factors involved are so numerous that placing and moving people in the organization according to some kind of *plan* often seems impossible. The task takes on the character of a human chess game to be played within the dimension of time as well as place.

Despite the apparent complexities, a certain amount of simplification is possible. Devising the best ways to use people is a chore that should be looked at from two separate perspectives: the company's perspective and the individual's perspective.   Let us tackle them one at a time.

The Company's Perspective

The order in which I have stated these perspectives is no accident. Today there is such a tendency to stress *worker* benefits, incentives, and satisfactions, that the goals of the company are sometimes overlooked.   Do not mistake what is being said here for advocacy of a return to the early conditions of the Industrial Revolution; I am simply pointing out that pleasing the *worker,* in material terms at least, is not necessarily satisfying the *company's* needs.

The following five points constitute the minimal necessity for satisfying the company's goals through the use of people:

1. *The means to cast a worker in the right role.*   Obviously, he can make his best contribution only in a job he is suited for.   But what he is suited for may change as he matures and gains experience. Thus the accepted techniques of tests and interviews, necessary before his first job assignment, should be continued and supplemented by performance reviews with superiors and co-workers at *periodic intervals* throughout his career.

2. *The means to prepare him for higher roles.*   This responsibility should be approached from the top down, with the men at the highest level specifically preparing those below for *their* jobs, and so on down the line.   Two additional approaches are: (*a*) "multiple management"—in which a second "board of directors," for example, is designated from among junior personnel, who function just as a real board would, grappling with the same problems and reaching "decisions," but without actual authority; and (b) job rotation—in which managers and supervisors trade departments, so that the head of Department A is required to run Department B for a given time, and vice versa.   Further training would include attendance at special seminars, business or art school courses, lectures, etc.

3. *The means to keep him.*   While this involves items that are of paramount importance to the worker himself—compensation and other benefits—the matter must be given serious consideration by the company for its own benefit.   Otherwise, the organization may find itself serving as a preparatory school for another company, quite probably a competitor.   This question should be thought through *prior* to hiring the man, to whatever extent is possible.   If, for rea-

sons of budgetary limitations or whatever, you see only a dim chance of retaining a man beyond a year or so, your company may be better off in the long run foregoing the sizable contribution he might make in the short haul.

4. *The means for dealing with problems.* Dealing with the worker's problems is, of course, a method of retaining him. But we must look at the matter from a wider view. It is not enough to satisfy one man so that he will continue to make his contribution to the organization. We must also deal with his grievances to prevent his dissatisfactions from spreading to his co-workers. The "open-door" policy is one of the most effective methods yet devised, every man knowing that he can gain access to his superior's office, and ear, for the airing of reasonable grievances. Regular staff get-togethers (the informal kind are usually more productive); specially called meetings, with "problems" constituting the agenda; private interviews; confidential questionnaires—these are other important devices in the repertory of the successful personnel manager.

5. *Procedure for removal.* When the cost of keeping a man in the company is greater than the loss from letting him go, someone in the organization has to face the matter and make a decision. No two specific cases will ever be exactly alike; hence no precise formula can be set forth regulating firing decisions. But in any case, the *procedures* should not be improvised. Once the decision has been made, the sequence of events should proceed generally as follows: complete determination of all matters pertaining to severance, benefits, etc.; advising of immediate superior of date that notification is to be made; actual notification; discussion immediately thereafter with appropriate representative of personnel concerning all terminal matters; provision for vacation of office or other area occupied at the earliest opportunity thereafter, with special care being taken to obtain all confidential material, keys, files, work in progress, and so on.

This is a job nobody relishes, but recognition of two guiding principles will serve to make things smoother: First, the company is seldom doing any man a favor when it keeps him on beyond the point where his continuation is not in the company's interest. The longer this situation continues, the more difficult it may be for him to relocate when the inevitable happens. Second, even dismissal for reasons of his incompetence or downright wrongdoing can be handled without rancor on the part of the company's representative. This should be strict policy, not only to avoid working emotional hardship on those dismissed, but to minimize the damage that a man tending to vindictiveness may accomplish.

The Individual's Perspective

With the company's perspective duly considered, the successful personnel manager has to be able to put himself in the employee's shoes and see things from the *individual's perspective*. Here are the minimum essentials:

1. *Compensation.* In reality, compensation is simply a dignified euphemism for *money*. A company may feel it is better public relations, when advertising for people, to couch its approach in euphemistic terms, but there would not be many replies if readers did not think the term meant cash. And even the package that contains many peripheral benefits should be analyzed by the personnel man with regard to their monetary value—either as hard-nosed information to support his bargaining position (if bargaining becomes necessary), or to avoid the shock of return to reality when the candidate says, "Never mind the trimmings, what am I going to be paid?" I suspect that some personnel people need a reorientation on the subject of compensation; they have read and heard so much about the satisfaction demanded by that "inner man" who apparently lurks inside each employee, that somehow they think less of the candidate who equates his ability with dollars. True, there are many things to hold a man to a job besides money, but he still has to pay his bills, and the fully equipped gym on the second floor is not much help in that direction.

2. *Additional incentives.* Having made certain that the horse is kept before the cart, by realizing that money is the foremost reason men work, we can proceed to a recognition of *other* reasons, and the part they can play in attracting and holding good men.

Among these, of course, are all the items usually lumped together as "benefits"—including stock options, profit-sharing, life insurance, bonuses, etc. When presented properly, in a way that does not make them sound like substitutes for the salary the man should be getting but is not, they can go a long way to convince him to join your company; and when they begin to appear later in more tangible form, they will naturally provide an added inducement for him to stay. On the less tangible side, but equally compelling when presented properly, are such things as good working conditions, ability to associate with top professionals in the field, interesting assignments, etc.

3. *Promotion opportunities.* Obviously, not every man who comes in at the bottom can get to the top of his company; if he could, there would probably be a new president or chairman every few days. Even the most ambitious employee knows he has to live with this fact of corporate life. At the same time, once a man *knows* he cannot go up, the adjustment required will generally result in one of two things: his settling into a routine performance of the job; or the mere biding of time until he can move to greener pastures. Often, the personnel man will be in no position to resolve this situation; there are only so many successively higher jobs into which persons can be moved. Not to recognize the consequences is to risk losing strong people by disregarding one of their primary motivations.

4. *Growth opportunities.* This is not necessarily synonymous with promotion opportunities. Any man worth hiring will appreciate opportunities to grow while on the job—to expand his horizon, to attain higher standards of professionalism, to develop new skills. These will not only be important to him for their own sake, but also will help toward the next essential.

5. *Ability to make the maximum contribution to his company.* Between two men who are both receiving adequate compensation for their work, you will often find that one is much happier in his job, and therefore much more inclined to stay on it and to keep others on theirs. This will almost invariably be the man who is making the bigger contribution to the success of his company. When a man realizes that his contribution is having a positive, worthwhile effect on the progress of his company—in short, that it is putting his talents to good use—he is seldom in any mood to leave.

In many of the impersonal entities known today as corporations, where any output is apt to be dehumanized by the sheer number of operations that go to produce it, not to mention the effect of automation, it is increasingly difficult for the individual employee to identify any particular contribution to the output as uniquely his own. As this tendency to a diminished sense of participation continues, the importance of finding ways for individuals to contribute—and to let them know they are contributing—mounts. Any manager, personnel or otherwise, who can open such opportunities for his people is truly devising the best means of using his personnel.

A brief comparison of the items listed as essential from the *company's perspective* with those listed as essential from the *individual's perspective* will indicate a certain amount of overlapping.   In that overlapping is the real *raison d'être* of a worthwhile personnel program.   The more the goals of the company and the individual can be made to coincide, the better it is for both.   When the company can progress toward the attainment of *its* objectives by creating conditions in which the employees can progress toward the attainment of *theirs,* both are headed for a most successful future.

CHAPTER SEVEN

Structure and Functions of the Advertising Agency*

JOHN CRICHTON   *President, American Association of Advertising Agencies*

NATURE OF AGENCY BUSINESS

There are either 7,000 or 9,000 advertising agencies in the United States, depending on whether one uses the arithmetic of the U.S. Census of Business or the listings in classified telephone directories of cities over 20,000 population.   Significantly, if one applies the test of payroll, the 7,000 figure becomes 4,500.   That is to say, 35 per cent of the agencies counted by the census are one-man operations.

Even among the 4,500 establishments, many are very small businesses.   For example, 1,400 establishments have an annual volume of

---

* Much of the material in this chapter is drawn from a publication of the American Association of Advertising Agencies called "Advertising Agencies: What They Are, What They Do, and How They Do It."   This booklet is in turn based on a lecture by Frederic R. Gamble, then president of the association, at the University of Missouri School of Journalism, in 1958.

business of less than $100,000 and have an average of two employees.   Another 1,900 establishments have annual volume between $100,000 and $500,000, and on the average have five employees.

Finally, there are 550 establishments (not agencies, since this figure would include branch offices) which bill more than $1 million.

It is a small business.   It employs, the census says, 65,000 people.   An informed guess is that, since the last census covered the year 1963, a current number might be 68,000.   This is fewer people than work for Boeing Aircraft.

They range in size from one-man agencies to multioffice companies with 3,000 employees in this country and 8,000 worldwide.   They manage to serve 15,000 regional or national advertisers, and many additional thousands (no one knows the number, even for estimate) of local advertisers.

WHAT AN ADVERTISING AGENCY IS

An advertising agency is (1) an *independent* business organization (2) composed of *creative and business* people (3) who *develop, prepare, and place advertising* in advertising media (4) for *sellers seeking to find customers* for their goods and services.

An agency may do a good many other things related to advertising, aimed at helping to make the advertising succeed, but if the agency does not prepare and place advertising, it is *not* an advertising agency.

Let us examine the definition, since each of the four points has relevance.

1. Independent

An advertising agency is an independent business organization, independently owned and not owned by advertisers or media or suppliers.

Independent so as to bring to the clients' problems an outside objective point of view made more valuable by experience with other clients' sales problems in other fields.

Independent of the clients so it may always be an advocate of advertising—trying to apply advertising to help clients grow and prosper.

Independent of media or suppliers so it may be unbiased in serving its clients, who are the sellers of goods and services.

2. Composed of Creative and Business People

An advertising agency is composed of creative and business people. They are writers and artists, showmen and market analysts, and merchandising men and women. They are research people, sales people, advertising specialists of all kinds, ranging from fashion to typography. They are also business people, running an independent business, financially responsible, applying their creative skills to the business of helping to make their clients' advertising succeed.

3. Who Develop, Prepare, and Place Advertising in Advertising Media

The advertising agency is a specialist organization. It seeks to apply advertising to advance its clients' businesses. What goes before the advertising in the way of preparation, and everything that comes after the advertising in follow-up to make the advertising succeed, is in a sense subsidiary to the advertising. To prepare and place advertising—successful advertising for the advertiser—is the primary purpose of the advertising agency.

4. For Sellers Seeking to Find Customers

The advertising agency does this, not for itself, but for sellers seeking to find customers for the sellers' goods and services.

WHAT ADVERTISING AGENCIES DO

In this discussion, most of the description is drawn from the "Agency Service Standards" of the American Association of Advertising Agencies (AAAA), first published in 1924, and widely copied and adapted by agency associations around the world.

Service Standards

The service standards delineate fundamentals of successful agency operation, and they enable advertisers and media to know what to require, and agencies to know what may be expected of them, in dealing with the problems of advertising.

Agency service, the service standards say, consists of interpreting to the public, or to that part of it which it is desired to reach, the advantages of a product or service.

Four Key Elements This interpretation is based on four key elements:

1. A study of the client's product or service in order to determine the advantages and disadvantages inherent in the product itself, and the relation of the product to its competition.

2. An analysis of the present and potential market for which the product or service is adapted, taking into account location, extent of possible sale, the seasonal sales pattern, the trade and economic conditions, and the nature and amount of competition.

3. A knowledge of the factors of distribution and sales and their methods of operation.

4. A knowledge of all the available media, and the means which can profitably be used to carry the interpretation of the product or service to the consumer, wholesaler, dealer, contractor, or other factor. This knowledge of media would include pertinent facts about the medium such as its character, influence, circulation— quantity, quality, and location—physical requirements, and costs.

Based on the analysis and knowledge explained here, the agency makes recommendations to the client, these recommendations are formulated into a plan, and the plan is presented to the client. (This plan is discussed later.)

Execution of the Plan When the client has approved the plan, the agency proceeds to execute the plan. This entails:

1. Writing, designing, and illustrating advertisements, or other appropriate forms of the message

2. Contracting for the space, time, or other means of advertising

3. The proper incorporation of the message in mechanical form and forwarding it with proper instructions for the fulfillment of the contract

4. Checking and verifying insertions, display, or other means used

5. Auditing and billing for the service, space, and preparation

Finally, the agency will cooperate with the client's sales work, to ensure the greatest effect from the advertising.

Into this pattern fit the personnel of the agency: the account executives who contact the client, the art directors, copy writers, space and time buyers, researchers, print production people, television and radio production people, and others who work in advertising agencies.

Additional Agency Services

In addition to advertising service, many agencies are willing to assist the client with other problems of selling and distribution.

Agencies will do special work for the manufacturer in such fields as package designing, sales research, sales training, preparation of sales and service literature, designing of merchandising displays, public relations, and publicity.

A key point to remember is that the agency must justify such work by doing it more satisfactorily than can either the manufacturer himself or a specialists firm in one of the fields—a competing expert.

THE ADVERTISING AGENCY PROCESS

It will be recalled from the four-element interpretation stated previously that two of the key points were a knowledge of the factors of distribution and sales and a knowledge of media.

Knowledge of Distribution

The knowledge about distribution and sales factors is usually acquired through study, reading, and experience—with special emphasis on experience, since factors and methods of distribution vary widely from industry to industry (hence from client to client) and also because they are constantly changing.

Accordingly, agency personnel are expected to visit and study a wide range of retail and service outlets: supermarkets, service stations, warehouses, banks, restaurants, hotels, railroad and bus terminals, airline offices.   They travel with salesmen, talk with clerks and store managers, visit consumers in their homes—probing, studying, observing, analyzing, looking for up-to-date knowledge of distribution, sales, and methods of operation which they need to know.

Knowledge of Media

Something of the same process applies to the knowledge of media. There are some 600 consumer magazines and 150 farm publications in this country, each with a different combination of characteristics, and often with different editions, regional, geographic, or demographic, which may be bought in various combinations; there are approximately 2,300 business publications, serving different fields of business, and different kinds of specialists within the fields; there are roughly 1,800 daily newspapers, and 8,900 weekly newspapers, each serving a geographic area; the national television and radio networks spanning the country; the 800 commercial television stations and 6,500 radio stations which serve local areas; the 700 outdoor plants in the country which post their panels along high-concentration traffic arteries; there are about 70 companies in the transit advertising business—car cards and posters in buses, subways, taxicabs, trains, stations, airports. This incredible variety of media, the complex of communications in a large industrial country, requires constant attention and study in order for one to be able to analyze and recommend advertising investments.

But there are also highly specialized media about which the agency needs to be knowledgeable—window and store displays, direct mail, premiums, and sampling. The agency needs to be current in knowledge about the available media and the means which can be used to carry their clients' messages to potential customers or trade factors.

Media are constantly changing. Their character, audience, physical specifications, and costs require continuing study by hundreds of agency specialists and researchers whose main responsibility is being current with this information.

There is much more information about media—in both a quantitative and qualitative sense—in the United States than in any other country in the world. More information is constantly being sought.

So much for the two things agencies know and how they go about keeping what they know current.

Research

The first three things they do involve *research*—the agency is studying the product or service; the agency is analyzing the present and potential market; from this study they formulate a definite plan, and after client approval (and changes, in many cases), move on to execution.

Research provides the solid floor of facts on which to practice the art of advertising.

Before plans can be made for an advertising program, and before advertisements can be created, facts are needed on many points, including:

1. What are the uses of the product; what form of the product is

more useful, and would changes or proliferation of form or a change in packaging be useful?

2. What are the product's advantages and disadvantages compared with competing products?

3. What kinds of people can use it and where are they situated? What is their frequency of purchase and rate of use?

4. What will (it is hoped) persuade them to buy it?

THE ADVERTISING PLAN

The most important function and the high point in agency operation is the making of the advertising plan. It might be said that the first half of the agency's work consists of making the plan; the second half, of putting the plan into operation.

Into the plan go—as recommendations to the client—these basic points:

1. Market or markets to be reached
2. What distribution changes to make, if any
3. What needs to be done about prices and discounts, if anything
4. What media channels in general to employ in carrying the message to the customer and the channels of trade
5. What appeals to employ
6. What to say—what the appropriate message in each channel is
7. What merchandising factors—salesmen, dealers, distributors —need to be contacted, educated, and brought into the work

After the agency has client approval of the plan, the execution of it begins.

EXECUTION OF THE PLAN

One of the points under discussion in the plan is a decision on media channels to be used. When that is agreed, copy writers and art directors for print media, and television and radio creative people, put the advertising into words and pictures.

Writing Copy

Agency copy writers for print media certainly need to be skilful in the use of words, but perhaps primarily they need to understand people and the motives which cause people to act.

They need the skill to present the advertiser's message forcefully and in good taste. Copy writers often do more than write headlines and text; they frequently sketch the layout or illustration or develop the idea on which it is based. There has been a blurring of the line of responsibility in creative work, largely induced by media such as television and magazines which depend heavily on photographs, so that copy writers tend to do things formerly done by art directors. The reverse is equally true: art directors frequently produce both the idea and much of the text for the copy.

Television and radio require special techniques. So television and radio messages—program commercials or spot announcements—are almost always handled within the agency through the joint efforts of writers, art directors, and broadcast producers.

Writing and production of television and radio *programs* is today most likely to be done by outside specialists—free-lancers, package producers, motion picture companies, or broadcasters themselves.

There are about 6,500 writers employed in advertising agencies, working in all media.

Making Illustrations

Agency art directors and artists work with the agency copy writers, account executives, or the advertising manager of the client company to suggest ways to arrange illustrations and text in the print advertisements. They make layouts or visuals to show how the finished advertisement will look. Sometimes they make the drawing or painting that is reproduced in the advertisement, although most finished artwork is bought outside the agency from individual free-lance artists or art studios.

Agency artists and art directors customarily work on the storyboards, the layouts for television commercials. They also do lettering, layouts, and sometimes finished artwork for booklets, folders, displays, labels, and other printed materials.

The trend to visualization in advertising has made the art director's influence more powerful and pervasive. As America is an increasingly visual society, the art director's role has become progressively more important. Abroad, where advertising has to leap language differences, the art director and the visualization of advertising have always been key elements in advertising's success.

There are about 5,400 people employed in agencies in all phases of visualization.

Contracting for Space and Time

Once the decision is made as to media to be used, when it is to be used, and in what amounts, the agency contracts with the publisher, broadcaster, or other media owners for the space or time desired.

Most agencies voluntarily use, and media in the vast majority accept, the order blanks copyrighted by the American Association of Advertising Agencies. These order blanks were developed to facilitate the placing of business by agencies and the acceptance of it by media. The order blanks in use are: Copyrighted Order Blank for Publications; Copyrighted Contract for Spot Broadcasting; Copyrighted Contract for Spot Telecasting; and Copyrighted Order Blank for Transportation Advertising.

Print and Broadcast Production

When the copy is written and the artwork is finished, and when they have been approved inside the agency and at the client organization, the production department converts them into printing plates or other mechanical material used to produce finished advertisements in publications or other print media.

These mechanical materials are usually purchased from outside suppliers, under the supervision of the print production manager. For this work a thorough knowledge of printing, engraving, typography, electrotyping, photography, and other technical processes and materials is necessary. To supervise such an operation requires creative ability, technical knowledge, and administrative and purchasing skills.

Broadcast production is a rapidly growing and rapidly changing field. Since agency men and women do most or all of the creative work on the commercials, the responsibility for the finished product —live, tape, or film—also rests with the agency, although the products may be bought from tape and film producers, or in smaller cities from stations. In almost all cases, the production will be done outside the agency.

Shows and programs are increasingly created outside advertising agencies, although there are still some shows created entirely by advertising agencies. More programs nowadays are purchased from either the networks, stations, or independent show producers.   In most cases, the show is shared with other advertisers.   In the programing area, the agency aims at building or selecting the program which will best attract good prospects for the product, at the most advantageous cost.

Checking, Billing, and Paying

It is part of the agency's responsibility to check media invoices against its orders, to be sure that the advertiser received what was ordered for him; the advertisements are measured in print, or checked against affidavits or monitoring reports in broadcast media, and adjustments are requested where advertising either failed to run or failed to run properly as ordered.

The agency then proceeds in its auditing and billing to collect from the client, usually several days in advance of the date when the agency is required to pay the medium.

A cash discount, allowed by almost all publications and by a number of broadcast media, and passed along by the agency to clients when they pay on time, serves to stimulate prompt payment by advertiser to agency and agency to media.

The agency's other bills for work or materials—e.g., artwork, mechanical materials—are sent to the client either when the job is finished or periodically as may have been arranged with the client.

Cooperation with Sales Work

It is usually necessary for the agency to work with the client, cooperating with his sales work, in order to ensure the greatest effect from the advertising.   This phase of agency service has been considerably expanded in recent years and has led to discussion about advertising agencies becoming "marketing agencies."

The nature and the extent of this cooperation will vary from client to client, and may well vary with the client from time to time over the years as his needs change.   But it is part of the agency's responsibility to help maximize the effect of the advertising prepared and run on the client's behalf.   In marketing and merchandising, agencies employ some 1,400 people.

Contacting Accounts: Client Service

While the other functions of the agency are being performed, the agency maintains liaison with the client, and this close rapport with the client's business, knowledge of the client's problems and the people and responsibilities within the client's organization, is a crucial element in the relationship of agency to client.

This liaison may be performed by an account executive, who is a specialist. He will frequently have experience which is of direct benefit to the client, and in any case he has the responsibility of representing the client's problems and viewpoints within the agency, as he usually represents the agency's thinking and facilities to the client. He will also usually have the responsibility for getting from the agency the talents, planning, and execution necessary to the client's projects, and it is his responsibility to adhere to timetables and budgets.

In a smaller agency this important function will probably be performed by the agency head. In a larger agency it will be handled in an account group, with one or more account executives, headed by an account supervisor.

AGENCY MANAGEMENT

There are three kinds of ability, generally speaking, which are needed in the advertising agency—sales ability, creative ability, and management ability. These three diverse talents are infrequently found in one person. Occasionally an agency principal combines all three, but more often two or more management people join in supplying the needed talents.

Most larger agencies today are corporations, because of advantages adhering to the corporate form in our tax law. Relatively few agencies are partnerships, although among smaller agencies some are sole proprietorships or unincorporated. There are a substantial number of agencies operating as "Sub-Chapter S" corporations, which are permitted a number of tax practices resembling partnerships.

Types of Agency Organization

Advertising agencies are organized in many ways—no two, perhaps, in precisely the same way. Also, most agencies are fluid in their organization, and change their structure from time to time as clients' needs, office requirements, and individual strengths and opinions may dictate. The agency organization will reflect as well contemporary technology and thinking.

Agency management may elect to organize the larger agency in either of two major ways—as a group agency or as a departmental-ized or concentric agency.

In a group agency (and they are usually larger agencies) a group of people handles the contact, planning, and creative work for one or more clients or products, drawing on service departments for such support as is needed.   Similar groups in the agency handle other accounts.

The second type of agency, departmentalized or concentric, is completely departmentalized by the functions performed.   Each department serves all clients.   The account executive calls upon the copy department for the copy writing on his accounts, on the art department for the layouts and illustrations, etc.

Some agencies are a mixture of group and departmentalized types, incorporating certain features of each.   There are countless variations, and frequently the determining factors are the size, character, and location of the client accounts.

Problems: Quality Control and Service Costs

Whether the agency is departmentalized or group in concept, it has the problem of assuring that its service and creative product meet its standards.

As the agency grows, the usual solution is the use of review boards —groups or committees formed from senior members of the agency to study the advertising or marketing plan or the creative work before presentation to the client.   Service work on the accounts may be dealt with less formally, through management supervisors or a special management committee formed to supervise account service.

Service costs are a concomitant of readiness to serve.   The agency must be prepared to handle advertising in any medium for a client, even though he has never used it before, if the agency recommends the medium for the client's purposes.

The agency must be prepared to serve a client whenever and wherever his advertising should run—and the advertising of many advertisers has seasonal peaks, reflecting the seasonal peaks of the client's business.   The agency therefore has to have adequate personnel, with specialists in many fields.

The expense of this readiness to serve is an important factor in agency costs, and it contributes to the sometimes precarious profit picture of the agency business.

Getting Business

Most agencies are justly proud of their record in holding clients. Average account tenure is around eight years, rising to twelve among larger agencies, and many agency-client relationships endure for many decades.

Nonetheless, a vital function of agency management—as in most business enterprises—is getting new business.

Some agencies advertise in newspapers, magazines, and advertising business papers. Some write letters to selected prospects, or send regular mailings of their work or critical acclaim of it. Third, and most general, is personal solicitation.

In this practice, American agencies are differentiated from those of many other countries. In other countries, the solicitation of new business from an advertiser who already has an agency is considered unethical. Some other countries also have agency association prohibitions against speculative presentations—the offering of creative work and planning to a prospective advertising client, frequently in competition with other agencies. In the United States, both solicitation and speculative presentation are ethical, although they may be inadvisable for business reasons.

An American position, sketched in the AAAA's "Standards of Practice," is that the advertising agency should compete on merit. It should not deprecate a competitor or his work, circulate harmful rumors about him, make unwarranted claims, offer credit extension or banking service, or seek to obtain an account by hiring a key employee away from another agency.

Major Cost: People

The crux of the problem of agency management is that the agency business is essentially a business of people. People are the strength of an agency, and an agency tends to be successful largely on the basis of the kind of people it can attract, train, motivate, and retain. The art of agency management is largely the art of hiring and developing the right people, and astutely supervising the deployment of their time and talent.

Approximately two-thirds of the gross income of an agency is paid out in salaries and other compensation to those who work in the business. It is far and away the principal cost of running an advertising agency; the next closest item of cost is rent, and rent is apt to be about one-tenth the cost of people.

Changing Agency Functions

One of the important responsibilities of the agency management is to analyze and anticipate the change of agency functions.

Historically the agency business has initiated some common functions in the advertising and marketing business, and displaced them—spun them off—when it became more practical to have them performed by specialist organizations.

As an example, many agencies owned type fonts and operated typesetting services before enough advertising volume was created to make the typography company an independent resource for all agencies. Many agencies operated art departments which produced finished art, until the advertising volume was sufficient for independent art studios to be formed to serve all agencies (in some United States cities, where the volume is not sufficient to support art studios, agencies still have departments large enough to do finished art). In the early days of research, agencies had research departments and their own field forces of interviewers; then the volume of research business rose to the point where independent research companies could be created which would assume responsibility for maintaining the field interviewers. Finally, in the early days of broadcasting and continuing through the start of the television era, it was customary for agencies to have broadcast program departments capable of creating and supervising broadcast programs, something now largely purchased from other sources.

AGENCY COMPENSATION

Nearly all major media—newspapers, magazines, television, radio, business publications, outdoor plant owners, and transit advertising companies—allow commissions to advertising agencies, which media recognize individually.

Larger advertising agencies receive, on the average, about 75 per cent of their income in the form of commissions allowed by advertising media, 20 per cent from the agency's own percentage charges on purchases (which they specify or supervise for their clients), and 5 per cent in fees of various kinds for special services.

Among medium-sized agencies the corresponding figures would be 70 per cent commissions, 20 per cent from percentage charges, and 10 per cent special service fees.   Among smaller agencies, the figures would be 60 per cent, 25 per cent, and 15 per cent.

Fee Basis

In a fairly recent study of close to 10,000 clients of AAAA agencies, about 3½ per cent of clients paid their agencies on an overall fee basis, the fee agreed upon in advance or based upon the agency's cost plus an agreed overhead and profit factor.

In the same study, on 5 per cent of the accounts (so small, however, as to represent less than 1 per cent of total billing) the agencies received only media commissions, with no additional income from percentage charges or fees.

On the remaining 91½ per cent of accounts AAAA agencies received as their compensation various combinations of media commission, agency percentage charges on purchases of materials and services for clients, and supplementary fees.

In an historical sense, most agencies now derive a higher proportion of their gross income from "agencies' own charges" (i.e., percentage charges on materials and services purchased or supplied, plus fees of all kinds) than they did twenty years ago.   These charges now average more than a third of total agency gross income.   Part of this development has been the growth of increasingly sophisticated cost accounting systems to enable agency managements to determine client profitability.

THE AGENCY-CLIENT RELATIONSHIP

Advertising agencies have enabled many small companies to prosper and grow into large ones.   Agencies hope and expect to be able to help a client to grow; the growth of the agency comes in money and reputation based on what it has achieved for clients.

Today there is scarcely a sizable advertiser who does not rely on an advertising agency for expert, objective counsel and unique creative skills.

Because advertising agencies render professional service adapted to each client's needs, there is much flexibility and variation in the working agreements between agencies and their clients.

Working Agreements

Several basic principles have been established through custom and trial and error:

1. When an agency undertakes to handle the advertising of a product or service, it is usually understood that the agency will refrain from handling at the same time the advertising of another advertiser of a directly competing product or service without the first client's consent.

In turn, the client generally agrees not to engage a second agency to handle part of the advertising of the product or service without the first agency's consent.

2. The agency customarily secures the client's approval of all expenditures connected with his advertising.

3. The client is obligated to pay promptly the agency's bills for publication space and broadcasting time.

It is a fundamental principle that the client must pay the agency in time for the agency to pay media by their due dates.   It is *not* a function of agencies to finance the advertising of their clients, since any extensive financing of clients by agencies would involve so large an amount of capital as to preclude from the agency business people with high talent but modest funds—people whose creative work might do much to increase the volume and success of all advertising.

4. The agency regularly passes on to its client any cash discounts allowed by media, providing that the client pays the agency's bill by the discount date.

THE AGENCY-MEDIA RELATIONSHIP

Agencies and media have had a long relationship.   In the early days, agencies were space brokers for media, buying space for what they could and selling it to whomever they were able, at whatever rates were obtainable.   Today the agency has distinct media responsibilities.

The Agency's Impartial Position

An advertising agency looks with an impartial eye upon all media available for use by its clients—magazines or newspapers, television or radio broadcasting, outdoor posters or painted bulletins, posters in subways, buses, or streetcars, motion picture screens, or direct mail.

The agency is impartial among media.   It seeks to develop advertisers—not newspaper advertisers, nor television advertisers, nor direct-mail advertisers, etc.—nor any other sort of advertiser differentiated by medium.

The agency aims to use advertising to develop the client's business.

What Media Say Agencies Do for Them

Most media managements, most advertising principals and directors of media, have largely grown up with the present advertiser-agency-media structure, and largely accept it as it is.   But when studying that relationship, this is how media views the agency's contributions:

1. The advertising agency develops new business.

2. The agency reduces the hazards of advertising and thereby the mortality rate in the medium's business.

3. The agency advocates the idea of advertising.

4. The agency creates the advertising messages which are an essential element in the sale of space or time which media wish to sell. This is the conversion of white space or blank time into advertising influence.

5. The agency develops and improves advertising techniques and thereby increases the productivity of advertising.

6. The agency simplifies the medium's credit operations and reduces the cost of these operations.

7. The agency carries the risk and cost of credit losses.

8. The agency simplifies the mechanical preparation of advertising and reduces the medium's cost in these operations.

9. The agency reduces the medium's cost in following up advertising schedules to meet publication or broadcasting deadlines.

ETHICS, STANDARDS, AND THE PUBLIC

This particular section is placed last because it does not affect the structure of the agency business and its functions only insofar as economic longevity in our time is likely to be closely related to how well public needs are served.

Over the years, advertising agencies through the AAAA have put high emphasis on ethical standards.   Some of the standards of practice of advertising agencies are defined in contracts between media and agencies, some in agency agreements with clients.

Part of the standards of practice is a "Creative Code," which applies to AAAA members and asserts that member agencies "will not knowingly produce" advertising containing:

1. False or misleading statements or exaggerations, visual or verbal
2. Testimonials which do not reflect the real choice of a competent witness
3. Price claims which are misleading
4. Comparisons which unfairly disparage a competitive product or service
5. Claims insufficiently supported, or which distort the true meaning or practicable application of statements made by professional or scientific authority
6. Statements, suggestions, or pictures offensive to public decency

The code goes on to say that these are areas which are subject to honestly differing interpretation, that taste is subjective and may vary from time to time, as well as from individual to individual. It says finally that "we agree not to recommend to an advertiser and to discourage the use of advertising which is in poor or questionable taste or which is deliberately irritating through content, presentation or excessive repetition."

Perhaps more firmly among advertising agencies than among any other part of the advertising community, there is a conviction that advertising and the public's interest must coincide. As a generalization, one of the roles of the advertising agency is to interpret to the public the product, service, or character of the manufacturer; on the other hand, the agency must frequently interpret to the manufacturer how the public views his product, practices, or reputation. This two-way responsibility cannot be discharged without rapport with and concern for the public.

Further, of the advertiser-agency-media trinity, perhaps only the agency can be said to be fully in the business of advertising. The advertiser is in the chemicals, computer, or cosmetic business, or whatever; if he wished, he could conduct his business without advertising. He does not, largely because costs favor his using advertising. If they did not, he would not use it. Media can exist without advertising, although neither their content nor their circulations would be so large or of such quality. But the agency is wholly in the advertising business. It is, as has been said, an advocate of advertising. It is, as well, in its own best interest but also in the best interest of clients and media, an advocate of truthful and tasteful advertising.

PART THREE

Advertising's Role in Marketing

CHAPTER EIGHT

How Advertising Works

PAUL E. J. GERHOLD   *President, Advertising Research Foundation*

ADVERTISING: A COMPLEX FORCE

This chapter is a description of how advertising works, of the things it does to benefit the advertiser.

The author's original aim was to produce a simple explanation of the advertising process.   As you will see, the explanation has turned out to be less simple than we would all like.

To describe how advertising works has proved to be a little like describing how language works or how music works.   Like language and music, advertising is a form of communication, with certain distinguishing qualities and some distinctive ways of achieving effects. But just as "music" may cover a concert by the New York Philharmonic or a riff on a recorder, so "advertising" may describe an automotive campaign of multimillion dollar, multimodel, multimedia dimensions, or a classified ad that reads: "Wtd: 2½ Rms nr Bus."

Advertising, in the real world, works for many different advertisers, with varied resources and goals and strategies.   And it works for them in many different ways.

Some Simple Statements

In spite of the many forms advertising takes, there have been made available, over the years, both by people in advertising and by opponents of advertising, a number of very neat, very simple descriptions of the advertising process.

We have repeatedly heard, for example, that an advertisement works by creating attention, interest, desire, and action.   More recently we have heard that campaigns work by moving the consumer, over time, through a sequence of brand attitude steps that go from unawareness to purchase.   We have been told that advertising works by building brand images, or by developing and registering unique selling stories.   To some, advertising works by segmenting the total market and particularizing the brand for the chosen segment.   It has been said to work through symbols, through ambiguity, through dissonance.

From the critics of advertising we hear that it works by playing on people's hidden fears and motivations, or by manipulating consumer demand for the advantage of the advertiser, or by distortion or misrepresentation.

So there is no shortage of simple statements about how advertising works.   And there is almost surely some enduring or occasional truth in each of them.   But unfortunately, the simple explanations do contradict one another, and every uncomplicated idea about how advertising does its job seems to have dozens of exceptions, exceptions that cannot be reconciled without destroying or at least complicating the original, simplistic description.

Works in Contradictory Ways

Advertising, in the real world, does its work in marvelously contradictory ways:

Advertising works on the consumer, to change consumer purchasing.   (But the campaign can also affect distribution and how much push retailers will give the brand.)

Advertising works indirectly.   Advertising changes attitudes; it makes people feel more favorably disposed toward a brand.   The sale is made in the store, but the buy is in the mind. (Yet a single mail-order advertisement may make the whole sale, from the first exposure of the product concept to the completion of the purchase transaction.)

Advertising works by conversion, by changing brand preference. (But some campaigns sell hardest against the brand's regular customers, to keep them loyal, or to induce them to buy more, or sooner, or a more expensive model.)

Advertising is a form of salesmanship.   (And yet advertising also is used by people who don't want to sell anything, but want instead to buy, or rent, or hire, or make an investment.)

Advertising, to say it again, is a complex force which does a lot of things, in a lot of different ways, for a lot of different people.   That is why you are now facing a description that tries hard to cover all the things advertising does and all the processes involved in doing them, rather than the uncomplicated explanation you may have expected.

Not only will this discussion not be simple; it will also be less precise and less scientific than you might like it to be.   After thousands of years of advertising and after the expenditure of several decades and many millions of dollars on advertising research, we should know, and we do know, a great deal about the processes of advertising.   But still there are many things about advertising, and especially about how it works in the human mind, that have not been determined, and about which our ideas are still partly speculation.   So it is conceded at the outset that this discussion is going to be somewhat theoretical as well as somewhat complex.

What Advertising Does

A reasonable way to start the discussion is to list some of the different things that advertising does.   We can then use the list as an outline for discussing or speculating about how advertising works in performing each general function.

To work at all, advertising has to do at least some of these things, and generally speaking it probably does most of them:
  1. It gets planned and brought into existence.
  2. It is reproduced, and delivered, and exposed to people.
  3. It is received and assimilated.
  4. It affects ideas and intentions.
  5. It affects product consumption.

6. It responds to time and repeated exposure.
7. It affects trade effort and supply.
8. It affects buying.
9. It changes sales and profits.
10. It changes the market.

These advertising accomplishments will be discussed in sequence, with a hope that, taken together, they will form a coherent, reasonably complete statement on how advertising works.

HOW ADVERTISING COMES INTO EXISTENCE

An ad or an advertising campaign normally starts with a period of planning and preparation.   Before the advertising can appear there must be the creation of a master copy, an original, of the advertising that is to be run, plus some decisions on expenditures and ad sizes and media and timing.

Nature of Advertising Planning

There is no standard set of steps by which the origination of advertising is accomplished.   Planning may be a disciplined process, or telescoped, incomplete, and impulsive.   If it is done systematically, it may include a preliminary investigation, extensive research and analysis, specification and consideration of possible strategic courses, and decisions on direction, followed by studies of budgets and ad sizes and media, the formulation of media plans, and finally contracts or agreements to use certain vehicles to carry the advertising.

Early Creative Activity   Whether the planning is systematic or not, there is always, in the origination of advertising, some kind of creative activity, some exploration and development, some writing of copy, plus possibly some rough art or storyboards.   Usually there is also some discussion and evaluation of alternatives, and then finally production of the plates or tapes or films or recordings in which the master ad or ads are embodied.

By the time these early stages of planning and preparation are completed, the emphasis and direction of the advertising will be rather well determined.

What happens at the start of the advertising process will, by act or omission, influence, for example, whether the advertising will work harder against:

Developed or undeveloped markets

The brand's own customers or its competitors' customers

The retail trade or the ultimate consumer

Early Communication Strategy Early decisions will affect the communication strategy of the advertising:

Broad reach or frequency of contact

Continuity through time or peaking

Emphasis on getting attention or on persuasion

Reliance on emotional or on rational appeals

The planned advertising also will reflect which of several alternative results the advertising should produce:

Increased brand awareness or improved brand opinion

An attitude change, or actual shopping or buying

Short-term or long-term financial payout

There can be few completely clean, uncompromised decisions in any of these areas. Advertising usually cannot affect only the trade, or only consumers; to some degree it will reach both. Similarly, no matter what strategic options are exercised, advertising will usually change both awareness and opinion; it will have some short-term and some long-term payout; it will have both emotional and rational impact.

Also, the execution of an advertising plan almost always changes the plan, at least to some degree. A case in point is how the final advertisement alters the theme or the selling proposition, which usually is decided (if it is decided at all) early in the advertising process.

Media and Copy

Even if the medium is not literally the message, it must be recognized that the medium, the mood, the milieu of the message all have a great deal to do with how the message is perceived and with what the final message actually is. How we say something both conveys and is what we really say.

The style and execution of a print advertisement, or in a television commercial, the casting and lighting, the camera work, and the tempo and feeling may transcend the basic idea, the claim or theme or stated appeal of the advertisement. In a sense the advertisement digests and assimilates the promise around which it is constructed.

This relationship between the theme of an ad and the ad itself is like the relationship between a popular tune and its recording. In the pop music field many songs have little or no existence apart from the hit record that made them popular.   The rendition alters and actually becomes the music; in impact and meaning and feeling the tune finally is what it has been made in its most popular version.

Two ads, presumably from the same campaign, can differ greatly in what they say to the same consumer; and two campaigns for competing products can make the same claim or deliver the same promise, but differ in impact and in response because they differ in how the statement is constructed.

The point to register about this first step in advertising is that setting the budget, choosing the media, and preparing the advertisements strongly affect the way the advertising finally performs even though what happens does not exactly follow our plan or fulfill our expectations.

No General Answer

So the answer to the question of how advertising works is not going to be a general answer.   It is unique to the individual insertion.   It is a function of what the particular advertising is and how it fits the brand and the market at the time it makes its appearance.

HOW ADVERTISING IS BROUGHT TO PEOPLE

In a normal advertising process, copies of the master ad are produced and carried to and exposed to people.   The copying, carrying, and exposing are done by advertising media, and different media do these jobs in quite different ways.

Functions of Advertising Media

The processes are familiar to all of us.   Print ads, we know, are reproduced with plates and inks and paper and the copies are moved physically from where the printing is done and physically circulated.   In broadcast media the master ad is converted into an electrical code and then converted again into a radio signal which is transmitted over the air.   The copies are made after distribution, when the signal is picked up and reconverted by individual receiving sets.

In the case of print advertising, the processes of copymaking, transmission, and exposure may require several hours, or days, or weeks or longer, depending on the specific print vehicle involved.   But for radio and television all these steps take place almost simultaneously, and when live commercials are used, the time sequence may be further foreshortened, since there is then no separate recording of the master ad; distribution and exposure of the ad are simply coincidental with the last step in the creative process.

The quality of reproduction of master ads differs among media vehicles and among ads in the same medium.   There often are variations in quality even between copies of the same ad in the same vehicle; copies as exposed show especially wide differences in radio and television.

Some media vehicles, notably certain painted or animated signs, do not work through a copying process at all.   In these cases only one ad, one unique sign, is actually constructed, and exposures take place because people come near to the master ad, rather than because copies of the ad are brought to people.

In spite of such idiosyncrasies of specific media, it is still true that all media, in one way or another, serve to convey advertising, to offer ads in a place where they can be exposed to people.

Differing Values of Media Audiences

In politics, some individuals are unimportant to a candidate, because they are too young to vote, not registered to vote, don't make their own or affect others' choices, or wouldn't change their minds under any conceivable promise, appeal, or argument.

In the same way and for comparable reasons, some consumers covered by advertising are without identifiable value for a particular advertiser.   Most of the people in the audience of a media vehicle, however, range between marginal and excellent prospects for most advertisers, being neither totally valueless nor, by any logical criteria, completely ideal advertising targets.   (In most cases their value can be judged only roughly, on the basis of inexact and subjective standards, which is one reason why media selection is less than a precise science.)

Differences in the potential value to the advertiser of the people reached by media reflect how they vary in such characteristics as their financial resources, their geographic location, their interest in and normal consumption of the brand and the product category, their general responsiveness to advertising messages, their exposure to prior advertising for the brand, and their saturation by competing campaigns. Not all these differences are widely recognized, regularly measured, and invariably considered in media selection.

Differences in Advertising Exposure

A media vehicle makes all the ads it distributes reasonably available to all the people it covers. But out of the whole audience of the vehicle only the audience reached by the specific advertisement can be directly affected by the advertisement, and when a vehicle carries a number of different ads, less than all of the audience for the whole vehicle will be exposed to each one. Even though an ad is accessible, an advertising exposure may not take place, if we assume that for an ad to be exposed, a person must physically confront it in such a way that only attention would be required for the ad to be noticed.

Number of Exposures Varies   Under this definition, the number of exposures from a single copy of an advertisement can vary tremendously. For a television set playing in an empty room, or an unopened newspaper delivered during vacation, the exposures per copy must be zero. But for a billboard at a busy intersection, the exposures for each day of posting may be numbered in the thousands.

In general, the total exposures of an ad and the kind of people exposed depend mostly on the media vehicle that carries the ad. (Secondarily, they also depend on the size of the advertisement and its placement within the vehicle.) The vehicle gets an audience, and some part of that audience is exposed to the ad.

Many media vehicles, including most television, radio, magazines, and newspapers, use content other than advertising to attract an audience and generate ad exposures. But it also is true that the ads people expect to find in such media may add to their attraction, and that in some other media, such as catalogs or shopping guides, skywriting or direct mail, the advertising operates without any real editorial environment, and creates its own exposures by its own interest or visibility or intrusiveness, or proximity to other advertising of the same kind.

Varying Values of Exposure   Every now and then we need to remind ourselves how different the circumstances of exposure, and hence the potential value of exposure, can be in different media. The differences are too often overlooked in the effort to find a level of comparability or commonality in media performance, even though the search for a universal yardstick does not change, for example, the fact that a look in passing at an outdoor poster is inherently different from a minute watching a television commercial, or from a conscious search for information in a newspaper shopping section.   No argument that each happens to be, by common agreement, an advertising exposure can alter their visible and extraordinary points of differentiation.

The differences are in the place, the conditions, the mood, the active senses involved in the exposure.   They are in the whole complex of the timing of the exposure, in who controls when the exposure occurs, in the relationship of the exposure to the purchase cycle, in the duration of the exposure, and in what happens when it is over. They relate to other exposures of competing ads, and of ads for the same advertiser.   Finally, they derive from the fact that exposures from certain advertising vehicles tend to occur in bursts or clusters, as when an individual leafing back and forth through a magazine passes an ad several times, or when he watches a television program with several commercials for the same brand.

Media, in other words, do more than make copies of ads and carry them to and expose them to people.   The media type, the media vehicle, and the media ad unit not only determine who will be exposed, they also determine, in many ways, how much effect the exposure can have.

HOW ADVERTISING IS RECEIVED AND ASSIMILATED

Whenever an advertisement is exposed, an opportunity is created for it to start working for the advertiser.   But exposure is only one first step; before a benefit can possibly be realized, something must be communicated from the ad to the person, which means that things like this have to happen: The ad must get itself *noticed.* Some content must come in through the *senses, be edited, encoded, put into storage,* and *referenced* for later access.

When we describe this phase of how advertising works, it is tempting to suggest that what happens is like the operation of a message center, or a master file, or the storage, access, and retrieval functions of an EDP system.   Because we know so little about what actually does take place, efforts at objective description tend to dissolve into analogies and imagery.   But if we must think partly in comparisons, we should also admit at the start that nothing in library or computer science is really very much like the uniquely electrochemical, uniquely human system by which the senses and the nervous system and the brain of man receive and assimilate, among other things, the content of advertising.

This is a highly personal business; the communication, the direct and immediate effect of advertising, is exerted on mass audiences only through the individuals who comprise those audiences.

Nature of Responses

It must be apparent that a person does not have to take note of or become involved in an advertisement simply because he has been confronted with it.   With the great volume of advertising that is now exposed to the consumer, with the bath of advertising in which the consumer typically lives, he has usually devised defenses against taking in and assimilating much of the advertising he could be aware of.

Some understanding of parts of this process can be gleaned by observing people's activities and psychophysiological reactions at the time of exposure.   Personal involvement with an ad is sometimes indicated by obvious physical behavior, by coming nearer to the ad, or by an attentive posture, or conversely by talking or moving about, by turning the page or changing channels, or by turning from the medium.   Certain other physical responses may indicate more consistently (if less obviously) whether or not an exposed ad is being noted.   These may include changes in pupil size, eye movements, blinking, opening or narrowing of the eyelids, facial changes, changes in skin moisture or color, and possibly even changes in pulse, heart rate and blood flow, temperature, muscular tension, and the rhythm and depth of breathing.

Most Critical Responses

However, the most critical responses of people during communication are ones wholly inaccessible to direct observation.   These are the changes in the mind, in the packing in of information, the absorption of ideas, the whole complex of intellectual and subjective, cognitive and affective responses that may take place independent of either overt, controlled behavioral responses or measurable involuntary physiological changes.

Perception

Exposed advertising is received first through one or more of the senses, normally the sense of sight or the sense of hearing, or a combination of the two. (Some advertising may involve other senses, like the sense of smell or the sense of touch, but this is comparatively rare.)

If the advertising contact is to be successful, signals received from the senses must be noted and accepted for passage so that at least some of the content can be carried back and given further evaluation.

It seems likely that what takes place in many cases is a superficial and quickly forgotten noting and screening, a kind of perceiving and rejecting at almost a subconscious level. We know that people often are exposed to advertising without consciously noting it, and surely without becoming lastingly aware of it. Still, some kind of scanning may be taking place; if the individual's name or some other interest-triggering word or picture is inserted into an ad, it will draw more attention and recall than we would normally expect.

This is a continuing check, not a single decision; the mind maintains control over what it will receive from an ad as long as the ad is exposed. For any substantial amount of material to be taken in, the brain must both assume and retain a receptive posture. When its receivers are open, the mind accepts a large proportion of the available impressions; when the receivers close, very little material can enter and be put into storage.

The Brain a Control Point

In this operation, the brainstem operates a control point that is not unlike a self-closing gate. The normal condition finds the gate almost closed, so that the cortex is not assaulted with impressions it has no intention of retaining. If the person wants to remember what he sees or hears, controls can keep the gate open for the material to continue to come in, but in the absence of continuing orders to keep open, the gate will automatically swing to the nearly closed position and very little information will be brought into the areas of the brain where it can be processed and retained.

When the material has passed the control point, it enters parts of the brain where it will be prepared and stored. This initiates a process that includes, in some kind of sequence, the editing, adapting, translating, encoding, relating, and referencing of what has been taken in.

When an advertisement comes into the brain, it is like a mixed load of building material dropped into the middle of a construction project.   If the contents of the advertisement are to be useful, they must be sorted and organized so that what is wanted can be found when the time it is needed occurs.

It is a reasonable assumption that in this process the mind discards or rejects some content, and that it may modify what remains.   What is played back in recall tests, for example, often shows that ads have been changed, presumably to fit existing orientations and preconceptions.   The brain, in other words, does not see what the eye sees nor hear what the ear hears.   It sees and hears what it likes and what makes sense and what it can absorb and retain and relate and recover, based on its existing field of reference and what it expects (logically or illogically) to use in the future.

At some point in the sequence, what is left or has been rebuilt from the advertisement is converted into chemical codes or electrical charges, and stored in a network of the tiny brain cells called neurons, until it is brought out again, usually for review, reconsideration, or renewal, or possibly for use in connection with a personal brand evaluation or market decision.

Mental Conversion Processes

The conversion processes by which the brain receives and retrieves advertising impressions may be, in some ways, analogous to the kind of sequential translation and retranslation that takes place in television, where a visual image is converted into an electrical code and the code into a radio wave and then back into an electrical code and a visual image.   The comparison, however, is faulty, since the transmission and reception of broadcast material, once done, is completed forever, and the end message is made to be as close as possible to the original.   In contrast, the processing by the mind takes place over an unspecified, indefinite period of time, and what is available for retrieval is fragmented or reassembled or reconverted into a more personalized, more useful form.

Advertising material that actually gets into the brain may still be changed or discarded.   The process of editing and adapting the information continues after the exposure has passed, or it may be resumed at a later time.

Some psychologists say that the mind tends to rehearse, during quiet periods, the information it receives, to practice retrieving it, to make or strengthen the references and connections that help to keep it accessible. It does this, they say, at times (including when the body is asleep) when it is not occupied fully with other tasks.

Limited State of Knowledge

All this, of course, is very obscure and also very important; we know comparatively little about the inner aspects of the communication processes, and yet it is on all these responses that the reactions to advertising ultimately depend.

At some future time, we will probably understand more about the communication of advertising than we presently do. Now, we can only wish that we knew more about what people look at and what they actually see when they notice advertising. We can wish we had better ways of finding out what they listen to and what they hear, and what they are thinking and sensing and how they are responding during and after exposure.

The limited state of our present knowledge becomes most apparent when we try to generalize about the factors that make communication successful. For one thing, we can guess that chance, or unidentified cause, plays a part in any consumer's noting and taking in of particular ads. Partly this is because luck has some influence on whether the ad happens to be exposed; partly it is because unplanned distractions or accidents of timing affect whether the exposed message is noted and received.

Effect of Media on Communication

Besides luck, we must assume that how an ad is communicated is affected by other circumstances, including the medium in which it appears.

Broadcast media, we know, produce their exposures only at prearranged times. The duration of the exposure is to a large degree involuntary, although the individual may turn off the set or exercise controls over his involvement. After the exposure, the advertisement no longer exists (except in the mind) for study or consideration.

These characteristics naturally influence the communication of all broadcast advertising.

Print media, and especially magazines, contact people differently, mostly at the option of and with the cooperation and help of the person who is exposed.   Exposure of an ad will usually take place when the person chooses to open or happens to open the magazine to the place the ad appears.   More importantly, the exposure may be stopped instantly, or made to continue for as long, and with as much study and attention, and as many references back, as the person wants.   So, in print, the quality of the contact between an ad and an individual is largely set by the individual, once the first exposure is accomplished.

Unfortunately, it is easier to describe differences in the circumstances of contact in different media than to generalize about their meaning.   We know from experience that, while people's typical behavior during exposure may be a function of the medium, individuals may adopt a receptive or a defensive posture, they may respond actively or passively, toward an advertisement in any vehicle.

Size of Advertisement

The size of an ad should also be important in communication, since size affects whether the ad is exposed and noted and also how much content the ad is able to carry.   Generally, we can assume that larger ads produce more communication.

Yet it is abundantly clear that size in no sense guarantees how much content an advertisement actually will register, or how vividly or lastingly the communication will be accomplished.   Very likely the heavy information loads (and the intricacy) of some advertisements actually make them hard to absorb, and hard to store, organize, and cross-reference.   With the limited time and the limited number of circuits available, the brain (or the small fraction of the brain tending the receipt of the advertisement) may find itself inadequate for this complex task.   With too much to do in too short a time, at some point the mind simply resigns—a kind of circuit breaker shuts off the operation.   As a result an ad designed to communicate a great quantity of information may get relatively little usable content into storage.

Quality of the Advertisement

In addition to whatever effect the vehicle and the ad size may exert, the quality of the advertisement, its message and appeal, its freshness and importance, has great relevance to its successful communication. Confronting an ad is like seeing another person; a momentary glimpse, an instant of exposure to a celebrity or to a striking beauty, may have more meaning than an hour across the aisle from a fellow commuter.

Over time, many thoughtful rules have been written about how different factors affect the process of communication, but solid, general criteria for success are still hard to come by.

Influences on Communication

At this point we can say safely only that the perceiving and receiving of advertising is personal and widely varied, that for most people the number of advertisements exposed and subconsciously rejected is considerably greater than the number for which reception at the conscious level actually takes place, and that advertising communication reflects the interactions of a number of influences including:

The intelligence and background of the exposed individual

His interest in the product and the brand

His immediate orientation

The nature and impact of the media unit and the media vehicle

The timing and physical circumstances of exposure

And, of course, the impact and interest of the ad

In a culture heavy with advertising, how well an advertisement works depends directly on how much communication it achieves. The successful ad must do more than be received, but if it is not received, it surely can do nothing at all.

HOW ADVERTISING AFFECTS IDEAS AND INTENTIONS

Up to this page, we have tried to describe how advertising is created, and how it is exposed and communicated to people. Below we will discuss how it affects purchasing, selling, consumption, dollar volume and profits, and the overall market situation.

We have reached, then, a kind of midpoint in this description of how advertising works.   Now we are at the key process where input becomes output, the pivot between, on the one hand, how advertising reaches people and, on the other, how it works for the advertiser through the people it reaches.   This is the area of interaction, where the customer converts the communication, and the communication converts the customer.

Effects on Person Reached

We are still describing, at this point, the effects of an advertising exposure on the person directly reached by an advertisement.   For the time being we also are concentrating on the responses of consumers, of possible buyers or users of what is advertised, leaving till later the consideration of how advertising works on sellers or suppliers, of how it can change distribution or merchandising.

Once advertising is registered, once content from an ad is put into the brain, it can go to work in a number of different ways.   It can create a great variety of responses, a whole spectrum of changes in ideas and feelings and attitudes and intentions that are derived from the communication.

Naturally, some communication of advertising to some individuals does nothing at all that benefits the advertiser.   Common instances are when an ad simply fails to identify clearly what brand it is for, or when a person finds an ad arresting or involving, but for reasons completely unrelated to the product.   And there are cases when an ad reaches someone not in the potential market (he is bald, and the ad is for hair tonic), so no kind of registration can beneficially change his feelings or actions.

Some Responses Negative   Some responses, inevitably, will be negative, reflecting the experience or mood of the individual or his reactions to the content, argument, or style of the ad.   A consumer may resent a claim that contradicts his experience, or react negatively to particular words or to their spokesman, to a mood or a tone of voice or a media environment.   An ad can be ascribed to and work for a competitor.   Advertising can generate negative reactions even when most people have a favorable response; to certain customers, an ad announcing a price reduction may make the brand seem less, not more, appealing.   Any claim based on market segmentation probably reduces the favor with which the brand is viewed in some quarters. Suggesting that a brand is strong or fast or modern can diminish its appeal to people who want their product gentle or slow or old-fashioned.

In evaluating how an ad works we must eventually balance negative against positive reactions, and always recognize that for some ads the net change may not be favorable. But, for an ad to work, it must produce positive responses. So, these are what we will consider to start this discussion.

Range of Responses It is pointless to try to put together a complete list of productive things that can happen to people following the communication of advertising. The range of responses is altogether too wide. But, as examples, we can visualize that, after an advertising contact, a person might:

Identify pleasantly with the people in the ad
Keep humming the jingle
Become more conscious of the brand name
Associate the brand with a symbol
Recognize the package more easily
Check up on something the ad said
Keep thinking about the arguments for the brand
Tend to forget an old dislike for the brand
Speculate about trying this kind of product
Imagine being known as an owner
Put to use supplies already on hand
Think about a bigger size or better model
Decide maybe to give the brand a trial
Mail in a coupon or inquiry
Ask somebody to shop for the brand
Go to a store to make a purchase

The listing is so varied because what happens depends both on the ad and on the person. It is easy to see the importance of the advertisement; one ad may start building a pleasant association for the brand name, while another might prompt the same consumer to make an immediate trip to a store. Differences among people are equally important; an ad that brings to one housewife her first awareness of a brand brings to another an amusing association that could, under the right circumstances, lead to an impulse purchase, while to still another housewife, perhaps to a regular user, it suggests a promising new use that will almost surely increase the size of her next purchase.   So the same ad can get different responses from different people, just as different ads can elicit different responses from the same person.

Effect of Responses on Buying

Favorable changes coming as a result of an advertising contact may have an immediate and direct effect on buying, or they may be only remotely related to possible future purchasing.   To simplify our understanding of these varied and complex interactions, we need some general term, some concept broad enough to cover all the ideational and attitudinal effects an ad can have on someone who has been exposed to it.

Generation of Personal Demand   Such a concept is attainable if we can isolate something that all these changes have in common, if we can identify a similarity in how these effects work to the advantage of the advertiser.   And they all do have a common quality, since they all tend, sooner or later, directly or indirectly, to improve the size or timing or the likelihood of future purchases of the advertised brand by the person affected (or by someone acting for him).   They all tend to create added demand for what is advertised.   Once we accept this idea, we can define the central function of most advertising in these terms:

The key process by which advertising works is the generation of personal demand.

"Personal demand," as it is used here, is a state of mind favorable to purchase.   It is the consumer's tendency toward buying what was advertised.

This needs some elaboration.   What is meant by "personal demand" might be clearer if it were called "personal demand probability."   As it is used here, "demand" means tendency rather than certainty, and so it might well be expressed as a statement of the odds that, during some reasonable future period of time, the individual will be disposed to buy the advertised product or service, or in different words, as the mathematical chance that, if supply and selling influences could be eliminated, the individual would purchase or cause the purchase of the brand.

Description of Responses in Mathematical Terms   At first, the suggestion that the basic responses to advertising ought to be described in mathematical terms may sound like a way to complicate an already overly involved discussion. But such a descriptive approach can have important advantages.

For one thing, the concept of "demand" as a mathematical probability avoids sorting customers into groups with names that mean different things to different people; it helps us avoid the use of plateaus to describe continuous slopes of differentiation. It can permit us to look, in equivalent terms, at both positive and negative responses to an ad. It can help us describe how the effects of an exposure change over time, and how successive exposures from a campaign may work together. But mostly it can give substance and meaning to what might otherwise appear as a forced effort to throw together in one semantic bag called "demand" all the things about consumers that advertising can change to the immediate or ultimate benefit of the advertiser.

The various direct or indirect effects of advertising, the gains in such areas as salience, favorable opinions, rationalizations for purchase, emotional wants, decisions to act, and urges to consume only benefit the advertiser (according to this generalization) if and because they involve some kind of gain in the consumer's likelihood of buying or inducing buying.

Gauging Personal Demand

The personal demand of an individual for a brand is suggested by the individual's opinions on what brand he thinks he will buy, what others he may consider, and what brands he might someday try. Demand is also indicated by the consumer's intentions to buy at all, the expected time till his next purchase, the quantity and model he thinks may be bought, where the purchase is likely to be made, and how much effect he personally expects to have on the decisions.

When questions of this kind are asked before and then after an advertising exposure, or of carefully matched samples exposed and not exposed to advertising, the answers of some people change, clearly as a direct response to the advertising contact. (The changes show up even in tests that are honestly designed not to clue people on what their answers should be.)

The evidence from such research is support for the demand generation concept, for the conclusion that a key reaction to an advertising contact is an often limited but immediate change in the likelihood of buying the advertised brand.

While in many cases personal demand may seem to change easily as a result of an advertising contact, usually it does not change very far. There are, after all, a lot of constraints on how much gain can follow from a single exposure. The consumer has his own routines of thinking and behavior, and his own ideas on ways to spend money, his own set of brand experiences, and his own frame of reference.

So, a gain in demand after an advertising contact may often typically be of the magnitude associated with a modest, short-term increase in brand awareness. A firm and final decision to buy can result from a single ad exposure, but except for retail or mail-order advertising, this probably does not happen too often.

When Demand May Be Reduced   In explaining the brand demand generation concept, it is important to remember that while advertising works by increasing demand, some advertising contacts with some people do reduce demand. It is also critical that when one brand gains demand after an advertising contact, other brands will often lose demand; a successful advertising contact for one brand may reduce the likelihood that the person will buy a brand competitive to it.

This is not always so, for some ads do help the whole product category. But advertising ordinarily does affect how predisposition divides between competitive brands, and when this is the response, a gain in demand for the advertised brand will be balanced by losses in demand for one or more of its competitors.

Demand Stems from Successful Communication

At this stage of the discussion there is probably no need to say that, in the working of advertising, generating demand is one whole process beyond the registration of advertising content. But it is important to remember that the gains in the chances of buying must derive from the successful communication of something from the ad. Increases come about because the mind processes advertising ideas into behavioral ideas, because, as the mind takes in ideas from the advertising and works them over and stores and retrieves them, they come to affect favorably the individual's thinking about buying what was advertised.

Just how this happens, like much of the brain's response, is obscure. On the surface, it seems sometimes to be a subjective and unpredictable process. We can assume that it varies with the exposed individual, and with his mental state and going interests at the time of exposure.   How much a person's demand will change because of an ad surely also depends on the brand and the product category; some brands and some kinds of products are more easily advertised than others, at least to specific consumers.

Most importantly, we know that the content of an ad directly affects how much demand it generates.   Differences in productivity between ads, as we have already noted, reflect, in the first place, how well each succeeds in communicating its content.   But they must also relate to how well the content of each ad motivates the consumer in the direction of buying.

This is a singularly critical level of advertising accomplishment. Between two ads, the better is generally the one that, through a combination of communication and motivation, generates more personal demand for what is advertised.

HOW ADVERTISING AFFECTS PRODUCT CONSUMPTION

We have been discussing a concept that identifies the key component in all the various consumer reactions following an advertising exposure as the generation of a change in personal demand for the advertised brand.

This combination or condensation of processes was proposed to provide a needed simplification of some very complex occurrences. It was also meant to emphasize the idea that different effects of advertising on consumers have a relevance to how advertising works only if they somehow increase the likelihood of people buying the advertised brand.

Initiation of Purchase of a Product

Having made this point, perhaps we can now back off a little, and look at some parts of the process in greater detail.   Specifically, it seems useful to look more closely at the effect of advertising on initiating purchasing of the product class and on increasing consumption of the product.

Advertising achieves these results in a number of specific ways. An ad may increase a consumer's general probability of buying something from the field of which the brand is a part.   It may speed purchase of the advertised brand by a customer who would eventually buy it anyway, or escalate the probable size or value of the next purchase, without disturbing the distribution of preference among brands.

An ad for a durable product, like a home, an automobile, a major appliance, or an industrial plant may escalate the value of the total purchase by trading the customer up to a more expensive model, or by encouraging the inclusion of optional extras.   These are major and recurring purposes of advertising for products of this kind.

Consumer Product Inventories   An ad may affect consumption by affecting consumer product inventories.   Many packaged products go through a period of consumer storage or inventory between purchase and ultimate consumption, while durable products are bought specifically for use over an extended period of time.   A candy bar can be bought to be eaten immediately, but for most products in most cases, purchasing is not with the anticipation of immediate total consumption, but for inventory or possession.

An ad can affect this process in two ways.   It can increase the customer's holdings of the product, and it can stimulate or encourage the consumption of existing inventories or products on hand.   In other words, an advertisement can operate to increase inventories or possession and it can work to decrease them.

When it encourages the using up of existing inventories, an ad helps to accelerate the individual's buying cycle and possibly to increase the size of the next purchase.   When it acts to increase the quantity on hand, it may actually have much the same effect; it may increase, coincidentally, the quantity included in the next purchase, and increased availability of the product may then tend to increase the rate of use and the total quantity consumed.

Preconditioning of Expectations   There are other ways in which an ad can affect consumption and the consumption process.   For one thing, ads will often precondition the expectations of the consumer, change the satisfactions he gets from use of the product, and so affect his probability and rate of repurchase.   Advertising helps to instruct people in how to serve and wear and use products, and there is little question but that it changes for many people how things seem to taste or appear and the satisfactions they give.

Many of these effects of advertising tend to be somewhat indirect, at least as they change product purchasing, yet they do serve to generate demand, and they are important.

Demand Probability

In analyzing this effect of advertising, we can go back to the demand probability idea, and the suggestion that personal demand should be defined as the likelihood that the individual would voluntarily buy or induce buying of the particular brand during a specified future period of time, assuming that trade stocks and selling had no effect on the decision.

With this kind of definition, a mathematical probability of buying can be assigned for each of the brands in the product category, and the total of the probabilities for all the brands will have to be the probability that some purchase of some brand will be made by or for the individual during the specified time period. We will call this summation of individual brand demands *buying probability* and then see what we can learn from an examination of this new concept.

Buying probability, quite simply, is an estimate of the likelihood that some purchase in the product category is going to be made, within the period specified, by or for the individual. The chance of a purchase taking place has to depend on a number of influences, which may include, for a specific person and product class, such questions as:

General economic conditions
The time and the season
The fashion, style, and use cycle
The individual's needs, interests, and predispositions
His personal impact on the family decision process
The consumer's financial resources
The amount of product currently on hand
The interval since the last purchase
The rate of consumption
Reactions to ads for products in this field

At any moment of time buying probability will reflect the overall likelihood of a purchase in the product category. This total figure could be redivided into the probability for different retail outlets, or that for different models or qualities or the inclusion of optional features, or by the value and size of possible purchases. In each analysis, all the probabilities would still add to the same total, always representing the going probability that there will be some purchase in the field.

Increase in Dollar Values of Future Purchases   But certain possible distributions—for example, those with heavy probability of purchase for an expensive model or for more units—can suggest that future purchases for the individual consumer will have a high dollar value.   Achieving such an increase in the probable value of the next purchase is an obvious goal of much advertising, and a secondary or incidental result in the case of other advertising contacts.   This is, then, one way that an ad can increase the volume or value of consumption in a product class.

An advertising contact also can affect, either purposefully or incidentally, the whole level of the individual's buying probability. The increase in buying probability can come about because the chances of buying a single brand are increased, and there is no compensating reduction in the chance of buying other brands in the same category, or it can happen if the chances of buying for a number of the brands go up because there has been, after the contact, a general increase in the individual's curiosity about, or interest in, or decision to buy the kind of product.   Some ads (and specifically retail advertisements) work to accelerate purchasing by giving a price or other incentive for buying now.

Acceleration of Next Purchase   Finally, a real, if somewhat delayed, increase in buying probability can result if, because of an advertising contact, a consumer uses up inventory on hand (if he drinks up a beer already in his refrigerator) and accelerates, in this way, the timing of the next purchase.

For products ranging from chewing gum to color television sets, the major advertising opportunity may be less in the development of competitive brand preference, and more in inducing purchase or in speeding the day a purchase will be made.   Many advertisers, without significantly changing the number of customers predisposed to their brands, have scored significant gains in volume year after year simply by selling more units to essentially the same customers.   In many industries, equivalent advertising efforts sometimes nullify the chance of making lasting competitive gains, yet all the brands enjoy increasing volume, presumably in part as a collective result of all their advertising.

Importance of Buying Probability   Still, a good many advertisers concern themselves less with these effects of advertising than with the impact of ads on the division of preference between brands.   The processes involved in building personal buying probability seem indirect and somewhat obscure.   But they are nonetheless important, both to the individual advertiser and to the economy, since it is largely through these effects of advertising that new products are accepted, new industries developed, new generations of consumers conditioned, and high levels of consumption maintained.

HOW ADVERTISING RESPONDS TO TIME AND REPEATED EXPOSURE

We have been concentrating up to now on an individual's immediate reactions to a single advertising exposure.   Now we must introduce the factor of time, and the effects of repeated advertising contacts.

Time as a Factor   Time is a factor in every process of advertising, from the planning stage to the calculation of payout.   Advertising appears at a point in time; it does its work over a period of time; it is changed by the passage of time.   Time affects the amount of personal demand generated by an advertisement and by a campaign, and time determines the residual demand effective at the moment of purchase decision.

Time has its simplest relationship to the one-time ad, to a want ad, a political announcement, or a retail ad for seasonal merchandise. Such an ad usually aims for an immediate response, so there is no need to think about how repeated advertising contacts over time will generate sustained communication or continuing brand demand. And since there is no campaign, there are no arguments about continuity or pulsing, reinforcement or wearout.   Yet timing is a factor in performance, even for such a disassociated ad; there is often a time element in consumer and brand marketing and competitive and trade activities.   While there are no complex interactions of advertising cycles and buying cycles, the time of exposure can still change both the consumer's receptivity to the ad and the chances that he will buy as a result of it.

The effects of time get even more critical when an ad is part of a series or a campaign, or an element in a continuing process of advertising and selling.   In such cases, it is necessary to take account of the whole complex structure of the accumulation and the decay of what happens to a person as a result of advertising.

Time-related Phenomena   To relate time fully to the advertising process, we must consider at least four time-related phenomena:

Changes over time in personal readiness to buy and receptiveness to advertising

Change in the interest in an ad or campaign with the passage of time and with repetition

Decay, over time, of the personal demand generated by an advertising exposure

Regeneration and accumulation of demand during a series of contacts with the same person

Advertising and selling, buying and use, are all dynamic processes; coordination in timing between these processes can strongly influence the success and the efficiency of marketing operations. The productivity of advertising, in particular, depends on how well its timing relates to the time dynamics of shopping, buying, and consumption.

Receptiveness to Advertising   Basic decisions on advertising strategy frequently are tied into such matters. The direction selected depends on how the advertiser reads the advertising opportunity at the time the advertising appears.

Consider, for example, automotive advertising, which is closely adapted to changes in the perceived interest, mood, and behavior of consumers. Comparing the beginning and the end of the model year for automobiles, there are not only large shifts in the volume of advertising done, and in the media used, but also in copy emphasis (from the styling and features story of the introductions to claims of practicality, proved performance, and bargain prices at the end of the season).

Differences in the perceived advertising opportunity are by no means restricted to seasonal variations in consumers' buying readiness and interest in advertising. For example, some airlines have standing orders to cancel all advertising in the event of a serious accident. The volume of ads for certain products changes by day of the week, depending on common buying cycles, and possibly even by hour of the day (morning may be thought of as a better time to sell mouthwash, and late afternoon a better time for beer).

For most people and most product categories, personal demand is characteristically fluid, rather than static over time. It is subject to some major and to many minor shifts, to both losses and gains, to short-term as well as more lasting changes induced by a variety of advertising and marketing, personal and external, brand-originated and competitive influences.

A consumer asked at different times about his readiness to buy and about the brands he is likely to consider often will give substantially different answers, even when there are only a few days between his responses.   Behavior of this kind demonstrates how brand disposition and personal demand change over time, and suggests how unstable some of the factors are that go into consumers' decisions to purchase.   It also suggests how time can change the opportunity to advertise effectively.

Change in Interest in Advertising   A second way that time affects advertising is in the changing communication of ads and campaigns. As ads and ideas grow older and more familiar, the interest they have for the person who is exposed to them changes, sometimes negatively, but sometimes positively, too.   Familiarity, in the case of advertising, can breed disinterest or resentment, or it can reduce resistance and make for friendlier feelings.

The issue of how many times an advertisement can appear and still be interesting and persuasive is often raised in planning advertising, since advertising people (with the important exception of certain mail-order advertisers) are quite concerned about the problem of wearout.   Fewer people, seemingly, consider build as an equally serious issue.   Yet some advertisements do gain communication values with repeated exposures; jingles and ideas fail from too little support; efficiency can be lost by too few, as well as by too many, uses.

An aura of expectancy develops around some ads; they become so liked and so enjoyed that people will go out of their way to find and come in contact with them.   What an ad communicates may be improved by repetition.   Claims that are first viewed with suspicion may build credibility as they are repeated.   And some ideas are too complex, or too subtle, to register well with one exposure; an idea or a mood can strengthen as it becomes familiar.

So an ad can either gain or lose effectiveness over a series of exposures or over a period of time.   Or, it may gain for a while and then start to lose.   But if it is used repeatedly, it is not likely to hold a constant value per contact for very long.   Even though it has the same engine and the same cars at both stations, the 8:10 from Stamford and the 8:18 from Rye is not really the same train, with the same services or meaning; the change in time and place and occupancy and convenience means that it is perceived in Stamford and in Rye as having quite different values.   An ad or a campaign, in much the same way, changes meaning as it reaches consumers at different moments of time.

Decay of Advertising-generated Demand   The third concept describing how time influences the workings of advertising is the decay, over time, of advertising-generated demand.

With the passage of time, the personal demand of an individual influenced by an advertising contact reverts toward its preexposure level; the added demand generated by any single advertising contact deteriorates and tends to disappear.

Unless the demand generated by advertising is put to use quickly in a purchasing decision, or (as we will note later) unless it is regenerated by added advertising contacts, a large part of its effect will be wasted.   The loss of effect can be reduced by better timing, and by new exposures of brand advertising to the same individual.,   But a large measure of waste simply is inherent in the time dimensions of advertising.

The reversion of personal demand after advertising is a difficult and not very inviting idea, one that is much easier to overlook than it is to understand.   As a result, many of us prefer to think of advertising as something that keeps pushing public opinion forward, that keeps brands going ahead, that acts as an energizer propelling brands in the direction of success.   We like to learn about advertising from the study of successful new products, which tend to improve over time in volume and acceptance, rather than from old brands that must fight to keep their share of market.

We think of advertising as a hammer that drives home the nail of consumer loyalty.   But the advertising process is, in reality, less like hitting a nail and more like pushing a pillow.   A short while after the contact has been completed, there often is little of a permanent nature still remaining.

The demand added by an advertising contact usually is greatest at the time of the exposure or shortly after the contact has been completed.   From then on the added demand tends to disappear.   This deterioration is in part a natural return to normalcy, a restoration of the status quo, but it probably also comes about as a result of the distracting effect of other events, other interests and other stimuli, including specifically the nullifying effect of competing ads in the same product category.

All brands in a class of products or services are, of course, competing directly for the favor of the individual, and advertising is a major tool of this competitive process.   A direct and immediate result of any brand's advertising is often simply counteracting the gains made at the expense of the brand by the advertising contacts of competitors (even though all brands may finally benefit as the competing advertising encourages new buyers and accelerates consumption).

While there is a certain inevitability about the reversion of demand in the period following an advertising exposure, the rate at which the deterioration takes place and the proportion of the original gain, if any, that is finally retained are both highly variable.

In one limited test series it was found that of the gain in demand measurable shortly after an advertising exposure, half had been lost by the next morning.   The actual amount and the rate of loss after a specific contact must reflect several influences, however, including the level of personal demand for the brand and the quality of the consumer's interest in the content of the ad, as well as the intensity of competitive advertising efforts.

The level of demand both immediately before and just after the exposure is probably quite critical.   When demand for a brand is at a high level because of the brand's general reputation, personal use experience, or very productive advertising, the demand seems to decay less rapidly and be less vulnerable to competitive displacement than when it is at lower levels.

Thus the brand that has achieved high demand may have a stronger, more durable demand position than the simple estimate of its chance of being bought at the next purchase might suggest.   The invulnerability of highly preferred brands to decay in demand may be a factor in their common ability to sustain volume with relatively modest advertising support.

How Interesting the Advertisement?   Another important influence on the durability of the demand gained after an advertising contact is how interesting the person has found the advertisement.   In the discussion of how advertising is assimilated, it was noted that some advertising material lingers in the mind, that the mind brings it back to the conscious level, or near that level, and considers it again.   Obvious cases are the jingle that the person can't stop humming, or the print ad the consumer goes back to look at again. And there are many other cases of ads the mind finds it hard to relinquish.

To be chosen for review, reconsideration, or practice retrieval, an advertisement needs special relevance or character, or intrigue or importance. Again, the importance of creative quality becomes apparent; the ad that has something that originally kept the receiving circuits of the mind open may well have also the quality that makes the mind find and reexamine it, and this can be a great advantage in making it work over a longer time for the advertiser's benefit.

In considering time and its relationship to advertising, we have covered changes in consumer interests as they affect the timeliness of advertising, changes in the communication qualities of campaigns and individual ads, and the change in effect during the period following an advertising contact.

Effect of a Sequence of Exposures

The fourth and possibly the most critical consideration involving time is the buildup in effect that can come as the result of a sequence of advertising exposures.

Gains in demand induced as a response to advertising and lost after a lapse of time may be recovered by additional contact with the same individual. But, what is more important, there can be a reinforcing or synergistic effect on an individual from a related series of brand advertising exposures; when the effect occurs, the total gain resulting from the series will be greater than the residual gain remaining after the first exposure, multiplied by the number of exposures that took place.

Training the mind to prefer a brand is possibly like creating a path through a wilderness. The conditioning of the mind, like the path, may become evident only after it has been traveled a number of times.

It is interesting that some productivity models for advertising apparently assume that, in a specified period of time, a second exposure to an individual consumer is less valuable than a new contact with someone previously unreached, as though ad exposure were the critical measure of advertising accomplishment. But when the processes of communication and demand generation are considered, and normal decay is taken into account, it seems likely that a better assumption would be that it is usually advantageous to deliver multiple advertising contacts against the same person.

A continuing advertising effort is likely to be most productive when the contact is with someone who has been reached before, or who will be reached again; thus, the productivity of advertising contacts may be a classic case of the whole being greater than the sum of the parts. An advertising exposure can have both a retroactive and a proactive effect; a generative advertising contact not only reinforces the effect of past advertising; it also enhances the demand created by future advertising.

To try to explain the nature of this reinforcing effect of advertising, we may pose what is a difficult concept, specifically that some kind of effect actually remains after an advertising exposure that is not identifiable or measurable unless and until some additional contact with the same individual takes place.

Dormant Response To give this a label, we can call it a *dormant response,* or a *dormant gain in demand.* We can say that when the gain in demand that has come about as a proximate effect of an advertising exposure fades, something inactive is left that can be restimulated by another contact with the same person.

If we were to chart these responses over time, the chart might look something like a rising sawtoothed curve. After the exposure of an ad there would be, as we have discussed, a gain in demand for the advertised brand. As time passes, the effect of this exposure would tend to fade, and the demand for the brand would tend to revert to its previous level.

But now, if another advertising contact can be accomplished with the same person within a short interval of time, demand for the brand may rise, not just to the level it reached following the earlier contact, but to an even higher point, suggesting that this new advertising contact was building on some kind of no longer measurable, but still existent demand.

The process is, in some ways, like that involved in learning unfamiliar material. After a lapse of time following one learning session, the mind may not be able to recall anything at all, and yet, after a second exposure and a third and a fourth, more is obviously remembered than was retained after the first contact.

Perhaps attitudes and predisposition, what we have called "personal demand," may also be "learned" in a similar way. If this is what happens, we can assume that the level of demand achieved after a particular exposure is somehow a function of both the active demand just before the time the exposure took place and an unidentifiable dormant demand from earlier contacts.

Demand Generation and Learning   The analogy of demand generation to learning can be deceptive if it is carried very far.   If we try to generalize about the impact of advertising from what we know from learning experiments, if we try to develop demand theory solely from observations about learning, we face serious problems.   Learning is motivated, it takes place in a reasonably tangible and progressing sequence; learning is a forward and upward activity.   Demand formulation, on the other hand, is unsystematic if not irrational, largely unmotivated, fragile, transient, buffeted by competitive and other forces.   It moves, like the wind, first in one direction, and then in another.   Learning can be permanent, but demand is always vulnerable to decay and to evaluative or competitive destruction.   In the formulation of demand, the gains are often accomplished within a limitation or a ceiling; existing loyalties and the demand for other brands restrict how much gain can be accomplished.

Advertising does not work at a disassociated point of time or in a logically elegant system.   Advertisements involve communication, awareness, predisposition, purchasing, and consumption, all individually sequential, all time-related, all subject not just to positive changes but to decay, reversion, and competitive reversal.

Importance of Sensitive Timing   Still, the critical aspect of time in relationship to advertising is not the limitations it places on accomplishment.   Nor is it the universal tendency of attitudes and responses toward deterioration.   The really important points are the advantages that come through sensitive timing, through the ability of some campaigns to grow stronger as they become familiar, through the potentially multiplying effects of repeated contacts, and most importantly, through the great advantages in sustained returns when an advertiser is able to build a brand, over time, to a high demand level.

HOW ADVERTISING AFFECTS TRADE EFFORTS AND SUPPLY

Up to this point we have discussed mostly the effect of advertising on demand and buying behavior, and only occasionally how advertising can also influence what the seller may do to change the outcome of the decision process.   Here we will summarize how advertising can affect this second half of the purchase-decision apparatus.

Varied Effects on Selling

The ways advertising can affect selling are quite varied.   Advertising can reach and impress wholesalers so that they are more disposed to handle and push the brand.   It can change the interests and the ideas of retailers so that they are more likely to stock the product, and to carry more stock or more models or give the brand additional facings, improve its shelf position, run tie-in retail ads, set up window and store displays, and price the product on a reduced or even a loss-leader basis.

Distribution and Trade Stocks   The effects of advertising on distribution and trade stocks may anticipate, coincide with, or follow the reactions of consumers.   Planned consumer advertising campaigns are often merchandised in advance to the trade, and become an element in persuading retailers to stock or to feature the brand.   Or, retailers may themselves become aware of a heavy volume of brand advertising or of an especially telling copy treatment and decide to exploit the effort by their own actions.   Or, increased brand movement resulting from successful advertising may cause a reevaluation of the brand by the dealer; a common response to successful advertising is an increase in the size of the retailer's normal order, with a resultant gain in retail inventories.

Stimulation of Buying for Inventories   One interesting parallel between the effect of advertising on the trade and its effect on consumers is in this stimulation of buying for inventories.   Just as increases in consumer inventories tend to encourage gains in consumption, so additions to trade inventories tend to be followed by special selling efforts on the part of dealers, to stimulate more aggressive selling at the retail level, and hence to encourage the overall movement of products into the hands of consumers.

How Trade Prices the Brand   Advertising often has a direct effect, also, on how the trade prices the brand.   Successful advertising may help to protect the trade's markups, and eliminate the need to cut prices in order to move the stocks on hand.   On the other hand, retailers will often themselves choose to give special reduced pricing to brands with successful consumer advertising campaigns.   Pricing then becomes part of a broad special effort, which may also include retail displays and promotions, to build traffic and volume at the retail level by capitalizing on the brand's strong consumer demand.

Brand advertising can improve the interest in and knowledge about the brand at the retail level (as well as the consumer) so that sales people are better informed and more competent in discussions with their consumer prospects.

Advertising can increase the likelihood and the effectiveness of trade endorsement of a product. For example, it can increase the chance that a pharmacist will say something favorable about a particular proprietary, and the chance that such an endorsement, when it is given, will be relevant to the product and reinforcing to ideas already in the consumer's mind.

Retail Advertising

One important area of advertising (much more important to advertising and to advertisers than its brief emphasis in this discussion would suggest) is the advertising for retail stores.

Advertising of the brand by a respected retail store can add to the brand's acceptability and so contribute directly to the generation of demand, even though the purchase may actually be made through an entirely different outlet. But retail advertising affects more directly other important aspects of product purchasing, specifically the consumer's selection of the store or stores at which the purchase decision will be considered and the time the decision is reached.

Retail advertising tends to bring buying decisions to a head, it emphasizes availability and specifies price, and hence becomes a critical influence in the initiation and development of the purchase situation.

National advertisers, recognizing the importance of retail advertising, may spend money to stimulate cooperative advertising, to finance ads at the retail level, to encourage price specials, and to generate joint promotions with related products.

Besides media advertising, retail advertising efforts often include the use of a variety of point-of-purchase materials, some of them created and provided by the retailer, many of them developed and paid for and supplied by the national manufacturer. Such advertising, too, has an important effect in calling products to the attention of potential buyers and hence in encouraging movement of the consumer toward a purchasing decision.

Advertising at both the local and the national level distributes coupons, offers samples, identifies dealers, builds traffic, invites inquiries, and develops leads for salesmen. Mail-order advertising actually supplants important trade selling functions.

Various Effects in Distribution and Other Selling Efforts Quite obviously advertising, in addition to its effect on consumer demand, often has an effect on distribution and availability, and on pricing and other selling efforts supporting the advertised brand.

In thinking about these effects it is important to keep in mind the impact of advertising specifically aimed at retailers and wholesalers, as well as the possibly incidental but nonetheless important effects on the trade of advertising aimed primarily at influencing consumers.

How much effect advertising will have on the various marketing and selling forces will depend on the strength of the advertising strategy, on how well the strategy is executed, and on how forcefully the strategy is brought to bear against the organizations and the people who sell.

HOW ADVERTISING AFFECTS BUYING

The purchase of a brand comes at the end of a series of activities in which an individual's personal demand for the brand:

Is transferred to a buying agent
Is affected by supply and selling forces
Is instrumental in starting active purchasing
Is subject to a reappraisal by the buying agent
Counteracts any impetus to buy competing brands
Survives a final review and decision

These processes are usually irregular and quite individual, but we still need to comment on them and on the effect of advertising on the various activities.

We have described the communication of advertising and the generation of demand as activities affecting individual people. Buying and use, however, are not commonly individual processes, but activities that are shared with others.

Use Groups and Buying Agents

Each person may be a member of several different purchase, or consumption, or decision groups. (Here we will call them all simply *use groups.*)   In some he may be the only important member, as when he buys chewing gum or cigars largely for his own use.   In others the group will cover only his own household, and in yet others he may be in a temporary or lasting association with people outside his household (a car pool, a club, a business, or two couples on a trip).

The most common example of a use group is the household, where products bought by individuals are often consumed by members of the whole family.   Meals, for example, are eaten together; the whole family lives in the home; various members drive and enjoy the family car.

One Member Buying for Family   It is common in this kind of family (and in social or commercial "families") to have one member serve as the buying agent and final decision maker for the group as a whole. In a factory, for example, one individual or a committee of individuals may finally order the brand of pencil to be purchased or specify what drill press will be installed with what features.

Personal demand of other group members is asserted in the buying decision through this *buying agent,* who may or may not be the individual in the use group with the highest level of personal demand. The controlling demand is often contributed by an individual who does not personally make the buy: the wife may make up the shopping list and suggest the brand, while the husband makes the purchase.

The buyer, even in such cases, is usually not without important influence, particularly when supply and selling forces cause a large recasting of effective demand, or when the buyer's reappraisal indicates that the demand transferred from someone else could lead to a bad decision.

Personal demand, as we have defined it, already reflects the probable impact of the individual on the group purchase decision.   If the individual has almost no voice in what the group buys, his personal demand will be very low; if he dominates the decision, it will be comparatively high.   When an individual is the buying agent, his own predispositions are discounted to reflect the effects of other people.

Since personal demand is already on this basis, there is no need to change it in merging it with the demand of other members of the use group.   As the demand of the individual is transferred to the buying agent, it is simply added to that of the other members, creating a new buying probability and a new combined demand for each separate brand.

The Purchasing Process

Once a buying agent has been designated for a particular use group, the purchasing process can begin.   In describing the process it may help to imagine that it occurs in some kind of sequential steps, that there is first of all a period of activation, a kind of a decision to start deciding about purchasing.   We can visualize that this is followed by a period of consideration, which may include physical shopping, or some kind of shopping through the buyer's mind, in an effort to take some account of the alternatives of purchasing or not purchasing, and of considering the brands that may be involved in the purchase decision.   The decision itself comes, in concept, at some time in the process, but even after it is made it may be challenged, reevaluated, and reconsidered.

Finally, the purchase itself may be consummated, an actual purchase transaction may be concluded, although even after this has occurred the buyer may have second thoughts and act on a decision to reverse the decision that was reached.

We are certain to describe all these processes in more organized, orderly terms than they deserve.   The real buying process in many cases is instantaneous and disorderly, depending on chancy associations and motivations the consumer does not consciously credit, and of which he may not even be aware.

Demand and the assertion of demand often are not very logical matters, even in industrial and governmental purchasing where they are supposed to be rational and highly organized.   Demand involves the processes of the brain, and the brain stores and uses a lot of information that is irrational, sensory, and emotional, which no amount of logic can really force out of existence or keep from participation in the decision process.

Initiation of a Purchase   The initiation of a purchase transaction may be completely spontaneous (some people even buy houses on the spur of the moment) or it may involve a regularly scheduled routine procedure or an elaborate routine of investigation, experimental shopping, and tentative decisions before the purchase is actually consummated.

It has already been suggested that at a number of points in the purchasing process the buyer may decide to buy or reach a decision to defer purchase.   There is in the whole process a considerable degree of irresolution, at least for many buyers, and this brings us back, again, to the need for emphasizing how full of chance and uncertainty the process as a whole may be.

Tendencies Rather than Certainty   Early in this description we considered the values of defining personal demand in probability terms. Here again, at the moment of purchase decision, it is important to recognize that what the buyer brings to the transaction is a collection of tendencies rather than any certainty of behavior.   Some buying is going to be done by people with a very low probability of buying, and a brand does have a chance to be selected even though it is not the one with the highest preference.

The uncertainty of action and choice from the buyer's point of view is complicated by the important fact that purchasing is an interaction, a compromise between buying and selling forces.   The simple availability of a brand or a model or a class of product at a time that is favorable to purchase inevitably has a great deal to do with whether a purchase transaction is completed.   Beyond this, the amount of effort expended by the sellers will have an influence on what is finally decided.

If a buyer has an equal demand for a dishwasher and a set of golf clubs, but cannot afford to buy both, the intensity of selling effort for each kind of product may have a controlling influence on which one will be bought at that time.   As between two brands, more aggressive displays, broader distribution, and more favorable pricing often tip the decision toward one brand or the other.

Influence of Supply and Selling Forces

When supply and selling forces react with personal demand, they may increase or decrease the likelihood that a brand will be purchased, depending on the relative advantages or disadvantages it has in the areas of distribution or selling support.   If the brand has limited distribution, or if other brands are being pushed more actively by the trade, obviously, its chance of purchase will be reduced.

An important influence on the recasting of brand demand at this stage is any price manipulation at the retail level.   Along with other selling forces, special price advantages can be important in increasing the likelihood of purchase.

Personal Appraisals Possible   In many cases, particularly where at least one of the available brands is unfamiliar to the buyer, the buyer will make a personal reappraisal of the brands, judging on the basis of feel, packaging, and appearance which one should be bought. The process is important for brands that are not known to the buyer on the basis of experience; generally it will not change the evaluation of a familiar brand.   In many buying situations, of course, there is little change as a result of this personal judgment, but in some cases it can lead to a sharp revision in a brand's chance of purchase.

Advertising Influences Selling Activity   Advertising, even advertising not directed to the trade, as we have noted, substantially influences brand availability and selling activity.

It also, as we have seen, affects demand and buyer behavior; it tends to encourage the tendency to purchase, to affect the choice of brands, to influence the buyer's thinking about the quantity to be purchased, and in some purchases to influence the grade or model that is selected and the store at which the purchase is made.   Advertising can help to escalate the purchase to a higher level and accelerate the time of decision.

Advertising is by no means the only factor affecting purchasing, since the individual purchase is the culmination of the interactions of so many different forces.   But there is almost nothing involved in the act of purchasing that cannot be affected, in one direction or another, to a major or to a minor degree, by a brand's advertising.

Advertising Counteracts Buying of Competitive Brands

Some purchase decisions, once made, tend to have exceptional longevity.   A printing press, once bought, is operated over a long period of time, a house is lived in for a number of years.   Even some decisions that are reconfirmed regularly are not easily reversed; people tend to live with their selection of an insurance policy or a savings bank, or their choice of a home hair-coloring preparation.   A really bad experience can always bring the decision up for reconsideration, but normally a change is difficult to accomplish.   There are no hard and fast rules about this, however.   Cigarettes, once a classic case of lifetime brand loyalty, currently show all manner of brand-switching patterns.

But consumers, having once bought a brand, do tend, through a kind of inertia of choice, to avoid the problems of selection by buying the same brand again.   If the brand performs well in consumption, it is likely to have and hold a distinct gain in demand following its first purchase.

Purchase Triggers Reevaluation of Brand and Advertising

The impact of the purchase is far more critical than this. Purchase triggers reevaluation both of the brand and of its advertising, with positive reinforcement if the experience is favorable, or negative if it is not. The reinforcement may mean a stronger, more emphatic likelihood of future purchase, and it may also stimulate greater interest in and acceptance for future ads. If the experience is bad, not just the brand but its advertising as well may be in for a long period of rejection.

All this may suggest yet another area of advertising effect, because what the ads say can sometimes help to predetermine the consumer's expectation; it can change how the product seems to taste, or look, and the satisfactions it delivers.

Some people in advertising like to refer to it as a multiplier, implying that while it increases or speeds up the success or failure of the brand, the success or failure would in some measure and at some time occur even in the absence of advertising. The concepts presented here assign to advertising a more primary and active role. Advertising, in this view, is more a generator than an accelerator. The concepts ascribe to the individual advertisement the ability actually to create consumer demand, and suggest that product purchase and consumption act to reinforce or correct this process.

Whichever analogy is better, there is little question that finally brand evaluation based on personal experience can act as an effective governor on a brand's success and on the productivity of its advertising, if the brand does not live up to the consumer's expectations.

HOW ADVERTISING CHANGES SALES AND PROFITS

If a consumer makes a purchase of the brand that he would not have made if a certain ad or ads had not appeared, the advertiser has realized a tangible return from the advertising.

If we add all the purchases of this kind, and subtract any purchases lost as a result of the same advertising, we have made a start on the question of how advertising changes sales and profits.

Sales as a First Yield

These net gained sales, the sales that would not have been made if the advertising did not appear, are the logical first measure of yield for most brand advertising.

To many people, the simplicity and correctness of this idea may be self-evident. Yet, because objections seem to be raised almost routinely against any effort to relate sales and advertising, some points about this concept may need comment.

It must be acknowledged again that not all advertising tries to make sales of the brand, since some is designed to enhance the value of the company stock, or to help the company in negotiating a labor contract, or to recruit engineers, or to explain why the product is in short supply. These cases, while numerous, are exceptions to the most common general advertising purpose. Today, most of the advertising that is done is paid for by companies and people who are selling something, and its obvious aim is to make additional sales.

Some notice should also be taken of the familiar comment that sales reflect the operation of so many different factors that they cannot show the effects of advertising. It is important to say that the measure suggested is the difference between sales, over time, with and without the advertising, and that this estimated difference is independent of whether sales are high or low, or going up or down, or influenced by other factors or not.

Profit as a Justification

Beyond sales, there is an even more basic and universal rationalization for advertising, and one that is even harder to compute. The real justification for advertising is not volume, but profit.

The profitability of a particular unit or program of advertising is the difference between its cost and the present worth of the overhead contributions and profit on all the gained sales it produces.

Again, this is a logical concept, but a difficult calculation, not just because of the initial problems of estimating gained sales, but because of the complicating effects of time on the whole operation.

Because time affects the reinforcement and the decomposition of the response to advertising, and because time relates to the market behavior of each individual, time also measures the total payout from advertising.   Today's advertisement will potentially influence brand volume over an extended sequence of profit-and-loss statements. There is no very logical or defensible deadline on payout for most continuing brands.   One purchase is linked to another, attitudes and experience beget attitudes and experience, and the payout chain, in reality, is endless.

In practice, estimating the profit contributions of advertising is usually based on quite arbitrary assumptions.   But if, because of the nature of the market or the financial resources of the advertiser, the payout must be short term, then some limited kinds of advertising (loading current customers, for example) may be the only approaches that are possible.   If long-term payout is considered, a broader spectrum of strategies can be employed, and the real return from the advertising may be greater, even though it is slower.

The financial and economic problems of evaluating advertising are very real ones.   But the idea, at least, is simple.   Advertising is done in the expectation of gained sales, and the belief that the profit on those sales will exceed what the advertising costs.

HOW ADVERTISING CHANGES THE MARKET

We have now traced the workings of advertising through a sequence from conception to the calculation of payout.   We must still describe some of the defensive responses advertising activates from competitive brands, note its impact on the volume and growth and sustained success of whole categories of products and services, and mention certain other effects on the public and the market.

Retaliatory Action

Very often, a successful advertising campaign will produce strong marketing responses from competing brands.   Almost inevitably, if a campaign begins to injure a competitor's volume or share of market, vigorous action will be taken to nullify what the advertising has accomplished and to protect the competing brand against further losses.

Retaliatory action may take a variety of forms.   The competitor may increase his advertising budget, or move aggressively into the specific media the successful brand is using, or adopt an imitative creative style. Frequently words or phrases will be added to the competitor's advertising to counter or cover successful claims. (Not all these advertising reactions are successful, and in some cases there is evidence that imitative responses have turned out to benefit the original brand.)

Competitive reactions often are in areas other than advertising. Frequently a brand that is seriously hurt will respond with deals, with specials of one kind or another and with outright price reductions. Successes also tend to stimulate competitors' product research and to accelerate the introduction of competitive products and packaging.

All these actions are intended to limit the sales that a brand can gain as a result of advertising, and they often do succeed in constraining the amount of change that is accomplished.

Effect on Volume of Products

Another important effect of advertising is its impact on the popularity and total volume of a category of products and services.

In an economic system in which many of the leading brands are advertised, it is not too difficult to rationalize some benefits of advertising for the individual brand. Its defensive aspects alone may seem to justify the appropriation. (Sales not lost are surely considered as gained sales under our definition.) Even if it were not for this consideration, advertisers often conclude that advertising is a more efficient and productive way to develop brand volume than price reductions, dealing, dealer incentives, and other merchandising activities, or they have decided that advertising is an indispensable supplement to these programs.

The broader economic case for advertising has to do with its effect on the overall volume of products sold by an entire industry, with the development of consumption, with the generation and spread of product usage. Sales made as a reflection of these changes must also be considered as gained sales. But they are singularly difficult to identify.

There remain now certain other effects of advertising that are too indirect or too irregular to fit, at this time, into an orderly system, but that are still important aspects of some advertising operations. Some of these relate to the consumer and the generation of demand,

and some to market conditions not directly related to normal areas of advertising accomplishment.

Word-of-mouth Communication

No discussion of advertising would be complete without some comment on how it affects word-of-mouth communication about the brand.   One thing that happens could be called recommunication of content.   This is when an individual passes along to other people advertising words and ideas, very much in their original form.   It is a process which sometimes reaches striking proportions; sometimes phrases or slogans fall into the public jargon, are picked up by entertainers and writers, dramatized, made into jokes, and repeated endlessly by the young and the general public.

Somewhat less dramatically, advertising can, as it makes a brand more popular, also make it more worthy of discussion; it can add to the incentive to speak about the brand from personal knowledge and personal experience, and encourage person-to-person communication of ideas and impressions and intentions.

Beyond normal word of mouth, advertising can help generate product endorsements from various authority figures and from opinion leaders not involved in the selling process, from teachers, doctors, home economists, and writers.

Effect on Consumer Product Values

Sometimes, the success of a brand's advertising campaign seems to be able to change the whole structure of consumer product values, appeals, and expectations.   Over the years, there have been a number of cases when advertising was able to change markedly the apparent segmentation of the market.   This suggests that segmentation is often not so much a reflection of inherent differences in the needs of different people as it is a description of created differences in their emphasis and orientation.

For example, for a long time before Crest, it was not easy to sell a dentifrice with an all-out anticavity story, and for a long time after Crest, it was hard to sell without a claim of this kind.   (Sometimes, of course, advertising does not change the public so much as it changes the style cycle in copy emphasis, and sometimes it is impossible to decide whether all the leading brands in a field really should be making almost the same claim at the same point in time.)

The emergence of many new products and new product classes is evidence that what come to be accepted as basic consumer needs and wants are, at least in some measure, reflections of ideas implanted or articulated or emphasized by advertising.

Advertising, which can be used to segment a market, also may serve to desegment the brand to broaden its appeal. Again and again, a brand, having achieved large sales through exploitation of a special quality or product satisfaction, then succeeds in offering alternative products, with widely different markets and different performance characteristics, under the same trademark.

Special Advertising Campaigns

Special advertising campaigns can have even broader effects than these on companies and their various publics, and sometimes these changes result from successful brand advertising as well as from corporate-image or other special-purpose advertisements.

Successful advertising can change the whole level of public opinion about a corporation or an industry; it can have the effect of changing laws, governmental regulations, and the activities of the bureaucracy.

Advertising may change a company from an unknown to a known employer, and this can affect the level of employee morale and the success of employee recruitment. It may stimulate the company's own people to work harder, and affect the movement of people from one company to another.

It affects the brand's advertising budget even though it also is a result of the budget; it changes expectations and decisions on financial payout; it affects the financial situation not only of the advertised brand but of the company as a whole. A successful brand-advertising campaign can affect the corporate credit rating and the price of the corporate stock.

It can have an impact on product research and development, not only because successful campaigns stimulate interest in additional products and product modifications, but because successful competitive campaigns may emphasize the need for a parity product or for one with an advertisable point of difference.

Summary

Beyond its effect on selling and supply, on personal demand and buying activity, and on sales and profits, advertising can generate a variety of effects on the market as a whole, on the company and its competitors, on the top managers of the corporation and their attitudes, on all the people who make, sell, buy, and finance the product.

It is clear that advertising is complex, that the roads through the mind and the market are devious and tortured and often uncharted, that advertising does not reduce to a few clean rules or limit itself to goals that disregard whole levels and orders of achievement.

We have not said here as clearly as we someday must how advertising works.   But there is hope that we may yet understand it, that we may see it in full perspective, that it is not so arcane nor so infinite as to defy always all efforts at useful description.

Some of the theory of how advertising works embodies the following concepts:

That a key process by which advertising makes sales is the generation of personal demand through direct advertising exposure

That responses to an ad will vary; of the people contacted, some will experience no change in demand, and the reactions of the others will differ in extent and even in direction

That the media type, the vehicle, and the advertising unit affect the occurrence of an advertising exposure, and the demand generated by the exposure; that chance, or unidentified cause, plays a part in an individual's exposure and response to an advertisement; that the content of an advertisement directly affects how much demand it generates

That individuals in a user group differ in their influence on buying; that advertising, as a way of generating personal demand, may activate an individual to assert his demand in purchasing and brand decisions

That an advertising contact may be reinforced by the effect of past advertising, and it may, in turn, enhance the demand created by future advertising

That the yield of a brand's advertising affects, and is affected by, the advertising yield for competing brands; that a brand may lose predisposition because another brand has gained it

That personal demand, once changed through an advertising contact or other stimulus, tends subsequently to revert toward its preexposure level

That when personal demand for a brand is at high level, it generally decays less rapidly and is less vulnerable to competitive displacement than when it is at lower levels

That advertising can affect the quality of satisfaction derived from owning, using, or consuming a brand; that it may stimulate product use and the consumption of existing consumer inventories, accelerate the buying cycle, and increase the quantity per purchase

That advertising, in addition to its effect on demand, may have an effect on availability, price, and other selling efforts supporting the advertised brand

And that the logical measure of yield for brand advertising is gained profit, the profit that would not have been made if the advertising did not appear

CHAPTER NINE

How Consumers Behave

ROBERT J. WILLIAMS *Manager of Consumer Products Marketing Research, The Dow Chemical Company*

WHAT IS CONSUMER BEHAVIOR?

Very nearly every human being (even an infant) can be regarded as a consumer. And virtually all of our behavior (even sleeping) involves the consumption of some product or service. It follows that a comprehensive discussion of "consumer behavior" would come very close to being a discussion of the whole of human activity. Our ambitions for this chapter are, however, somewhat less grandiose.

We shall assume that the marketer (whatever may be his academic curiosity about human nature in general) has a particular professional interest in those behaviors which lead to the tingling of the cash register bell, and ultimately change the bottom line of his profit-and-loss statement. For our present purposes, therefore, we shall confine our attention to one particular class of behavior: the decision behaviors which precede and control the buying of goods and services for the consumer's own use.

The Advertiser's Interest

The advertiser's interest in consumer behavior stems from his interest in controlling that behavior.   He wants to know, of course, what strings he must pull, what magic gestures he must make, in order to have the consumer behave in a way that will enhance his own sales and profits.   Of course, no one really expects to discover some magic formula that will force the consumer to part with his money unwillingly.   The consumer is no more subject to hypnotism than the advertiser himself.   There are no hidden coercive springs to be pressed, no secret nerve mechanisms to be triggered, that will make the consumer see a sow's ear as a silk purse.   However, most of us acknowledge the efficacy of one not-so-secret formula which successful marketing and advertising men have been using for a long time—build a better mousetrap, and beat a path to the consumer's door with it. Some knowledge of consumer behavior may help in designing that better mousetrap, and in charting some of the paths to the consumer's door.

A Much-studied Subject

Consumer behavior has been a subject for study by psychologists, sociologists, economists, anthropologists, mathematicians, and of course, businessmen.   Professionals in each of these disciplines tend to use the language and constructs of their own fields of specialization, and quite naturally select for study that aspect of consumer behavior which lends itself most readily to analysis in their own terms. In the discussion which follows I have been shamelessly eclectic, and have borrowed freely from thinkers in all these fields, but have tried to avoid their jargon.   For the most part, however, I have yielded to a personal bias, and have described consumer behavior as it appears to the marketing researcher.

An individual consumer generates an income by exchanging his own time, effort, skill, or property for money.   That money would, of course, be just so much wastepaper except for the fact that it can, in turn, be exchanged for objects which are useful to the consumer, or for the time, efforts, and skills of other people.

The Nature of Values

The value of a dollar bill to an individual consumer derives entirely from the value to him of the goods or services for which it can be exchanged. (This statement does not necessarily presume that the individual is completely informed about all the ways in which he can possibly spend a dollar, but only that he has spent a few of them in the past and has developed some generalized notion of the pleasures and benefits of doing so.) The value of these goods and services, in turn, derives entirely from their usefulness to the consumer in satisfying his needs. (I shall use the word "needs" in this chapter to stand for all the concepts included in the phrase "needs, desires, wants, wishes, urges, and motives.")

The Kinds of Needs

Not all the consumer's needs are equivalent, of course, because he feels some more deeply or more intensely than others. Some he feels as "inescapable demands," some as "urgent requirements," some as "strong desires," others as "interesting possibilities," and still others as "whims." This order of importance is not established by the individual as a self-conscious decision, but is developed by all the "character-molding" forces at work in his environment. It constitutes his "sense of values."

Given a set of needs ordered into a priority hierarchy, certain uses of the consumer's money—those uses directed at satisfying high-priority needs—become invested with very great utility. Other uses—those directed at satisfying whims—are invested with less utility. In general the consumer will be willing to spend more money for those goods and services having greater utility than for those having lesser utility.

UTILITY OF A PURCHASE

However, the total utility of a single purchase does not derive from the satisfaction of one single need, but from the satisfaction of a great variety of needs, some important and others trivial, which may have no logical relation to one another. To illustrate this point, let us consider the process by which a hypothetical consumer, whom we shall call Mrs. Jones, came to serve chocolate cake to her family for dessert at last night's dinner.

We will have to assume that the "need to feed and care for her family" has a fairly high priority among all Mrs. Jones' needs, and in the course of her day, this need prompted her to a bit of menu planning.

During her menu planning, Mrs. Jones was made acutely aware of the vast number of ways in which she could "feed her family," all of which seemed equivalent for the purpose of satisfying that need. Although her need to feed her family precipitated the act of menu planning, it could not help her choose among the equivalent alternatives which she faced in that planning. Her menu choice, then, was guided not by that need, but by other needs, such as her need to avoid repetition and boredom in her meals, and her desire to derive pleasure from certain congenial combinations of food.

A Primary Decision

At one point in her planning she had to make a decision about whether to serve dessert or not, which may have been partly governed by her need to give love or pleasure, or to secure the praise and approval of her family. Having made an affirmative decision on that issue, she had to choose from among the various equivalent dessert possibilities, such as pie, ice cream, fruit, cake, pudding, etc. That decision may have been determined by her desire to acquiesce to the preferences of a particular family member.

Having chosen to serve cake, Mrs. Jones then had the options of buying a cake at the bakery, or preparing one from the raw ingredients, or preparing one from a packaged cake mix. Her desire to save time and effort narrowed her choices to the bakery cake and the packaged mix. But her need to make at least a token gesture of attentiveness to her family led her finally to choose the cake mix. She was then faced with the choice of a brand and flavor. She chose the more familiar brand because of her need for assurance that the cake would turn out the way she wanted it, but selected a flavor she had not tried before, called "Chocolate Ripple," to satisfy her curiosity about it.

Various Choices

Figure 1 summarizes the various choices and decisions which Mrs. Jones had to make in order to get cake on her dinner table, and also the various needs which we have presumed were operative in those decisions. Needless to say, if Mrs. Jones were as self-conscious or as deliberative in making her decisions as we have been in talking about them, she would be too overwrought after planning the meal to be able to prepare it! Actually Mrs. Jones passes easily and quickly from one decision to the next, and arrives at the end point often without even recording in her own mind the intermediate steps.

This does not imply that the needs (or motives) which shaped her decision are "suppressed" because they overwhelm her emotionally, nor that they are a part of her "subconscious" which she is unwilling to acknowledge. She simply does not clutter her consciousness with

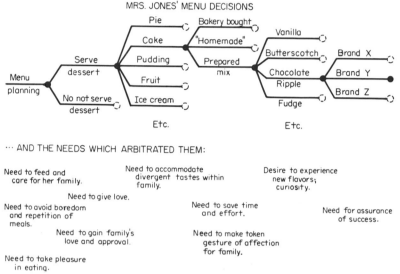

Figure 1

the details of a decision which is so trivial an event in her day, nor introspect about needs and motives which are so much a taken-for-granted part of the fabric of her life.

For example, if Mrs. Jones serves dessert at three out of four evening meals then her decision to do so on this occasion is actually easier than a decision not to do so. The selection of cake rather than pudding, pie, or fruit may seem to her to be a straightforward interpretation of her family's preferences, qualified by consideration of the fact that she hadn't served cake at any meal for over a week. The brand decision she would probably describe as "habit" (a default of decision), and the flavor decision may have actually been made days earlier, when, in response to a neighbor's chit-chat, she said, "I'll try that the next time I have a cake." But however facile Mrs. Jones may appear to be in tossing off these decisions, we cannot deny the reality of her needs, nor the control which her needs exert in her decision behavior.

"Rational" and "Irrational" Terms Meaningless

To separate the forces which shaped Mrs. Jones' decision into categories of "rational" and "irrational" motives would be unnecessary, arbitrary, and meaningless. Mrs. Jones would be behaving "irrationally" only if she made choices which were inimical to the satisfaction of her needs. However, even though she may sometimes incorrectly anticipate the consequences of her choices, all her decisions are made with the *intention* of satisfying her needs. *We* may make a mistake by trying to interpret her decisions in terms of *our* needs, or by trying to interpret her choice at one level in terms of a need which in fact governed her choice at some other level. From such mistaken points of view her decision may appear to be "irrational." But Mrs. Jones is not a party to our interpretive errors.

The point to be remembered is that Mrs. Jones' overt economic behavior of buying this product or that is almost certain to be the end result of a rather long chain of decisions and choices, and that each decision in that chain may be influenced by a different set of needs from the one preceding or following it. Each decision reduces one need, but exposes a new set of options, among which the choice will be determined by some other need.

When Is Marketer's Influence Effective?

At what point in this elaborate chain of decisions can the marketer intrude his influence most effectively and most economically to obtain a decision in favor of his product? Before we seek a positive answer to this question let us first eliminate from consideration those junctures in the decision process at which the marketer's influence is likely to be *least* effective and *most costly* to apply.

Needs Cannot Be Created

No ordinary or acceptable marketing action can create a need (or motive) in a person who previously did not feel that need. Needs and motives have their source within the individual and probably have not changed very much since man first appeared on this earth. Our culture controls the manner in which we express (or suppress) our needs, and we work endless variations and refinements on our manner of satisfying our needs. But the needs remain very much the same. Psychologists used to amuse themselves by showing how even our most patently social needs—such as our need for attention and approval—are derivative from more fundamental needs; and how *all* our needs ultimately derive from a most primitive need for individual and species survival. In all likelihood such speculations come fairly close to the fact—and in any event suggest the extremely low probability that new needs will burst in the human psyche as a consequence of advertising or marketing efforts. In short, advertising does not create motives.

Relative Importance of Needs

Nor is any marketing action capable of producing any profound or lasting change in the hierarchy of importance which an individual consumer has established among his needs. The importance which a person assigns to the satisfaction of a particular need depends in part upon his early training, the cultural complex in which he lives, his biological makeup, and all those forces which contribute to what is sometimes called "his value system." Some people value short-term amusement more than others; some people derive more pleasure from food than others; some divert themselves with sensory delights and others with intellectual pursuits; some are selfish and others generous. These are aspects of personality and character on which advertising operates only to the extent that it is one of many forces operating in our culture. As a character-molding force, the importance of advertising must be judged relative to the importance of parental training, schooling, religious influences, literature, the total impact of all the media in which advertising is imbedded, and all the other forces operating in our culture. In short, advertising is not efficient for increasing the importance of one need relative to all other needs.

Relative Utilities of Options and the Marketer

The marketer has the best chances of influencing the decision process at those points where the consumer makes a judgment about the relative utilities to the various real options presented in the world external to himself. Looking back to our case of Mrs. Jones and the chocolate cake, those junctures were (1) her choice in planning her menu between serving dessert or not doing so, (2) her choice of cake among the many possible desserts, (3) her choice of a prepared cake mix rather than bakery cake, or a cake made from "scratch," (4) her choice of Chocolate Ripple flavor over the other flavors available, and (5) her choice of a particular brand.

Importance of Market Position   The juncture at which a marketer should choose to exert an influence on this decision process depends upon his market position.   A marketer whose brand commands a minor share of the market should probably concentrate his efforts on influencing the consumer's flavor or brand choice (junctures 4 and 5).   The minor brand has more to gain by shifting users from other brands into his own, or by encouraging use of his own unique flavors, than by persuading nonusers to enter the product class.   A marketer whose brand dominates the product class, on the other hand, may have more to gain by trying to bring people into the product class than by attempting to influence movement among brands.   This marketer would concentrate his efforts on influencing the consumer's decision to serve cake made from a prepared mix rather than bakery cake or homemade cake (juncture 3).   A trade association for all cake marketers, if one existed, would direct its efforts at influencing the consumers' menu-planning decision and choice of cake over alternative desserts (junctures 1 and 2).

Help in Discerning Differences in Utility   Clearly, not every marketer will benefit equally by trying to appeal to the consumer's "deep-down, underlying motives" for using the product class.   Indeed, in most markets none would benefit from doing so.   If a marketer seeks to influence a brand choice, then the motives to which he must appeal are those which enable the consumer to discern differences in utility among the brands within the product class.   The fact that these motives may be irrelevant to the motives for using the product class should not be a consideration.   A consumer's desire to "get something for nothing" may exert a powerful influence on his choice of the brand which happens to be offering a premium, even though this motive is quite unrelated to his motives for using the product class.

I have refrained, so far, from attempting to draw up a catalog of "basic human motives," as was the fashion in discussions of consumer behavior just a few years ago.   The reason for this is that these basic motives (such as sex, fear, and self-preservation) rarely operate in the kinds of decisions the marketer is seeking to control. Brand-choice decisions are determined by relatively shallow versions of these motives, or by their remote derivatives.

Decision as the Result of a Personal Calculus

Moreover, the utility of an object, such as a package of cake mix, is not appraised in a single dimension. Mrs. Jones' final decision about her family's dessert was based on a complicated addition of utilities in several dimensions, including the utility of the time and effort saved by using the mix, and the utility of being able to obtain a flavor which she did not know how to duplicate in her kitchen. These utilities may have been available also in a bakery cake, but the prepared mix afforded her the additional utilities over the bakery cake of enabling her to serve a "just-baked" cake and to make some of the same gestures of love toward her family that would have been involved in making a cake from the raw ingredients.

The calculus by which Mrs. Jones combined and compared these various utilities is known only to Mrs. Jones. At the very moment she was making her decision in favor of a particular kind of cake mix, her neighbor may have been deciding to bake a cake "from scratch." The decisions of the two women differ because of differences between them in the value which they place on convenience, and their enjoyment of the act of baking. To put it another way, in their calculus for combining utilities, each woman assigns different weights to the utility of saving time and effort, and the utility of a particular class of play behavior.

BEST COURSE FOR THE ADVERTISER

The advertiser who attempts to alter the consumer's calculus for combining utilities in a way that would favor the selection of his brand will almost certainly face an uphill struggle. A cake mix manufacturer, for example, who would try to educate adult women to perceive additional utility in "convenience" than they now do, would probably have to contemplate expenditures comparable to those which were made to teach those same women to spell correctly and add sums correctly when they were young and flexible children. And he could expect no better results. One sage manufacturer, whose identity is lost in antiquity, is said to have remarked, "It's easier for me to make what they want, than to make them want what I've got."

Give Consumer What He Wants

The real wisdom of that remark is that it suggests the most direct and powerful influence which an advertiser can bring to bear on the consumer's decision process: to provide the consumer with what he wants, and make it more useful than the competitor's alternative— that is, to build a better mousetrap.   Needless to say, even that effort will be wasted unless the better mousetrap is made available to the consumer and he is made aware of it.

Concept of Brand Loyalty

Observations that some consumers buy the same brand on many successive purchase occasions while others buy several different brands have given rise to the construct of "brand loyalty."   When an advertiser talks about consumer "loyalty" to his brand he is probably referring to the consumer's feelings that the brand affords him more utility than other brands at the same price.   This attitude is indeed a very dilute version of an individual's feelings of "loyalty" to his country, his lodge, his family, or his school.   Almost any consumer would, in truth, rather switch than fight.   Nevertheless, however faint the advertiser may judge the feeling to be, he thinks of brand loyalty as an *attitude,* and this attitude is presumed to be a precondition for persistent brand-choice *behavior.*

In actual practice, the *attitude* is usually inferred from observations of persistent brand-choice *behavior.*   The usual inputs for such a study are diary records, in which a panel of consumers record their brand selections in certain product classes over a very long period of time.   These diaries are behavior records, and do not attempt to evaluate attitudes.

The advertiser should, however, be extremely cautious about inferring the existence of loyal attitudes from observations of brand-choice behavior, and conversely should be quite hesitant to predict the behavior from measures of attitudes of commitment to various brands.

Variable versus Random Choices

A consumer's choices of brands may show considerable variability without, however, being random choices.   For example, a smoker

may divide his patronage among four or five different brands of cigarettes. This seemingly labile brand-choice behavior may arise from
fluctuations in that person's needs which, in turn, alter the utility to
him of the collection of product characteristics which distinguishes
each brand from all the others. For example, a day of excessive
smoking of his regular cigarettes may incline the smoker to select a
mentholated brand the next day. When he carries the cigarettes in
the pocket of his suit coat he may prefer the collapsible softpack, but
when he carries them in his trouser pocket on the weekend he may
prefer a crushproof box. His brand choices, though variable, are
purposive.

On the other hand, another smoker's choice of brands may be truly
random. This does not necessarily suggest that he is unable to evaluate the total utility of each of the various available brands, but may
imply only that (1) the available brands do not, in fact, objectively
differ in any dimension which is meaningful to that particular consumer, or (2) that the consumer is incompletely informed about the
differences among the brands, or (3) that he does not believe in the
reality of the alleged differences. To such a person, one smoke is as
good as another, so he accepts whatever brand comes to hand. One
of the important functions of advertising is to provide the consumer
with believable information about those differences among brands
which make them unequal in their utility to him.

The fact that still another smoker always selects the same brand is
not necessarily evidence that he discriminates it as providing him
more utility than the other brands available to him. Selecting or
asking for a different brand would require just a little more delibera-
tion and attention than selecting the brand he habitually uses. If he
discriminates no differences among brands, this slight extra effort is
unwarranted.

A fourth smoker may also persistently use a single brand, but for
the reason that he truly believes that it affords him more utility than
any other. The attributes which make the brand useful to him,
however, are not related to needs which fluctuate in intensity with
time or circumstance. In all likelihood the attributes for which he
selects the brand do not afford an immediate benefit as the cigarettes
are smoked, but some more remote benefit which is partly accepted on
faith, such as "less tars and nicotine."

ATTITUDES AND BEHAVIOR

We can systematize these thoughts by performing a small "mental experiment." Let us divide the users of a particular product class into two groups: (1) those who always buy the same brand (the behaviorally loyal), and (2) those who divide their patronage among several brands (the behaviorally fickle). Let us further divide both of these groups into two subgroups: (*a*) Those who perceive significant differences in utility among brands and feel committed to the brand they are using (the attitudinally loyal), and (*b*) those who feel that all brands are about the same (the attitudinally fickle). We would thus create four distinct classes, or *loyalty types,* as shown in Figure 2. If

Consumers may be divided by their

PURCHASE BEHAVIOR
into these two groups···

		1. Always buy the same brand. LOYAL	2. Sometimes buy different brands FICKLE
and by their ATTITUDES into these groups	(a) Feel it's important to use a particular brand (LOYAL)	Group 1a Behaviorally and attitudinally loyal.	Group 2a Behaviorally fickle but attitudinally loyal.
	(b.) Think one brand is about as good as another (FICKLE)	Group 1b Behaviorally loyal but attitudinally fickle.	Group 2b Behaviorally and attitudinally fickle.

Figure 2

behavioral loyalty were intimately associated with attitudinal loyalty, then the subgroup of "behaviorally loyal but attitudinally fickle" would be empty. Nor would any consumers be found in the subgroup "behaviorally fickle but attitudinally loyal."

In fact, however, the two loyalty measures are quite unrelated. For most product classes the proportion of consumers who are attitudinally fickle is about the same in the behaviorally loyal group as it is in the behaviorally fickle group.

Four Loyalty Types

The existence of these four loyalty types has been verified in numerous studies covering a large number of product classes. The four groups differ sharply from one another in the manner in which they assess the utility of the brands they purchase, as typified by our four smokers. The following paragraphs give a synoptic description of the groups, and the kinds of reasons an individual in each one might offer to account for his brand selection.

Group 1a: Behaviorally and Attitudinally Loyal   These consumers buy only one brand and claim that it is important to them to use that brand. Since they do not afford themselves the opportunity to make comparisons among brands, they are probably responding to a feature of their brand which is not accessible to immediate experience, such as the reputation of the manufacturer, or the fact that it is a "prestige" brand, or that it is endorsed by an authoritative person or celebrity, etc. If we should take an inventory of the brands that they are using, we would find that they tend to buy the higher priced brands, since price may be accepted as evidence of quality.

When asked why they choose that particular brand, they reply simply that "It's the best." If pressed to say in what way it is best, they respond that it has "superior quality" or that it "performs better" (without, however, being able to say *how* it performs better or *how* the superior quality can be detected). They also cite the "reputation of the manufacturer" as a reason for their choice. In other words, this group appears to respond to an assumption of "quality" in a particular brand which is not necessarily evident in surface features, but is established by reputation and tradition. This group seems to be most aptly described by the name *quality conscious.*

Group 1b: Behaviorally Loyal but Attitudinally Fickle   Although these consumers always buy the same brand, they do so without any conviction about its superiority over other brands. Apparently their selection is based largely on habit, or ignorance of the alternatives. They take the easy course of choosing the brand they know about, whose name they can pronounce surely, and the one that requires a minimum of thought and reflection to remember.

Consumers in this group are fairly casual users of the product class. They use the brands that are so closely identified with the product class that they have become almost generic (e.g., Kleenex, Scotch tape, etc.).   When asked why they selected that brand they usually do not have any ready answer other than "Just always use it," and may even counter with the question, "Well, what else is there?"   We might call them *habit bound*.

Group 2a: Behaviorally Fickle but Attitudinally Loyal   Although consumers in this group move from brand to brand, they nevertheless feel that the brand they are using affords them some particularly useful benefit.   They choose among brands wisely, selecting the one which is best adapted to the current state of their needs.   They are very well acquainted with the features which distinguish one brand from another, and are discriminating in their choice.   They tend to be heavy users of the product class, and consequently have ample opportunity to try and evaluate the various offerings of the market.   Of the four groups, this one is the first to learn of a new brand on the market, and the most willing to try it, particularly if it offers an unusual feature.

When asked about their reasons for brand selection, they talk at length about the particular features of the product.   They tend to be unimpressed by the reputation of the manufacturer, or sales gimmicks such as contests or premiums.   They are willing to pay a slightly higher price to obtain a brand with a particular feature, but do not consistently use high-priced brands.   Because of their alertness to the differentiating features of the various brands, they should be called *feature conscious*.

Group 2b: Behaviorally and Attitudinally Fickle   These people shift from brand to brand, but are nevertheless insensitive to the differences between brands.   Their interest in the product class is low, and is limited to performance in the defining function of the products. They are obviously unimpressed by peripheral features.

They have little basis on which to choose among brands other than price or availability.   When asked their reasons for brand selection they say, "It just happened to be on sale," or "It's the cheapest," or "It happens to be the brand the store carries."   Obviously they will be the most responsive of all groups to price-off deals or special sales. The name *bargain hunters* seems appropriate for this group.

Since some products are more important to more people than other products, the distribution of consumers into these four loyalty groups will differ from one product class to another.   In general, products which are purchased for the individual purchaser's personal use tend to generate more attitudinal loyalty than products that are purchased for someone else's use or for shared use.   Products necessary for survival or which contribute greatly to health, comfort, and well-being also seem to inspire strong loyalties.   Thus, medicines and drugs would generate more attitudinal loyalty than toiletries, say, and toiletries more than household cleaners.

If the differences between brands in a product class are easily discriminated (e.g., food products), we would expect more consumers to be feature conscious with respect to that product class than to one where the differences are not easily discriminable.   If the differences between brands are such that the consumer cannot easily assess them, such as differences in purity (e.g., medicines), nutritional value (e.g., vitamins), or durability (e.g., appliances), then we would expect more consumers to be quality conscious with respect to that product class. If considerable price variability exists in a product class, then those consumers who do not consider the product important will behave like bargain hunters.   If there is no price variability, they will become habit bound.

Attitudes and Behavior among Product Classes

An individual consumer's behavior and attitude with respect to one class of products is not necessarily indicative of his behavior and attitude with respect to some other class of products.   A homemaker may be habit bound in her choice of a brand of frozen orange juice, but feature conscious in her selection of a brand of baby food.   A man may be a bargain hunter when he is buying undershirts, but quality conscious in his selection of a suit.

A person's behavior and attitude with respect to a product class depends, for the most part, on the importance of the product to him. This, in turn, depends on the intensity of his need for it, or the amount of satisfaction he can derive from it, or in some cases from ambivalent feelings toward the product arising from fear or guilt concerning its use.   For example, a person who suffers from very severe and frequent headaches will probably choose his brand of headache remedy with great care.   He will learn to discriminate differences in the kinds of relief he obtains from using different brands.   If he fears that excessive use may result in dependence, or tolerance, or be habit-forming, he may vary in his brand choices, choosing at one time a brand which he is certain will give relief, and at another time a brand which he regards as safe.   If he is concerned about the purity of the product, but is unable to distinguish differences in purity himself, he may simply stick with the brand which has the best reputation for quality.

On the other hand, a person whose headaches are mild and infrequent will probably find that all brands of headache remedy are sufficiently effective to provide relief in his case.   Since he uses headache remedies infrequently, he will probably not become concerned about the likelihood of their being habit-forming or of developing tolerance for them.   When he buys a headache remedy, he may simply ask for the brand he knows best—the one he "has always used"—simply because it is the easiest to recall and the easiest to say.   He may not, in fact, even trouble to discover that alternatives exist in the market. He may never even discover that the other brands which he sees are indeed brands of headache remedies!   However, if his habit of buying the same brand again and again is disrupted because, say, that particular brand becomes unavailable, he will be forced to choose among the alternatives.   We can safely predict that he will choose then on the basis of the only difference which is evident to him: price.

A Manufacturer's Decisions

A manufacturer's decisions about how to spend his marketing money should be influenced by the distribution of consumers in the four loyalty groups for his market, as well as his position in that market.   If the majority of consumers, in their behavior and attitudes with respect to his product class, are classified as bargain hunters, and if his product has a shelf price about equal to his competitors, then he would be wise to invest most of his marketing money in deals and promotions which have the effect of lowering his price to the consumer.   If he cannot be price competitive, then he must be content to serve the minority of the consumers who are classified as feature conscious or quality conscious.   (This may not be an unattractive position, if his is the only brand in his market which is serving this minority.)

If the majority of consumers exhibit feature-conscious behavior with respect to his product, the manufacturer might consider increasing his R&D expenditures.   These expenditures may be directed toward either the improvement of his brand (if it is not widely preferred among the feature-conscious consumers) or the development of a second brand having a set of features different from his present one. His advertising should, of course, be feature-oriented, and should stress those characteristics of his brand which distinguish it from the others.

If the dominant consumer attitude toward a product class is quality consciousness, then the advertising for a brand within that class should stress the reputation and dependability of the manufacturer and the great care which he takes to assure a uniform, high-quality product.   Advertising of unique features is not inconsistent, if the features can be presented as evidences of underlying quality.   For certain types of products, written guarantees may provide the necessary assurance to quality-conscious consumers.

If most consumers are habit bound in their behavior toward a product, the manufacturer of a brand within that class should spend a part of his money for trade deals and the kinds of promotions which will obtain as large a share of the shelf space as possible.   He should, of course, avoid out-of-stock conditions, or even poor shelf positioning of his brand.   Such situations may result in a disruption of the habits on which he depends.   His advertising should stress package and name identification, and he should spend his advertising money to buy high frequency of exposure for short and simple messages.

MARKET SEGMENTATION

Although I have not yet used the words "market segmentation," the classification of consumers into four loyalty types, as we have been discussing, is clearly one way of dividing a market into segments.   A market segment is usually thought of as a group of consumers distinguished by a common perception of utility in a particular attribute of a product.

Ways of Segmenting a Market

Loyalty behavior and attitude is, of course, only one way in which a market may be segmented.   Other consumer interests may interact with other product attributes to create another set of segments.   For example, we might think of the scissors market as containing a segment of consumers who accept left-handed scissors but reject right-handed, and another segment who accept right-handed scissors but reject left-handed ones.   These two segments need not together con-

stitute the whole market, since a group may exist for whom handed-
ness is not an issue (the truly ambidextrous, or those left-handed persons who, by dint of necessity, have learned to use right-handed tools).
Other markets may be segmented in other dimensions.   For example, the chewing gum and the ice cream markets may be segmented in
terms of flavor preferences; the clothing market in terms of conserva-
tism versus faddism, and so forth.

Many marketers are turning away from a policy of "pleasing most
of the people some of the time," to one of "pleasing some of the people
all of the time."   That is, they are diminishing their efforts to create
products for some hypothetical "average consumer" in favor of making products for people who have some specialized product interests
—that is, a market segment—even though the segment may be relatively small.   Their notion, of course, is that it's better to be the exclusive supplier to a small segment than to buck a welter of competing brands for the attentions of the crowd.   This trend benefits both
the consumer and the marketer, since it leads to products which are
more useful to the individual and for which he is consequently willing to spend more money.

However, the trend creates the marketing problem of recognizing
market segments and determining their size and the kinds of products
most appropriate for them.   Early attacks on this problem were limited to interpreting the different requirements of groups defined in
terms of observable characteristics, such as men versus women, city
versus suburban versus rural dwellers, young people versus older
people, and so forth.   Somewhat later, marketers became attentive to
groups defined in terms of personal characteristics and psychological
traits, such as "sophistication" and "venturesomeness," which are observable only by using some fairly specialized measuring techniques.
More recently marketers have been attempting to define groups in
terms of their interests in various specific product attributes directly.
Once such a group has been identified, no further research nor in-
ferential leap is required to make use of the knowledge for product
development.

Example in Laundry Bleach Market

In order to illustrate how new-product possibilities can be identified
with market segments, let us imagine a miniature marketing experiment contrived to explore a new-product possibility in the laundry
bleach market.

In this experiment we will consider just two attributes of laundry bleach: (1) its effectiveness in making white clothes whiter, and (2) its ability not to fade colored clothes.   (In a real experiment we would be concerned with many other attributes, of course, but these two will serve for our example.)   In most bleaching systems these two benefits are in conflict, since improvements in whitening effectiveness can only be obtained at some sacrifice of color safety.   We would expect that whitening effectiveness would be important to some degree for all bleach users, since it is the defining function of a bleach.   Color safety could also be an important benefit to some users, since it would make possible the use of bleach when laundering white and colored clothes together, or clothes made of part white and part colored fabrics.   The importance of color safety to a homemaker would depend upon her laundry habits, the composition of her family wash, and her anticipation of accidental damage to colored materials.

Suppose, then, that we ask a sample of homemakers which one of these two benefits would be more important to them in selecting a brand of bleach.   (If we were considering many attributes, we might ask our homemakers to rank them, or locate them on a scale of importance.)   The results of our imaginary inquiry show us that 70 per cent of the homemakers consider whitening effectiveness more important, and 30 per cent consider color safety more important.

We conclude that the homemakers can be divided into two groups which differ from one another in the kind of product which would be most useful to them.   This is indicative of segmentation in the market, but not necessarily indicative of a product opportunity.   Before we can decide if this segmentation affords a product opportunity, we must know to what extent the homemakers consider that these desired benefits are provided by the products which are presently available to them.

Conspicuous Product Benefits

We can, however, ask another sample of homemakers which of the two benefits is more conspicuous in the product which they are most accustomed to using.   Suppose that 90 per cent of them say that whitening effectiveness is more descriptive of their present brand, and 10 per cent say that color safety is more descriptive.   We would be forced to the conclusion that some women (about 20 per cent) are less than perfectly satisfied with the product they are now using, since 30 per cent claim to be more interested in color safety than in whitening effectiveness, while only 10 per cent perceive color safety as the more conspicuous feature of the product they are accustomed to using.   This information is sufficient for us to recognize a dissatisfied market segment, assess its size, and define the type of product to which it would be vulnerable.

In our hypothetical experiment we considered only two benefits, so that there were only two ways in which homemakers could order those benefits.   Three product attributes, however, could be ordered in six ways, four could be ordered in twenty-four ways, five in 120 ways, etc.   The inclusion of additional attributes, therefore, somewhat complicates the analysis of the experiment.   However, since market segments are often defined by a special interest in certain peripheral benefits, the value of the experiment is enormously increased as we expand the number of attributes which are considered together.   Fortunately, a bit of mathematical legerdemain (called *factor analysis* and *discriminate analysis*) enables the marketer to group consumers in terms of their common product interests and to group products in terms of similarities in their perceived characteristics, even when the number of attributes to be considered is quite large.

This seemingly magic procedure does not, of course, discover consumer interests, nor does it invent product attributes to satisfy those interests.   It can only assess benefits and features which have been conceived by the wit and creativeness of the marketing man or technical researcher.   However, it is quite effective in assessing the potential market vitality of products based on those benefits, once they have been conceived, and often suggests a new marketing strategy for some already existing brand.

Attitudes toward Cleaning   Many of the markets for household cleaning products can be divided into three fairly distinct segments in terms of women's attitudes toward the cleaning chore.   We might characterize the attitudes of the three groups as "compulsive," "casual," and "cautious."

Some women approach the cleaning task with an almost compulsive desire to make the house spotlessly clean.   Although they do not take particular pleasure in the cleaning activity itself, they do not begrudge the effort which is required to do a thorough job.   They tend to eschew convenience products because they do not believe that thorough cleaning is possible with so little effort.   They demand complete cleaning effectiveness in the products they use, and are willing to take a little extra care, or risk a slight hazard, or make an extra effort, in order to get results. We would expect to find paste wax, scrubbing brushes, and strong soap in their cleaning cupboards.

Another group of women views the cleaning chore as a necessary evil—something to be put off as long as possible, and then done with a minimum expenditure of effort and time. They are too busy with outside-the-house interests to be very much bothered with cleaning. That is not to say that they are slovenly, however. They are, in fact, frequently fastidious in their personal grooming. They sincerely wish to present a clean home to their neighbors and guests, but would prefer to achieve that effect by the wave of some magic wand or by the employment of servants, rather than by their own efforts. These women, of course, choose convenience products even when such products are less effective cleaners. They give very little thought to the possible hazards involved in cleaning with strong chemicals, so long as they are quick and easy to use. Paste wax and scrubbing brushes have given way in their cupboards to the one-step liquid self-polishing wax and cleaner, and a long-handled applicator.

The third group of homemakers is distinguished by an interest in the safety of the products they use. A woman in this group avoids the strong soap that might roughen her hands, the strong bleach that might weaken the fibers of her clothes, the flammable, the corrosive, the poisonous. She is willing to take a little extra time, or expend a little more energy in her cleaning chores, and even to tolerate a less-than-perfect job of cleaning, in order to avoid "taking a chance" with harsh cleaners. Her cupboard may contain either paste wax or liquid wax—but whichever it is, it will bear the Good Housekeeping Seal and Underwriters' Laboratory approval.

These three segments are true "market" segments, in that each requires a particular kind of product; and the attributes which cause a product to be acceptable to one group may cause it to be rejected (or accepted reluctantly) by the other two.

No doubt many other groups of homemakers could be described in terms of their attitudes toward household cleaning. For example, we could probably identify a group of fastidious homemakers and distinguish them from another group of careless or slovenly homemakers. However, while membership in these latter groups determines the use and nonuse of cleaning products, or the frequency of use, it does not determine the type of product which will be acceptable within the user group. However interesting such groupings may be from a sociological viewpoint, they are not "market" segments, in that they do not demand specialized products.

CONTROL OF CONSUMER BEHAVIOR

I began this chapter with the thought that the marketer's interest in consumer behavior stems from his interest in controlling it. I have tried to point out that controlling the behavior from "within the consumer"—for example, by creating new needs or motives in him, or changing the importance to him of some particular needs, or by altering his sense of values—would be difficult and costly, and indeed may be impossible. However, the advertiser can exert control over consumer behavior from "outside the consumer," by controlling the stimuli to which he responds. The marketer achieves this control by his control of the kinds of products he offers and what he tells the consumer about them.

A consumer imputes value to a product precisely to the extent that he perceives it as satisfying his needs. But consumers differ from one another in the nature of their needs and in the importance which they assign to the satisfaction of one need relative to another. Therefore, consumers differ from one another in the types of products which they value most. A group of consumers who value products in more or less the same way constitutes a segment.

Consumers and Marketers Benefit

This variability among consumers can afford an advantage to the marketer who chooses to serve one or more consumer segments. He does this by formulating products to meet the particular needs of those segments, or by presenting his products to them in terms of their unique interests. He can then be assured that his products will be perceived by consumers in the selected segments as having more value than his competitors' products, and that they will therefore be more often chosen or will command a higher price.

This type of market specialization not only profits the marketer, but benefits the consumer, too, by providing him with products better adapted to his own idiosyncratic tastes and desires.

OTHER VIEWS ON CONSUMER BEHAVIOR

BRIM, ORVILLE G., JR., DAVID C. GLASS, DAVID E. LAVIN, and NORMAN GOODMAN: "Personality and Decision Processes," Stanford University Press, Stanford, Calif., 1962.

BRITT, STEUART HENDERSON: "Consumer Behavior and the Behavioral Sciences," John Wiley & Sons, Inc., New York, 1966.

CLARK, L. H. (ed.): "Consumer Behavior: The Dynamics of Consumer Behavior," New York University Press, 1955.

COX, DONALD F. (ed.): "Risk Taking and Information Handling in Consumer Behavior," Harvard University Press, Boston, 1967.

CUNNINGHAM, R. M.: Brand Loyalty: What, Where, How Much? *Harvard Business Review*, vol. 34, no. 1, pp. 116–128.

FARLEY, J. W.: Why Does Brand Loyalty Vary over Products? *Journal of Marketing Research*, vol. 1, no. 4, pp. 9–14.

GROSSACK, MARTIN M. (ed.): "Understanding Consumer Behavior," The Christopher Publishing House, Boston, 1964.

HOVLAND, CARL I., and IRVING L. JANIS: "Personality and Persuasibility," Yale University Press, New Haven, Conn., 1959.

KATONA, GEORGE: "The Mass Consumption Society," McGraw-Hill Book Company, New York, 1964.

———: "The Powerful Consumer," McGraw-Hill Book Company, New York, 1960.

RAMOND, CHARLES K., and LESTER KRUEGER: "Are There Consumer Types?" Advertising Research Foundation, New York, 1964.

SCHOENFELD, DAVID, and ARTHUR A. NATELLA: "The Consumer and His Dollars," Oceana Publications, Inc., Dobbs Ferry, N.Y., 1966.

TUCKER, W. T.: The Development of Brand Loyalty, *Journal of Marketing Research*, August, 1964, p. 35.

ZALTMAN, GERALD: "Marketing: Contributions from the Behavioral Sciences," Harcourt, Brace & World, Inc., New York, 1965.

PART FOUR
Planning

CHAPTER TEN

The Marketing Plan

CORNELIUS DuBOIS *Consultant in Research*

There is a legend in the advertising business that the idea for an annual marketing plan sprang full-grown from the brow of Clarence Eldridge of General Foods on March 6, 1951.

There has been talk that the annual marketing plan died in obscurity, sometime in the late 1950s or early 1960s, of a strange combination of obesity and malnutrition.

Both the legend and the rumor are nearly true.

It was on March 6, 1951 that then vice president and general manager of the Post Cereals Division, Eldridge, circulated a bulletin to his General Foods marketing organization specifying that there should be an annual marketing plan for each advertised brand, outlining in detail what the plan should contain, who should prepare it, how it should be used.   It is also true that since 1951 the marketing plan tended to become fat, unloved, and neglected.

Eldridge had been formulating his marketing plan concept and specifications for a long time before that launch date, and he has given public recognition to good planning that went on long before him. As to that funeral, it has not happened yet and it may not happen—although it is likely that annual marketing plans in the future will be somewhat different from what they have been in the last eighteen years.

Current importance of the annual marketing plan, indicating that it is by no means moribund, is the announcement of seminars being given in New York, Chicago, and Los Angeles. ·

WHAT IS THE MARKETING PLAN?

If you look upon what is called a marketing plan as a forward-looking statement of strategy and tactics, you are only partly right. The marketing plan, as defined by Eldridge and his followers, and by many others is indeed a statement of tactics and strategy, but its distinguishing feature is that it is based on a statement of goals and objectives, which in turn is based on an analysis of the problems and opportunities facing the company and the brand, which in turn is based on a statement of facts.   The framework of a plan, then, is

    I. The facts
   II. The problems and opportunities
 III. The objectives
 IV. The program

With that kind of framework one could have a sales promotion plan, a pricing plan, a sales incentive plan, a public relations plan, or an advertising plan.   Important, however, is that this is a *marketing* plan, based on the total marketing concept that all aspects of a marketing effort are interdependent and must be looked at together and planned together.

ELEMENTS OF A MARKETING PLAN

In attempting to define the plan I indicate the important main elements that must be included if a marketing plan is to be what it says it is, but there are infinite ways of filling the outline.   You will find it helpful to prepare your own outline in detail, and you will want to refer to it every now and then to make sure that the plans you are involved with are covering the essential points.   You will also find that you need flexibility.

The outlines that follow illustrate different ways of filling in the basic four- or five-part outline.

The first of these is abstracted from Clarence Eldridge's legendary 1951 memo (which actually did exist).

    I. Statement of facts
        Sales history (factory)
        Sales history to consumer
        Share history to consumer
        Price history
        Product history
        Competition
        The market
        Consumer attitude trends
        Franchise strength and weakness
        Distribution trends
        Gross profit history
        Advertising expenditures, year by year
        Selling expense year by year
        Advertising history (media, themes, etc.)
        Selling history
   II. Listing of problems and opportunities
  III. Objectives
  IV. The plan

The second outline is from Maurice Mandell's "Advertising," [1] in which Dr. Mandell credited Herbert West [2] with the facts or "situation" part of the outline.

    I. The situation
      A. Size, scope, and share of the market
        1. Sales history of all manufacturers, and share of the market, in dollars and units
        2. Market potential and major trends in supply and demand of this and related products
        3. Pricing history through all levels of distribution and reason for principal fluctuations

[1] Maurice I. Mandell, "Advertising," Prentice-Hall, Inc., Englewood Cliffs, N.J., 1968, pp. 133–139.

[2] Herbert West, How to Select Facts for a Master Planning Blueprint, *Advertising Agency* magazine, Mar. 15, 1957, p. 61.   Reprinted with permission of *Advertising Age*.

B. Sales, costs, and gross profits on the firm's product
   1. Sales history, by size or models, by sales districts
   2. Cost history, including cost of goods delivered, selling, advertising, administrative, and all other expenses
   3. Gross profit history (net before taxes), including competitors if known
C. Distribution channels
   1. Identification of principal channels; sales history through each type, including competitors if known
   2. Buying habits and attitudes of principal channels; the firm's product versus competitors', including data on shelf frontage, inventory, turnover, profits, and out-of-the-stock situation
   3. Firm's selling policies and practices, in comparison with competitors
   4. Firm's forcing promotion, in comparison with competitors
   5. Trade advertising, literature, and exhibits
   6. Point-of-sale display material
D. The consumer or end user
   1. Identification of persons making the buying decision, classified by age, sex, income level, education, occupation, geographical location, etc.
   2. Consumer attitudes on the firm's product versus competitors', on quality, price, packaging, styling, etc.
   3. Consumer purchase habits, including such factors as time of purchase, place, cash or credit, frequency
   4. Consumer use habits; how, where, when, by whom
   5. Firm's advertising history; expenditures, media and copy strategy, measurements of effectiveness; similar data on competitors
   6. Publicity and other educational influences; strategy and effectiveness
II. Problems and opportunities
III. Strategy
A. Objectives
B. Methods
IV. Tactics

The third outline is one of several versions used by Foote, Cone & Belding.[3] This one dates from 1959.

[3] For detailed discussion of a similar FCB outline see Cornelius DuBois, What Does the Advertiser Need to Know about His Market? in *University of Georgia Bulletin*, Sept. 15, 1958, pp. 62–73.

I. Review
   A. The industry
      1. Definition and description
      2. The market
         a. Trade channels
         b. Consumer
      3. Changes and trends
      4. Intangibles and attitudes
   B. The company or brand
      1. What it is
      2. How it has been advertised
      3. Marketing policies, methods, structure
      4. Marketing and advertising budgets
      5. Pricing and profitability
      6. Distribution
      7. Sales trends
   C. Competitive comparisons
      1. Product virtues and weaknesses
      2. Competitors' marketing and advertising methods
      3. Competitors' potential
      4. Share-of-market trends
      5. Trade franchise
      6. Consumer franchise
         a. Who and where
         b. Images and attitudes
         c. Share of mind
      7. Share of pressure
         a. On the trade
         b. On consumers
II. Appraisal
   A. Problems
   B. Opportunities
III. Goals
   A. Long term
   B. Next year
IV. Strategy
V. Actions
   A. Budget and its allocation
   B. Selling and merchandising
      1. Sales
      2. Consumer and trade promotions
   C. Product, pricing, packaging

      D. Advertising
        1. Copy
        2. Media
      E. Research

The fourth outline is Eldridge's again. This is his 1966 version.[4]

    I. Statement of facts
      A. Appraisal of the product itself
      B. Sales history
      C. Competitive situation
      D. Pricing
      E. Marketing expenditures
      F. Past advertising strategy
      G. The people to whom you wish to sell
      H. What the consumer wants
      I. Trade relations
   II. Problems and opportunities
  III. Objectives
   IV. Complete marketing program
    V. Recommended marketing appropriation
   VI. Forecast of volume profit

It would not take very much digging to produce a dozen more, all somewhat different, all based on the same general principles. All these outlines contain explicit items for the statement of facts. None tries to spell out an outline for the statement of problems and opportunities or for the objectives. To do so would be to trammel the thinking of the man or men preparing the plan. Nor can anyone attempt to specify for all plans, what items ought to be covered under the heading of "tactics." One plan outline does provide a checklist of the kinds of things that ought to be included. The others cover in textual descriptions (not quoted here) the necessity for including many aspects of marketing tactics, not just the advertising program.

WHAT HAPPENED TO MARKETING PLANS?

Regardless of which outline was being followed, the tendency in the 1950s was for elephantiasis.

What happened to marketing plans throughout the industry?

[4] Clarence E. Eldridge, "The Role and Importance of the Marketing Plan," Association of National Advertisers, New York, 1966, pp. 6–8.

The same thing that happens to a mammal or a goose when it over-eats: it gets too fat for its own good. In company after company, plans reached the point of surfeit where the advertising manager and the marketing director would say very complimentary things to the man or group who prepared the plan, and then the fat impressive book would progress from the corner of the boss's desk to the table behind his desk, to a file somewhere, without ever being read thoroughly, without ever accomplishing its purpose unless somebody prepared a summary in order to get action.

Another thing that happened in many other companies was the use of the marketing plan to impress or brainwash a board of directors. You can hold a board at close attention for an hour or more while you summarize the facts with slides, and then hand each a copy of your book. But you can do that only once. Next year the board members who stayed in the room would begin objecting that you were covering much the same ground all over again.

The fatter the books became, the less useful they proved to be. Along with obesity came a sluggard's pace. The big plan took so long to prepare that brand managers, copy writers, account men, media men, merchandising men (and all the others who had to plan and act) couldn't wait; they perforce prepared their own plans for their own spheres of action. Thus the big plan defeated itself. It failed to coordinate advertising with total marketing.

Nevertheless, the principle remains a sound one. It can be applied without self-defeating detail.

STATEMENT OF FACTS

Plan Book versus Fact Book

What had happened to marketing plans was a tendency for both executives and researchers to confuse a plan book with a fact book. There is an important distinction. A fact book is a big compilation of facts about a product and its market designed to be consulted as a reference source. A plan book is a device to be taken to other persons in order to convey recommendations. More specifically, it is a particular systematic way of arriving at these recommendations and presenting them.

Every account group in an agency, every product group in the client's office, should have a fat and handy compilation of the facts about the company, the product, and the particular brand, including all the kinds of facts that could influence a marketing plan.   The fact book will be useful if you:

1. Keep it separate from the plan book
2. Keep it where you can refer to it
3. Keep it up to date
4. Keep the responsibility for maintaining the book in the hands of someone with knowledge

In this day of computers you might also put your facts on magnetic tape or microfilm or both and let the computer retrieve what you need when you need it.

The separate fact book, loose-leaf, of course, should be organized exactly the same as existing plans, since the two go together.

You add material in full detail as you get it.

At the same time, you make the briefest possible summary, with reference to detail and source, and put it in another loose-leaf binder in preparation for the next marketing plan.   In both cases you will be using the outline headings of the most recent plan, modified when new facts come in that do not fit the old outline.

If you operate this way, an effective marketing plan can be put together quickly and readably.

While you are digesting the new facts, write down your thoughts on interpreting them and how these facts confirm, modify, or totally change your statement of the problems and opportunities.

If the new data spark an idea for action of any sort, write that down too, right away; don't lose it by letting it cool off.   If the idea does get cold after you have written it, you'll notice that yourself and kill it later on.

Four Areas of Knowledge and Understanding

What is important is not the facts as facts, but the knowledge and understanding that the body of facts can provide when viewed and interpreted in perspective.

This knowledge and understanding can be compartmentalized into four broad areas.

Facts about the Product We're Selling   We must define what the product is physically; what it is designed to do for people; how it works; how it compares physically and functionally with its competitors; how it is sized, priced, packaged; and what are the trends and developments in the area of product progress, both for our client's brand and for competitors.

The Market We need to know and understand the people to whom we are selling. We might begin this factual analysis with discussion of the trade channels through which our product reaches the public, and the habits and prejudices of the dealers, wholesalers, and brokers on whom we must rely. Then we'll devote our main emphasis to the people in the market. How many are there? Who are they? Where are they? What is the difference, if any, between those who use a lot of the product and those who use a little? What is our share of market for this product, our competitive situation in the home as well as over the counter? Devote some particular emphasis to the people who are using our particular brand—their numbers, their characteristics, their locations, together with what we know about how they use the product.

In characterizing people, be concerned with their ages, incomes, education levels. Ideally, go beyond this, to define personality characteristics of the users. We must always remember that the marketplace is constantly changing; we must keep track of trends and developments.

Attitudes and Motivations In this area, the first thing we need to know is the direct interaction between people and our product. We need to know the extent to which people feel the need for our product, and why. We need to know how they perceive its benefits; how they see its differences from other brands. We need to know their satisfactions, dissatisfactions, and loyalties for our brand and for competitors. We need to know direct reasons for using or not using our brand or our type of product, and we need to be able to draw at least reasonable inferences about our brand's psychological benefits and potential emotional appeals. We need to know what trends and developments have been occurring in brand reputations and images, what impact new products and new developments have on consumer attitudes.

Competitive Environment We need to know what competitors are claiming, and with what weight and through what media. We need to know and guess their strategies, tactical habits, and capacities for retaliating and counteracting our moves in pricing, dealing, promoting. Unless we're launching a totally new brand, we need to review our own past budgets and media and copy emphases. We must understand the taboos, restrictions, and mandatory inclusions that apply to this particular brand. We need to review evidence of the effectiveness or ineffectiveness of our own and competitors' past advertising.

(For a checklist of the types of facts pertinent to an understanding of each type of situation, see Exhibit A, below.)

With understanding of our product, our market, the mental or emotional interaction of product and people, and the competitive environment, the agency and client can define the problems and opportunities, establish advertising and marketing objectives, and build the specifications for strategy.

PROBLEMS AND OPPORTUNITIES

If the advertiser knew all the facts just as facts, in segments, he still would not know very much. He would still be like the student of history who has a perfect memory of all the dates, battles, names, congressional debates, and Supreme Court decisions—all the facts necessary to answer the true-false questions on an examination—but no comprehension of history. The facts about a market are important only if they mean something and if the meaning is understood.

To find meaning in the facts we must now look at them in relation to one another. Actually, much of the work of setting forth the facts systematically has served to segregate a number of unimportant facts, which we can now safely ignore. Note that certain kinds of facts, as I have classified them, are related only to certain kinds of advertising actions.

The facts come at us gradually, and we can see them one at a time, see them fall into the patterns of what we already know—and if the facts are important, they will change the patterns.

In practice, the most important facts almost always become apparent.

The most important part of a marketing plan, the key to its implementation, is the statement of problems and opportunities, in which facts are interpreted and put together into a meaningful pattern. This is never a one-man statement. It is an agreement, after a review of the facts, of what kind of situation we are in.

This is the section in which you *use* the knowledge and understanding that the facts provide.

As Eldridge puts it: [5]

> What is meant by problems?   Well, the problem may be the product itself or its price or its packaging.   It may be inadequate distribution or unsatisfactory point-of-sale support.   It may be dissatisfaction on the part of the trade with the marketer's customer service, or his policies with respect to cooperative advertising or cash discount, or the mark-up the trade is able to take.
>
> Some of these "problems" may not lend themselves to correction or solution, but their disclosure in the plan brings them into the open and subjects them to critical examination of their potential solvability.   At the same time, many of the problems are susceptible of solution, and that is the point at which the problem is converted into an opportunity.   There may be problems of an entirely different nature.
>
> Maybe too few customers are aware of the product.   Still more may not know of the merits of the product, or of changes that may have been made in it to make it more responsive to consumers' wants.   Perhaps advertising has placed emphasis on product attributes which are of little or no concern to consumers, and conversely has failed to emphasize —or at least to "sell"—the attributes which consumers do want.
>
> Here, again, a recognition of the problem is the first step in creating an opportunity.   And out of the combination of problems and opportunities comes the next part of the plan.

OBJECTIVES

As everyone says who has written about a marketing plan, it is important to be specific.   Don't just say you want to increase sales this next year, but by how much you are going to increase them.   Don't just say you want to improve consumer awareness of such and such a facet of your product, but by how much you aim to increase this awareness in this next year.   The vague, more general objectives can be put as a long-term goal, but for the period for which you are planning, set a goal that is both reasonable and specific, something that may be attainable, something that might even be measurable if you get there. [6]

[5] Eldridge, *op. cit.*, p. 9.

[6] See also Russell Colley, "Defining Advertising Goals for Measured Advertising Results," Association of National Advertisers, New York, 1961.

STRATEGY AND TACTICS

It is often necessary to show how basic strategy is geared to a larger long-range objective, and then how the tactics are geared to the overall strategy and to the one-year objectives. Whatever is done must stem from our previous discussion.

Remembering that this is a marketing plan and not just an advertising plan, you will want to include your tactics on pricing, couponing, displays, package design, contests, other forms of merchandising, as well as the advertising that will go into traditional media.

It is important that the tactics part of the plan be boiled to a bare minimum. If the media persons in the agency want to submit a detailed justification for all the dollars in their media plan, let them do it separately. You will have, in the marketing plan a criterion to make sure that the media plan fits. That goes for the creative and the merchandising persons, and the rest of them. You will have given them the framework, the rationale, the direction toward which to apply their talents for the accomplishment of the company's objectives.

WHO IS RESPONSIBLE?

Who should be responsible for preparing the plan? That question is moot. It has to be someone whose job requires him to be familiar with the facts and the problems with which the plan will deal. It has to be someone with the intuition and reasoning power to see what the facts mean. It has to be someone who is sophisticated enough in marketing operations to know what actions are possible. It has to be someone who can write English clearly enough to convey the facts, problems, and strategy to people who are not so familiar with them, but who have to approve actions and budgets. It must be someone capable of forgetting previous attempts to reduce marketing plans to a formula, if the formula doesn't fit. If you have such a person at your service, it doesn't matter whether his title is brand manager, account executive, market researcher, assistant advertising manager, or vice president—marketing. He'll probably have a bigger title soon.

One final reprise on brevity: The plans that almost killed marketing plans used to run from 1 to 2 inches thick, not counting the impressive bindings that surrounded them. If yours is more than ⅜ inch thick, put it on a diet.

EXHIBIT A. CHECKLIST OF FACTS

What follows here is not intended as an outline to be followed for each marketing plan. Consider it instead as a checklist of the facts that might be organized in your fact book and cited (where pertinent) in a plan to help achieve each main type of knowledge and understanding.

---

1. KNOWLEDGE AND UNDERSTANDING OF THE PRODUCT

Product Class	*Our Brand and Major Competitors*
What is it or what made of?	What is it or what made of?
How does it work?	How does it work?
How different from related product classes?	How different physically from other brands?
The need: Consumer problems it is designed to solve.	Do we serve this need?
	What special need do we satisfy?
General benefits.	Do we provide the general benefits?
a. Major	*a.* Major
b. Others	*b.* Others
	What unique or special benefits do we provide?
	a. Major
	b. Others

---

2. KNOWLEDGE AND UNDERSTANDING OF THE MARKET

Product Class	*Our Brand and Major Competitors*
Wholesale channels.	Wholesale channels.
Penetration: Per cent carrying.	Penetration: Per cent carrying.
Who uses this kind of product?	Who uses this brand?
	(If new) Who would use?
Who are the frequent or big-volume users?	Are we strong or weak with frequent users of the product?
	(If weak) Who does dominate the frequent users and who *are* frequent users?
Where are the users?	Where are our users?
Extent of brand loyalty, switching, multiple brand use.	

Nonusers of the product class: Who and where?	Nonusers of brand: Who and where are our best pospects? *a.* What kinds of users of other brands? *b.* What kinds of nonusers of the product class?
Size of total market (in dollars, in numbers of people).	Brand share of the market.
Recent growth?	Recent growth?
Future growth?	Future growth?

---

3. KNOWLEDGE AND UNDERSTANDING OF THE INTERACTION BETWEEN
   PEOPLE AND PRODUCT

Product Class	*Our Brand and Major Competitors*
Is the need for this kind of product widely recognized?	Is the need for the brand's version of the product recognized?
Are its general benefits perceived?	Are the brand's unique benefits perceived?
Are they seen as important?	Are they seen as important? Is the brand seen as sharing the general benefits?
Are the mechanics or ingredients known?	Are the unique mechanics or ingredients known?
Are they important to people?	Are they important to people?
Why do people use this kind of product?	Why do people choose this brand?
Why don't people use it?	Why don't people choose it?
What do users like about the product?	What do users like about the brand?
Why?	Why?
What don't users like?	What don't users like?
Why?	Why? Brand reputation Elements of image, imputed attributes, etc.
Basic human motives underlying purchase or use.	Do these motives apply to this brand? What other basic motives can apply uniquely?

---

4. KNOWLEDGE AND UNDERSTANDING OF THE COMPETITIVE ENVIRONMENT

Product Class	*Our Brand and Major Competitors*
Trade support?	Trade support?
Pricing?	Pricing?

Price promotion?
Other deals?
Other promotion?
Total weight of advertising.

Industry media patterns.

Advertising taboos and restrictions (legal or self-imposed).

Price promotion?
Other deals?
Other promotion?
Budget and what it buys.
Evidence that brand responds to advertising weight.
Media emphasis.
Evidence that media used are effective.
Advertising taboos and restrictions (legal or self-imposed).
Mandatory inclusions.
Major appeals now being used.
  a. Direct sales argument.
  b. Emotional and motivational overtones.
What past appeals have worked?
Why dropped?
What appeals have not worked?
Why?
Slogans
Words "owned."
What evidence that appeals are:
  a. Interesting?
  b. Communicable?
  c. Believable?
  d. Persuasive?
What evidence on presentation of the appeals?

Though you will see holes where data needed for your situation are not included, the checklist is much too complete. Use it to select the most pertinent items—and in the process, be brief. Remember that you are not writing the *Iliad*. You're writing a plan.

CHAPTER ELEVEN

The Advertising Plan

EDWIN W. EBEL *formerly Vice President, Advertising Services, General Foods Corporation*

COMMENTS ON THE PLANNING OF ADVERTISING

While for my own convenience I have chosen to write this chapter about the advertising plan in four sections, you, the reader, will find I have not adhered strictly to this method.

The four sections are

    I. Comments on the Planning of Advertising
    II. Purpose of a Written Plan
    III. Where Marketing Stops and Advertising Begins, or Vice Versa
    IV. Suggestions for Contents of an Advertising Plan

You may find something in Section I that might better be in Section III. Perhaps something that is covered in Section III will be covered in Section IV, or vice versa. You may find I've touched on the same subject in more than one section.   If all this be so, I ask you to regard this dissertation as a single text.

There is another point to be made at the start of a chapter on the advertising plan which is part of a "Handbook of Advertising Management."   How can an advertising plan be conceived, prepared, and written without almost every subject in such a handbook being involved?   It could be that unintentionally this chapter is encroaching on numerous chapters of the book.

Since the preceding chapter is concerned with the marketing plan, I shall in the course of this chapter point out some of the areas where the advertising plan may conflict or cross wires with the marketing plan.   The general practice today is to integrate the marketing and advertising plan—or to make the advertising plan a chapter of the marketing plan.   This practice is a natural outgrowth of the advent of the brand manager or product manager, who has charge of both marketing and advertising.

Following are some broad observations on the *planning of advertising*—whether there is to be a written plan or not.

Efficiency versus Effectiveness

The first thing to bear in mind is that even a good advertising plan does not guarantee good advertising.   It does help in the execution of an advertising campaign.

In the way many marketing-advertising plans are conceived and written, they are apt to be more helpful in terms of *efficiency* than *effectiveness.*

When we speak of *efficiency,* we usually are thinking of cost per thousand, of reaching the right demographic audience in the right geographic places at the lowest cost.

When we speak of *effectiveness,* we are concerned with *reaching people's minds* with an advertising message that attracts their attention, interests them, and moves them in favor of the product or service.[1]

I like to think in terms of the planning of advertising rather than in terms of a document called "the advertising plan."   It is a

---

[1] My entire experience has had to do with consumer products.   Therefore, I shall use the word "product" rather than "service."   The principles outlined may apply to both.

broader, more comprehensive approach and therefore more likely to result in good advertising.

I also like to think in terms of the thought that must go into the planning of advertising—and the things that stimulate that thinking. This, of course, includes the absorption of statistical facts which can guide the thinking.

The Wealth of Statistics

Today, thanks to marketing research and its handmaiden, the computer, the planner of advertising has a large fund of statistical information available to him.

This is, of course, a great help, but it also places a great responsibility on the planner to avoid letting statistical data rule the roost.

To quote from an article by Arnold Gingrich in the July 10, 1967, issue of *Advertising Age:*

> At this early phase of the space age, it is already possible to cite a number of instances where the computer has already out-thought man, both as to the speed and the complexity of the thought process. So it is probably safe to say that the machine can think as well as or better than a man can, over the entire range of *tactical* thinking—the situations where prior knowledge of past problems solved, infallibly retrieved and applied, is sufficient to be controlling. Where the machine can't go is only where very few exceptional humans can go successfully—into the upper reaches of thought, the level of *strategic* thinking, where hunch, insight, intuition, or inspired guesswork can make the difference between winning and losing, between invention and disruption, between creation and destruction—in other words, into the rarefied strata of *creative* thinking.

J. B. McKitterick of General Electric had some cogent thoughts which he expressed in a business talk:

> . . . Our planning has tended to become a mere administrative process of endless criteria, and the creative quality of the alternatives examined is scarcely worthy of the sterile perfection of the decision system applied. As a result, imaginative ideas entailing some real element of uncertainty tend to be cast aside for safe trivia.

To bring these two comments even closer to the subject at hand, I am going to paraphrase David Ogilvy's famed remark, "The consumer is not a moron; she is your wife." My paraphrasing is: "The consumer is not a statistical digit; she is your wife."

Consumers Are Human Beings

So the first—and very vital—thing in the process of planning advertising is to discipline yourself to think of consumers as living, breathing, pulsating human beings with all the unpredictable attributes, whims, and caprices of a human being. While a statistical digit may *represent* a human being, it is a fixed thing. A human being is not.

The next step is to put yourself in the role of the consumer. To do this, you actually use the product. This should be the initial step in learning about consumer behavior as it relates to the product in question.

Talk with Likely Prospects

Next, leave your desk and office behind you and go out and talk to people who your common sense tells you are the likely prospects.

This will serve two purposes:

1. It will stimulate your thinking. In this connection, I suggest you forget the old taboo about preconceived notions. Preconceived notions are really thoughts that stem from your own mental computer bank. These thoughts will form the premises which you will verify or deny through consumer research.

2. It will equip you to interpret (humanize) the statistical information which will be available to you through consumer research.

Think of Consumers as Individuals

Along with disciplining yourself always to think about consumers as human beings, not digits, discipline yourself to think of them as *individuals,* not masses.

It is true that in advertising circles we use the phrases "mass appeal" and "mass media." However, masses do not go into a store, go up to a shelf, and pick out a product. Individuals do. Masses are merely the sum total of individuals.

It is *individuals* we must keep in mind and address ourselves to.

So while you are in the process of planning advertising, avoid getting trapped in common denominators. A statistical common denominator may be a convenient thing, but it is an inanimate thing.

An individual is a living being. A common denominator is a shortcut to mediocrity; it has aptly been called "calculated mediocrity."

As I write this I do not have at my disposal evidence from "recall," "attitude change" or other data to prove this. However, from the memory bank of my own cranial computer comes a print-out which shows that the most effective advertisements are those addressed to individuals rather than to a composite. At best a composite is a synthetic person—a simulation. Who can get creatively inspired by a simulation?

Don't Sell the Human Mind Short

The best way to summarize these introductory remarks and to stress their importance is to quote one of advertising's most able practitioners, Charles L. Whittier. In connection with a project on which he and I worked called "The Power of an Idea," he commented on: ". . . the tremendous power that can be generated by that most wonderful of gifts with which man's Creator has endowed him—the human mind."

So my final admonition in these introductory remarks is: In the planning of advertising, don't sell the human mind short.

PURPOSE OF A WRITTEN PLAN

My introductory remarks urged you to do some uninhibited and inventive thinking before you tighten up and organize your thinking in order to put it into a *written* plan.

There is, of course, good purpose for a written plan.

Forces Consideration of All Problems

The most important purpose is to force the advertising manager and his agency to give consideration to all the problems and opportunities involved in marketing and advertising the product, and to put together in an orderly way all the available information bearing on these problems and opportunities—along with all the imaginative thinking that those involved can come up with.

Four Other Reasons

Some other reasons for a written plan are:

1. Objectives To establish reasonable and measurable (within reason) objectives. It is not enough to have as an objective "to increase sales." More will be said about this later.

2. Agreement To obtain agreement (and approval if necessary) of all the parties involved on the plan which will determine the course of your advertising (marketing).

3. Continuity To keep the advertising manager and his agency on the line of attack which has been decided upon. Continuity is a vital part of successful advertising. This does not mean that once an advertising plan is conceived, prepared, and approved, it should be a frozen entity. It does mean that a written plan serves to prevent or at least discourage change purely for the sake of change—in other words, to avoid impulsive change.

It is only natural for an advertising manager new on the job to want to prove his worth by doing something new or different. It is also natural for an ambitious advertising manager to expect his agency to keep coming up with new approaches. Controlled by a written plan, this can be a great asset. Without control it can have a disastrous effect on the continuity of the advertising, and hence a disastrous effect on its success, to say nothing of needlessly sapping the agency's strength.

Therefore, a company policy which forbids, or at least discourages, the advertising manager from deviating from the approved advertising plan without designated higher authority avoids the running of advertisements which may be brilliantly provocative but not on the target—and also ensures against the deterioration of continuity.

4. Timing The timing of a written plan is closely related to its purpose, especially the purpose of protecting continuity. For budgetary purposes, advertising plans are usually prepared on an annual basis, tying into the company's fiscal year. This, of course, is sound business practice, but there is one thing wrong with it, and that is the temptation to develop a new advertising strategy or theme when preparing the new annual plan to fit the fiscal year.

Bookkeeping and accounting are done on an annual basis in order to coincide with the annual report to stockholders. But people's buying habits and attitudes and tastes do not change on an annual basis.   Therefore, the time for changing advertising strategy cannot be a fixed annual date.   Marketing conditions change suddenly. New competitors enter the field; somebody starts a price war; somebody else comes up with a new give-away gimmick.   Such events naturally call for prompt change.

Unexpected media opportunities often make a change desirable. For example, an exceptional television "buy" becomes available. However, in such an event, it should mean only a media change. The right strategy could be to continue the "unique selling proposition" (borrowing from Rosser Reeves) that you have been using.

Balance between Continuity and Expediency   The question of whether or not to change an advertising strategy (annually or at interim periods) will always involve maintaining a balance between continuity and meeting current or expedient needs.   At times there will be call for doing the expedient to meet a current problem, but also important is maintaining the continuity that is building your brand image and your continuing business.

In any case, to avoid hasty change, just as the original plan was approved by higher authority, change should be similarly approved. It's a good check on impetuosity.

WHERE MARKETING STOPS AND ADVERTISING BEGINS, OR VICE VERSA

In discussing suggestions for the contents of the advertising plan, we should recognize the probable duplication or conflict between the marketing plan and the advertising plan.

Marketing is the originating, designing, producing, distributing, and advertising of products *with the consumer's interests at heart.* Add to that the manufacturer's justifiable interest in serving the consumer at a profit.

Advertising is communicating with the consumer for the purpose of moving him—changing his attitudes, making him buy.   This includes television, radio, magazines, newspapers, direct mail, outdoor advertising, transit advertising, theater programs, local social programs, skywriting, signs on trucks, personal correspondence—and, if you wish, osmosis and subliminal perception.

I regard store traffic as circulation; therefore, I regard packages, store signs, and displays as advertising. Any contact with the consumer is advertising.

A highly admired associate of mine used this statement: "Advertising takes people to the product. Merchandising takes the product to the people." Perhaps this could be a way to distinguish advertising from marketing, but I don't think so.

For after all, *markets are people, and it is people to whom we advertise.*

What is it about the product that will make people want it? Would it sell better if its consumer satisfaction were increased—if a change were made that would make it more attractive to consumers? Is this advertising or marketing?

Who are the people who represent the best potential for the product? Aren't these the people to whom we wish to advertise? What is the nature of these people, demographically or geographically? Is this advertising or marketing?

Will it be more productive to get present users to use more of the product, or to find a way to make new users? This may be a marketing decision, but it is a task for advertising.

The pricing of a product is generally regarded as a marketing decision. But it is axiomatic that if a product is overpriced, it will have a negative effect on advertising productiveness. So is pricing an advertising or a marketing function?

This could be a continuing dialogue. But this is enough to make it clear that separate plans on advertising and marketing are not always practical.

For one thing, there is this constant dilemma (on a new product or on an old one in a new territory): Do you get distribution first and then advertise, or do you advertise first to force distribution?

In the mid-1950s, General Foods, by using all television properties to introduce a new product, accomplished in terms of distribution and repeat sales in one week all that would normally have taken months to do. The question remains, do you start with distribution (marketing) or do you start with communication (advertising)?

In the case of an established product when sales start to slip, it could very well be that it is not a fault of consumer advertising. It could be that the channels of distribution need oiling so that the product moves smoothly to the retail shelves and is available to those motivated by advertising. By oiling the channels of distribution, I mean use of the proper lubricant. Under certain conditions this might be an advertising or promotion allowance. So, when is this part of the advertising plan, and when is it part of the marketing plan? Is it not really a part of an integrated plan?

In the January 27, 1969 issue of *Advertising Age,* James Button of Sears Roebuck stated that the company had "added a new dimension of *marketing*" (italics mine). He referred to measuring the results of *advertising.* So advertising? So marketing?

Separate plans on advertising and marketing are not always feasible, if indeed possible.

SUGGESTIONS FOR CONTENTS OF AN ADVERTISING PLAN

Here I should confess that I have never written an advertising plan —that is, a formal advertising plan.

I am in the position of a theatrical critic who has never written a play but has criticized many. I have been the critic of a great many advertising plans and, I hope, always seeking to be constructive.

As a result, it has been my observation that in order to write a good advertising plan you have to be something of a schizophrenic. On one hand you must be constantly aware of all the facts and figures that bear on the case, and on the other you must remain ready to let your imagination dominate your thinking. Advertising is a creative enterprise.

The advent of the computer, as helpful as it may be, does not make intuitive judgment obsolete. In fact as the use of the computer increases, judgment and ingenuity will be of increasing value. Perhaps to fit into computer jargon we'll find a new way to describe those attributes. It might be "humanizing the print-out"—putting the breath of life into it.

A Document Reflecting Thinking

After all, an advertising plan is a document reflecting the *thinking* that has been done in the process of advertising planning—mixing painful and exhaustive and original thinking with available facts.

It is doubtful that there could be one formula for an advertising plan that would fit all products and situations. Hence my suggestions for an ideal plan all have to be generalities.

A short time ago in the vain hope of improving my duffer's golf game, I studied a book in which top pros presented the basics of a good swing for each club.   One thing that intrigued me was that each pro said that the height, weight, and temperament of the player might warrant deviations from the ideal swing.

An Ideal Advertising Plan

And so on that premise, I shall give you what I believe is an ideal advertising plan.   I will be lengthy because I am trying to be comprehensive.   I might add that all the items or subjects which I include in this section on the contents of a plan may not find a place in *your* written plan, but with a few exceptions, all these items and subjects are things to which you should have carefully given consideration when, first with no inhibitions and later with disciplined thinking, you were conceiving your plan for advertising.   It is worth repeating: To write a really good advertising plan, you have to be something of a schizophrenic.

You must treat with great respect all the facts and figures that are available or can be made available to you—but not worship at their shrine.   You must counter your respect for facts and figures with an equal respect for imaginative and creative ingenuity.

My prescription for an ideal plan will not be mine alone, but a synthesis of what I have absorbed from association with many able advertising men.

I have already stated that in many, if not most cases, advertising plans and marketing plans are one document.   Hence I find it difficult to choose the subjects which belong only in the advertising plan.   So I am going to include all (admittedly I may miss some) the subjects which I believe have a bearing on advertising.   The marketing plan will no doubt contain many of these and others besides.

1. Product Personality   First, the advertising plan should describe the product.   Not just its physical dimensions, but what the manufacturer believes it will do for its users.   Every product has a personality.   What is there about it that gives it its personality?   What is the image the manufacturer wishes to achieve for it?   Is it a masculine or feminine product, or both?   Is it a high-priced product with a limited market, or a low-priced product with value appeal?   Or is it a low-priced product that might do well to have a high-priced image? Ad infinitum. You might call this a *statement of the advertising philosophy.*

2. History What is the history of the product, assuming it is an established product? There is probably no need to go back to its origin. Conditions change so rapidly these days that it is safe to assume that only events of the past three years (or five, if need be) will have a bearing on next year's plans. What has been the practice may not be so important as what is likely to be the practice. Today more than ever before, it is likely that the future practices will not be found in history. (This in itself puts a caution on the use of case histories. The conditions which existed at the time of the "case" may no longer exist.)

(If a lifetime history of the product is regarded as necessary, do not make it a part of the advertising-marketing plan. Make it a separate document and bring it up to date each year. In this way you avoid making the annual plan a tome and do not impose on those who have to read it.)

Generally speaking the following subjects should be included in the history. Sometimes the advertising-marketing history is called a *statement of facts.*

a. What is the growth record of the category in which the product falls?

b. Have any new products developed which directly or indirectly compete with the category?

c. How does the product which is the subject of the plan stand in relation to its direct competitors? What is its sales growth?

d. What is the pricing history of the product in relation to competition? Have there been any recent changes in pricing, and what effect have those changes had on sales?

e. What has been the basic copy appeal or copy policy? Any changes and evidence of the result of change? What have been the basic copy appeals of competitive products? Relate this to relative sales positions.

f. A record of packaging—both design and sizes. Any changes in packaging that were utilitarian rather than artistic? What were the results of changes, if any?

g. Have any changes been made in the product itself? What results did this have on sales—or consumer attitudes? Changes in competitive products?

h. In general, what is the record of consumer attitudes? Any marked changes, positive or negative?

i. If there is seasonal consumption of the product, are there any changes taking place in this?

j. What is the record of regional distribution and sales? What advertising or promotion has been done to correct this? What have been the results? (Assuming, of course, that regional distribution is not caused by "outside" factors, i.e., freight or other distribution costs, inappropriateness of product to climate, etc.)

k. What is the record of advertising expenditure in dollars and in relation to sales or gross profit (or whatever the accounting procedure of the company may be)?

l. What is the record of advertising expenditure in relation to advertising expenditures by competitors?

m. What consumer promotions have been employed in the past couple of years? What results? How about consumer promotions engaged in by competitors?

n. In the last year have there been outstanding advertising or promotional events for the product? For competitive products? What result?

o. Have there been any major changes in the use of media? Any recognizable results?

If you have all this information, you will have a rather comprehensive history. But as stated, in these days of rapid technological, economic, and social changes, a history of more than several years may not be of practical value.

3. Problems and Opportunities The phrase "problems and opportunities" could represent either a section of a plan, or a spirit permeating the advertising and marketing thinking of the plan's writers.

The problems will become apparent in a study of the history or statement of facts. Identify the problem and you have the first step toward its solution.

The opportunities may also be in the statement of facts. They may be apparent or they may lie dormant, only to be brought to life by imaginative thinking, by indulging in uninhibited freewheeling.

Included in *opportunities* is the matter of what people comprise the most productive market. Is there opportunity to widen the market by product, package, or price change? If the product is one subject to seasonal consumption, can this be changed? Are there regions or districts where, in relation to category sales, it is reasonable to expect an increase in the product's share of market?   Is it possible that a different copy approach should be used in different regions? And on and on.

4. Copy Policy   Obviously this is the essence, the hard core of advertising.   Rosser Reeves calls it "the unique selling proposition." Tom Ryan called it "the provocative idea."   Call it what you will, it is the be-all and end-all of successful advertising.   Hence it is no doubt the most important item in your advertising plan.

Since Part Five of this book is devoted to copy, there is no need here to do more than position it in the advertising plan.   In your plan you should give the reasoning and documentation for the selection of the copy theme or themes.   If there is more than one theme and one is regarded the more important of the two, the reasoning for this should also be included.

5. Media   Having arrived at a copy policy, the next step is, naturally, exposing it to the right people.   There are two steps: Determining who are the right people (already discussed under opportunities) and determining what is the *best* way to reach them.

I have deliberately used the word "best" rather than "efficient" or "effective."   To me, "efficient" implies least costly.   "Effective" implies greatest impact.   Naturally both are important.

We often use the word "reach."   Unfortunately "reach" has two meanings.   One is a matter of delivering a message to "Resident, 311 Sidestone Road, Vernon Cascades, U.S.A.," and we usually refer to this as *circulation* or *audience*.   The other meaning is reaching a person's mind, and we think of that as *penetration* or *impact*.

The impact of an advertisement can be influenced by its surroundings.   Hence in your advertising plan you should give consideration to the *character* of the medium as well as its size, coverage, and other efficiency quotients such as geography and demography.   There are separate chapters on media, so there is little need to say more here.

6. Promotions   For the reason that premiums, couponing, sampling, and other promotions are so often used to combat some situation that arises unexpectedly, it is difficult to include plans for such activities in an annual document.   However, in preparing the annual budget, it is well to make provision for such events.

7. Product Change   Initiating a product improvement is undoubtedly a marketing venture, but it is hard to think of a product improvement that does not provide an opportunity for advertising. It therefore at least deserves mention as a possible item for the contents of an advertising plan.

8. Packaging Changes   In these days of self-service not only in supermarkets but in hardware stores, etc., the package is advertising. It is the most potent form of reminder advertising.   A commercial or a magazine advertisement can impel a desire—but no form of advertising can say, "Here I am; here's what I can do for you," the way a package can.

Hence packaging is advertising, and what you plan to say in your commercials and other advertisements should be reflected in your packaging.   People who look at television are referred to as *audience;* people who get magazines are referred to as *circulation;* people who move around stores are called *store traffic.*   They are all the same people.   Therefore, stemming from your copy policy, an examination of your packaging belongs in your advertising plan.

(Here I have been referring to package design and copy.   The utility of the package in helping the consumer put the product to use is also a matter to be given consideration in your advertising plan.   It may offer an effective copy theme.)

9. Pricing   What a product costs in relation to what its advertising promises is certainly a factor in consumer decision to buy or not to buy.   Price determines value, and value is one thing in which the consumer is interested.   Little more than this can be said in a chapter on advertising planning that encompasses *all* consumer products.

What establishes worth or value?   It is not merely an intrinsic consideration.   To try to simplify this: Is Heinz Ketchup worth more than XYZ Catsup—in the consumer's mind?   Even admitting equal intrinsic value, is Heinz Ketchup at 37 cents a greater value than XYZ Catsup at 37 cents—or even 30 cents?

I shall leave the question of pricing with the statement that brand reputation is as much a factor as intrinsic worth in determining value in the consumer's mind.   This is a factor that warrants consideration in the writing of an advertising plan.

10. The Budget   To say it lightly would be to say that someone has to add up what all the advertising ventures will cost, and so there must be a budget.   However, to say it seriously, every company has its own method of accounting, and therefore, to each his own.   A general chapter on advertising planning can do no more than say that an advertising plan should include a budget of costs that can be fitted into the company's budgeting of all business expenditures.

11. Objectives and Measurement   The concluding statement of an advertising plan could very well be the objectives of the advertising. There are those who say this should be the opening statement.   For purposes of this chapter I refuse to take sides.   This discussion has to deal in generalities, as advertising plans will range from plans on Campbell Soup to Steinway Pianos.   As stated, there can be no constant formula.

There is, however, one universal rule.   The stated objective of an advertising plan should be something more definite than "to increase sales"—that is, when it is believed there should be a statement of objectives.

The objective might well be to increase the awareness of a given quality of the product; the introduction of a product change; the launching of a new package design or a new size; the increase in distribution in a specific geographic area (for example, bringing all areas up to an agreed-upon norm), and so on ad infinitum.

The measurement of the accomplishment of an objective, when it is possible to make such measurement, will be covered in Part Seven on research.

The planning of marketing-advertising is a comprehensive consideration of all factors involved in marketing-advertising.   Without recognizing the cohabitation of advertising and marketing, I would not have attempted a chapter on the advertising plan.

An appropriate closing is a quotation from a document by Peter Langhoff: [2]

> Since one of its purposes [planning] is to coordinate all marketing operations, thus embracing sales management, copy writing and media buying, it must be effected above that level. . . . These policies cannot be formulated independently any more than the Air Force, the Army, and the Navy can independently conceive top-level plans.

[2] President, Advertising Research Bureau, and former chairman, Advertising Research Foundation.

CHAPTER TWELVE

How Much to Spend
for Advertising*

MALCOLM A. McNIVEN *Vice President, Marketing Research
Department, Coca-Cola USA, a Division of the Coca-Cola
Company*

IMPORTANCE OF ADVERTISING
BUDGETING RESEARCH

Advertising has been an important part of our economic system for
many years. Growing levels of expenditures ($18 billion in 1968)
have been allocated to advertising over these years despite the fact
that most advertisers know little about how to establish an appropriate level of advertising expenditure. There is perhaps no other part
of the business to which we allocate resources that provides so little
justification for their use.

This is not to belittle the role of advertising in business. Far from
it. Advertising is one of the major motivating forces in our consumer economy and, therefore, has contributed to its dynamic

* Based upon the introduction to Malcolm A. McNiven (ed.), *How Much to Spend
for Advertising?* Association of National Advertisers, Inc., New York, 1969.

growth. But while we can accept advertising's contribution to the vitality of any consumer economy, any conscientious manager has to ask, "How much should I spend?"

As financial commitments to advertising budgets increase and as management becomes more sophisticated in the procedure of making decisions, the time has clearly come to study seriously how advertising budgets should be established. A similar statement was made ten years ago at an annual Advertising Research Foundation meeting by Prof. Jay Forrester of MIT. It is still appropriate. It is high time that procedures were set up to assure top management that the recommendation to spend a given number of dollars for advertising is based on something other than sheer judgment or intuition. Progress has been made. As the technology of quantitative problem solving has gradually found its way into the field of marketing, some old decision-making methods are being replaced by new ones. However, all the new methods have not yet proved themseves capable of handling the complex decisions of advertising allocation, so the old methods are slow to disappear.

In an attempt to limit the scope of this chapter to a manageable size, I have not included any information on the other two main decision areas of advertising: media and copy. While there is an obvious payoff for improved decisions here, there has been a great deal done in these areas and a great deal written about them. In contrast to this, there has been relatively little written or done in the area of advertising budgeting research.

In the course of assembling this chapter, I reviewed many books and papers dealing with the problem of allocating advertising funds. There is no clear-cut agreement on the best method for evaluating advertising expenditures, and it is unlikely there will ever be a single approach used for all problems. Instead, I offer a number of good procedures which the advertiser may test and apply to his particular advertising problems.

This chapter thus exposes the reader to a wide variety of methods and opinions about allocating funds to advertising. These are, in my opinion, the best examples of the respective methodologies they espouse. I have tried to summarize only those approaches presenting a clear procedure for estimating advertising levels. These methods may be used now in the solution of an advertiser's own problems of advertising expenditures. I am quite aware of the diverse types of problems that different readers will bring to this book, and assume they will select those methods most appropriate to their own problems, and use the particular skills available in their advertising evaluation function.   If a specific method arouses interest, information may be obtained through correspondence with the author of that method.

METHODS OF ESTIMATING ADVERTISING EXPENDITURE LEVELS

There are three basic methods of estimating advertising expenditure levels: (1) guideline; (2) theoretical, and (3) empirical.   Each has its advantages and disadvantages.   I shall discuss each and note the papers which relate to it.

Guideline Methods

Guideline methods are those usually developed through attempts to identify some measure or characteristic in the marketing system by which budgets can be compared and set.   The National Industrial Conference Board's 1963 survey of advertisers found guideline methods used by most of them.   Several guideline methods are described by Hurwood in a paper from that survey.

Ratio of Advertising Expenditure to Sales Volume   The most popular guideline in setting advertising budgets is the ratio of advertising expenditure to sales volume.   Although this is usually not a rigid or fixed procedure, the general area of advertising expenditure is arrived at by using a standard percentage of the sales in the prior time period, or of the sales forecasted for that budget year.   Says one executive: "Budgets are generally established at 2 per cent of gross sales, or when extra heavy demands are known this could go as high as 3 per cent of sales, and conversely, be lowered if not needed."

The obvious fallacy in this guideline is that when a company is having a good year, it may spend more money on advertising than it should.   It may be to its advantage to save that money for the contingency of a bad year which may follow, or to use the funds for other corporate investments.   A company should be able to capitalize on its successful marketing policy by making increased profits, rather than by spending additional amounts for advertising.   Conversely in bad years, a company should be willing to sacrifice some profits in order to maintain its position in the industry by advertising at higher levels than the per cent-of-sales guideline would suggest.

Increase over Past Year   Another guideline is some percentage increase over the preceding year's expenditure.   This allows the company to take into account increases in advertising costs and ties it to planned growth in company sales.   At the same time, the guideline fails to recognize the needs of the market in that particular year, and there is no assurance that last year's budget was near optimum.

Task Method   A third guideline is called the *task method,* where the advertising manager and his agency counterparts estimate the advertising coverage they will need to reach various target groups with the desired frequency.   This again is based on subjective estimates of what reach and frequencies are required, but allows them to add these estimates to reach an annual national figure.   This method is responsive to the needs of the marketplace and the needs of the product, but ignores the other claims on company resources in their relation to the advertising budget.   In practice, task-method estimates are usually revised by management to conform to some existing guidelines.

Advertising and Market Share   A fourth guideline method is described by Peckham in his paper "Can We Relate Advertising Dollars to Market Share Objectives?" in which he describes relationships between share of advertising and share of market (Figure 1).

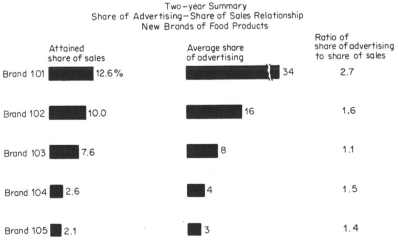

Two-year Summary
Share of Advertising—Share of Sales Relationship
New Brands of Food Products

	Attained share of sales	Average share of advertising	Ratio of share of advertising to share of sales
Brand 101	12.6%	34	2.7
Brand 102	10.0	16	1.6
Brand 103	7.6	8	1.1
Brand 104	2.6	4	1.5
Brand 105	2.1	3	1.4

Figure 1 Can we relate advertising dollars to market share? (*Courtesy of James O. Peckham.*)

The obvious advantage of Peckham's procedure is the ease with which one can establish an advertising level by deciding on a share of the total product-class advertising one wishes to attain.   His data show that the share of advertising over a two-year period is approximately 1½ times the share of sales obtained by each brand.   This does not necessarily mean that the advertising share has caused the growth in share of sales, but only that it is correlated with it.   In fact, this type of analysis fails to consider the other marketing variables affecting sales.

There is a common disadvantage in using any of these guideline methods to establish an advertising budget.   The major goal of establishing the advertising budget is to obtain a good profit advantage over competitors, to spend as much as is necessary to maximize his current or long-range profits, and to do this better than his competitors.   This implies the use of advertising as a competitive tool, and the advertiser must do better with his advertising strategy than his competitors if he is to gain a marketing or financial advantage.   By using the guideline methods, such as per cent of sales, or share of advertising, the advertiser is "running with the pack" and merely duplicating their efforts.   This does not give him a competitive advantage, and it is unlikely to be the most profitable level of advertising for him.   One could say that it is a safe but inefficient way of establishing an advertising level.

THEORETICAL METHODS

The second group of methods are theoretical models.   These attempt to estimate the most profitable level of advertising for a specific advertiser by using econometric or marketing models based on historical data.   Certain records of an advertiser's business operations are used as input, and the model estimates the most profitable level of advertising for him.

Marschner's Model   "Theory versus Practice in Allocating Advertising Money" by Donald Marschner attempts to demonstrate the wide gap between theoretical models, as developed by professionals in universities or in marketing organizations, and actual practice in terms of allocating advertising funds in business today.   He first describes a normative model of the relationship between sales and advertising, including many of the agreed-upon functions supplied by other papers in the field (Figure 2).

Suggested Allocation Model, Based upon the Adaptation of Various Concepts Appearing in Literature Which Describe the Theoretical Relationship between Sales and Advertising

$$X_i = X_j \left\{ \frac{D_{bi} \cdot V_{bi} + U_{bi}(V_{pi} - V_{bi})}{D_{bj} \cdot V_{bj} + U_{bj}(V_{pj} - V_{bj})} \right\} \cdot N_p \left(\frac{Q_{pi}}{V_{pi}} \div \frac{Q_{pj}}{V_{pj}} \right) \cdot F_p \left(\frac{E_{bi}}{E_{pi}} \div \frac{E_{bj}}{E_{pj}} \right) \cdot \frac{C_i}{C_j}.$$

KEY

X = Budget.

D = Rate of Sales Decay, established by market research.

V = Sales Volume, during time period $t - 1$.

U = Sales Opportunity for Brand "b," expressed as a decimal fraction. (This may be a specified "share of the available market," representing a practical estimate of the growth in sales volume to be aimed at as a sales goal; or, on the other hand, it may be the entire available market, less only such volume as has already been achieved, in which case the value of U would be 1, or 100 per cent.)

Q = Advertising Dollar Weight, during time period $t - 1$.

N = Conversion Factor, indicating the importance of dollars spent on advertising as a determinant of Sales Response, in relation to all other ingredients in the marketing mix; the values and nature of N are determined through market research.

E = Copy Effectiveness Indicator, determined through market research or motivational research.

F = Conversion Factor indicating the importance of advertising copy effectiveness as a determinant of Sales Response, in relation to all other ingredients in the marketing mix; the values and nature of F are determined through market research.

C = Average cost of reaching one prospect with one satisfactory message by means of the advertising medium or media normally used.

i (subscript) = Any specific market.

b (subscript) = Brand "b": our brand.

p (subscript) = All, or the sum of, or the total of, competing brands plus Brand "b" in a specific product category—that is, "the industry."

j (subscript) = All markets, or the total of all markets—that is,

$$j = \Sigma i_{1, 2, 3 \ldots n} .$$

Figure 2 Suggested allocation model. *Donald C. Marschner, Theory versus Practice in Allocating Advertising Money,* The Journal of Business, *University of Chicago Press, July,* 1967, *p.* 290.)

Marschner's model, which suggests a way of establishing a budget for each individual market, says that the advertising budget for a specific market should be determined by taking the national budget and then multiplying that by an expression which could be called the *sales opportunity* for a brand in that market, as it relates to the total market. This is then multiplied by an expression which indicates the importance of advertising as it relates to other marketing factors.

The third expression indicates the importance of advertising copy, how effective copy is relative to other marketing factors. Finally, this is multiplied by the cost efficiency of advertising in that particular market. Budget for the total market is established by merely using the national aspects of the equation, forgetting about the local market aspects. Of course, the data required for input in this model are hardly ever available, and this is one reason why it is strictly theoretical in nature, and only useful as a conceptual idea or to stimulate the generation of specific kinds of information as input to the model.

He then describes an oil company and a coffee company actually allocating advertising funds. His conclusion: theory and practice are far apart, for two reasons. First, theory tends to ignore one of the essential facts of corporate life, namely that businessmen must compromise in their search for the best solution. They are concerned with doing a job adequately, not optimally. Second, businessmen tend to think through the advertising-sales relationship to some logical conclusion. Their decisions are influenced more by rote and habit than by true problem solving, according to Marschner.

Marschner's criticisms are revealing and lead one to question present decision-making procedures. Of course, the use of theoretical models for decision making should be supplemented by judgment, but apparently this is rare also.

Econometric Method   Next is an econometric method developed by Robert Weinberg and published nine years ago by the ANA. At that time it represented the classical econometric approach to establishing advertising expenditure levels, and it remains the best example of this approach. It requires data which can be developed from existing company records. Then, with the recommended analyses, the advertiser may estimate the advertising exchange rates, and then calculate an advertising planning chart.

Figure 3 represents the output of the Weinberg method for planning advertising expenditures. The table shows, down the left-hand side, the expected level of residual industry advertising expenditures. In other words, these are the best estimates of what range industry advertising expenditures could achieve during the time period for which one is planning his advertising expenditures. Across the top are the company's marketing objectives in percentage share of the total industry market. These represent share-of-market goals for the time period one is planning for. The table then allows one to read off the advertising requirements to achieve that goal under various industry expenditure levels. It is essentially a share-of-advertising approach, only the manner in which it is derived is far more complete and appropriate for a specific company than was Peckham's share-of-advertising guideline method.

It is a strong approach that should be considered by major advertisers, since it is likely to produce better estimates of advertising levels than the guideline methods described earlier. It is weak in that it may be insensitive to specific marketing characteristics of a given product class. Also, the functional relationships between the variables in the historical data may result from a reverse causation (e.g.,

AN ILLUSTRATIVE ADVERTISING EXPENDITURE PLANNING TABLE FOR THE YEAR 1954 (TOTAL INDUSTRY SALES = 245.0 MILLION DOLLARS)

	Company Marketing Objective (Percentage Share of the Total Industry Market)										
Share of the Total Industry Market (Percent)	19.2	19.4	19.6	19.8	20.0	20.2	20.4	20.6	20.8	21.0	21.2
Net Change in the Company's Share of the Market (Percent)	0.0	0.2	0.4	0.6	0.8	1.0	1.2	1.4	1.6	1.8	2.0
	(1)	(2)	(3)	(4)	(5)	(6)	(7)	(8)	(9)	(10)	(11)
Expected Level of Residual Industry Advertising Expenditures (Millions of Dollars)	Company Advertising Expenditure Requirements (Thousands of Dollars)										
(A) 10.00	2,319	2,746	3,251	3,848	4,556	5,391	6,380	7,550	8,934	10,571	12,505
(B) 10.25	2,377	2,814	3,332	3,944	4,669	5,526	6,540	7,739	9,158	10,835	12,818
(C) 10.50	2,435	2,883	3,413	4,040	4,783	5,661	6,699	7,928	9,381	11,099	13,130
(D) 10.75	2,493	2,952	3,494	4,137	4,897	5,795	6,859	8,116	9,604	11,363	13,443
(E) 11.00	2,551	3,020	3,576	4,233	5,011	5,930	7,018	8,305	9,828	11,628	13,755
(F) 11.25	2,609	3,089	3,657	4,329	5,125	6,065	7,178	8,494	10,051	11,892	14,068
(G) 11.50	2,667	3,158	3,738	4,425	5,239	6,200	7,338	8,683	10,274	12,156	14,381
(H) 11.75	2,725	3,226	3,820	4,521	5,353	6,335	7,497	8,872	10,498	12,421	14,693
(I) 12.00	2,783	3,295	3,901	4,618	5,467	6,469	7,657	9,060	10,721	12,685	15,006
(J) 12.25	2,841	3,364	3,982	4,714	5,581	6,604	7,816	9,249	10,944	12,949	15,318
(K) 12.50	2,899	3,432	4,063	4,810	5,694	6,739	7,976	9,438	11,168	13,213	15,631
(L) 12.75	2,957	3,501	4,145	4,906	5,808	6,874	8,135	9,627	11,391	13,478	15,944
(M) 13.00	3,015	3,570	4,226	5,002	5,922	7,008	8,295	9,815	11,614	13,742	16,256
(N) 13.25	3,078	3,638	4,307	5,099	6,036	7,143	8,454	10,004	11,838	14,006	16,569
(O) 13.50	3,131	3,707	4,388	5,195	6,150	7,278	8,614	10,193	12,061	14,270	16,882
(P) 13.75	3,189	3,775	4,470	5,291	6,264	7,413	8,773	10,382	12,285	14,535	17,194
(Q) 14.00	3,247	3,844	4,551	5,387	6,378	7,548	8,933	10,570	12,508	14,799	17,507
(R) 14.25	3,305	3,913	4,632	5,483	6,492	7,682	9,092	10,759	12,731	15,063	17,819
(S) 14.50	3,363	3,981	4,713	5,580	6,605	7,817	9,252	10,948	12,955	15,327	18,132
(T) 14.75	3,421	4,050	4,795	5,676	6,719	7,951	9,411	11,137	13,178	15,592	18,445
(U) 15.00	3,479	4,119	4,876	5,772	6,833	8,087	9,571	11,325	13,401	15,856	18,757

Note: In the computation of the present table, the Company's advertising exchange was computed to four decimal places; for example, the advertising exchange rate for $\Delta M = 0.8$ is 182.2091. The advertising exchange rates employed in the derivation of Tables Eight, Nine, and Ten were computed to only one decimal place.

Figure 3 An illustrative advertising expenditure.

advertising was budgeted historically as a per cent of sales). This criticism can be leveled at most general econometric models, and yet the estimates derived from this approach will probably place the advertiser in the region of optimal expenditure, although perhaps not at the optimal level. Anyone interested in pursuing this approach will want to review the original document and follow the procedure from start to finish.

Hendry Method The second theoretical model described here is the Hendry method described in the paper by Ben Butler. This method is a theoretical approach which attempts to develop optimal advertising levels through an examination of the company's position in relation to its competitors. Share-of-market and advertising expenditures are examined in relation to the profitability of the company's operation. The output of the Hendry analysis is plotted on a chart shown in Figure 4.

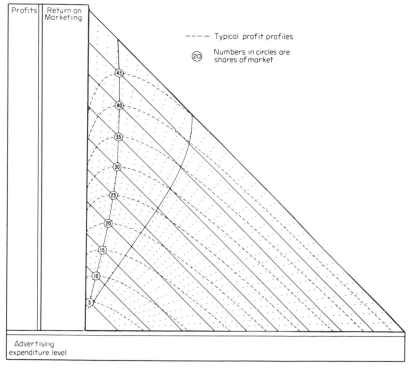

Figure 4 Hendrograph advertising expenditure analysis.

The curved dashed lines represent profitability levels for a brand at various advertising and market-share levels.   The solid line (with circles) indicates points of optimum profit at various market-share levels.   The solid line to the right indicates points of breakeven at various share levels.   In order to conduct the analysis, three items of brand information are required: (1) direct manufacturing margin, (2) the advertiser's expenditure level, and (3) share of market.   Once the program has been calibrated for the product being analyzed, the computerized analysis will then describe what share of market and resulting profitability would exist for any alternative level of advertising expenditures.   This determines a company's position on this chart.

The Hendry approach to estimating the most profitable advertising expenditure level is interesting because it is based on an attempt to develop fundamental laws of consumer dynamics, which were arrived at deductively and which are being tested on actual product sales and advertising data.   Based on the case history available for evaluating this method, it seems to be extremely useful in making general predictions about the effects of changes in advertising levels.   As these theoretical models become more specific, their results relate to more real activity.   They may demonstrate that the laws of consumer dynamics developed in this procedure do in fact explain consumer behavior.

This method makes certain assumptions about the relationships of advertising to sales which may or may not apply to a specific product class.   However, empirical testing of the model seems to indicate that it has wide generality, and as with the Weinberg approach, is very likely to place the advertiser close to the right expenditure level.

EMPIRICAL MODELS

The third way of estimating optimal advertising budgets is the *empirical model*.   There has been growing interest in this type of research, because these models are sensitive to the specific characteristics of the given product class and to the marketing factors acting on the product at the time the budgets are being set.   These models are built on the basis of experimental feedback from the marketplace, as opposed to historical data or assumptions.

Experimental Designs A paper by Seymour Banks shows how experimental designs can be used to study the productivity of advertising in the marketplace. The main point made by Banks is that only through continuous experimentation with advertising variations will the advertiser ever know the true effects of advertising on his product's sales. Other methods of data analysis may yield interesting results which will be helpful in moving in the right direction for advertising budgets. However, only experimental studies are able to parcel out the effects of advertising independent of other marketing variables and to measure this effect in the context of factors operating at the time the test is being made. He points out some of the terminology used in describing experimental studies and some of the models used for analysis of experimental data.

Advertising Experiments McNiven describes briefly some results of advertising experiments and the manner in which the right advertising level can be estimated from the results of these experiments.

One of the studies he describes, and one which has been described in other papers, is a study which tested three different levels of television advertising for Teflon-coated cookware. This study attempted to measure the changes in Teflon-coated cookware units per thousand housewives as a result of varying television advertising at high, medium, and low expenditure levels. The outcome of the study demonstrated the response of the Teflon cookware sales to the various levels of advertising, and allowed the advertiser to estimate the best level of advertising. Since several consecutive studies were done in this series, an estimated response function is shown which relates profitability to advertising level (Figure 5).

Another study is reported which describes an experiment that varies media, as well as level of advertising. This study demonstrates that the experimental approach can be used to test a wide variety of advertising problems. In this particular study twenty-seven cities were used and the advertising levels were varied as well as combining newspaper and television advertising in different combinations. The results of the study indicate that different media had different effects on sales. The media were then used in different combinations to allow the advertiser to tailor his media plan to that point which was best for his product at that time in its marketing history. The outcome of these studies was empirical models which were essentially the multiple regression equations used to analyze the results of the experimental design. These empirical models may have some degree of generality to other situations, but must be used with care. The weights of the variables may change from situation to situation.

Government Work   William Hoofnagle reports experimental designs used by the Department of Agriculture in evaluating effectiveness of advertising for various produce and commodity products. The use of experiments to measure advertising effects was first implemented in the Department of Agriculture, and has been developed by it over the last ten years. Hoofnagle summarizes the Department's experience and recommends implementing such a program in a more brand-competitive environment.

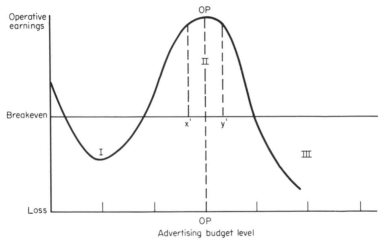

Figure 5   Advertising budget level.

A point that is clearly demonstrated by the Department of Agriculture studies is that the experimental method used to evaluate advertising effects works very well across a wide variety of products. Properly implemented, this technique is capable of estimating the amount of sales generated by different levels of advertising or promotion or in-store demonstration. The important thing for the reader to remember is that studies reported by McNiven, and those of Hoofnagle, cover many different kinds of consumer products, and it is very likely that this technique is appropriate for most advertised products. Of course, one of the main problems with these empirical studies is that they require time, money, and professional knowledge to complete them satisfactorily.   There has been an attempt to stimulate advertising programs on computers by various organizations. In these computer programs, advertising exposures are distributed across various segments of the population, and the response of these segments are estimated and thereby generate changing market shares.   So far none of these studies seems to have been able to predict the actual movement of products in the market, and there still remains a great deal to be done if this method is ever to be useful.

Combining Theoretical and Experimental   There has been an attempt to combine the theoretical model with the experimental approach in order to gain the best of both worlds.   This is described in Prof. John Little's paper "Adaptive Control Systems in Marketing."   His paper appears to be the most fruitful approach for measuring effectiveness of advertising.   He proposes continuing experimentation on the effects of advertising, from which one can construct and later modify marketing models which estimate the optimal advertising strategy for a company.   Experiments provide information about the relation of advertising to sales.   Then the model is updated, which allows one to estimate promotional rates of return, and these rates are installed in further experiments.   At any point the model estimates the most profitable advertising level from all information available to it at that time.

An Adaptive Control System   Let us describe an example of how an adaptive control system might work.   There are unlimited ways in which this could be arranged, but one system would be to install a checkerboard design in markets across the country.   This would entail dividing the country into two or more groups of markets and then placing alternative advertising programs in each of these groups of markets.   Then by looking at the sales and market-share figures from these groups of markets, one can estimate which strategy is more effective than others.   As one group of markets starts performing better, that strategy can be spread to the other groups of markets.   One can also use a more complicated design and gain the same kind of information with fewer markets.   In this case, one may wish to test more complex strategy in a relatively few markets, and again, feed the information back to the model which estimates the likelihood of having developed a superior strategy.   These studies can be run in a reasonably short time, since we are often dealing with products and advertising programs where the consumer response would be rapid. By continually running these kinds of experiments and feeding the information back into a model of consumer response to advertising, one is building a fund of knowledge which can handle many of the marketing decisions which will have to be made by a company on a continuous basis.

NEXT STEP FOR THE ADVERTISER

In order to determine the national advertising expenditure levels for a company, management must first decide how much money and talent it is willing to commit to such a program. If management is willing to commit enough money and spend enough time seriously to undertake the measurement of advertising productivity, then the course of action is fairly clear.

1. Hire adequate professionally trained personnel to cope with the difficulty of the problem with the technical methods that are required for such an evaluation.

2. Budget sufficient funds for the research.

3. Develop the patience required to learn about the complex problems of advertising.

A research program on advertising expenditures should attempt to provide quick results and at the same time attempt to develop sharper estimates of the profitability levels. To accomplish this a program goes through several phases. First, the company is probably using one of the guideline methods described in the first section of this chapter. It can quickly move to a theoretical model which will tell whether it is right. If not, it can move in the direction of optimal expenditures. At the same time it can undertake small-scale experiments wherein it varies levels of advertising. It can expand its experimental approaches as it gains experience. The results of these experiments will point the way to the development of a model of advertising effectiveness which will be specific to that company. The experimentation will have to continue for a long period, but as the model becomes better developed, it can be used to estimate advertising expenditures.

For a package-goods company to go through this type of research program will probably require three to five years and several million dollars. The company with a smaller advertising program, or whose management has less desire to explore advertising expenditures in such detail, might prudently hire a consultant, or an organization that conducts such studies, and use one of the theoretical models described here. The theoretical models are more likely to set the proper expenditure levels than the guideline methods currently being used by the company. Perhaps $1 million a year should be adequate to cover such a program, and it is bound to more than pay for itself in increased productivity of advertising.

ESTIMATING TOTAL ADVERTISING PRODUCTIVITY

All the discussions in this chapter pertain only to establishing the proper dollar expenditure level for advertising. They have ignored the problems of media allocation and development of advertising copy. Obviously, advertising dollars can be spent in a variety of media which vary in efficiency. Unusually good advertising copy can make an advertising dollar produce more benefit for the advertiser. But many publications discuss media allocation and copy testing. To place some boundaries on the material covered here, I have not dealt with these questions. If an advertiser establishes a near-optimum expenditure level for his current advertising program, he can further improve the productivity of his advertising by better media allocation and better copy development. This should then allow him to reduce his expenditure level, since it will in a sense produce the same advertising push for him at less dollar expenditure.

If marketing management asks, "Should I start a research program on copy, media, or advertising weight?" the quickest and largest payoff is in exploring optimum levels of advertising expenditure. To advertise in the same media, with the same copy approaches, while refining expenditure levels, should provide a quick payoff for management. Then to tune up the system further, it becomes necessary to find that combination of copy, level, and media which serves the company best and achieves the marketing goals for the company.

There is very likely to be a large payoff for discovering an outstanding copy approach, but there is a slim chance of finding such copy regularly.

As marketing becomes more segmented and localized, advertising spending practices will have to become more complex. Future advertising levels will probably be varied quite regularly and developed on a local basis to appeal to local conditions. This will require continuous feedback from adaptive control systems designed to modify the advertising programs in accordance with the conditions of the marketplace. As production and research become more similar among large companies, competitive advantages through efficient advertising allocation and production are bound to become one of the major focal points in American business. The companies that start now to prepare for that eventuality will find themselves in a stronger competitive position in the future.

BIBLIOGRAPHY

BANKS, SEYMOUR: "Experimentation in Marketing," chap. 1, Introduction to Basic Concepts, McGraw-Hill Book Company, New York, 1965, pp. 1–22.

BUTLER, B. F., P. M. THOMPSON, and L. A. COOK: "Quantitative Relationships among Advertising Expenditures, Share of Market, and Profits," The Hendry Corporation.

HOOFNAGLE, WILLIAM S.: Experimental Design in Measuring the Effectiveness of Promotion, *Journal of Marketing Research,* May, 1965, pp. 154–162.

HURWOOD, DAVID L.: How Companies Set Advertising Budgets, *The Conference Board Record,* NICB, March, 1968, pp. 34–41.

LITTLE, JOHN D. C.: "Adaptive Control Systems in Marketing," American Marketing Association, June, 1968.

MARSCHNER, DONALD C.: Theory versus Practice in Allocating Advertising Money, *Journal of Business,* July, 1967, pp. 286–302.

McNIVEN, MALCOLM A.: "Choosing the Most Profitable Level of Advertising: A Case Study," Association of National Advertisers, Inc., Workshop on Advertising and Planning and Evaluation, December, 1966.

PECKHAM, JAMES O.: "Can We Relate Advertising Dollars to Market Share Objectives?" Twelfth Annual Conference of Advertising Research Foundation, October, 1966.

WEINBERG, ROBERT S.: Developing an Advertising Planning Procedure: An Econometric Approach, "An Analytical Approach to Advertising Expenditure Strategy," Association of National Advertisers, Inc., 1960, pp. 22–44.

CHAPTER THIRTEEN

Budgeting and Controlling Advertising Expenditures

ARTHUR F. RUDY *Manager of Production, Control and Office Services, Advertising and Promotion Department, Armstrong Cork Company*

One of the most important tools required by advertising executives is an adequate system for budgeting advertising expenditures and for controlling these expenditures as budgeted. Such a system may be hand-operated and compiled in a small company or operated by electronic data processing equipment in a large, complex corporation. Either way, a satisfactory budgetary control system gives executives ready access to the information needed in planning advertising programs and administering their execution in the field.

BUDGETS

A budget means one thing to a newly married couple, and another to a corporation executive. For our purposes, a budget may be described as a careful estimate of the dollars to be taken in, available, or required by any particular part of the business complex during a given period of time. These include the expenses necessary to create a predetermined volume of sales and profits, cash for both fixed and working capital, and the like. A budget, then, should serve to coordinate the financial aspects of a business in such a way that sales income, expenditures, profits, and cash requirements will all be in the proper relationship.

Traditional business goals—satisfactory growth and profits—make budgets a very necessary monthly and yearly planning device.

Advertising budgets are generally made up for a minimum period of a year, because the very nature of the business calls for yearly contracts with magazines and networks to earn the maximum discounts. The frequency with which the entire advertising budget is reviewed or revised varies from company to company. Obviously, the more complex the business, the wider the range of products advertised, and the larger the number of projects involving large sums of money, the more often the budget should be reviewed.

Budgetary Control

Budgetary control involves not only careful planning (the compilation of budgets) but also the controlling of all functions of the business or department. In the case of an advertising budget, budgetary control requires the entire department, from the senior advertising executive to the copy writer and artist, to keep as close to the charted course as possible.

Budgetary control is a tool for the advertising executive to use in operating the department or section effectively. The control or system provides the manager with a means of living within a budget by keeping him informed as he goes along so that he can take whatever corrective action is necessary. Budgetary control is to a businessman what a road map is to a tourist. It gives him instant answers to the questions "Which way?" and "How far?"

Need for Budgetary Control

The amount of money spent for advertising varies from company to company depending on size and kind of products sold, but it is usually a major item of expense. Ratios of advertising expenditures to sales range from less than 1 per cent to more than 20 per cent.

The mere size of advertising expenses, however, is not the only reason why an adequate budgetary control system is necessary. The very nature of advertising expenses is such that waste and extravagance are greater possibilities than in most other areas of the business. Many of the goals of advertising are somewhat indefinite. The rapid flux of conditions affecting advertising makes it difficult to use the scientific and technical methods applied to manufacturing cost reduction.

Because of these situations, business must make use of budgetary control in planning and supervising advertising expenditures.

Responsibility for the Advertising Budget

A sound principle of good budgetary control is that budget responsibility should follow organization responsibility. The advertising budget should be compiled under the general direction of the senior advertising executive. The plans or budgets should be reviewed with the senior marketing executive who is ultimately responsible for the budget, and have his approval. This is very important because he is responsible for the distribution of the company's products, and everything that aids him in distributing them successfully should have his approval.

In many companies, advertising budgets are also submitted to the president's office for approval before they are compiled by the controller's department into the master profit-and-loss budget.

This step is a very wise one because the master profit-and-loss budget is eventually submitted to the president's office for approval. In this way, the president's office is cognizant of the advertising programs, and if any reduction of expenditures in the master budget is to be made, the advertising budget will not be reduced inadvertently.

Items Included in Advertising Budget

A word or so should be said about what items are to be included in the advertising budget. Many lists have been prepared, including all types of expenses, but only those expenses should be included that are the responsibility of the senior advertising executive and his department. No real control of advertising expenditures can be made if charges are made to advertising which really belong to sales or publicity expenses.

Obviously, varying organization structures and functions make any one "list" inappropriate. For our purposes at the Armstrong

Cork Company, Lancaster, Pa., the following charges are included in the advertising budget:

A. Advertising media (including production costs)
   1. Television
   2. Radio
   3. Newspapers
   4. General magazines
   5. Business magazines
   6. House organs
   7. Photographs
   8. Directories and catalogs
   9. Pattern books
   10. Pattern engravings and color shots
   11. Literature
   12. Dealer service
   13. Promotions
B. Sales promotions (trade shows, conventions, and affairs produced and administered by advertising department)
C. Department expense
   1. Salaries
   2. Indirect labor
   3. Vacation and holiday pay
   4. Supplies
   5. Maintenance labor and materials
   6. Freight
   7. Stationery
   8. Travel
   9. Postage
   10. Telephone and telegraph
   11. Rent
   12. Service outside firms
   13. Employee expense (education, meals, etc.)
   14. Subscriptions to publications
   15. Entertainment
   16. Employee benefits
   17. Association dues
   18. Depreciation
   19. Insurance
   20. Taxes—payroll
   21. Taxes—general

Control of the Budget by the Advertising Department

Once the advertising budget has been approved, it should be the responsibility of the company's senior advertising executive to control the expenditures within the limits of the budget.

At the Armstrong Cork Company, the advertising department handles its own advertising accounting with five employees: a control manager, supervisor, and three clerks. For more than twenty-five years this group operated a manual system.

Designed to show advertising budget balances and expenditures at a moment's notice, a manual clerically operated system of advertising budgetary control was put into effect in 1941. Despite the fact that the budget for which this manual system was originally devised has grown fifteenfold, and the nature of the advertising expenditures has undergone sharp change in the years since 1941, this system operated very smoothly with only a few minor revisions until 1967, when a new computer-based system was installed. The simplicity of this manual system would make it a valuable control tool for either large or small advertising departments, regardless of the number of products advertised or the media or promotional materials used.

MANUAL BUDGETARY CONTROL SYSTEM

The following explanation shows how the manual budgetary control system applies specifically to product advertising. The system is based on three interrelated accounting forms: control card, project initiation sheet, and job description card. Using these, the accountant responsible for administering advertising funds can see at a glance the status of budgets in such categories of product advertising as general magazines, newspapers, radio and television, business magazines, house magazines, product literature, and directories and catalogs.

The Control Card

The control card (Figure 1) is the basic accounting form used in the system. After the advertising budget has been completed and approved, a separate control card is made up for each individual cate-

JOB NO.	ITEM	DESCRIPTION	BUDGET		FUNDS RELEASED		FINAL COST	BALANCE
			Date	Amount	Date	Amount		
F1	"Decorate for living" Booklet		1/1	10,000	1/15	10,000	9,500	(500)

Account No. **226**   ACCOUNT NAME **Literature for dealer distribution**

Division **FLOOR**

BUDGET POSITION OR UNRELEASED BALANCE	
Date	Amount
Jan.1	150,000
1/15	-10,000
	140,000
3/1	+ 500
	140,500

Form 3756 6-48

Figure 1   Control card.

gory of advertising activity. Each such card shows the dollar amount budgeted in the upper right-hand corner.

In practice, this manual system of budgetary control is not brought into play until the basic creative work on a given project has been completed. This means that the copy has been written, the art layout made, the entire creative job approved, and cost estimates obtained from artists, typesetters, engravers, printers, and binders. This practice was possible because the company's advertising and promotion department includes a large staff of creative people—writers, artists, and designers—whose job is to prepare literature and promotional materials and to coordinate and check advertisements prepared by the company's advertising agencies. Thus, no funds budgeted as direct advertising expense are spent on the basic creative work. The salaries of the copy writers and artists involved in this work are budgeted as departmental expense, as are the equipment and facilities which they use.

In a firm which relies on advertising agencies or outside commercial art houses for initial copy or layouts, funds would have to be budgeted for this creative work, and the system of budgetary control under discussion here would go into effect just as soon as such expenses were incurred.

The Project Initiation Form

The project initiation form (Figure 2) must be filled out by the man handling the project before any expenditures are made. This form

```
        P R O J E C T   I N I T I A T I O N
           Advertising and Promotion
                                              No.  F1

     ■ PROJECT TITLE    "Decorate for Living" Booklet

     Date  January 15              Code No.  170-145-22-00-401-602

     Project Originator  Mahler              Section  Floor

     ■ SPECIFICATIONS                ■ COST ESTIMATES (including tax)

     Quantity  100,000   No. of Colors  4      Est. Production    $9,900

     Page Size 8½" x 11"  No. of Pages         Est. Art              100

     Paper Stock  Warren's Lustro              Est. Total        $10,000

     Cover Stock  Same                  ■ COMMODITY

     Method of Printing  Letterpress           Corlon - 401

     Printer  Donnelley Printing Company

     Composition

     Mechanical

     Packaging                          ■ BUDGETARY REMARKS

     Delivery to

     Transportation

     Mailing Requirements

     ■ DATES      Schedule  Actual   ■ PRODUCTION AND SCHEDULE REMARKS

     To Agency    _____  _____

     From Agency  _____  _____

     Revise Out   _____  _____

     Revise In    _____  _____

     Ok. Date     _____  _____

     Art Start    _____  _____   KEY

     Art Finish   _____  _____   White, Section Mgr.    APPROVAL

     Prod. Start  _____  _____   Buff, Budget Control   Section Mgr._____
                                      Blue, Attach to Project
     Prod. Finish _____  _____                          Budgetary_____
                                      Green, Production
     Dist. Start  _____  _____   Pink, Order & Inquiry  Director_____

     Dist. Finish _____  _____   Gray, Adv. Design Services

     Form 2755 7-64
```

Figure 2 The project initiation form.

(Reverse Side)

PROJECT INITIATION

■ INSTRUCTIONS CONCERNING ART PRODUCTION

Mechanical artwork for booklet including composition and reproduction

proofs.

Finished art for Decorating booklet - specifications of type

Lettering - "Decorate for Living"

■ ART

	Date out	Art rec.	Inv. rec.	Est. cost	Cost
Godfrey Agency	1/23	1/25	1/30	–	$100.00
Lanc. Composition	1/23	1/24	1/25	–	25.00
Proof Room - 1/16					

Figure 2 The project initiation form. (*Continued*)

initiates the first budgetary step to be taken, checking on the availability of funds for the job.   In addition to its budgetary control function, the project initiation form includes the basic information about the job which is essential to those handling the art and production phases of the project as it moves toward completion.   The form shows the starting date and the copy writer handling the job.   Then there is a complete list of specifications, estimated costs, and production information. In addition, a detailed schedule permits close control.

Assuming that a company has art and production staffs operating within the organization, duplicate copies of the project initiation form are provided for these functions. (See key at bottom of the form.) The securing of all necessary approvals on the form results in funds for the project being made available so that production can get under way. The reverse side of the form provides space for instructions concerning art production, art schedules, specifications, and further production information.

With the project initiation form completed, the accountant handling the advertising budgetary control function now has adequate information to enable him to earmark funds for this particular project on the control card of the respective product line. He learns from the budget information on the project initiation form the estimated total cost of the project. This amount is recorded on the control card in the column "funds released." This released amount is then deducted from the original budgeted figure shown in the upper right-hand column of the card marked "budget position or unreleased balance."

As funds for each new job in this category are released during the year by means of subsequent project initiation forms, these funds are deducted, and the balance remaining in the right-hand column of the control card will show at all times the funds still available in this account. Thus, by adding the funds remaining on each control card, one can compute in a matter of minutes an accurate balance of advertising money still on hand—and the purposes for which it is earmarked.

The availability of this balance and the ease with which it can be computed are the key factors in providing the advertising executive with an up-to-the-minute record of the funds available for his use. If a decision is made to spend more money in one category than originally budgeted, funds from one control card can be transferred to another or to a card for an entirely new account that is established.

Job Description Card

As funds are released from the control card, a subsidiary job description card (Figure 3) is started to show an accumulation of all the expenses incurred in the course of completing a particular project.

ORDER NUMBER	DATE OF ORDER	VENDOR	DESCRIPTION	ESTIMATED COMMITMENTS	Art Production	ENGRAVING	COMPOS. ELECTROS PRINTING	AUTHOR'S ALTER.	REPRINTS	MISC.	PARCEL POST EXPRESS FREIGHT		DATE OF INV.	NO. PAID
1	2/1	Godfray	Artwork		100									
2	2/5	Lane Comp.	Repro Proofs		25									
3	2/5	Royal Electrodes	Electro Types	~~1,000~~			1,100							
4	2/5	Graphic Arts	Engraving	500		600								
5	2/10	Donnly Prtg.	Printintg 100,000	7,500			7,675							
			copies 8-1/2" X 11											
			8 Pages, 4 Covers											
			Totals		125	600	8,725							
							Total			9,500 or 9-1/2 c ea.				

DESCRIPTION OF JOB "Decorate for Living" Booklet — JOB NO. F1 — YEAR — FUNDS RELEASED $10,000 — CODE 170-14522-00-401-602 — DIVISION Floor

Form 3757 1-60

Figure 3 Job description card.

The amount of funds released is posted in the upper right-hand corner of the ledger card. Separate columns are available for purchase order numbers, dates of purchase orders, suppliers, description of items for which expenses are incurred, and columns for recording the following information:

Estimated commitments

Actual costs of:

Artwork and photographs

Engravings

Composition, electros, printing

Author's alterations

Reprints

Miscellaneous

A copy of every order or contract placed with a supplier by the production section of the company's advertising and promotion department is routed daily to the budgetary control section. If the value of the purchase order is more than $100, it is entered on the job description card, and the cost, as estimated by the member of the production section who placed the order, is posted in the column "Estimated commitments." When the invoice is received, it is posted in the proper column, and a line is drawn through the estimated commitment. If the amount of the purchase order is less than $100, no record is made on the job description card until the invoice is received.

The most important advantage of keeping a running cost record such as this one is that up-to-date expenditures for any given project can be checked at any time during its production.

As various advertising projects are completed, the detailed job description cards are totaled, and the sum entered on the control cards, with the entry under "Budget position or unreleased balance" adjusted accordingly. Job description cards for completed projects are closed out and placed in a file. This file is used to compile a monthly recapitulation of each completed job. The monthly recapitulation report is set up under the following headings:

Recapitulation of Project Initiations with Actual Expenditures

Name	Job No.	Amount released	Total cost	Over or (under) release	Art cost	Production cost	Product manager

This recapitulation provides the accountant with information on: (1) the jobs that have been completed, (2) the final costs of each job, and (3) the effect of these costs on the budget balance. In addition, the filed cards are valuable for analyzing the cost of a given job and are a convenient reference in building subsequent budgets, preparing forecasts, and estimating similar jobs.

Summary of Manual System

Through this manual budgetary control system, the advertising executive can be kept informed of his budget position at all times. He can also balance overages in one account by making savings in another. On the other hand, if it becomes evident that major savings will be made in a number of accounts during the year, these savings can be used either for additional projects within the budget period or as a cost-reduction contribution. But, most important, this relatively simple method of recording expenditures gives the accountant in charge of advertising budgetary control a means by which he can, at any time, make a speedy accounting of uncommitted funds.

BUDGETARY CONTROL BY ELECTRONIC DATA PROCESSING

As stated earlier, control of the advertising budget changed from a manually operated system to a system of control by electronic data processing equipment at the Armstrong Cork Company after almost three decades of satisfactory performance by the manual method.

There were four main reasons for the changeover:

1. *Speed.* Under the manual system, several key reports were twelve to fifteen working days after the fact because the information was dependent on reports from other areas of the company. Computer reports are available much more promptly.

2. *More usable reporting.* The advertising executive will receive a monthly summary for each product group exactly as he has set it up in the original budget. This is only possible via the computer as will be explained later.

3. *More interrelated reporting.* Because the computer has an un-limited "memory" or storage system, the three basic monthly reports given to the department management will be far more interrelated one to the other than was possible with a manual system.

4. *More accurate reporting.* Theoretically, the computer should be more accurate, because in companies where electronic data pro-cessing is used by the controller's department, the advertising depart-ment will be using much of the same data. The information may be used in a different manner by the advertising department, but be-cause the data have already been carefully checked by the department responsible for the keeping of the company's records, they should be more accurate.

In summary, budgetary control by electronic data processing is much faster, far more complete, and much more usable reporting than was possible with a manual system.

The Revised Project Initiation

The changeover from the manual system to the computer system began by redesigning and revising the project initiation. The "purse strings" for the advertising budget under the manual method, this vital tool had to contain information necessary to program the computer.

This was done (Figure 4) by inserting the square rectangular box on the upper right-hand corner of the project initiation.   Here all the pertinent information needed by the key-punching section of the

PROJECT INITIATION
Advertising and Promotion

■ PROJECT TITLE

Date _____

Project Originator _____

Section _____

■ SPECIFICATIONS

Quantity _____ No. of Colors _____

Page Size _____ No. of Pages _____

Paper Stock _____

Cover Stock _____

Method of Printing _____

Printer _____

Composition _____

Mechanical _____

Packaging _____

Delivery to _____

Transportation _____

Mailing Requirements _____

PROJECT NO. -

INFORMATION FOR DATA CENTER

CPD - Cont. So. - Dept. - Comm. - Media

____ ____ ____ ____ ____

Released Amount - _____

Commodity Distribution:

1. _____   _____ %
2. _____   _____ %
3. _____   _____ %
4. _____   _____ %
5. _____   _____ %
6. _____   _____ %
7. _____   _____ %
8. _____   _____ %
9. _____   _____ %
10. _____   _____ %

■ COST ESTIMATES (including tax)

Est. Production _____

Est. Art _____

Est. Total _____

■ DATES   Schedule   Actual   ■ PRODUCTION AND SCHEDULE REMARKS

To Agency
From Agency
Revise Out
Revise In
Ok. Date
Art Start
Art Finish   KEY
Prod. Start   White, Section Mgr.
Prod. Finish   Buff, Budget Control
Dist. Start   Blue, Attach to Project
Dist. Finish   Green, Production
Form 3755 5-67   Pink, Order & Inquiry
                   Gray, Adv. Design Services

APPROVAL

Section Mgr. _____

Budgetary _____

Director _____

Figure 4   Project initiation form revised for computer system.

data processing center is summarized so that funds can be released from the budget and a project started.

Specifically, this information is:

1. Project number
2. Accounting code
3. Dollar amount
4. Product distribution

The revised project initiation for the computer method serves basically the same function as in the manual system. The project is identified by type of expenditure, starting date, copy writer handling the job, a complete list of specifications, estimated costs, and production information as well as a complete schedule.

Signatures are required in the lower right-hand corner by those executives controlling the budget, indicating that funds are available, that the job has been approved, and that production can start.

Tabulation of Project Status

With the use of the revised project initiation form in the data center, it is now possible to compile a tabulation that itemizes all charges against individual projects. This can be done for the preceding month plus period to date. This form is called a *tabulation of project status* (Figure 5) and provides:

1. Specific information on the individual transactions that have affected each project during the preceding month

2. A list of prior-month charges shown in total only, month by month

This tabulation can be obtained weekly or bimonthly, or at any time conditions warrant running the report.

This report gives the budgetary control section a detailed account of the various types of expenditures released against each individual project. In this way, every current project can be analyzed in terms of expenditures, income, and budgetary status. At the far right side of this report, the voucher numbers of all paid invoices are listed so that the charge can be very easily verified in case there are questions.

The tabulation of project status is not circulated beyond the budgetary control section because of the very size of the report. Advertising executives are far too busy to analyze these data, and the report remains in the budgetary control section for checking and reference purposes only.

Figure 5 Tabulation of project status.

Project No.	Month	Coding Comm.	Coding Class	Art	Compos. electros Printing	Misc. source 22	Other So.	Other sources amount	Actual total	To-date total	Released amount	Unspent balance	PM.	Ref No.
14912	5	401	801				51	490—					12	00021
14912	5		801				51	5—					02	05569
	Total month							495—						
	Total project			401 100%				321	495—	321	1,000	679		
	Distribution													
14965	2	400												
	Total project			361	365				726	726	725	1—		
	Distribution			401 38%	409 41%	402 21%				726	725	1—		
Closed														
14990	1	400												
	Total project			499		499			499	499	500	—		
	Distribution			401 28%	409 17%	499 / 402 32% 403		404 2%	408 10%	405 7%	500	—		
Closed														
15076	2	401												
	Total project			83	587				670	670	670			
	Distribution			83	587				670	670	670			
Closed				401 100%										
15098	1	404				447			447	447	1,000	553		
15098	2	404				209—		159—	368—	79	1,000	921		
15098	3	404				458—			458—	379—	1,000	1,379		
15098	4	404				17			17	362—	1,000	1,362		
	Total project			404 100%		203—		159—		362—	1,000	1,362		
	Distribution													
Closed														
15110	1	409				19			19	19	100	81		
	Total project			409 100%		19				19	100	81		
	Distribution													
15121	1	400				7,913		686—	7,227	7,227	20,000	12,773	31	11980
15121	2	401				862		2,050—	1,188—	6,039	20,000	13,961	11	04730
15121	3	401				23		228	251	6,290	20,000	13,710		
15121	4	401	401			15		191	206	6,496	20,000	13,504		
15121	5	401	401			24	15	59	83					
	Total month					24		59	83					
	Total project					8,837		2,258—		6,579	20,000	13,421		
	Distribution			401 30%		402 26% 403	10%	404 17%	405	6,579 4%				
15147	4	401		184	542				726	726	725	1—		
	Total project			184	542				726	726	725	1—		
Closed				401 100%										

13-15

Tabulation of Media Projects

The computer now takes the information assembled from individual projects and reassembles it in a new tabulation by media (Figure 6).

This forms the basis for the final report which is given to each divisional and product advertising executive.

However, the report does serve another very useful purpose. It is given to all advertising executives so that they can quickly see in summary form the progress of each of their issued projects. Actual expense and income for the prior month are listed, as well as a comparison with the amount of funds released. If current expenditures exceed the funds released, the computer prints an asterisk at the far right of the report, notifying the executive that an overage exists.

What can be done if such a situation arises? If the overage is significant, an additional release of funds should be made by the advertising executive against the same project number so that his accounts are in order. If the overage is inconsequential, then it can be ignored in order to minimize red tape. The following variances from the released funds offer a good guideline as to whether the overage should be ignored:

Size of Job	Variance Permitted
$1– $500	50%
501– 1,250	$250.00
1,251– 2,000	20%
2,001– 4,000	$400.00
4,001–10,000	10%
10,001–20,000	$1,000.00
20,001–over	5%

Product Advertising Expense Report

We now come to the most important report which the computer compiles: a tabulation that goes to each advertising executive who is responsible for the control of expenditures by product groups.

The computer is able to prepare this report because of the storage of information furnished to it in the two previously described reports, tabulation of project status and tabulation of media projects.

Perhaps we should go back to the very beginning, the time when the budget has been approved. Let us assume that an advertising executive has the following budget to operate with for the next fiscal year:

Product	Budget
ADVERTISING	
1. Television	$774,900
2. General magazines	296,270
3. Business magazines	125,410
4. House organs	14,400
5. Photographs	900
6. Directories and catalogs	48,528
7. Pattern books	130,180
8. Pattern engravings	18,000
9. Literature for dealer distribution.	58,280
10. Dealer service	21,760
11. Promotions	286,163
12. Bureau of interior design	9,600
13. Dept. expense (projects only)	68,252
	$1,852,643
Sales promotion (share of several shows produced and administered by advertising)	$66,960
Dept. expense (share of many types of expense, salaries, employee benefits, etc., as detailed earlier in this chapter).	$145,638
Total	$2,065,241

What the advertising executive needs on a weekly or monthly basis is a comparison of his original or revised budget with expenditures and income, released funds via the project initiation, and what is left in his accounts, the unreleased budget.

The product advertising expense report (Figure 7) gives him just that information. The computer is programed with the original budget information on the left side. The various media selected appear spelled out with the money budgeted adjacent to this detail.

Actual expense and actual income for each medium budgeted appears on a monthly and year-to-date basis. As project initiations are accumulated they are tabulated under another column, "Released funds." Naturally, it is this total which is then subtracted from the original budget to arrive at the unreleased budget balances.

Actual expenses and income data appear on this report only as a guide to the progress of the media projects.

When a project has been completed, the overage or underage from the original amount released is summarized in a report of all such

Media projects	Budget or revision	Actual expense Month	Actual expense Year to date	Actual income Month	Actual income Year to date	Released funds Month	Released funds Year to date	Compl. OV-under releases	Unreleased budget
Night TV:									
10012		160	235				500		
10013		1,118	5,535				10,000		
10014		2,780	4,362				9,400		
10636		55,300	275,500			7,000—	275,500		*
15310		3,778	45,993				41,524		*
15405		1,146	1,146				1,030		
Total	774,900	64,282	332,771			7,000—	337,954		436,946
General mags:									
10002		39	335				700		
10003		339	1,934	17—	134—		2,800		
10006		45	235				350		
10140		62,380	107,609			62,380	107,609		*
10147			19,281				19,279		
14965			152				152		
15208		51	671				660		
15268		32	7,408				7,500	11 OV	
15413			3				1,683		
15433			236				8,500		
Total	296,270	62,886	137,884	17—	134—	62,380	149,233	11 OV	147,026
Business mags:									
10141		524	3,210			524	3,210		
10143		10,930	32,814			10,930	32,814		*
10144		1,848	9,118			1,848	9,118		* *
15167			119				144		
15249			1,032				1,120		
15256			2,074				2,656		
15277			675				1,032		
15278			864				920		
15287			2,485				2,248		
15290			135				160		
15291			1,289				1,030		
15292			305				180		
15315			418				432		

15327			272			171	*
15338			254			250	*
15356			1,030			1,080	
15363			1,243			1,140	*
15387		908	964			1,260	
15391		863	1,065			1,080	
15400			941			1,030	
15401			258			192	
15402			313			290	
15404		32	186			126	*
15409			287		112	272	*
15411			385			384	*
15429		77	242			280	*
15434		3	107			1,080	*
15437		603	603			424	
15438		77	81			198	
15442							*
15444		55	55			1,432	
15456		255	255			1,070	
15468		25	25		1,260	1,260	
15470		39	39		48	48	
15478					1,320	1,320	
15487					1,080	1,080	
Total	125,410	16,239	63,143		17,122	70,531	54,879
Pattern books:							
10033			87—			160	
15121		21	2,617	909—		5,200	
15219		18	22,499	1,110—		22,800	
15376			1,860	96—		2,160	
15436		5,451	5,451			5,696	
Total	130,180	5,490	32,340	2,115—		36,016	94,164

Figure 6 Tabulation of media projects.

Media projects	Budget or revision	Actual expense Month	Actual expense Year to date	Actual income Month	Actual income Year to date	Released funds Month	Released funds Year to date	Compl. OV-under releases	Unreleased budget
Night TV	774,900	64,282	332,771	17—	134—	7,000—	337,954	11 OV	436,946
General mags	296,270	62,886	137,864			62,380	149,233		147,026
Business mags	125,410	16,239	63,143			17,122	70,531		54,879
Pattern books	130,180	5,490	32,340		2,115—		36,016		94,164
Patt. engraving	18,000		6,868				8,000		10,000
Dir. and catalogs	48,528	2,593	10,246		61—	2,593	10,281		38,247
Literature			1		1				
Lit. dealer	58,280	2,493	4,334	259—	963—	1,092	17,018	2 OV	41,260
House mags	14,400	945	4,886	40—	140—	928	5,984		8,416
Dealer service	21,760	1,377	12,884	36—	141—	462	13,126	12 OV	8,622
Promotions	286,163	1,194—	208,737	5,468—	29,642—	8,952	263,222	72 OV	22,869
Other media	10,500	1,142	3,814	93—	5,834		7,590		2,910
Total	1,784,391	156,253	817,888	5,913—	27,361—	86,529	918,955	97 OV	865,339
Other expenses:									
Salaries etc.	145,638	15,387	76,994			12,137	60,685	16,309 OV	68,644
Dept. operating	68,252	7,875	38,391			5,687	28,435	9,956 OV	29,861
Sales prom	66,960	3,787	9,878		82—	5,580	27,900	18,104	57,164
Total	280,850	27,049	125,263		82—	23,404	117,020	8,161—	155,669
Total	2,065,241	183,302	943,151	5,913—	27,443	109,933	1,085,975	8,258—	1,021,008

Figure 7 Product advertising expense report.

projects completed and sent to the data center. In this way, the unreleased budget balance in this report is kept current and accurate. Incidentally, the reasons for significant deviations from the budget or project releases are provided in another report to the advertising executive.

Each Armstrong division has a product advertising expense report for every product having its own profit center or profit-and-loss statement.

For example, one division has seven such reports coming to its senior advertising executive.

The computer can then take all the data for these seven different product areas and summarize them into one final report for the division. Such a report is prepared for each division within the company.

Summary of the Computer System

As stated earlier in this chapter, a demand arose for a more complete budgetary control system than could be provided for in the manual system—a system in which the advertising executive receives not only a progress report of his media costs but also a summary of all the costs of his operation. This includes the department costs of freight, postage, salaries, etc. This information is extremely important to advertising executives because their distribution costs (postage, air express, and freight) often equal or exceed the media costs.

It was also important that costs pertaining to sales promotion activities which are the advertising department's responsibility be included in the monthly commodity report.

All this information is very easily obtained from the data center because the controller's department is also using the same facilities for the compilation of cost data as the advertising department. It is simply a matter of reassembling the information and reprograming it for the advertising department.

How has the computer method of budgetary control been of help in forecasting expenditures for the balance of the year? These preliminary "estimated actuals" are usually calculated in September or October (if the budget is on a calendar basis), based on eight months' actual figures plus the latest estimates for the final four months.

The budgetary control accountant can arrive at a good estimate for the year by analyzing the product advertising expense report in two different ways.   If his answer in both cases is nearly the same, he can feel reasonably sure that the factors which he used were accurate. He does this:

1. By extending the actual expense figures, less the actual income, by a factor for the time remaining in the year, adjusted to the rate of activity for each medium for that period.   After this is done for each specific medium and all other expenses in the report, a reasonable "estimated actual" figure can be obtained.

2. By assuming that the budget or revised budget figure is correct for the period to date (this can safely be assumed after possible additions and deletions or transfers from one commodity to another have been made for the year).   The unreleased budget figures should then be adjusted for the number of jobs remaining to be done.   This figure should then be deducted from the budget or revised budget amount.   This second estimate should reasonably be the same figure as that calculated by the first method.

Usually this study is made just prior to the compilation of the budget for the new year.   The reasons for the differences of the "estimated actuals" from the budget or revised budget are noted, and the facts thus revealed become extremely useful in preparing the budget for the following year.   As a matter of fact, it would be almost impossible to bridge the gap from one budget to another without this interim review.   The computer has made this operation faster and more efficient.

SUMMARY

Controlling advertising expenditures by either the manual method or electronic data processing equipment is a necessity in today's business world.   With the tremendous growth that most business will experience in the years ahead, budgetary-control methods must provide fast, accurate, and usable reports.

Depending on circumstances within the specific company, either of these two methods should help solve budgetary-control problems.

PART FIVE
Copy

CHAPTER FOURTEEN

Copy Strategy

WHIT HOBBS *Senior Vice President, Benton & Bowles, Inc.*

We are in business to communicate effectively with our customer. That is our all-important function. To understand our customer, to get to know him well, to like him and be his friend, to help him and inform him and entertain him and challenge him and make him feel good about us and our product and convince him—with enthusiasm and with absolute honesty—that we have something for him that he needs and wants. Something (a product or service) that we believe in and are enthusiastic about—and want to get *him* enthusiastic about, too. And so our job is to get results, to sell a good product to a good customer.

Changes in Advertising Approach

This is not the way it has always been. When I first went into advertising, it was a loud, jingly business. We were convinced that the average mentality of our audience was low, which meant that the only effective way of reaching people was by talking down to them.   Yelling at them, nagging them.   The twelve-year-old mentality—that was our big hang-up a quarter of a century ago.   And in those days a twelve-year-old wasn't the sophisticated youngster he is today; we were convinced that he didn't know much of anything about anything.   So we said to ourselves in our great wisdom, "Let's not do advertising that *we* like, that *we're* proud of; the boobs out there will never get it; it'll be way over their heads."   We practiced what we preached; we talked to the crowd rather than to the customer, and we were very wrong.

Selling in the Singular

Since then, advertising has grown up, and so have the people in it, and our whole attitude toward the public has changed.   Instead of selling in the plural, we have learned to sell in the singular.   Instead of trying to reach everybody, we have learned that it is better to say something special to *somebody*.   It's a tremendous difference.   We have learned to raise our aim and lower our voice and talk to people one at a time.   We have learned how to get close to the customer; today we know him better.   And because we know him better, we *like* him better.   And because we like him better, we *treat* him better.

He feels the same way about us.   He likes us better.   People don't enjoy being hit over the head.   They don't like to be scolded.   They like the personal touch.   It's friendly and flattering.   In this lonely, cold, computerized world, they like being liked.

Advertising Is More Relaxed

And so advertising in the last decade has grown a great deal friendlier and more relaxed.   More conversational.   More involving.   More fun.   More like one friend communicating with another.   This friend of ours, this customer—we have trained him all too well.   He sees through half-truths; he sneers at rigged demonstrations; he has an inner blab-off that tunes out dull, routine messages.   He likes (and *deserves*) advertising that is bright and contemporary and imaginative.   But there has to be more to it than that.   Winning the customer's attention is not enough; we also have to make a selling point, and it has to be the *right* point, and we have to make it stick.

Finding Out the Problem

Which brings us to creative strategy: the all-important first step in effective creative selling.   Creative strategy is getting in close—*first*.   Finding out what the problem is, first, and *then* finding a brilliantly creative way of solving it.   There is all the difference in the world between brilliant advertising that solves a problem and advertising that does not solve a problem and is just brilliant.   How often are we doing it the hard way, the right way?   For my money, not often enough.

You see, there are cycles in our business, and we are currently in a creative cycle.   Creativity is king, and creative people are getting the royal treatment these days.   Anyone who would impose restrictions, discipline, on them is hampering creativity.   And obviously, working to a creative strategy is a very severe discipline.

Thus it follows that a lot of foolish advertising is being done in the name of creativity.   By a lot of foolish, undisciplined people.   And, what's worse, it's being *run*.   Sappy, smart-aleck headlines.   Far-fetched, far-out illustrations.   Posters that are more concerned with making a pun than making a point.   Silly, empty, nonsense commercials that don't *sell* anybody anything.   (My wife says, "I love that funny commercial about the goofy girl who . . . ," and I say, "What was it selling?" and she says, "I don't remember.")   They make the guy who did them look like a genius to his wife and kids; but in the marketplace, they make the advertiser who is paying big money to run them look like a jerk.

Creativity Needs Direction

I am 100 per cent for creativity in advertising, but not total creativity.   What I am against is lack of direction, lack of strategy, lack of *thinking the problem through first*.   I am against advertising that is created in limbo, rather than as a specific answer to a specific selling problem.

I am against turning creative people loose, with no guidelines, no aim; I believe in *directed* creativity.   Which is another way of saying that I believe in doing it the hard way.   I believe in saying to creative people, "Here is the creative selling strategy that has come out of the marketing data and research data, and that has been agreed upon by the client.   Here is the direction.   Here is the job that advertising has to accomplish, the ground it has to cover.   However you do it, this is the target you *have* to hit."

First, carefully define the problem.

Second, determine the creative selling strategy that is going to solve that problem.

Then, and *only* then, turn creative people loose.   With complete freedom.   With no restrictions, no holds barred.   With cotton-pickin' hands kept off.   With all the facts they need.   All the time they need.   All the encouragement they need.

Translating the Strategy into Advertising   They now have the specific problem of taking a specific strategy and translating it into dynamic advertising: into a strong, simple selling idea, brilliantly executed. They have the specific problem of getting people who now think A to think B.   And in order to get that B in a woman's already crowded bonnet, they have to do it in the simplest, boldest, freshest, most original, most compelling, most memorable way possible.

This is the kind of creativity I'm for.   The *directed* kind.   Done by creative professionals who, once they know exactly where they're going, keep coming up with wonderfully ingenious ways of getting there.   Let us look at some examples of what I'm talking about, case histories where strategy made a big difference.

Case History on Furniture Wax

Once upon a time, the top manufacturer of waxes and polishes (S. C. Johnson) came to the agency with a furniture wax that had a clear advantage over competition: it offered speed and convenience because it came in an aérosol dispenser instead of being a paste.   So did the agency immediately assign a creative team to the task of turning out exciting speed-and-convenience advertising?

No.   Instead, the agency immediately began to gather the necessary data from which it would develop marketing and creative strategies.   Step 1: The agency took a long, hard, professional look at the product, the market, the competition, and (most of all) the customer. It wasn't a healthy market.   It was sliding downhill.   What was the problem?   The problem was that women hated to wax their furniture.   It was a chore and a bore.   They did it once or twice a month, and they wished it were even less often than that.   On the other hand, research pointed out that women *dust* their furniture nearly every day.   And (to make a long story very short) this fact led to a strategic question: What would happen if you could somehow find a way of getting that once-a-month furniture wax onto that once-a-day dust cloth?

What happened was a remarkable sales success.   The creative team took this get-it-on-the-dust-cloth creative strategy and came up with the promise of "waxed beauty instantly as you dust."   The results were amazing.   The Johnson product, Pledge, did not stop the decline in furniture waxes; it doubled the market.   It was the right selling idea, the right strategy, the right words and demonstration, all at the right time.   The point is that what happened *couldn't have happened* without the strategy.   And the strategy couldn't have happened without first getting close to the customer and getting a clear understanding of the problem.

Strategy on Disposable Diapers

Procter & Gamble came along with an exciting new product: a disposable diaper that was demonstrably better than the competition. This was the first disposable that was truly flushable; what a great advantage!   What an opportunity!   Over 350 million diapers are used every week.

So did the agency lock the doors and turn on the creative brilliance?   Not until a few facts were faced—and the customer's hang-up was uncovered and carefully analyzed.

Disposable diapers were not new.   They had been around for twenty years or more, and they had been advertised and promoted, and yet, in all that time, they had never been able to capture more than one-half of 1 per cent of this huge market.   Why not?   One reason was because the advertising had always done the obvious; it had positioned the product as a boon and a convenience for the mother.

What did this do for the mother?   How did she feel about the product?   She perceived paper diapers as "a sometime thing" that she used away from home, on motor trips and vacations.   But not all the time.   She had inner feelings about paper diapers.   Mostly it was a feeling of guilt: yes, they made life easier and pleasanter for her, but using them made her feel that perhaps she was being a lazy, extravagant, self-indulgent mother.   She said that if she were using paper diapers and her mother-in-law came to call, she would quickly hide them in the closet or kick them under the bed.

So the agency went to the client with a revolutionary strategy: don't feature your big, competitive advantage—bury it at the very end of the commercial.   Instead of making Pampers better for Mother, demonstrate to her—*prove* to her—that this is a modern diapering system that is superior to cloth.   A better system.   Not better for Mother, better for Baby.   Softer, more absorbent, to keep Baby drier without plastic pants.

Interesting situation: the client comes to the agency with an exciting new technical breakthrough.   The agency does its homework and strongly recommends a strategy that all but ignores this news.   The client finally said, "Okay, it's your baby," and the strategy led to remarkably involving advertising that is changing mothers' minds about paper diapers.   Very successful advertising.   Very successful product.   Thanks to a very successful strategy.

Enough about babies; let's go to the bar!   (From drier babies' bottoms to drier tastes in drinks.)

Problem on Sherry

Harvey's Bristol Cream was a high-class, high-priced cocktail sherry with lagging sales.   Question: Couldn't some of those bright creative guys and gals at the agency come up with something very *clever* that would get people talking about the product—and buying it?

Answer: Yes, bright creative people can always dream up a lot of nifties, but there is more to ringing the cash register than ringing prose.

Instead, the agency decided to figure out the problem.   Why were sales declining?   Why weren't younger customers buying the product?

Changing tastes and fashions and lack of sophistication among younger customers turned out to be the problems.   The trend was to drier drinks at the cocktail hour—bourbon and Scotch and gin.   The trend was to on-the-rocks drinks—in old-fashioned glasses.   ("Is a cocktail sherry a cocktail?   Could you drink it on the rocks?")   Research pointed out that a cocktail sherry was too sweet to hold its own at the cocktail hour.   Creative people could have written headlines that were real winners without the guidance of a sound creative strategy, but left entirely to their own devices they never would have come up with the campaign that ran—and worked.

The creative strategy that developed was this: "Let's reposition the product in time.   *Let's move it* from 5 o'clock to 9 o'clock—from before dinner (where it is too sweet) to *after* dinner (where it isn't so sweet as the liqueurs that are the competition).   Besides, there was an increasing interest in after-dinner drinks.   Rich, heavy desserts were going out of vogue; more and more dinner parties were ending with cheese and fruit and coffee—and a liqueur.

So, working to this new after-dinner strategy, the creative group came up with a very memorable, very competitive selling theme for Harvey's Bristol Cream in its strategic new time slot: "Never serve the coffee without the Cream."   Clever?   Yes, but not just clever for the sake of being clever; clever with a purpose.   What is *really* clever about it is that it is a fresh, memorable way of expressing a timely selling idea that immediately increased sales.   This is the best kind of cleverness there is, the kind that enhances a sound selling idea, strengthens it rather than obscuring it.   The point is that brilliant execution is not enough: great advertising has to be built on a great idea.   Where do great ideas come from?   Very seldom out of thin air, out of the blue.   Most of the solid ones come out of solid facts and hard work and digging.   And teamwork.

On-target Advertising

In today's overcrowded, overcompetitive, overpriced world, there isn't room for empty, show-off advertising that takes up space and doesn't sell anybody anything.   It doesn't stand a chance.   It's a waste of money.   Great advertising has to do more than light up the sky—it also has to hit the target.   It has to be a one-two punch: one, a big idea; two, a brilliant execution.   Which means beginning at the beginning and doing it the hard way.   First, know everything there is to know about your prime customer and about your product and your competition and your market.   Then carefully develop a direction, a strategy; and once you satisfy yourself that it is the *right* strategy, stick with it.

Let your rule be: If it isn't advertising that has a compelling idea, that is on strategy, don't run it.   If the strategy isn't boldly, excitingly executed, don't run it.   If it doesn't grab you, doesn't involve you, challenge you, flatter you, make you feel good, stir you to action, don't run it.   The money you save will be your own.

CHAPTER FIFTEEN

Execution of Copy Strategy in Print Media*

WILLIAM D. TYLER *Creative Consultant*

PROPER EVALUATION OF CREATIVE WORK

The most important function of the brand manager is one for which he has the least training. This is the proper evaluation of creative work the agency submits.

At business school he has learned to measure, grade, and analyze almost every other aspect of his work. Anything that deals with facts and figures is something he is trained to handle. But very little he has learned provides him with guidance when it comes to judging the power of a given creative idea or the potential effectiveness of a creative execution.

Worse, there is no place he can go to learn how to judge creative

---

* Some parts of this chapter are based upon the author's column in *Advertising Age,* copyrighted 1967–1968 by Advertising Publications, Inc.

work, no school, no definitive text.   There probably never will be, so volatile are trends in creative advertising.

This is ironic.   Here he is, bright, educated, ambitious, and well versed in marketing, yet when it comes to making a decision that usually involves his greatest budgetary commitment, one that can do more to influence sales than any other, he is alone and unassisted, untrained and unsure.

Because he is oriented numerically, he is apt to commit a cardinal error.   Rules, formulas, and slide-rule calculations provide him with answers to the other decisions he has to make.   So, very understandably, he looks to similar dicta to help him solve the creative-decision problem.

What he does is to look for a set of rules he can apply to creative work.   He has choice of several.   Each has its merit.   Each has proved its worth in certain situations.   But each and every one is both limited and limiting.   This is because no two advertising problems are identical.   They change with the times, what competition is doing, economic conditions, and even the fact that a given approach has been used before.

Study of Accepted Rules

What is the brand manager to do?   Two seemingly contradictory things.   First, he should study every single set of accepted rules. Second, he must make up his mind that none applies to every situation.   Unlike any other facet of his job, the study of what constitutes success or failure in advertising is an unending one.   It can never be neatly capsulated into a single set of rules, to be pulled out whenever he has to pass a judgment on a creative submission.

By the same token, he must immerse himself in not one, but all the recognized copybook rules of advertising.   He must study Claude Hopkins' "Scientific Advertising."   He must read Rosser Reeves' "Reality in Advertising."   He must read David Ogilvy's "Confessions of an Advertising Man."   He must read William Bernbach on the subject of advertising as an art rather than a science.

He must keep aware of Starch figures on ad readership and Gallup-Robinson impact studies to know how people react.   He must know the principles of the hard-sell school.   And those of its archenemy, the soft-sell school.   He must even keep up with commentators in the trade press for new trends, views, and the reasons behind them.

Personal Involvement   All this is because creative evaluation is the one subject that one never quite learns.   The man who goes furthest is the one who digs deepest.   More than study, it requires personal involvement.   Before one can trust his own reactions to any given advertising, he must include something of himself in that judgment. In other words, he must have a chemical reaction to advertising as well as a rational one.   Successful advertising elicits from the viewer both a logical and an emotional response.

There has never been a time when the need for great proficiency in creative evaluation has been so important.   What has brought it about is that in the past ten years, the advertising "explosion" has resulted in a 65 per cent increase in the volume of advertising.

Has this increase in the advertising noise level lessened the opportunity for the individual ad to be acted upon?   In a word, it has.

Volume Up, Efficiency Down

A Nielsen finding shows that it takes twice as many advertising dollars to gain one share point as it did ten years ago.   As the volume goes up, the efficiency goes down.

Let me state the problem a little more frighteningly.   Figures compiled for General Foods some years ago showed that the average family is exposed to more than 1,500 advertising messages daily.   No doubt the figure is some 65 per cent greater today.   But that is not the point.   The point is that research by the AAAA shows that, of all this barrage of ads, the consumer consciously sees or hears only eighty.

Of those eighty, only 8.4 leave the consumer with a positive or even favorable feeling about the product or service.   So what we are facing today is the realization that it has never been so hard to get through to people by advertising.   It will undoubtedly get harder.

ADVERTISEMENTS THAT BROKE THE RULES

So you can see how important it is to get the best creative work possible from your agency every time.   One way to do this, as I have said, is to take care not to rely on any single set of criteria.   Such reliance serves more as blinders than as illuminating guides.   Here are some examples of advertisements that broke sales records as they broke fundamental creative rules.

Complete Information

A generally accepted rule of creative strategy is this: When you have a product that constitutes a once-in-a-lifetime purchase and a major investment, your ad should supply complete information.   Yet when the depression of the 1930s hit, and piano sales plummeted downward, the most expensive make reversed the trend and actually increased its sales.   It did it with a campaign that gave the prospect no facts or buying information whatever, just a mood picture of a pianist at the keyboard of a Steinway and the slogan, "Instrument of the Immortals." (See Figure 1.)   Copy was assumptive of leadership and quality, leaned on claims like, "the chosen instrument of the masters."

Why did this work?   Evidently the strength of the Steinway, in the public mind, was prestige.   It didn't need factual backup.   So, this approach made the Steinway seem a better value than a cheaper make.

But you might say that the same factor is true in the case of Rolls Royce.   Yet the ad shown in Figure 2, packed with detail about dozens of Rolls features, described in the fullest manner, sold $350,-000 worth of cars in Chicago after one insertion in the *Chicago Tribune.*

Why was this approach successful for Rolls when the opposite was true of the Steinway?   In this case, Americans had a great curiosity about the Rolls, which they knew more for its reputation than for any of its specifics.   So this ad satisfied that curiosity as it sold readers on the quality of the Rolls itself.

Competitive Advantages

Should, then, a good rule be to include competitive advantages in your ad?   Usually, but not always.   Shown in Figure 3 is the most successful auto-loan ad to run in New York over a five-year period. Yet there is not even a hint of a competitive advantage in this ad for Manufacturers Hanover.   No reason is even implied for going to this bank instead of another for your car loan.   Why was it successful? Simply a triumph of creativity; people couldn't get the car with the sponge body out of their minds.   In fact, the bank ran it around town and got added publicity value out of it.

You will notice, however, that at least the headline ("Are You Driv-

STEINWAY
The Instrument of the Immortals

There has been but one supreme piano in the history of music. In the days of Liszt and Wagner, of Rubinstein and Berlioz, the pre-eminence of the Steinway was as unquestioned as it is today. It stood then, as it stands now, the chosen instrument of the masters—the inevitable preference wherever great music is understood and esteemed.

STEINWAY & SONS, Steinway Hall, 107-109 E. 14th St., New York
Subway Express Stations at the Door

Figure 1 (Steinway Pianos) This ad reversed a declining sales trend in the 1930s.

The Rolls-Royce Silver Cloud—$13,550.

"At 60 miles an hour the loudest noise in this new Rolls-Royce comes from the electric clock"

What _makes_ Rolls-Royce the best car in the world? "There is really no magic about it— it is merely patient attention to detail," says an eminent Rolls-Royce engineer.

1. At 60 miles an hour the loudest noise comes from the electric clock, report the Technical Editor of THE MOTOR. The silence of the engine is uncanny. Three mufflers tune out sound frequencies—acoustically.

2. Every Rolls-Royce engine is run for seven hours at full throttle before installation, and each car is test-driven for hundreds of miles over varying road surfaces.

3. The Rolls-Royce is designed as an owner-driven car. It is eighteen inches shorter than the largest domestic cars.

4. The car has power steering, power brakes and automatic gear-shift. It is very easy to drive and to park. No chauffeur required.

5. There is no metal-to-metal contact between the body of the car and the chassis frame—except for the speedometer drive. The entire body is insulated and under-sealed.

6. The finished car spends a week in the final test shop, being fine-tuned. Here it is subjected to ninety-eight separate ordeals. For example, the engineers use a stethoscope to listen for axle-whine.

7. The Rolls-Royce is guaranteed for three years. With a new network of dealers and parts-depots from Coast to Coast, service is no longer any problem.

8. The famous Rolls-Royce radiator has never been changed, except that when Sir Henry Royce died in 1933 the monogram RR was changed from red to black.

9. The coachwork is given five coats of primer paint, and hand rubbed between each coat, before fourteen coats of finishing paint go on.

10. By moving a switch on the steering column, you can adjust the shock-absorbers to suit road conditions. (The lack of fatigue in driving this car is remarkable.)

11. Another switch defrosts the rear window, by heating a network of 1360 invisible wires in the glass. There are two separate ventilating systems, so that you can ride in comfort with all the windows closed. Air conditioning is optional.

12. The seats are upholstered with eight hides of English leather—enough to make 128 pairs of soft shoes.

13. A picnic table, veneered in French walnut, slides out from under the dash. Two more swing out behind the front seats.

14. You can get such optional extras as an Espresso coffee-making machine, a dictating machine, a bed, hot and cold water for washing, an electric razor.

15. You can lubricate the entire chassis by simply pushing a pedal from the driver's seat. A gauge on the dash shows the level of oil in the crankcase.

16. Gasoline consumption is remarkably low and there is no need to use premium gas; a happy economy.

17. There are two separate systems of power brakes, hydraulic and mechanical. The Rolls-Royce is a very safe car—and also a very lively car. It cruises serenely at eighty-five. Top speed is in excess of 100 m.p.h.

18. Rolls-Royce engineers make periodic visits to inspect owners' motor cars and advise on service.

19. The Bentley is made by Rolls-Royce. Except for the radiators, they are identical motor cars, manufactured by the same engineers in the same works. The Bentley costs $300 less, because its radiance is simpler to make. People who feel diffident about driving a Rolls-Royce can buy a Bentley.

PRICE. The car illustrated in this advertisement—f.o.b. principal port of entry—costs $13,550.

If you would like the rewarding experience of driving a Rolls-Royce or Bentley, get in touch with our dealer. His name is on the bottom of this page. Rolls-Royce Inc., 10 Rockefeller Plaza, New York, N.Y.

JET ENGINES AND THE FUTURE

Certain airlines have chosen Rolls-Royce turbo-jets for their Boeing 707's and Douglas DC8's. Rolls-Royce prop-jets are on the Vickers Viscount, the Fairchild F-27 and the Grumman Gulfstream.

Rolls-Royce engines power more than half the turbo-jet and prop-jet airliners supplied to or on order for world airlines.

Rolls-Royce employs 42,000 people and the company's engineering experience does not stop at motor cars and jet engines. There are Rolls-Royce diesel and gasoline engines for many other applications.

The huge research and development resources of the company are now at work on many projects for the future, including nuclear and rocket propulsion.

ROLLS-ROYCE AND BENTLEY

Figure 2   (Rolls Royce) Sold $350,000 worth of cars from one newspaper insertion.

ing a Sponge on Wheels?") contained an urge to buy.   And it is generally agreed that a headline should do this—or at the very least, say something favorable about the product.   Yet in the original Hathaway Shirt ad, the one that was so wildly successful that the client had

Figure 3   (Manufacturers Hanover) Resulted in sizable increase in car-loan business.

to build a new factory, the headline said nothing about the shirt (Figure 4).

It is generally agreed that the strength of "The Man in the Hathaway Shirt" lay in its positioning of Hathaway as smart and fashion-

Figure 4   (Hathaway Shirts) Response was so great a new factory had to be built.

able through understated "snob appeal." Here again a rule was broken for a sound reason. A blatant appeal to buy would have destroyed the image of fashion and quality.

Brand Name In Headline

However, the shirt ad at least had the brand name in the headline, and you would think that this was one rule that should be routinely followed. But occasionally you should break this rule, too, as in the case of the ad for Pretty Feet (Figure 5). This headline, "What's the ugliest part of your body?" not only omits any product reference, but is as indirect as it could possibly be. Yet 50,000 women wrote in for a sample as a result of the offer contained in the last paragraph. More importantly, the ad gets a large share of credit for the widespread national distribution that followed its appearance. The reason for its success was an approach that went all-out for reader interest, and got it.

Parenthetically, when this indirect approach fails, it is a total failure. If the advertiser fails to get the audience for total readership, he is left with nothing. He has failed to register his name, his product benefit, anything. So when you use the "readership" approach, make sure you're going to get it.

The Positive Approach

You would think that one rule should never be broken. That is the one that says you should always take a positive approach. Never accentuate a negative about your product.

Yet when the 3M Company undertook to tackle mighty Eastman in the area of camera film, it simply showed the package and headed it, "so what if the box isn't yellow?" (See Figure 6.) Copy went on to point out that most people think that if film doesn't come in a yellow (or Kodak) box, it just can't be so good. It went on to challenge the reader to buy new Dynachrome and find out for himself, while he saved money at the same time. This approach worked so well for 3M that this unknown brand went to second place in the field within a year or two of introduction.

Single Out Product Category

Another rule it is hard to argue against is the one that says your headline should at least single out the product category. Yet Clairol went on to fame and riches behind a stet headline that gave the reader no clue as to what the subject matter was: "Does she or doesn't she?" (See Figure 7.)

You could say, however, that at least Clairol showed beautiful hair, and no one could ever run a successful ad for a hair product without showing beautiful hair.   You could even be wrong here.   An ad for

What's the ugliest part of your body?

You just said, "my feet", didn't you?
That's typical.
Most women feel their feet are the least attractive part of their body.
Up until now all a woman could do was hide them.
But now there's something you can do to make them pretty.
Not just passable. Pretty.
Now there's a product named, appropriately enough, Pretty Feet.
Pretty Feet is a pleasant roll-off lotion.
Pour a little on your fingers every day of the week and rub it into your feet.
Then see the rough, dead skin roll right off.
Soon you'll have beautiful feet that can wear open sandals...lovely feet that won't hide in the sand at the beach...smooth feet that won't run stockings...soft feet that will be as sexy as the rest of you.
If you're genuinely interested in making the ugliest part of your body pretty, we'll be happy to start you off with a free sample bottle of Pretty Feet.
Just write to Pretty Feet, Dept. H2, Chemway Corporation, Fairfield Road, Wayne, New Jersey.

Figure 5   (Pretty Feet) Buried sample offer brought 50,000 requests.

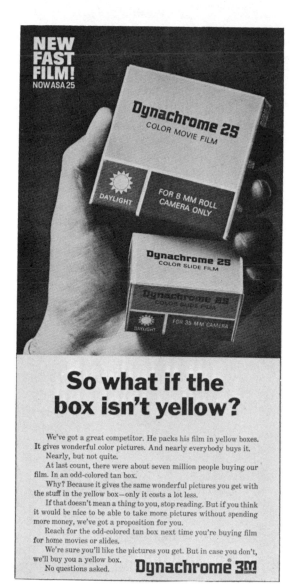

Figure 6 (Dynachrome) Helped put unknown brand into second place in first year.

Figure 7 (Clairol) This approach credited with having built the huge business.

Prell that simply showed a woman wearing a lather hairdo (Figure 8) was not only the best-remembered ad to run in *Good Housekeeping* over a five-year period, but Prell's share hit an all-time high during the time it ran.   Before it did, however, a panel of admen was asked to pass judgment on it.   To a man, they said, "Forget it!"   Fortunately, it was also shown to some women who weren't admen, and they said, "Wonderful!"   What they realized was that, in total, the

Lather hairdo shaped by Enrico Caruso

Drench your hair in luxury
with Liquid Prell...
the extra-rich shampoo!

Figure 8   (Prell) Best-read ad in *Good Housekeeping* in five-year span.

ad said luxurious lather, in a highly memorable and incisive way. That was the advertiser's sole objective.

Short Copy

There is also a rule we will discuss further to the effect that copy, to be read, and to be most effective, must be short.   This is based on the fact that the volume of advertising is so great that people have less time than ever before to spend with any one ad.

Yet an ad for a diet-control product, Ayds, contains well over a thousand words (Figure 9).   One month after this ad appeared, the company had to put on an extra shift.   The reason: When your subject matter, in this case how to get slim, is one the prospect is intensely interested in, you err in *not* giving him a complete story.   He wants to know all you can tell him.

Those are enough examples of the need for keeping free of inflexibility when viewing a creative submission.   What works in one situation does not necessarily work in another; no two are exactly alike. Yet there is a certain body of creative "truths," if you will, which though not infallible, generally obtain in advertising.   I will not attempt to list them here, since I have given several sources already. Having made your selection, a good rule to follow might be to match them against any creative work submitted to you and then, if you find any violation, dig for the reason for the omission.   In other words, don't go on the assumption that since a rule has been violated, the ad is wrong.   The opposite may very well be the case.

CURRENT TRENDS IN COPY

Once you have decided on a body of rules, you must next turn your attention to a more nebulous and volatile set of criteria.   These are current trends.   The advertising business is a hotbed of new trends. It is faddish.   Its practitioners are constantly looking for the new and the different.   As a result, the brand manager is constantly being confronted with advertising that is hard to judge, since it is based on either a fad or a trend which is only now emerging.   It is important for him to know which, because if the approach is based on a fad, it is a passing fancy and may well be passé by the time the advertising appears.   If it is a genuine trend, he may ride on a wave of new interest. So the following section will concern itself with new trends in ad-

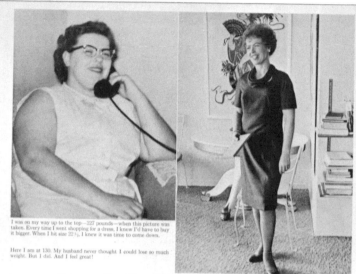

I was on my way up to the top—227 pounds—when this picture was taken. Every time I went shopping for a dress, I knew I'd have to buy it bigger. When I hit size 22½, I knew it was time to come down.

Here I am at 130. My husband never thought I could lose so much weight. But I did. And I feel great!

I stopped crash dieting and lost 97 pounds

By Edith Henderson—as told to Ruth L. McCarthy

I never thought when I went to work in the bakery that I'd turn into a 227-pound cream puff. But that's exactly what happened. Of course, it didn't happen overnight. For fifteen years, I'd been overeating. My job, however, was what tipped the scales. From nine to three, I lived in a world of Danish rolls, sugar-coated doughnuts and plump apple turnovers. The temptation was terrific. And I had little will power. When I wasn't selling, I ate. And when I went home, I didn't stop. In fact, I ate even more.

My husband is a baker. He and I and our three children live on a small farm in Rice Lake, Wisconsin. We have ten acres. On six, we grow corn and oats. On the rest, we have livestock. There's always plenty to do, but the exercise I got doing chores only helped to build up my appetite more.

Our evening meal was the big one. And I really mean big. Meat. Heaps of potatoes, smothered in gravy. Sometimes macaroni and cheese or spaghetti. And plenty of pastry—prune kolachy, berry pie or my favorite, homemade chocolate layer cake.

You can see what made me fat. It wasn't heredity. My six sisters are all slim. It wasn't glandular. It wasn't lack of exercise. It was simply my own oversized appetite that was to blame for the shape I was in.

What made me decide to do something about my weight? Strangely enough, my job, the very job that was helping to make me fatter. You see, at the bakery I was "out in public." I was no longer seeing just chickens and rabbits and calves every day. I was seeing people. And they were seeing me. That's when I began to see myself. There I was—Edith Henderson, in my early thirties, wearing a size 22½ dress. The other girls I worked with were all slim. The contrast was enough to move me to action.

I'd tried dieting before, but never with much success. Once, many years ago, I took a drug. It wasn't for me. Later, I tried crash dieting. Eggs and grapefruit . . . day after day after day until I couldn't stand it anymore. I was so ugly with my family, even they encouraged me to go back to my chocolate layer cake.

This time, however, I was determined to take off the weight gradually and sensibly. I knew, though, that I'd need help. That's when I turned to a vitamin and mineral reducing-plan candy to curb my appetite. I'd read in a magazine about it would help me. Oh yes, one thing more: Misery loves company. So I called a few of my overweight friends to ask if they wouldn't be interested in trying to reduce along with me. They were. So we formed the "Chub Club." Some took reducing drugs. Others tried liquid diet drinks. Still others used will power alone. I was the only one to take the candy, Ayds. And I was the only one to achieve a major weight loss.

What did I have to do on the Ayds Plan? It was really quite simple. The candy contains no drugs. There's nothing in it that made me nervous. I just followed directions — took one or two Ayds before meals, with a hot drink. For me, that was usually a cup of coffee or tea. Fifteen minutes later, I was able to sit down at the table with the rest of my family and eat what they ate. Only I ate less, because my appetite had been curbed and I wanted less.

Where cake and coffee used to be routine when we watched television in the evening, I now take a cup of coffee and an Ayds. It comes in two flavors, you know. There's the caramel kind. And there's the chocolate fudgy kind. I like the caramel kind best, because it's chewier. I have to have something to chew when I'm reducing. I just can't drink a meal.

How much weight did I lose in all? 97 pounds! And I've maintained the weight loss, too. My husband told me later that he never thought I could do it. But I did! And I feel great. I felt good-natured, too, all the time I was on the Ayds Plan. Not irritable like the other times when I dieted. My whole family is just delighted with the new "me." And so am I. I seem to be more popular and have more friends than I ever did. My new figure has caused quite a lot of talk in the town where I was raised, too. A few months ago, I went back for a visit. Someone who'd known me for years stopped me on the street. Only she thought I was my sister. My "skinny" sister. What a compliment that was for me! And so it would be for you, if you'd gone from a size 22½ to a size 12! Thank you, Ayds.

BEFORE AND AFTER MEASUREMENTS		
Before		After
5'4"	Height	5'4"
227 pounds	Weight	130 pounds
40"	Bust	36"
38"	Waist	29"
40"	Hips	36"
22½	Dress Size	12

Figure 9 (Ayds) One month later, factory had to add an extra shift.

vertising.   It is concerned with reader reactions, techniques of execution, and new approaches.

Is Advertising Gaining or Losing?

As advertising has become big business, better brains and more attention have been assigned to it.   The creative people have never been
so talented, nor so highly paid.   There has never been so much research to guide them.   It would seem to follow that advertising
would be more effective today than ever before.

But there is a physical law to the effect that every action produces a
reaction.   The greater our efforts to persuade, the more firmly the
consumer digs in his heels to resist.   And, today's consumer is being
badgered as no human being ever was before him.

In self-defense, he has learned how to screen out ads that do not
pertain to his immediate wants.   The question is: Is he doing a better job than advertising is?   Is the defense stronger than the offense?
The answer seems to be a reluctant "Yes."   The figures for magazine readership indicate a slight decline over the past several years.

However, the noting, or observation, of those same ads has been
rising.   What this seems to say is that we have been smart enough to
pack more of our message into headline and picture, rather than relying on copy blocks, thus obviating the effects of a shorter span of
reader attention.

The message is clear.   We must say what we have to say faster and
with greater impact just to stay even.   (See Figures 10 and 11.)

Copy Writers Who Don't Write

The legendary campaigns of the past were characterized by long
copy.   Pepsodent became the leading toothpaste behind Claude
Hopkins' copy-heavy ads which averaged around 400 words.
Odorono built the underarm deodorant market with an ad by Jim
Young 1,200 words long (Figure 12).

The strength of these ads lay in their *persuasive* quality, something
that requires a total presentation to an unhurried reader.

The major emphasis today is on arresting visual concepts, jarring
headlines, terse copy; elimination of the secondary, sharp focus on a
single selling point.   (See Figure 13.)   What this has tended to develop is a new breed of copy writer; one who does little actual writing.
When he does, it comes in short spurts.   He is taught less how to

write than how to shorten, pare, and excise.   He often sells through inference rather than declaration.

Here the gentle art of persuasion is in danger of being lost.   These ads register their point; they challenge, they influence.   But they do not sell.   Selling requires time and close attention on the part of the

Please hold this newspaper a little further away if you're smoking Benson & Hedges 100's.

AS ADVERTISED IN OVER 100 NEWSPAPERS IN MAJOR U.S. MARKETS.

Figure 10   (Benson & Hedges) Example of a telegraphic delivery of a specific feature.

Figure 11 (Lowenbrau) Example of instantaneous impression of a quality image.

There isn't a girl who can't have the irresistible, appealing loveliness of perfect daintiness

Within the Curve of a Woman's Arm

A frank discussion of a subject too often avoided

A woman's arm! Poets have sung of its grace; artists have painted its beauty.

It should be the daintiest, sweetest thing in the world. And yet, unfortunately, it isn't, always.

There's an old offender in this quest for perfect daintiness — an offender of which we ourselves may be ever so unconscious, but which is just as truly present.

Shall we discuss it frankly?

Many a woman who says, "No, I am never annoyed by perspiration," does not know the facts — does not realize how much sweeter and daintier she would be if she were *entirely* free from it.

Of course, we aren't to blame because nature has so made us that the perspiration glands under the arms are more active than anywhere else. Nor are we to blame because the perspiration which occurs under the arm does not evaporate so readily as from other parts of the body. The curve of the arm and the constant wearing of clothing have made normal evaporation there impossible.

Would you be absolutely sure of your daintiness?

It is the chemicals of the body, not uncleanliness, that cause odor. And even though there is no active perspiration — no apparent moisture — there may be under the arms an odor unnoticed by ourselves, but distinctly noticeable to

others. For it is a physiological fact that persons troubled with perspiration odor seldom can detect it themselves.

Fastidious women who want to be absolutely sure of their daintiness have found that they could not trust to their own consciousness; they have felt the need of a toilet water which would insure them against any of this kind of underarm unpleasantness, either moisture or odor.

To meet this need, a physician formulated Odorono — a perfectly harmless and delightful toilet water. With particular women Odorono has become a toilet necessity which they use regularly two or three times a week.

So simple, so easy, so sure

No matter how much the perspiration glands may be excited by exertion, nervousness, or weather conditions, Odorono will keep your underarms always sweet and naturally dry. You then can dismiss all anxiety as to your freshness, your perfect daintiness.

The right time to use Odorono is at night before retiring. Pat it on the underarms with a bit of absorbent cotton, only two or three times a

week. Then a little talcum dusted on and you can forget all about that worst of all embarrassments — perspiration odor or moisture. Daily baths do not lessen the effect of Odorono at all.

Does excessive perspiration ruin your prettiest dresses?

Are you one of the many women who are troubled with excessive perspiration, which ruins all your prettiest blouses and dresses? To endure this condition is so unnecessary! Why, you need *never* spoil a dress with perspiration! For this severer trouble Odorono is just as effective as it is for the more subtle form of perspiration annoyance. Try it tonight and notice how exquisitely fresh and sweet you will feel.

If you are troubled in any unusual way or have had any difficulty in finding relief, let us help you solve your problem. We shall be so glad to do so. Address Ruth Miller, The Odorono Co., 719 Blair Avenue, Cincinnati, Ohio.

At all toilet counters in the United States and Canada, 60c and $1.00. Trial size, 30c. By mail postpaid if your dealer hasn't it.

Address mail orders or requests as follows:
For Canada to The Arthur Sales Co., 61 Adelaide St., East, Toronto, Ont. For France to The Agencie Américaine, 38 Avenue de l'Opéra, Paris. For Switzerland to The Agencie Américaine, 17 Boulevard Helvetique, Geneve. For England to The American Drug Supply Co., 6 Northumberland Ave., London, W. C. 2. For Mexico to H. E. Gerber & Cia., 2a Gante, 19, Mexico City. For U. S. A. to The Odorono Co., 719 Blair Avenue, Cincinnati, Ohio.

Dr. Lewis B. Allyn, head of the famous Westfield Laboratories, Westfield, Massachusetts, says:

"*Experimental and practical tests show that Odorono is harmless, economical and effective when employed as directed, and will injure neither the skin nor the health.*"

Figure 12   (Odorono) Ad that built the underarm deodorant market.

Figure 13 (Mobil) Example of new trend based on arresting visual and jarring headline.

15-20

prospect.   But these ads are pragmatic.   They know they won't get that kind of loving attention, so they make the most of what they can get.

Just So They Know Our Name

However, this trend toward limited objectives can go too far.   The newest trend is the one that does nothing but burn in the name of the advertiser or the brand.   Such a peculiar trend could never have come into being had it not been for today's advertising explosion.

This proliferation of ads gave birth to a new and negative philosophy that says all a less-than-million-dollar advertiser can hope to accomplish today is to get his name known.   So, be realistic, he is told.   Don't try to sell your product.   You won't even be heard above competition's roar.   Concentrate on just one thing, and you stand a chance of getting that across.

That one thing is name familiarity.   It is true that a well-known name can open doors for salesmen and get acceptance for a brand in a product-parity field.   But still, this is an objective too limited for my taste.   Not, however, for such advertisers as Ron Rico Rum (Figure 14), assorted stockbrokers, mutual funds, and even an insurance company.   More power to them.

Chinese Fireworks

The worst thing about today's cult of creativity in advertising is that it puts the emphasis on spectacular individual ads instead of campaign successes.   Since advertising success depends on continuity and repetition, a single ad, no matter how inspired, cannot be depended on to do anything more than start the ball rolling.   It takes a series, where every ad contributes to the same image or sales message, to ring the cash register in an important, sustained way (see Figure 15).

However, you can't blame the creative man for going all out for variety.   He worries that he will run out of ideas if he has to confine himself to making the same point in a new and brilliant way every time.

He knows that a proof book (or sample reel) full of an eye-popping variety of goodies is his best door opener to a more lucrative job.   A book full of look-alikes, even though backed by sales-success stories, is not so impressive in the marts of creativity today, sad to relate.

Figure 14   (Ronrico) Campaign that succeeded through establishing name familiarity.

The trouble is, there are agencies that encourage the Chinese-fireworks type of campaign.   *And* clients who allow themselves to be bowled over by scatter-gun brilliance rather than insisting on adherence to the agreed-upon strategy.

What Is Happening to the Headline?

Ad makers spend a lot of time worrying about the illustration. They knock themselves out polishing the copy.   But it's the headline that gets read by five times the number who read the text.   And it's

Figure 15   (Marlboro) This series was successful for at least 15 successive years.

the headline that can translate an outstanding picture into buying action.

Finally, if, as someone said, the headline is 80 per cent of the advertisement—shouldn't we stop and see what's happening to it?

There are three things.   First, we have the "delayed take" trend. That's the headline that's divided in two—usually by a picture or an expanse of white space.   Ideally, the second half is not used to complete the thought, but rather to add an unexpected snapper. This snapper may simply reinforce the message in the first half— or it may add another dimension.   (When used incorrectly, as it often is, it is nothing more than a gag, added for laughs.)

Figure 16 is an excellent example of the delayed take at its best: "Don't wait to order a Sau-Sea Shrimp Cocktail."   This appeared over the picture of a ready-to-serve shrimp cocktail with the lid off. Second half of the headline read: "Open one."   This to underline ease and convenience.

The second major trend is variously called the "verbless headline" and the "*the* headline."   Examples are all around us: "The Paper Car," "The Whichwatch," "The Bathing Suit Shave."   They range from just great ("The Panic Button" for Whirlpool air conditioners) to something else again ("The Quiet Drink" for some whiskey).   (See Figure 17.)

As a trend, this is a dangerous one.   Reasons: Such headlines are passive (because verbless), product-oriented (no obvious self-interest to the reader), and ask no action from him.

Best Headlines Offer Rewards   What characterizes the best headlines today?   The same thing that has always provided the number-one base for a great headline: A reward for the reader in terms of a benefit or a promise.   Four out of five of the best ones last year (in this writer's opinion) held out such a promise.   Of these, one out of five did so obliquely, while the rest offered a reward directly.

The third important trend is the "incomplete headline."   This is the headline that addresses itself to the picture.   Without the picture, it is meaningless.   With the picture, the circuit is completed, and the bulb lights up.   This is a technique that can result in great advertising.

Examples: A picture of two Volkswagens parked in a single parking-meter space is headed, "It's perfectly legal" (Figure 18). Blue Cross shows a nurse tenderly cradling a newborn baby.

Don't wait to order a shrimp cocktail.

Open one.

Figure 16 (Sau Sea) Example of the "delayed take" headline approach.

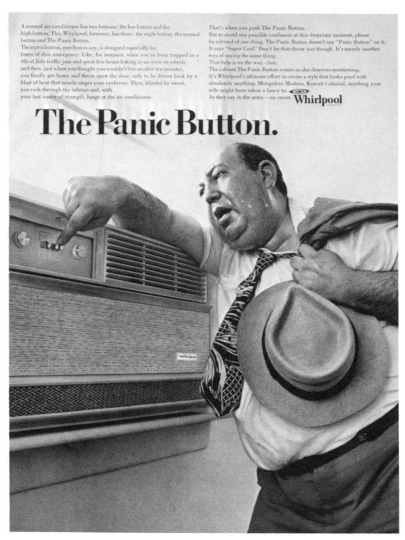

A normal air conditioner has two buttons: the low button and the high button. This Whirlpool, however, has three: the night button, the normal button and The Panic Button.

The extra button, needless to say, is designed especially for times of dire emergency. Like, for instance, when you've been trapped in a 4th of July traffic jam and spent five hours baking in an oven on wheels and then, just when you thought you wouldn't live another ten minutes, you finally get home and throw open the door, only to be driven back by a blast of heat that nearly singes your eyebrows. Then, blinded by sweat, you rush through the inferno and, with your last ounce of strength, lunge at the air conditioner.

That's when you push The Panic Button.

But to avoid any possible confusion at this desperate moment, please be advised of one thing. The Panic Button doesn't say "Panic Button" on it. It says "Super Cool." Don't let that throw you though. It's merely another way of saying the same thing.

That help is on the way—*fast*.

The cabinet The Panic Button comes in also deserves mentioning. It's Whirlpool's ultimate effort to create a style that looks good with absolutely anything. Mongolian Modern, Kuwait Colonial, anything your wife might have taken a fancy to.

As they say in the army—no sweat. **Whirlpool**

The Panic Button.

Figure 17 (Whirlpool) Example of the "verbless headline" at its best.

It's perfectly legal.

In New York City, it's often possible to get two VWs into one parking meter space.

And both are within the law. So long as both are within the meters.

(Who pays the dime? It doesn't matter, just so that one of them does.)

We're telling you this for two reasons:

If you're a VW owner, we want you to know it's okay to keep on doing what you've been doing all along.

And if you're not a VW owner, we want to let you in on some of the ways a VW can make little problems out of big ones in New York.

For instance, you spend less time driving around and around and around the block in a VW. You can usually pull into a place the big cars had to pass up.

You learn to take leftovers. (The end of a block, odds and ends next to building entrances, etc.)

Parking attendants will sometimes wave you in when the sign says 'Lot Full.' (And if you rent garage space by the month, you can often get it for less because a VW takes less.)

In short, one of the nicest things about driving a Volkswagen in New York City is parking it.

It gives you the feeling you're getting away with something.

Even when you're not.

Figure 18 (Volkswagen) An "incomplete headline," i.e., requires picture to complete sense.

Headline, designed to make the point that Blue Cross is a nonprofit enterprise: "All the profit we need." And a one-word headline, "California," does not say much without the picture. That shows two cars passing in opposite directions, one with skis on back, the other with a surfboard on the roof.

This marriage of words and picture into a single, meaningful, jolting expression of a selling idea, is creativity at its peak.

Farewell to the Old "One-Two"

A venerable and once highly regarded school of advertising is finally and grudgingly biting the dust.

This is the old one-two. One, the ad strained to reach out and grab the reader. Not to make a point, you understand; just to get his attention any way it could. Two, once you had that, you embarked on your selling story.

The one-two approach made eminent sense in its day. That day was when ads were fewer, and there were less demands on the reader's time. It made for intriguing ads, and if you weren't too rushed, you'd wade through and rather enjoy them.

There's too much going on today; too many ads, too many media, too many things to buy. So the old one-two has lost its punch.

What is taking its place is a telescoping of one and two into a big fat one. Your attention getter today has to make your selling point. Or, put another way, your selling point has to be presented in a highly arresting way. It has to be the star of the show. You have only one shot at your prospect, so you cannot waste it on a light, warm-up jab. You've got to hit him with your Sunday punch with no preliminaries. Or risk not reaching him at all.

There is no one best way to do this. It can be done facetiously or seriously, factually or imaginatively. (See Figures 19 through 22.) It isn't so important how it's done—that's up to the creator and his particular talent—as that it be done. This is the most difficult and demanding challenge the creative man has ever faced—to deliver the product's prime advantage in such a way as to do three things: interrupt, make memorable, and finally, burn in. Never before has so much been asked of creative people.

The "We're Not Perfect" School

There is a new wave of copy that pokes fun at the product. In amateurs' hands, this results in a sickeningly Uriah Heepish pose.

Worse, the self-kidding can take over the ad and bury the favorable claims.   Finally, it takes a stouthearted client to sit still for a pie in the face.

Once having overcome these obstacles, as so many have, the benefits are several.   Credibility, for one.   If you come clean about your

Figure 19   (Metrecal) Crystal-clear presentation of theme: "Indulgence without penalty."

Figure 20 (Du Barry) Device allows reader to make a self-demonstration.

15-30

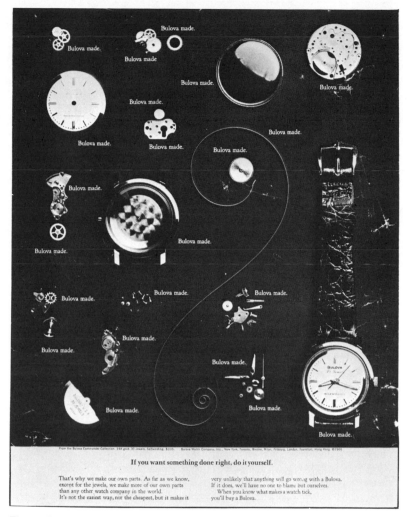

Figure 21   (Bulova) Objective: to establish Bulova quality at a glance.

weaknesses, the reader is more inclined to believe your claims about strengths.

Another is the shock value of belittling oneself in a world of self-awarded encomiums.   You're sure to get attention.   That is, until everyone starts following suit.   Still another virtue of this new school

Figure 22   (Schaeffer) Even a promotion ad can deliver its message with telegraphic speed.

is that it wins friends and disarms enemies as it presents the product realistically and modestly instead of heroically and belligerently.   In a word, this is the approach based on candor.

Some examples: Volkswagen all but started the whole trend with an ad several years ago headed: "Lemon." The point: VW inspectors have very rigid standards and occasionally we have to turn back a car that doesn't meet them (Figure 23).

Volvo took an even bigger chance. It illustrated the car in the most unfavorable image it can have. That occurs when a city car is being dug out of a snow pile after having been buried for a week on a side street. Headline: "If you don't have a garage you should have a

Figure 23   (Volkswagen) Example of the "we're not perfect" school.

car that doesn't need one." A good way to visualize toughness and resistance to unfavorable conditions.

Dynachrome, in the ad cited before, hailed its ". . . great competitor. Packs his film in yellow boxes. Ours comes in an odd-colored tan box." Such an approach conditions the reader to a thoughtful consideration of the claim that follows. That claim, in effect: just-as-good pictures for less money.

Avis manages to convince you it tries harder because it is number two. Horn & Hardart used to say, "Come on in. It's not fancy. But it's good." Canada Dry reversed the order: "Our Quinine Water is less bitter, has more bubbles and is the largest seller. . . . Otherwise, it's like any other."

But when all is said and done, Volkswagen is the master of this technique. A car on its back is titled: "Will we ever kill the bug?" Copy: "We experimented with a bigger beetle, but it was something awful. True, we make an ugly little car and keep getting away with it. But that's no reason to make an ugly big one and press our luck." Against a background of Detroit bombast over the years, this approach has been highly successful.

End of an Era

The Lava ad shown in Figure 24 is the one that could never have run. Yet it did.

It was bought and paid for by the one client in the world who has stood foursquare down the years against everything this represents. Procter & Gamble built advertising's mightiest juggernaut on strict adherence to one principle: the positive approach.

Never be indirect, never be negative, never admit a shortcoming. Say something superlatively positive about the product, and say it in the clearest, most unmistakable way you can. Don't rely on humor; it may distract the reader.

If you can make your point more ingratiatingly through implication, don't. State, claim, assert, never infer.

With all that doctrine in their upbringing, plus a record of advertising successes unmatched by any other advertiser in any field, how could this headline happen in a Lava Soap ad: "World's worst bath soap."

It is indirect, negative, unclear, lighthearted, and without even an implication of product virtue. The reason this ad is so important has nothing to do with whether it is any good or not.   Its importance is solely historic.   It bangs shut the door on one era and puts the official stamp on a new one.

The days of advertising success through mere assertion are about over.   The public has become more selective in the products it chooses and the ads it reads.   There was a time when sheer weight and repetition of a claim could assure success.   No more.   Now you

Figure 24   (Lava) The ad that ended an era.

have to do a better job of interesting and convincing the prospect than your competitors do.

No longer are dollars and rate per thousand the controlling factors. The one that is, is *un*measurable. It is the skill of the creative man.

If the Shoehorn Fits

There is a lot of bad advertising in magazines today that can be blamed on television.

What has happened is that advertisers are trying to shoehorn television techniques onto magazine pages. The reasoning goes like this: My TV campaign is successful. Therefore, I should adapt the same approach to print. Not only should it be equally successful there, but it will serve to reinforce my TV messages.

Just one flaw. A technique developed for television often just does not translate to the printed page. Procter & Gamble had a fantasy character for Ivory Liquid named Mary Mild. She was a Mary Poppins dressed as an Irish housemaid, and she floated around the television screen symbolizing, hopefully, the help your hands get from use of Ivory Liquid for dishes.

Transferred to a magazine page, she looked as though she were dangling from a tree, and the whole thing looked preposterous.

For Comet Cleanser, there is a highly effective trade character named Josephine. On television, this gravelly voiced lady plumber comes to fix stopped-up drains and incidentally show the housewife how to get rid of sink stains with Comet. But transferred to print, she becomes merely an endorser of the product, and a rather incongruous one at that (Figure 25).

Van Heusen Shirts ran an absolutely hilarious commercial in which an entire family of Chinese laundrymen struggled vainly to iron out the permanent crease in the shirt. But when this appeared as a print ad, it was just another quite good ad.

On television, Polident, a denture cleaner, has an arresting demonstration in which an egg is stained with iodine only to have Polident slowly dissolve that stain before your eyes. The print version, somehow just lays there.

Tide had an exceptionally fine demonstration campaign, consisting of having a woman put one garment inside another, then knot the bundle and throw it in the washer. Later it was removed, un-

Figure 25 (Comet Cleanser) Example of poor adaptation of good television campaign into print.

knotted, and the inner garment came out spotlessly clean, to illustrate the product's unusual cleaning abilities. In print, this same sequence comes out as a tedious and rather boring collection of pictures and captions.

Moral: The proponents of adaptation intend to gain penetration through repetition. But penetration and repetition of what? In most cases, they are trying to burn home a technique of presentation. But that is not the point. What you want to sink in is the basic selling message itself. To do that best requires the technique that best fits the medium, not shoehorning a technique from one medium to another.

When Is "Derogatory" Advertising Derogatory?

A crackdown on derogatory advertising is under way. The industry has gone on record against competitive references that are either "untrue or unfair." Watch that word "unfair."

It stems from a justifiable fear that today's trend toward direct comparisons with named competitors in ads, as in Figures 26 and 27, can eventually lead to name-calling, mudslinging, and finally, unfair denigration of others.

But what is the line that separates fair from unfair? And who is to judge? Is Ford unfair to Rolls when it advertises, "Quieter than a Rolls Royce?" Or do both benefit from the publicity? And is the public the eventual winner? Or loser?

The Gordian-knot way to solve the "derogatory advertising" problem is simply to forbid any direct reference to a competitor. Yet this could be the worst thing that ever happened to advertising.

Most advertising down the years has done little more than say sweet nothings about a product. As a body of reading matter, it must be just about the dullest ever compiled. It has contained less information, fewer facts, than almost any service material ever written. It has relied mainly on adjectives, on charm, on manner of presentation, coupled with unspecific, unsupported claims of superiority.

It has, nevertheless, served us and the community well. But times have changed. Advertising that does nothing but heap praise on a product begins to lose effectiveness when either of two things happen. The public becomes ad-sophisticated. Or the volume becomes so huge that it is impossible to get people to focus on a nonsubstantive message. Since these two conditions have simultaneously converged upon us, advertising must make a violent adjustment.

Some advertisers have found the way. By coming right out and naming names, making side-by-side comparisons, talking frankly about their competitive advantages in specific terms, they have made their ads stimulating, informative, and rewarding to the reader. True, there's a terrible risk there. In the hands of unscrupulous practitioners, this will inevitably lead to "unfair" comparisons.

Figure 26   (Personna Blades) Example of calling a competitor by name.

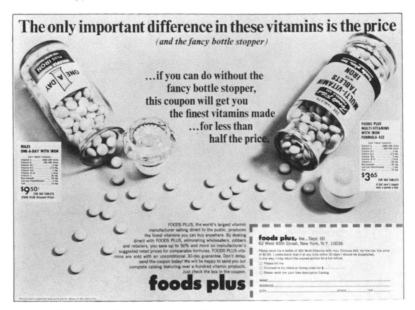

Figure 27   (Foods Plus) Example of combative approach designed to pit a brand against a leading competitor.

"Untrue" ones, of course, can be handled legally. But there will be borderline cases involving "unfairness."

Advertisers generally want to hold on to this method of communication. It may well be the most vital new creative weapon to have come into their hands in many years—the direct reference to competition, fairly handled. Cut it off, and they lose. Let it run amok—everyone loses. This is the most intricate problem the business has ever faced. It must be solved in such a way as to permit us to continue this combative, outspoken, challenging advertising approach without at the same time fouling our own nest.

The easy answer is to legislate out of existence all references to competitors. (Remember, *any* reference can be termed "unfair.") A course of action is needed to obviate this. Its lack may put an end to the most lively, creative movement in advertising history.

CHAPTER SIXTEEN

Execution of Copy Strategy in Broadcast Media

DONALD BRIGHT BUCKLEY *Director, Kahn/Buckley*
Associates Inc.

It is vital that we start this chapter with a strong disclaimer.   This is
not a "how-to" essay that can help you turn out sales-producing, prize-
winning, talk-provoking broadcast commercials by next Tuesday.
That's the job of a specialist within your agency who lives or dies
by his reputation for doing just that (and perhaps only that) day in,
day out.   If anything, this is a "how-not-to" treatise that, it is hoped,
can help you help him to help you—by understanding him and his
job rather than attempting to do it yourself.   Many a good brand
manager has alienated both his agency and his own management by
the understandable but erroneous belief that anybody can write a
commercial.

DIFFERENCE BETWEEN BROADCAST AND
PRINT EXECUTIONS

There are many ways to differentiate between execution in print and
broadcast.   My favorite is fairly Freudian.   Imagine yourself sitting

on a bench in the park. To your left is a statue. You can sit and stare and study just as long as it holds your interest. If you like you can come back tomorrow and look some more. But to your right, walking past you is a beautiful dame. In less than a minute she'll walk through your life and disappear. Maybe you'll see her walking by again sometime. But even if you do, you only have a fleeting impression. The depth of that impression depends upon the dame. Print ads are like statues. Broadcast commercials are like dames.

Maybe that's why you can load up a print ad with lots of information when it's pertinent and interesting. Back in 1948, my old boss, Wilbur VanSant, used to say, "A man with a bellyache will read a whole column on paregoric." And it's true. But when it comes to broadcast, remember, nobody stares at fat ladies.

You'll find we'll come back to the dame analogy a couple of more times. That's because broadcast executions are elusive, tender, and easily crushed. It fits.

Sins in Execution

In my opinion, there are many deadly sins in executing broadcast commercials. Number 1 is the mere exposition of the strategy in toto. Number 2 is totally ignoring the strategy.

Sadly, the 1950s saw too many of the former. And sadly, the 1960s were bent upon the latter. Yet happily, there seem to be enough dedicated, talented, experienced (and hardheaded) creative men around to turn out solid advertising with a brilliant flair no matter what the trends and fads may be. And let us not ignore the courage, confidence, and judgment of that elite group of clients who buy the good ones.

Radio and Television: Similar yet Disimilar   Let us consider some more deadly sins. Number 3 is the belief that radio commercials and television commercials are just about the same except that one has visual aids. No dice. If a TV sound track works as a radio commercial, there's too much going on in the TV version. You're not letting the pictures work for you. And it follows that a good radio commercial can't convert to TV just by adding film.

Actually, nowadays, both are graphic mediums in a sense. One has visible pictures, the other has mental pictures.

It follows therefore that television is the medium of demonstration. And radio is the medium of imagination. Let's clarify that one before it's wildly misinterpreted.   This concept was horribly abused in the early days of TV.

Demonstration does *not* mean a mandatory side-by-side comparison of your product and Brand X.   Rather it means *show* the viewer your story, your idea, your product, its benefits.   Show instead of tell. Demonstrate to speed up the learning process.

By the same token, *imagination,* in terms of radio, does *not* mean everything must be far-out fantasy.   Rather it means stimulate the theater of the mind instead of sitting there talking.   After all, the listener doesn't have to listen.   And most of the time, he's doing something besides just listening: waking up, working, or driving a car.   Radio's strength is its weakness.   While it's the constant companion, it seldom demands exclusive attention.   So the degree to which you stimulate the listener's imagination has a lot to do with the depth of penetration and remembrance of your story.

Of course, there are exceptions to these generalizations.   In this business rules are constantly broken rather than written.   Great presenters, celebrities, showmen with a knack for "telling it like it is" can often do just that.   And bona fide news, if it's really news, should be presented as news, not hidden under a slick production number. Case in point: the introduction of True cigarettes.   Within three days after the Rosewell-Park report on tar and nicotine content was released showing True to be a significant winner, both radio and television carried taped, low-pressure, "Honest John" reports of the news.   News treated as news.   In fact, one commercial so resembled a news bulletin, the networks required the addition of a disclaimer supered over the opening of the commercial.

Fluid Media   Radio and television are fluid media—multilevel fluid media.   They exist only in film or tape *or mind.* The printed word, the script, the storyboard, the shot list, the fact sheet, and the strategy *are not* the commercial.

There is no perfect way of presenting broadcast commercials.   But there surely is a wrong way: read them.   Never!   That's deadly sin number 4.   Listen.   Dream.   Imagine.   Talk them out.   And don't be shaken by surprises.   They happen.   Usually for the good. But watch the face and moisture on the palms of the man who carried the seed in his brain.   If he's ecstatic and he's good, bet with the house, but don't drag out a limp, folded, spindled, and tattered storyboard and think that it's a commercial.   It's a blueprint of sorts and

a communications tool.   But it's a long way from perfect because it
doesn't move.   It's a statue, not a dame.

THE TOOLS OF THE CREATIVE MAN

Nevertheless, before we go any further, let's spend a few paragraphs
on the most familiar tools, no matter how inadequate they may be,
that are used in dealing with commercial ideas before they actually
become commercials.

The Script

The script is common to both radio and television, even though the
two scripts may look somewhat different.   Classically, the radio
script is a double-spaced paragraph in the neighborhood of 120 words
per minute with sound and music instructions tossed in as they fall in
caps and parentheses.   (Dialogue scripts resemble plays.)
    The television script is usually divided into two vertical columns.
The left is typed in caps giving picture or video instructions.   In
the adjacent portion of the right-hand column the script and audio
instructions appear.
    Nowadays not enough people bother to write out a bona fide televi-
sion script, but go directly to rough storyboards.   Frankly, I miss
them.   I remember the early days of Revlon's historic television era
when *all* commercials, even some of the shade promotions for lipstick
and nail enamel, were shot *live* just from scripts, set designs, and cos-
tume sketches.   No storyboards.

The Storyboard

Since the beginning of television, the storyboard has been the basic
blueprint and communications tool for the production of the television commercial.   There exists much controversy today as to
whether the storyboard is a help or a hindrance.   In my opinion,
much of the answer rests in whether emphasis is given to the first or
second half of the word: "story" or "board."
    The mere physical existence of a series of drawn frames with video
instructions and audio copy typed under them can be of no value unless the *story* clearly emerges.   The *story* is important, the *board* is
not.
    Oddly enough, the man who taught me most about storyboards

had never worked in television.   Back in 1949 I had occasion to work with Will Eisner, president of American Visuals Company, on a series of training manuals.   Although he hates the phrase, these were done in "comic strip" form.   Prior to this commercial venture, Will had been the daddy of a cartoon strip called "The Spirit" (among others). The distinguishing characteristic of this strip was the incredible amount of action implied in Will's drawings and the limited amount of balloon copy.   Things happened in "The Spirit," and you sensed it by merely scanning the page.   So before the true growth period of television even began, Will Eisner was turning out magnificent action-packed storyboards.

Purpose of the Storyboard   Bear in mind that you are holding an inanimate object that does not move, lacks the plasticity of film, makes no sound, has no music, and is generally crudely drawn.   It is not a commercial.   It is a tool which is often inadequate, but perhaps the most inexpensive and rapid way of gaining understanding and agreement among the many persons who will be involved in the production of the television commercial.

I guess Will's favorite story about the cavemen sums it up best. Od and Ug were having a heated discussion one day and were faced with a complete failure in communication.   Finally, in desperation Od said to Ug, "Leave me draw you a picture."   That's how we got the famous cave drawings in the south of France.

Often the television writer will make a rough "miniboard" to help communicate to his art director what he has in mind.   Just as often, nowadays, the television art director may start the process with a rough graphic concept, calling in his writing counterpart for help. (And in some cases there are renaissance guys who can do the whole thing by themselves.)   As the writer and art director work together, a more polished storyboard emerges where the design of the commercial becomes more apparent and the action implications are sharpened.   At this stage, the storyboard helps the agency account group understand the intent of the commercial.   Next, it helps the many echelons of the advertiser.   The storyboard also provides a basis for communicating with production companies in obtaining bids. Their initial attention to the storyboard deals primarily with technical requirements that emerge, size of set or location, types of equipment required, talent costs, length of shooting, and so on.

After approval is obtained on a commercial, sometimes the first step in production is to create a shooting board in which finer attention is given to camera moves, opticals, and editing techniques while in the stages of preproduction with the film company.   This can be a waste of time or a great advantage, depending on the complexity of the commercial.   If the desired technique is intricate, involves extreme cutting, montages, color communication, or great imagery, it can be a help, but only to the people who are sufficiently technically oriented to understand it.

Hindrances of the Storyboard   Once again let me emphasize that this is a blueprint and communications tool—not the commercial. Whenever an advertiser or an agency directs his production house to "shoot the board," he is depriving himself of the immense potential creative contribution of the "hot" director and cameraman he has haggled so hard to get for the job.   The other extreme can be equally disastrous.   Certainly, this is no time to start from scratch on a basic idea.   Under any circumstances, the finished commercial must reflect the strategy and intent implied by the storyboard.   A middle ground must be reached through the strength of the agency people who have the trust and confidence of the advertiser.   When this ideal relationship is established, beautiful nuances can be built into a commercial by intent or even by "happy accidents."

Some years ago, one of the major soap companies experimented with a storyboard which had three typewritten sections under each drawn frame: (1) video instructions, (2) audio, (3) objectives.   A hue and cry went up among the creative people in their stable of agencies that this was mechanistic, busy-work, and unnecessary.

Upon reflection, however, the idea has great logic.   Often, by stating what it is you are trying to accomplish by a given sequence of film, you not only refine your picture content and audio at the conceptual stage, but also communicate more clearly to your production house what you are trying to say and do and why.   The longer you work with this system, however, the more you realize that such a statement of objectives is more easily accomplished and with stronger results, if instead of attempting to write objectives for each frame, you prepare an overall statement of objectives.

Different Types of Storyboards   Historically the storyboard has consisted of from twelve to eighteen pictures, each of which is accompanied with a written video section explaining what is in the picture, camera moves, optical effects, etc., and an audio section explaining music, sound, and script.   Some agencies prefer to lay them out one frame per page and present the commercial in flip-chart form. Others lay them out horizontally with approximately twelve frames per page.   Still others lay them out vertically with four to six frames per page.   In many cases, it is a matter of personal taste.   Yet there are advantages for each of these techniques.   One frame per page helps everyone discussing the storyboard concentrate his attention on what is being discussed at that precise moment without wandering forward or backward to other frames.   While the horizontal technique of twelve frames per page has the danger of permissive wandering, on the other hand it often provides a better overall grasp of the graphic concept.

THE SIX-FRAME BOARD.   This type is very much in vogue today, and works best where there is a good working relationship between a top agency TV team and a knowledgeable client.   It reduces the concept to a simple clear-cut representation of the real key graphics. It leaves out the editing-room pyrotechnics, because the team instinctively knows how they're going to put it together.   They're after agreement on the solid skeleton.

THE ONE-FRAME BOARD.   This method is best applied when the commercial is truly built around one powerful graphic idea.   You use one drawing or scrap photograph to indicate the central idea, then talk your way through the commercial with a script.   It works well where a commercial depends heavily on a central-character study or an interesting location or set.   Another variation is an actual sketch of the set—and you walk your fingers through it to communicate your idea.   Some agencies I've known use this with paper dolls of the lead characters, moving them around.

THEN THERE'S THE NO-BOARD BOARD.   The cycle now completes itself and you're back to a script and a key prop and a great presenter. Sometimes, the theater of the mind can more clearly understand a commercial concept this way than with all the rough or comprehensive drawings in the world.

THE ALMOST-FINISHED-COMMERCIAL BOARD.   There's a great temptation to shoot a series of stills or test film or tape to show commercials that are almost air quality.   It frequently backfires.   You're almost finished—but not quite.   You've come so close but are missing the final polish of professional production nuances.   I've seen it work like crazy—or fall on its face.

Now that we've glanced over the mechanical tools, let's take up the far more important creative and psychological tools, rules, theories, and practices in broadcast execution.

THE INCREDIBLE IMPORTANCE OF EXECUTION IN BROADCAST

You can construct the most perfect marketing plan, product profile, competitive analysis, and creative strategy—and still blow the whole bundle.   The only thing the consumer sees and hears is the execution.   Think about that for a minute: The thing the marketers know least about and the creative man knows most about is often dominated by the introspective view of a marketer.   And all the groundwork can be meaningless if the intimate, convincing moment of communication is self-serving to the advertiser instead of the consumer.

To make things worse, we live in an age of parity products.   By the time you've innovated your product, your competitor's lab has stuck it under a spectroscope (or hired your top guy in R&D) and is hot on your heels with virtually the same thing.

And now, let's consider that we have spent all the postwar years with the marketing maw chewing up every unique strategic or positioning idea that an entire industry can offer.   There may be no totally new ideas—or at least not enough to go around.   All that is left to separate your product or service from the industry cliché is the uniqueness and excellence of your execution.   So if it requires consideration of something unfamiliar or expensive—consider it.   It may be the only fuse that can detonate the swamp.

The Endless Debate: Creative versus Media

One can build a strong case for either side: (1) Write the best commercial you can.   If it comes out as 30 seconds, run a 30-second commercial.   If it takes 60 seconds, run minutes.   Or (2) figure out the best possible media buy.   If 30-second commercials are more efficient, write 30-second commercials, etc.

Neither is totally realistic.   One ignores the money realities.   The other ignores the communications problem.   Somewhere in between with professionalism and mutual respect, the answer must be found in each case.

The most efficient media plan can't work with a weak 30-second commercial. Neither can the world's best minute commercial deliver enough customers if not enough people see it. And the real dilemma is that this is one of those decisions that research can't solve because you're adding apples and oranges.

Nevertheless, "target" length should be discussed before your first attempts at execution of your strategy. It makes a difference in the "mind clock" which every good broadcast copy writer has developed. You simply think differently in trying to solve a problem in 30 seconds as opposed to 60 seconds. And this preapplied discipline can help you from becoming embroiled and in love with an idea that simply can't live in 30 seconds.

Don't, however, dismiss the other side of the coin. If a great minute commercial emerges and your best pro's simply can't bring off a strong 30—it's time to go back for a heart-to-heart talk with your media director.

SIX STRATEGIC DECISIONS

Every creative director has his favorite form of organizing strategic information. But most strategies include at least six critical decisions:

1. Who's your friend? Or whom are you talking to and trying to convince?

2. Who's your enemy? Is it a competitor or some other obstacle—even apathy?

3. What's good? Or what real consumer benefit exists in people terms?

4. Why should I believe? Or what's in or around the product or service that substantiates the benefit above?

5. Who's talking? Or what personality are we projecting for the advertiser, tone of voice, etc?

6. Anything else? Are the "musts" and lists really necessary or merely cluttering up the air?

Strategies are seldom briefer and often longer. Sometimes they even start defining execution ideas. I find these needlessly limiting. Nevertheless, it brings up an interesting disclaimer. No one I know can accurately and clearly define where strategy stops and execution begins. Nor can he define where execution ends and production begins. With any good commercial they flow into each other smoothly and the seams never show.   They are like dissolves instead of cuts.   But that's production talk.   And I hope to limit this chapter to a minimum of technical production, dwelling mainly on the creative philosophies of execution of strategy.

Without needlessly rehashing how one arrives at strategic decisions, let's take a moment to understand the critical importance of these building blocks as we enter the stage of broadcast execution.

Personal Form of Communication

First, remember, you're dealing with a highly personal form of communication that is part of a person's life.   His nightly bout with television can soothe away a hectic day, transport him to a stadium or bring the horror of war crashing into his den—while her daytime hours can be lightened by a soap opera or enlightened by history in the making.   And radio, the constant companion, lessens the loneliness in the kitchen or the car.   Because broadcast offers so vast a choice, it becomes an extension of the personality of the viewer or listener as he or she expresses that choice with the dial.   So you see, it's terribly personal.

Arthur Godfrey's greatest contribution to radio (and later television) was the impression that he was not addressing the masses but talking instead to one woman at a time.   He may very well have been the first to articulate this philosophy.   Many grasp it today as a matter of course.   Yet many still fail to understand it.   This is another deadly sin.

But these observations may help build a foundation for the importance of truly understanding the prime target—not just demographically, but psychologically as well.   Once having understood him, you must talk to him in his frame of reference and his idiom, not yours.   So if you absolutely hate the music of the day, and feel that fashion is becoming downright indecent, you'll never reach today's young market unless you check your personal bias and let someone who's with it turn the young set on for you.

Never Talk to Strangers

My mother always taught me never to talk to strangers.   I can't think of better advice for the creative adman.   That advice is based on protection of your paycheck and pension plan.

The simple truth is that almost everybody's strategy *starts* with some sort of profile description of a market target or prime prospect or user or consumer. If he (or she) is changing with the times, either evolutionary or revolutionary, yesterday's awareness of his psychographic profile can make him a stranger today. Or worse, it can make you a stranger in his eyes! So don't talk. Not until you've digested today's breed of cat—or maybe even tomorrow's.

Let us make it clear that this is not a plea for the cold-blooded murder of the English tongue. It is not a plea that we all master and use the language of either the jet set or the beat generation, the patois of the recording artist or the idiom of any ethnic group. Rather, it is a caution that people may very well think differently, feel differently, respond differently today. (And tomorrow.)

Life is changing. Values are changing. Miles are disappearing. Drudgery is diminishing. Mammoths are being miniaturized. Moments are being minimized.

Can the human race survive this environmental about-face without reflecting some symptomatic changes in personality and philosophy? I doubt it.

There's no question in my mind that an intimate understanding of your key market target (or your personalized consumer) is the most vital contribution creative people bring to broadcast execution. That's because it influences the way you handle all the other building blocks of the strategy.

From the Culture into the Product Once upon a time all claims seemed to radiate from the product and into the culture. Nowadays the most telling claims seem to radiate from the culture and into the product. And if I may abbreviate the dictionary, "culture" means the accumulated knowledge, whereas "society" means the accumulated restrictions. To understand the culture, you must understand the people *as* they are accumulating. And this braintwister has given rise to advertising which is much more people-oriented and emotional than advertising which is product-oriented and factual.

This requires the realization that he who would pursue creative execution must have a split personality. On the one hand he is part philosopher, psychologist, sociologist. But because it's a real world he must also be alert to the practical side, realizing that much of what his people are accumulating comes from the total effect of all the advertising to which they are constantly subjected.

KNOW WHAT'S GOING ON

While I earnestly believe that imitation is the downfall of an advertiser, I am equally convinced that intensive exposure to other advertising is critical for the creative man.   I cannot tolerate the lost arty souls who make a living in the advertising business while defaming it in toto, parroting the dissenter's favorite battle cry: "I never watch television."   I've never known a really top creative man who didn't average a couple of hours a night with the TV tube and a couple of hours a day with the radio.   He must—just to know what's going on.

In the first place, it gives an instinctive picture of what constitutes par for the course.   You get a feeling of the total fabric of the medium.   You get a rather clear picture of what the major advertisers of each industry are saying (or more importantly what they are not saying).   You're better prepared to search out preemptive campaign strategies and executions.   You avoid the embarrassment of coming up with a marvelous campaign idea only to discover later that someone else is already doing it.

Duplication of Ideas

On this latter score, don't ignore the distinct possibility of ESP (extra-sensory perception) or the fact that other professionals faced with the same problem may come up with the same answer.   Many years ago I was on a train from Baltimore to New York.   Just before leaving I checked the first run on some 24-sheet posters we were doing for Betholine-Sinclair.   The subject was faster winter starts.   The poster showed a woman's foot in a white fur-trimmed snow boot pressing down on the starter.   The copy said, "Just touch and go . . ."   It had a blue background and an orange station sign.

The train was drawing into 30th Street Station in Philadelphia.   I looked out the window and got the surprise of my life.   There atop a building was a giant spectacular in the process of being painted. Workmen on a scaffold were putting on the finishing touches.   It had a man's foot pressing the starter.   The copy said: "Just touch and go . . ."   On the right was the green-and-white Cities Service sign.

Things like this can and do happen.   But with the exception of

ESP, they happen far less often when you know what's going on. And the only way to do that in broadcast media is to look and listen —a lot.

Exposure to the Best

In addition to the everyday awareness of these media, it's equally important to expose yourself to the cream of the crop, the best of what's going on. This sharpens your perspective, elevates your benchmarks, and helps you spot trends in the growth of the art of communicating and convincing.

There are several opportunities open to you. Some for free, some for fee. First, the sample reels of film and sound production companies contain what they believe to be their best contemporary work. Usually, their judgment is rather sound. They're anxious to play them for you as a means to get some of your business.

There are several excellent reels put together annually or more often by the industry's most informed historians, observers, and awards directors. The ones I find most helpful are listed below. You can write them for additional information.

American TV Commercials Festival, Wally Ross, director, 6 West 57th Street, New York. A reel of the television winners and a record of the radio winners is available each year following the awards. Fees vary depending upon usage, and schools receive a special discount.

Harry Wayne McMahan, 620 Esplanade, Pelham, New York. This invaluable service can be tailored to your own needs. Periodically McMahan and his associates put together a master reel, industrywide reels, reels showing trends, etc., for television commercials. In addition they produce "The Ambros McMahan Radio Briefing" records which contain their selections of the best up-to-date commercials. A wide range of services are available for varying fees. Most worthwhile.

Maurie Webster, vice president for development, CBS Radio, 51 West 52nd Street, New York. In an effort to demonstrate the new vitality and versatility of radio, Webster produces a most informative and entertaining tape of what's going on that's important and refreshing. If you're heavily involved in radio, this is a must.

There are other excellent sources, but these are the ones I rely on most heavily.

Once you have armed yourself with insight into the typical couple at the other end of the airwaves, *and* become current with what's going on, what do you do with it?   I like to think of it this way.

PREPARE THE MIND—THEN FREE THE MIND

Someday I'd like to have that translated into Latin and cast in bronze as the motto of creative advertising people.   I honestly believe that it is the key to contemporary, creative execution.   It justifies and positions the discipline of strategy.   It legitimizes the climate of creativity.

Creative Man's Four Hats

Perhaps the best way to understand it is the story about the creative man's four hats.

Every good creative man has one head and four hats.   He has a miner's cap with its lamp, a green eyeshade with accompanying paper cuffs, the winged helmet of a Viking, the powdered wig of jurisprudence.

First, he dons the miner's cap.   And he digs out every scrap of ore in the vein.   He is not selective.   He simply exhausts the vein he is digging and tosses every possible nugget into his cart.

Second, he replaces the miner's cap with the clerk's green eyeshade and paper cuffs.   He examines the load from the miner's cart, sorts it, and enters the valid pieces in his ledger, totals his columns, balances his books, and prepares his statement (strategy).

Third, he casts off his bondage from the countinghouse and places the Viking's winged helmet on his head.   He is free.   The open sea beckons.   He will fly under sail, sometimes running free with incredible winds, sometimes becalmed, but everlastingly exploring uncharted seas.

And fourth, when his voyage is over, he removes his helmet and takes on the wig of jurisprudence, coldly to evaluate the discoveries of his previous self.

But remember, he has but one head.   He would look absurd if he wore more than one hat at a time.   If he were to wear the green eyeshade of the clerk with the miner's cap, he might be trying to evaluate while exhausting the vein.   He could outsmart himself and miss the mother lode.   If he were to wear the wig of jurisprudence along with the Viking's winged helmet, judgment might restrain him from the risks of the greatest adventure.

This grim little fairy tale is merely a graphic way of saying that the creative mind must accept, develop, and defend a four-way split personality that many a skilled marketer may find alarming. You can help him while he wears the first two hats. You can help him with the fourth after he has had a chance to evaluate and judge his own work and even prepare a defense. But when he reaches the point of winged flight with the third hat, leave him alone. That's when the creative mind is at work. That's what execution is all about.

MAN'S MOST VERSATILE CREATIVE TOOL

Many attempts have been made to define creativity beyond the concept of talent or gift. Unfortunately, most of these attempts have been made by psychologists and researchers who do not possess the same brand of creativity or work at it every day of their lives. This is not to say that their work is not creative, rather that it is a different form of creativity. I doubt if the best male gynecologist really knows precisely what it feels like to have a baby. He knows every facet of the process, but he has never experienced it in fact.

So we are faced with a dichotomy. The scientists can be much more precise in their explorations of the process. The creative man may not be so technically articulate. But he has experienced it. And in my opinion, the part of him that experiences it most intensely is his *subconscious mind.*

The Subconscious Mind

That's the reason I cling to the motto: "Prepare the mind—then free the mind" and its accompanying "four hat" theory. In essence it uses the *subconscious mind* as the real working tool.

In other words, if you absorb all the pertinent information and then formulate the objectives and strategy, your best bet at this point is to walk away from it and let it cook. Staring at blank paper is demoralizing. And an overt attack at execution at this point often turns out a commercial that is nothing more than the strategy statement set to pictures and music. On the other hand, if you suffer with the pieces in your subconscious mind while doing something else to break the monotony, ideas begin to spill out.

No matter what degree of creativity you may have started with, no matter how you have refined it, I believe it is at its optimum if you let it work for you rather than forcing it.   Disciplines are important in every other stage, but this phenomenon can have no disciplines except those a good broadcast writer has accumulated from experience.

His mind works on a plane different from that of the print writer. He is not so concerned with a stopper headline and illustration.   He is concerned with the passage of time—a story that will move from something interesting and relevant to a favorable conclusion. There are more tools at his disposal and more arts to be mastered.

How Ideas Emerge

Sometimes a commercial may come out full-blown.   Other times pieces begin to emerge.   And every writer is different.   One of the best ad-women I ever knew had the nickname "58-second mind"— because every commercial idea she ever turned out was timed instinctively to fit.   She used to start doodling until the doodles became delightful primitive drawings which became a sequence which became a commercial.   Another successful writer did all his actual creative thinking on weekends while riding a tractor on his farm.   He used the normal work week for digging, sorting, and evaluating.   I personally find that if I devote the weekend to manual work at my country place, the ideas start spilling out much faster on Monday morning.

This may explain why writers often stare out of windows, seem near to napping with their feet on their desks, do all manner of seemingly unproductive things which exasperate their managements. But if they are at the third-hat stage, forcing them to conform can force your commercials to conform to mediocrity.

Perhaps I've used the term "writers" indiscriminately.   I really mean to imply "commercial builders" regardless of their primary specialty.   The break-through idea may be a picture sequence, a piece of music, a casting or location idea, a word, a slogan, anything that opens up a new path.   More of these nuggets seem to pour out of the subconscious because it is free of inhibition and the need to evaluate.   So we're now at the point where ideas are beginning to emerge. Is there any way to help them along?

EXPLOIT THE TRENDS BUT EXPLODE THE CLICHÉS

Too often the urge to imitate overshadows the urge to innovate.   In my opinion this comes from fear, laziness, and the urge to be "in." When it happens on the client side it's usually caused by overreaction to the advertising of competitors.   When it happens on the agency side it's usually the result of who won what awards in the last competition.   In either case it creates a massive cliché.

The Industry Cliché

This is the costly phenomenon where virtually all the advertisers of a given industry turn out advertising that is so similar the poor consumer has difficulty in telling one from the other.   Generally it starts with pressure from the sales department when they're falling behind the quarterly prediction, and you hear a question like, "Why can't we have stuff like the XYZ Company is running?   That's really working out in the field."   Before you know it, the pressure mounts and you're dealing with a stated objective to duplicate their campaign when what is really needed is a campaign that separates you from them.

Perhaps the most classic industry cliché was in the tire industry in the early 1950s.   The name of the game was color spreads in the late-lamented *Saturday Evening Post* showing the largest possible head-on retouched exaggeration of one's tread.   Suddenly one advertiser had the wisdom to switch his campaign from strategy to execution to media.   Goodyear blasted the swamp with the now-classic multi-awarded "Go Go Goodyear" campaign from Young & Rubicam. There was excitement and urgency and realism—and most of all an implicit consumer benefit in their television commercials.   They also established an important musical theme which was to become a valuable continuing property for the future and a vehicle for radio "magnification."

Look at what has happened to tire advertising since then.   Once the industry cliché was broken, other advertisers used their new free-dom with such distinguished examples as Gulf's "Rolling Tire" com-mercial created by Erwin, Wasey, which tied for Best: Auto Acces-sories in the 1965 American TV Commercials Festival—and

Uniroyal's "The Rain Tire" created by Doyle, Dane, Bernbach, also winner of the Best: Auto Accessories in the 1967 American TV Commercials Festival.   These are just a few examples of distinguished television execution from an industry whose advertising used to be very, very dull.

In the proprietary drug industry, Contac Cold Capsules from Menley/James Laboratories put an end to the "belly-and-bowel" school of drug advertising with "pleasant sell" and "tiny time pills."   Since then Allarest, Alka-Seltzer, Excedrin, and others have turned out advertising that is rewarding to everyone, including the consumer.

In light of today's fresh airline advertising, it's difficult to remember the dreary "destination schedule" commercials that ran in the early 1960s.   Today the list is almost endless, but as one set of clichés is broken another begins to emerge.

The Technique Cliché

This cuts across industry lines and ranges from parody to plagiarism. (For obvious reasons no specific examples will be cited.)   Nevertheless, this is what happens when one advertiser has a breakthrough commercial and other advertisers in other industries adopt part or all of it for their own use.   It can be as innocently simple as the rush to use *the* hot announcer or *the* hot director or *the* in sound or hand-held camera throughout or machine-gun film cutting or multi-image montage or whatever is new and different at the moment.   (Remember it was only new for the first that did it.)

Slightly more serious is the case where one advertiser grabs something timely such as a movie plot or cast and suddenly six others are reshooting the same script with a different product shot.   Parody of other commercials also seems to be very much in vogue.   While it's often entertaining, I wonder if in the final analysis it's really cricket. Doesn't it "soil the nest?"   Doesn't it split the sponsor identification? I honestly don't know, but it concerns me.

It's also been charged that some agencies have "a look"—that all their ads for all their clients look alike.   In some cases, I think this is true, but not of the agencies at whom the charge is usually leveled.

The moral of the twin clichés discussion is simply this: If you wish your advertising to stand out, then by simple logic it has to be new and different from the rest.   So while it's a lot easier to imitate, the name of the game is innovate.   And since production costs in broadcast are usually a lot higher than in print media, you're twice as obligated to make the grade.

PREEMPTION IS PRICELESS

Earlier (and later) I refer to preemption.   This applies to strategy as well as execution.   In its simplest form, preemption merely means talking about something (or talking about it in a manner) that competitors could talk about—but ignore.

In today's climate of parity products this becomes critical.   It requires insight and guts.   But let's assume that some basic factor is common to your product and the products of all (or many) of your competitors.   Because you, and your counterparts as competitors, are extremely close to the technology involved, you assume it is a standard operation or feature of that product category.   *If* you can back off far enough and become totally philosophical, you may realize that here, at last, is an uncovered base.   Your management may scoff. After all, all the competitors *could* say the same thing the day after you chose to break your campaign.   But you are blessed with lead time.   Under normal circumstances it will take them weeks to come to the realization, weeks to come to the decision, and more weeks to approve advertising to counter you, and still more weeks to produce and air what they have approved.   By now you have developed a consumer awareness (if you've put your money where your mouth is) and the idea is yours.   Every nickel competition spends in saying "me too" may only serve to reinforce your identity with the concept or execution.

How Preemption Pays

Sometimes preemption pays off with a totally new idea.   Often it works with an old idea the industry has discarded ten or twenty years ago—and it's time for a rerun.   Take, for example, the case of Macleans.   Twenty years ago the toothpaste people discarded whiteness for more competitive and narrow positions.   Macleans actually retreated to a generic toothpaste strategy, but did it with fresh, compelling television executions and shocked the industry virtually overnight.   In its simplest form they said: Strong taste equals strong cleaning power; strong cleaning power equals strong appeal; whiteness wins.

Preemption is one of my favorite techniques. It often involves strategy more than execution, so I shall not dwell upon it too heavily. But preemption (when it works) makes the management team at an advertiser's headquarters feel smug and smart. It demoralizes competitors and makes them self-conscious. If you don't get too hung up on those factors and keep the real target in mind, it can make consumers sit up and take notice.

Where executional preemption really reaps benefits for you is when you look back at the industry cliché. If everyone else is working with fun and games, be quietly authoritative. If everyone else is presenting documentary proof, charm their pants off.

In the final analysis, preemption is just another form of burying the clichés. And it's one of the most effective.

ANIMATION AS A MEANS TO PREEMPTION

Probably no form of video communication has been less understood or more maligned than animation. There are those who will tell you it's unrealistic, unbelievable, expensive, time-consuming, child-oriented, and bad. I differ.

Animation can be an important tool in preemption. It can break through an industry cliché. It can bring charm and warmth to a situation that might otherwise be mundane. And it can ruin a good idea that ought to have been shot in live action but seemed too tough.

If I were to attempt to compose a rule, it would stem from print advertising. A shocking graphic idea in which two incompatible elements are juxtaposed for the attention value of their incongruity *must* be photographed. After all, you can draw *anything*—and the incongruity is not so important in a painting as it is in a photograph. On the other hand, if you wish to characterize or humanize static or unpleasant things or exaggerate bigger than life, a cartoon or painting may work much harder. Think of animation in these terms.

What Works in Animation

In my opinion, powerful demonstrations do not necessarily work well in animation. Demonstrations (in the hard sense of the word) are presenting fact before your eyes, and nothing short of it's-happening-now-without-help conveys your true intent. If you have to resort to animation to prove a point, chances are your point is just a little stretched.

On the other hand, the right kind of animation can warm and humanize a crotchety stomach as in the recent Alka-Seltzer debate twixt man and his abused adversary—or bring charm to the chauvinistic pride of Easterner and Westerner in TWA's "Cultural Exchange" flights from coast to coast—or make the overly protective wife a living angel in Contac's "Loving Couple" commercial (also known as "Poor Baby"). Are these stupid examples? Not in my opinion. All three were phenomenally successful. All three earned awards. All three were natural candidates for animation.

But, were they expensive? Did they take forever to produce? I can only speak with authority about two of them, but I'm given to understand the same is true of the third. They cost no more than the average live commercials normally produced by the same advertisers. At least one was done in *less* time than the average live-action commercial produced for the same advertiser. And they were a joy to work with.

It's interesting to note, however, again using the same three advertisers, that Alka-Seltzer did not resort to animation on its previous "No matter what shape your tummy's in" commercial. TWA did not resort to animation for its "Atlantic River" commercial. Contac did not resort to animation for its summer colds sequel to the ugly animal called "Pursuit Plane." Each was tougher to produce with live action, but it was required for the power of inherent incongruity.

So once again: There are no real rules. What works, works. It's part intuition, part judgment, part experience. If you're right, you're a hero. If you're wrong, you'll find another job anyway.

MUSIC, THE MAGNIFIER

I'm appalled at the way so much commercial music is mishandled or ignored completely. Maybe it's because I started out blowing sax and clarinet for name bands. But it seems that those advertisers who use it well put a powerful added selling tool to work for them, put a memory halo on their product, and build a synergism into their total campaign. Those who merely sneak it in badly (and cheaply) detract from what they are trying to say. The point is they use music as an afterthought.   It's as critical a building block as any other in most good commercials.   Leave it out by intent but never by oversight.

Greater Importance of Music

While music has always been important (and controversial) in broadcast commercials, it's even more so today, because today's music itself has undergone great changes and attained greater importance.   It is not only a barometer of the changes we're undergoing in the cultural revolution, in many ways it is also an instigator of these changes.   All of which makes it more important and more difficult to handle well.

Long before the birth of television, radio commercial music consisted mainly of jingles—a few of them great, many of them mediocre, a lot of them just plain bad.   As a result, certain researchers formed the conclusion that music in general was a bad selling tool, totally ignoring some of its great successes.   Then when the infant video tube dealt radio a severe body blow, music sank further into the background.   Radio was in trouble and budgets were cut.   Television was new and advertisers were fascinated with stand-up announcers, spokesmen, side-by-side demonstrations, and a take-it-all-too-seriously form of selling.   There were notable exceptions, of course, but the air wasn't very musical in that era.

Maybe it was the radio renaissance that brought music back—because when radio found its powerful new niche as the constant companion instead of the family's evening entertainer, its format was music and news, not situation comedy, variety shows, and dramas. If you wanted to match your medium, music became a must.   Television music at this point lagged behind radio, perhaps because advertisers were suddenly faced with unfamiliarly large production costs and settled for the economy of stock music, and this was treated solely as a background element which in many cases only interfered with the balance of the commercial.

New Forms of Music

Perhaps it was the tobacco industry that led the way with R. J. Reynolds out in front.   But when music came into its own again in broadcast, it came back strong and in a different form.   It was more than mere jingle.   It had more stature and better quality.   It took on characteristics of theme music and signature music in much the same way that the old radio programs had themes.   It was written into commercials as a full-fledged element, as an articulator of pictures, as counterpoint to words.   Recently, in some cases, it has become so memorable and identifiable with its product that it has even replaced the words.   Where this has happened the music in question was a full-fledged song, not a jingle.   In other words, it had beauty and mood and contemporary appeal to a music-minded young America.   It was not a ditty written for catchy early memorability with forced rhymes and many repeated mentions of the sponsor.   In some cases it barely mentioned the sponsor, and utter clarity of lyric was not so important as the total musical communication on all levels.

There are some who say it has even led to an identity crisis where it's hard to tell whether the song or the commercial came first.   On the one hand there is Diet Pepsi's "Girl-watcher's Theme" which went on to become a hit record.   On the other is the hit record, "Up, Up and Away" which became TWA's 1968 advertising theme.

The significant thing is that nothing could more clearly point up the incredibly important role of music in broadcast execution today.   As a result, there are still a lot of "jingle" writers around, but there is a growing number of commercial music experts whose thinking reflects this new trend.   Their work is expensive but impeccable.   The sooner they are brought into the picture, the better the finished commercial, not just because it gives them more time, but because their contribution may influence the total concept.

The technical aspects, rules, codes, rights, etc., to commercial music today are more than enough to fill a major textbook—which would be obsolete by next Thursday.   I shall make no attempt to cover any of these.   Rather this is a plea to consider music as an important conceptual factor in broadcast execution.

Think for a minute of the advertisers you know who have a strong, identifiable piece of commercial music.   Try putting a price tag on its value to them.   It's a true capital asset.   For if you accept our earlier definition that radio is the medium of imagination, music can replay a whole television film through the theater of the mind, while a listener keeps his eyes glued firmly on the road ahead.

Hints on Using Music

There are no bona fide rules about how or when to use music.   There are, however, some bits of advice on how to avoid the deadly sin of breaking its magnifying power.

Don't Smother Music   Give it air.   Let it breathe.   If it's fighting with your announcer, either the band or the announcer has too big a part.   Usually it's too many words for the announcer.   Softening the music in the mix until the brass sounds like tin will only make it worse.

Don't Patronize with Music   A youth market commercial doesn't necessarily call for loud rock.   The kids have some beautiful songs, too. An ethnic appeal doesn't always cry for soul.   But if you use rock or soul or any other new sound, do it with an expert in the same way you hire a good conductor if you choose a symphony.   At least one advertiser this year spent a bundle on a hit song and rewrote the lyrics in the idiom of yesterday.   It was both ridiculous and insulting to the market he was after.

Don't Look for Bargains in Music   This is no place to save money because you went over budget on film.   If the sociologists are right and commercials must not only compete with but also surpass programing, your music can't sound cheap.

THE FOURTH HAT, FIRST STEP IN EVALUATION

We've come almost full-cycle to where we began in attempting to explore some personal biases on broadcast execution.   It's time to back off and look at your commercial ideas and apply your own judgment before someone grabs them and copy-tests them.   To be perfectly honest, I loathe copy testing, not because I don't believe it is necessary, but because I have yet to discover a method that is close enough to being infallible.

Nevertheless, having come full-cycle, let's return to an analogy we started with about *commercials* and *dames*—and add another dimension to it.

You've seen it happen at every party you've ever attended.   A dame walks into the room and every guy present goes "Wow."   With some dames, this seldom happens.   With others, it just does.

You can't really explain why.   And worse still, if you try to analyze it, you can end by destroying the whole illusion.

Picture in your mind one of the new Italian starlets.   Wow! That's a woman.   But get a grip on yourself and see if there isn't something you could pick apart.

Nose . . . a little long.   Better have it bobbed.   Uh . . . those teeth. Full caps. Hair . . . it needs some highlights. It won't photograph well that dark. And style it. Restyle it. Of course that means we'll have to change her make-up.

Now she's a little hippy. Three days on nothing but skimmed milk will take care of that. And that dress has to go. Take her to Bergdorf's and get something marvelous. And shoes while you're at it, those little heels make her feet look big.

And do you think you could find a good voice coach . . . there's a little too much accent there for my money.

So you fix all these things—but how does your Pygmalion creation turn out? All the parts are perfect. But maybe the "Wow" is gone. Maybe you've just wound up with a beautiful dame that looks like every other beautiful dame—but she's not great anymore.

So you learn a lesson. Before you start picking apart the parts, give yourself a chance for an overall "Wow." If you've got it, easy on the changes. If you don't, chances are the changes won't fix it anyway.

Commercials are like dames—remember?

It's kind of sad in this day and age that so many people spend so much time scrutinizing the pieces, picking the parts, before they've given themselves the chance to say "Wow" or "No wow."

This doesn't mean I'm against all the blood, sweat, and tears it takes to build a great commercial, or that I think the first script is always the way to go. Not on your tintype.

This doesn't mean that I believe there is a woman (or a commercial) in this brave new world that can't be improved upon with the right kind of professional help. But I underscore the term *professional*. A great hairdresser can do as much for a woman as a great copy writer, art director, or producer can do for a commercial. But when this role is delegated, or for that matter usurped, by a part-time creative expert who doesn't live and breathe and suffer with this specific craft day in and day out, you're courting disaster.

This doesn't mean that I believe everyone but the creative man should be deprived of an opinion.

Rather, this is a plea that every level of the advertising business reinstate the pause for reflection—a "wow break."

Think of the good ideas that could have been saved that way. And think of the money that could have been saved in not pursuing things that weren't real ideas after all.

You see, without the "Wow break" we're forced to resort to other

ways of determining whether an ad has it or not.   There are all sorts
of ways of measuring different parts of an ad.   They can measure just
about anything statistically, except the "Wow."

That's why it's so important to make your first evaluation step the
"Wow break."   It's just as important a measure as any scientific tool
you can employ, and best of all, it's free.

DO AWARDS COUNT?

Another chronic debate that seems never to end is awards.   In my
opinion they count very heavily.   But just as I deplore advertising
that is written to a specious formula to score well on a given method
of research, I think writing for the singular purpose of winning
awards leaves a lot to be desired also.   It's a matter of balance.

A good commercial, written with understanding of your target
audience, simple in concept, believable in claim, excellently produced, stands a very good chance of scoring and winning.   But neither a recall number nor a plaque is the reason for being of any commercial.

Nevertheless, nowadays as the industry, its arts, and its people
become more and more mature, awards are starting to represent
achievement in the eyes of one's peers.   They have become a vital
part of creative morale.   They have produced in some cases certain
salary escalations which some find unfortunate and others find over-
due.   In the final analysis, properly positioned, they make people try
harder.   And they're here to stay.

Awards are most often criticized by people who haven't ever won
them.   I've seen hardheaded antiawards businessmen grin like
schoolboys when they held their first Clio in their hands.

CHAPTER SEVENTEEN

Execution of Copy Strategy in Direct Mail and Out-of-Home Media

(Direct Mail) HARRY B. WALSH *Creative Director—Direct Mail, Ogilvy & Mather Inc.*

(Outdoor Advertising) G. EMERSON COLE *Vice President—Creative Director, Institute of Outdoor Advertising*

(Transit Advertising) DANIEL E. CALLANAN *Vice President and General Manager, Mutual Transit Sales*

(Point-of-Purchase Advertising) HOWARD STUMPF *President, Point-of-Purchase Advertising Institute, Inc.*

DIRECT MAIL

Good direct-mail copy strategy often starts with arithmetic. Last week I received a mailing that illustrates this point neatly.

It was from a company that wanted to sell me a business service. It came in a number 10 envelope that cost about ½ cent, and it carried 6 cents first-class postage. The list from which it got my name (I recognized the imprint) had charged 3 cents for the one-time rental. The process of inserting, addressing, sealing, and metering had probably cost another ½ cent. The enclosure was a simple black-and-white folder, one-half of which briefly described the service. The other half was a business reply card. This piece had cost, at the very most, 1 cent.

So of the total 11-cent cost, 10 cents (91 per cent) had been spent sending the message.   Only 1 cent (9 per cent) had been spent selling the product.

Just suppose that, instead of the black-and-white little folder, the writer had included a four-page black-and-white letter describing the service in detail (1½ cents), a pictorial brochure showing the service in action (1½ cents), a leaflet with several testimonials from users (½ cent), and a separate business reply card (½ cent)?   This mailing would have had not one but three separate selling pieces, plus a reply card.   It would have had room for ten times as much selling copy as appeared on the original folder.   It would have had space for pictures of the product and of people who had used the product.

These additions would have added only 3 cents—about 27 per cent—to the original's 11-cent cost.   But they would unquestionably have increased response, and might well have *multiplied* it many times.

So, when blocking out your direct-mail packages, always examine the balance between what you are spending in sending the message and what you are spending in selling the product.   You may find you can add important selling material that will increase your response —and do it for peanuts.

Tips for Effectiveness

Here are some other tips that can help make your direct mail more effective:

1. *Write the letter first.*   The letter, not the brochure, is the foundation upon which most successful direct-mail packages are built. So tell your complete story in your letter, and let the other pieces in the mailing reinforce it.   Make it look like a letter.   Use typewriter type and avoid big headlines and pictures.   When the feeling of the mailing is informal and personal, it sometimes helps to emphasize important passages with simulated pen marks.

2. *Start with a short, provocative sentence.*   The first sentence in your letter is almost as important as a headline in an ad.   Keep it short, like a headline.   Two lines or less is a good rule to follow. Make sure that it says, in one way or another, that the letter that follows is interesting or important or both.

3. *Move the reader along with you.*   The easiest thing in the world to do is to stop reading.   So don't let the reader "get off" at a fold in the letter or at the bottom of a page.   Where the letter folds,

be sure you have a run-on sentence that forces him to open up the letter and continue.   End the first page in the middle of a particularly provocative sentence that will carry him on to the second page. Make a promise in the beginning of the letter (a gift or a special offer or a revelation of some sort) that you don't fulfill until the end.

4. *Indent important material.*   The best way to emphasize important material is to paragraph it and indent it on both sides.   But don't overdo indenting or you will lose its effect.   I usually select the single most important sentence on the first page—probably a strong promise or offer—and indent that.   The rest of the page remains in full margin.   That way the reader who is skimming the letter will catch the key point.

5. *Use crossheads.*   Underlined or capitalized crossheads serve to break up solid copy and make it look more inviting.   They also serve as topic sentences, of course.   Their main function is to make the copy look open and readable.   When I use them, I put one on the first page and then two on each succeeding page, placed roughly one-third and two-thirds down the page.   It also helps to paragraph your copy frequently.

6. *Restate your offer completely at the end of the letter.*   When reading third-class mail, many persons glance briefly at the first paragraph and then go to the end of the letter to see the offer.   If it looks like an interesting proposition, they may read the entire mailing. Don't make them hunt for your offer.   Be sure it is stated plainly in the closing paragraphs of the letter.

7. *Use a postcript.*   Postscripts get high reading.   After all, reading a postscript is a lot easier than reading a whole letter.   It is fair to say that *every* letter should have a postscript.   Use it to emphasize important copy point, or to give a cutoff date for your offer, or to ask for the order again.   There is something in every letter that merits repeating.

8. *Identify your reply device.*   Whether you're using a business reply card or a reply form with an envelope, tell your reader what it is and what you want him to do with it.   If postage is prepaid, tell him that.   If there are a number of pieces in the mailing and it looks as if your reply device might get lost in the shuffle, print on colored stock and ask your reader to look for the "blue card" or the "green order form."

9. *Restate your offer on the reply device, if possible.*   Some people

who have been sold by your mailing will set the reply card or form aside, planning to mail it later, and throw the rest of the mailing away.   Unless your offer is plainly restated on the reply device, they may come to it later and not remember what it was for or why they saved it.   A stub on a reply card or an extra paragraph on an order form cost next to nothing, and they might pick up a few extra replies for you.

10. *Don't be afraid to offer a gift.*   Never say "we can't afford to give gifts" until you have analyzed your response figures with the proposed gift in mind.   Suppose you are mailing to purchasing agents to develop sales leads for an office copying machine.   Your standard offer is a booklet, and it pulls 1 per cent returns.   If your mailing costs $100 per thousand, you are buying leads for $10 each.   If you were to offer a $2 pen-and-pencil set as a free gift to those replying and requesting a demonstration, you might increase your response to 2 per cent.   At this level, the cost of the mail is $5 per response.   Add to this the $2 cost of the gift and you have twice as many leads for only $7.   While the quality of the leads will be somewhat lower (some people will respond just for the gift), the lower lead cost has a good chance of lowering the cost of the final sale.   Consider, too, that the gift will provide the salesman with a good door-opener when he delivers it.

11. *Use a big brochure.*   Your brochure should cover about the same ground your letter does, but it will do it in pictures and type, rather than in letter form.   (Some persons like to read brochures. Others like to read letters.   Because of the nature of direct mail, you can oblige them both.)   Where there is any question about the size of the brochure, choose the larger rather than the smaller.   The cost of enlarging a brochure by 50 or 100 per cent is usually negligible when set against the total cost of the mailing.   The mailing with the larger brochure will almost inevitably outpull the one with the smaller brochure.

12. *Demonstrate the product in your brochure.*   For some reason, many mailers simply show a large, static picture of the product in their brochure.   It is much more effective to show the product in action, as you would show it in a television commercial or a magazine ad.   (The manufacturer of a leading garden tiller has made a fortune with a mailing showing a simple, old-fashioned before-and-after picture.)   Sit down with your writer or your art director or your photog-

rapher and decide how best to show the advantages of your product or service in pictures.   If possible, do it in pictures that tell a story.

13. *Use testimonials.*   The best copy you can possibly find is written by satisfied customers.   If you are in the habit of saving complimentary letters, you might have a gold mine of great copy sitting in your files right now.   Pull them out and see what you have.   Perhaps you can excerpt ten or twenty or even more paragraphs for use in your next direct-mail piece.   If you can, use a few in the body of your letter, and add the rest to your brochure.   Some mailers like to set testimonials in typewriter type to give them a personal appearance. If you have no testimonials stored up, it is easy to go out and get them.   For example, suppose you are selling an industrial stamping machine.   Select a cross section of existing customers and send them a questionnaire asking their opinions and suggestions about your stamping machine.   Ask leading questions with simple "check one" answers: "Does the machine operate fast enough for your needs? ——Too fast ——Too slow ——About right."   Then, at the end of the questionnaire, ask for the customer's general comments, and leave space for a handwritten or typed note.   I have pulled between 15 and 20 per cent response with a form like this—and gotten hard-selling believable copy that I couldn't have bought at any price.

14. *Use envelope teasers—sometimes.*   When you are doing a hard-sell, commercial-looking mailing—and when you have a really good offer, print your offer on the envelope.   Often you can make your envelope selling promise even stronger by using windows that show some of the contents—picture or headlines.   Go slow on this technique when you are trying for a dignified, personalized feel for your mail.

15. *Personalize your mailings as much as possible.*   Often it is impossible to get any real personal feeling into direct mail.   But when the list ·you are mailing to is small, you can sometimes add a valuable individual touch simply by handwork, such as handwritten envelopes or short penned notes which include the name of the addressee.   When the list is somewhat larger, a so-called process letter duplicates typewriting so exactly that, when the address and individual salutation are added, the result is almost indistinguishable from a real typed letter.   When the quantity to be mailed is really large, and when the list to be used is on computer, "computer letters" can be used quite economically.   This space-age technique enables you to

insert any number of personal references based on the addressee's name and address and Zip Code number.   Although more expensive than ordinary offset copy, computer letters have more than pulled their weight in hundreds of mailings.

16. *Sample your product, if you can.*   Often you can add tremendous additional impact to your mailing by enclosing actual samples of the product.   Samples of fabrics and metals and fluids have all been used with considerable success.   One mail-order house which sells winter coats has, for many years, enclosed in its mailings a sample swatch which dramatically shows the quality construction of the product.

17. *Test and test and test.*   It is easy to test one mailing against another.   You simply key the reply devices and then count the returns as they come in.   If you want to get basic information from your tests, you must test only one thing at a time: Letter A against Letter B, Offer A against Offer B, etc.   Don't draw any large conclusions from small results.   Even when you pull 300 or 400 returns, there is still a built-in random error of plus or minus 10 per cent!   So keep mailing and *accumulate* returns.   That way you can build an accurate index of the success or failure of your direct mail.

18. *Make your offer painless.*   Remove all the obstacles that may cause your customer to decide not to reply.   For instance, if you are going for a cash sale, be sure to offer a money-back guarantee.   But don't just throw in a line saying "money back if not delighted."   Make it important.   Frame your guarantee in a bank-note border and give it all the specifics you can: the number of days for which it is good, how the money will be refunded (airmail, perhaps?), why it is company policy to make such a guarantee, etc.   If you approach your guarantee as if yours was the first company ever to make such an astonishing offer, you will probably end with good guarantee copy. If you are going for inquiries and no salesmen will call, make that plain, too.   If your reply device is postage paid (it ought to be), tell them they don't have to stop and look for a postage stamp.

19. *Include a telephone number.*   Lots of people, businessmen especially, prefer the telephone to the mails.   If it is practical, include a telephone number they can call to order or inquire.   If you are expecting a really large volume of replies, special numbers should be set up.   If you can handle the calls in your own office, simply key each mailing by asking them to call "Miss Jones" or "Miss Smith."   Add-

ing the option of a telephone reply in the letter and brochure and reply device will increase returns almost every time.

20. *Get referrals from your responders.* People respond amazingly well to a simple, modestly worded request for help. After you have your order or inquiry, follow with an inexpensive thank-you mailing in which you ask for the names of others who might be interested in this product or service. Don't be surprised if the names you get back turn out to be the best list you can mail.

OUTDOOR ADVERTISING

Outdoor advertising exists for the purpose of communicating a message to the public in as effective and efficient a manner as possible. There are, however, certain differences between outdoor advertising and other media with respect to the execution of copy strategy. So, let us first explain the medium itself.

There are, in the United States, more than 60 million signs which are located out of doors. About 300,000 of these conform to what is known as "standardized outdoor advertising" structures. These structures are situated within business and commercial areas in scientifically designed patterns to provide coverage of entire markets. In this respect, they are similar to radio, television, newspapers, and magazines.

The two basic forms of outdoor advertising are the poster panel and the painted bulletin (Figure 1). Although the poster panel is a proportion of 1 by 2¼ and the painted bulletin of 1 by 3½, there is no real problem in creating advertising which will fit either or both.

The Creative Demands of Outdoor Design

It is quite possible that no other advertising medium places such a premium on *creative discipline* as does the creation of an effective outdoor design. The message to be communicated must be pared to the bare essentials if we are to develop impact and memorability upon an audience which is in motion, at a distance, often occupied with the problems of weather, visibility, and perhaps youngsters raising a rumpus in the back seat. In short, we must say it quickly and clearly. Perhaps the nearest problem of a similar nature in other media would be the creation of a 10-second station ID in television.

Considerable research has shown that, regardless of the medium used or the length of exposure, a single advertising message will leave a consumer with a maximum of *two ideas*.   What should these ideas be?

1. Name of product
2. Reason to buy

Recognizing this, many creative directors start to develop a campaign or even an individual advertisement as a poster design.   They have found that, if they are able to communicate their message within the confines of good outdoor, they can convert easily into other media, because it is always easier to expand than to cut.   They say: "If it will work in outdoor, it will work anywhere."

Once the idea is in the concentrated form of a poster design, the advertiser and the agency can visualize the impact of the idea and agree upon the basic selling message.

The Design Concept in Outdoor Advertising

It has been found, through the experience of hundreds of creative people and thousands of designs, as well as by research conducted by

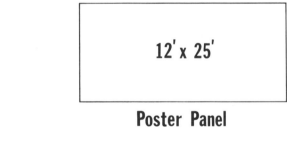

Poster Panel

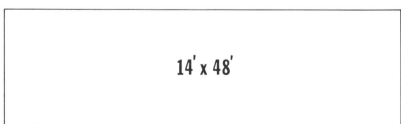

Painted Bulletin

Figure 1   Types of outdoor advertising.

Alfred Politz Research and Schwerin Research Corporation, that an outdoor design, to be effective, must contain no more than the three elements shown in Figure 2: identification, copy, and illustration.

These three elements may be combined into a single unit, or separated as shown in Figure 3.   To use more than three units in a design will confuse rather than communicate.

Quite often, particularly in the field of package goods, the identification will be on the package itself.   The Fab design is an excellent example of this type of identification.

Identification in Outdoor.   Identification in *any* advertising can be achieved in several ways.   Some companies or products have a logotype which is instantly recognized by the public and needs no explanation.   A few examples are shown in Figure 4.

Many corporations have logotypes or forms of identification which are *not* well known.   In most of these instances, they add a word or two of explanation to ensure identification (Figure 5).

Because identification is the number-one *idea* to be registered in any advertising, care should be taken that the identification is of sufficient size in an outdoor design.

Copy in Outdoor   Whatever words are used in an outdoor design, they must convey the message quickly.   Therefore, the words should be short and mean one thing only.   Usually, the copy will contain the all-important reason to buy.

There has long been a misconception of the number of words allowable in a poster design.   The easiest way to judge their effectiveness is to read them out loud.   If you can read the copy in less than eight seconds, and understand the message intended, the copy is all right.   Again, here is a similarity between outdoor and a 10-second station ID on television.

Type should be simple and easy to read so it does not obscure or slow communication of the message.   If possible, upper- and lowercase letters are preferable, because they force the reader to grasp a phrase, an idea, rather than just a word at a time.   See Figure 6.

To be legible at a distance of several hundred feet, no copy should be less than 12 inches in height, preferably 16 inches.   This means copy should be about one-eighth the vertical height of the design.   If the corporate or product name is used as the identification, these letters should be as large as possible.

Illustration in Outdoor   Outdoor offers the largest physical size of any

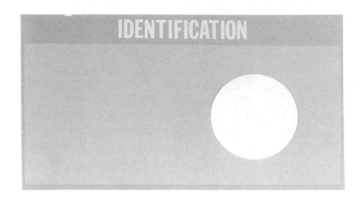

Figure 2 Three elements of outdoor design.

17-10

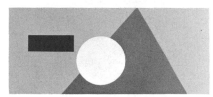 

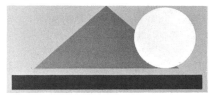 

Figure 3   Combinations of the three elements of design.

Figure 4   Well-known logotypes.

advertising medium.   In outdoor, an aspirin tablet can be as large as a car, and a car can be shown full-size and in full color.   Sheer size is dramatic.   If only a portion of a face or object is shown, by use of judicious cropping, startling dramatic effects can be attained as in Figure 7.

Figure 5   Logotypes with explanatory copy.

Bold colors befit outdoor design.   In magazine advertising, subtle colors offer wonderful possibilities, but in outdoor designs, seen from a distance and while in motion, these subtleties may disappear.   The same artwork can be used, it is true, but cropping, color value, even retouching must be considered to attain the maximum impact.

Figure 6   Simple typography so message comes through.

If one color can be singled out to consider, it would be red.   Under the conditions by which outdoor is seen and has the opportunity to communicate, red often bleeds, visually.   Thin white lettering on a red background will dissolve into illegibility.   Red against a black background will disappear.   Yet, red lettering on a white background grabs attention and impresses the viewer.   So, be careful of the use of red.   Make certain it is in the foreground, not in the background.

While on the subject of background, keep in mind the fact that people are moving when they see outdoor advertising.   Therefore, a background which is complicated will serve only to obscure the message, not enhance it.

Figure 7   Dramatic effect achieved by cropping.

Pay particular attention to silhouette.   The shape of a person or an object gets indistinct as you move farther away from it.   Quite often, the selection of the background can mean the difference between effective and lackadaisical outdoor design.   Background shapes which fight visually with the foreground, package, or logotype should be avoided.

How to Order an Outdoor Advertising Design

Today, in most agencies, the creative people work in all media. This is good, because they then have to think in terms of the overall communication problem.   However, all too few creative persons have had experience in the design of an outdoor poster or bulletin. Because outdoor demands such high degrees of creative discipline, copy writers and art directors usually attack the outdoor problem last, as they assess a campaign.   Much too often they attempt to adapt a magazine layout to outdoor advertising.

An advertiser, once he has reached the decision that outdoor advertising is an important part of his media mix, should make it clear to his agency that outdoor should be considered separately.   Quite often, the European feel for outdoor posters offers an opportunity to American advertisers to stand out from the crowd.   Those who have used illustrations created specifically for outdoor rather than adapting illustrations made for other media have found they obtained impressive results.

Carefully organized market tests have been made by leading national advertisers to determine the impact of truly outstanding outdoor designs.   In each case, not only has brand awareness gone up dramatically, but so have sales.   Therefore, it behooves an advertiser to request special creative attention be paid the work on his outdoor campaign.

When the advertiser (who is paying the bill) insists that outdoor designs be given primary attention, the results will usually affect his advertising in other media as well.   Why?   Because the creative people have exerted a maximum of *creative discipline* to produce the poster designs.   These can then be expanded into longer forms in other media.

Figure 8 shows some examples of excellent outdoor designs which can be converted easily into effective magazine, newspaper, or television advertising.

How To Get Effective Outdoor Advertising

Once the advertiser has arrived at the decision to use outdoor advertising as a part of his media plan, he will request the agency to prepare outdoor designs.   It is at this stage that complete agreement on the approach must be made.   Once the basic selling proposition has been agreed upon, the agency can then exert the discipline necessary to produce effective outdoor advertising.

The agency will prepare renderings of the proposed designs. These should be examined in light of the principles and techniques that have been described.   Once final approval has been granted, the quantity of posters or painted bulletins to be used will determine the mechanics of reproduction.

For example, if the design will appear on less than 200 panels, it will probably be silk-screened for reasons of economy.   If more, it may be lithographed.   In either case, fidelity of reproduction will be of the highest quality.   The same holds true of individually painted bulletins.

Special Considerations in Outdoor Design

Recent developments offer effects which can enhance an outdoor design.   The use of Da-Glo inks and paints provides a dimensional effect when used properly.   It should be noted that Da-Glo should be used against a dark background in order to achieve maximum effect.

Figure 8   Outdoor designs which can be converted for use in other media.

A new process combines Da-Glo inks and lithography to provide a translucent effect.   This is most effective for the promotion of liquids.

Quite often, the extension of certain elements of a design beyond normal borders of the poster or bulletin increases the impact and memorability of the design (Figure 9). These extensions are called *embellishments.* They may consist of cutout letters or extensions of the design itself. In either case, the standardized outdoor advertising industry has established standards limiting the distance of extension of these embellishments.

Figure 9 Extension of design beyond the borders of the poster or bulletin.

A special unit which is available from many outdoor plant operators is called *tri-vision,* or *multi-vision.* As the name implies, these structures offer a change of copy, three different designs, every few seconds. As shown in Figure 10, a theme can be varied to hold interest, demonstrate variety, and achieve impact.

Another way of attaining variety and thus increasing impact is by the use of snipes and teasers. Snipes are specially printed pieces of

Figure 10   Variations of the same theme.

paper which are posted on a panel after the initial posting, to change the message in some way. A teaser is simply an incomplete design which becomes complete with the use of snipes. Interest can be created and sustained using a combination of these elements. See Figure 11.

Figure 11   Use of teaser.

Definite economies can be effected in large runs of paper by taking advantage of specific printing patterns. In many instances, a portion of the design, if laid out properly, can be printed in four colors. The balance can be printed in one or two colors, usually a copy line, and then combined with the more expensive portion. (Figure 12.)

Aids for the Advertiser

Outdoor advertising offers a challenge not just to the creative person preparing the designs, but also to those using the medium. Outdoor advertising provides flexibility, the opportunity to pinpoint an ad-

Figure 12   Combination of printing processes.

vertising message to reach a specific age group, income group, or ethnic group. Demographic data are now available in new research by W. R. Simmons & Associates, A. C. Nielsen, Alfred Politz, Advertising Research Foundation, and others.   This material has been compiled and analyzed by the Institute of Outdoor Advertising and is available to advertisers and agencies, so that advertising messages can be tailored to the precise market for a product or service.

The Institute of Outdoor Advertising also provides creative services to help produce the most effective designs possible. Designs for outdoor advertising can now be pretested by Schwerin Research Corporation in the same sessions in which television commercials are pretested.

Through the combination of showings tailored to a specific market, designs which take advantage of the many possibilities in paper patterns and printing methods, rotary bulletin plans, and creative discipline to whittle down the selling message to its essentials, outdoor advertising offers a challenge to make the most of the marketing opportunities it provides.

TRANSIT ADVERTISING

Transit advertising is truly a mass medium. It utilizes each metropolitan-county area's public transportation system as it communicates advertising messages to people who are out and about, frequently on their way to buy. Like the vehicles on which it travels, transit advertising moves through all areas in a market, reaching each segment of its population and passing most retail outlets. It offers last-minute impressions near point of sale, and keeps both dealers and distributors mindful of a promotion.

There are three types of transit advertising: *interior, exterior,* and *platform posters.* Although the same person could be counted among the viewers of each, his receptivity to messages changes as he moves from the station platform onto a transit vehicle, or from driving behind one bus carrying advertisements to waiting for another to cross at an intersection.

Sizes, Copy, Color

Before creating a transit advertisement in any of these three types, it is well to be aware of the conditions under which it will be seen, of the frame in which each advertisement is placed, of the remaining live-copy area, and of the fact that we are discussing only the seven standard sizes. Other sizes are available in only a few markets (as those on cable cars, subway clocks), and are frequently sold only for twelve-month showings.

Interior Transit Advertisements Interior transit advertisements (Figure 13) are situated above the windows on both sides of practically every bus and subway car in America. Until the mid-1960s these stood side by side in racks 11 inches high. Their widths varied, although most were (and still are) 11 by 28 inches. Brightly colored cards were then inserted between the ads to showcase each message, and two or more 22- by 21-inch frames were installed over the 11-inch racks on each side of many transit vehicles. Most subway cars have two additional 22- by 21-inch frames inside each end. One bus manufacturer is now delivering vehicles with twelve individually framed advertising spaces—two 22- by 21-inch frames and four 11- by

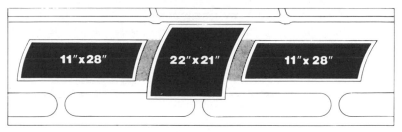

Figure 13   Interior transit advertising.

28-inch frames on each side.   (Incidentally, in transit advertising all measurements are expressed in terms of height by width—never width by height.)

Eye level to the standing rider and facing two or three seated passengers, the interior transit ad provides diversion during the 23-minute average ride.   Long copy is recommended—but in type large and legible enough to be read from a seat across the aisle.   Full color is recommended—particularly when one considers the need for product identification and appetite appeal.   Magazine and supplement artwork are frequently adapted to interior transit ads which advertisers print on five-ply stock and ship to those markets selected for the campaign.   Incidentally, printers must be told that the stock's grain should run horizontally for 11 by 28 inches and vertically for 22 by 21 inches.

In a few United States markets a small portion of each fleet is framed for backlighted interior transit ads, most of which are printed on styrene (0.010 gauge).   When specifying stock, check to learn if your ad will be featured in any of these markets, order the correct number of styrene ads (0.010 gauge) for each, and let the operator know that he will be receiving the balance printed on five-ply stock.

Although copy is changed monthly, some advertisers run two and four ads simultaneously—each running in half or a quarter of the fleet.   They know that the average rider seldom travels in the same vehicle or sits in the same seat twice during the same week.   They know, too, that a rider must walk down the aisle to his seat.   They have different recipes, points, models, or views to feature and feel that each should be showcased for the long ride.

Other advertisers use this 23-minute commercial as they use 10-second television spots—to register quick product identification.

For such flash impressions we recommend exterior transit ads on the front, back, or side of whatever number of buses the market's transit advertising operator feels is necessary to cover properly his entire area (Table 1.)   Many transit advertising operators have docu-

TABLE 1   Number of Buses Recommended to Carry Your Exterior Transit Ad in Fifty Top Markets

Akron.	40	New Orleans	60
Albany-Schenectady-Troy	40	New York	400
Atlanta	100	Norfolk-Portsmouth	80
Baltimore	120	Omaha.	60
Birmingham.	40	Philadelphia	300
Boston	300	Phoenix	40
Buffalo.	100	Pittsburgh.	200
Chicago	400	Portland, O.	40
Cleveland	200	Providence-Pawtucket.	100
Columbus	60	Richmond.	60
Dallas	200	Rochester	100
Dayton	40	Sacramento	40
Denver	100	St. Louis	200
Detroit	300	Salt Lake City.	20
Flint	36	San Antonio	80
Grand Rapids	40	San Bernardino-Riverside.	20
Greensboro-Winston Salem	36	San Diego	60
Houston	100	San Francisco-Oakland	220
Indianapolis.	80	San Jose	20
Kansas City	100	Seattle-Everett	100
Los Angeles	400	Syracuse	40
Louisville	80	Tampa.	20
Memphis.	60	Toledo.	40
Milwaukee.	120	Wichita	20
Mobile	40	Youngstown-Warren.	24

mented the reach and frequency values of such No. 100 showings in their respective markets, and the difference (in cost-per-thousand exposure opportunities) between fronts, backs, and sides does vary a bit from market to market.

Exterior Transit Advertisements   After working within the 11- by 28-inch frame of an interior transit ad, one needs to change his approach before creating a 30- by 144-inch exterior ad for the side of a bus (Figure 14 *a* and *b*) or a 21- by 72-inch for the frame between its taillights (Figure 15*b*).   The extra-wide dimension is unique among measured

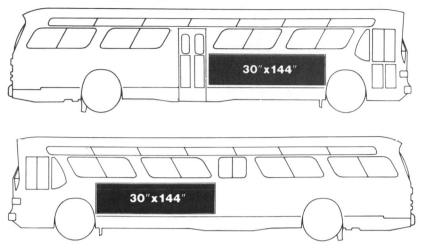

Figure 14   Exterior transit advertising, side.

media and a creative discipline is required to tie together the featured elements.

We've seen advertisers use hammocks, long canoes, dachshunds, and lounge chairs to tie elements together.   Others have simply "laid

Figure 15 Exterior transit advertising, front or back.

the bottle on its side."   Occasionally, an advertiser panels off the right end of his ad to name or price the product pictured within the rest of the frame.   The automobile advertisers do this well, letting their well-known logotypes identify the featured product.

Here, one may turn to the preceding section on outdoor advertising for guidance, because the ingredients of a good outdoor poster are basically the same as those for a good exterior transit ad—name the product and give a reason for buying it.   Some suggest using bold colors, thick type (in upper and lower case), contrasting backgrounds, strong silhouettes, never more than five words, etc.   Others urge advertisers to identify, demonstrate, excite, sell, and ask for the order— and read the words out loud, as you ask close associates to tell you what they mean.   Before even thinking about what should go into your exterior transit ad, try to imagine how receptive each viewer will be each time he has the opportunity to see your message.

Exposures at Intersections   Research has shown that these "moving billboards" provide most of their exposure opportunities at intersections—not only to pedestrians, but also to bus riders, motorists, and their passengers.   Test the medium yourself as you pass through your next ten to twelve intersections.   See how many exterior transit ads you can read on moving buses while you're waiting—and how many you can read while you're moving and the buses are waiting.   Two-word and three-word messages come across the first time, and their meaning begins to make an earnest impression after four or five exposures.

It should be remembered that the transit advertising operator pastes your 70-pound opaque paper on Masonite or Duron, delivers the finished boards proportionately to the garages in his market, and installs them in frames that are designed to fit in with the styling of the bus.

When the same copy is scheduled to run for more than the usual twenty-eight days, some advertisers print directly on Masonite.   Such boards are discarded at the end of each showing, unless the advertiser makes other provisions.

Other Sizes of Exterior Ads   Two other sizes of exterior transit ads should be mentioned: the 22- by 144-inch backlighted rooftop and the 21- by 44-inch headlight (Figure 15a) which is also featured with the 30- by 144-inch frame on the sides of many United States buses.   The smaller 21- by 44-inch frame is efficient at bus stops and in those situations where traffic is moving slowly.   It is usually printed on 0.050 waterproof cardboard or 0.040 styrene.   Sometimes it is also varnished after printing.

Frequently these 21- by 44-inch ads are purchased in No. 200 showings, although a few recent advertisers have been renewing their combinations of a No. 100 showing of 30- by 144-inch ads and a No. 100 showing of 21- by 44-inch ads—always with the understanding that both ads would never be posted on the same vehicle, thereby extending the reach and almost doubling the frequency when the creative approach is similar in both sizes.

Others ask to have such a combination of sizes posted on the same vehicle—like a full-page ad and a quarter-page ad in the same issue of a newspaper or magazine. Here the advertiser sees both ads enjoying the same circulation, and because one size is not increasing the reach nor frequency of the other, he strives to increase his impact (his total recognition and awareness) by using a related (not similar) copy approach.

The 22- by 144-inch backlighted rooftop ad (Figure 16), known in

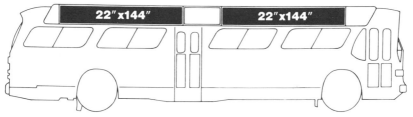

Figure 16   Bus-O-Rama.

the business as a *Bus-O-Rama*, offers exposure during evening hours, as well as during the day. Two are featured on each side of many new buses. They are usually assigned to routes which require service until midnight. Most production is on 10-gauge vinyl and laminated to plexiglass or lumasite. Some is silk-screened directly on the plexiglass or lumasite. Either way it stays in the frame for twelve weeks. Again, we recommend two or three words in easy-to-read type and sharp contrasts between colors used in any artwork. We also recommend the practice of a few advertisers who stretch their ad messages across both 12-foot panels—jumping over the vehicles' route number which is featured between the two 22- by 144-inch frames.

Except for 22- by 144-inch backlighted rooftops and the 30- by 144-inch king-size, exterior transit ads are printed on one sheet. If the campaign is scheduled for only one market, a silk-screen process is usually the most economical means of production. Larger runs are handled more efficiently by lithographers who handle the 30- by 144 inch posters in two or three sections. Cost-conscious advertisers save considerable production dollars by concentrating their four-color elements in one of these two or three sections—leaving the one-color or two-color copy in the rest of the ad. Moviemakers promote their features in two of the three sections, and leave a portion of the third for local theaters to tie in with their silk-screened opening dates, prices, curtain times, etc.

The Platform Poster The third type of transit ad is the platform poster (Figure 17). Here 70-pound opaque stock is supplied, taken

Figure 17 Platform poster.

to location, and installed in 46- by 60-inch frames. Located underground, elevated, at ground level, in terminals, and at transfer points, they are seen by commuters while they're waiting to board a transit vehicle.

Successful users of platform posters eye-test each ad at an average location, agreeing that the type is too small when it cannot be read from across the track. Frequently, their magazine art is edited and enlarged, thereby extending the frequency of what they intended to be the original message. (Sometimes this tactic actually works in reverse—with the transit ad preselling close attention to particulars when the rider encounters a more detailed ad in a magazine.)

Transit Ads with Other Media

National advertisers usually delegate these creative ad production details to their advertising agencies.   In this way their transit ads are integrated with the same campaign scheduled for other media in the designated markets.   For product introductions, seasonal promotions, contests, etc., point-of-purchase display material is also integrated with the advertising campaigns.   People who design point-of-purchase material frequently know how their displays can be adapted to transit ads.

In most markets, transit advertising operators honor requests for eye-testing copy on one or two vehicles.   Before printing and distributing a huge quantity, it is well to see how your transit ad looks in the environment for which it was created, and to watch how people notice it.

Picture files are maintained by many transit advertising operators and their sales representatives.   A quick look through a tray of slides can be most rewarding—particularly when the salesman has some knowledge of the history and success of each campaign.

Points To Check

For any of many reasons, the most beautiful ad on the bus might never sell its product.   Nobody can accuse the medium which delivers exposure opportunities at fantastically low costs per thousand. So ask for help as you begin planning strategy for your next transit ad.

Check Availabilities   The size you want might be sold out for two of those six months in one of the markets on your list.

Integrate Copy   Since you're including transit ads in your media mix, it's logical to integrate elements of the same copy used in other media.

Discipline Yourself   It's not easy to sum up an idea to fit into a transit ad.   But once you've done it, you'll find it easy to express that idea in other media.   Some creative people start with transit or outdoor, and go from there.

Follow Specifications   Your transit ad will miss the bus if it doesn't fit the frame, or doesn't arrive in time, or doesn't get printed on the right stock, and so on.   Ask for production specifications.   Most operators are striving toward standardization, and their sales representatives can be most helpful.

Consider Field Salesmen   Some would like to carry copies of your transit ad to each dealer in their territories—advising the retailer of your upcoming promotion and leaving the ad there as a window banner or wire banner.   With buses passing most retail outlets (and stopping in front of many to discharge shoppers) dealers like to stock products promoted with transit ads.   Make sure somebody shows them your transit ad before it begins going by their stores.

Use Available Help   This medium has been revitalized since the mid-1960s, and the desire to help advertisers and their agencies is shared by most transit advertising operators and their sales representatives.

POINT-OF-PURCHASE ADVERTISING

There is one unique element present in the point-of-purchase medium—immediacy.   The product is either in, on, immediately adjacent to, or in nearby proximity to the signs or displays for which copy is to be written.   Only enough needs to be said to prompt the customer to do one of the following three things:

Reject the item as not of current interest.

Purchase the item based on prior experience.

Stop and consider purchasing if the item is unknown.

Rejection can be from previous unpleasant experience with the product, or from dislike of the image of the product given in mass media, or from indifference.   Purchase can stem from the present reminder of pleasant experience with the product, from a favorable image created by mass media or word of mouth, or from factual reading about the product.   The stop-and-consider reaction is desirable possibly to overcome rejection and to make the customer into an automatic purchaser another time.   All copy should be developed with these three possible shopper reactions in mind.

Copy for the point-of-purchase medium can and should be ultimately specific, because it is an "on-target" medium.   For example: A display for snow tires will be utilized only in those stores which carry the particular brand featured in the display, in those state areas or regions where there is snow, and only at that time when protection against snow is of high interest to the customer.   Such specificity and timeliness create the need for highly effective copy.   It should be generated by the fact that this sale can and should be made here and now.   It can be expressed through every known system of printing, since these are all available to this medium.

Types of Copy

The use of copy on signs and displays is an integral part of the very function of the unit.   In most media, copy has a function of its own, apart from the rectangular space it occupies, and it bears no direct relationship to its environment beyond that of getting someone to notice it.   Copy on signs and displays, however, does have a direct relationship to its environment.   It is designed to call attention not to itself, but to some factor in the environment—a retail outlet, an area or department, or goods offered for sale at or in the outlet.   As such, it has three main duties to perform:

1. Identification   This is a prime duty and one which must not be subdued.   Some signs and many displays perform only this duty. Copy for this purpose consists only of the logo and whatever few words are necessary to characterize the outlet or manufacturer concerned, or the product at hand.   The words elected for this purpose must be clear, concise, and to the point.   They must be words which are well understood by most people and have connotations in keeping with the image desired for the retail store or the product.   Together with the logo they must immediately convey the wanted impression.   Such copy seldom goes beyond a single descriptive phrase. For example:

Norge—Quality Home Appliances
Hush Puppies—for truly comfortable feet
Haig—The Oldest Name in Scotch
Ace—The Sign of Service

In many cases the identification logo and its support are completely crystallized by time and usage.   Adaptation to signs and displays becomes a sole matter of placing these elements in the environment or adjacent to the product with maximum consideration for tastefulness and visibility.   Both of these qualities involve design of the unit which will carry the message, especially determination of size.   An identification unit for a brand of gasoline may have to be 36 feet tall in order to be visible from a sufficient distance to allow an approaching truck to slow its speed, change lanes, and come to a complete stop at the station with maximum traffic safety.   A product identifier to be used in a jeweler's case may be limited to a few inches. Location determines the size and complexity every time.

2. Advertising   For all signs or displays which also do an advertising job, it is important to retain the identification function, but to add to it the special features of a specific product or sale.   Here copy not only identifies, it also sells, informs, directs, explains—all of which assumes close-up reading.   The consumer has reached the point of purchase.   The sign or display has already captured the customer's attention.   Now this attention must be held and intensified for a brief moment more.

a. SELLING COPY.   This is a more or less inclusive idea which stimulates the impulse to "lift" advertising copy from whatever media and transfer it to the spot where the goods will be sold.   The impulse should be resisted, however, since such copy is generally not suited to the situation.   Mass media copy is "remote sell."   Sign and display copy is immediate sell.   The products are at hand.   The customer is in a buying mood.   Flowery phrases designed to arouse latent interest have no time to operate with immediacy.   Selling copy on signs and displays must be variations of "Buy me because . . . ," "You need me (or this product) now," "Here I am; come and get me." The more direct the copy, the more successful the sell.

b. INFORMATION COPY.   This is the kind of copy wanted by store customers, the kind that answers questions where the store provides no one to ask or where those persons the store does provide do not know the answers.   Customers are grateful for signs and displays which say: "This store carries a full line of____," or "This special store-wide sale ends Friday," or "It's time to think of back-to-school items."

c. DIRECTIONAL COPY.   Also much appreciated by the customer is that this copy directs traffic outside or inside the store.   In addition, special signs or displays direct the customer to where a particular product may be located or a particular class of products.   For many small items, apt to be overlooked, this may be the single most productive form of display.

d. EXPLANATORY COPY.   Such copy would include explanations of store policy, store hours, product guarantee policy, who may or may not purchase certain products, credit terms, and many other general types of explanation for which signs and displays are used.   In general, this kind of copy differs from *information copy* in that the customer usually views it from a closer position, and it therefore concerns itself with more detail.

All these types of copy should be kept simple and direct.   The message should be conveyed in as few words as possible—always keeping in mind the factor of visibility.   Where will the sign or display be placed?   From where will the customer view it?   It should be remembered that the customer is not sitting at a desk or in an easy chair, but is afoot, walking, often at a somewhat hurried pace.   What the message is about should stand out clearly.   Key words need to be prominent.   A good test for such copy is to have it set up at about the distance at which it can be assumed to be seen and have four or five persons walk by and then tell what it is about without closer examination.

3. Merchandising   This is the third duty of a sign or display. There are many merchandisers used in and outside of stores today where all the merchandising is done by the physical conformation of the display, and absolutely no copy is used except for the identifying logo and supporting phrase.   Advertising copy is completely eliminated.   This is particularly true of the most permanent types of displays which are designed to remain in use for a year or longer.   More promotional types of display, however, use considerably more copy. The types involved parallel those outlined above in the paragraphs on "Advertising."   Identification is, of course, too important to underplay, both for immediate and residual effects.   The differences for the various types of copy are as follows:

a. SELLING COPY.   Here, where the product is easily within reach, copy must sell by involving—"Smell me," "Touch me," "Pick me up," "Hear me," etc.   Or, selling copy which merchandises can involve the customer imaginatively instead of physically by suggesting a use for the product—"Picture this in your living room," "Your family needs the vitamins contained in____," and so on.   Imagination can also be stirred by appealing to emotions—"Your child will enjoy this," "Make father happy on his day."   The important point to remember is that the product is always within easy reach of the customer's hand while the copy is being read.   Actually, "being read" is not exactly the right expression.   The customer does not read this copy in the same sense that he would in a magazine or newspaper, or even on a television screen.   It might be more accurate to say that the customer absorbs it as a whole, in one instant.   It may never come to full consciousness.   Thus, the importance, again, of keeping selling copy brief and sharply to the point.

b. INFORMATION COPY.   Here is copy which the customer will really read, putting some effort into the reading.   However, this process depends upon product interest already being present, or having already been aroused.   Information copy should be just that—information about the brand, product, or service.   The customer resents being sold while seeking information.   Information copy should be as clear and concise as possible, and easy for the reader to grasp.   In setting out information, it is easier for the reader if the various points are numbered or in some fashion separated and given a boldface lead.   The customer can then skip over points he already knows and go directly to the point or points in which he has an interest.   Remember that when the customer is reading information copy, involvement is already a fact.   The sale can depend on how well the information is given.   A sale can be lost if the customer's particular question is not answered, or is answered in an obscure way.

c. DIRECTIONAL COPY.   This kind of copy, when the merchandise is at hand, is often confined to the product itself: "Open this end," "Tear along here," etc.   Sometimes, however, it is necessary or desirable to put such directional copy on the display: "Ring here for meat service," "Turn this lazy susan for further selection."   The need for brevity and clarity of this type of copy is obvious.   What is not always so obvious is the necessity or desirability for its inclusion.   Only careful consideration from the customer's point of view (one must always assume the customer is unfamiliar with the situation faced) will resolve the matter.

Another type of *directional copy* is that of "How to assemble," "How to open," or "How to operate."   Sometimes such directions, because of some feature such as ease of function, are in themselves a selling feature.   When this is so, it may be an advantage to dramatize the feature on the display rather than simply including it in or with the package.   Still another type of *directional copy*—"How to enter this contest," or "How to obtain this premium"—is more often than not printed on a tear-off pad which is attached to the display.   This is always advisable whenever the promotion or offer gets more complicated than "Mail in this box top for____." Besides, it is important for the customer to have a tangible reminder of the offer. (Remember to include tear-off directional copy to the customer immediately above the pad.) Here again simplicity and reading ease are important. Print that is too small looks complicated. Slack printing or poor-quality paper says "junk."

d. EXPLANATORY COPY. We may think of *selling copy* as creating the *dynamics,* and the other types of copy as giving the *specifics,* as follows: *information copy* as telling "what," *directional copy* as telling "where" and "how," and *explanatory copy* as telling "when," "why," and "how much" in terms of choices of color, size, shape, design, or dimension. Successful merchandising displays often take care of assorting for color, size, shape, design, or dimension, without any copy being needed. They do it by the very design and engineering of the unit. "Why" is also, in many cases, dramatized by the display with the copy itself doing a supplementary job.

Inclusion of Copy

From all the above it can be seen that the philosophy of copy and its use is very different from that of copy in other media. In the various forms of print media, copy is the master, even when a strong visual is included. In radio, copy and its delivery are all. In television, copy and delivery are still vital despite the strong visual. In signs and displays, the environment is the master; the form and substance are determined by it, and the copy becomes an accessory, albeit a strong accessory.

Because it is an accessory, it can very easily become excessive. Signs and especially displays do their utmost with three-dimensional form, while disciplining copy. The process of copy inclusion is therefore a major consideration.

Step 1: Research. The design of a sign or display begins with a survey of the general (and sometimes particular) environment in which they will eventually be placed, and a study of the way in which the customer moves about in that environment.

Step 2: Verbalization. What do we want to say to that customer? How much is necessary? How much can be eliminated?

Step 3: Crystallization. How much of what needs to be said can be said by the medium—the sign or display itself? How much is left over which must be said in words?

Step 4: Location and limitation. Where on the sign or display will the remaining necessary messages be placed? Will it be best if concentrated in one area, or perhaps separated for emphasis? What size limitations are thus created and how does this affect what must be said in words? How does what must be said in words affect, in turn, the design of the sign or display?

Step 5: Type consideration. Once the copy distillation has been made, and the design restructured to accommodate what must be said, what type will be selected for maximum visibility at the proper distance? Should the face selected be chosen for harmony or contrast with the general feeling of the unit? How readable is readable?

Step 6: Color considerations. A standard for maximum visibility has been determined to be black lettering on a light yellow background. Obviously, from the point of view of monotony alone, this is not an appropriate choice for every sign or display. What colors can be used? Almost all colors can be used in some combination and still achieve visibility by varying the light values of the colors used. For example, red and green, though brightly contrasting in hue, have similar light values and so offer short-range visibility. Dark red and pale green, or dark green and pink offer good visibility.

It will be seen that the copy writer's skill in sign and display writing must be an integral part of the designer's art. If the copy writer is not himself the creative designer or the design engineer, he must work very closely with him.

Dynamics of Copy

The ever-present need for simplicity and clarity of copy for signs and displays does not relieve the writer from the necessity for force and intensity. Instead, it highlights the need. Puns, homonyms, "cute" words, and trick spellings have a questionable place in copy for signs and displays. In this medium, as in no other, the copy writer must "tell it as it is" in carefully lined phrases with heavy emphasis on verbs and nouns and with but sparing use of adjectives. An adjective, almost any adjective, is a glaring anachronism to a customer with a hand on the product. "Feel the soft touch of this ____" is open to so many interpretations of the word "soft" that the result is likely to start the customer questioning, "Is it really soft?"

The *prospective* customer sitting in a chair, reading, watching, or listening, may be able to anticipate a vague idea of "soft" which will at some future date be encountered. The *moving* customer, at or in the store, who can touch the product, does not have to be told it is soft, may even resent being told it is soft if it does not meet a personal idea of softness. Better simply to say, "Feel it," and let the customer make the decision.

The same principle applies to any sensuous response. Such responses are personal. Only the customer can judge them. Only the customer knows that internal feedback which will bring to consciousness the desired response—"I must have that."

This also applies to certain nonsensuous statements—price, for example. The customer in the store knows how much money he has in his pocket. "Inexpensive" to one customer may be "expensive" to another. The point of purchase is the point of final decision, the moment of truth, where the customer will either buy or not buy, and the time is right now. The main feature should always appeal to that. If it is price, put it first. If it is the volume per package, let it precede. Always give the major selling point top billing. Be sure to avoid weakening your strong selling point by saying too much. If you include a weak feature, you detract from the others.

One final advantage of point of purchase is that it seldom, if ever, appears where it is unrelated or out of context. The shopper must go to the point of purchase. It never approaches the shopper. Therefore, when the shopper confronts your copy he is usually in a position and in a mood to buy the product offered. The situation has been reduced to one of choice or decision. The sign or display is there to do its part in resolving the 40 per cent of buying decisions which are made in the store in favor of its particular brand, product, or service. It is there to do the selling job.

PART SIX
Media

CHAPTER EIGHTEEN

Media Planning

RICHARD P. JONES · *Vice President, Director of Media,
J. Walter Thompson Company*

NEW PRECISION IN MEDIA PLANNING

The process of developing a recommendation for the allocation of media dollars entails a series of steps which are logical and simple in concept, but require a great deal of analytical skill, media expertise, and sound judgment to execute successfully. This chapter will outline the allocation procedure and explore in detail some of the more important elements of a sound media plan.

A good deal of pertinent information is now available from syndicated research services such as W. R. Simmons, Brand Rating Index, and others, which was not available a few years back. This information, together with the advanced analytical techniques made possible by the application of electronic data processing equipment, has introduced a degree of precision into the media selection process that was not possible a few years ago. There are still many areas where judgment must be applied, but these judgments can now be based on a more solid foundation of knowledge.

Changes in Media Research

As background, it may be worthwhile to review briefly the changes that have taken place in media research and explain how they have affected media planning techniques.

First, and most importantly, the new research *is more relevant to the critical job of matching media to markets.*

The key element is that it combines research into the media habits of people with product-usage data.   Information on both is taken from the same people, making it possible for the first time to assess the product-purchase rates of a medium's audience in meaningful and specific terms.   This is a big step forward.

Second, the new data provide a better *identification of audiences in terms of people* rather than households.   Until a few years ago, most media audience research reported on the coverage of media vehicles by the number and kind of households reached.   But obviously households do not read or view media; people do.   With the old research, it was not clear whether it was the housewife, the husband, or the teen-age daughter who was being exposed to the magazine or television program once it got into the home.   Today, the trend is toward measuring the media habits of individuals, who can then be qualified as prospects according to either personal or household characteristics or individual purchase patterns—a much tougher assignment for the researcher but an essential step forward in defining media values in meaningful marketing terms.

Third, we are now getting *a better fix on the interaction of various kinds of media.*   These new services are finding out from the same people the extent of their exposure to the various types of media, television as well as magazines, and radio, and newspapers.   While this still does not tell us which media form is the most effective, it is now possible for planners at least to assess the numerical contributions of various media to a media problem more accurately than ever before.

Finally, *much of the new research is available on computer tape,* making it possible to utilize the incredible speed and memory capacity of the computer in data analysis.   For those agencies that do not have their own computer installations, service bureaus or shared-time operations are available.

The computer, however, has contributed much more to media planning than a superior computational capability. It has enforced a more stringent discipline on the decision makers. Because the computer is, in fact, a "logic machine," it has forced us to define and evaluate audience objectives more carefully, to proceed in a rational step-by-step fashion throughout the analytical process, and to make explicit decisions with regard to the relative values of media forms and media vehicles which were sometimes evaded in the past.

Importance of New Advances

The importance to the advertiser of this improved information and new-found analytical expertise is self-evident. Budget requirements have multiplied, and the role of advertising as a marketing tool has increased over the past two decades. Advertisers have quite understandably come to expect a more careful accounting of dollars allocated for media. They want a well-reasoned rationale and documentation for the specific media proposed and the plan for using them most effectively.

The reason is simple. The media decision is critical to the success of the advertising campaign. It determines, for example, the characteristics of individuals exposed to the advertising, and it controls the place and the circumstances, form, timing, and frequency of advertising exposure.

Beyond exposure, the media decision influences the whole complex of advertising perception and communication. It selects the senses through which communication takes place. It affects their response to the advertising.

Beyond its direct effect on consumers, the media decision may even affect distribution, dealer interest, and the kind of retail selling support the brand receives.

It is obvious that a decision of this magnitude must be approached in a carefully reasoned, highly disciplined way. While the kinds and amounts of information that will be appropriate will vary from problem to problem, and the analytical techniques required may change, it is possible to set down a general procedure that will serve as a guide to the media planner and a checklist for the advertiser. Such a procedure is outlined at the end of this chapter.

Areas to Be Explored The remainder of the chapter will examine the most critical problems and decisions to be faced in media planning and describe some practical methods for resolving them. Specifically, these areas will be explored:

1. Setting the media objectives
2. Fulfilling creative requirements
3. Defining audience goals
4. Allocating advertising dollars geographically in relation to sales opportunities
5. Scheduling the advertising
6. Establishing reach and frequency goals
7. Test marketing
8. Media plan outline

SETTING MEDIA OBJECTIVES

The media objectives are, in effect, a listing of all the things the media planner must take into account in selecting the components of his plan. Carefully expressed, they serve two basic purposes: They are the means of arriving at complete agreement on the part of everyone involved as to what is to be accomplished, and they provide guidelines for the actual purchase of media time and space.

Unfortunately, media objectives are often couched in such vague terms as to be inadequate for either of these purposes. Generalities such as "provide broad national coverage," "deliver maximum reach with adequate frequency," are crutches for the careless or superficial thinker. They obviously provide neither a specific goal for the execution of the plan nor a yardstick by which to measure results.

They Must Be Consistent with the Advertiser's Overall Marketing Objectives and Strategy The successful media plan is not an end in itself but a means to an end. An objective that calls for "the lowest possible cost per thousand" is irrelevant unless the goals against which this cost per thousand are to be measured are spelled out and are consistent with the product's marketing targets.

They Must Be Consistent with the Copy Strategy and the Requirements of the Creative Approach There is little argument that the most important element in an advertising campaign is the message. Thus the media specifications must take into account the requirements for an effective message. Obviously, a discussion between the media planner and the creative supervisor is highly desirable before the process of media selection begins.

They Must Give Adequate Consideration to Competitive Activities In making media decisions, we should consider the likelihood that the individuals covered by each medium will be heavily or lightly reached by competitive advertising.   On occasion, alternative media choices may be about equally desirable, except that one is being used by competitive brands.   If these are brands against which our product will have no special advantage in copy or dollar expenditures, the competitive advertising may largely nullify the response to our own advertising and diminish its profitability.   If good alternative media are available, we should seriously consider using them.

On the other hand, if we are in a position to dominate other competing advertisers in a particular medium, or if a consumer comparison of copy will leave our brand with a clear advantage, we may profit from direct media competition.

In some cases, where media serve a sort of shopping-guide function, i.e., the so-called shelter magazines in home decoration, it is desirable for competitors to group together.   Or, when the market saturation for a product category is low and promotional funds are limited, the total market may best be expanded by parallel competitive efforts.

Expert media selection requires a knowledge of competitive activity, and the proper use of this information involves imaginative thinking and a good sense of strategy.

They Must Take Realistic Account of Budget Restrictions All media plans are a compromise between the ideal and the practical.   Large space and time units may be creatively desirable, but their high cost may defeat their value because of a critical reduction in exposure levels.   Budget will also affect the definition of the audience target, whether the advertiser can afford to reach the total market or would be better advised to direct his limited funds toward a high potential segment.   The size and shape of the media plan will depend upon the bolt of cloth from which it must be cut.

Critical Specific Questions

These are the general requirements.   More specifically, the media objectives should contain concisely summarized answers to the following questions:

1. To whom should the advertising be directed?   (Demographic description of target groups, and indication of relative value assigned

to each.   Male versus female?   Users versus principal purchasing agents?)

2. Where should the advertising messages be delivered?   (Nationally?   Regionally?   By client sales territories?   Are geographic or major market variations in message weight desirable?   If so, what levels, by area?)

3. When should the product be advertised?   (Taking into account seasonal requirement, anticipated competitive activity, etc.)

4. What creative requirements must be taken into account? (Does the copy strategy dictate certain media capabilities, such as color, sound, motion?   Is a special frame of reference or editorial environment needed?   What units of time or space are needed and affordable?)

5. What are the special requirements or priorities for reach, frequency, or frequency distribution?

6. What other marketing requirements must be met?   (Is retail merchandising support required?   An unusual degree of budgetary or timing flexibility?   Support for consumer promotions?   Other?)

As indicated earlier, the answers to each of these questions usually require considerable analysis of market and media data, a thorough understanding of the overall goals of the advertising campaign, and the application of a very large pinch of judgment based on this knowledge.   The critical need throughout is to be as precise and specific as possible in order to provide guidelines that will help maximize the efficiency and effectiveness of the advertising dollars in accomplishing the objectives of the campaign.

Following sections will describe some methods for becoming more proficient in the art of being specific.

CREATIVE REQUIREMENTS

Advertising is *communication,* and effective communication depends on the presentation of the message.   One of the media planner's most important responsibilities, therefore, is to provide the most appropriate vehicle for the advertising copy.   All the advantages gained through a careful allocation of dollars in the marketplace can be wiped out if the message does not come across to the potential consumer.

Communication between Media and Copy

As mentioned earlier, close communication between the media planner and the copy group is highly desirable in the early stages of plans development.   A discussion at this time will serve two important ends:

It will help the copy group understand clearly the exposure opportunities and limitations which will result from the use of various media forms or units of time or space.

It will provide the media planner with an understanding of the intended creative approach which will guide his thinking in the selection of media.

Impact versus Exposure   An understanding of the limitations which the use of large units of space or time imposes is always important. An actual situation comes to mind in which a better assessment of this factor could have made a difference to the success of the product.

A well-known advertiser in the household-products field introduced a new colored brand (Brand A).   The creative group devised an excellent campaign using four-color, full-page magazine advertisements.   The objective of this approach was to dramatize the new colors and give the product a high-quality, "decorator" image. Copy tests revealed an excellent reaction and good playback of copy points.   Initial reaction in the marketplace was also good.

The strategy might well have worked except for one factor.   A leading competitor came out with a similar product (Brand B) shortly thereafter.   Ignoring the "need" to show the product in color, the second advertiser elected to use 20-second and 30-second television spots.   With about the same budget he was able approximately to double the amount of exposure against the primary target group.

The gamble on greater exposure at the sacrifice of a more dramatic creative approach paid off.   A decreasing brand share indicated trouble for Brand A.   Field research revealed that consumer familiarity with the advertising campaign was low, though it was well liked by those who claimed to have seen it.   Most distressing, many who claimed familiarity with it actually attributed Brand A copy to Brand B.   Obviously, the more frequent repetition of the Brand B name had enabled it to attain a substantially greater *share of mind*— a critical factor in the marketplace.

In this case, the Brand A budget was obviously inadequate to provide for both expensive units and competitive frequency.   An otherwise excellent campaign had failed for lack of exposure.

The relative importance of creative impact through expensive space or time units versus greater exposure through less costly units must be resolved on the basis of judgment, experience, and a full awareness of the media alternatives.   Little progress can be made on the media plan until a decision on this point has been reached.

Once this decision has been made and the creative strategy settled, the media planner is in a much better position to select media which will (1) provide the physical characteristics needed to present the message most effectively, and (2) take full advantage of the general media environment.

Media Environment   Much has been written and little has been proved about the ability of a medium to enhance the impact of the advertising it carries.   A majority of advertising men believes that a medium does act as something more than a simple carrier; that an advertisement seen in the environment of a reader's favorite magazine or a viewer's favorite program will have an edge in terms of both perception and response over one seen in a neutral or unfavorable environment.   If the copy approach is congenial with the spirit and the content of the medium, so much the better.

This phenomenon, if real, is the result of two factors: (1) the amount of attention given the media vehicle by the individual exposed, and (2) the psychological rapport between the medium and the reader or viewer.   In door-to-door selling, a salesman will find that his success depends on both the degree of interest his prospect has in the product and the amount of customer rapport he is able to achieve.   The same may be true of a media vehicle, which, like a salesman, has a definite style and personality.

Demographic audience information, based as it is on simple exposure, is only partially useful in analyzing this subtle aspect of media selection.   The medium may reach many people, but it will probably be most effective among those viewers or readers who find it congenial enough to absorb their full attention.   Syndicated attitudinal studies such as TV Q, Magazine Q, and several studies done by individual media, all shed a glimmer of light if not a full beam on the media preferences of different kinds of people.

However, whether the media planner uses research or simply judgment, the important thing is for him to make an explicit decision regarding the value of the medium as a *communicator* of the advertising to appropriate target groups.

DEFINING AUDIENCE GOALS

The most critical job the media man must face is the establishment of audience objectives.   Once an advertisement has been put into finished form, the next step is obviously to see that it gets adequate exposure.   Every advertising exposure costs money.   Thus, the determination of how many exposures should be bought, and who should receive them, occupies a great deal of the media planner's time.

Dangers of Generalization

We know, of course, that not everyone uses the product or service to be advertised, and that many people can never be induced to use it either because it does not fit into their way of life, they cannot afford it, or because it simply does not appeal to them.   There is a temptation to generalize about such people—to say that single persons or old or rural people or some other broad groups are not prospects and therefore should be eliminated from consideration.

Such oversimplification can be dangerous.   Market studies usually show that there are some exceptions to the nonbuying rule in any group.   Some Cadillacs are sold in the ghettos, senior citizens do drink Pepsi-Cola.   It is really a matter of degree.

Index of Soft-drink Usage

Age	Male	Female	Total
Total United States	100	100	100
12–15	117	97	107
16–19	174	112	143
25–29	125	108	115
45 and over	81	95	88

Any hard-and-fast definition of prospects that fails to take this phenomenon into account almost certainly will result in the exclusion or underweighting of a substantial potential market concealed within the "nonprospect" segments of the population.

By the same token, there are certain to be many individuals who are not users or potential users in the groups defined as "best prospects."   An efficient media plan must also recognize this fact.

Establishment of Audience Goals

What is needed, then, is a method of establishing advertising audience goals which takes into account the elusive nature of the prospect group.   If the market data are reliable, such an approach should enable the media planner to improve the efficiency of his media selection by helping to identify and evaluate potential consumers, and to select media which are most efficient in reaching those potential customers who have been selected as targets for the advertising.

It is important at this point to face one of the more frustrating aspects of the media planner's job.   That is the knowledge that no matter how precise he is in setting his audience targets, the nature of media is such that he will inevitably reach many individuals who are of little value as customers.   Mass media are by definition nonselective.   They offer something for everybody and thus cut across the demographic segmentations that determine product usage.

As Dr. Leo Bogart points out in his excellent book "Strategy in Advertising": [1]

> There is no perfect case of media and marketing matching.   Any medium, no matter how selective, will reach some people other than the ones who are prospects for a manufacturer's product.   Any market of heavy users, no matter how concentrated, will include many people beyond the reach of a selective medium.
>
> In any attempt to correlate media and consumption habits, some very important simplifications have to be made.   To the extent that there is a relationship at all, it is rarely a direct relationship between the two.   Instead, it usually arises because of the intrusion of a third element which reflects such things as the consumer's age, education, or income, or more subtle matters of personality and taste.

Recognizing that a perfect market and media match is unattainable, the media planner must nevertheless make every effort to minimize the waste circulation by carefully describing his consumer target in terms that can be related directly to his knowledge of media audiences.

How to Identify Targets   There are two methods of identifying audience targets and evaluating media which are in general use today:

[1] Leo Bogart, "Strategy in Advertising," Harcourt, Brace & World, Inc., New York, 1967, p. 203.

First, a *demographic-matching* approach. Under this system, market and media audience characteristics are matched in an effort to put messages in front of designated prospects with minimum cost. This is the traditional approach, but it has recently become much more scientific as a result of computer technology.

Second, the so-called *product-user* (or *direct-match*) approach. With this method the number of actual users of a given product in a medium's audience is taken into account as well as the approximate volume they consume in a specified period of time. Different media can then be compared on the basis of their efficiency in reaching users or "heavy users" of a product category, or when information is available, of the advertiser's own brand or competitive brands. In some cases, the total volume of product consumed by each medium's audience can be measured.

The principal weakness of this approach is that it cannot be used to analyze the demographic components of the current market—an essential first step in pointing the direction toward market expansion opportunities. Neither is it of value in the selection of media for the introduction of new or drastically altered products.

On the other hand, it is a very useful measure of the efficiency of media when the marketing strategy calls for either (1) increasing the volume of product used by present customers, or (2) increasing brand share within the present market.

The demographic approach has some value in almost any situation. An understanding of the demographic characteristics of users is basic in developing the overall advertising strategy and determining the best copy approach. However, as a media selection tool, demographic matching also has its weakness.

This weakness lies in the implicit assumption that for any demographic group there will be about the same percentage of users in a medium's audience as in the population as a whole. This is not always true. For example, let us assume that a product is bought by 40 per cent of all housewives aged twenty-five to thirty-four years and living in middle-income families. A given media vehicle may reach 25 per cent of such housewives. The trouble is that there is no real assurance that a *proportionate* share of the 40 per cent of these housewives who are *users* are included in the 25 per cent of similar women covered by the media vehicle.

This variance is the result of the selectivity of media vehicles. A family's product usage will be strongly influenced by its demographic characteristics—its size, income, age of children, etc.—but the *media exposure* of the family's chief purchasing agent is the result of such subtle matters as personality and taste.   Thus there can be no assurance that two women who are equally heavy users of, say, bacon are also interested in the same magazine or television show.

Researchers are attempting to improve current methods of relating purchasers and media audiences through a new measurement which involves a blending of demographic and psychological characteristics.   This new measure is currently referred to as *psychographics,* or in a slightly different form, *attitudinal segmentation.*   It promises to lead a step closer to the goal of matching media to markets, but as yet it is in a very elementary stage of development.   Until further progress is made, media planners must utilize as best they can the two current systems described earlier.

A demonstration of how each of these two approaches may be applied follows.

Demographic Matching

This approach requires the type of information currently made available through syndicated research services such as Simmons, Brand Rating Index (or, through the blending of market data from any one source with media data from another).   Data must be drawn from a sample of the population which is reasonably representative of the whole and is large enough to be statistically stable when broken down into the required number of subsegments.   The following information is needed:

1. A description of each individual in the sample in demographic terms—his or her age, household income, education, family size [2]

2. A record of each individual's usage of the product or brand to be advertised over a specified period of time

3. A record of each individual's media exposure

By relating the product usage history of each individual in the sample to his or her personal or family (demographic) characteristics, it is possible to identify those characteristics which separate users from nonusers or heavy users from light users—the characteristics, in

[2] A list of demographic breakdowns recommended for researchers is available in a document published by the American Association of Advertising Agencies entitled "Recommended Breakdowns for Consumer Media Data."

other words, which serve as *predictors* of the potential of each person as a customer.

Contribution of the Computer   The important contribution which the computer has made to this process is to enable us to take into account the complex correlations which exist between different characteristics.   For example, it is useful to know that women aged eighteen to thirty-four have an above-average probability of purchase, but it is more useful to know that within that large group, those women with two or more children are twice as valuable as the remainder, and of those with two or more children, the segment having a family income of more than $8,000 a year is 25 per cent more likely to buy.

The computer, with its capacity to perform thousands of calculations in a matter of seconds, can identify subsegments of the market in multidemographic terms and specify the value of each group in relation to the average of the entire sample.   It thus enables the planner to be far more precise in defining and evaluating his audience targets, and as a consequence, to develop a more efficient media plan.

Market in Multidemographic Terms   In this example, an analysis of the purchase patterns of the respondents (adult women, in this case) disclosed that the most important predictors of usage of Product A were age, income, and family size.   By dividing the universe into seven *mutually exclusive* groups (that together account for the total adult female population) based on these characteristics and relating the usage levels of each group to the *average* for the entire sample, it was possible to assign each group a relative value, expressed as an index, with the overall average expressed as 100.

This first step provides an important insight into the productivity level of each group.   However, it could be misleading unless the *total* potential of the group is taken into account.

For example, in Figure 1, Group 1 has a high productivity index (245), but since it contains only 8.2 per cent of the households, its total consumption (number of people times average purchase rate) represents only 20.2 per cent of national total.   On the other hand, Groups 6 and 7, each with a relatively low productivity index, nevertheless account for 25.9 per cent of total consumption.

As pointed out earlier, this approach reduces the likelihood of oversimplification.   If the planner had generalized that younger, larger, upper-income groups were the "best prospects" and set these people as his audience target, he might have unwittingly overlooked

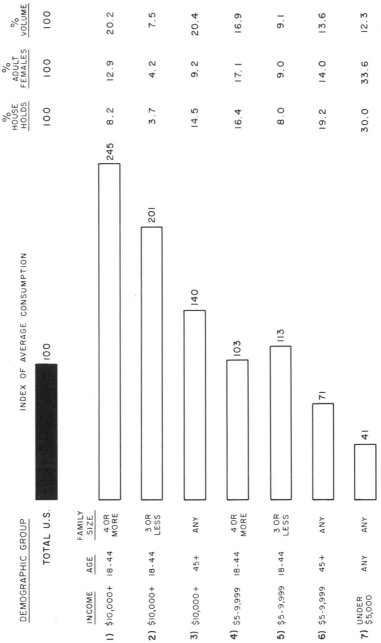

Figure 1 Product A: Analysis of consumption by demographic groups.

or undervalued the older or less affluent people (Groups 3, 6, and 7) who together account for almost half of the total. By showing the value of each group in terms of both their productivity and their overall importance in the marketplace, such a generalization is unlikely to be made.

This is not to say that the media plan should necessarily strive to distribute advertising impressions against prospect groups in direct relation to their current usage rate. Other factors such as budget, recent or expected changes in the market situation, competitive considerations, or a change in the advertising approach may dictate an entirely different strategy.

For example, if the budget is too small to develop competitive impact against the whole market, it may be more sensible to attempt to concentrate advertising weight as much as possible against a relatively small, potentially productive segment (such as Groups 1, 2, and 3 in Figure 1).

Again, if a drop in the price of the product is about to take place, the under-$10,000 groups may assume a new importance. Strategy may require an "overweighting" of Groups 4, 5, and 6 in that case.

If it is determined that the greatest current opportunity lies in expanding the market as a whole by increasing consumption on the part of light or moderate users, a quite different allocation of advertising weight may be in order.

Positions of Competitive Brands On the other hand, if the market is mature and approximate "saturation usage" has already been achieved, the advertiser's main marketing task may be to attract customers away from his competition. In this case, an analysis of the relative position of competitive brands within each group can often reveal an opportunity in one or more areas of the marketplace which the shrewd media strategist can turn to his advantage. Figure 2 is a good demonstration.

In this product category, a packaged food product, three brands have a 70 per cent penetration overall.

Brand A and Brand C are competitive in price and are the leaders in the field. Brand B is a "price brand," relying heavily on trade and consumer promotions.

In advertising, Brand A features quality and taste using media aimed at housewives. Brand B is highly promotional. Brand C has

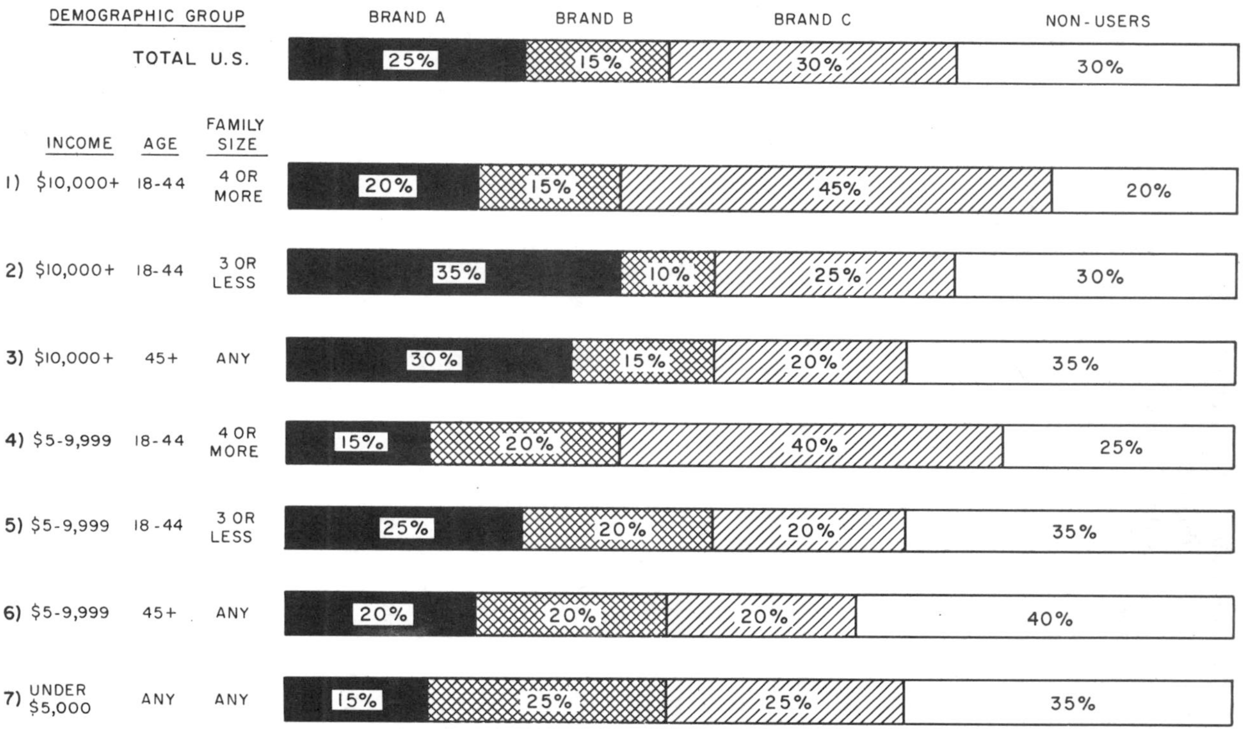

Figure 2 Product A: Brand penetration by demographic groups.

divided its effort between housewives and children, stressing quality but in a much lighter vein.

A study of brand penetration by demographic groups points up some interesting differences as a result of these varying strategies. Brand B, as would be expected, has its highest share in the lower income, older groups. This is a function of price promotion. Advertising can probably not do a great deal about it, nor are these groups productive enough for the product category as a whole to justify a major effort by Brands A and C.

Brand C, however, is considerably stronger than Brand A in Groups 1 and 4, both of which have above-average product penetration and are worth cultivating. These groups contain large families, and after further study, it is apparent the success of Brand C is because of its appeal to children.

Brand A, which does well among smaller, middle- and upper-income families, might well decide to invest some of its dollars in media aimed at young people, children's television shows or comics, for example.

The point is that such a demographic analysis provides a good basis for making a marketing strategy decision because the decision maker knows the rate at which different people currently buy. Once this marketing strategy is set, it should be reflected in the statement of media objectives where it will serve as a guide in evaluating alternative media plans.

A short discussion of this media evaluation phase may be in order here before we move on to a discussion of the product-user approach.

Alternative Media Combinations A truly meaningful analysis of the delivery of alternative media combinations against various subsegments of the market involves complex mathematical computations, the volume of which calls for the use of the computer. This assumes that the planner wants to know the reach and frequency against each group as well as the simple gross-rating-point count the plan delivers. An example of the results of such an analysis is shown in Figure 3.

Before any media analyses were undertaken, the following decisions were made:

1. The advertising would be directed to adult females within the groups specified.

2. The objective would be to distribute advertising weight as

Income	Age	Family size	Percent Current volume	Plan 1 7 magazines day net. TV (75 GRP/wk)			Plan 2 10 magazines prime net. TV (30 GRP/wk)			Plan 3 8 magazines day net. TV (20 GRP/wk); fringe spot TV (30 GRP/wk) 26 A mkts			Balance U.S.	
				Imps %	Reach.	Ave. Freq.	Imps %	Reach	Ave. Freq.	Imps %	Reach	Ave. Freq.	Reach	Ave. Freq.
1. $10,000+	18–44	4 or more	20.2	10.4	79	3.7	17.3	85	3.7	13.1	86	3.8	83	2.8
2. $10,000+	18–44	3 or less	7.5	3.3	74	3.9	5.4	89	3.2	4.6	90	4.0	88	2.6
3. $10,000+	45+	Any	20.4	7.1	77	3.7	10.1	85	3.2	10.1	87	4.3	83	2.6
4. $5–9,999	18–44	4 or more	16.9	19.1	78	5.1	20.1	78	3.4	18.1	87	3.9	84	3.0
5. $5–9,999	18–44	3 or less	9.1	9.5	79	4.8	10.2	85	3.0	9.7	90	4.0	88	2.8
6. $5–9,999	45+	Any	13.6	13.8	78	4.7	13.6	74	3.1	15.9	87	4.5	83	2.7
7. Under $5,000	Any	Any	12.3	36.8	72	5.6	23.3	63	2.6	28.5	80	3.5	75	2.6
Total impressions, in thousands..........				238,566	76	4.8	152,184	75	3.1	182,057	85	4.0	81	2.8
Total cost............				$345,600			$350,000			$349,700				
CPM women............				$1.45			$2.30			$1.92				
CPM potential............				$0.19			$0.23			$0.21				

Figure 3 Product A: Analysis of the distribution of advertising impressions by demographic groups.

nearly as possible according to the current sales potential of each demographic group.

These decisions having been made, it was then possible to determine which of several media combinations would meet the objectives most efficiently.

There are, of course, computer models in use which will select the *one* most efficient plan. These so-called maximization programs are not infallible, however, owing to the many areas requiring personal judgment. It is frequently desirable to supplement such an analysis with additional evaluations which include other media or revised judgmental decisions.

In this example, three combinations of magazines plus daytime and nighttime television were run off. Five factors were considered in evaluating the plans:

1. Total message weight
2. The distribution of messages by groups
3. The reach and frequency against each group
4. The cost per thousand adult women
5. The cost per thousand units of potential (women weighted by their usage rate)

The tables in Figure 3 demonstrate the following points:

1. Plan 2 (magazines and prime evening network TV) does a better job than either Plan 1 (magazines plus day network TV) or Plan 3 (magazines plus day network TV and fringe spot TV) in distributing advertising impressions in relation to sales. (All three plans place more emphasis than desired against Group 7, which is inevitable when mass media are utilized. This points up the fact discussed earlier, that a perfect plan is seldom attainable.)

2. While Plan 2 has the best skew, it is the least efficient of the three plans in reaching women. It does place more actual impressions against all those groups with above-average sales indices (Groups 1 through 5), and yet, in spite of this, the lower-cost media used in Plan 1 (daytime TV as opposed to prime evening TV, and less magazine space) which has resulted in substantially greater advertising tonnage against all women has given Plan 1 an efficiency advantage in coverage of "units of potential." This emphasizes the need, where two or more media forms are involved, for an explicit decision as to the relative worth of each type of impression. Is an exposure in magazines equal to one delivered by television, is it half as valuable, or worth

twice as much?   In totaling impressions, such differences must be taken into account if one plan is to be equated with another.

3. Plan 3 provides greater reach and frequency than Plan 2 in the twenty-six Nielsen A counties in every demographic group.   However, it gives slightly less reach and substantially lower frequency in the remainder of the country in Groups 1 through 3.   The choice between these two plans would depend on the geographic distribution objectives (discussed in detail in a later section).

While an analysis of this type based on a demographic-matching approach does not solve all the problems of the media planner, it does substantially narrow the areas of choice in deciding on the most appropriate media strategy.

The Product-user Approach

This system for evaluating media is more direct than demographic matching.   It eliminates entirely the need to determine the demography of the customer.   The information required is (1) knowledge that a given respondent in the research sample is a user of the product or brand under consideration; (2) some measure of the quantity of usage; and (3) a report on his or her media exposure over a period of time.

With this information (which is provided by the syndicated research services) it is possible to identify media known to be read or viewed by people who have purchased the product and to compare them on the basis of lowest cost per thousand users.

Figure 4 provides an example of the results of such an analysis. The product in this example is in the alcoholic-beverage field. Magazines have been ranked in order of the cost per thousand adult male readers, with each magazine's relative position on this basis indicated in parenthesis.   It is easy to see that substantial differences exist in the two rankings.

A refinement on this type of analysis is to categorize all individuals in a medium's audience into groups labeled "heavy," "medium," "light," or "nonusers," and rank each vehicle on its efficiency in reaching one or more of these categories.   If the marketing strategy calls for a high degree of concentration against "best prospects," the heavy-user approach would be the best method for the problem.

An even more exact measure of media value is usually possible through a further step in this type of analysis, based on the total volume of product usage.

In most cases an estimate of the volume of usage for each individual in the sample is available. It is thus possible to compute the total volume accounted for by the audience of each vehicle and develop a ranking based on cost per thousand "units of potential" covered.

	(1)	(2)	(3)
		CPM	*CPM*
		Product	*Adult Male*
	Rank	*Users*	*Readers*
Magazine A	1	$11.94	$3.85 (9)
Magazine B	2	17.34	2.76 (2)
Magazine C	3	17.91	3.55 (6)
Magazine D	4	19.92	2.97 (3)
Magazine E	5	20.25	3.31 (4)
Magazine F	6	23.45	3.62 (7)
Magazine G	7	23.86	3.96 (10)
Magazine H	8	25.56	3.70 (8)
Magazine I	9	27.79	4.00 (12)
Magazine J	10	30.28	3.41 (5)
Magazine K	11	31.02	2.74 (1)
Magazine L	12	38.51	3.98 (11)

SPACE UNIT: Four-color page.
SOURCE: 1967 Simmons Magazine Report.

Figure 4 Product B: Alcoholic beverage. Magazines ranked by CPM total product users and adult male readers.

The mechanics of this are simple. The computer identifies users in each medium's audience, multiplies each user by the number of units of the product purchased or consumed (cans of food, bottles of beverage, number of trips, etc.), totals these, and divides the sum into the cost of the unit of space or time selected.

This figure is important because it not only demonstrates each vehicle's relative efficiency in delivering "users," but also takes into account the amount of product used by these people.

Figure 5 provides an example of the results of such an analysis for a household product sold largely to women. The medium under consideration is network daytime television. In columns 1 through 4 are given (1) the name of the program, (2) the cost per thousand adult women, (3) the cost per thousand units of consumption represented by the audience (CPM potential) and (4) the selectivity indicator.

This final column is an important additional piece of information. It is useful to know how heavily concentrated the media vehicle's audience is among the prime categories of users, regardless of cost. The selectivity indicator reflects the vehicle's ability to skew toward the heavy-using segment.   (The higher the indicator, the greater the percentage coverage of heavy users relative to coverage of all adult women.)

Program	CPM Women *	CPM Potential *	Selectivity Indicator
A	$1.53	$0.14	104
B	1.78	0.17	102
C	1.55	0.18	82
D	1.73	0.18	92
E	1.68	0.19	85
F	1.63	0.20	83
G	1.95	0.20	97
H	1.75	0.21	83
I	1.77	0.22	78
J	1.78	0.22	82
K	1.79	0.22	79
L	1.80	0.22	81
M	1.80	0.23	75

* Based on 60-second unit cost.

Figure 5   Product C: Household package goods. Daytime network performance.

The decision as to which system will yield the best results depends, as always, on (1) the strategy for selling the product, and (2) the availability of appropriate and reliable information.

Influencing the Channels of Distribution

There are occasionally secondary audience targets of considerable importance to the advertiser.

For example, if retail distribution is a problem or shelf space is being encroached upon by competition, it may be of particular importance to impress the store manager or distributor with the size and nature of the consumer advertising being put behind the product.

Advertisers frequently attempt to do this by describing their campaigns in appropriate trade magazines. However, actual exposure of the retailer to the consumer advertising is even more effective. In addition to convincing him that the advertiser really means business, it enables the retailer to judge for himself the effectiveness of the advertising copy and form some estimate (hopefully positive) of probable customer response.

Where such firsthand exposure is considered important, the planner will attempt to include in the schedule media which provide exposure to the trade. Newspapers are generally considered to be effective for this purpose (most retailers use them for their own advertising), as are outdoor, general magazines, and prime-time television.

With the growth of chains and discount houses and the concomitant development of central buying committees and automatic inventory control, the need for special pressure at the store-manager level is somewhat reduced. Nevertheless, many advertisers consider a media plan which can be merchandised to the trade a definite plus, while recognizing that this should never take precedence as an objective over effective impact against the consumer.

ALLOCATING ADVERTISING DOLLARS GEOGRAPHICALLY

In addition to evaluating the market demographically, it is essential that one thoroughly understand geographic sales patterns and establish a strategy of area allocation of advertising dollars. Although the development of such a strategy, which involves a knowledge of current sales and recent trends, product distribution, transportation costs, long-range plans for expansion, competitive maneuvers, etc., is not primarily the responsibility of the media planner, its successful implementation is. He must plan media strategy in such a way as to place advertising dollars where they will be most productive.

This assignment is complicated by the fact that marketing strategy will frequently dictate a pattern of expenditures which is at odds with the audience distribution of the national media under consideration. It is indeed a rare situation where this is not the case.

The media planner must utilize techniques which give him maximum capability to take into account the advertiser's unique sales pattern. He must consider these variations both by geographic region and by market size, sometimes on an individual market basis.

Media Expenditure by Sales Area

Perhaps the least complicated approach to the problem of matching media dollars to sales potential by geographic region is to take a map of the advertiser's total sales area, describe on it the boundaries of each regional marketing division (which, it is hoped, can be defined in terms comparable to media coverage, such as whole counties, television areas, census regions, or the like) and within each of these areas develop a media expenditure goal which reflects the marketing strategy.

This goal is often expressed in terms of dollars (or messages) per thousand homes, or people, or housewives—whatever the target audience happens to be.

If the market is basically national in character, alternative national media plans can be analyzed on the basis of their audience delivery in each area.   Such an analysis will show the fit of each plan, and demonstrate where major weaknesses occur.   These can then be corrected through the addition of local or regional media.

Use of Television in Sales Areas   An example of such analysis and adjustment (in this case performed by computer) is shown in Figures 6 and 7.

In this case the advertiser has provided the agency with sales forecasts by market area for each quarter of the year.   Estimates of the advertising-sales ratio (A/S ratio) on a national basis have been developed and the agency media department instructed to try to approximate that same A/S ratio in each area.   (This is a rather unusual approach to local market allocations.   While it is important to know what the A/S ratio will be, local dollar allocations are usually influenced by considerations such as developmental potential, distribution, competitive problems.)

The primary medium for all products in this case happened to be nighttime network television.   Brands were rotated through a sizable stable of corporate program buys.   The media planner's first step then is to determine the distribution of net television dollars by market area.

Figure 6 demonstrates the advertiser's problem in a sample group of sales districts.

The coverage of all programs Product D will participate in during the quarter has been ascertained, and the network television expenditures have been allocated to each of these sales districts on that basis.

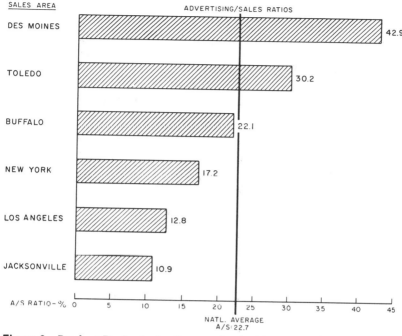

Figure 6 Product D: Analysis of network television expenditures by advertiser sales area.

Those figures have then been related to sales forecasts for each area and the A/S ratio established.   The line down the center represents the national ratio of 22.7 per cent which is the goal, but as the horizontal bars show, the net television does not distribute itself that way.

The range runs all the way from a 42.9 per cent A/S ratio in Des Moines down to 10.9 in Jacksonville.

This does not, of course, reflect only the fluctuations in the network television coverage, although these can be considerable.   It reflects primarily the fact that the variation in sales potential (and therefore advertising requirements) by market area is quite substantial.   Any medium, no matter how even its geographic distribution, would almost certainly result in the same kinds of variation in A/S ratios across the country.

With the national pattern established, it remained to estimate the number of dollars required to bring each underspent division up to a point where the A/S ratio would approximate the national average.

This amount of money was then translated into the number of television spots (or rating points) it would buy in that particular area.

As can be seen in Figure 7, the number of spots varied substantially —sixteen 30-second television spots in New York, forty spots in Los Angeles, and fifty-eight in Jacksonville.

The overspent divisions, such as Des Moines and Toledo, could only be corrected by reducing the total network effort (requiring even more spot television in the underspent areas) or running cut-ins for other products—an expensive business because of station cut-in charges. In this case, since the overspent markets were relatively small and the amount of overspending nominal, no action was taken.

Variations by Market Size   A similar approach can be taken in cases where the problem involves variations in sales potential by market size.

The following tables describe a situation in which consumption levels of the product vary by Nielsen county size. Indexed against the average United States consumption level (index: 100), A counties have a relatively high level of consumption (index: 130) and D counties a very low level (index: 33).

Per Capita Consumption

Total United States County Size	Per Cent Individuals 100	Per Cent Consumption 100	Index (100)
A	40.9%	53.0%	130
B	26.5	30.0	113
C	17.5	12.0	69
D	15.1	5.0	33

Let us assume that it has been decided that network television and magazines will be used for national coverage with local market support supplied by spot television. Three alternatives are described below:

Gross Rating Point * *Delivery—Adults*

	Schedule A	Schedule B	Schedule C
Network TV	125	250	275
Magazines	100	100	100
Spot TV—A markets	350	150	150
B markets	250	100	—

* GRP = Adult impressions divided by adult population.

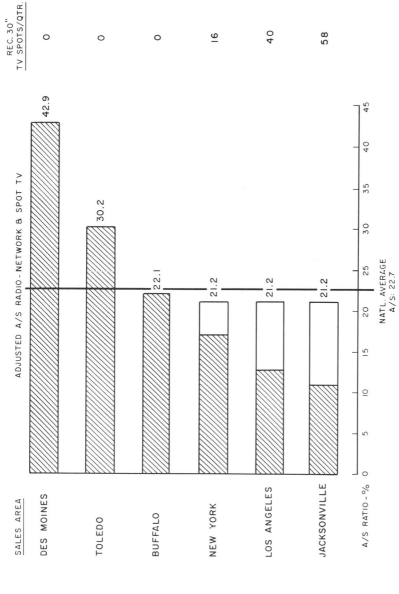

Figure 7 Product D: Analysis of spot television requirements by advertiser sales area.

It can be seen that each of these schedules contains varying amounts of the three media components measured in terms of gross rating points.

If we were to analyze the combined United States delivery of each of these alternatives on the basis of (1) GRPs, (2) reach of the total adult population, and (3) average frequency per persons reached, the result would be:

	Schedule A	Schedule B	Schedule C
Gross rating points	435	429	436
Reach, per cent	84	88	88
Average frequency	5.2	4.9	5.0

Using this technique, there is little to choose between the three plans.   Obviously, a more careful analysis of delivery *by county size* is needed to determine which will best match the advertisters' marketing objectives.

An intermediate step might be to evaluate the delivery of each plan within each group of spot markets versus the remainder of the country.   The following tables reveal striking differences in audience delivery between A and B counties and between these and the nonspot areas.

A Markets	Schedule A	Schedule B	Schedule C
GRPs	575	500	525
Reach, per cent	92	90	91
Average frequency	6.3	5.6	5.8
B Markets			
GRPs	475	450	375
Reach, per cent	88	89	87
Average frequency	5.4	5.1	4.3
Nonspot Markets			
GRPs	225	350	375
Reach, per cent	72	86	87
Average frequency	3.1	4.1	4.3

Finally, it is necessary to relate the delivery of each alternative in these various areas to the consumption pattern.   This comparison is made below:

County Size	Consumption Index	Index of Impressions, Alternative Schedules		
		A	B	C
A	130	132	117	120
B	113	109	105	86
C and D	52	52	82	86

From these tables it is possible to select the plan which most closely matches the advertising objective, in this case Plan A.

Dollars Invested and Advertising Messages Efforts are often made to translate dollar investments in each area into advertising messages generated. This is theoretically a far more precise measure of advertising input since it takes into account such factors as local rating levels (in broadcast media), readers per copy (for magazines), and variations in market by market media costs. In cases where media audience surveys are both frequent enough and accurate enough, such a refinement can be made.

It should be kept in mind, however, that in cases where a combination of media forms is involved (as in the preceding example), a decision to base the comparison on message input carries the obligation to place a value on messages derived from different media forms as well as on different units of time or space. Is a 1-minute television commercial equal to a black-and-white magazine page? Should a 30-second commercial message be given a value of one-half the minute, two-thirds, three-quarters? How about a magazine spread versus a color page?

An analysis based on dollar input assumes that equal dollars generate equal impact. It implicitly accepts the theory that the law of the marketplace, which has governed the pricing of media forms and units of space and time over many years, has taken into account the buyers' combined judgment of the value of the media product. Full-color reproduction, for example, would not be salable at its premium cost unless in the experience of advertisers the value of color justified the price.

This is undoubtedly an overly simplified view, since it does not take into account the creative requirements of individual campaigns. Nevertheless, many advertisers feel that after eliminating certain obviously unsuitable media, this approach is as realistic as attempting to assign a relative weight to each different kind of message delivered.

It is also pertinent to keep in mind that the profitability of the brand is based in large part on the dollar expenditure required to market it.   A careful marketer, therefore, cannot afford to lose sight of the dollar investment required to support the product in each area. If he finds the advertising costs in one market to be so far out of line as to make the market unprofitable, he will either reassess his media approach or eliminate the market in favor of another, more profitable area.

There are many possible variations on the allocation procedures described above.   But regardless of the technique, it is essential that advertising dollar allocations bear a direct relationship to the requirements of each geographic area based on the advertiser's judgment of its current value or future potential.

SCHEDULING THE ADVERTISING

Of all the problems the media planner must cope with, one of the most complex has to do with scheduling advertising.   This problem must be considered on several levels.

Timing Least Complicated

The least complicated level is timing the advertising.   For example, for those products which have a clear-cut seasonal sales curve, it generally makes sense to time the advertising when most people are in the market.   However, even this axiom should be subjected to careful scrutiny.

Coca-Cola decided in the 1930s to attempt through advertising to develop an almost nonexistent winter business.   It introduced a new sales theme, "Thirst Knows No Season," and plugged it hard off-season (when competitive advertising was at a minimum) with considerable success.

Charts of new-car sales show relatively moderate variations by season.   Yet automobile companies spend from one-third to one-half of their total budgets on the two to three months new models are introduced.   The theory is that during this period consumer interest is at a peak, and the advertising will work harder to build a predisposition toward the particular line advertised.

These exceptions, and there are many others, prove that in media scheduling no traditional pattern should be accepted without a careful analysis of the possible results of breaking the mold and trying a new approach.   While the cases cited represent an advertising and marketing decision as opposed to a strictly media consideration, an alert media man can often, from his own knowledge of media usage, suggest similar opportunities to steal a march on competition.   For example, where no important seasonal variations occur, a study of competitive advertising patterns may reveal an opportunity for a low-budget advertiser to dominate the field at a given time of year.

Timing can also mean taking advantage of the availability of the desired audience to the medium.   For example, running a food ad in newspapers on the traditional Thursday or Friday grocery shopping days when women are "shopping" the food pages.   Or reaching teenagers on weekend radio.   Or businessmen in the early morning or evening drive times.   A study of the times and days when the target audience is likely to be the most available and most receptive is an important ingredient in media planning.

Need for Flexibility

An additional consideration in scheduling is the need, on occasion, for *flexibility*.

In a highly competitive market there is often a need for quick tactical maneuvering to take advantage of a competitive weakness (loss of distribution in a major chain or outlet, for example) or to capitalize on a favorable market development (a new package, favorable publicity, etc.).   The likelihood of such a contingency should be assessed by the media planner and provision for the necessary flexibility made in advance.

Such provision can take the form of a contingency fund to be held aside until the need arises.   However, unless there is a reasonably strong probability that such action will be needed, it is usually wiser to incorporate the funds in the media plan in such a way that they can be transferred on short notice.   Newspapers, spot radio, and spot television are examples of media where minimal contractual commitments are required and funds can be shifted in time or place on short notice.

Rate of Advertising

A much more complex scheduling problem involves the *rate* of advertising—the knotty question of scheduling on a continuous basis versus short flights of advertising spaced at intervals throughout the year.

Again, there is no rule of thumb to follow.   The size of the advertising budget related to that of competition is a key factor, and this in turn must be related to the product itself and its current position in the marketplace.

The gravest risk is to spread the advertising too thin—to fail to break through the "noise level" and attract the attention of the potential consumer.   At the other extreme is the possibility of wasting costly impressions after the job has already been accomplished.

In examining this problem, it may be useful to see what happens when an equal number of television spots is spread over a thirteen-week period, or concentrated in shorter "flights," say, nine weeks or six weeks.

First, if the program schedule is the same, the total gross rating points in a given quarter will produce the same reach, average frequency, and frequency distribution by viewing quintiles whether the GRPs are spread over the entire thirteen weeks or concentrated in a shorter period.   A flighting pattern does not increase the proportion of total impressions delivered in the heaviest quintiles during the total advertising period.

(This is true, of course, only if the same number of announcements is spread over the same number of different programs with the same distribution of GRPs by day part.)

Following is an example of how such a schedule, spread over three-day parts, might be condensed from thirteen weeks to nine weeks and finally to six weeks.

	Approx. No. of Ann's. Total Quarter	*Approx. No. of Announcements per Week*		
		For 13 Weeks	*For 9 Weeks*	*For 6 Weeks*
Prime evening network	22	2/wk x 9 wks 1/wk x 4 wks	3/wk x 4 wks 2/wk x 5 wks	4/wk x 4 wks 3/wk x 2 wks
Day network	20	2/wk x 7 wks 1/wk x 6 wks	3/wk x 2 wks 2/wk x 7 wks	4/wk x 2 wks 3/wk x 4 wks
Fringe spot	30	2/wk x 9 wks 3/wk x 4 wks	3/wk x 6 wks 4/wk x 3 wks	5/wk x 6 wks

Since the total number of exposures does not change as a result of adopting a flighting pattern, the effect of compressing the same total number of exposures into a shorter period is to increase the average number of exposures a week during the advertising period.

Figure 8 illustrates graphically the increase in the number of average weekly exposures during the advertising period when the schedule is condensed from thirteen weeks into nine weeks and then into six weeks. The data are based on total adults, and are shown for all adults and then separately by quintile. The chart represents the area where spot television and the network schedule are both running.

Share of Advertising

While no one as yet has been able to shed much light on "how much is enough," most strategists will agree that the *share of advertising* is a key factor in arriving at a judgment in any given situation.

If competition is spending at a level which is substantially greater than is affordable on a continuous basis by the brand to be advertised, it is usually wise to move in periodically with bursts of sufficient intensity to assure awareness of the advertising.

In the example given, the determination of which period of time is most appropriate will depend on judgment, which in turn will be based on knowledge of such factors as:

The purchase cycle of the brand
The brand-switching probabilities
The anticipated level of competitive activity
The life cycle of the brand

Varying Scheduling Patterns

With so many factors involved, it is safe to say that the same flighting pattern would not produce the same results for a different product or for the same product in every situation. The dynamics of media require that the dimension of time be carefully considered. There is some laboratory evidence that consumers can be *unsold* by a barrage of advertising extended beyond a given point; there are indications that at a certain point in the life cycle of a product, it is wise to withdraw all advertising to allow the public a "period of gestation," and then to come back with renewed vigor; there is evidence that for some products short bursts of advertising (one or two weeks in, one or two weeks out) will produce more sales than the same amount of advertising run every week.

The effect of timing, or *periodicity* as it is sometimes called, is one

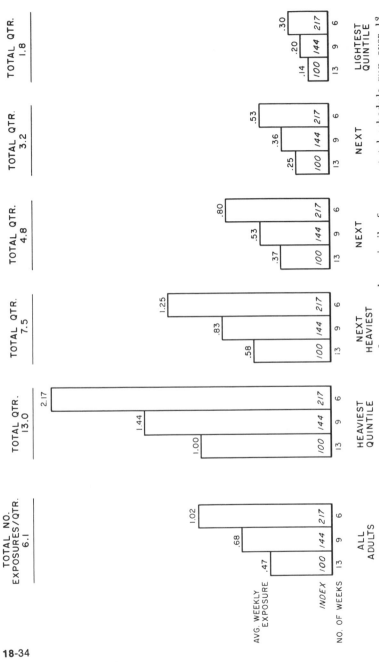

Figure 8 Comparison of average weekly frequency of exposure by quintile for same total schedule run over 13 weeks versus 9 weeks versus 6 weeks, total adult basis, total network and spot in spot area.

which requires more study. In the meantime, the creative media planner should not close his mind to the possibilities inherent in experimentation with varying scheduling patterns.

ESTABLISHING REACH AND FREQUENCY GOALS

A key decision in any media plan involves the proper balance of reach and frequency. It is seldom possible within any specified budget to reach as many people as often as one would like. Since a compromise is usually required, a decision must be reached as to whether a plan should be designed which will maximize coverage of the total defined market without much regard to how many impressions any individual receives, or conversely, whether a frequency goal against a prime segment of the market should be set up, with secondary consideration given to expanding coverage beyond that segment if funds turn out to be available.

Figure 9 demonstrates the results that might be achieved by applying these different strategies.

Two Different Plans

Plans A and B both cost approximately the same. Plan A might be classified as a *reach* plan, while the objective of Plan B is to obtain heavier *frequency* against a smaller audience. Plan A reaches 89 per cent of all women; over two-thirds receive five or fewer impressions, while only 6.4 per cent are contacted more than eight times. Plan B, which emphasizes frequency, reaches 69 per cent of all women, but of these more than one-third are exposed eight or more times.

It is apparent from these differences that the choice of alternative media plans must depend heavily on the reach and frequency strategy established at the outset.

This decision would be relatively easy if there were available some empirical data which indicated how many advertising messages are required to ensure maximum consumer response. Obviously, no such certain knowledge exists. Advertising works differently on different people—and may work differently on the same individual from time to time depending upon the message, the media, and the individual's stage in the decision process. Thus, it is impossible to say that X number of impressions is just the right number to put against a single individual, much less an entire "prospect group."

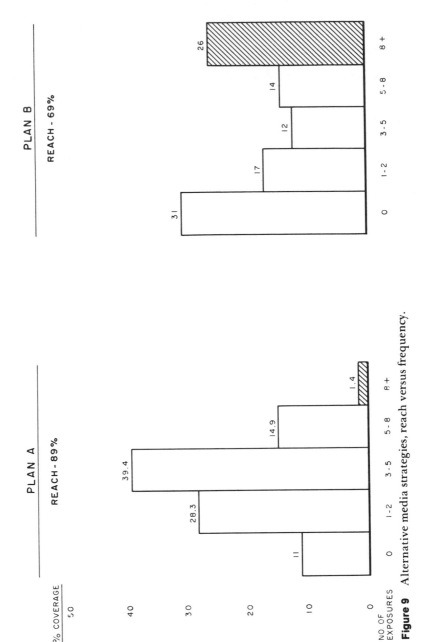

Figure 9 Alternative media strategies, reach versus frequency.

Elements in a Decision Nevertheless, an explicit decision on this critical question must ultimately be made and a number of considerations will be involved in the decision. First among these will be *the budget available relative to the size of the potential market.*

Ideally, a media budget would be fixed only after a careful assessment of the goals of the advertising plan and the estimated cost of meeting those goals. Unfortunately, in the real world, the budget is more often based on an arbitrary percentage of sales or sales quota and is frequently subject to alteration, up or down, as the year progresses. The media planner's options under these circumstances are limited. He is not in the ideal position, as a rule, of saying how much reach and frequency should be delivered; rather, he must assess the objectives of the plan in the light of the dollars available and recommend the most effective *practical* plan. In doing this, he will of course analyze a number of alternatives to arrive at the one which will come *closest* to the ideal distribution of impressions he would like to achieve. This is often a hard decision and requires a careful assessment of several other factors.

A second key consideration will be *the competitive environment in which the advertising will be working.*

A study of competitive media schedules will provide a reasonably accurate estimate of the volume of advertising being put against subsegments of the potential market by competing brands. It should also be possible to estimate the monthly reach and frequency achieved by these schedules.

With this information it will then be possible to form a judgment as to where advertising dollars have the best chance of achieving a positive response, or conversely, where competitive advertising may largely nullify response to our own advertising and diminish its profitability.

If there is no real alternative but to meet competition head-on, such information will indicate what level of advertising is needed in order at least to rise above the "noise level" of competing copy claims. We can then circumscribe the "reach" goal in order to achieve the frequency level necessary to get into the range of optimum effectiveness.

Another consideration which will affect this decision is *the degree of brand switching or brand loyalty in the product category.*

Information on the intensity of consumer loyalty to the particular brand and other brands in the product class is available from consumer panel studies and from special surveys of brand attitudes and brand switching.

Where brand loyalty is naturally high and it appears that a heavy weight of advertising may be required to induce switching, an advertising strategy concentrated against only a fraction of the total market may be very productive, and only such a policy may, in fact, produce the frequency required for effective communication.

Finally, it is necessary to take account of *the stage in the product's life cycle—is it in a growth period, sustaining, or on the decline?*

A new product building its market will probably set as its advertising goal brand awareness among the maximum number of potential users. A strategy of broad exposure, therefore, may seem appropriate in the first year or two of its development.

Once the product becomes well known, the market has stabilized, and inevitably, competition has moved in, a strategy of maintaining competitive weight against the best customer groups may be more productive. Such a strategy change will lead to more emphasis on frequency of impression delivery against the selected market segments.

In the declining phase a gradual retrenchment in spending may further circumscribe the reach objective. Maximum affordable frequency against enclaves of loyal customers will be the objective in an effort to stave off the inroads of new, more dynamic competition.

Selection of Media   Once a reach-frequency strategy has been agreed upon, the media planner has the responsibility of selecting those media which, in combination, offer the greatest potential for successful implementation. Media audiences differ in their extent and rate of duplication, and these differences must be taken into account.

A valuable attribute of the computer in media selection is its ability to do just this. One system in use at J. Walter Thompson and perhaps at other agencies provides the opportunity to place differing values on a first impression going against an individual in the simulated population as opposed to the second, which in turn can be evaluated differently from the third, etc. If a first contact is given a greater value than any subsequent exposure to the same person, the computer will be forced to search for media vehicles which add the greatest number of new viewers or readers at each stage in the selection process. The result maximizes reach.

On the other hand, if subsequent impressions are given ascending values, the computer will be forced to search for media vehicles with considerable overlap of audience in the selected groups, thus maximizing repeat impressions (frequency) and minimizing reach.

The computer, however, is not able to set the strategy. This can be done only by the media decision makers on the basis of a careful evaluation of each specific situation.

Reach-Frequency Pitfalls

In the actual selection of media vehicles, there are certain pitfalls in the analysis of reach and frequency which must be avoided.

How to Evaluate Reach

a. COVERAGE VERSUS SELECTIVITY. If the media strategy calls for "maximum coverage" of a carefully defined target-prospect group, it will be important to implement that strategy as efficiently as possible. A television program or magazine with mass appeal may well provide excellent coverage of the selected market segment but be a very inefficient vehicle because of the additional *waste* circulation which the advertiser must buy.

On the other hand, a selective vehicle which at first glance may appear to have a high cost per thousand in terms of its total audience may be comparatively efficient when measured against potential prospects only.

The three factors to be considered are (1) coverage, (2) selectivity, and (3) efficiency against prospects. Figures 4 and 5 showed how vehicles can be ranked in order to provide a clear comparison of their relative performance on each of these bases. Efficiency in reaching the selected target is, of course, the result of selectivity related to cost and is the key criterion.

It should be reiterated here, however, that reach cannot be rigidly controlled. The relationship between market goals and media audiences is tenuous at best. Except for those specialized media aimed at such select groups as flower growers, boating enthusiasts, or skiers, or those few publications offering demographic editions (such as *Time*'s doctors' edition, etc.), it is not possible to pinpoint a target group exactly. Thus, there are always practical limitations on our ability to achieve reach goals, and alternative media plans must be evaluated on their *relative* capabilities in this area.

b. THE HIGH COST OF ADDING REACH. A second important

consideration is the cost of adding a few percentage points of reach to a schedule.   As can be seen in the following table, a daytime network television investment of $32,000 might provide a reach of 40 per cent of all housewives, for example.   A 100 per cent increase in dollars would be required to build that reach to 51 per cent, an increase of only 27 per cent.   The dilemma the media planner faces is where to draw the line between efficient and inefficient reach levels.   In making this decision he must also consider the value of the added frequency against those already covered.

*Comparison of Incremental Reach Versus
Dollar Investment in Daytime Televison*

Weekly Daytime GRPs	Estimated Reach	Per Cent Increase	Dollar Investment	Per Cent Increase
40	40		32,000	
60	47	17	48,000	50
80	51	27	64,000	100

c. THE QUINTILE DISTORTION.   Every individual tends to spend more time with one medium than another.   Television has its devotees, as do magazines.   Some people spend an hour or two with the daily newspaper; others race through it in a few minutes.   While the demographic characteristics of individuals may have some influence on these predilections, the connection is tenuous at best.   Thus a heavy investment in any one medium will create imbalances in the distribution of impressions among market segments or demographic groups.

On the other hand, the addition of a second medium will almost invariably tend to level these imbalances.

Figure 10 illustrates what happens in a fairly typical situation. The evening network television schedule (in this case a "scatter plan" involving six programs) provided a reach of 47 per cent of all adults in the United States over a four-week period.   However, if these viewers are divided into quintiles on the basis of number of hours of television viewed per week, it can be seen that 79 per cent of the heaviest-viewing quintile is exposed to the message as contrasted with 10 per cent of the lightest-viewing quintile.   Frequencies are also heavily skewed, ranging from 1.0 to 1.6.

The addition of a second medium, in this case magazines, leveled the reach substantially.   As can be seen in Figure 10, the magazine

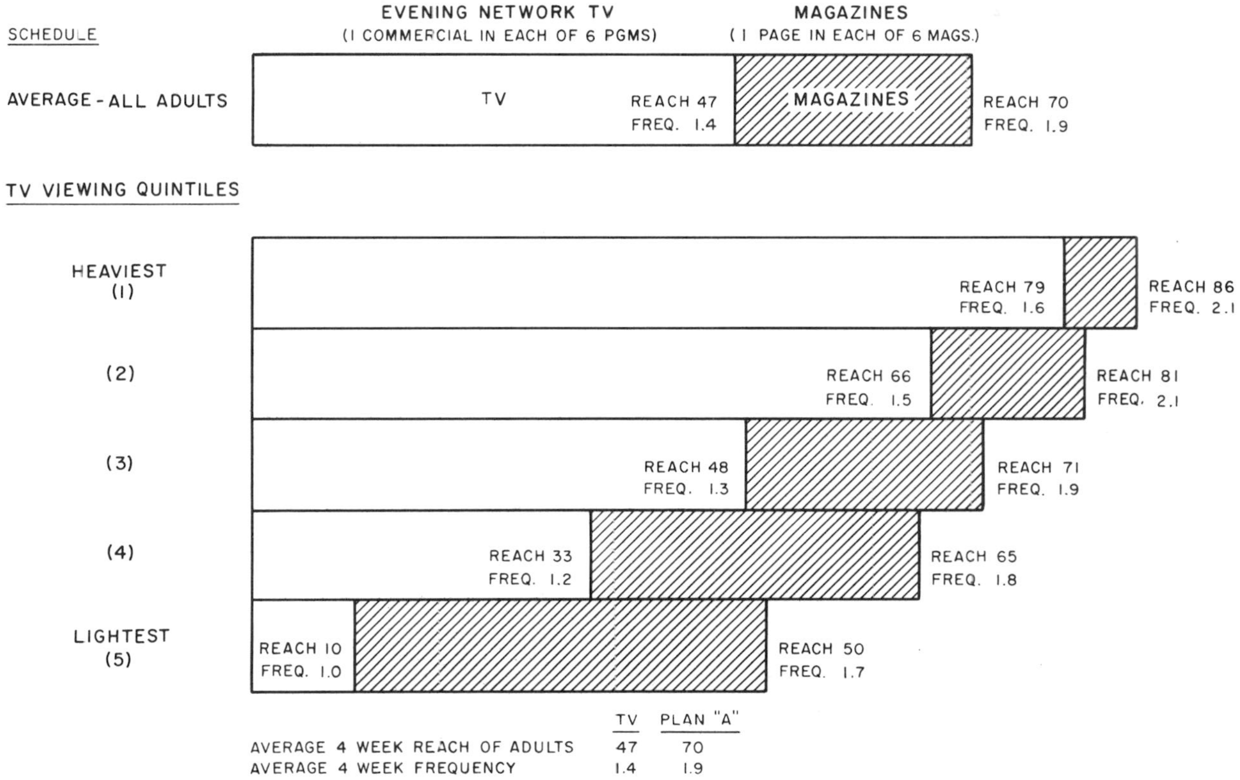

SCHEDULE

EVENING NETWORK TV
(I COMMERCIAL IN EACH OF 6 PGMS)

MAGAZINES
(I PAGE IN EACH OF 6 MAGS)

AVERAGE - ALL ADULTS

TV

REACH 47
FREQ. 1.4

MAGAZINES

REACH 70
FREQ. 1.9

TV VIEWING QUINTILES

HEAVIEST
(1)

REACH 79
FREQ. 1.6

REACH 86
FREQ. 2.1

(2)

REACH 66
FREQ. 1.5

REACH 81
FREQ. 2.1

(3)

REACH 48
FREQ. 1.3

REACH 71
FREQ. 1.9

(4)

REACH 33
FREQ. 1.2

REACH 65
FREQ. 1.8

LIGHTEST
(5)

REACH 10
FREQ. 1.0

REACH 50
FREQ. 1.7

	TV	PLAN "A"
AVERAGE 4 WEEK REACH OF ADULTS	47	70
AVERAGE 4 WEEK FREQUENCY	1.4	1.9

Figure 10 Analysis of reach and frequency distribution by television-viewing quintiles.

18-41

schedule added 400 per cent to the reach of the lightest-viewing television quintile and 10 per cent to the heaviest.

While magazines tend to complement television particularly well (intensive viewers tend to be light readers and vice versa), any other medium added to the television schedule would have had the same effect to some degree.   It is safe to say that if level coverage of any target audience is desired, a mix of more than one medium will achieve the objective better than a single media form used exclusively.

On the other hand, while there undoubtedly is a point beyond which it is economically unsound to pile more impressions against an already overexposed quintile of viewers or readers, it is not always easily determined when the addition of a second media form to balance the skew is desirable.   The excitement and impact that can be engendered by a concentrated effort in a single medium may, in fact, be the secret ingredient which makes the total campaign a success. A degree of "overexposure" may be critically important to tip the scales in favor of the product advertised.

Sound media planning will certainly include an analysis of frequency distribution within a medium's total audience, but the proper use of this information involves imaginative thinking and a good sense of advertising strategy.

TEST MARKETING

When a company introduces a new product, its principal objective is to realize a profit on the investment required to launch and maintain the product in those areas of the country where it can be sold.

To determine whether the product is likely to produce a profit, it is necessary to estimate a level of sales believed to be attainable when the product is in full distribution.   The funds generated by this level of sales obviously must be sufficient to cover the costs of marketing as well as to leave a profit balance.

These forecasts then become the basis for deciding whether or not to go ahead and what amount to commit to advertising and promotion.

Once the advertising-and-promotion budget is established, a theoretical "national" marketing plan is decided upon.   The ultimate profitability of the product will be determined by the ability of this marketing plan to create and maintain awareness, interest, and sales momentum at the levels forecast.

Since this theoretical national plan is drawn up without benefit of actual market conditions and reactions, it is prudent to test its effectiveness in a limited area before a major commitment is made.

This test marketing will minimize the risk of failure by determining whether the product can be sold and the sales levels that can probably be achieved.

Also, by employing test markets, the advertiser has the opportunity of testing the various elements of the marketing plan and making adjustments in the mix or timing of these elements where changes appear necessary or desirable.

It is important that the test-marketing plans be an accurate reflection or simulation of the plan that will be used by the product once it is national because:

1. The advertiser is then in the best possible position to gauge whether the sales and profit forecasts for the national plan are attainable.

2. He is assured that the test-market results are based on realistic schedules that the product will be able to afford after it completes national distribution.

The Test Area

The selection of the test area is critical, and marketing considerations normally take precedence over media considerations in the selection of appropriate test markets.   However, this is not to imply that media considerations are unimportant.   A test conducted in media situations which are atypical may well muddy the waters to the point where projectability of the results is severely impaired.

What then are the media criteria for the selection of a test market? The following is a general guide:

Market Size   Tests are sometimes conducted in a single geographic region which contains a mix of various-sized population centers or in a group of widely dispersed markets.   There are pros and cons for each approach, but it is most important that the test area be large enough so that results can be projected nationally, and yet not so large as to be economically impractical.   An area containing at least 2 to 3 per cent of the population is desirable, and some experienced marketers insist that 5 per cent is minimal for a safe projection.

Demographic Characteristics   The market(s) selected should be reasonably typical of the nation as a whole—not too industrial or too rural, too rich or too poor, and if possible, should not represent too strong a sectional bias.

Market Definition   There should be a close correlation between the area to be audited for test results and the effective coverage area of the media used.   This will affect not so much the selection of markets as the definition of the sales-audited area.   For example, if the basic medium is television, the audited area should include all counties effectively covered by the stations used.   However, if the basic medium should be daily newspapers, the audited area might be the city zone or metropolitan area.

Media Availability   The mix of media available in the test areas must be similar to that available in the nation at large, with reasonable flexibility as regards closing dates and cancellation privileges. There should be no important spill-in from media originating outside the area or spill-out to areas where the product is not yet in distribution.

Media Costs   Rates charged by local media carriers should not be unusually high.   Because of the variations in local media rates, markets of similar size often have substantially different costs.   There could be important savings, therefore, in the proper selection of markets.

Category Development   In the case of an established product category, the areas selected should be reasonably typical in terms of product consumption, distribution, and competition.   Significant differences in brand shares or abnormal pricing or promotion patterns should be taken into account.

Media Translation Concepts

There are two basic methods of approaching the translation of a national media plan into test-market areas:

1. To simulate in the test markets the amount of advertising weight which would be developed on a national basis of average impressions per household.   This is often called the "Little U.S.A." approach.

2. To approximate as closely as possible the media weight and media mix that would be delivered into the *specific markets* by the

national plan.   This is known variously as a "take it as it falls," "slice of life," "let the chips fall as they may" approach.

The decision as to which of these two methods should be used must depend on the circumstances of the test and the selection of test markets.

The whole point in test-market translation is to duplicate as exactly as possible the media weight and media mix that will support the national introduction of the brand in order for the test results to be nationally projectable.   The more variables introduced into the test situation, the less reliable the projection of results is likely to be.

Thus, ideally, the combination of markets selected for the test would be representative of the national picture in terms of (1) demographic and economic characteristics; (2) product-category development; (3) distribution possibilities; (4) media characteristics and usage.   Under such an ideal set of circumstances the media scheduled to run nationally could be permitted to run normally in the test areas with only the minimal adjustment necessary to simulate a locally unavailable vehicle.   The resulting media schedule would mirror the hypothetical national plan.

Unfortunately, such a geographic "Little U.S.A." is seldom feasible in test-market selection.   Compromises dictated by marketing facts usually result in a selection of markets for the test which do not reflect the national delivery of the media plan.

For example, network television rating levels vary widely from market to market.   Test-market ratings could, by coincidence, be substantially lower or higher than the national average.   The same type of variation could exist in print.   An introductory newspaper ad might reach 60 per cent of the population nationally, but in a given test area reach only 40 per cent.   Such variations in advertising input could distort the results of the test.

When the markets selected are not representative of the national media situation, it is desirable to control this media variable within the test area.   For example, if the national television plan is expected to deliver 100 gross rating points, an equal number would be purchased in the test areas and dispersed by day part to equate with the national effort.   (This is of particular importance if tests at different weight levels are being executed simultaneously in different markets to determine what spending level is most productive.)

An obvious exception to this approach of simulating the average national weight in test areas occurs when a special local effort is planned in certain markets—for example, a "heavy-up" spot television effort in Nielsen A markets.   In this situation it is desirable to simulate both the A county plan and the national plan in different markets to determine the effect of the added local weight.

Test-market Translations of National Media Plans

In translating a national plan to test market, an advertiser has the option of using as a basis:

1. Advertising message weight
2. Advertising expenditures per thousand population

Most advertisers use the test-market translation of media weight as a basis for setting test-market appropriations.   One reason for preferring this method is that most test markets tend to have media rates which exceed the national average, and by allocating expenditures on a per capita basis, the weight that will be translated into test market will be significantly lower than the level set forth in the national advertising plan.

An even more important reason is that such variations between the cost of local media and the cost of national media falling into the same markets could create a serious problem in assessing the profitability of marketing the product nationally.   Profitability must be determined in test areas by relating sales to the expenditures that will be incurred in the market when the national plan is operational, not to local market expenditures required to simulate that plan.   Thus a ratio of advertising to sales based on local costs where those costs are substantially out of line with national media will be both irrelevant and misleading.

In the next few paragraphs, some of the problems of test-market translation medium by medium are reviewed as well as the commonly accepted methods of solving them.

Since the test-market schedules are a test of the effectiveness of the proposed national plan, the local schedules must duplicate as closely as possible the *media weight* and *media mix* that would be delivered into the test markets by the national plan.

Obviously when a national plan incorporates local media, such as spot, ROP, or outdoor, it is possible to achieve an exact duplication in test markets simply by a direct duplication of that part of the national plan.

Local Simulation of a National Plan However, when the national plan calls for national media, exact duplications are rarely possible, and we have to rely on *simulating* the weight the national plan would deliver into the test markets. Here are the various means by which national media can be simulated locally.

Network Television or Radio Cut-ins in the test markets in existing corporate programs can be considered a reasonably accurate simulation of a national plan calling for network. The drawbacks to this approach are:

1. The advertiser must pay for the physical cut-in, thus investing funds that do not produce advertising weight. For a schedule calling for many announcements, such nonadvertising costs can represent a sizable sum of money.

2. The cut-in eliminates the incumbent network brand commercial from that market. Frequently this forces the test brand to pay back the preempted brand plus paying for the cut-in; or to purchase replacement weight for the preempted brand as well as paying the cut-in charges.

The alternative to network cut-ins is to *simulate* the network schedule by means of local spot announcements. These spot announcements are purchased to provide the same audience levels and composition that the network schedule would provide. Frequently it is desirable to purchase more weight to compensate for the probably reduced attention the "between-program" spot receives relative to an "in-program" commercial.

Magazines For those magazines offering individual market circulation breakouts, it often is possible to translate directly the national plan that calls for those magazines.

However, some magazines do not yet offer individual market circulation breakouts, and it is necessary to simulate that coverage by means of other magazines, local supplements if they are available, or local newspapers. Supplements and ROP usually are not very satisfactory simulation vehicles for magazines because of the differences in penetration, audience composition, and reading life.

Where such a translation is necessary, the adjustment is similar to that for television—establish the "print rating point" level of the national plan (impressions per household) and attempt to duplicate that level as nearly as possible.

Supplements The Sunday group is the only "national" supplement available locally, and therefore a direct translation of a national supplement plan calling for *Sunday* is possible. However, the other national supplements (*This Week, Parade, Family Weekly*) would have to be simulated locally either by locally edited supplements or ROP.

One word of caution in conclusion. While rating-point levels are the basis for determining the accuracy of the simulation, a sharp eye should be kept on reach and frequency levels as well. A test plan which provides an equal number of GRPs but grossly distorts the reach and frequency of the national plan may be quite misleading in its overall effect.

OUTLINE OF A MEDIA PLAN

The following outline indicates the type of information and reasoning expected in a media recommendation. This list does not necessarily cover all the points which should be considered in planning media strategy. Moreover, since conditions differ for each product, every point may not have to be covered for every plan.

    I. *Media Objectives.*
        A. *General.* What are the broad media objectives? Are these consistent with the product's overall marketing objectives and strategy? Are they consistent with the copy strategy and the requirements of the copy plan? Do they give adequate consideration to competitive activities?
        B. *Specific.* In order to focus more sharply on the media target, what are the specific media objectives (in such terms as the following):
            1. *Whom* does the product want to reach? (Men, women, children, housewives? Age groups? Income groups? Family type? etc.)
            2. *Where* does the product want to deliver its messages? (Nationally? Regionally? Metropolitan areas, suburban areas, rural areas?)
            3. *When* does the product want to advertise? (All year? Variation by quarters? Seasonal peaks?)
            4. *What* message does the product want its media to deliver? (What are the media requirements and limitations dictated by the copy? What product image and consumer attitude are desired?)
            5. *Why* are these objectives important? (Detailed supporting data and sources should be included in an appendix.)

II. *Statement of Strategy to Meet the Objectives.*
   A. Listing of general principles which will apply to plan.
      1. Reach versus frequency.
      2. Necessity to meet or dominate competition in share of advertising.
      3. Relation of advertising dollars to sales on an area-by-area basis.
   B. Selection of primary medium and why.
   C. Selection of supplementary medium and why.
   D. Principles of media usage.
      1. Specific types of media within the media form (day or night television, network or spot) and why.
      2. "Fill-in" media weight requirements to offset audience fluctuations on a market-by-market basis.
      3. Efficiency standards (maximum CPMs).
      4. Scheduling—i.e., acceptability of piggybacking, single or multiple exposures per broadcast, flighting versus continuity.
   E. Discussion of alternative possibilities that have been considered and explanation of rejection.
III. *The Tactical Plan.*
   A. Budget summary.
      1. Tables showing total dollars and per cent of total for each media classification.
      2. Tables showing difference with preceding year.
   B. Outline description of plan.
      1. Brief description of the major elements included in each media classification.
         a. Identification: i.e., name, network, and time period of shows; magazine titles; general identification of other elements too lengthy to list in detail.
         b. Number of stations, newspapers, markets, etc., involved.
         c. Description of space or time units to be bought and per cent of total represented by each.
         d. Duration of schedule.
      2. Explanation (in tabular form when possible) of how each element of the plan performs in relation to stated objectives of the plan.
         a. Quantitative information: i.e., reach and frequency by groups; gross impressions.
         b. Quantitative information: i.e., nonstatistical factors such as environment, emotional impact, authority of medium in a special field, etc.

            c. Competitive considerations: i.e., how current competitive activity has influenced recommendation, any suggested adjustments in case of a changed competitive environment.

            d. Flexibility provisions; i.e., action that is recommended in case of budget adjustments.

        3. Reasons why stated tactics are considered better than possible alternatives.

  IV. *Summary Tables (Appendix).*

    A. *Expenditures in Relation to Sales Patterns.*

        1. Tables comparing planned dollar media expenditures with consumer sales volumes, by the most appropriate indices of market potential.

        2. A table comparing planned dollar media expenditures (and per cent of annual national total) with sales volumes for each quarter of the year.

    B. *Media Coverage, Frequency, and Other Statistical Data.*

        1. *Print media.* Tables giving such information as the following for each publication and in total, where applicable.

            a. Circulation and total audience.

            b. Number and size of insertions.

            c. Gross messages delivered.

            d. Costs (per insertion and for entire schedule).

            e. Cost per thousand (for magazines, supplements, comics, etc.) against appropriate audience targets.

            f. Per cent coverage of families.

                i. Nationally.

                ii. By regions, districts, or territories.

                iii. By county size.

                iv. By appropriate demographic breaks.

        2. *Broadcast Media.* Tables giving such information as the following for each network broadcast program, for each spot campaign, and for all broadcast activity in combination:

            a. One-time basis.

                i. Per cent coverage of families, television homes, radio-only homes, etc.

                ii. Estimated Nielsen average-audience rating.

                iii. Homes reached (Nielsen average audience).

                iv. Number and length of commercials.

                v. Gross messages delivered.

                vi. Cost (total and per minute or per commercial unit).

                vii. Cost per thousand per commercial minute (or commercial impression); total homes reached; women only (if appropriate).

    viii. Regional or county size breakdowns, if available.

  b. A four-week audience basis (Nielsen total audience)

    i. Per cent coverage of homes or other appropriate target audiences.

    ii. Average frequency against the same groups.

    iii. Breakdowns by appropriate geographic areas.

3. *Alternative Plans.* Comparison of statistical data for other plans with the recommended plan.

CHAPTER NINETEEN

Uses of Print Media

WARREN A. BAHR *Executive Vice President and Director of Media Relations and Planning, Young & Rubicam, Inc.*

IMPORTANCE OF BRANDS AND BRAND MANAGERS

In this chapter we want to discuss the communications links between products and their various publics that are provided by print media, and to examine media characteristics and strengths and how these can aid in the progress of a brand toward its market. We shall consider consumer magazines and newspapers, as business publications are discussed in Chapter 28 and farm publications are examined in Chapter 29.

As so ably stated by William Colihan of Young & Rubicam in an office memorandum:

> We are living in a world of brands, whether viewed by an advertiser or an agency. Strong brands make strong companies, and not *vice versa*. Each brand lives in its own competitive world, where it must fight its own battles and bury its dead. What it gets from the corporation is an input of research and resources, facilities and support in a

dozen or more areas. The brand is entity, asset, profit center—past, present, future. The whole philosophy of package goods is based upon this concept. Companies are restructured for it, divisions created, subsidiaries spun off. All this is to improve the opportunity for brands, because they, not the corporations, make the profits. This is why any consideration of how advertising works must stress that it is important for a corporation to look at media selection on a brand basis.

I do not say that there are no good corporate decisions. Some time ago, corporate investment in television programs was clearly one. It gave the brands certain values, and at the same time, offered extra values for the corporation. However, when the decision seems to help the corporation at the expense of the brands, it should be reconsidered, re-tested, and probably rejected.

Agencies get assignments by brands; they are paid by brands; they are penalized by losing brands; they are often thought to be living in sinful polygamy with two brands of the same client. Even when agencies get corporate assignments, these are always of secondary consideration to the welfare of the prime factors, the brands. Obviously, the brand should be of prime consideration when selecting media.

Disadvantages When Brands Are Slighted

What are the disadvantages when a brand is not given prime consideration? There are several, and they affect the planning and buying functions.

Planning Area   In the planning area, nonbrand purchases affect adversely or discourage strategic planning for a brand because they suggest accommodation to an existing structure, rather than the encouragement of free thinking, experimentation, or innovation to a more specific prospect goal.

Buying Process   In respect to the buying process, corporate purchases must subjugate prospect specifics to gain defined values, usually economic, that on a weighted-value basis might well result in decreased selling effectiveness for any brands concerned. Of four opportunities available in the media market, A might be best for Brand A; B for Brand B; C for Brand C, based on individual brand prospect potential, but the consolidated buy could be D for reasons of overall pure audience cost efficiency which dilutes any specific brand advantage. When D is selected, we usually deify a single numerical definition of limited validity as justification instead of using other equally valid guides whose yield in terms of communication values would be higher for the individual brands concerned.

Meaningful Aspects of All Media   All media have attributes. Important to consider is what each medium will do for a brand in respect to use of their audiences, definable by examination of demographic and geographic characteristics, coverage in depth, timeliness, and most importantly, the subjective interpretation of their editorial identification. These are the meaningful aspects of media. The criteria to measure them, such as reach and cost factors, are less significant than the power of the vehicle itself, and the mood and environment it provides, to display the brand to its audience which it has culled in a specific purpose from the consumer universe.

Rise of the Product Manager

As brands and communications channels have proliferated, there has been an equal proliferation of marketing personnel. The kind of person who is making a decision in this area has changed. There has been a great foreshortening of experience, and of necessity, a correspondingly increased reliance on proved systems of analysis based on formularized generalities. These well-conceived and generally well-executed guidelines are specifically geared to minimize loss possibilities, and in general succeed very well. They sacrifice, however, independence of thought and penalize creative opportunism. This becomes a major factor in print sales consideration when we realize the fact that most of the numerical criteria imputed as value norms are in terms of television or electronic delivery potentials.

One of the major problems confronting print has been the rise of the product manager, who must manage all businesses entrusted to him from only two points of perspective: (1) profitability from expansion in terms of packages and/or dollars, or (2) goods sold at reduced cost ratios. This combination of systems and limited goals makes difficult the acceptance of the subtleties that print offers in terms of more specific audiences, more responsive prospect pools which could be cultivated into long-term loyal consumer adherents.

Long-term Benefits from Use of Print Media

A major contribution that advertising can perform for a brand is a feeling of confidence by the consumer in the quality its name possesses. In general, this form of long-term benefit can be built best in the print media because of their self-selective nature and the believability that the medium imparts to them.

Print is unique in that it lends through its permanence an enhancement of quality. One of the major objectives of corporations has been to build strong family brand names. The rationale has been that the attributes in terms of satisfaction, quality, and responsibility possessed by the parent brand will aid newer offshoots to prosper and at a more economical advertising-sales ratio in today's competitive marketplace. In general, the genesis brands of the successful families of products operating under this type of prestige transfer umbrella were built originally in print media.

The very nature of the print media and their strength in building a more lasting image of quality, however, work against them. If the qualities we ascribe as being great advertising benefits of print—prestige, confidence, believability, etc.—are true, it must be recognized that it takes longer to build these consumer reactions because the periodicity of print and frequency of audience exposure limit it to a slower but longer-lasting accumulation of brand consumer empathy. Once accumulated, however, the brand could well be in a much better position, less vulnerable to price shifting and competitive new-product introductions, and better able to keep its image intact with minimized advertising expenditures. A basic problem of print, however, is this element of longer-term development. Test-market results for go no-go decisions, week-by-week budget attainments, product life spans, and collapsed time between innovation and imitation are powerful forces that mitigate against prolonged time sequences between advertising effort and consumer action.

Short-term Solutions   In general, then, the brand manager's solutions to most problems have to be on a short-term basis, and this makes the selling of a print vehicle very difficult. There are exceptions. He is receptive to newspapers because they appear daily and offer him a way to get an idea across quickly. They can also deliver local price differentiation. A quick-action device common to both newspapers and magazines is the coupon drop. Promotional and event selling pridefully or defensively can be classified in the immediate-action category. In general, however, the conditions of quick turnover do not permit use of the power of the print vehicle in its truest sense—the building of the believability and the establishment of the dominance of the brand in various segments selected by the editorial content and the nature of the printed vehicle itself.

I shall attempt in this chapter to heighten the perception of the advantages to be derived through the use of print by advertisers for their brands by highlighting the meaningfulness of magazines and newspapers in terms of vitality, communicative links, depth and breadth of exposure, penetration, and judgmental dynamics. I ask my readers to act as catalysts, being the combining force between product energy and needs and the communication channels (audiences and physical and psychological dimensions) reported on.

It goes without saying that all that is pertinent is not pointed out, for as I award you the task of selection and rejection, I ask you to choose from the potpourri of information presented, that which is meaningful to your specific and immediate brand-advertising needs. I am serious in this wish that your approach to this chapter be in this character because only through your specific involvement of interest can I be of service.

Since print is by nature informative and long lasting, I hope as changing situations occur, remembrance of other facets beaming on your changing involvement in problem solution will be recalled. The advertising product is after all in its purest sense a combination of two elements—the message created and the message communicated. The closer these two elements are to each other and to the product requirement, the better the result. It stands to reason that if product, problems, prospects, opportunities, and objectives are individual and definable, then message creation and communication implementation must be in concert and in tune with each other to attain maximum effectiveness.

PROLOGUE TO PRINT

It seems somewhat strange (and disappointing) that in perusing various books in which today's scientists and sociologists prognosticate the myriad changes we should expect in decades to come, one finds virtually nothing about change in print communications. Yet, print will record and describe every other change and will be called upon to expand drastically in order to encompass every other type of growth—psychic and intellectual, as well as physical and material.

Could it be that print has by now been around long enough to survive and defy the forecasts of preceding generations of prognosticators to the point where most of today's soothsayers find it easier to ignore than to predict its future?

Print has a long and a fascinating history which space here does not permit us to explore in depth.   However, following are a very few of the historic highlights which will at least suggest that print has a long and direct attachment to the progress of civilization.

Origin of Newspapers

We know that newspapers are basically journals relating to matters of public interest.   In this context, it is interesting to note that "Columbia Encyclopedia" attributes the origin of the newspaper to Julius Caesar, and that the earliest recorded effort to inform the public on current events was the Roman *Acta diurna* which was posted daily in public places.   China's oldest newspaper began in the eighth century, and in the fifteenth century, manuscript news sheets were issued in major cities throughout Germany.   In 1556, the Venetian government posted the *Notizie scritte* for which readers paid a small fee or *gazetta;* it became so popular it was finally printed in quantity.

The Earliest Magazines

Magazines, under the broader generic term of *periodicals,* have also been with us for hundreds of years.   The French *Journal des Savants* commenced publication in 1665, and its successor publication is still being printed today.   The first English periodical, *Mercurius Librarius,* began in 1680, and like *Journal des Savants* its articles were devoted to scientific and literary subjects.

In 1731, with the publication of *Gentlemen's Magazine,* the word "magazine" was first used in the sense of a periodical for entertainment.

Flow of Writing Talent

It is fascinating in tracing the evolution of the periodical to note a complete turnaround in the flow of writing talent.   Magazines and newspapers were the starting place of practically every great literary light of the nineteenth and first half of the twentieth centuries; e.g., Jonathan Swift, Samuel Johnson, Sir Walter Scott, Charles Dickens,

Benjamin Franklin, Washington Irving, Poe, Hawthorne, Whitman, Lowell, Mencken, on up through Dylan Thomas, whose first poetry appeared in Welsh newspapers.

Now the pendulum has swung to the point where after a reputation has been established in other literary forms, today's great authors, instead of emanating from, are gravitating into contemporary print media; e.g., Truman Capote, James Michener, Norman Mailer, and others.

This then, albeit too briefly, indicates how deeply newspapers and magazines are ingrained in human progression for the most recent 2,000 years of history.   Little wonder then that most scientific and philosophical crystal-ball gazers with one notable exception do not wish to presume that print media existence is doomed or that its social significance is in danger within the foreseeable future.

CONSUMERS' VIEWS OF PRINT AND BROADCAST

Consumers' views of the relative values of advertising in print and broadcast media have been examined in several studies, notably "Advertising in America: The Consumer View." [1] This book is based upon a series of studies sponsored by the American Association of Advertising Agencies that began in 1964.

Magazines

The least-criticized major medium is consumer magazines. Editorial content in magazines is aimed generally at a more sophisticated audience than is material in any other medium, and in some magazines (e.g., women's fashion magazines) the advertisements are *sought* by consumers as much as is the editorial matter.

Criticism is occasionally directed at consumer magazines for the large number of pages devoted to advertising, especially prior to the Christmas season.   In respect to individual advertisements, some attention-getting devices, such as semidraped females, are sometimes criticized.   Because pages of magazines are used largely by estab-

[1] Raymond A. Bauer and Stephen A. Greyser, "Advertising in America: The Consumer View," Harvard Graduate School of Business Administration, Boston, 1968, 474 pp.

lished major advertisers, there are relatively few attacks on magazines in respect to sleazy products and deceptive copy. (This situation could be in the process of erosion as more and more mail-order ads find their way into the medium.) As in any print medium, however, the self-decision element is present—that is, the ability of the reader to avoid unrewarding advertising by turning past pages of ads or by concentrating on nonadvertising content. This characteristic of advertising in magazines makes commercial messages in them less intrusive.

Thus, neither the nature of consumer magazines nor their advertisements are subject to much specific criticism. There is a single exception. Precisely because they are mainly directed at a more adult group, and because exposure to children can in part be controlled, there is less restriction on the types of *products* that can be advertised in magazines. Hence, persons who object to the advertising of magic cures, and prosthetic devices, for example, will and do have an opportunity to find ads in magazines which are offensive to them.

Newspapers

Like magazines, newspapers are seldom criticized for the intrusiveness of their advertising, inasmuch as page flipping and selective scanning allow the reader to bypass as many of the advertisements as he wishes. Because of the inherently local, low-cost, and daily nature of newspaper advertising, content of newspaper advertisements is distinctive in several ways.

They are a prime vehicle for local store advertising that informs readers of the time, place, and price at which products and services can be bought. However, these same characteristics result in more "bait" and deceptive advertising than in higher-cost media and other media that can check more carefully the sources of the ads and their specific product claims.

Broadcast

Both the intrusiveness of broadcast sound as well as the specific techniques of attention getting and selling invite the attacks of critics.

Broadcast advertisements are intrusive, breaking directly into the listener's consciousness, and moreover, they interrupt the program content.

WHY MAGAZINES EXIST

In embarking on this description of magazines to advertising management, it is highly appropriate to point out that every major American corporation, whether it makes chewing gum or automobiles, is

Reactions to Advertisements in Four Media

| | | *Nature of Reaction* | | |
	Annoying	*Enjoyable*	*Informative*	*Offensive*
All media	23%	36%	36%	5%
Magazines	9	37	48	6
Newspapers	12	23	59	6
Radio	24	33	40	3
Television	27	38	31	4

SOURCE: Raymond A. Bauer and Stephen A. Greyser, "Advertising in America: The Consumer View," Harvard Graduate School of Business Administration, Boston, 1968.

itself actively engaged in magazine publishing.   Regular weekly and monthly sales and production reports are actually periodicals which are indispensable to brand and corporate management.   Annual reports are, in fact, magazines edited toward current and prospective shareholders.   Thus, the indispensability of magazines for the pur-

Relationship of Media to the Reasons Ads Are Considered Annoying

	TV	*Radio*	*News-papers*	*Magazines*	*All Annoying Ads*
Stimulus qualities	79%	92%	34%	53%	73%
Intrusiveness	46	63	16	17	42
Insult to intelligence	22	20	7	14	19
Content impact	11	9	11	22	12
Informational failure	33	28	48	42	36
Moral concern	8	9	13	10	10
Evaluative	8	6	13	13	9
Other	4	4	7	8	5
"Just annoying"	5	3	3	6	5
	137%	142%	118%	132%	138%

SOURCE: Raymond A. Bauer and Stephen A. Greyser, "Advertising in America: The Consumer View," Harvard Graduate School of Business Administration, Boston, 1968.

poses of conducting the corporation's business has been fully established.

However, the purpose here obviously is to go beyond this internal communication sphere and to approach the proposition of magazines and our consumer public.

Preference of Advertising in Media

	With Advertising	Without Advertising	No Opinion
Magazines	73.7%	15.0%	11.3%
Newspapers	92.4	11.9	5.7
Television	36.2	52.5	11.3
Radio	37.1	45.9	17.0

SOURCE: Gallup, 1959.

At this point, it is necessary to develop a detachment from our own personal attitudes toward magazines. We cannot properly develop a clear understanding of the relationships between magazines and their publics and our brand objectives with the intrusion of distorted individual experiences and introspections.

Advertising people are communicators; therefore, every magazine the advertiser reads, no matter what its nature or its subjective purpose to him, is invariably viewed in an additional and singular dimension—that of a communications force. In addition to their individual preferences in the vast field of consumer magazines, advertising people are exposed to numerous publications by virtue of their profession; and magazines and competitive communications media are a daily preoccupation.

Accordingly, the advertising professionals' reactions to magazines, individually and collectively, are highly atypical.

How Magazines Began

To understand the contemporary magazine and its potential forces as communicator and motivator on behalf of the brand, it is vital to explore how and why the magazine began.

Magazines (as opposed to broadcast, which was basically the child of technology) had editorial need for universal appeal, and therefore, they restricted their content empathy to entertainment of all forms.

The magazine basically began as a phenomenon of nineteenth-century minority groups—people who could be called the literary aristocrats. This occurred at a time when there were much greater polarities in literacy levels; in a sense, these were social units that could be related to Plato's theory of the Republic which dictated that society should be led by the learned. For them, the preexistent newspaper form was not (and in many senses, it still is not) sufficiently erudite and specific in terms of their knowledge levels and interests.

This was the way magazines were first used as an advertising force; a device to skim across the buying public and to reach the leadership or affluent element in society—these factors along with education comprising the backbone of nations, the strength of progress, are the hallmark of magazines.

The magazine began essentially by accomplishing those things which newspapers could not do. Newspapers were, for the most part, controlled by government or by unilaterally and narrowly attuned special interests. Even where they were not controlled, newspapers had involvements which were totally parochial—even more parochial than today—long-range, instantaneous transmission of news matter being nonexistent. The newspaper was completely chauvinistic; it had a high level of urgency and a need to create devices, real or otherwise, which sold copies each day. Newspapers had to generate an appeal to the masses to the exclusion of fully feeding the special interests and intellects of individuals and groups.

In these and other senses, the existence of newspapers as the only communications form implicated a perpetuation of isolation and the social status quo.

This is basically history; yet, as in so many areas, that which is historic has a contemporary significance and offers pertinent insights into the conditions of today. Perhaps the most simplistic definition of the role of magazines as opposed to newspapers in relation to man can be stated as follows:

The total life of a man and the circumstances under which he lives can be delineated from the pages of his local newspapers, between the dates of birth notice and obituary. The kind of person he is and the character and style of his existence can be defined by those magazines he chooses to read during the various stages of his life.

MAGAZINE DIMENSIONS

Magazine publishing today represents one of America's largest industries, even if we judge it just from the standpoints of dollar volume and physical output.   (These, by the way, do not begin to reflect the values of the creative, informational, and motivational benefits of this product which cannot be measured in conventional terms.)

For example, 186 magazines comprising twelve general categories developed 132,594 pages of editorial matter alone in 1968; if laid out in three-column format, this original and unduplicated material would fill a press sheet of the width of *Time* magazine in a length of 2,451 statute miles.   Measuring another way, if we placed each 1968 issue of these 186 magazines side by side, we would fill 37.3 feet of shelf space, the length required for eleven complete sets of "Encyclopaedia Britannica."

Another rather dramatic dimension is based upon what two national magazines—*Life* (fifty-one issues) and *McCall's* (twelve issues) —must produce in order to fulfill their circulation for 1969.   The total physical output of just these two publications stacked side by side in an area of 10 square feet would create a solid tower 100,000 feet high and weighing 270,750 tons.   Expressed in terms of raw paper, inks, engravings, printing and production equipment, power, transportation, and postage, in addition to total man-hours for editorial, advertising, circulation, and promotion, these two magazines provide an indication for our comprehension of the immense proportions of the magazine industry in toto.

MAGAZINE INGREDIENTS

In 1949, S. I. Hayakawa, America's foremost semanticist wrote:

> Although in real life communists are sometimes charming people, they are never presented as such. . . . Although in real life Negroes often occupy positions of dignity and professional responsibility, in magazine stories they are never permitted to appear except as comic characters or as servants, because by intentional orientation, Negroes should never be anything else.[2]

[2] S. I. Hayakawa, "Language in Thought and Action," Harcourt, Brace & World, Inc., New York, 1949, p. 260.

Obviously, a great deal has changed, and even the learned scholars did not foresee the dramatic social and attitudinal changes brought about by such significant events as the Army-McCarthy hearings and the Supreme Court Civil Rights rulings.   However, people react to history; magazines, as manifestations of social interest and enlightenments also react.   In fact, magazines are themselves often the means by which trends and movements are accelerated.

"Columbia Encyclopedia" states that the term *magazine* is usually limited to periodicals designed primarily for entertainment.   However, World War II and ensuing involvements have made Americans more world-conscious.   The launching of Sputnik in 1957 shocked both government and public into a sudden sense of urgency for informational, educational, and technological proliferation.

At the same time, other communications forms began to fulfill many of the escape and entertainment functions which had primarily been equal in the twin forces of magazines; editorial information being the other.

The magazine industry had long been involved—some publications regrettably too heavily—in a dual state of entertainment and escapism as a primary circulation gatherer.   However, television soon became the principal entertainment form in terms of broad masses, and escape and entertainment are much more available today in other forms.   (Other media were also profoundly affected by the advent of television dominance in this area.   The novel, theater, and movies reacted by broadening their sophistication levels and permissive standards.)   Radio became the ever-present companion who whispers in your ear anytime, anywhere.   The magazines reacted by changing their directions, by accenting with increasing purposefulness their informational stance in society.

Editorial Shifts
Per Cent of Editorial Matter—Fiction and Stories

Magazine	1950	1960	1967	1968
McCall's	33	18	12	11
Ladies' Home Journal	29	30	14	13
Redbook	56	47	40	40
Good Housekeeping	20	24	18	18
Family Circle	19	7	—	—
Woman's Day	24	10	4	4
Esquire	24	11	6	8

SOURCE: Lloyd Hall.

During the same time that public appetite for magazine fiction has quantitatively changed relative to its desire for factual content, its tastes in what fiction it sought to assimilate have become infinitely more sophisticated.

In 1949, Hayakawa portrayed magazine fiction as follows:

> The reading of the average magazine story . . . requires no extensional checking whatsoever, neither by looking at the extensional world around us nor by furrowing our foreheads in attempts to recall opposite facts. The story follows nice, easy paths of *already established intentional orientations* . . . the expected judgments are accompanied by the expected facts. The straying hubby returns to his mate, and the little wife who is "true blue" triumphs over the beautiful but unscrupulous glamour girl . . . the big industrialist is "stern, but has a kindly twinkle in his eye." Such stories are sometimes cleverly contrived, but they never, if they can help it, disturb anyone's intentional orientation.[3]

Even what Hayakawa reported then relative to other magazine content is no longer pertinent, but is repeated here because it provides a benchmark for how much has changed:

> In the magazines of mass appeal, the writers rarely rely on the reader's ability to arrive at his own conclusions. In order to save any possible strain on the reader's intelligence, the writers *make the judgments for us.* The "slicks" do this less than the "pulps" while in the "quality" group, the tendency is to rely a great deal on the reader, to give no judgments at all when the facts "speak for themselves," or to give enough facts with every judgment so that the reader is free to make a different judgment if he so wishes.[4]

However, it would be grossly misleading to oversimplify the nature of change in magazine editorial. While we live in a society which has ceased to contemplate its own navel in the interests of other contemplations, where permissiveness threatens to become a virtue, and where technology has etched man's footprint on the moon, the most remarkable aspect of change lies in its astronomical varieties. Thus, greater predictability of information and audience creates for magazines a singular opportunity and a need for more unpredictability in communicating with this audience.

[3] *Op cit.*, p. 128.
[4] *Ibid.*

The Stewardship of Individuals

In this context, one of the constants of magazines is the fact that magazine stewardships largely remain in the hands of individuals.

To illustrate this, I refer to the *Writer's Handbook,* a highly respected authority on creative writing which is directed at tyros and professionals alike. Following are quotations in that publication from the editors of three major magazines:

> The editor . . . is in much the same position as the captain of a ship: his word is law, and he may do as he pleases in deciding to buy or not to buy a story . . . he must always live with the realization that the responsibility is ultimately his. If the magazine runs on a rock or shoal, if it founders or runs aground, there is only one person to blame, and he is that one.

> For fiction and full-length articles, the final decision is made by the editor or the executive editor.

> By this time, the stories in question have passed everybody but the pay-off man.

Therefore, the end product is still based upon editorial judgment, and the judgments will vary interestingly and significantly, even from magazine to magazine within the same field.

For example, there's an interesting little distinction in the outdoor books: *Outdoor Life's* fiction is all in the first person: "I saw the bear coming and I reached for my gun." *Sports Afield* edits all its fiction in the third person: "John saw the bear coming at him and he reached for his gun." There are a million people who prefer it one way and another million who prefer it the other. Important is to know the factual point of difference and relate this distinction in a meaningful way to our communication strategy in these vehicles.

There are similar differences among women's books, men's books, and service books. All these similarities and dissimilarities demand constant observation and review in terms of communicating with optimum closeness to the audiences of each of these publications.

Editorial Analysis When we talk about communication strategy in this sense, we are getting right back to depths of editorial analysis. Unfortunately, this kind of analysis cannot always be quantitative. It is not really a matter of rating a single value on a one-to-ten scale.

It is a matter of describing and differentiating values which, if it can be done at all, can be done only in words.   In fact, we cannot even begin to make editorial comparisons and editorial evaluations until we make discriminations for our continuing frame of reference.

Considering the subtleties of editorial discernment, the large number of properties to be observed, and the ever-changing psychological posture of the total public and its magazine-audience components, as well as those changes which occur in the strategies of the brand, this is an art which is and should be the responsibility of the advertising personnel, both agency and client alike.   The agency because it is structured to utilize its uniquely close and highly voluminous contacts with the producers of the various magazine products, as a function of perceiving and interpreting the implications on the advertiser's behalf.   The client because he is ultimately responsible for the product's welfare, and is the most qualified to select the direction it should take.

WHY PEOPLE READ MAGAZINES

We have briefly traced the history of the magazine product and touched upon new human enlightenments and appetites.

However, it would be presumptuous and even wrong to presuppose that the existence of thought hunger and food for thought should automatically result in purchase, consumption, and enjoyment of the product.   A man desires more than raw knowledge, and even if this were not so, there are many other avenues from which he can acquire knowledge.

To communicate most effectively within magazines, we must have some idea of not only who is exposed, but why they are exposed.   Or to be more precise, why the reader has elected to commit himself to the magazine.

Power of Conscious Selection

The editorial contents of magazines take down certain barriers to perception; they force the reader to take down certain of his own mental barriers.   To an extent, a magazine has done this even before the cover is opened.   A reader is prepared to ingest certain kinds of facts, certain kinds of ideas, presented in a certain way.   If he were not, he would not be preparing to read the magazine.

This power of conscious selection is a force you have to apply an effort against in that you make the specific act.   It requires an input on the part of the consumer, and once having initiated motion, he will be much more willing to expend more effort such as by going after the product he has seen advertised.

This commitment factor is at work before reading even begins.   If we know which barriers the reader has taken down, we can present our commercial message in such a way that it will enter that opened aperture to the mind more easily and with longer-lasting effect.

We must consider human motivations and drives and how these are acted upon by the astute magazine publisher.   In this way, we can gain a usable understanding of the atmosphere within which the magazine communicates to its public; hence, how magazine advertising can optimumly operate within the magazine-reader framework.

Community of the Magazine Audience   Earlier, magazines were described as an outgrowth of literate minorities and their deep desires for informational exchanges which could not be derived from any preexistent form, be it books or newspapers.   As an extension of that, it should be said that magazines are the connective interest threads between those individuals who comprise these various intellectual and interest groups.

While newspapers are parochial in respect to place, magazines are parochial in respect to interests in a manner which is not physically or arithmetically discernible.

They bring people together on ideas and informations, and in so doing, create a homogeneous audience force—much in the manner of the mystics communicating with spirits and levitating tables.

In this sense, then, the magazine relates to a community—based on the inescapable similarity of personality complexes and interests which have necessarily no basic foundation in geography, but rather are based upon various sets and combinations of psychological conditions which were described by Freud and others many years ago.

They offer the reader an opportunity and fulfill his innate need to be selectively expansive, even when he cannot physically expand beyond his present state of income, location, and influence.

Magazines Provide Authority   Magazines also satisfy the desire for authoritativeness by drawing from the very top skills and disciplines. Magazines can pursue a contemporary theme with thoroughness, enhance and expand upon the picture of the theme, and give it permanence—the pill, youth problems, social change, whatever. Highly expert print interpretations often mean more to the individual than social conversation or consultations with family doctors, lawyers, and the like, because they are on the record and subject to rebuttal from the magazine audience.

Audience Homogeneity It has been proposed that as the country grows smaller through mass transportation and broadcast communication, the need for this extraction of audience homogeneity out of geographic heterogeneity will decline. However, in my opinion, magazines will thrive because as the country becomes more intrarelated, it will become more segmented; within growing homogeneity, there will be an intensification of desire and search for identity and individuality. Relevant to this, then, is the fact that brands are not single-faceted; each has a variety of qualities and personality characteristics.

Appeals of Different Kinds of Magazines

Readers go to some magazines because they are comfortable in that they have a constancy of theme and personality, a predictable consistency of approach and appeal, as well as a singleness of purpose. They approach other magazines for the shock value they expect and receive. The exposé journalism form, of course, generates a different set of psychic reactions; therefore, the reader mood in relation to the totality of that kind of magazine, including its advertising, will be different from reaction to those publications which function basically to reaffirm and expand upon previously known and relatively noncontroversial subjects.

Mass Magazines Mass magazines encompass both journalistic styles, thereby enabling the reader to shop for editorial matter based upon his mood of the moment. In this manner, the mass magazine appeals to more of the total man; hence, it should be called *mass* not only in terms of circulation and audience size, but also in reference to the scope of information types and styles and the variety of methods in which it is presented.

However, "mass" is an often missued word. Mass implies everyone or almost anyone; if any magazine appealed to the total social complex, it would have circulation comparable to the total unduplicated audience of United States newspapers or the maximum audience of all prime-time television shows in the aggregate. Obviously, this is not the case.

The fact that they do not achieve this level of penetration demonstrates that the mass magazine does not really appeal to the total man. Instead it deals with a definite approach or a specific which is present in all men, but much more prevalent in some. Therefore, even mass magazines, in a sense, are selective; however, as opposed to the special-interest books, they deal within a broader group.

Selectivity among Mass Magazines   In a general sense, for example, *McCall's* relates to women; *Look* applies itself to the family unit and then relates its basic editorial approach to the selective group against a broader group.   *Reader's Digest,* in a sense, is more security-oriented and appeals to the nostalgic, the convenience-minded, and those who are concerned about health and personal welfare.

This dedication to a point of view has its impact upon the audience, particularly in relation to measurements of magazine audiences for a brand campaign.   Often in making these measurements, there is concern with overlap and duplication between the various books being used; actually because of these differences of involvements generated by the various mass books, duplication is far from totally wasteful.

Each of the so-called mass magazines, in fact, has a singularity of purpose which is unique unto itself.   Therefore, selectivity exists even in mass.   For example, there are readers who love *Reader's Digest,* but will never enjoy *Life;* and there are *Life* readers who are strong nonreaders of *Look* and *Reader's Digest.*

Depth of Analysis   Generally, larger magazines also appeal to other aspects of human personality.   In relation to specific and measurable events which have already been reported and to a degree analyzed in other media, the magazine offers greater depth of analysis.   It provides this in a much more permanent form; it allows the reader to reconfirm and reconclude on the basis of a broader knowledge of the subject.   In this sense, it adds to his weaponry in expostulating, expanding, and at times, deepening his own personal perspective.

Magazines as Status Symbols   Beyond this, many magazines feed other facets of the human psyche.   Magazines also serve as status symbols and ego builders, and as a reflection of man's aspirations beyond his present attainments.   Beyond this, magazines comprise a tangible confirmation of attainments already achieved; in this sense, they reinforce ego and go even further in that they provide the reader with assurances that his attainments have been worthwhile.   As he has progressed professionally or economically, he seeks new spectra to satisfy his concurrent growth of informational needs, materialistic wants, and economic leverage.   This is the graduation, so to speak, from *Argosy* to *True* or from *True* to *Esquire* and *Playboy;* in addition, it is the supplementation of the individual's original magazine complex with business books and news weeklies which enable him to live up to his larger and broader status in life.

(One meaningful demonstration of this is that before a party, the magazine consumer will lay out his "better" magazines side by side and will discreetly hide all others.   This display signifies a pride of possession, and in fact, a pride in self.)

Effect of Psychic Factors on Communication

Relating these and other psychic factors to the proposition of advertising communications in magazines is a subtle art.   We can suppose that various kinds of magazine editorial create subliminal as well as the more obvious and direct conditionings by which motivations can be generated.   Stating this very broadly, it could be said that the pill sells cosmetics; cancer sells travel; Elizabeth Taylor sells wigs; unisex sells exercise machines.

This is a manifestation of several factors.   For example, in relation to the pill, there is a simultaneous interest in technology.   In connection with new interests in travel, we encounter opportunities to sell those brands which are prestigious and which are compatible with the emotional complex which evolves from the desire for travel.

Opportunities for the Advertiser

Here, of course, we have cited some of the indirect manifestations of editorial environment; there are more direct ones which are applicable to great advantage if we seek them out.   This involves constantly investigating editorial, and fluctuations and trends within editorial, because these continually provide the opportunistic advertiser with new direct-line brand potentials and with futures in terms of related lines.

Emotional Differences   In relation to the sex revolution which we expect will continue, it should be added that of all media, magazines alone maintain polarization of the sexes, all other media being basically bisexual.   However, perhaps more dramatic than the demographic differences between audiences of magazines in the same field are the emotional differences.

One example is *Vogue* magazine.   This publication has a rigid editorial policy in that it will feature only fashions which are new and have not been published elsewhere.   Therefore, the reader going to *Vogue* knows that everything she will see, at least in the editorial sense, will be completely new.

To some types of women, this is an attraction in that they are more susceptible to original ideas and to change.   This factor can and should be exploited from an advertising standpoint in that the advertising execution should be attuned to this editorial concept.

On the other hand, there are other types of women who do not choose to be completely confronted with things not seen before; instead of interpreting them in the context of being new, they consider them to be foreign and disruptive to their basic frame of reference. Other magazines cater to this trait in the ways they present fashion.

Therein is a demonstration of how emotional variances and relative receptivities to different advertising executions can largely be predetermined through a deeper understanding of the editorial philosophy of the individual magazine.

Identification of the Reader with the Magazine

Of course, no explanation of why people read magazines would be at all complete unless we alluded to the great identification that individuals feel with magazines relating to special and highly specific interests.

The individual needs a high degree of fulfillment, attainment, and appreciation (back patting).   This is manifested in the explosion which is occurring in special-interest magazines, which is a single-dimension extension of knowledge; i.e., you get some information on skiing and music in a general way in general-interest publications, but you buy a specialized magazine in order to increase and deepen this knowledge.

Special-interest magazines   There is a paradox really in describing the special-interest magazines, in that they are generally described as being "narrow."   However, this is a misinterpretation in that there can be broad applications of special interests, and even where the subject matter involved does not have mass appeal in the numerical sense, it more than compensates for this by having a deep appeal in an involvement sense.   This has several implications for the advertiser.

Value to the Advertiser   First, copy content can be tailored to the psychic group as opposed to the general practice of designing a single copy execution which is applicable to all magazines used in the campaign.   This approach, of course, is a great deal harder and more expensive to fulfill than to expostulate.   It is for this reason that selection of magazines to fit existing creative product communications is the primary method of achieving advertising-communications empathy.

In addition, the much greater depth of involvement in the special-interest group substantially offsets the higher costs per thousand inherent to these publications.   Specifically, in operating against a much higher attention and receptivity level, a half page in a special-interest magazine can probably generate at least as much attention and motivation as a full page or a spread in a publication of more general interest.   Therefore, while the page CPMs are vastly different, the involvement and communications CPM is very much in line.   Obviously, the reverse attitude insofar as ad size and CPM justification is concerned is the better route to take once you have rationalized the audience's value; that is, that the more valuable the prospects, the greater the concentration of them in terms of a percentage of the vehicle's audience and the better advised you are to maximize your advertising impact against them through size, frequency, or promotion.

Wrapping up the subject of why people read magazines, we again refer to Hayakawa, who states that:

> Human beings, for the purposes of their own well-being, and survival, insist upon getting knowledge from as many people as possible, and also insist upon disseminating as widely as possible whatever knowledge they themselves feel may have been valuable . . . power presses, cheaper methods of printing . . . make possible the quick finding of practically any information people might want—these and many other devices are now in operation in order that we need not depend solely on our own experience, but may utilize the experience of the rest of humanity.[5]

UNIQUE QUALITIES OF MAGAZINES

In exploring the qualities of the medium, we are attempting to relate what it is that sets magazines apart within the total media spectrum.

Long Life Spans

Men, women, and children do not discard magazines in the same way as they do other print media.   Newspapers, and even the most elab-

[5] *Op cit.*, p. 239.

orate direct-mail pieces, are thrown away with relative ease; they have no lasting significance. However, magazines have incredibly long life spans.

The explanation for this phenomenon probably begins in early history when man first used print to record major events. While man has changed, he has consistently paid homage to scrolls, manuscripts, and all other varieties of print communications through which knowledge, beauty, and higher ideals are transmitted from one generation to another.

Magazines, in their relatively short existence, have substantially increased in those qualities which readers value: personally oriented and timeless content incorporated into highly creative and appealing packaging. Whether or not these values or attachments are consciously perceived by the reader, the fact remains that he does not want to destroy the magazine—he reads it thoroughly, refers to it again, and passes it along.

More Time Spent with the Magazine   There is a major benefit here for the advertiser in that when a magazine generates these values, it transmits advertising messages within a psychological and editorial environment that will serve the brand long and well. The reader spends more time with the magazine; second exposures are generated; better advertising readership occurs; and in a variety of ways, the magazine develops a cumulative effect upon brand consumers that goes far beyond the expectations that are implied by the numbers which are reflected by circulation.

For example, in terms of passing the magazine along, and thereby expanding its capacity to accumulate an audience, it is interesting to examine what occurs in *Life* magazine on an issue-by-issue basis. The following statistics convey some interesting information:

LIFE (*Circulation: 8,150,000*)—*1969*

Issues	Net Audience, in Thousands	Per Cent Reached	Frequency
1	36,687	29.3	1.0
2	49,009	39.2	1.5
3	56,011	44.8	1.9
4	60,637	48.5	2.4
5	64,262	51.4	2.8
6	66,888	53.5	3.3
7	69,138	55.3	3.7

LIFE (*Circulation: 8,150,000*)—*1969* (**Continued**)

Issues	Net Audience, in Thousands	Per Cent Reached	Frequency
8	71,014	56.8	4.1
9	72,639	58.1	4.5
10	74,014	59.2	4.9
11	75,264	60.2	5.3
12	76,390	61.1	5.7
51	91,768	73.4	20.4

SOURCE: Young & Rubicam estimates.

Starting with the circulation base of slightly more than 8 million, a single issue of *Life* accumulates an audience of more than 36 million adults (4.2 per copy).   For a great variety of reasons, the audience of this weekly magazine is relatively volatile as is demonstrated by the fact that ten consecutive issues of *Life* accumulate a total net audience more than twice as great as its single-issue net.

Over a fifty-one–issue span, *Life* reaches 73.4 per cent of all United States adults, and its accumulated audience is 2½ times as great as its single-issue audience.

We find a completely different pattern when we examine comparable data for *Reader's Digest:*

READER'S DIGEST (*Circulation: 17,438,000*)—*1969*

Issues	Net Audience, in Thousands	Per Cent Reached	Frequency
1	43,583	34.9	1.0
2	53,010	42.4	1.6
3	58,011	46.4	2.2
4	61,262	49.0	2.8
5	63,637	50.9	3.4
6	65,638	52.5	4.5
7	67,138	53.7	4.5
8	68,513	54.8	5.1
9	69,638	55.7	5.6
10	70,639	56.5	6.2
11	71,514	57.2	6.2
12	72,264	57.8	7.2

SOURCE: Young & Rubicam estimates.

Operating from a circulation of just under 17.5 million, a single issue reaches 43,583,000 adults (approximately 2.5 per copy). This indicates that even though *Reader's Digest* has a much longer chronological life than *Life* magazine, there is less of a tendency to pass it along. Also, the *Reader's Digest* audience tends to be relatively stable on an issue-to-issue basis. Whereas *Life* has less than one-half the circulation of the *Digest* and its first-issue audience is only 80 per cent that of the *Digest,* after five issues, *Life* has accumulated numerically a much larger net audience than the *Digest;* in fact, over a one-year span (twelve issues of *Digest* and fifty-one issues of *Life*), the *Life* audience is 25 per cent larger.

Other considerations aside, these two examples demonstrate how each magazine accumulates its audience differently as an outgrowth of each magazine's editorial and audience individuality.

Advertising within these structures has a unique meaning and an essence of its own that can be used in a variety of ways to reinforce the marketing activity of any brands. In this sense, we can exploit the unique magazine proposition of timelessness and the individual's desire to retain that which is timeless longer than that which is generically connected with a specific point in time; i.e., the newspaper.

Change in the Usefulness of a Magazine   In relation to these phenomena and other characteristics of magazines and their audiences on a single-issue basis, as well as over a broad span of time, it is pertinent to touch upon the history of *National Geographic*. For many years, it was stored and kept by a small audience. These were those in the higher-than-median age groups to whom it appealed from a nostalgic point of view and those younger elements of the audience who looked to it as a geography reference source. This guided how it was used as a brand book.

However, the world changed and the topics encompassed within *National Geographic* suddenly became more apparent and important, and the pass-along versus retention character of the book changed in accordance with changes in tastes and patterns of the country (in fact, circulation actually increased more than preexistent pass-along). People began to travel more; conversation and other geographic elements attracted infinitely broader interest; and therefore, *National Geographic* was operating within totally new dimensions. Because of changes in social mores, it moved from a reference book and a memory stimulator to a very live position piece.

In purely chronological terms, it does not very often occur that a magazine is a harbinger of social interests and habits. Yet, ski books have been with us for many years, while the skiing explosion is a rather recent phenomenon; and there are other areas where this is happening now, still others where we should anticipate it will occur in the future.

Retention versus Pass-along

We can draw several conclusions from these ideas, facts, and examples:

Certain magazines (particularly in the monthly field) have much greater opportunities to pick up more subscriber circulation because they are not passed along. The consumer who has strong desires to read these publications regularly cannot presume that he will receive them (regularly) second- or third-hand.

On the other hand, the larger the pass-along factor, the more difficult it becomes for the magazine to achieve a rise in its actual circulation.

There are those magazines which are subject to drastic change in terms of being pass-along vehicles as opposed to retention vehicles. These two characteristics should not be presumed to be constant; therefore, optimum planning and development of long-range advertising franchises in specific magazines involve constant reevaluation of each vehicle individually in terms of its own character changes, as well as the character of its audience and of the society in toto.

Specific and Coincidental Appeals of Magazines

Magazines generally, in order to succeed (and in order to provide a platform for successful brand advertising), must have a purpose and a reason; specifically, they must appeal to a specific group.

The successful magazines are historically the ones which are positioned in accordance with changes in our society. These are the magazines which apply themselves to communities of interest, ideas, and information exchange, and which address themselves with empathetic compatibility to the population segment selected for them by editorial planning and execution. This is necessary to prolonged success in the highly competitive publishing field.

It also explains why those magazines which are created for an existent *coincidental* audience pool (charge cards, mailings to top-level homes, etc.) have less value and are less likely to succeed. Within this coincidental audience, there exist vast differences, regardless of the supposed advantages of having a so-called captive audience and an easily facilitated circulation procurement. The case of *Dare* magazine trying to develop a circulation universe around the barber chair is a specific example of this.

Reader's Involvement with Magazines

Another singular quality of magazines, alluded to in our introduction, is that the kind of person a man is and the character and style of his existence can be defined by those magazines he chooses to read during the various stages of his life.

To explain this further, various moves and changes in the individual and the family life-cycle vein (as opposed to the geographic move) will alter, sometimes dramatically, the pattern of magazines which will be read. The most obvious example of this are the baby books which are embraced and, in fact, sought out by the expectant mother. Similar changes occur when the family moves to suburbia and house and garden books become a new and vital part of the reading habit.

This phenomenon of evolution occurs most dramatically in the magazine area, broadcast viewing habits and other communications exposures remaining essentially the same. (The newspaper the family reads will be either the same metropolitan newspaper or the suburban paper, which is still a newspaper per se in terms of character and the informational services it performs.)

The new magazines represent a totally new dimension of readership and involvement. This, by the way, happens concurrently with multitudinous needs in terms of home-oriented products as well as those less direct items which serve as affirmation symbols of the family's new status and identity.

Even within the professional area, we find a highly direct manifestation of magazine exposures and involvements dramatically altering as our life-style changes.

For example, everyone who is engaged in the advertising function has had the experience of picking up *Advertising Age* for the first time; this is almost as much a case of necessity as it is desire. Almost invariably in this first exposure, there is a newness, starkness, and a basic unfamiliarity with the content and format of this publication. Therefore, most first exposures to *Advertising Age* (and to other magazines, either of a consumer or a business nature) entail a fundamental superficiality of involvement.

However, as we cultivate the *Ad Age* habit, so to speak, its predictability of format, style, and interpretation, together with our increased feeling of confidence and our growing reliance upon the publication, generate involvements which become infinitely deeper than those which occurred the first time. Therefore, in terms of communicating in magazines in depth, it is important to understand that the reader's inherent motivational dimensions deepen as the involvement chronologically lengthens.

Reading Ease Increases with Knowledge   At the same time, there is an increase in reader ease as the reader acquires more knowledge about the subject matter encompassed within the magazine, as well as increased familiarity with the vehicle itself. This injection of the reader's own knowledge into his relationship with the magazine represents an advantage; the reader, in a sense, becomes a participant within the magazine content; he puts something into it. This makes the magazine more meaningful to him as time increases, and at the same time, increases the advertiser capability to generate deeper motivation to the prospect as this time span lengthens.

These are just a few demonstrations of some of those characteristics which make magazines unique as compared with other media forms. They have a definite and definitive place within the brand-advertising spectrum. However, here it should be stated that one of the great deterrents to the return of magazines as a major brand-advertising medium is the fact that they still think of themselves as the primary medium.

Are Magazines a Primary Medium?

Once magazines recognize their relative position within the total communications framework and tailor their selling efforts accordingly, everyone, including the magazines themselves, will benefit. Optimum contemporary usage (and optimum selling) has yet to be developed because the magazine is a new medium in today's more enlightened (and more communicated-to) society. This enlightenment is to the magazine's benefit; because of the broader market, magazines have more positions within which to become meaningful.

However, if they elect to try to become all things to all people, they encounter an obvious impossibility; and there have been too many attempts in the magazine business to do this.

It is unrealistic, and in fact, impossible to be the sole medium, or in many cases, the primary medium.   It would be much better to recognize that since the best part of product prospects are the smaller part (and these are becoming increasingly more recognizable), they should seek to go after this group—and then sell their saliency of communications to this group.

To this point, magazines have consistently applied their greatest sales weight against top management.   This is probably not where the decision is made.   If a change is effected, it is probably an *obstructive* rather than a *constructive* decision. However this is pursued sometimes to the exclusion of conveying individual and collective magazine merits at the level of the brand, be it the brand manager or the agency personnel responsible to the brand.   The track record of this approach, as defined by magazines' shrinking share of the total brand advertising dollar, should at some point demonstrate that this singularity of selling at the top is not the road to advertising success.

Magazines have their unique proposition.   It is hoped this will be properly interpreted and conveyed to those levels of actual advertising decision making which are pertinent.

Dynamics of Magazine Seasonality

If magazines would highlight their important aspect, then here is a device they should use.   Unique brand-advertising opportunities exist in the sense of exploiting "seasons" within the magazine medium. The considerations here involve:

Conventional climatic seasons

Selling seasons, including holidays, etc.

Seasons of currently unrealized potential for cyclical products

Seasons which exist within the lifetime of each brand

Psychic seasons which are germane to special types of magazines

(In the section on newspapers later in this chapter, it will be demonstrated how astute retailers have perfected the art of exploiting actual seasons, and in addition, creating seasons of their own where none previously existed.)

Climatic Seasons   In terms of the climatic seasons, magazines have obvious limitations, as opposed to local media, because of their geographic leverage; the sequence of seasons in the Southwest, for example, being entirely different from that of the Northeast.   However, in examining actual magazine advertising programs, it appears that there still remain opportunities to draw a much closer relationship between ad placement, content, and timing to the various seasons of the year.   Regionals do this for advertising, and editorial is sometimes done in these regional forms as well.

Creating a relationship between *when* the ad appears and *how* the ad appears develops the backdrop for drawing a closer involvement with the brand prospect.   We can presuppose that there is an opportunity to gain greater *attention* during hot-weather periods with advertising strategies which have hot-weather connotations, even of the subtlest nature, and that the same would be true for the winter months.

Selling Seasons   At this point, the selling seasons per se seem to be the best utilized of all the seasonal opportunities in magazines.   For example, there is an almost direct relationship between broad-appeal magazines published in September and October, which are the new-car introduction months, and the physical characteristics of car dealerships themselves.

The magazine, in a sense, becomes a reflection of "automobile row," where it has long been established that dealerships situated adjacent to other dealerships enjoy better selling opportunities than those which are totally isolated from all competitors.

In an advertising sense, the increasing number of ads designed for a particular audience creates and then sells a better marketplace. People shop the ads and want to see a variety of purchase opportunities in relation to a product category or a specific buying need.   It is conceivable that these things feint for attention in the marketplace and even benefit by being at a spot where goods are exposed when people are looking for them; but, it does not mean that we are always in favor of the advertising well.   The editorial rub-off is the important thing.

Again, relating this to the automotive industry, the development of automobile row enabled the consumer to look at competitive brands together within a short period of time and to make a purchase commitment—where in some cases, the end result would have been no purchase commitment at all for any brands or models.

It should be pointed out here that each calendar season—Christmas, Mother's Day, etc.—seems to precipitate what could be called *advertising clutter*. However, as opposed to other media forms, clutter in print is a phenomenon which, under certain circumstances, is sought after rather than rejected by the product prospect; therefore, this clutter has positive rather than negative values.

The climatic and the selling seasons are therefore those which offer the most apparent, and to this point, the best-implemented opportunities for brand promotion within magazines.

Competition being as it is, optimum exploitation of the more obvious seasons, confronted with optimum exploitation by competitor brands, can result in a type of stand-off from an advertising seasonality standpoint. Therefore, we explore additional phenomena which could provide greater seasonal opportunities for advertising the brand in magazines—and here again, certain lessons will be drawn from retailer usage of newspapers.

Seasons for Cyclical Products There are various products which would appear to be locked into seasonal cycles, principally because of historical factors; yet, prospect tastes and desires can be changed by astute marketing and advertising merchandising.

A classic example of this is the pattern of developing year-round tourism in Florida.

In less obvious forms, the same thing occurs within the automotive industry each year. The cars do not always change so drastically; instead they change a little at a time by new chrome designs, safety features, and accessories with each year's model. Automobile advertisers use this as an opportunity to build a consumer-predictable season in magazines by promoting a new style feature—each year a change in something totally familiar.

This practice by the car people actually spans two of the types of seasonalities listed previously. In addition to communicating a calendar season by way of the autumn introduction of new models, at the same time they capitalize on the seasons which exist in the lifetime of the brand; that is, the new model is in effect a new stage of brand life.

Seasons within the Lifetime of a Brand This technique can be applied much more broadly in that practically every brand in each product category has several stages in its own life cycle.

There is the state of newness which requires an advertising strategy attuned to wide dissemination and broad interpretation of the unique properties of an unfamiliar brand.

Once established, and having achieved an identity franchise and a user core, the brand proceeds to another stage, this being the conservation of current users and the broadening of acceptance among prospective new users. The advertising techniques involved should be altered accordingly.

All brands, of course, hope to achieve an extremely high level of acceptance, and when this occurs, the subsequent strategy involves conserving users and generating frequency of purchase and consumption.

Further, there are often instances of improvements to the brand, where the strategy in part sensibly reverts to broader exposition and the description of new properties.

Finally, there is the mature brand in a dwindling product market, where holding or increasing share is the main strategic consideration.

These are just some of the stages through which a brand may progress over a period of time. Each has a direct bearing on magazine selection and advertising execution within these magazines—from the standpoint of size, frequency, and advertising content.

There are no pat patterns for advertising executions relative to each of these brand life cycles. Rather, they are matters of judgment specifically related to each brand and to each of its seasons on a highly individualized basis. However, from a very general standpoint, it is obvious that the total magazine universe lends itself to a multitude of brand-season combinations. Also, in a more specific sense, even within a given set of demographic criteria, there are those magazine combinations which relate most to newsworthiness; others which are more compatible to reassurance; still others which implicate innovation and experimentation, etc.

Here, as was related earlier, the selection of vehicles which will perform best in terms of the state of the brand is a media art form. It again involves a continuing examination of each magazine group and of individual entities within groups. They will change in their natures, and therefore in their environmental and motivational properties, and finally, in their ability to transmit the brand-advertising message in that genre which is most compatible to the current state of the brand and to the advertising task at hand.

Psychic Seasons of Magazines   Finally, in relation to the dynamics of magazine seasonality, there is the proposition of the psychic seasons which occur within certain kinds of magazines.   This is a much more nebulous area than any of those described above, but it is important enough to deserve mention.

Quite often, special-interest magazines are related to activities for which there is a definable calendar season—yet the magazine is published on a year-round basis.   The ski magazines are an excellent case in point, in that the great preponderance of skiing occurs within a five-month span (with the exception of those skiers who have the dedication and wherewithal to indulge regularly their habit during the summer in the Alps or South America).   Therefore, in the case of a ski magazine, the winter months comprise a reader season of *participation,* and the summer months, a season of *anticipation.*   Consequently, the current or prospective ski buff acquires these magazines and reads them in an entirely different light during one time of the year as opposed to the other.

The editorial environments are basically the same.   The demographics are unaltered.   However, the deep and basic reader attitude goes through an extremely wide cycle—participatory at one time as opposed to anticipatory at the other.   As the ski magazines and other similar special-interest books inevitably become more important for communicating deeply to certain brand-prospect types, an examination of the ramifications of their own peculiar seasonalities will become more and more relevant to planning.

All Seasons Are Exploitable

The seasons described here and their pertinence to the proposition of advertising planning do not encompass all the great variety of seasons which exist.   Nor should they be construed as representing, in themselves, paramount considerations.   However, the fact is that they do exist.   They are exploitable.   The purpose here is to demonstrate that this is so, and to crystallize cognizance of this fact and stimulate further exploration into this phenomenon.

DYNAMICS OF THE MAGAZINE

Here we proceed beyond raw numbers and facts to an examination of how readers' psychological involvements combine with the unique characteristics of magazines to establish the stage for advertising the brand.

Magazines, by maintaining printed communication to those widely separated units which together comprise an interest segment, can react with great and consistent depth; at the same time, they can lend the subject at hand a level of permanence and attractiveness which is exceeded only by that of a book. Conversely, other major media, even in much newer forms, are basically tied to those executions which are philosophically universal, and mechanically historic.

This places greater demands upon the magazine publisher in that he must maintain sensitivities and special perceptions to society in flux, and specifically, to those sometimes subtle changes that occur within his widely dispersed audience. The publisher—therefore, the publication—must keep pace, but at the same time neither overinvolve nor overreact.

In magazines, the forces of constancy and change are not to be considered incongruous. That pulp which did not become somewhat slicker has disappeared; this is a condition of literacy improvement and taste elevation.

Yet, that in the mass field which has not become somewhat more explicit, controversial, and contemporary loses its sense of urgency and the ability to maintain attention and respect in the contemporary society; this is a manifestation of growth of enlightenment, and the phasing out of social and conversational taboos through new art forms, music, and particularly, the modern theater.

However, the most pervasive danger of all is to overreact and thereby forfeit the magazine's basic *raison d'être*. Periodical performance of the communications function to the same audience within a changing society demands an extremely high sense of editorial balance. A loss of this delicate equilibrium portends deep consequences to the publisher, and ultimately, to the advertiser.

Therefore, while it is the consumer who comprises the end manifestation of magazine dynamics, it is the magazine publisher who, through expertise and deep dedications to audience attunements and planning, must lay the groundwork through which the dynamics can materialize.

Accordingly, in any in-depth analysis of individual magazines, we are consistently concerned with the management of the publishing enterprise itself in relation to brand advertising: Is it progressive and dynamic?   Is the publisher alert to new opportunities and prepared to generate new ways of doing business?   Only through intelligent and continuing evaluation of these and other areas of the publishing operation can we hope to determine properly the values which it can contribute to our overall communications objectives and to the specific needs of brands.

The magazine publisher is (or should be) fully aware of the importance of these principles.   In fact, this is how the medium has progressed historically.   Primitive and yet very direct explorations into life-styles, attitudinal studies, and egotistics research have existed since the nineteenth century as an outgrowth of publisher-reader interaction on an issue-to-issue basis.   The publisher needs only to measure news circulation in-flow (and the character of its sources), circulation renewal (and the character of renewal lapse), newsstand sales and their variations, and mail from readers.   He must then make the correct interpretations in order to measure, and if you will, measure up to the changes within his audience universe.

Finally, in terms of dynamics, as the society becomes more interest segmented while it is physically homogenizing, there are demands and needs for new types of magazines.   This is reflected by the fact that among magazines carrying advertising, there has been an average of twenty-five live births as opposed to eleven deaths per year over a twenty-year span (in one recent year alone, we tabulated eighty new magazines ranging from *American Politics* to *Hog-Farm Management,* and we were treated to such *au courant* titles as *Flip, In, Go See, Tempo,* and *Clyde*).

In relating magazine dynamics to brand objectives, we attach great importance to proliferation and change.   On the other hand, it is obvious that other media are proliferating; but in this context, it is pertinent to recognize the completely different nature of the proliferation and change which are occurring in magazines as opposed to other forms.

MAGAZINE AUDIENCES

Now that a description has been made of the magazine as a product itself, it is appropriate to place under meaningful scrutiny that commodity which the magazine purveys to the advertiser—its audience and its ability to communicate within its audience structure.

This encompasses not only dimensions and demographics (psychographics have been touched upon earlier), but also the important factor of how people obtain their magazines—all these factors being relative to advertising considerations.

Magazines comprise their own vast complicated but orderly communications universe. Within this universe, there are giant stars whose energy and influence are impressive. This is indicated by Figure 1.

While the actual statistics are often startling, we are constantly

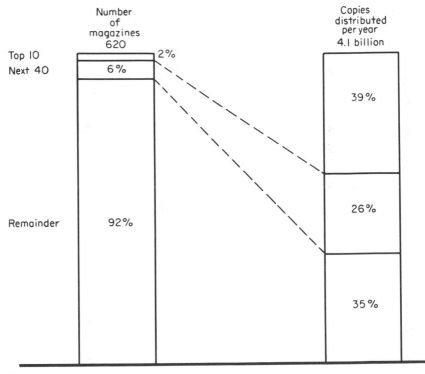

Figure 1

aware of the fact that the magazine field is broadly dominated by a few units. However, it would be a great mistake to underestimate the influence and growth of smaller and more specialized magazines.

Today there is a magazine for almost every sport, hobby, and intellectual leaning one might have; as leisure time continues to increase, these magazines have predictably grown. However, the growth rate of special-interest publications far outpaces growth in leisure time, travel, or hobby participation.

For example, one study shows that over the past twenty years, circulation of idea books has increased more than 500 per cent; sports magazines by 368 per cent; and hobby magazines by nearly 300 per cent.

Aside from the circulation increases of these publications, it could be assumed that with a modicum of publisher expertise, the narrower the magazine's subject scope, the deeper the dialogue with its reader; also, the more definitive and predictable its audience, both arithmetically and psychologically. Potentials for specific products or specialized creative strategies within these magazines is self-evident —and these potentials should continue to grow almost astronomically. Herein lies a stage for future, if not present, action.

Heavy Magazine Readers

In marketing, we have a necessarily high preoccupation with the heavy user. Therefore, it is appropriate to begin a description of the magazine user with a look at the heavy magazine reader. The following table clearly demonstrates that there is a direct correlation between degree of magazine exposure and education and income of adults:

Magazine Exposure *	Median Years of Schooling
Light	9.2
Medium	12.2
Heavy	12.7

Magazine Exposure *	Median Income of Household
Light	$5,819
Medium	$8,212
Heavy	$10,212

* Light—five or less issues (none included); medium—five to ten issues; heavy—eleven or more issues (out of fifty-six issues studied).

Virtually everyone can read, and therefore can read magazines. However, there are differences in literacy levels which are generally based upon education; that is why rises in education and magazine-reading levels are so closely aligned.   It could further be stated that education is the common causative factor affecting both magazine reading as well as income; that if we have an elite in this country, it is probably an education elite; thus, socioeconomic status, income, education, and magazine reading are all closely interrelated.   During the past twenty years, per-issue circulation of magazines has increased at approximately four times the rate of population growth; it has shown a remarkably close correlation with rise in education levels.

Dedication of the Readers   The dedication of the magazine-reader household to the medium is demonstrated by the following facts:

With an average issue of the 35 magazines measured in a particular study (of the total 652 magazines published), one can reach 82 per cent of all United States women and 79 per cent of all United States men.   On the basis of individuals, the *average adult reads 2.8* of these 35 magazines; if we eliminate non-readers, the *average reader reads 3.5*.

On a per household basis, the overall average is 4.1 of the measured magazines; when we segregate magazine-reading households, the average rises to 4.7.

Being based on only 35 publications, these figures, of course, do not reflect readership of smaller magazines, including those which appeal to the vast spectrum of special interests.   Yet, there has been a discernible rise in individuality and specificness of purpose and approach.

Six Publications per Household   Accordingly, it has been estimated, while not documented, that the average magazine household reads more than six publications on a regular basis, and copies per household are very much on the increase.   Actually, because some of these publications are weeklies, the total copies of magazines which enter these heavy-reader households within a given month is even greater —the figure probably approaching eight.

One major factor here relates to the so-called enfranchisement of youth in America, and the propagation of child habits by parent habits.   Now, with the existence of magazines on which youth can rely for information and support, these magazines seem to find greatest acceptance within those households which are magazine-oriented. This is already adding another important dimension to the concept of the heavy-magazine-user household. Parenthetically, it is also creating a more deeply involved magazine-reader base for the future.

Factors of Age, Education, Income Some types of magazines are much more selective in reaching particular population segments than others. In terms of age, outdoor and sports magazines are effective in reaching people under thirty-five, as are the news weeklies. The business books tend to be much more selective among thirty-five to forty-nine year olds.

In relation to education, people who attended college, although less than one-quarter of all people in the United States, constitute over half the readers of the news weeklies; and almost three-quarters of the audiences of the quality magazines, such as *Harper's-Atlantic, Saturday Review, The New Yorker* (68 to 84 per cent of these readers have incomes of more than $10,000).

When considering books by household income, the business books, news books, and quality magazines excel with a generally high reading index in the $10,000-plus household income group. Moving higher, individuals with incomes over $15,000 account for about 25 per cent of the readership of business books, while less than 3 per cent of total population falls within this income group.

Particular Demographics Even within certain magazine types, there are specific magazines that stand out according to particular demographics. *House Beautiful* when compared with *House & Garden, Better Homes & Gardens,* and *American Home,* has quite a different and more selective profile. It tends to have a younger audience, with a substantially higher index among eighteen to twenty-four year olds, and it reaches a substantially better-educated and higher-income reader than its counterparts.

Within the broad sports category, with its wide scope of editorial appeal, *Sports Illustrated* is outstanding among college graduates, individuals with incomes over $15,000, and professionals and managers.

These are just a few demonstrations of the fact that oversimplifying the magazine medium into various homogeneous categories can sometimes be more distortive than enlightening.

Circulation Growth in General

In 1968, the 677 magazines constituting the magazine industry averaged 315.8 million copies per issue, which aggregates to slightly more than 5.39 billion copies for the year. This represents 89 copies of magazines annually for the average household (314 for families with an income of $10,000 or more).

While the net number of magazine titles published increased by only 37 in the eight years between 1960 and 1968, average circulation per issue increased by 26.3 per cent and revenue by 66.9 per cent.

Another demonstration of magazine vitality lies in analyzing those 287 of the total 677 magazines which are audited by the Audit Bureau of Circulations; these account for more than 70 per cent of all magazine circulation:

Year	Circ. per 100 Adults
1940	95.8
1950	133.3
1960	153.7
1967	168.4
1968	168.8

This growth occurred during the period that saw the greatest growth of television and its competition for time and attention, as well as for presentation of entertainment and news interpretation.

Variations in Growth by Type   Relative circulation gains need to be viewed with all the usual cautions, especially when one is trying to read implications into them. Large circulations will be hard put to show the percentage gains of smaller ones (also, there is always the problem of precise, mutually exclusive group definition). However, to proceed with some highlights on growth for a recent five-year period:

Women's magazines show the smallest gain—up 5.1 per cent; including young women's magazines within this group raises the gain factor to 7.9 per cent, but is still the lowest (they represent, of course, the biggest block of circulation). Following the common practice of lumping the young women's magazines into this total group hides their own 22.3 per cent gain. While their growth rate is projected from a smaller circulation base, the primary reason for their gains is the greater number of young persons in the country, as well as their increasing interest in and awareness of the world around them.

The four large general books had a 9.8 per cent circulation increase during this same five-year period; and the home-and-shelter magazines increased by 11.2 per cent.

The sharpest gainers among the major classifications were business magazines (up 32.4 per cent) and news weeklies (up 28.7 per cent). This was probably caused by the rapid broadening of the size of the middle-management level, higher education in general, and increased interest in the stock market and related business elements, among other reasons.

Of course, none of these growth figures in any way approaches the doubling, tripling, and quadrupling of special-interest magazine circulations which were described earlier.

Magazines by Circulation Method   There has been a tremendous amount of hypothesization about the relative merits of newsstand versus subscription circulation, and paid circulation versus free and controlled circulation; a proper and impartial presentation of these arguments could comprise a chapter of its own.   Here we will deal with only the basic and relevant known facts.

Of the total industry's circulation, 66 per cent is by subscription. The figure is a little higher (70 per cent) for the ABC magazines.   As one might suspect, there is a wide variation between individual magazines in their subscription levels.   For example, store-distributed magazines (*Woman's Day* and *Family Circle*) have no subscriptions; *Playboy* and *Seventeen* are more than 75 per cent single-copy sales; and *TV Guide* sells over two-thirds of its copies on newsstands.

At the other end of the scale, we have the general weeklies, news weeklies, and women's and home books, which are high in ratio of subscribers to single-copy sales.   General weeklies sell 96 per cent of their copies by subscription, and the figure among news weeklies and business books is even higher (*Business Week,* 100 per cent subscription; *Forbes,* 97.8 per cent; and *Fortune,* 96.3 per cent).

Although there is a wide variation among major magazines in their subscription to single-copy ratios, there is not so great a difference in terms of proportion of total circulation in metropolitan areas.   Of thirty consumer and business books measured, the range was from a low of 61 per cent to a high of 78 per cent.

Circulation Rate Base One of the changes that has taken place in the circulation area is the increased move toward a circulation rate base as compared with the guarantee. Only twenty-seven of the ninety-nine magazines currently reported by Publisher's Information Bureau offer guaranteed circulation (and of these, twenty are either small-circulation or very specialized publications).

The reasons for this recent trend are probably several. For example, with most circulations today at more than a 90 per cent subscription level, the need to reassure an advertiser that a certain circulation is being achieved becomes infinitely less. Also, with the great preponderance of contemporary media buying on a total-audience basis (where one's total audience can inexplicably fly high or fall low on someone's error margin), it could be argued that a publisher should not have to rebate on the basis of a factor that was not considered in making the magazine buy.

Family Circle and *Woman's Day* are examples of what can happen to even good books in the negative sense. Through their January and February circulation drop-offs, they reinforce the existence of the constant danger inherent to the lack of a subscriber base. (*TV Guide,* on the other hand, with its September circulation peaking at newsstands, represents a predictable positive opportunity.)

Then, too, a guarantee could be called a one-way thing. During a recent eighteen-month period, only one of twenty-two major magazines was off (2.3 per cent) in circulation versus the rate base or guarantee. The twenty-one others were over in their delivery from 1 to 15 per cent each. In fact, some magazines such as *TV Guide* and *Reader's Digest* provide close to a million "free" circulation—more than the total circulation of many magazines.

Sources of Circulation In connection with circulation bases, something should be stated about circulation source. The vast majority, three-quarters, of subscriptions sold are ordered by mail. The next largest source of subscription, 10 per cent, is generated by the publisher's own salesmen. An additional 9 per cent emanate from schools, churches, fraternities, and other nonprofit organizations.

Of all new subscriptions, 77 per cent are sold for from one to two years' duration and 12 per cent are sold for three years or more. This establishes a relatively firm circulation base (newspapers, for example, are generally subscribed to on a month-to-month basis); and at the same time, this indicates the extent to which the reader is willing to commit himself to his magazines once the selection has been made.

Controlled Circulation   Controlled or free circulation is a facet of the magazine circulation picture that deserves a few words.   Analysis shows more than 130 magazines having controlled or free circulation, in whole or in part.   Their circulation is in excess of 52 million.   Most of this circulation is free; the rest simply controlled.   While nearly 30 per cent of them started in the 1960s, and so can be considered a modern happening, several go back to before the turn of the century.

Three-fifths of these are relatively small in circulation—under 100,000; with the next largest number in the next larger circulation group—100,000 to 250,000.   Only fourteen are over one million—and some of these are groups rather than a single magazine.

Media Seasonality   Finally, media seasonality is an area of primary concern to the advertiser.   In this connection, magazine circulation is virtually flat across each twelve-month period (in marked contrast to the large summer dip and winter peaking of television).   Specifically, the fifty magazines that lead in advertising revenue show a circulation variation (compared with the year-round average) which reaches a plus 3.2 per cent in December and a dip of only 2.5 per cent in January, May, and July.

EVOLUTION OF ADVERTISING FLEXIBILITIES

All that has been said about magazines in earlier pages is fundamentally applicable to considerations of the medium as an advertising force on the national level.   However, the contemporary nature of brand development, distribution, and promotion has long since made it impractical to consider magazine advertising exclusively in the nationwide sense.   The extent to which characteristics of brand propositions and problems have changed has made this approach inadequate.

Also, within the communications arena, we have experienced the emergence of multimedia complexes, in terms of physical facilities. This has created a major reaction upon how people receive and seek out informations, and makes the interweaving of various media forms both desirable and practical.   Provided that proper physical availabilities were created, magazines could play an important supportive role in brand promotion, operating in concert with other basic media forms.

In addition, developments within the marketplace, exclusive of our own considerations on behalf of the brand, have created an urgent need for the breaking down of the magazine from a national medium into one which the advertiser can segment. As the magazine audience in its totality has vastly deepened from the historic literary aristocracy of the few into a dynamic communications force for the total consumer spectrum, it has concurrently developed much deeper and more identifiable structures within each magazine audience universe. Because of the tremendous increase in buying power of the total marketplace, from an advertiser's point of view it becomes necessary to plumb deeper into these structures.

Depths of Readers' Characteristics

Whereas in the past magazines were used for skimming across the top, it becomes a matter of urgency today to utilize magazines to plumb the depths of groups of people within the context of their place of residence, their mode of life, and their specific and mutually unique interests.

Isaac Walton was the first of the famous sports fishermen; today there are 40 million licensed fishermen. As opposed to that point in time when all rural communities were highly similar and all cities basically alike, the leisure-time expansion and the educational explosion, together with much higher levels of person-to-person intercommunication, have led to greater manifestations and interrelationships of group identities. This again occurs in respect to interests and geographically actually much more so than through the coincidence of demography.

At the same time, new media methods erupted upon the scene. Therefore, the magazine industry was faced not only with the facts of the evolution of American life, but also with the stark reality that there were new means by which the brand advertiser could extract his audience type and audience place on a selective basis which had not been the case in the pretelevision era.

Geographic Splits

Accordingly, in the early 1950s, the agencies and manufacturers were finally able to persuade first one and then another of the major magazines to split out the West, the South, and the rest of the country for the benefit of the client.

This ability to segment within mass magazine circulations became necessary also because of the expansion of new products and the methods by which they were presented to the public.   For instance, there was a deep need to make magazine advertising availabilities adaptable to product roll-outs and to test markets; and the first fractionalizations of magazine circulations were directed toward the Nielsen regions.

It should be added that coincidental with all these evolutions and events, there were new developments in production technology which made flexibility development physically feasible.

In terms of the historic sectional breakout, a national page was still required, but there was either a two- or three-way split per magazine. Ironically (and perhaps somewhat to the occasional frustration of the magazines), clients sometimes changed their minds, and this advertising never ran.   However, other efforts proceeded, other advertising did run, and thereby, magazine splits and regionals were started.

In 1955, there were only seven magazines which offered regionals. Within five years, the number had grown to 124.   By 1965, 186 magazines offered regional flexibility, and by the end of 1968, this number had grown to 235.

Regionalization in Look   As a demonstration of what can be accomplished in terms of splits, it is interesting to examine the history of regionalization in *Look* magazine.   In 1959, *Look*'s regional editions were considered an innovation within the major magazine field.   In that year, its regional plans started with seven geographic zones ("MagaZones"), and were quickly extended to eight.   By 1962, *Look* was offering fifty-two zones; in 1965, individual "MagaCities" were added, making a total of fifty-nine different breaks in *Look*.   By 1965, still more "MagaCities" were offered, increasing the total to seventy-five—but with the overlap considered actually eighty-two different editions of *Look* were involved.   In 1968 (just nine years after its first regional break), *Look* added a demographic edition called *Top/Spot*.   While this added one more national buy to "MagaMarket" 75, it meant 144 different editions of each issue for the editors and production people—plus any special or test breakouts that might be involved.

The example of *Look* should demonstrate that in today's advertising climate, you can be assured that as greater regional flexibility is required, it can be accomplished. However, it should be emphasized that chances are that an almost exact split to fit regional needs for brands in magazines already exists to answer any current problem.

We have been told that although the number of regions available in a major magazine may be in the low hundreds, this would mean at least a million different regional combinations for one magazine when used in combination with others.

Market for Regional Advertising   There was and is a ready market for regional magazine advertising.   In examining the general and farm group of ninety-six magazines for 1968 versus 1959, regional advertising dollars increased 369 per cent compared to a total advertising increase of just 52 per cent. Of course, it is always easier to have a larger percentage increase when starting from a smaller base. Nevertheless, raw-dollar figures are impressive; investment in regional advertising went from $43 million to $200 million in 1968. Also, each year regional revenue increased as a percentage of total advertising in these magazines, from 5.4 per cent of total in 1959 to 16.7 per cent in 1968—and this trend continues to be upward.

Of course, like all other "averages," this could be misleading in individual cases, because the percentages can be very high for some while relatively low for others. One six-months study covering twenty-two major consumer and business publications reveals that regional advertising accounted for 39 per cent of total revenue for *TV Guide,* 24 per cent for *Time* magazine, 23 per cent for *Life,* and 21 per cent for *Look.* Of the twenty-two books measured, only in one instance did regional advertising account for less than 10 per cent of total revenue—*U. S. News* was at the low end of the scale with its regional pages accounting for 0.9 per cent of total revenue.

One emerging form of further magazine flexibility is based upon the new highly distilled management levels and the concurrent abilities of some magazines to break out these circulations.

Remnant Space   Before proceeding to other flexibility forms, mention should be made of remnant space, an opportunity that has developed out of all these regional editions.   Few magazines offer it. However, there are those publications which offer a reduced rate if an advertiser allows leeway of issues in which to utilize unused portions of various regional editions in order to put together a "national" circulation.   *Life,* for example, offers 25 per cent off.

Demographic and Occupational Groupings

As stated in the preface to this section, the considerations in terms of the interest of the brand go far beyond matters of region and geography. There has been a growing awareness by magazine publishers and brand advertisers alike that great potentials exist in terms of demographic and occupational groupings. We predict that demographic editions are bound to expand in the near future, both by type of split-out and by the number of magazines offering them. This again will be a case of the desires of advertiser and agency providing the incentive; and at the same time, magazine-publisher computerization of subscription lists will increase, providing much greater means of identifying individual units of their audience.

Today, a half dozen major magazines offer such editions. *Farm Journal,* for example, offers three "extra" editions (dairy, beef, and hog); *Reader's Digest* breaks out high school circulation; *Fortune* offers subscribers in manufacturing; *Time* offers three editions—college students, educators, and doctors. *Newsweek* also has a doctor's edition, and a special section called *Newsweek Careers,* which features classified display ads for high-level recruitment advertising.

Look offers *Top/Spot,* which is a national geodemic edition. This is comprised of subscribers living in Zip Code areas where (1) median income is high, and (2) there is a large physical concentration of people in that Zip Code area. These Zip Codes were initially split across forty different markets and have now been expanded to eighty.

Look has added an interesting dimension to this particular breakout; they have added editorial matter in the *Top/Spot* sections of the magazine which is designed to appeal more to upscale subscribers. Finally, *McCall's* is offering a demographic edition to reach upper-income subscribers called *V.I.P.-ZIP.*

Exploitation of Technology This flexibility of magazine advertising availabilities in terms of numbers of forms involved, the technology which has been harnessed, and the accomplishments which have been achieved is highly impressive when we consider that it has occurred in the most recent fourteen years of the 200-year history of the medium.

To place the future values of this flexibility evolution in their proper perspective, it should be understood that technology will, in fact, continue to grow. However, it was *not* technology in and of itself which created the phenomenon of the geographic, regional, and demographic splits.   Rather, it was the exploitation of technology as a tool in order for magazines to meet competition from other media, and more importantly, to answer the demands and needs of innovative and imaginative brand advertisers and their agencies.

Meanwhile, we are experiencing the production of advertising packages based upon editorial-advertising themes in a variety of magazines.   This provides an opportunity to harness the overall corporate-dollar commitment within the magazines to produce a desired brand environment and to generate special selling propositions at substantial discounts.

As brand-consumer identification proliferates through computers and other technological devices, we anticipate the identifications of new opportunities whereby further aspirations of brands within the increasingly competitive marketplace can be realized.

Increased Costs   However, this leads us to one of the major problems of flexibility—that is, the increased costs that are created by breaking the total audience structure down into smaller units in order to provide better marketing values.   While the physical capabilities are very much existent, the incremental cost factors make taking advantage of these further breakdowns less feasible.

Therefore, there develops a need to go beyond the process of further and further fragmentations of the circulations of single vehicles.   Instead, we face the need to increase this definable, highly fragmented, and very desirable circulation entity through the combining of comparable circulation fragments among several different magazines.   This leads us directly into another area of magazine flexibility.

The Magazine Network

This network addresses itself very directly to two propositions which were covered earlier.   First, generally speaking, the more specialized the interests which are encompassed by individual magazines, the more intense will be readership and consumer involvement.   This is an inherently positive factor.

On the other hand, the specialized magazines attract smaller audiences, and therefore, do not individually offer us a sufficiently large segment of the total brand-prospect complex; at the same time, buying them individually involves an extremely high cost factor.

Over many years, attempts were made to sell these magazines in special combinations and packages. However, this was not successful because even when discounts were offered, the rate structure on which the discounts were based was so exceptionally high relative to larger magazines, that even at discounted rates, they were seldom attractive enough.

Therefore, as in the case of regionals and demographic editions, there was a distinct need and an opportunity as yet unrealized, and concurrently there existed technology which had not been totally exploited.

The experience of *Time* magazine, with its special college-student, educator, and doctor editions, provided a clue to the solution of these problems and established the basis on which the magazine-network concept was formed—supported by the appropriate (and indispensable) economic incentives to the publishers of these smaller specialized books.

Begun in Baby-book Field The magazine network, as we now know it, first came to fruition in 1966 in the baby-book field, which encompasses a large number of small publications. These have a great variety of distribution methods, but regardless of how it reaches its reader, each has a deep and unique involvement with the new mother or mother-to-be.

No single one of these magazines dominated this field, and none was large enough in circulation to provide attractive advertising-cost structures to the brand advertiser with a need in this particular market. Also, because of their own physical and financial limitations, these magazines could not afford what was needed in terms of graphic reproduction.

However, the potentials were great—so great that we decided to make a total effort to overcome the problems of small circulation size, high CPMs, and limited graphics. There was a period of many months during which planning and experimentation took place. Without detailing this background work, we will address ourselves to the end product of the baby-book experiment, which became the basis for the magazine-network concept.

Specifically, we were able to coordinate the advertising efforts of a number of brands that had an interest in the baby-book market, and in fact, despite all preexistent disadvantages, some of these brands were already using the baby books. By coordinating and pooling the efforts, schedules, and advertising resources of these various brands, we were able to produce, by high-quality four-color printing, four pages of four-color advertising. Appropriate quantities of each of these were provided to the individual baby books.

Inasmuch as the agency, on behalf of its clients, had developed all the graphics in terms of printing, we were able to negotiate the baby-book space rates for these particular inserts down to a level where the total cost to the advertiser (production and space combined) was substantially lower on a CPM basis than would have been possible by any other method. These brands had the further advantage of four-color advertising in publications which heretofore had had no color-printing facilities whatever; accordingly, the high quality and impact of four-color bleed pages added another dimension on behalf of the brand.

By mass printing, we were able to effect economies and at the same time maintain quality control; therefore, it was possible to place an attractive advertising form into as many of these magazines as was needed for the purposes at hand. In the total sense, this gave us complete flexibility within an area of highly specialized and individualized, but compatible publications.

The only minor problem involved was the extent to which the advertiser was willing to live with the fact that he would be facing or back to back with another brand ad; this developed to be a minor consideration in relation to the tangible benefits of the baby-book network.

Expansion of Concept and Technique   This concept and technique have now been expanded into a military-magazine network, which is comprised of the military circulation of *True, Sports Illustrated, Stereo/Review,* and ten other small-circulation magazines; and there is also a military wives' network.

Through the developments of these segments of magazine circulations, we have been able to demonstrate to the mass magazine publishers, as well as to advertisers, the viability of the magazine-network principle.

Further Opportunities   There are further opportunities for magazine networks in the smaller-publication field. For example, the same factors can be applied to those various "city" magazines which are proliferating with great speed. We expect to see the ability to skim off the class audience on a local basis through magazines such as

Philadelphia, Washington, Baltimore, and *Phoenix.* It will be made possible through the same technique which was initiated in the baby books; that is, the providing of all these magazines with pre-printed four-, eight-, and twelve-page inserts which can be leafed into the body of their magazines.

However, this is just a beginning.

We believe that as the magazine network achieves acceptability and recognition for what it can accomplish in terms of in-depth penetration within a reasonable cost discipline, we will reach the point where we can actually create new magazines where magazines do not now exist.   For example, we could develop a composite advertising entity which would be comprised of a teen-age New York, teen-age Chicago, teen-age Los Angeles, etc.   These would be independently edited magazines insofar as relating to the teen-agers and their unique interests within each of these cities; however, as a sufficient number of brands develop a concurrent commitment to reach teen-agers in top markets through this unique vehicle, we can utilize the already established production economies and space-rate formulas inherent to the magazine-network operation.

Creation of new magazines   Therefore, we would in a sense be creating magazines through advertising—this would be the total completion of the circle from the point where advertising was essentially created through magazines.

Looking toward the future, we could presume it is highly possible that by applying the principles which brought the original magazine networks into existence, many of the new magazines which will be presented to the public will, in fact, be magazines created by agencies and ad managers.   They promise to be the new magazine initiators of tomorrow.

Certainly, there is sufficient available editorial expertise; there is a ready pool of capable writing talent; and as has been demonstrated through massive growth of special-interest magazine circulation, there is a ready audience at hand on almost any subject.   All that need be done is to select audience groups and interest complexes and to develop on their behalf an editorial direction with which they can become involved.   This can be done on a national basis or in terms of regions or even individual localities.

Through the harnessing of the technology perfected by magazine networks, we can be totally local; on the other hand, we can address ourselves totally to the very narrow special proclivities of individuals or interest groups, no matter how widely dispersed. We can then combine all those audience segments which are demographically and psychographically compatible to the objectives of the brand, and through the magazine-network technique, we can develop the supportive advertising which can perpetuate this type of publication.

This then is one of the magazine dimensions we see for the future —the fact that the next magazine-publisher complex will likely emanate from the conference rooms of various farsighted and opportunistic American corporations.

NEWSPAPERS: AN IN-DEPTH EXAMINATION

In opening the section on magazines, we dealt with magazine dynamics in terms of the total numbers—dollars, vehicle count, circulation, and audience. We did so because an understanding of magazines in the total-dimensional sense is indispensable to a comprehension of the arena in which magazine advertising operates in competition for reader attention and appeal. However, the character of newspapers is such that a viable comprehension of this medium demands a different thought discipline.

It would not be totally inappropriate to begin this discussion of newspapers by expanding at length on the following facts:

In 1968, more than 21 billion copies were purchased by consumers; they spent more than $2.25 billion for these newspapers (compared with $766 million in 1945); and despite large-city newspaper failures and mergers, and competition for public attention from other communications forms, the number of daily newspapers in the United States exceeds 1,740 (the number of daily newspapers which existed in 1945); and there are now more than 8,000 weekly newspapers.

These figures are dramatic in talking about this medium in terms of total dimensions. However, while this box-car-number approach would not be entirely incorrect, it does not in itself approach the challenge of describing the relevant dynamics of this media form as they are concerned with our much more pertinent objective—developing a stage of understanding from which we can optimumly operate in our effort to motivate consumers on behalf of the singular propositions and objectives of the brand and the corporation.

Purveyors of newspaper "white space" so often rest their cases on these numbers, and from them conclude that newspapers are the basic advertising medium for today and tomorrow, just as they were in the pre-World War II period.

While it is awesome to realize that in 1968 *The New York Times* used 384,000 tons of newsprint (cut from more than 6 million trees), box-car numbers and awesomeness should not be the salient determinants of the merits of this or of any medium in terms of motivating our public.   Instead, we direct ourselves to the proposition of going beyond "whats" and asking for the "whys"; and by so doing, we will much more closely approach the relevant truths we are seeking.

Newspaper Ingredients

What are the ingredients of the newspaper as they nourish the public, and therefore, as they have a concurrent potential for nourishing the needs of advertising management?

There is an inherent danger in confining our thinking to what is now; but what is now will not be so in two years.   Accordingly, we shall consider the classic, but not widely known, values of the newspaper and what the newspaper has demonstrated in terms of fluidity and its response to spontaneous events and gradual changes in the social and marketing complex.

Basically, newspapers are perhaps the least understood of the various major media.   They are like milk on doorsteps—we have become so accustomed to having them around that they become almost an unconscious habit.   It is not a commodity that consumers consciously evaluate and reevaluate as they do in the case of a television program, or in buying your brand as opposed to that of your competitor.

Newspapers Are Products of the Community   Newspapers are very much the indigenous communications vehicle of the community.

Here we must make that critical distinction on those things which are unique to New York, for example, and make it so typical a community, in contrast to the much larger national market mosaic— those thousands of other communities, many of which resemble one another, but none of which is at all like New York.   To understand properly a medium which is so local in nature and character, it is vital to drop from our thinking the mystique of New York and its leading newspapers because this mystique is, in truth, a potential mistake in developing the depth of insight which becomes increasingly vital as brand-advertising competition intensifies.

Of all communications vehicles, newspapers are perhaps the most parochial in terms of concerning themselves with that which is germane to the specific community within which they are published. In this sense, the newspaper responds to and is a manifestation of the culture of the individual community.

While we sometimes regard America as a homogeneous mass, in reality it is made up of many mutually exclusive subcultures.   This is true of geographic, psychological, regional, and local levels—Los Angeles, Yankeeism, tourism in Florida, St. Louis, the Southwest, the Pacific Northwest.   The medium which comes closest to reflecting and conveying the tone of each specific community culture is the daily newspaper.

Dynamics of the Newspaper   To appreciate how newspaper advertising works on the reader, it may be helpful to understand the atmosphere in which it is created.

Each day's newspaper starts calmly, almost blandly, with "canned" crosswords, comics, advice to the lovelorn—and then the action begins.

A local man advertises a house; a downtown merchant advertises a sale; a national airline advertises wanderlust.

Revolution erupts in Asia; scandal breaks in Washington; and a grand-slam homer is hit in Chicago.   A friend marries; a son is graduated; and a birth or a death occurs within our own neighborhood.

These are the commercial, factual, and psychological forces that feed the pulse of the newspaper, piped in by international wire, long-distance phone, or the desk in the newspaper lobby.

And then the race with time begins.

Commercial matter flows from the advertising department, and news reportage and commentary from the editorial department (where it has been rewritten, edited, and headlined), into a central control area where it is "made up" and "laid out" into an instantaneous design of what the issue will look like.   From there it is routed through rows of typesetters and photoengraving tanks, after which it comes together like several massive metal jigsaw puzzles on individual-page galley forms.   Each completed page form is rushed to a matrix machine which, through tons of pressure, creates a plastic mat (or mold).   Each mat is then cast into a curved metal plate which is put on a high-speed conveyor belt and rolled directly to the pressroom where it is bolted on to the press. A small button for this page is pushed, and the numbered red light flashes on the control panel boards in the offices of the mechanical superintendent and the publisher. When all the red lights are lit, the press foreman pulls the master switch, presses roll, and within seconds, newspapers are moving up the conveyor belt into the mailroom, and the first edition is on its way to the reader.

In a large sense, the newspaper is a manufacturing miracle. As hours progress, it is revised and replated, edition by edition, in reaction to spontaneous news breaks—and it is totally redesigned, retooled, and remanufactured as a brand-new product every day.

While the specifics of mechanical technology vary and are rapidly changing, the same intensities and senses of urgency are constant and universal, and comprise the atmosphere in which the national newspaper advertisement is presented to the public.

Examining Newspaper Power While people and marketing structures and techniques will change, and media of necessity will react to these changes, there are classic conditions and inherent truths underlying past, present, and future media considerations.

Specifically, "power of the press" has been with us for many years. Yet, at times the phrase and what it implies seem to have become blunted; particularly the incisive power of the newspaper press in an era of heavy proliferation of other journalistic forms. This supposition of press-power deterioration can be a distortive line of conjecture for the marketer.

In brand promotion, all of us are sensitive to the importance of attaching ourselves to marketing and advertising forces which provide a maximum level of communication strength, public influence, and economic power. In this context, it is pertinent here in our discussion of newspapers to explore their own singular communications, influence, economics, and power factors.

How Profitable Are Newspapers?

You do not have to be unusually well informed to know that there are some newspapers which had severe problems over the past decade. We have seen failures and mergers in New York, Boston, San Francisco, Los Angeles, and Pittsburgh. It sometimes seems as if the newspaper world is collapsing economically. This can create a feeling of doubt about building brand futures in this medium. However, just as New York newspapers are not typical of the total medium in terms of reach and parochial involvement, newspapers in the highly publicized major markets are not typical of the total medium in the economic sense.

In the course of examining newspapers, we look at the profit-and-loss figures of the average so-called hometown daily newspaper of 50,000 circulation. It might be interesting if here you were to estimate what the annual profit or loss of an average newspaper of 50,000 circulation might be. We did this with some acquaintances, and their estimates ranged from a loss of $20,000 to a profit of $100,000 a year.

Actual figures show that in 1965 the average newspaper of that circulation had a before-taxes profit of $916,000; in 1966, this profit had risen to $1,209,000; in 1967, to $1,263,000; and in 1968, to $1,393,400. This is not at all bad for a small-city commercial operation.

Going further up the circulation ladder, we find that the profit of the average newspaper of 250,000 circulation in 1965 was $2,700,000 before taxes; in 1966, $3,300,000; in 1967, $3,500,000; and in 1968, $3,700,000. In markets where 250,000-circulation newspapers are published, the combined profit of all three television stations was $1,500,000.

Most of this revenue comes from advertising. Total newspaper-advertising revenue has approached the $5 billion mark, and has grown by almost 150 per cent since television became a major commercial medium in 1950. Most of the increase is in the form of local advertising, up 165 per cent since 1950, versus a 75 per cent increase in national advertising revenue.

It should be emphasized here that a great deal of advertising which was national eighteen years ago is now classified as local. This reflects monies that have been diverted from national advertising campaigns into cooperative allowances which have been spent in newspapers through retailers. It also reflects reclassification of certain categories of advertising from national-rate to a local-rate basis or to special in-between rates; for example, in the automobile dealer association and appliance distributor areas.

Whatever the source, or the advertising-rate rationalizations, the newspapers are enjoying unprecedented profits.

"The Lords of the Press"

In the vast majority of American cities, the newspaper publisher is the community's most powerful individual, and generally the most influential in terms of molding thought.   Yet, his is a sensitive power in that continued consumer influence and profitability by his newspaper depend on its being attuned to the community; to maintain its franchise, the newspaper must, in most cases, appeal to 70 to 85 per cent of the people who live there.

Therefore, while operating from a seat of power, the publisher must be sensitive to all that goes on in the marketplace—its culture, politics, economic changes, and social moods.

Ultimately, then, the newspaper is mainly the product of the community, rather than the product of the publisher.

To state the publisher phenomenon in its most simple terms, the green eyeshade of the pre-Depression publisher has been replaced by the journalism and business school diplomas of his offspring, and new business disciplines and varieties of communications expertise have replaced the kerosene-lamp editorial as the dynamic newspaper function.

Editorial versus Advertising Orientation

One of the major problems of advertisers, and national advertisers in particular, is based on the orientation of newspaper publishers and the evolution of newspaper power structures in general.

Before the turn of the century, the newspaper subsisted almost totally on circulation, and each day's circulation, in turn, was dependent upon the vividness and opportunism of the editorial function; in those years, the publisher also occupied the editor's chair.   As recently as a generation ago, most newspaper revenues came from circulation, and while the newspaper operator had delegated many editorial authorities to salaried editors (philosophically compatible, of course), he remained almost exclusively concerned with the editorial functions.

Now, however, the newspaper economic pendulum has swung to the point where advertising occupies 65 per cent rather than 45 per cent of total space, and advertisers provide 70 per cent of the newspaper's revenue, instead of 25 per cent.   Yet the principal interests of the people who control many newspapers still relate heavily to editorial. To paraphrase a Biblical quotation, newspaper editors, like holy men of old, speak as if they are moved by the Holy Ghost. This comprises the paramount problem in our dealing with newspapers— of all major media, newspapers have the least dialogue between the people who develop the editorial product and those who sell and who buy advertising.

A New Generation of Publishers

We may soon see an end to this problem, in that the stewardship of major newspapers is moving into the hands of a new generation of publishers. Contemporary newspaper management is recognizing that it has circulation problems, and that it must justify its franchise to the community in order to survive. At the same time, it is keenly aware that broadcast is siphoning off rapidly increasing amounts of advertising dollars from retailers—whereas publishers had historically considered their position with retailers to be almost invulnerable.

Accordingly, more publishers are beginning to concern themselves much more directly with advertising and the problems of advertisers. Also, they are much more aware of the fact that advertising serves a dual purpose for newspapers in that it is not only a producer of revenue, but it also has extremely important editorial values and circulation attractions of its own.

However, we must recognize that this advertising-awareness level has barely passed the glimmer stage—and much remains to be accomplished. It behooves all of us in our dealings with top newspaper management to remind them constantly that when we purchase newspaper white space, we not only provide revenue, but through the character of nearly all national advertising, we also materially enhance the newspaper product itself.

It is unfortunate that many newspaper editors still consider advertising to be an intrusion into the product and a barely tolerable evil, when it is, in fact, the only means by which the modern newspaper can survive. It has been estimated, for example, that if *The New York Times* had to exist without any advertising, the daily paper would have to be priced at approximately $1, and the *Sunday Times* at $5, in order to meet all their cost-overhead factors—and thus, the product could be priced out of existence.

Multifaceted Foundation

In concluding the foregoing, it can be said that the newspaper medium operates from a multifaceted foundation of publisher concern and expertise, profit orientation, and reaction to the local public pulse.   Taken together, these factors present the broad outlines of our contemporary newspaper medium.

Now we proceed to consider what the newspaper performs arithmetically and psychologically, how and why it uniquely communicates to the reader and brand consumer, and then relate these factors to present and future newspaper-advertising considerations.

HOW THE MEDIUM COMMUNICATES

The following figures and interpretations will give some indication of how this medium communicates with its readers:

Daily Circulation over 60,000,000

Year	No. of Morn. Papers	No. of Eve. Papers	Total M&E	Total M&E Circulation
1920	437	1,605	2,042	27,790,656
1940	380	1,498	1,878	41,131,611
1945	330	1,419	1,749	48,384,188
1950	322	1,450	1,772	53,829,072
1955	316	1,454	1,760	56,147,359
1960	312	1,459	1,763	58,881,746
1965	320	1,444	1,751	60,357,563
1968	328	1,443	1,771	62,535,394

SOURCE: Bureau of Advertising, ANPA.

Substantially more copies of newspapers are sold today than ever before.   While circulation has not kept pace with population, this is primarily because of mergers and consolidations within the medium.   Penetration of newspapers today is increasing, and should continue to do so as population rises and literacy levels and social awareness expand.

Not Read by Everyone

Now we confront the general overstatement of the newspaper as the complete-market medium and the resultant supposition that newspapers blanket the entire consumer universe. This, by the way, is a

Consistently High Coverage by Region

Region	Per Cent Households	Per Cent Readers		
		Adults	Men	Women
New England	95	90	90	90
Metro New York	93	87	91	84
Middle Atlantic	90	87	89	85
East Central	90	82	82	82
West Central	90	83	83	82
Southeast	80	73	71	74
Southwest	78	71	73	69
Pacific	89	83	84	82

SOURCE: Bureau of Advertising, ANPA.

fallacy which was originated by the newspaper industry. The fact is that newspapers do not reach everyone.

Instead, the medium has its own level of selectivity which is related

Highest Coverage in Nielsen A Counties

County Size	Per Cent Households, Any Adult	Per Cent Readers		
		Adults	Men	Women
A	91	85	88	82
B	89	84	84	84
C	88	80	81	80
D	77	69	68	70

SOURCE: Bureau of Advertising, ANPA.

to education, income, awareness, and consequent interest by the individual in what is happening in the world around him.

A revealing way to look at the newspaper audience is to measure people who *do not* read newspapers:

Per Cent of Households Not Reading on an Average Day

Administrators 2
Higher executives, managers 3
Major professionals 4
Semiprofessionals. 6
Clerical, sales, technician. 6
Small-medium proprietors 8
Skilled manual workers. 10
Machine, semiskilled 11
Unskilled labor. .17
Retired 19
Part-time employed 21
Unemployed 26
Farmers, farm labor 28

SOURCE: Bureau of Advertising, ANPA.

Now to examine people who *do* read newspapers—how they obtain them and when and how they use them, and other basic data relevant to the reader-newspaper relationship:

Per Cent Delivered to the Home

Home-delivered 71
Store, newsstand 19
Self-service rack 1
Other sources 9

SOURCE: Bureau of Advertising, ANPA.

The 71 per cent home-delivered factor becomes particularly significant when we recognize it as a national average, which includes the newspapers published in New York and Chicago. In New York, for example, the *Daily News,* currently the country's largest newspaper, reports less than 1 per cent of its circulation as home-delivered. Chicago's evening newspapers have an extremely high level of newsstand sales because of the character of Chicago as a major commuter market. It has been estimated that the top three markets aside, nearly 80 per cent of newspaper circulation is home-delivered, and that the average in markets below the top ten is well above 85 per cent home delivery.

Here we see the portability quality of the medium and an interesting phenomenon.   While newspaper reading in the total sense is considered a habit per se, the largest group of respondents to readership research report they have no habitual reading time.   Therefore, it can be surmised that the newspaper is programed in and out of the

Per Cent Read at Home

At home 90
At work 6
Visiting 3
On way to work 2
In restaurants 1
Other places 1

  SOURCE: Bureau of Advertising, ANPA.

Most Often Read after Dinner

A.M.—before or with breakfast 10
A.M.—after breakfast 11
Noon—mealtime 2
Afternoon 12
P.M.—after dinner 32
Other times 3
No habitual time .36

  SOURCE: Bureau of Advertising, ANPA.

twenty-four-hour time span at the whim and convenience of its consumer.

In the face of competition for time and attention, the newspaper is well read.

Per Cent Average Time Spent Remaining Constant
(Average Reading Time per Paper)

40 minutes or more .42
30–39 minutes 23
Up to 30 minutes 34

  SOURCE: Bureau of Advertising, ANPA.

Here again, national-average figures can be misleading.   It can be properly assumed that *The New York Times, Chicago Tribune,* or *Los Angeles Times* reader will spend substantially more time with his newspaper simply because it has broader content. On the other hand, in the smaller markets, all the newspapers' high spots can be consumed by the reader in less than a half hour.   In this sense, thirty minutes spent devouring a twenty-four-page suburban newspaper can actually be more significant than sixty minutes of scanning *The New York Times*.   Page-by-page editorial and advertising exposure levels could be substantially higher and involvement factors much deeper—and here it should be emphasized that the time spent should not, in any way, be construed as a measure of involvement.

Reading by newspaper "department" reveals opportunities to maximize traffic and ad exposure.

	Reading *Per Cent of Those Who Open the* *Page Who Read One or More Items*	
	Men	*Women*
General news	64	63
Sports	60	38
Food, fashion	42	70
Business and finance	54	42
Radio, TV	68	65
Society	43	68
Amusements	62	52
All other	52	60

SOURCE: Bureau of Advertising, ANPA.

Reader Traffic Patterns   In reviewing reader traffic patterns, it should be pointed out that too often there is much more concern with right-hand pages and far forward positions than there probably should be.   Limitations of space here do not allow for extracts from scores of studies which indicate that in some cases, left-hand positions are actually superior to right-hand positions; and that less-than-full-page national ads far forward in the main news section are often completely overwhelmed by full-page local advertisers who have daily franchises for pages 3, 5, 7, 9, etc.   There are times when it would be advantageous to get away from this front-of-paper clutter (where, by the way, most news stories are of secondary nature) and to have a potentially greater attention-getting position toward the back of the main news section (where many high-interest front-page stories are continued).

A Review of Reader Arithmetic

Let us take a quick look at the arithmetic of this medium.

It gives massive coverage of ourselves and our neighbors: 86.5 per cent of all homes, 80 per cent of all adults, 72 per cent of all teen-agers are exposed to a newspaper every day of the week.

Eighty per cent of homes buy and read a weekday newspaper; more than 86 per cent read one or more newspapers each day of the week; and 88 per cent read at least one in the course of five days.   Across the country as a whole, nine out of ten homes in the city and suburbs—white and nonwhite—read a newspaper every day.   Whether we are talking about cities of a half-million population or more, cities of from 50,000 to a half million, or in the burgeoning suburbs, coverage ranges from 89 to 93 per cent.

Ninety-eight per cent of our population who are college graduates read newspapers, as do 99 per cent of those in the $10,000-and-more income bracket.   Nine out of ten read our newspaper at habitual times, and we and our wives each pick up the newspaper on an average of 2.4 times every day.

Thorough Reading   We read our local newspaper thoroughly—71 per cent of us read it page by page.   Another 21 per cent scan, but eventually go through it from beginning to end.   Only 2 per cent cease reading after looking at a specific section or item in which they are most interested.   This delivered-at-home, read-at-home newspaper is a uniquely important part of our lives, and 49 per cent of us tell researchers we would feel quite lost without it.

In talking with people who have lived in cities which have suffered from prolonged newspaper strikes, it seems that when the newspaper is, in fact, taken away from them, almost all people feel quite lost without it.   They have grown to feel close to the newspaper.   In fact, of all those who indicated a closeness to any medium—this includes "no preferences"—almost 50 per cent felt closer to newspapers than to any form of broadcast.   It seems that in the course of devouring our newspaper, we not only do so with our minds, but also with various cutting devices—53 per cent of readers have clipped some editorial item during the past three months.

Newspapers—All Similar, Yet All Different

This then tells the story of the American daily newspaper medium in toto.   However, there is no *real* newspaper medium in toto—it exists only as a hypothetical national communications force made up of hundreds of different, individualistic publishing enterprises.

All of our some 1,700 newspapers are quite similar in what they attempt to do and what they contain.   All work with the same fundamental ingredients—news, editorials, and advertising; and many, in fact, use identical wire services and syndicated features.

Yet each newspaper is different in a number of key ways:

There are vast differences among newspapers in editorial interpretation.

Each newspaper has a deep involvement in the news and events of its own unique community.

The localness of retail and classified advertising will make any one paper quite different from all others.

Finally, the face and format of each paper is distinctive.

We seldom appreciate these subtle differences until we find ourselves in strange cities, looking at the "faces" of strange newspapers. Yet, it is through these differences that the individual newspaper communicates so directly to the parochial interests and involvements of the individual reader.

WHY PEOPLE READ NEWSPAPERS

Those who are least able to explain why people buy newspapers are newspaper purchasers themselves.   Our product public is more reflexive than reflective.   It rarely knows why it reacts as it does; stimuli, both gradual and spontaneous, trigger into action various psychic preconditions which are most often subconscious in nature.

If you were to ask the average newspaper publisher to explain concisely why people read his newspaper, he would say for details, verification, and interpretation.   While these three words tell the story fairly well, and are the most concise explanations of the reader-newspaper relationship, they are by no means the whole story, particularly in terms of contemporary marketing and communications processes.

(Later, we will trace those changes in how newspapers approach people which have resulted from changes in the structure of the marketplace and the character of its components, and measure the results of those changes in terms of how and why people approach newspapers.)

New Journalistic and Informational Values

Now that reportage of immediate events and news breaks is so capably presented by broadcast, the newspaper has assumed new journalistic and informational roles. These are highly important within the framework of a more aware and information-conscious public, and they are all based on needs which would have emerged even without the incursion of broadcast into the realm of news.

Social Changes

A few decades ago, it was enough to know that something had occurred. In a relatively noncommunal society, where each family was basically an isolated unit, there was neither a general need nor a desire for broader informations and interpretations.

Social policies and philosophies were generally constructed at the individual family level, and for all intents and purposes, the only information and opinion discourses took place outside or within houses of trade or worship. Basically, all else was transmitted by word of mouth.

However, new phenomena developed in America—heavy polarization toward urban centers, fluidity of population, mass transportation, and perhaps most significant of all, the near-universal presence of the telephone, our threshold of person-to-person and family-to-family dialogue. Coincidentally, we experienced an acceleration of the movement toward higher education for all.

These forces brought dramatically higher literacy levels, and at the same time, an infinitely greater need for individual and total-community comprehension of the facts and forces behind news and events. Thus, the American family was pried from the insulation of its historic hearth and home; and within a short time, each family and individual found itself to be a discernible part of an interrelated total public.

Accordingly, the public concern became the business of the individual, and the individual concern the business of the total public. With these new human exposures and changes came responsibilities —unrelenting responsibilities to hypothesize, philosophize, and to arrive at decisions involving much deeper implications than ever before.

The individual as a new member of this new public had to seek out information sources or to create new sources where none had existed before. It became obvious that the two-minute announcement of the town crier, or any variation thereof, would not be adequate; there were urgent desires and needs to go beyond the event itself and to develop meaningful verifications and interpretations.

Newspapers Adjust to Change

Newspapers, which in earlier days had devoted major amounts of space to fiction and features, began more and more to replace this entertainment matter with deeper reportage and news evaluations; this, in fact, brought about the interpretative syndicated columnists. Hence, as broadcast has perfected the art of reporting the raw news, newspapers have moved further into satisfying the desire for exploration and explanation in depth.

Other Motivations   In addition to the more apparent ways in which the newspaper helps its reader—confirmation, interpretation—it satisfies other, more classic, human desires.   These include the basic appetite for reading things, for minutiae, and for the one-upmanship that one can only practice by knowing as much of what is in the newspaper as a neighbor does.

The unique content of the local newspaper also appeals to other facets of the readers' psyche.   These include the appetite for gossip, and the desire for titillation and the compulsion to peek; also, the bravado and braggadocio outlets, and the need for the individual to feel that he truly belongs.

In these respects, it can be said that the unrelenting newspaper reportage of traffic violations, divorce and bankruptcy proceedings, advice to the lovelorn, high school home runs, and calendars of club meetings provide as much of a motivational backdrop for advertising as do major international events.

This medium comprises and will probably continue to remain the singular diary of the community as complete with exposure and reportage of the sins and the shortcomings of its component people as with the good that they individually and collectively accomplish.

This then creates a series of satisfactions and involvements which are totally unique in that in these areas, the newspaper becomes that single stage upon which each town's own "Spoon River Anthology," "Peyton Place," and "Main Street" is played every day before each of the diverse members of the community.

This is an involvement syndrome which is highly singular, which is exploitable, and which deserves consideration when thinking in terms of aiming toward the deep motivational processes of the brand prospect.

A Sensitive Medium   It often seems that if there is any communications form which has been static and will remain static, it would be the newspaper.   In the context of great social changes and technological advances in other communications forms, newspapers on the surface appear to be the least likely to react to change, let alone exploit change.   However, closer examination of this medium shows that it has a high sensitivity to what is happening in the marketplace in terms of arithmetic dynamics, population shifts and changes, and the ever-evolving attitudes of population segments and individuals.

Reactions to Population Shifts

In the area of markets themselves, it is a well-known fact that in most major urban centers, central city cores are declining and deteriorating; at the same time, smaller markets and suburbs are booming in size, quality, and sales potential.

A major factor or manifestation of this drift to the suburbs has been the great growth of shopping centers and the concurrent decline of metropolitan midtown as the primary selling arena.   Some major newspapers are already offering advertisers the option of urban-suburban breaks.

During the twenty years following World War II, selling space in newly built major shopping centers alone was said to have exceeded the total amount of selling space which had existed in the United States prior to 1945.   In this relation, it is interesting to measure what has happened to the circulation of those newspapers published within the large metropolitan markets as opposed to circulations of those which are published in the smaller communities, including suburbs:

*Daily Newspaper Circulation Changes
by City Size—1968 versus 1950*

City Population	Per Cent Circulation Change
1,000,000 and over	−14.9
500,000–1,000,000	−1.2
250,000–500,000	+38.8
50,000–250,000	+32.8
Under 50,000	+33.3

SOURCE: Bureau of Advertising, ANPA.

It should be pointed out that much of the circulation decline in the million-plus population markets has been caused by newspaper consolidations. On the other hand, the major factor in the rapid growth of smaller-city newspapers is the shift to suburbia. This point is given more support by a study prepared on community versus metropolitan newspapers in the top ten markets:

*Circulation in Top Ten Markets
Community Versus Metro Newspapers*

	Per Cent Change, 1962 vs. 1945
Community dailies	+94
All weeklies	+81
Metro dailies	+2

Changes in Distribution of Newspapers   These circulation figures, together with the earlier data on shopping-center activity, indicate that as the family moves away from the central city core, there is an almost automatic change in shopping habits, and the development of a suburban parochialness of interest. All of us are aware of the fact that the suburban phenomenon has expanded to the point where brand-new cities have been created around either factories or commutation points. In this context, it is interesting to note that there has been a dramatic change in the distribution of the newspaper product.

To put this in the vernacular of marketing, we would say that since 1945, about 25 newspaper brands have been dropped—the New York *Herald Tribune*, Boston *Post*, Pittsburgh *Press*, Los Angeles

Mirror, among others.   However, during the same period, 104 new brands have hit the marketplace in the sense that 104 more cities have their own daily newspaper in 1968 than did in 1945.

As mentioned, most of this germination of suburban communities and subsequent suburban publications has to this point been generated by the movement to the suburbs of factories and businesses and by the growing preference of consumers to commute to work rather than endure the growing problems of the central urban area.

Shopping-center proliferation was mentioned as another manifestation of these population trends.   However, the pendulum is swinging even further.

Shopping-center Newspapers   We are, at this point in time, beginning to see the creation of a completely new type of newspaper— again, the result of the medium's reaction to changes in the social and market structures.   As the huge shopping centers continue to dot the landscape and to become dramatically more important in terms of their share of total retail sales volume, there is the beginning of a proliferation of shopping-center newspapers, just as more and more shopping centers are now including civic auditoriums and churches. Therefore, becoming an urban-type complex of their own, they are manifesting a newspaper.   Here it should be pointed out that the newspaper, for all practical purposes, is more than any other medium a manifestation of its own parochial public.

Reaction to Changes in Social Awareness and Concern   While the foregoing is highly important to marketing planning for the present and future, it would be a gross overinterpretation to underestimate the vitality of the metropolitan city itself and the great communications needs which exist therein.

Dialogue within the heterogeneous community which is trying to approach viable homogeneity is indispensable.   In addition to having a constitutional press freedom, the newspaper editor also has a singular in-depth community-wide editorial franchise, as well as an obligation to be the forum for this community dialogue.   The implications here in terms of social futures are enormous, and the metropolitan newspaper publishers with whom we have had occasion to discuss this are well aware of what is at stake.

The specific handling of this intracommunity dialogue, the sifting out of fact from rumor, and the overall stabilization of relationships among community segments are the primary local editorial functions of today's big-city newspaper. An organ of this type attaching itself to these problems with a sense of urgency has become almost indispensable to a city in the face of the many forces that are trying to effect a great variety of changes, not every single one of which is in the best interests of the welfare of the total community or even of those individual groups on whose behalf they are originated.

A Stabilizing Force While this hypothesis seems somewhat platitudinous and at the same time irrelevant to the act of advertising and marketing, such is not the case.

A rather dramatic demonstration of what happens when all newspapers are removed from a large city during the period of social flux occurred in Detroit throughout the summer of 1968 during a prolonged newspaper strike.

Within several days after cessation of newspaper publication, Detroit was rife with rumors. Almost daily, the city was astir with stories of imminent violence of various kinds. Mayor Cavanaugh and other city officials of Detroit appeared regularly on the city's broadcast outlets in an attempt to quash the rumors, to maintain dialogue between city administration and residents, and to eliminate the constantly recurring fears of the community.

After a period of time, the Mayor concluded that it was not totally possible to maintain stability within Detroit in the absence of its newspapers; he reported this to the Michigan legislature several times.

It was the conclusion of sociologists, as well as of the Mayor, that the absence of the newspaper removed the single most important stabilizing force within the community.

Changes in Reader Interests and Attitudes

The contemporary newspaper publisher must reckon with change of another kind—*the evolutionary changes in the interests and attitudes of individuals* who comprise his newspaper's audience. Accordingly, the publisher must be tuned in to his readers. He does this by constant and massive (yet relatively unsophisticated) reader research.

Interviews among Readers Each day literally tens of thousands of interviews are conducted among readers by various newspapers developing information we very seldom are allowed to see. Readers are asked whether they would like the paper to give more or less emphasis to local or national or international news.   Their interests, attitudes, and desires on a number of subjects are recorded and measured.   Scores, similar to broadcast ratings, are tabulated on each individual comic strip, feature writer, and local columnist.

One result of this concern with divergent reader points of view can be seen on editorial pages of newspapers which now carry side-by-side conservative with liberal columnists.   Social issues are always with us, and people look for an interpretation of a social issue which is compatible with their own points of view.

This really gets to one of the things that has happened in newspapers.   For example, in the days of the old Hearst press, we had a Hearst point of view; and *The World* had a Pulitzer point of view. Newspapers today, in order to survive, have to maintain 75 to 80 per cent penetration of the marketplace; to do so, they must present some semblance of consensus of points of view, and editorially they are doing this.

This, then, is change in newspaper philosophy, which while not as apparent as change in circulation, is just as dramatic, and from the consumer-motivation standpoint, just as important.

The Newspaper Umbrella

From an advertising standpoint, the strength of newspapers is demonstrated by media reactions to market change.   While there is great fragmentation in other media forms, the newspaper has, in contrast, shown a strong tendency to polarize.   This has even occurred in the major metropolitan centers where by way of mergers and consolidations, larger segments of the market are brought under single newspaper umbrellas—demonstrating that the medium's apparent weakness is, in fact, an inherent strength.

Concurrently, other media have had to fragment.   This makes it increasingly difficult to command large market segments through other media with the ease we have enjoyed heretofore.

Phoenix as an Example   A case in point is the Phoenix, Arizona, market, which in many ways is a growth leader in terms of the national market mosaic.   Marketing analysts suggest that the growth pattern which Phoenix has enjoyed during the past decade, while unique in terms of the present, actually foreshadows what will occur throughout the country—it is happening in Phoenix first because of its obvious advantages of climate, land availabilities, topography, etc.

Taking Phoenix as our case in point then, we examine changes in its media outlets during the brief period from 1960 to 1969.

The number of television stations increased from four to six; the number of radio stations went from twelve to twenty. This aggregates to an expansion of broadcast outlets, vying for listener and viewer attention, from sixteen to twenty-six.

During this same time span, the number of newspapers has remained the same. Phoenix continues to support a strong morning and a strong evening newspaper (which the national advertiser generally buys in combination) and combined circulation has grown by 30 per cent.

Fragmentation of Broadcast Audiences Many of us anticipate that the broadcast fragmentation problem will become much deeper within the next few years.

To this point in time, station proliferation and fragmentation has mainly occurred through entrepreneurial exploitation of market growth patterns, affluence, and channel availabilities. However, dramatic forces are at work which could accelerate broadcast proliferation and fragmentation:

Government is exhibiting intense interest in opening the publicly owned airwaves to a wider and more diversified group of operators. Specifically, there is a definite intent to make television and radio station operations affordable and available to socially oriented market segments with particular emphasis on the ethnic groups.

The sudden and recent (as of this writing) increase of broadcast advertising by retailers represents a relatively untapped dollar cornucopia for the prospective broadcast operator. It should be anticipated that these locally oriented and locally directed revenues will accelerate development of new broadcast facilities.

Technology will continue to be the backdrop against which these various economic, marketing, and social forces will be at work. Greater ease and lower cost of getting on the air will stimulate technological development and vice versa. For example, the number of CATV systems is increasing dramatically—640 existed in 1960; approximately 2,250 are anticipated for 1970.

Fragmentation by Interests Looking further into the future, it appears clear that as competition for listener and viewer attention intensifies, there will be an increasing tendency to move from raw numerical audience fragmentation into fragmentation by interest. In this sense, perhaps broadcast will more and more begin to resemble the magazine medium in that universal-audience and total-appeal program forms will of necessity be augmented or even replaced by demographically, psychographically, or sociographically disciplined broadcast formats.

Should this occur, we can anticipate two potential results: First, it would become substantially more difficult and inefficient to accumulate mass audiences at the various local levels through broadcast. Second, as the retailers, who will have been major contributors to station proliferation, become more conversant with the art of using the medium and through more sophisticated research become more knowledgeable about their various publics, they will apply their local influences and their unmatchable local dollar leverages toward franchising the prime local broadcast availabilities.

In this area, the parallel can be drawn to what has happened in the newspaper medium, where the retailers have what are considered to be all or most of the prime position franchises. Unavailability of position franchises and prime availabilities is a much more serious matter in broadcast than in print due to the very nature of the two media forms. Newspapers and magazines have scanning and flip-through reader patterns, and the reader is conditioned to look for the ads. In broadcast, there is no physical retention. In addition, there is the advertising-avoidance factor which was touched upon earlier in this chapter.

Therefore, it seems clear that the relative values of franchises in broadcast and print are facing imminent and dramatic changes, and deserve constant reevaluation; and the proposition of newspapers as the singular community-communications umbrella merits continuous consideration.

Newspapers and the Urban Negro

To finish with newspapers and change, one of the problems of newspapers that can be turned into an advantage is the movement of the Negro into the central city and the fact that this then causes great schisms in the prospect definition of a newspaper's audience, because a newspaper by nature covers the total city. It is highly conceivable that this can be turned into one of those truly strong points of newspapers, as far as advertising is concerned in the future.

Advertising and brand names are with us only because they give a confidence to the purchaser, and the purchaser then has a reference or a framework that says that the company or item has integrity and it produces a good product.   This has traditionally been a fact that has been relied on more by people with less money to spend than by people with more money to spend.

It has been said that the Negro market per se probably represents the greatest concentration of people with a desire to buy and a need to be informed of what they are buying, and a need to have confidence in what they buy.

All these factors related, along with the social developments in the city and the changing nature of the Negro in the economy, can mean that one of the most potent buying forces the country has ever seen will be available in the newspaper form, especially for brand items.

NEWSPAPER ADVERTISING

Most of what comes to corporate management about advertiser usage of newspaper are homogenizations of box car totals, with little or no interpretation of component parts.   Here, as elsewhere in our business lives, there are numbers behind numbers, and a variety of diverse forces which affect all the numbers.

The fact that newspaper-advertising revenues now exceed $5 billion and were 2½ times as great in 1968 as in 1950, when commercial television moved into full gear, is admittedly dramatic.   However, these figures, which are salient selling tools of the newspaper industry, have little real meaning to the agency and the corporation in our constant effort to comprehend properly the specific newspaper-advertising proposition.

Accordingly, here we will subject these figures to a brief but essential microscopic examination and proceed to the more relevant whats and whys and hows of newspaper advertising.

Advertising-volume Trends

The figures which follow are the raw-dollar-volume figures mentioned above.   In the interest of space, every fifth-year figure (plus the year 1968) has been extracted from the year-by-year data which are available to us:

Newspaper Advertising Volume, in
Millions of Dollars

Year	Local	National	Total
1940	652.4	163.0	815.4
1945	710.4	211.0	921.4
1950	1,542.2	533.4	2,075.6
1955	2,344.5	743.3	3,087.8
1960	2,866.7	836.1	3,702.8
1965	3,565.0	870.0	4,435.0
1968	4,245.0	992.0	5,237.0

SOURCE: Bureau of Advertising, ANPA.

These figures show a constant growth pattern in all areas, despite a variety of forces and events which have worked against newspaper-advertising growth. In addition to the obvious diversion of dollars into the television medium, aggregate newspaper revenues have been adversely affected by the following:

Cessation of publication by over a dozen important newspapers in New York, Los Angeles, Boston, San Francisco, Pittsburgh, etc.

Emergence of regional editions of national magazines as a new and highly effective competitor for advertising by brands which were nonnational in nature.

Conversion in major newspaper categories—i.e., automotive, tire, appliance—from the national rate to the substantially lower retail rate. The rationale and ramifications of this conversion will be described in subsequent pages.

Considering these and other factors, then, newspapers on the whole appear to have held their own extremely well, at least in terms of raw totals.

However, converting these totals into individual indices for local and national revenues develops a basis for much more relevant insights into what has been occurring in the ad columns of the newspaper—as well as some clues to the future (Figure 2).

Here we see, by way of advertiser usage, a demonstration of newspapers, inherently local in character, becoming increasingly more local. This becomes particularly clear when we consider that 65 to 70 per cent of total newspaper content is advertising.

Our chart of indices reveals other interesting facts, and the oppor-

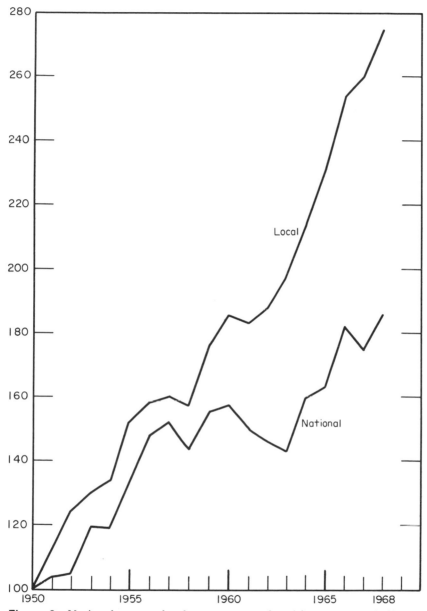

Figure 2 National versus local newspaper advertising revenue indices (1950-100).

19-77

tunity to relate various segments of the trend lines to outside forces and events should not be allowed to pass.

Relationship to Economic Trends   For example, it is fascinating to trace the line movements in relation to the recessions of 1958 and 1961–1962.   In the immediate prerecession period, the indices rise sharply, indicating a buildup toward the need for an economic "correction."   Then the recession period itself has a predictable effect on newspaper advertising.   (Here it should be noted that national declines more sharply than retail.   The national advertiser, being locked into other media on a long-term basis, makes his most immediate and drastic cuts in the newspaper budget.   This is a case where newspaper time flexibility works against the medium.)   Finally, following each recession, the dollar-index trend resumes an upward course slightly steeper than that which immediately preceded the recession.

This conjecture of relating newspaper-advertising trends to the national economic situation gains support here in 1969.   Economists in government and the private sector are deeply alarmed about runaway inflation, and severe economic brakes are being applied; in this connection, it is interesting to trace the newspaper-advertising indices, particularly retail, from 1963 through 1968.   Perhaps newspapers are a barometer, or even presage economic episodes.

A second interpretation of this chart is based on relative year-by-year growth of the local and national revenue indices from 1957 on.   Previously, they were generally parallel, but in a rather sudden sense, as of 1958, retail began to grow at a much more rapid rate.   For every ensuing year, without exception, the gap between the two indices has widened.   This is the kind of phenomenon that demands a reason: what occurred in 1957?   The answer could very well be in the fact that 1957 was the year of the General Motors "consent decree," whereby for all practical purposes, GM and the other automobile manufacturers relinquished control over a large portion of the automotive advertising budget.   Briefly here (the matter will be expanded upon later), this led to a far-reaching chain of events that has permanently influenced the advertising content, and therefore, the character of the daily newspaper.

Newspaper-advertiser Performance

We have traced, tracked, and where possible, measured a broad series of interactions from the basic proposition of newspapers to news, through the medium's reaction to changes of marketing and emotions, to the threshold of newspaper-advertising dynamics.   We have tried to define, understand, and interpret each of these functions in terms of the demand for optimumly actionable evaluation and implementation of viable newspaper fact and theory.

Now we approach our subject in another, equally vital perspective —an examination of the newspaper advertiser himself and how he reacts to and exploits change in the society in toto, and in relation to the newspaper medium in particular.

The following table was developed from a study conducted among 178 newspapers by Dr. Kenneth Byerly of the University of North Carolina School of Journalism.   While certainly not conclusive, the figures are quite revealing, particularly in comparing national advertisers' activity with that of local and retail and classified advertisers.

The Byerly Study of 178 Daily Newspapers

Per cent of total ad linage:	1950	1964
Retail	66.0	67.9
Classified	18.3	22.3
National	15.7	9.7
Per cent of total ad dollars:		
Retail	60.1	63.6
Classified	19.6	22.6
National	20.3	13.8
Rate trends: *		
Retail	100.0	171.6
Classified	100.0	160.5
National	100.0	176.9
National linage by city size: *		
Over 1,000,000 population	100.0	110.3
50,000 to 100,000	100.0	65.5

* Based on 1950 index = 100.0 per cent.

These data lend themselves to many interpretations on linage and dollar trends, some self-apparent, which space here does not permit. However, the last set of figures is particularly interesting.   Earlier we traced the circulation decline of large-city dailies and the remarkable growth of newspapers published in smaller cities.   A real paradox lies in the fact that national-advertising linage has seemingly moved in the opposite direction.   More recent information, as it becomes available, will no doubt show a continuation of these trends.

How Retailers Use Newspapers

To approach an understanding of the critical subtleties necessary for harnessing newspaper dynamics (to our own interests), it is vital to investigate the advertising whys and wherefores of the retailer.

In the typical newspaper, retailers place seven times as much space as all national advertisers combined. Today's retailing giants grew up almost exclusively in newspapers (in fact, Richard W. Sears first made contact with Alvah C. Roebuck through a help-wanted ad in the Chicago *Daily News*).

It is common practice, yet a gross oversimplification, to describe retail advertising as a proposition of price, size, and place. It is a much more deliberate art. To project properly retailer newspaper performance toward our own comprehension of the medium, it is vital to appreciate the overall retailer proposition and then to interpret it in terms of the diverse types of retail advertisers—an exploration of the highly variegated to discover that which is common and relevant.

Advertising Objectives First, we have the unique, yet highly pertinent phenomena of almost every retailer and his advertising strategies and objectives as related to his needs:

Inventory turnover out of stockrooms and warehouses and to the consumer is indispensable to his business existence, let alone success. Merchandise stocking is the constant weight around his neck, and dead shelf space is disaster.

Advertising must generate action for the retailer. He builds his image in his logotype, art style, and typography, but copy execution, timing, and other devices must move merchandise.

Much retail advertising appeals to the compulsive proposition that to spend is to save—to truly save, you must spend less for that which you may or may not have previously intended to buy.

Retailing Seasons and Events Retailers perfected the art of creating their own seasons and events through astute advertising. A mental review of the retail year will demonstrate how the American consumer's calendar has been completely restructured by retail newspaper advertising: January—white sales; February—furniture sales; March—pre-Easter; April—pre-spring; May—Mother's Day; June—Father's Day; July—clearances; August—back to school; September—fall fashions; October—winter clothing; November and December are the two months of Christmas. The last week of the year is devoted to gift exchange and "While you're here, there's our year-end clearance," which is invariably extended into January—by newspaper ads.

These retailer-created national "seasons" are augmented by those events and occasions which, in each local context, are just as vital and community-involved—rodeo days in the Southwest, Pilgrim's Day in the Northeast, *ad infinitum*.

Types of Advertising   Now, to categorize the various types of retailers in terms of their advertising.

That which comes to mind most quickly is the price-and-place type of ad such as used by food stores and discount houses.   Much of this copy is a proposition of developing instantaneous consumer reaction. It has little apparent subtlety because the grocers long ago determined that in the weekly ritual of selling household staples, there is no necessity for creating a commodity desire; these items are matters of day-to-day family sustenance.

Since the desirability factor is eliminated by the existence of hunger, the consumer is totally committed to buying the commodity before seeing the advertising.   Therefore, the fundamental advertising proposition gravitates to price (although in some retail food advertising, factors of convenience, service, and quality are also included).

Transient Retail Advertising   The second basic retail-advertising form consists of promotions by small and infrequent "transient" local businesses.   Because of a basic lack of advertising knowledge and also because so much is at stake in terms of developing a payoff from each individual ad, transient retail copy takes on a relatively crude character.   It is more memorable for this than for anything else.

However, the great bulk of retail advertising falls into a third category of execution which encompasses consistency, subtlety, and sophistication—that highly creative and purposeful newspaper advertising which is developed by the large retailers.   With them, there is not quite the same sense of urgency as exists with their smaller competitors.   Accordingly, the Marshall Fields and Lord & Taylors of America develop their advertising to serve a dual purpose.

Sale of Specific Items   First, of course, is the need to sell specific advertised items.   However, because they can be in the newspaper with tonnage and consistency, the advertising is also designed to develop the image and futures of the corporation.

These retailers who, to a large extent, dominate the columns of the newspaper use their continuity to develop a written message to the newspaper reader.   To enhance this, they will nearly always advertise on specific days of the week, and quite often their advertising will be in the same position within the newspaper.   In this manner then, they develop predictability.

For example, a reader of the Chicago *Tribune* knows where to look for Abercrombie & Fitch, Marshall Field, and Carson Pirie Scott ads. By adhering to this same-day-of-week and same-position pattern, these retailers assume (and capitalize on) the character and function of newspaper editorial features.   In fact, at the beginning of this chapter, there are figures which relate to the fact that people want advertising in newspapers—there is less tangible but very convincing evidence that they want to know where and when to find specific retail ads.

Distinctive Visual Styles   In examining several weeks' issues of any newspaper, you will note that each leading retailer develops a distinctive visual style.   This goes far beyond the regular use of the distinctive store logotype; it involves the use of specific art styles, typefaces and sizes, as well as an overall consistency in total appearance; i.e., some retailers use large illustrations exclusively; others use a great deal of white space, and some will use bold type while others will regularly use the lighter typefaces.

In a sense, this retail advertising is somewhat like sign language, in that it triggers an identification through graphic styles and devices. It is interesting to speculate that retail newspaper advertising has long since passed the point where even someone who is illiterate can comprehend most of the ads; this is a rather unique accomplishment.

Consistent Copy Techniques   There is even a consistency in terms of copy techniques; Abercrombie & Fitch copy is a good and readily available demonstration of this.   The retailers use the continuity-predictability technique consciously and with good purpose.   They know that newspaper readers in general, and their own store customers in particular, have become accustomed to and therefore react to this adjudicated sameness and regularity of communication.

As for intrusiveness, a term now exclusively related to broadcast, this was first employed on a broad scale in the aisles of a Dallas department store, long before commercial television. Specifically, Neiman-Marcus, perhaps the paramount pacesetter in newspaper advertising, aligned (or purposely misaligned) their counters in an interlocking herringbone pattern so that customers had to walk around several merchandise displays before reaching their newspaper-advertised specials.

Of course, there are variations within the overall theme, and you will find that some retailers are highly innovative. Neiman-Marcus, referred to above, will, for example, use discordant colors and modern art forms to enhance the appeal of the most mundane products.

Generally speaking, it can be said that weight, continuity, consistency of style, localism, and opportunism are the basic elements of successful use of newspapers by retailers. Further, all the advertising by an individual retailer has a degree of sameness, while retail newspaper advertising in the aggregate is highly varied; but at the same time, all this advertising does have a single common denominator—which is localness.

This, then, is the advertising arena and the physical environment which together with editorial comprise the universe within which the national newspaper advertiser functions.

How National Advertisers Use Newspapers

The great bulk of national newspaper advertising today evolves around new-product introductions, special promotions including coupon drops, and that advertising which appears in newspapers largely through default. This includes advertising for liquor (which is limited in terms of the media which will accept it), automotive advertising (where, for a variety of reasons, there must be an identification with the local dealerships).

Generally speaking, the character of the national newspaper ad differs from retail in several respects. First, it is relatively more impersonal in that it is seldom geared at the individual local marketplace. Also, national advertising, with the exception of that for proprietary drug items and certain other commodities, tends to be, if you will, slicker. Also, for the most part, national advertisers do not use the consistency of format, art, and type styles such as are successfully employed by the local retailers.

Rate Differentials We must submit here that retailers use newspapers with the great dominance that they do mainly because of the cost differential between local and national rates. This rate differential which so deeply disturbs all of us exists for two reasons. First, it developed as an outgrowth of a long-past marketing and advertising structure, and second, it has been perpetuated because the newspapers find it economically infeasible to eliminate it spontaneously.

Its origins lie in the days before chain-store retailing, in an era when the general store or the drugstore had a single outlet, located somewhere in the central part of the city. The proprietor was able to obtain advantageous rates somewhat on an emotional basis, in that he was neighbor, friend, and fellow club member of the newspaper publisher. In their mutual parochialism, the agreement was made to protect this friendly retailer from the competition of "foreign" advertisers (in most newspaper representative contracts today, the term "foreign advertising" is still used in referring to national advertising).

In the initial stage of newspaper rate development, the retailer was also able to negotiate a distinct rate advantage over the national manufacturer because of the relative manner in which he and the manufacturer sold goods in relation to where the newspaper was circulated. The retailer argued with considerable merit—in pre-mass transportation and toll-road days—that he received value only from newspaper circulation in the city and its immediate environs. He contended with conviction that the national manufacturer, on the other hand, with his universality of distribution, received value from all the newspaper's circulation. Therefore, he syllogistically concluded (and convinced the publisher) that the national advertiser should pay for total circulation, but that he, at the same time, should pay for only that portion of the circulation which was geographically related to his own customer prospects. Thereby, the rate differential came into existence.

These causative factors no longer exist, and yet rate differentials have remained. While chain-store retailing, mass travel, shopping-center proliferation, and the growing inclination of consumers to travel further to buy value have replaced the corner store and the horse and buggy—and all publishers recognize this—hard facts of economics and cold emotional fears about diversion into other media have resulted in the publishers' retaining their rate differentials.

Effect on Use by National Advertisers   This has had an unfortunate effect on the use of the newspaper by a great many national advertisers; and in general, has led to other devices—the establishment of local retail basis and the use of co-op advertising.

For example, as a result of General Motors' consent decree in 1957, many automobile manufacturers lost control of the total automobile national-advertising budget. It was discovered that dealers could form local and regional associations, and they could use their local contacts and combined leverage and obtain the local rate. Thereby, control of a large portion of automotive advertising dollars was lost by manufacturers and their agencies and went into the hands of the dealers.

The same thing occurred in the tire field a few years later. The result has been that, through lack of control, advertising in the automobile, tire, and appliances classifications has lost the basic character, direction, and quality that is so vital to manufacturers in terms of the long haul.

It is a case when the expedient has worked in terms of dollars (and significant dollar consideration was involved); however, in terms of prestige and so-called image making and long-term respect for product and type advertising to which the public is exposed, there has been great suffering, and it will continue until such time as the rate inequity ends. This is a key problem that newspapers face, and a key problem that corporate managers face.

Various forces are operating at an increasing pace to make retail and national rates more equitable, but progress has still been slow. Perhaps at some point in time, government will step in—there are indications that it is investigating the issue now. Perhaps, on the other hand, because newspaper-advertising revenue is 80 per cent local, we may get rate equalization simply because the national part will phase out and all advertising will gradually convert to some form of retail. As the volume of national diminishes, the dollar loss to a newspaper by converting to a single rate is much less. So, in effect, we may see the development of a single-rate structure by metamorphosis.

EXECUTION-OPPORTUNITY EXPANSION, COMPUTERS, AND DECISIONS

Recognizing that there is less than ever a single ideal formula for frequency, size, or content, we must approach the planning proposition on what we call a "what-if" basis. Here again, application of judgments within budgetary limitations is the fundamental planning chore, but our abilities to interpret various rationales become immensely broadened through the use of a properly programed computer operation.

This tool, in this sense, becomes increasingly indispensable; that is, to the extent that we understand that it is a tool which reflects the relative results of various judgments and is not in itself an absolute developer or executor of the media plan.

If not already, we are approaching the point where the sheer number of frequency, size, and continuity combinations defies arithmetic interpretation:

As was demonstrated earlier, we have infinitely more vehicles than ever before; and number of vehicles should tend to increase at an accelerated pace rather than diminish or remain static.

Also, within each media form, we have dramatically increasing flexibilities in physical techniques and availabilities going far beyond the old regional breaks which at one time, in themselves, seemed to comprise a complicated multiplicity of choices.

These factors are further compounded by the great growth definitions within each of the media forms—it is in this area, more than in any other, that we will most likely see the heaviest proliferation of choices in years to come.

Therefore, the number of possible combinations, which once could be counted in the hundreds, are more likely to be in the hundreds of millions.

Applying the "What-Ifs"

In spite of all the capabilities of today's computers and the promise of technology to come, we cannot foresee any immediate opportunity to explore each one of those millions of "what-ifs" in connection with any brand campaign.

Therefore, the underlying and fundamental criterion is the judgment of the advertising planner to explore and utilize those various series of "what-if" situations which are most relevant to the task at hand.

This selection of potential solutions is, in turn, highly dependent upon arduous, objective, and yet imaginative examinations of all forces and factors which embrace the brand and its potential advertising approach to brand prospects.

Capable Personnel

This involves the employing and proper training of capable people to make these various explorations. This is important, and it is done in recognition of the fact that greater facilities for exploration and greater numbers of capable individuals applied against the multitudinous "what-ifs" provide a distinct competitive brand-advertising advantage.

In addition to enabling us to delve more deeply into potentially appropriate areas which would otherwise remain unexamined, this principle of applying technology and expertise in quantity against the advertising task extends itself to the proposition of media balance, as well as the critical sciences of optimum scheduling; i.e., phasing, periodicity, etc.

We have found this preparatory work and the examination of budget factors, competitive activities, brand-prospect variables, and trends within media forms to be indispensable to the final act of planning. It is from this basic-training phase that we can best arrive at those particular "what-if" solutions that are most promising and deserve deeper evaluation and comparison.

In turn, these solutions and all relevant accompanying materials are analyzed judgmentally as well as electronically; and hence, we extract from the hundreds of millions of possible individual advertising actions that which is singularly most appropriate.

"What-If" and Broadcast-Print Integration

Specifically, in terms of the proposition of print, we encounter some rather revealing sets of numbers when we explore what occurs in terms of *frequency distribution* through various scheduling alternatives. Here we will use four demonstrations.

The following is a breakdown of reach and frequency provided by a schedule where the budget is totally television—50 per cent day network (twenty announcements) and 50 per cent night network (four announcements):

	Day Network	*Night Network*	*Total Media*
	41/2.8	35/1.5	54/3.1
1	16.3	21.7	18.4
2	8.8	8.9	11.0
3	5.4	3.2	7.3
4	3.6	0.8	5.0
5	2.4	—	3.5
6	1.6	—	2.5
7	1.1	—	1.8
8	0.7	—	1.2
9	0.5	—	0.9
10	0.3	—	0.6
11	0.2	—	0.4
12+	0.4	—	0.9

This 54 reach and 3.1 average frequency is obviously concentrated among those who saw any of the commercials just once or twice.

However, when we examine what occurs when the budget is 50 per cent television (four announcements on night network) and 50 per cent print (one insertion each in five magazines), we note a number of dramatic changes:

	Night Network	*Print*	*Total Media*
	35/1.5	69/1.7	76/2.3
1	21.7	34.2	27.7
2	8.9	22.0	21.9
3	3.2	9.6	14.0
4	0.8	2.8	7.6
5	—	0.4	3.5
6	—	—	1.3
7	—	—	0.4
8	—	—	0.1
9	—	—	—
10	—	—	—
11	—	—	—
12+	—	—	—

First, reach becomes substantially higher in that this supplementary print schedule, by the nature of its audience composition relative to that of nighttime television, combines with the broadcast to provide an overall reach of 76.   Although the average frequency is about the same as when the total budget was committed to television, we find that more people are actually seeing the ad a greater number of times.

Taking the "what-if" exploration into another phase, we examine what occurs if the budget is 50 per cent spot television (60 per cent of this in fringe and 40 per cent in day spot), and the remaining 50 per cent is devoted to one insertion each in five magazines:

	Spot TV	Print	Total Media
	71/3.9	69/1.7	85.4/4.7
1	18.2	34.2	15.0
2	13.1	22.2	13.6
3	9.8	9.6	11.7
4	7.4	2.8	9.8
5	5.7	0.4	8.0
6	4.3	—	6.4
7	3.3	—	5.1 ·
8	2.5	—	4.0
9	1.9	—	3.1
10	1.4	—	2.4
11	1.0	—	1.8
12+	2.5	—	4.7

Here reach is even higher than in the preceding instance, while average frequency of 4.7 is substantially greater.

Finally, for the purposes of comparison, we examine the reach and frequency-distribution pattern of a campaign comprised of 50 per cent day network (twenty announcements) and 50 per cent spot television (thirty-two announcements in combination fringe):

	Day Network	Spot TV	Total Media
	41/2.8	71/3.9	86/4.6
1	16.3	18.2	15.3
2	8.8	13.1	14.0
3	5.4	9.8	12.1
4	3.6	7.4	10.0
5	2.4	5.7	8.1
6	1.6	4.3	6.4
7	1.1	3.3	5.0
8	0.7	2.5	3.9
9	0.5	1.9	3.0
10	0.3	1.4	2.2
11	0.2	1.0	1.7
12+	0.4	2.5	4.2

Here we predictably encounter still a different result; again, while both reach and frequency are substantially greater than in our first example of day and night network, the frequency-distribution pattern is skewed quite heavily toward those who are exposed to the advertising four times or less—this despite the fact that we have an aggregate of fifty-two exposure opportunities.

The comparisons of these tables should not be presumed to be in themselves totally conclusive demonstrations of any precise points. However, as a group, they represent one of many thousands of possible demonstrations of what could be revealed through application of various advertising contingencies against known facts relating to advertising-exposure opportunities, and the numerical contributions which can be made by the integration of print into the advertising program.

Relevancy of Input Characteristics

In the final analysis, computer output will be a manifestation of information input. Therefore, it must be emphasized that since input is basically numerical, there must be an understanding and appreciation of the kinds of media numbers we encounter in dealing with computers. The computer, in its mechanical isolation, cannot in and of itself make some highly critical interpretations between various types of numbers.

Specifically, there are different and significantly varying classifications of numbers one will encounter in relation to various media forms and advertising strategies; and it is vital that there be an understanding of these number types and of their relative values.

Numbers: Their Variations, Meanings, and Values

We break these numbers down into three basic categories—exposure potential, attention, and motivation.

Exposure Potential Those numbers which one most frequently encounters in dealing with media mathematics, and particularly data which emanate from media, fall into the area of exposure, or more properly, *exposure potential*.

This is the aggregate audience exposed to any part of a publication or broadcast operation. It is, as you will see, the largest of the three figures; this probably explains why it is the one most often presented to us by media representatives. In essence, it comprises the maximum number of people who have any physical opportunity whatever to be exposed to the advertising message within the vehicle being considered.

It should never be construed as representing the number of people who will actually perceive or react to our advertising within that vehicle; and in this sense, it falls far short (or perhaps overlong) in revealing any meaningful information on the action of the advertising against the prospect.

These are the box-car numbers; true, they are impressive, and in a sense, subliminally satisfying in that they allow those who wish to do so, to presume that they are reaching and selling audiences in vast numbers. However, in this sense, they can also be grossly misleading, and those satisfactions one receives from perceiving box-car figures can be far outweighed by the raw fact that not nearly all these people are, in fact, being communicated with to any degree which has any true meaning to the brand or to the advertising task at hand.

Recognizing the potential deception of exposure-opportunity arithmetic, we find it necessary to probe more deeply in our examination of the communications action between specific advertising and specific brand prospects. We are, in a large sense, searching out smaller numbers, but numbers which have more meaning.

Attention   Our next step then is to examine our arithmetic in terms of *attention*. This is much more elusive, in that it is not now universally available in acceptably documented forms; however, while not a finite measure, it is a much better guide. It extracts from all those who may have had any opportunity to perceive the ad, those who, in fact, did so; therefore, it indicates to whom we have transmitted the fundamental gist of the advertising message.

This, then, as opposed to the much larger audience of the advertising vehicle, is the audience of the advertisement per se; these are those prospects with whom we have a realistic opportunity to develop a communication.

In comparing actual advertising propositions, we have found that those media which deliver the largest prospect audience as measured by advertising *attention* are often quite different from those which offer the broadest and largest audience on the basis of *exposure potential*. Therefore, the constant quest for the ad-attention audience is highly worthwhile.

However, even this important step from measuring *exposure potential* to measuring advertising *attention* does not go far enough toward guiding the end judgments of vehicle selection, frequency, continuity, and ad size.

Advertising has long since moved beyond the point where it was created specifically to attract attention, and where it was presumed that attention development performed the ultimate purposes of brand advertising. Today, as opposed to the past, consumers have infinitely more choices between individual brands within product categories. Consequently, for the most part, specific brand names are becoming less synonymous with product categories; i.e., Ivory Soap, Ford Cars, and Wrigley's Gum. This raises the strong necessity for further refinement—the development, understanding, and measurement of still another dimension of advertising arithmetic.

For example, Figure 3 is a demonstration of the advertising pro-

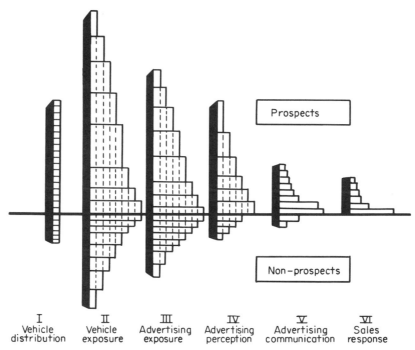

Figure 3 The advertising process.

cess. Its purpose is to dramatize the vast distance which actually lies between the first consideration, which is the physical distribution of the advertising vehicle, and the final consideration, which is the actual sales response.

While the relationships between the six segments in terms of size and the interpretations of weight against prospects and nonprospects will vary with different advertising executions, the principles inevitably remain constant. There is a long road between the tangible placement of the advertising message and the motivation of the consumer toward the actual purchase act.

Our recognition of this then leads us to our search for better though probably smaller numbers in the continuing effort to optimize advertising on behalf of brand versus brand.

It has probably been noted by now that throughout this chapter we have involved ourselves with the psychological aspects of the magazine and newspaper forms. We have purposefully avoided filling page after page with those data and statistics which, after all, have already been recorded and described in so many places, and are commonly available from several sources.

Motivation Instead, we have been addressing ourselves to the psychological qualities of the media, of their operators, of media and man, and the multiplicity of interactions and motivations which exist among people, and the manner in which they choose to assimilate information. We have done so because this most closely addresses itself to our final set of numbers, that being the measurement of advertising *motivation*—in terms of the numbers of people we can expect to motivate (synonyms: convert, actionate, re-sell, etc.) with given advertising strategies, in given vehicles and dimensions.

Motivation of prospects is the fundamental force that we constantly aim to develop. In each of our lifetimes, we have many acquaintances, but marry only one at a time. We watch many automobiles and slam many doors in showrooms, but we buy only one make and model at a given moment. We see great arrays of cereals on food-store shelves, but we choose to select certain types and brands.

It has by now been well established that man individually, as well as societies and communities, is governed more by his subconscious than by all the varieties of detectable environments that he encounters in his lifetime. He is *motivated* to buy the specific car or the cereal or the particular brand within any category.   On one hand, he does not select blindly, and on the other, he seldom selects for reasons of which he is fully aware.   Therefore, motivation becomes our central purpose.   Relative development of motivations among prime brand prospects will most often determine which of those brands with basically equal quality will develop greater acceptance; therefore, greater, more frequent, and more loyal purchasing.

Here we emphasize the loyalty factor and the principle that repeat purchase is the foundation upon which brand growth must be built. Therefore, the motivation principle must address itself very directly and deeply to the current user, as well as to those new prospects whom we hope to attract into our brand-user universe.

This, then, is why we seek for that most elusive arithmetic—the numerical measure of brand prospects who can be motivated by a given advertising strategy within a given set of media vehicles.   This can comprise the critical difference between optimumly successful advertising and that which falls short (to whatever degree we can precisely measure how closely we approach optimum success—as opposed to target success).

There are no perfect patterns for establishing perfect numbers to describe motivation values, and conceivably, there never will be. Earlier, it was pointed out that there are millions of possible variations and combinations of media usages.   This being the case, there are doubtless billions of variations of motivational values attainable through advertising executions.   All advertising confronts so many conditions and preconditions, dispositions and predispositions.   On an individual, community, and national basis, there are times of euphoria and of gloom, of boom and recession, excitement, apathy, involvement, distraction, progress, and regress; and all these will be reflected in media as well as in how people perceive media, and much more particularly, how they perceive and react to each advertisement and the advertising campaign in toto.

Hopefully, we have demonstrated the benefits of or at least aroused the desire for ascending those statistical-informational steps which become narrower numerically, but at the same time become so much stronger in terms of brand-advertising goals, present and future.

In relation to our specific topic here, it should be submitted that broad exposure, and to a lesser degree, attention are the primary functions of broadcast media.   These two factors, particularly that of exposure, are the most easily definable and measurable under present conditions.

However, in addressing ourselves to motivation, it might be said that this phenomenon in part involves manifestations of believability, verification, confidence, permanence, interest or community chauvinism, personal involvement, etc.   This combination of factors is infinitely more elusive in terms of the measurement process.   It is the most difficult in terms of establishing precise numerical values; instead, these facets of motivation are the most demanding of all the various considerations in terms of the application of judgment.

If it should be assumed that these characteristics of believability, verification, etc. are inherent to print, then it could follow that the basic strength of print is to some extent or another circumvented by the fact that the essences of print which relate to the primary objective of motivation are least measured and these are the areas where the least knowledge exists.

Again, while motivation is the least defined of all the actions we measure and is the most difficult to assess, it is the most important criterion.

Therefore, any examination of potential improvement of the advertising strategy by dominance or frequency lies in the area of understanding the motivational values concerned—and we should not let the biggest and first, and yet the lesser, unit of exposure opportunity be the end all (rather than the starting point) of our advertising examination, or we run the risk of defeating the purpose and promise of advertising.

CHAPTER TWENTY

Uses of Broadcast Media*

SAM B. VITT *Senior Vice President and Executive Director of Media-Program Department, Ted Bates & Company†*

SOME BASIC DATA

The average person, during his lifetime (to seventy years) will spend close to nine years watching television and six years listening to radio. This accounts for fifteen years of broadcast exposure. This time spent by the average person represents 80 per cent of his total hours spent with the four major media (television, radio, magazines, newspapers).

* This chapter is largely the work of the Ted Bates Media-Program Department. All departmental divisions, of which there are six, were involved generally; but particularly that of the Media Information and Analysis Division (M.I.A.D.). Nevertheless, I take full responsibility for any flaws which may have slipped in. I cannot do the same for any credit. That should be lodged with the department and divided among its superb personnel. A large slice, of course, being left for M.I.A.D. itself.—Sam B. Vitt.

† Mr. Vitt is now president, Vitt Media International, Inc.

The success of these electronic media in selling products influenced national advertisers to invest in 1968 better than $3 billion in broadcast.

Media Department Structure and Responsibility

The advertising department of a manufacturing or service company and the media department of an advertising agency are the units responsible for counseling on the selection and investment of client dollars in advertising media.   The heads of these units, the advertising director (advertiser) and the media director (agency), together supervise the final media recommendation presented to the advertiser's top management.   Communication between these two is essential to the success of the plan being finally approved.

Figure 1, represents an oversimplified organizational structure and

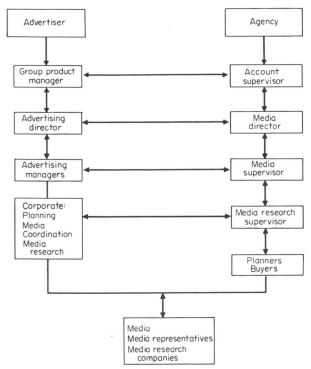

Figure 1 Basic media department organization and advertiser-agency communication.

communications flow.   In some cases there are specialists positioned at different levels within these media structures.   For example, the network specialist is primarily responsible for the commitment or coordination of corporate network dollars.

In addition to their internal staffs, there are outside personnel who assist in selection of media.   These are composed of persons employed directly by individual media, by media representatives, by media research companies, and by the various bureaus representing each medium.   Each in his own way supplies data, often significant, that contributes to a better advertising plan.

In all cases these individuals must be responsive to copy and marketing requirements and allocated budgets, in determining the selection of media.

Target Audience and Media Objectives

The staff involved in the planning and buying of media for a given brand should familiarize itself with all data available that will direct it to the brand's potential customers.   There are syndicated research sources (Brand Rating Research and W. R. Simmons, for example) that describe users (age, sex, etc.) of products in terms of degree of use and their media habits with magazines and network TV.   These data, together with special tabulations and brand sales information, assist in the selection of individual vehicles within the broad media.   However, buying objectives today tend to concentrate on evaluating vehicles that will deliver the primary target (women eighteen to forty-nine, teens, etc.) most efficiently, disregarding the sales contributed by other lower potential groups (e.g., women more than fifty years old) in the population.   There is a movement to assigning weight factors to different members of the population depending on their contribution to the overall sales success of specific brands or brand categories.

In addition, the media departments together with the group product manager and account supervisor must determine the major media objectives for a given brand.   The following illustrates possible objectives influencing media selection and strategy:

To reach efficiently and effectively as many potential product users as possible within the framework of the budget

To concentrate in those areas that represent above-average sales potential

To protect its current franchise in total United States markets, plus added weight in selected markets

To maintain national umbrella coverage and match major competition in selected markets

The form shown in Figure 2 was developed to help define the brand's target audience and establish the brand's marketing and media objectives. These questions, which are preliminary and basic, should be answered by the account supervisor and should be considered in developing the brand's media plan.

Basic Broadcast Facts

Since this chapter will direct itself to the broadcast media—television and radio—it is essential that the advertiser and agency media staffs, before planning and buying broadcast, familiarize themselves with the basic facts of these media and how they operate. We will review government licensing, the size of each universe, the potential audience, the kinds of people who view or listen, the hours of exposure, commercial time allowed and used, and station facilities and how they operate.

Government Control and Licensing

The Federal Communications Commission (FCC) is the government body responsible for the allocation of broadcast channels and for the granting of licenses for broadcast stations. Assigned licenses are not permanent. They can be revoked if the Commission finds that the licensees are not living up to their community or industry obligations. Even though the broadcast industry, through the National Association of Broadcasters, self-imposes good-practice regulations, the FCC often influences the establishment of commercial standards through informal communications with the broadcast industry (i.e., number of commercials per half-hour).

Currently there are 584 commercial TV stations that can collectively send picture signals to all the households in the United States. These stations can be purchased individually, market by market (spot), or they can be purchased as a group (network), since 490 are primarily affiliated with one of the three networks—ABC, CBS, NBC.

Types of TV Stations   There are two basic types of stations—VHF (very high frequency) with channel assignments 2 to 13, and UHF (ultra high frequency) with channel assignments 14 to 83. VHFs (440) generally operate on maximum power (100,000 watts—channels 2 to 7; 316,000 watts—channels 8 to 13) with antenna heights averaging 1,000 feet above average terrain (depending on local topography). These facilities enable a station to radiate approximately 75 to 85 miles.   UHFs (114) vary greatly in terms of power—500,000 to 5 million watts.   The majority generally are assigned around 1 million watts and radiate about 50 to 60 miles.   The UHF 5 million watts power can compete with the VHF 100,000 to 316,000 watts power and 1,000 foot antenna if all sets in the area are equipped to receive both V and U channels.   Most TV markets are either all V or all U.   However, there are a few that have both types of signals. The majority of top 100 markets (95) have three or more originating TV stations.   Each network has a primary or secondary affiliate in each of these markets.

Types of Radio Stations   There are 4,156 AM radio stations and 1,753 FM stations.   Approximately one-third of the AM stations are affiliated with one of the four networks—ABC, CBS, MBS, NBC. Recently ABC grouped and expanded its affiliates to create three different "programing" networks to reach specific target audiences—contemporary, informational, entertainment.   In addition, it has created, for the first time, a major FM network consisting of 173 stations.

There are two portions of the broadcast spectrum assigned to commercial broadcasting: Amplitude modulated (AM) operating on 550 to 1,600 kilocycles, and frequency modulated (FM) operating on 88 to 108 megacycles.   As in TV, the effective radius depends on antenna height and power in addition to position on dial.   Effective radius in radio can have a much wider range than in TV—20 to 150 miles.

Many stations (1,500) operate in the daytime only.   Because evening atmospheric conditions generally broaden coverage areas, it is necessary for stations that continue to broadcast at night to reduce power or narrow their signal to avoid station overlap.

The Federal Communications Commission has licensed a selected number of stations (76) to operate at maximum power (50,000 watts) in the evening.   These outlets are known as *clear-channel stations* and have unusually broad coverage patterns.

I. 1. *Product:* _____ 2. Date: _____

3. **Budget: $ (M)** _____ 4. Advertising period: Start date _____ ; End date _____

II. 5. *Purpose of Plan* (Check where applicable):

a. _____ Introduction b. _____ Annual c. _____ Heavy-up d. _____ Weight test: (_____ hi; _____ low)

e. _____ Other (pls. explain): _____

III. 6. *Marketing Objectives* (pls. describe briefly the two or three objectives you feel should govern the product's strategy. e.g., (a) where advertiser must use competitive pressure; (b) color a must):

a. _____

b. _____

c. _____

IV. 7. *Audience* (pls. check primary and secondary audiences by categories shown):

	Primary Audience			Secondary Audience		
	Female	Male		Female	Male	
7. Sex:	_____	_____		_____	_____	
8. Age (years):	_____ to 6;	_____ 6–11;	_____ 12–17;	_____ to 6;	_____ 6–11;	_____ 12–17;
	_____ 18–35;	_____ 36–49;	_____ 50+	_____ 18–35;	_____ 36–49;	_____ 50+
9. Income ($M):	_____ Under 5	_____ 5–9.9	_____ Over 10	_____ Under 5	_____ 5–9.9	_____ Over 10
10. Region *:	_____ NE	_____ EC	_____ WC _____ S _____ P	_____ NE	_____ EC	_____ WC _____ S _____ P
11. County size *:	_____ A	_____ B	_____ C _____ D	_____ A	_____ B	_____ C _____ D

* Nielsen

V. *Geographic Sales* (pls. first show per cent of product's sales by its sales territories; second, your best estimate of how per cents would fall if best *potentials* by sales territories could be realized:

	Per cent Total
12. Territories: _____	
13. Per cent sales: _____	100.0
14. Per cent potentials: _____	100.0
	100.0

VI. *Seasonal Sales* (pls. repeat same procedure as in V):

	J	F	M	1st Total	A	M	J	2d Total	J	A	S	3d Total	O	N	D	4th Total	Grand Total
15. Per cent sales:																	
16. Per cent potential:																	

VII. *Copy* (pls. check copy lengths and sizes available for consideration):

TV Per Cent	Radio Per Cent	Mags. Per Cent	Newsp. Per cent	Outdr. Per cent
60 sec.	60 sec.	P-4C	ROP	24
30 sec.	30 sec.	P-BW	Color	30

Other _____

VIII. *Media*

18. Reach and frequency (pls. check the relationship of reach to frequency you feel most pertinent to this product): _____ Reach more important; _____ Reach less important; _____ Reach and frequency equal

19. Competition (pls. list share of market, advertising budgets, and distribution among major media of product and its three largest competitors):

	Mkt. Share	Ad. Bud. $M	Per Cent Media Distribution						
			TV Net.	TV Spot	Radio	Mags.	Newsps.	Outdr.	Other
Prod.	.	.	—	—	—	—	—	—	—
A	.	.	—	—	—	—	—	—	—
B	.	.	—	—	—	—	—	—	—
C	.	.	—	—	—	—	—	—	—

IX. 20. *Other Considerations* (pls. check other items which must be considered in constructing this media plan):

a. _____ Corporate network support
b. _____ Ethnic and/or special market support
c. _____ Coupon and/or sampling promotion support
d. _____ Others

_____ (Signed) Senior Group Head

Figure 2 Target analysis form.

TV Universe

The basic fundamentals of the 1969 TV world (see Figures 3 and 4) are:

    58,000,000 TV homes, 95 per cent of all homes
    55 to 60 per cent equipped to receive UHF signals
    19,200,000 TV homes with two or more sets
    21,980,000 equipped with color

It is estimated that by the early 1970s 95 per cent of all TV homes will be equipped to receive all channels—both VHF and UHF.

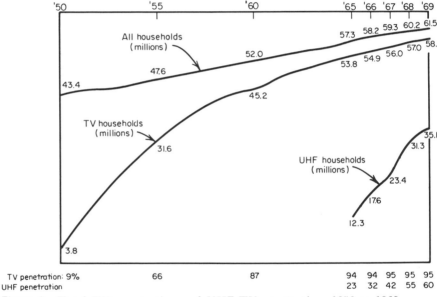

Figure 3　Total TV penetration and UHF TV penetration, 1950 to 1969. (*Derived from A. C. Nielsen Company estimates.*)

Radio Universe

The 1969 radio-world fundamentals (see Figures 5 and 6) are:

    59,000,000 radio homes, 97 per cent of all homes
    36,000,000 FM radio homes
    60 per cent of radio homes equipped for FM

282,000,000 radio sets
44,000,000 radio sets equipped for FM
1.5 radios per persons two years old and over

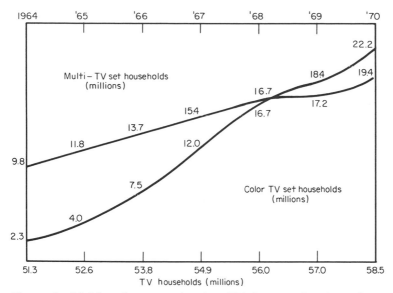

Figure 4   Multiset homes and color TV homes. (*Derived from A. C. Nielsen Company estimates.*)

TV Programing

The TV networks supply their affiliates with programing for daytime, 10 A.M. to 4:30 P.M. (Monday through Friday), and for prime time, 7:30 to 11 P.M. (Sunday through Saturday). They also supply network news (7 to 7:30 P.M., Monday through Friday, or 11 to 11:15 P.M., weekends), early morning shows (7 to 9 A.M., Monday through Friday), and late night shows 11:30 to 1 A.M., Monday through Friday). Affiliates do not always accept 100 per cent of the network fare. They have the option to select only those programs that they believe will do well in their areas. However, affiliates generally telecast a good portion of time supplied by the networks. The programing of the remaining time periods is planned and purchased individually by stations.

Independent TV stations (94) rely on movies, network reruns, and syndicated programs. There is no central source of programing for them. The larger stations with more capital produce their own shows and sometimes sell them to other independents.

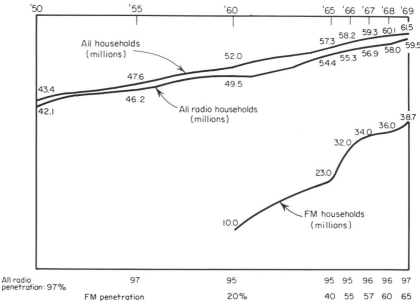

Figure 5 Radio penetration (1950 to 1969) and FM penetration (1960 to 1969). (*Source: RAB,* TV Digest, *NAFMB.*)

Radio Programing

The radio networks supply limited programing (2½ to 4 hours per day) to their affiliates, emphasizing national news and celebrities such as Arthur Godfrey. The stations tend to do their own programing (almost all of which is on tape), generally to reach a specific segment of the population. Primarily this programing is tied to individual musical preferences ranging from rock and roll to opera. In the major markets there are "talk" and "all-news" stations.

There are two kinds of FM stations. One is exclusively FM, the other is tied to an AM outlet bearing the same call letters. These AM and FM combinations broadcast identical programing (simulcast) approximately 35 per cent of the time and are sold as a package. The remaining 65 per cent is programed and sold separately. FM programing tends to be more sophisticated and, therefore, attracts better-educated and higher-income audiences.

Historically, merchandise and ideas have been demonstrated and sold on a person-to-person, door-to-door basis. Most sales experts agree that *man* is the most successful sales agent. He moves, he talks, he demonstrates the product or service to be sold. He gets his customers personally involved.

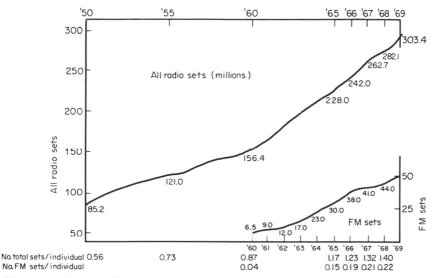

Figure 6 Total radio sets (1950 to 1968) and FM sets (1960 to 1968). (*Source: RAB,* TV Digest, *NAFMB.*)

Television is the closest thing to the ideal salesman—a real person—available within our current media environment. It moves, it talks, it demonstrates, it is in the home. It has all the live qualities of the personal touch effectively to sell a product.

On the other hand, radio capitalizes on its ability to create sound with special effects that stimulate a person's imagination into thinking that he sees a demonstration. In addition, radio listening is probably one of the last media exposures before entering a supermarket, a gasoline station, a drug store.

The broadcast medium delivers mass audiences efficiently. This, together with the unmeasured qualities of television and radio and their individual success stories, continues to encourage advertisers to invest in these media.

Investments in Broadcast

It is estimated that more than 55 per cent of 1968 national advertisers' investments in the five major media (almost $5.5 billion) was in broadcast (48 per cent in TV, 8 per cent in radio). Almost 60 per cent of television dollars were in network and 40 per cent in spot. Radio, on the other hand, was primarily used as a spot vehicle—83 per cent of its total.

In the same year the top ten package-goods advertisers invested $86 out of every $100 in the broadcast medium ($81 in TV, $5 in radio). However, within the top ten package-goods advertisers, there are wide ranges in the proportion of total investment assigned to broadcast. For example:

Per Cent Distribution of Total Ad Dollars

Media	Company A	Company B
Network TV	62.9	26.3
Spot TV	30.7	24.4
Total TV	93.6	50.7
Network radio	0.8	0.4
Spot radio	1.0	0.4
Total radio	1.8	0.8
Total broadcast	95.4	51.5

Further examination of actual schedules within the network TV area reveals that two different advertisers have each invested $1 million in the following pattern:

	No. of Commercials	No. of Minutes	No. of Programs
Advertiser 1	8	8	1
Advertiser 2	65	32½	8

This is an example of the possible variations that are available to advertisers. Advertiser 1 was seeking concentration; advertiser 2 was seeking dispersion.

TELEVISION

TV Usage Patterns

In order to invest effectively TV dollars to reach a brand's target audience, broadcast buyers must be acquainted with household and personal viewing patterns. These vary by hour of the day and by month of the year. The following charts reflect household tuning and total male and female viewing. In addition, there are viewing patterns of key age groups.

Households   The percentage of households tuning in television increases throughout the hours of the day, reaching a peak between 8:30 and 9 P.M., when approximately two-thirds of United States TV households are tuned in. From this point on there is a gradual drop-off for the remainder of the evening. (Figure 7.)

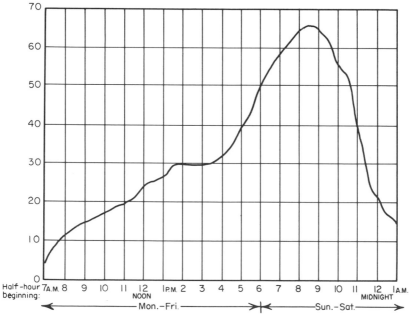

Figure 7 Percentage of United States households using television. (*Derived from A. C. Nielsen Company estimates.*)

Men   Levels of men viewing television are expectedly low during the weekday daytime hours.   Male viewing levels start to pick up during the early fringe-time period, reaching their peak between 9 and 9:30 P.M., similar to household tuning.   There is a sharp drop-off in late evening fringe.   With the exception of the late fringe-time period, the viewing levels of men aged eighteen to forty-nine are somewhat lower than those of total men.   (Figure 8.)

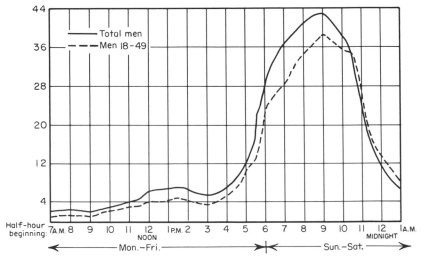

Figure 8   Percentage of men viewing television.   (*Derived from A. C. Nielsen Company estimates.*)

Women   Levels of women viewing television gradually build throughout the day, peaking from 12 to 2:30 P.M., with a slight drop-off in the late afternoon.   Viewing levels resume their growth around 6 P.M. and peak at 9 to 9:30 P.M.   Younger women's viewing patterns follow closely the viewing pattern of total women at slightly lower levels until 11:30 P.M., when their viewing slightly exceeds the level of all women.   (Figure 9.)

Teens and Children   During the major portion of the broadcast season (September to June), teen viewing is marginal during weekday daytime hours until approximately 3 P.M.   After-school hours exhibit a dramatic increase in teen viewing levels.   This viewing con-

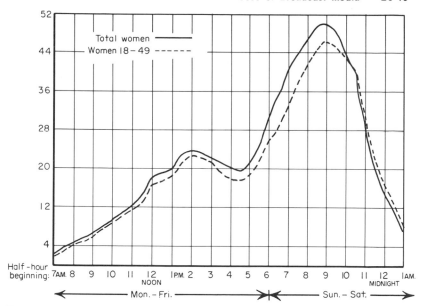

Figure 9 Percentage of women viewing television. (*Derived from A. C. Nielsen Company estimates.*)

tinues to accelerate until it peaks at 8 to 9 P.M. (early prime), and then drops off sharply for the remainder of the evening.

Children view television to a greater extent than teens throughout the day until 9 P.M.   During the daytime hours, their viewing peaks in the early morning, drops off in the early afternoon, and then builds rapidly until it peaks between 7:30 and 8:30 P.M.   There is some drop-off around 6 P.M., probably related to the dinner hour.

The previous usage charts indicate the potential within viewing groups by hour of the day.   Individual programs will vary depending on their share of the viewing potential.

Seasonal Variations The preceding data are based on the November to December period, and the levels indicated will vary by season.

Table 1 shows the seasonal variation of homes using television by broad dayparts for each month of the year.   In general, viewing levels within each daypart peak during the January to February period.   Early evening shows the greatest fluctuation from one period of the year to another, while late evening is the most stable through-out the year.

Seasonal viewing patterns among people follow closely the seasonal variations of homes using television with one exception. The patterns among teens and children will differ during the summer period when their viewing is not influenced by school semesters.

Levels of Attentiveness Homes using television or people using television are strictly quantitative measures relating to tuning or viewing activity.   Viewing activity is accompanied by a degree of interest referred to in Simmons as "attentiveness" (the degree to which a viewer is actively involved in paying attention to the program).

There is a wide variation in levels of attentiveness by time of day. Adult male viewers report higher levels of attention than women for all time segments of the day.   This difference is most pronounced during the weekend daytime hours when there is a preponderance of sports and male-oriented programing available.   Levels among women fluctuate to a greater extent than among men because of the

TABLE 1   **Seasonal Variation, United States Homes Using Television**

	Day	Early eve.	Prime eve.	Late eve.	Avg. early–late
Annual avg.	100	100	100	100	100
Jan.	119	128	115	108	121
Feb.	113	121	111	103	114
Mar.	103	110	108	97	106
Apr.	97	100	104	96	99
May	90	88	93	96	91
June	92	75	81	97	83
July	95	76	81	100	85
Aug.	97	78	84	100	86
Sept.	90	90	103	98	93
Oct.	96	98	104	100	99
Nov.	99	116	108	99	110
Dec.	108	121	109	104	115

SOURCE: Derived from A. C. Nielsen Company estimates.

greater influence of household activities on women's television-viewing habits.   Both men and women report their highest levels after 9 P.M.   See Table 2.

TABLE 2   Levels of Attentiveness,* By Daypart

	Women viewers	Men viewers	Index (women =100)
Weekday (Mon.–Fri.):			
6:00 A.M.–9:59 A.M.	37.4	NA	—
10:00 A.M.–11:59 A.M.	51.7	NA	
12:00 Noon–4:59 P.M.	63.9	NA	—
Weekend (Sat. and Sun.):			
8:00 A.M.–12:59 P.M.	41.0	56.3	137
1:00 P.M.–4:59 P.M.	52.3	76.0	145
All Days of Week (Sun.–Sat.):			
5:00 P.M.–7:29 P.M.	56.1	70.1	125
7:30 P.M.–8:59 P.M.	68.7	76.1	111
9:00 P.M.–10:59 P.M.	77.9	79.8	102
11:00 P.M.–11:29 P.M.	75.5	82.6	109
11:30 P.M.–12:59 A.M.	76.2	78.6	103

* Per cent of viewers paying full attention for most of time period.
SOURCE: W. R. Simmons, 1968.

Within any daypart there is a wide range of attentiveness for individual programs.   Evidence indicates that rating size and program type influence attention levels.

Attentiveness by Viewer Characteristics   High attentiveness levels are reported by adults:

Age fifty and over

In low-income, poorer-educated households

In smaller families

Conversely, the lowest attentiveness levels are reported by the younger, more active adults:

Age eighteen to thirty-four

In $10,000-plus, better-educated households

In larger families

NETWORK TV

Network television is principally telecast during weekday daytime hours of from 10 A.M. to 4:30 P.M. and the prime evening hours of from 7:30 to 11 P.M. (Sunday through Saturday). In addition to these basic network blocks, additional network programing is telecast during the weekend daytime hours (principally children's programs and sports) and in the early and late evening time period (news programs).

Network Telecasting Patterns

A network program is generally carried by a group of stations, each located in a different market and each usually referred to as a network *affiliate*. The list of stations carrying a program is called the *line-up*. The number of stations carrying the average daytime or evening network program approximates 190. This lineup will generally allow a program to be potentially seen by 90 to 99 per cent of all United States television homes.

The majority of the markets carry network programs on the same day. The following is an illustration of the standard evening telecast pattern.

Eastern time zone	8–9 P.M. local time (live)
Central time zone	7–8 P.M. local time (live)
Mountain time zone	7–8 P.M. local time (fed from Pacific time zone)
Pacific time zone	8–9 P.M. local time (3-hour delay)

This conventional telecast pattern does not apply to daytime network, especially in the Pacific time zone where each network currently has its own unique telecast pattern.

In some cases a market will carry a specific program telecast on a delay basis (on another day at another time). These delays influence normal programing environment patterns, and can have great influence on program performance in a particular local market.

Commercial time allowed within network programing is recommended by the National Association of Broadcasters. This is an organization made up of television and radio stations. One of the duties of this group is to set up allowable commercial time and positions within the broadcast day.   In the two network periods the general standards differ:

	No. of Minutes	No. of Positions
Daytime		
Half hour	6	6 *
Prime time		
Half hour	3	4
Hour	6	6 *

* Occasionally these positions can be increased to seven depending on program type and network negotiations.

This commercial time is generally purchased in 60-second units. However, there are many advertisers who split this minute into brand combinations of varying lengths—30/30; 40/20; 45/15; 50/ 10.   This practice is generally referred to in the industry as *piggy-backing,* and brand positions within these shared 60-second units are generally allocated by a corporate network unit (pool operation).

Sponsorship Patterns   Network minutes are sold on the basis of single sponsorship, alternate sponsorship, or participation.   (See Figure 10.)   The following outlines the various forms of alternate-sponsorship patterns.

EVENING NETWORK

	Sponsored Portion	
No. of Min. by Week 1 2 3 4	Hour Program	Half-hour Program
1 – 2 – 1 – 2	$\frac{1}{4}$ sponsorship	$\frac{1}{2}$ sponsorship
2 – 0 – 2 – 0	$\frac{1}{6}$ sponsorship	$\frac{1}{3}$ sponsorship
1 – 0 – 1 – 0	$\frac{1}{12}$ participation	$\frac{1}{6}$ participation
2 – 2 – 2 – 2	$\frac{1}{3}$ participation	$\frac{2}{3}$ participation
1 – 1 – 1 – 1	$\frac{1}{6}$ participation	$\frac{1}{3}$ participation

DAYTIME NETWORK

Weekly Pattern—60 Seconds	Sponsored Portion of Half-hour Program
1–5 commercials	$\frac{1}{30}$–$\frac{1}{6}$
5–10 commercials	$\frac{1}{60}$–$\frac{1}{3}$
10–15 commercials	$\frac{1}{3}$ –$\frac{1}{2}$

Note: Daytime assumes five programs per week.

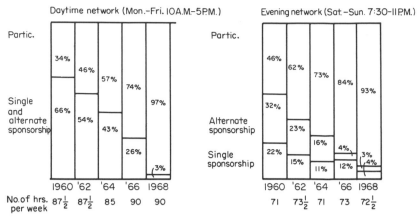

Figure 10 Trend of how network time has been sold, per cent distribution. (*Derived from A. C. Nielsen Company estimates.*)

Since the early 1960s there has been a great change in network buying. Participating minutes, which accounted for approximately 34 to 46 per cent of total network minutes in 1960, have shown a continuous increase and currently account for 93 to 97 per cent of total network minutes, at the expense of sponsored minutes.

EVENING

Sponsored Portion of—

Hour Program	*Half-hour Program*
¼ sponsorship	½ sponsorship * †
⅙ sponsorship	⅓ participation * †
½ sponsorship	⅙ participation ‡
⅓ sponsorship	⅔ sponsorship * † §
⅙ participation	⅓ participation * †

* Full product protection in half-hour program.
† Half-hour protection in hour or longer programs.
‡ Possible product protection depends on network negotiations.
§ Full product protection in hour program.

DAYTIME

Sponsored Portion within Half Hour	*Product Protection*
¹⁄₃₀ to ⅙	Scatter purchase, no PP
⅙ to ⅓	Quarter-hour PP
⅓ to ½	Full PP (within half hour)

Product Protection

Product protection is only granted on sponsored minutes. Some sponsorship patterns offer definite product-protection guarantees, while others are dependent upon network negotiations. The following tables indicate the degree of product protection involved in specific network purchases.

Network Cost

Wide ranges exist between day and evening commerical costs because of variations in time and talent charges. These variations are a reflection of audience potentials available in these dayparts. Figure 11 shows the trend of the average cost per commercial minute in these two time periods. Individual programs can fluctuate widely around these averages.

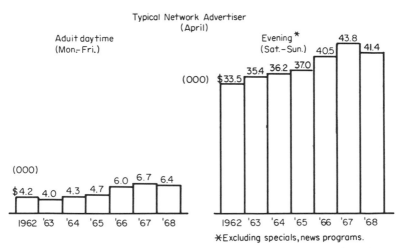

Figure 11 Network minute costs. (*Derived from A. C. Nielsen Company estimates.*)

Network costs also fluctuate seasonally and are dependent on whether it is a buyer's or seller's market. Advertisers who deem it essential to have franchise network position will commit prior to the season at premium costs. Additional dollars may be held in reserve for possible "opportunistic" buys as the season progresses.

Network minute costs have been increasing slightly in both day-parts.

Network Audience

In the section dealing with homes and people using television, we observed different levels of viewing activity by hour of the day. Network programs achieve varying shares of this available audience, resulting in wide ranges of audience performance for individual programs. Average household program performance for daytime and evening programs over the last several years is illustrated in Figure 12. This chart indicates daytime program ratings averaging some-

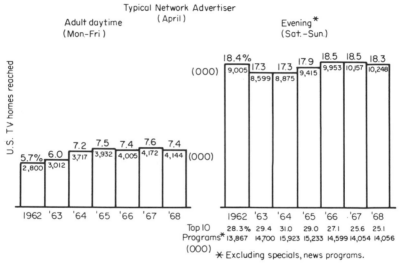

Figure 12 Network rating trends 1962–1968. Percentage of United States TV households tuned in average minute. (*Derived from A. C. Nielsen Company estimates.*)

place between 6 to 7 per cent, while evening is around 17 to 18 per cent. Although there has been little fluctuation in average ratings, the number of households has generally shown slight increases because of the growth of the television universe.

One interesting development observed from the Nielsen Multi-Network Area Reports—thirty top markets representing 50 per cent of all United States TV homes—indicates that evening's network share of total television activity is gradually decreasing (see table below).   Whether this is an indication of a growing disenchantment with network programing or a reflection of improved independent programing is difficult to assess.   If this trend becomes more pronounced, it would be reflected in lower evening network ratings.

Evening Network Share of Total Viewing
Nielsen Thirty-Market Multi network Area

Broadcast Season	Network Share	Independent Share
1965–1966	86.1	13.9
1966–1967	83.4	16.6
1967–1968	81.6	18.4
1968–1969 *	81.0	19.0

* Estimated on season-to-date information.   (September, 1968 to February, 1969).

Although programs achieve the average ratings shown in Figure 12 on a total United States basis, rating performance for these programs varies by location and characteristics of *household*.

Individual market ratings for a specific program can vary greatly from its total United States performance.   The factors that influence local market-rating levels are atypical programing environment because of delay factors, number of stations in the market sharing the available audience, and local programing appeal.

These local market variations in network rating performance result in the utilization of TV spot for network equalization.   Television spot will be discussed at length in a later section.

The foregoing discussion involved program performance on a household basis.   Program performance by age and sex will vary, dependent upon the availability of the specific demographic group within the time period as well as the individual program's appeal. See Figure 13.

Network Efficiencies

Interrelating audience levels and average commercial costs produces cost per thousand (CPM) or program efficiency performance.   These vary widely by program within any daypart.   Figure 14 indicates the average cost per thousand commercial minutes in network.   Although the daytime pattern is somewhat erratic, the evening pattern

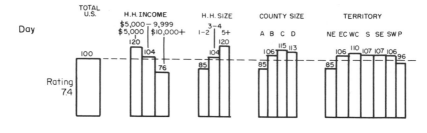

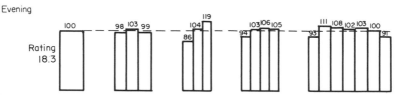

Figure 13 Characteristics of network audiences. (*Derived from A. C. Nielsen Company estimates.*)

has been relatively flat since 1963. The increases in cost per commercial minute appear to be compensated for by an expanding United States TV household universe.

The data in Figure 14 reflect efficiencies on a household basis. Efficiencies within specific viewer groups will vary greatly depending upon the available audience by age and sex and the program appeal. The following table shows current efficiencies within certain key demographic groups for the average evening and average daytime program.

	Daytime (*Mon.–Fri.*) *10*A.M.–*5*P.M.	*Evening* (*Mon.–Sun.*) *7:30–11*P.M.
Avg. audience rating, per cent	7.4	18.3
CPM minutes	$6.4	$41.4
CPM commercial minutes		
Homes	$1.56	$4.05
Women 18–49	3.06	8.10
Women 50+	4.11	11.25
Men 18–49	—	10.95
Men 50+	—	13.97

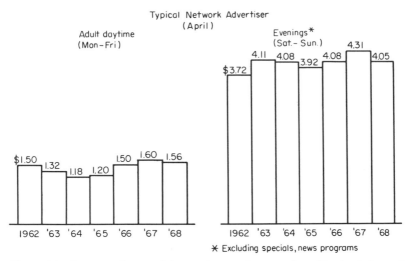

Figure 14 Cost-per-thousand home impression trends. (*Derived from A. C. Nielsen company estimates.*)

The network television programs with the lowest CPMs are not necessarily the programs that deliver the most homes.

As Table 3 indicates, Joey Bishop, ranking fourth on cost effi-

TABLE 3 Top Ten Evening Programs *

Name	Homes eff. CPM, in dollars	Rank	Homes, in thousands	Rank
Rowan and Martin	2.63	1	17,440	1
Newlywed Game	2.92	2	10,090	51
Jeannie	3.05	3	11,460	31
Joey Bishop	3.22	4	2,170	85
Lawrence Welk	3.26	5	11,630	26
Daniel Boone	3.31	6	11,630	26
Dating Game	3.32	7	9,010	59
Virginian	3.43	8	13,110	13
High Chapparral	3.48	9	10,320	48
Gunsmoke	3.51	10	14,140	8

* Excluding news programs.

SOURCE: Derived from A. C. Nielsen Company estimates, 1968 to 1969 Nighttime Network TV Schedule.

ciency, ranks eighty-fifth in actual homes delivered. Program performance within any demographic group would also show wide variations if ranked on efficiencies or audience size.

Cumulative Audience and Frequency

The total delivery of a combination of commercials represents the gross audience—for example, four commercials each delivering 10 million homes (17.5 rating) would total 40 million gross home impressions (70 gross rating points). However, some of the homes reached by any one commercial will also be exposed to one or more of the other commercials. The total number of different homes reached by a combination is referred to as the *cumulative audience* or total unduplicated reach of the schedule. The ability of pressure within daytime network versus evening network to reach different homes will be dependent upon the potential audience available in the daypart. As indicated in the following table, evening network —which reaches more than 90 per cent of homes in a week—will have a much greater capacity to extend the unduplicated reach of the schedule, since day has a ceiling of only 74 per cent in the average week.

Per cent *TV Homes Tuned*	*Day (Mon.–Fri.)* *10A.M.–5P.M.*	*Evening (Sun.–Sat.)* *7P.M.–11P.M.*
Average minute	23.5	57.9
Average day	55.9	79.2
Average week	74.4	92.8

Other critical factors influencing the unduplicated reach performance of a particular network schedule within daytime or evening relate to commercial dispersion by time of day, network, and program.

Figure 15 is an example of a specific budget level at typical cost efficiencies spent 100 per cent in day, 100 per cent in evening, or 50/50 day-evening. Since pressure delivered, and unduplicated reach achieved, will naturally vary dependent upon commercial length, we have illustrated the budget on a 60-second and a 30-second basis, as well as a split-dollar allocation in 60- and 30-second units.

The average frequency indicated in these illustrations is a result of the gross schedule delivery divided by the number of different homes reached. The figure reported may be expressed in terms of fractional frequency (i.e., 5.7), whereas in fact homes are exposed to a specific number of commercials, one, two, three, four, or more, up to a possible maximum of the total number of commercials in the schedule. At this point there are no studies on the relative value of homes exposed to one, two, three, four, or more commercials of a product. This is likely to vary by product class, and would be dependent to some extent on copy treatment and competitive frequency.

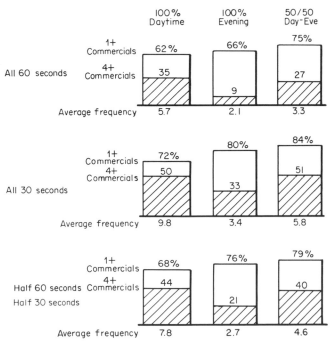

Figure 15 Example of estimated four-week reach and frequency with $4 million annual budget in TV network, percentage of United States TV households. (*Source: Ted Bates & Co. estimates.*)

In Figure 15 a $4 million budget using 60-second commercials in daytime network at typical efficiency levels will reach 62 per cent of TV households one or more times (35 per cent of TV households four or more times) in a four-week period. This figure illustrates evening's capacity to extend total reach and daytime's advantage on a frequency basis.

TV SPOT

TV spot refers to the purchase of a single unit of commercial time within a single market as contrasted to a network purchase where large groups of markets are purchased simultaneously. In effect, spot is a local medium, whereas network is a national medium.

TV spot expenditures are concentrated principally in the daytime and the early and late evening fringe-time periods. Spot is also purchased within prime time. Spot availabilities on network stations are generally limited to station breaks (10, 20, 30, or 40 seconds) while 60-second spot in prime time is principally sold on independent stations. The networks continue to offer an unsold network minute to their affiliates to be sold locally. The following table indicates the spot dayparts by time zone.

	Eastern Time Zone	*Central Time Zone*	*Pacific Time Zone*
Day	Sign on– 5:00 P.M.	Sign on– 4:00 P.M.	Sign on–5:00 P.M.
Early	5:00 P.M.– 7:30 P.M.	4:00 P.M.– 6:30 P.M.	5:00 P.M.–7:00 P.M.
Prime	7:30 P.M.–11:00 P.M.	6:30 P.M.–10:00 P.M.	7:30 P.M.–11:00 P.M.
Late	11:00 P.M.–Sign off	10:00 P.M.–Sign off	11:00 P.M.– Sign off

Selection of daypart is contingent upon audience target and potential offered by that daypart. Within any daypart, potential of a specific target group will vary by local programing.

Buying and Scheduling Procedures

Buying (agency) and selling (station) local television time is coordinated by sales organizations, each representing a different group of stations situated throughout the country. When purchasing spot, the agency buyer will make contact with the representatives for the stations in the particular market to secure the current availabilities on their stations that meet the brand's requirements.

TV spot decisions can be based on combinations of the following factors:

1. Efficiency in delivering households
2. Efficiency in delivering target audiences
3. Efficiency in delivering heavy product users
4. Rating size

5. Reach criteria based on dispersion over stations and dayparts

TV spots are sold in varying lengths generally ranging from 10 to 60 seconds.

Today there are many types of buys available within and between programs:

1. Participations in local syndicated programing
2. Rotating spots within varied dayparts over different days of the week (orbit plan)
3. Package buys—group of spots sold collectively
4. Station breaks—between programs (10- to 40-second commercials with some 60-second units available on independents)

In recent years there have been increased efforts to capitalize on the scheduling flexibility of spot TV. This flexibility enables advertisers to schedule in waves—also referred to as *flighting* (extra impact coinciding with special sales efforts)—or in limited selling seasons (toys at Christmas; cold remedies in winter).

Because of the complexity of spot buying today, some advertisers have elected to have spots purchased by a centralized pool. Spot positions within this corporate pool are then allocated to individual brands, with, at times, two brands sharing a location (30/30, 45/15, etc.). As in network, this technique is commonly referred to as *piggybacking*.

Among some of the major advantages to an advertiser using a centralized pool are:

1. Centralized administration
2. Allowance for longer-term commitments, and generation of a higher percentage of franchise locations
3. Improved merchandising cooperation from stations
4. Standardization of reporting formats to advertisers

These advantages generate economies for the advertiser which can be observed directly through improved CPMs and reduced operating costs. In addition, a corporate pool offers the advertiser better control over the spot-buying operation.

Advertisers often utilize spot TV as a means to simulate a national network TV campaign instead of using the more expensive network cut-ins. This is generally implemented in test markets projectable to the total United States or for new-product introductions.

Costs

Spot costs and discounts vary by market, stations, and daypart, principally dependent upon estimated audience delivery.

As expected, costs are higher in larger markets. Stations' costs within a specific market will be dependent upon their coverage patterns and their share of market audience. There are certain markets, because of demand, that establish higher-than-average rates.

60-second Spot TV Buying Guide
Average Cost per Market

Market Groups	Day	Early Eve.	Prime Eve.	Late Eve.
1–10	$195	$365	$325	$480
11–20	90	175	220	205
21–30	80	140	200	155
31–40	70	125	195	130
41–50	50	95	150	105
51–100	40	65	105	50

NOTE: Prime evening 60-second spots, of necessity, reflect a concentration of expenditures on independent stations and limited use of network affiliates.

The figures in the preceding table reflect the average cost per market within market groups. Individual markets within any market grouping can vary greatly from this average. Spot rate cards by market and by station are found in Standard Rate & Data Service. They are complex, comprehensive, and in most cases, spots are grouped by broad dayparts. There are a number of stations that establish costs based on estimated home audiences (known as *P* or *grid cards*).

Audience

The audience delivered by a particular TV spot (as defined in local rating services) is measured within three geographical areas.

1. Metropolitan areas or the standard metropolitan statistical area as defined by the Bureau of the Census

2. Television advertising areas (designated market area or area of dominant influence) which include those counties which are exclusively assigned to the market achieving dominant audience viewing

3. Total area which includes all counties that account for in excess of 95 per cent of a station's audiences

The cumulative coverage of markets grouped in order of prime-time quarter-hour audience delivery represents the following percentage coverage of United States TV households.

	Per Cent United States Coverage	
Market Groups	*Group*	*Cum.*
1–10	37	37
11–20	12	49
21–30	9	58
31–40	6	64
41–50	6	70
51–100	18	88

Audience levels for individual spot buys can show wide variations. The following factors influence the size of audience delivered by a specific buy:

1. Size of market
2. Station coverage
3. Station share (program popularity)
4. Day part

The TV homes (absolute numbers) delivered by a particular spot can be expressed in terms of percentage rating in either the metropolitan area or the television advertising area.

The average metropolitan ratings within various dayparts by market grouping are listed in the following table. Ratings generally increase for groups of smaller-sized markets because of more limited competition from other stations.

	Average Metropolitan Ratings			
Market Groups	*Day*	*Early Eve.*	*Prime Eve.*	*Late Eve.*
1–10	5.7	8.6	5.4	7.8
11–20	7.0	11.8	11.8	11.7
21–30	8.1	13.0	14.1	11.4
31–40	9.1	16.8	19.8	14.0
41–50	8.1	14.3	16.9	12.7
51–100	9.5	16.5	19.2	12.3

NOTE: Prime evening 60-second spots, of necessity, reflect a concentration of expenditures on independent stations and limited use of network affiliates.

In the case of local markets, household demography (i.e., income, education) is not so readily available as in the case of network. However, viewer information by age and sex is reported in individual local market reports. Table 4 reports average viewers per home by daypart. These averages reflect what is generally true

TABLE 4   **Audience Composition by Dayparts, Viewers per Average Home**

	Day	Early eve.	Prime eve.	Late eve.	Avg. early–late
Total	1.52	1.98	2.18	1.69	1.84
(2+)	100%	100%	100%	100%	100%
Men	0.24	0.52	0.69	0.64	0.58
(18+)	16%	26%	32%	38%	32%
Women	0.85	0.76	0.87	0.85	0.80
(18+)	56%	38%	40%	50%	43%
Ladies of House	0.72	0.64	0.73	0.73	0.68
	47%	32%	33%	43%	37%
Adults	1.09	1.28	1.56	1.49	1.38
(18+)	72%	64%	72%	88%	75%
Teens	0.10	0.19	0.21	0.12	0.16
(12–17)	7%	10%	10%	7%	9%
Children	0.33	0.51	0.41	0.08	0.30
(2–11)	21%	26%	18%	5%	16%
Men	0.05	0.14	0.20	0.20	0.17
(18–34)	3%	7%	9%	12%	9%
Women	0.29	0.21	0.27	0.30	0.26
(18–34)	19%	11%	12%	18%	14%
Adults	0.34	0.35	0.47	0.50	0.43
(18–34)	22%	18%	21%	30%	23%
Men	0.10	0.27	0.40	0.41	0.34
(18–49)	7%	14%	18%	24%	18%
Women	0.5C	0.41	0.52	0.55	0.48
(18–49)	33%	21%	24%	33%	26%
Adults	0.60	0.68	0.92	0.96	0.82
(18–49)	40%	35%	42%	57%	44%

NOTE: The above March-April audience composition can be considered a typical pattern of the entire broadcast year, except for some summer variances among youth audiences.

SOURCE: A. C. Nielsen Company.

within individual markets; however, specific program adjacencies (for example, childrens' programs versus news in early evening) would show wide differences in viewer profile.

Efficiencies

As in network, relating spot audiences to costs produces CPMs or spot efficiencies. The following table shows average 60-second spot efficiencies within daypart by market groupings.

Average Cost Efficiencies

Market Groups	Day	Early Eve.	Prime Eve.	Late Eve.
1–10	$1.65	$2.10	$2.40	$2.70
11–20	1.95	2.20	2.75	2.70
21–30	2.00	2.10	2.90	2.80
31–40	1.90	1.85	2.60	2.75
41–50	1.80	1.90	2.70	2.55
51–100	1.60	1.80	2.40	2.30

NOTE: Prime evening 60-second spots, of necessity, reflect a concentration of expenditures on independent stations and limited use of network affiliates.

The data presented above dealt with household efficiencies on a 60-second basis. In a piggyback situation, the cost efficiency of each 30-second portion would be half of the 60-second CPM. Because of this efficiency advantage, there has been an increasing tendency on the part of advertisers to use 30-second commercials, especially in view of the fact that research has indicated that the recall value of a 30-second commercial is approximately two-thirds the value of a minute.

There is evidence that the 30-second commercial length may replace the 60-second length as the basic purchase unit—at 50 per cent of the minute rate.

Typical 60-second efficiencies by specific viewer groups are shown in Table 5. These data reflect averages, and can vary within any market, station, or daypart, contingent upon buying criteria.

Cumulative Audience and Frequency

In the same manner as the combination of network locations delivers a certain gross audience which translates into an unduplicated audience reached at a specific average frequency, combinations of spot locations within a market or group of markets will also represent a specific level of reach, frequency, and gross pressure delivered. The only difference between network and spot is that, normally, network reach and frequency are examined on the basis of the total United States TV universe, while spot buys are evaluated in terms of individual market (or total market list), reach, and frequency. The size of the total market area is referred to as the *coverage of the spot list*. As in network, dispersion of TV spot locations will influence reach performances. Dispersion may be assured in spot through the use of different stations, different dayparts, rotation scheduling patterns.

TABLE 5 **60-second Spot TV Efficiencies (February–March), Cost per Thousand**

Demographic	Day	Early eve.	Prime eve.	Late eve.
Total homes	1.75	2.10	2.55	2.65
Total adults	1.55	1.60	1.70	1.70
Total men	5.65	3.65	3.95	3.85
Men 18–49	11.30	6.70	6.95	6.25
Men 50+	11.25	8.15	9.15	10.00
Total women	2.15	2.80	3.05	3.05
Women 18–49	3.65	4.95	5.20	4.90
Women 50+	5.10	6.50	7.25	8.20
Teens	11.55	7.60	10.55	20.70

Figure 16 illustrates reach performances of specific spot buys in a local market with different degrees of concentration or dispersion.

RADIO

In the previous section on television, we reported usage by household and key demographics. Since radio has become such a personalized medium, data are generally not available on a household basis. Listening activity is available for men, women, and teens. Because of the different listening patterns—weekday versus weekend—these are presented separately.

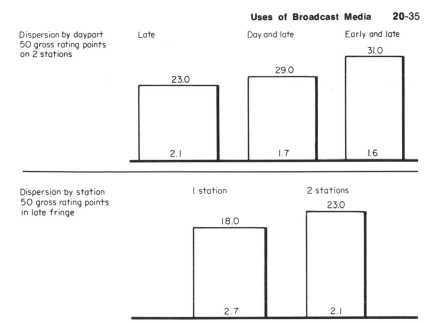

Figure 16 Weekly TV spot reach and frequency. (*Derived from A. C. Nielsen Company estimates.*)

Weekday Listening

Radio listening on weekdays can be divided into the following distinct dayparts:

Morning drive time	6–9 A.M.
Housewife time	9 A.M.–3 P.M.
Afternoon drive time	3–7 P.M.
Evening	7 P.M.–midnight

Figure 17 reports total radio usage (in and out of home) for men, women, and teens.

Listening of all age groups peaks between 7 and 8 A.M. when people turn to radio for weather, news, time, etc.

Women's listening gradually drops off until 11 A.M., when it levels off for the remainder of housewife time.

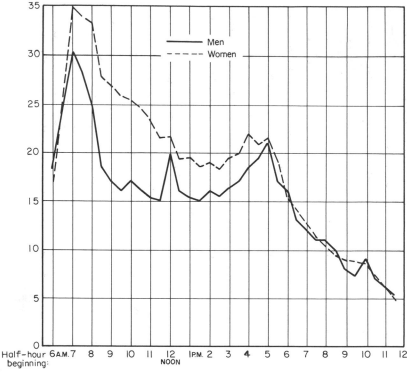

Figure 17 Percentage of adults listening to radio. (*Derived from Brand Rating Research–RADAR estimates.*)

Listening levels by men decline dramatically immediately after morning drive time, remain constant throughout housewife time, and increase slightly in afternoon drive time.

After 5:30 P.M. listening of both men and women drops dramatically to the lowest levels of the day when TV approaches its highest usage levels.

Usage patterns of the younger versus older adults are similar. Variations are slight.

Teen-agers' listening (based on the March-April period) fluctuates to a greater degree by hour of the day than adult listening. This reflects inability to listen to radio during the normal school hours. Immediately after school recesses, teen-agers' listening increases dramatically, and exceeds adults' listening in the afternoon drive time.

While adults abandon radio during television's prime-time hours, teen-agers can be reached in large numbers during this time period.

Variations in Weekend Listening

The weekend radio listening pattern for each demographic group varies from weekday listening patterns.

Usage peaks in midmorning and remains fairly consistent throughout the day (until 4 to 5 P.M.). Adults' listening falls off dramatically during the early evening hours. Teens, on the other hand, can be reached in large numbers all day including the early evening hours.

Seasonal Variation

There are slight seasonal variations in adults' radio listening except for the third quarter. In the morning (6 to 10 A.M.) quarter-hour usage falls approximately 15 per cent below the annual average, while the evening (7 P.M. to midnight) shows an increase of 25 per cent. See Table 6.

TABLE 6   Index of Seasonal Variation in Radio Usage by Daypart, Average Quarter-hour Usage (Mon.–Fri.)

	6–10 A.M.	10–3 P.M.	3–7 P.M.	7–Midnight
Annual avg.	100	100	100	100
Adult men:				
1st qtr	108	100	106	80
2nd qtr	108	100	98	107
3rd qtr	89	110	106	133
4th qtr	95	90	90	80
Adult women:				
1st qtr	109	103	106	80
2nd qtr	109	97	106	107
3rd qtr	84	103	98	120
4th qtr	98	97	90	93
Teens:				
1st qtr	107	39	113	93
2nd qtr	107	64	97	111
3rd qtr	88	245	97	111
4th qtr	98	52	91	85

Teen-agers' listening habits are also fairly consistent throughout the year, except for the midday time period, which shows a tremendous increase during the summer when school does not interfere with radio listening.

Where Listening Occurs

It is estimated that 70 per cent of all radio listening takes place within the homes, the remaining occurring in automobiles, backyards, etc.

This relationship, as expected, differs for men. During weekday drive time, men split their listening approximately fifty-fifty between in and out of home. This distribution remains fairly constant for both summer and winter periods.

Because women travel less during the weekday drive-time period, their listening tends to be concentrated more in the home (75 per cent). This distribution also is fairly stable throughout the year. Older women would have correspondingly less out-of-home listening because of their more limited activity.

A small portion of teens' listening is out of home during the winter (15 per cent), but this doubles in the summertime (30 per cent).

Profile of the Male and Female Radio Listener

Figures 18 and 19 describe radio listeners in terms of geographical location and socioeconomic characteristics.

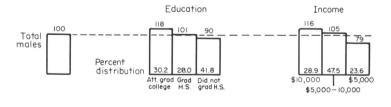

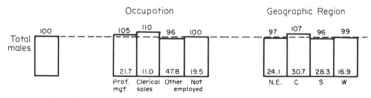

Figure 18 Characteristics of adult male listeners, by selected demographics. (*Derived from W. R. Simmons & Associates Research, Inc., estimates.*)

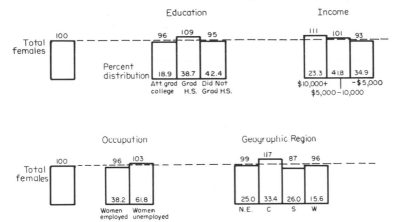

Figure 19 Characteristics of adult female listeners, by selected demographics. (*Derived from W. R. Simmons & Associates Research, Inc., estimates.*)

The better-educated, upper-income male listens more than the average male. Variations by occupation and geographical location appear to be minimal.

Women listeners also appear to be better educated and to reside in households with higher incomes. There seems to be strength in the Central Region and weakness in the South.

NETWORK RADIO

Programing

The networks supply a limited amount of programing to their affiliates ranging from 1½ to 4 hours per day. This is composed mainly of five-minute programs broadcast hourly that include national news, features, or sports. CBS Network also offers a half-hour of Arthur Godfrey.

Network radio took on a new complexion recently as the ABC Network grouped and expanded its affiliates to create four different programing networks to reach specific target audience—contemporary, information, entertainment, and FM. Programing still remains predominantly news and sports.

Since ABC Network affiliates provide the majority of their own programing, they are chiefly responsible for the audience profile of their stations.   ABC, by grouping stations with similar formats and inserting five-minute network news and sports, can provide advertisers with an opportunity to reach specific audiences.

The following table indicates the number of stations and the number of hours (Monday through Friday) recently offered by each network.   Each network will guarantee a 95 to 100 per cent station clearance which provides 90 to 95 per cent potential United States radio home coverage.

Network	No. of Stations	No. of Hours of Programing
ABC-Contemporary	163	1½
Information	292	2¼
Entertainment	205	1½
FM	173	1
CBS	244	4
MBS	500	1½
NBC	218	2½

Sponsorship Patterns

The five-minute program segments provided by the networks generally allow 1 to 1½ minutes of commercial time.   Ten-minute programs are allowed a maximum of 2½ minutes; quarter-hour programs, 3 minutes of commercial time.

This commercial time is usually sold in packages of 60- or 30-second lengths, or combinations of these.   Generally, the larger the package, the cheaper the unit cost.

These commercials can be scheduled in one of two different ways —within specific designated network segments or run-of-station (ROS) network segments.   Although the ROS buy offers less audience control, it is usually sold at lower unit costs.

Radio Costs

As previously mentioned, the limited amount of network time available is generally sold in packages of both 60- and 30-second commercials.   The following example of rates reflect a 95 to 100 per cent clearance guarantee, providing approximately 90 to 95 per cent potential United States radio home coverage.

These costs have not fluctuated much during the past 10 years. Today it would cost approximately 6 per cent more to purchase a network minute than in 1960.

Network	60-second Range	30-second Range
CBS	$750–900	$550–700
MBS	750–900	500–600
NBC	800–1,000	650–750
ABC-Contemporary	900–1,000	675–750
Information	550–600	400–450
Entertainment	450–500	325–375
FM	250–300	175–225

Network Radio Audiences

While costs have remained relatively stable, audience levels for network radio have increased, paralleling the growth in total radio homes (a 9 per cent increase from 1960 to 1969).

Audiences of specific programs range from approximately 400,000 to 3 million listeners age twelve and older. These audience levels translate into ratings of 0.3 to 2.0 per cent.

Network affiliates tend to broadcast programs appealing to older men and women. Consequently, network programs positioned in this environment inherit this type of audience. As Table 7 indicates, basic programs on each network are skewing toward older adults.

Several ABC subnetworks, incorporating stations with younger audience profiles, should enable ABC to deliver this audience segment. (National audience composition data are not currently available on these networks.)

Network radio audiences are currently measured nationally twice a year—covering the spring and fall seasons. These limited audience data related to network costs produce adult listener efficiencies which range widely. Network radio, however, is a highly negotiable medium. Individual packages can be structured to provide competitive efficiencies within the medium.

Network Radio Cumulative Audience

The increase in the number of radio stations and the trend toward programing directed at specific target audiences has served to fragment both network and spot radio audiences.

TABLE 7   Network Radio Audience Composition, Per Cent Distribution

	Total persons	Women		Men		Teens
		18–49 yr	50+ yr	18–49 yr	50+ yr	
Total United States·	100.0	28.5	15.9	25.7	14.5	15.4
Network and Program Type						
CBS Network:						
News:						
%	100	27.0	28.0	22.0	21.6	1.4
Index	—	95	176	86	149	0.09
Sports:						
%	100	19.7	28.9	22.7	25.9	2.8
Index	—	69	182	88	179	18
Arthur Godfrey:						
%	100	32.1	27.0	17.3	23.1	
Index	—	113	170	67	159	
Dear Abbey:						
%	100	29.0	30.2	18.7	20.4	1.7
Index	—	102	190	73	141	11
Dimensions in Health:						
%	100	27.1	28.1	21.7	22.2	0.9
Index	—	95	177	84	153	0.06
NBC Network:						
News:						
%	100	25.9	25.4	24.0	17.0	7.7
Index	—	91	160	93	117	50
Sports:						
%	100	29.6	17.4	24.6	19.3	9.1
Index	—	104	109	96	133	59
Mutual Network:						
News:						
%	100	28.3	21.0	25.2	12.3	13.2
Index	—	99	132	98	85	86
Sports:						
%	100	27.9	17.6	24.6	13.6	16.3
Index	—	98	111	96	94	106
ABC—4 Network		Not available				

All networks collectively reach 36 per cent of persons age twelve and older in the average day and 59 per cent in the average week.   In relation to radio's total reach potential (77 per cent daily, 95 per cent weekly), network delivers less than half daily and less than two-thirds weekly. These figures describe the maximum potential offered by network. To achieve these levels an advertiser would have to buy *all* network daily and weekly positions.

Each network independently delivers a relatively small unduplicated audience—2 to 11 per cent daily and 5 to 23 per cent weekly. To reach a broad cross section of the available network radio audience, it is necessary to employ multinetwork schedules.

RADIO SPOT

The proportion of total radio expenditures allocated to spot serves to position the importance of spot within the medium. More than 90 per cent of total dollars invested in radio represent local and national spot expenditures. This allocation is attributed to the large number of independent stations (2,663) and the limited amount of network programing.

Programing

Local radio programing has become more diversified in order to satisfy the interests of individual listeners. More stations are using uniform formats throughout the broadcasting day to attract particular segments of the population.

The majority of this programing is music, and the listener has a wide spectrum to choose from. An interested person, in a large market, can generally find a station with specific musical programing— jazz, folk, blues, country and western, show music.

The majority of the population relies on radio for late-breaking news developments; therefore, virtually all stations, regardless of format, regularly schedule news reports.

Since stations tend to follow a uniform format throughout the broadcast day, people select and are loyal to a limited number of stations.

	Average Number of Stations Tuned to per Listener				
	6–10 A.M.	*10–3* P.M.	*3–7* P.M.	*7–Mid- night*	*Total day*
Men	1.4	1.4	1.5	1.4	2.3
Women	1.4	1.4	1.4	1.3	2.2
Teens	1.4	1.3	1.5	1.4	2.1

Basically, radio station formats can be classified within the following broad categories:

Talk Programs and News   Reporting and discussing a wide range of topics.   Popular among older persons, college graduates, and professional people.

Music, Sports, News   Popular music, sports reporting, and news coverage.   Audience skews toward thirty-five years and older, and better-educated people.

Ethnic (Negro)   Generally geared to younger generation.   Programing includes predominantly contemporary music and commentary.   There are more than 100 stations programing exclusively for Negroes.   In addition there are hundreds of stations carrying such programing on a part-time basis.   Foreign-language radio programing has declined over the years, except in concentrated Spanish markets such as New York, Los Angeles, and San Antonio.

Contemporary   Synonymous with "Top 40," generally rock and roll, jazz, folk music.   Effective for reaching the youth market.

Popular Music   In some respects difficult to distinguish from contemporary—more prone toward standard-type music, film or show tunes, mood music.   General appeal with some skew toward younger, middle-class adults.

Good Music   Serious, semiclassical, and classical music, opera. Enjoyed by professional, better-educated adults.

Demographic characteristics are unique to individual stations. However, some generalization can be made by station type.

Allowable Commercial Time

Generally, radio stations, irrespective of affiliation or format, will conform to the recommended National Association of Broadcasters' commercial practices, calling for a maximum of eighteen minutes per hour.

Since radio does not have the advantages of sight and motion (demonstration values), most advertisers believe a full 60-second commercial is needed to communicate effectively the advertiser's message.   Stations themselves discourage the use of 30-second units by charging 80 per cent of the minute rate.

Costs

Over the past decade, radio spot costs have increased approximately 36 per cent, a much greater increase than indicated for network radio costs (10 per cent).   This is a reflection of the greater interest and demand for this segment of the medium.

Spot radio is generally purchased in "minute plans" (groups of six, twelve, or eighteen spots per station).   Discounts increase in accordance with volume.   The following table shows card rates using a twelve-plan across all dayparts.   Figures indicate the average cost for the top four stations per market.

AM Spot Cost per Minute within Market Group *

Market Groups	Costs
1–10	$623
11–20	352
21–30	305
31–40	214
41–50	234
51–100	704

* Based on average day and evening cost of top four stations in each market.

Based on these twelve-plan rates, a spot campaign in the top fifty markets, on the top three stations, would cost approximately $60,000 per week.   These costs would increase if an advertiser wanted to concentrate in prime radio time (drive time).

These data are based on rate card costs, and represent maximum figures for a radio campaign.   The actual cost of a campaign would be discounted to varying degrees depending upon the current buying environment and the negotiating ability of the buyer.

Coverage and Audience

The potential coverage of most radio stations ranges between 20 and 150 miles.   However, there can be a large differential between those who can listen and those who actually do.   Because individual markets usually have enough stations to offer the full spectrum of radio programing, and because listeners like to follow the local developments, they tend to listen to stations within their own market.

As a result of the fragmentation of the audience because of the wide choice of stations available, we see relatively small rating sizes, not only on a household basis, but also among individual population groups.

The following table shows typical rating levels within ranked market groups among key demographics.

Market Groups	Avg. Homes Ratings	Average Persons Ratings		
		Men 18–49	Women 18–49	Teens 12–17
1–10	2.4	1.5	2.0	1.2
11–20	3.7	2.3	3.0	1.7
21–30	3.3	2.1	2.8	1.6
31–40	3.4	2.2	2.9	1.6
41–50	3.2	2.1	2.8	1.7
51–100	3.0	2.0	2.7	1.6

The range of ratings, and the share of audience they represent, can vary greatly by market, by station. For example, the Los Angeles and Atlanta metropolitan areas both have the same usage level during morning drive time. However, the Los Angeles audience will be split among three times as many stations as the Atlanta audience.

Cost Efficiencies

Radio audience measurements in local markets are more readily available than audience data in network radio. Consequently, spot radio cost efficiencies can be estimated at least on a quarterly basis (top fifty markets—four reports per year from Pulse). The data below are based on averages of card rates and audience levels.

60-second AM Spot Radio Efficiencies, Cost per Thousand

Market Groups	Homes	Men 18–49	Women 18–49	Teens 12–17
1–10	$1.20	$3.40	$2.20	$ 6.90
11–50	1.70	5.50	3.40	10.60
51–100	2.60	8.00	4.60	16.00
1–100	1.70	5.10	3.20	10.70

NOTE: The above are based on averages and, therefore, can vary contingent upon buying criteria.

Advertisers directing a radio campaign to teen-agers would undoubtedly be able to improve the cost efficiencies on the table by positioning commercials on teen-appeal programing.

Cumulative Audience and Frequency

Radio has always been and still is recognized as a frequency medium.   Recent research has shown that radio also has the facility for delivering reach within a select target audience.   More than 90 per cent of all demographic groups are exposed to radio in the course of a week.   Since a large portion of radio activity is in non-network programing, these potential audiences would be available to spot radio advertisers.   Because of audience loyalty, it is necessary to buy many stations to achieve the reach potential of radio.

FM RADIO

Since AM listening accounts for approximately 85 to 90 per cent of radio listening, the preceding material has focused on an examina-

Characteristics of FM versus AM Radio Homes *

	Per Cent Total Radio Homes	100=Level among All Radio Homes	
		FM	AM
Household income:			
Under $5,000	32	64	126
$5,000–9,999	50	104	97
$10,000+	18	153	62
	100		
Age of head of house:			
18–34	24	98	102
35–49	39	111	91
50+	37	90	108
	100		
Education of head of house:			
Grade school	19	66	128
Any high school	54	94	105
Any college	27	137	70
	100		

* How to read table: Among homes owning FM, there is 53 per cent greater concentration (153 index) of upper income ($10,000+) households than among homes owning all types of radios.

tion of AM radio.   Because of the increase of FM sets, FM programing, and the forming of the ABC FM Network, FM is emerging as an important part of the radio medium.

Currently 60 per cent of all radio homes are equipped to receive FM.   This figure will continue to grow since a good portion of sets now sold include FM.

The 60 per cent now receiving FM skew toward the better-educated, upper-income households.

Because of the limited size of the FM audience and the techniques employed by local measurement services, it is very difficult to get reliable FM audience estimates.   For certain advertisers looking for upscale target audiences, FM could be a suitable medium.   However, the limited data available to evaluate buys may now deter advertisers from committing funds to FM.

CHAPTER TWENTY-ONE

Uses of Direct Mail and Out-of-Home Media

PAUL M. ROTH *Vice President and Director, Media, Radio and TV Programing, Kenyon & Eckhardt, Inc.*

Out-of-home media for purposes of this discussion are outdoor, transit, and point-of-purchase advertising. It may appear incongruous to put direct mail, which is the third largest medium in terms of dollar volume ($2.5 billion per year), in the same chapter with out-of-home media such as transit advertising ($34 million per year). However, what they all have in common is that while much can be said *for* them as media, there is remarkably little that can be said *about* them relative to broadcast, magazines, and newspaper media. The statistical information explosion has yet to engulf the subject media.

Each of these media will be discussed separately, following the same basic outline to the extent that information allows:

1. *Description of the media:* Typical facilities, basic units of sale, creative units available

2. *Cost of purchase:* Examples of typical costs, estimates of efficiencies achieved

3. *Research information:* Standard measures of criteria of evaluation, basic facts

4. *Users of the media:* Advertising objectives and strategies that the medium serves, major users.

Some general comments are worthwhile.

Some General Comments

Direct mail is beginning to offer a major new challenge to the advertiser because of the computer. There is a real concern today for what is being called a new invasion of privacy as the result of technological innovation. The tremendous information-storage and memory capacities of electronic computers combined with ever-increasing efficiency in electronic communication between computers are enabling a building of centralized information about every individual. These highly accessible data are becoming the basis for more effective and selective mailing lists. Better lists will make the medium more efficient.

Another trend for efficiency is that costs are going down because of the increasing number of group mailings. Direct-mail specialists are increasing commitments to such regularly scheduled mailings. Several advertisers share an envelope for their own purposes to a predetermined list, thereby reducing their individual costs. Because of these increased efficiencies, more direct-mail vendors are turning to advertising agencies to compete for the large media budgets, instead of just soliciting advertiser sales-promotion funds.

Out-of-home media are noted for expanding their display flexibility, with new units offering greater visibility and creative opportunity. A better understanding of exposure opportunity has also been developed by the application of new research concepts to traffic measurement. Also plants are being modernized and cleaned to provide more attractive display. Thus, the opportunities for an advertiser to follow more effectively the consumer in his or her daily travels to work or right into the supermarket are expanding at a rapid rate. The challenge still exists to understand fully the contribution these media make to maintaining consumer awareness or convictions created largely by the other mass media.

DIRECT MAIL

Description of the Medium

Direct-mail advertising is the use of the mail to reach preselected individuals with an advertising or sales message. It is the only medium which permits the advertiser to pinpoint recipients of his advertising communication with a minimal amount of waste circulation.

High degree of prospect selectivity and ability to personalize sets direct mail apart from other major media. When an advertiser uses any of the other major media—magazines, newspapers, radio, television, or outdoor—he purchases a circulation which includes individuals who are not necessarily prospects for his product. An automotive-accessories manufacturer whose product is used exclusively on station wagons, can, through direct mail, reach all or any portion of the station-wagon owners in the United States. If, because of budget limitations or marketing strategies, he must limit his circulation, he can do so by any number of demographic breakdowns. He may choose to reach only those station-wagon owners in a given geographic area, or only those owning a specific make or year, e.g., 1967 Ford wagon owners in New England. Thus, this advertiser can be certain of the names and addresses of the prospective buyers he will reach. He can, if he wishes, reach 100 per cent of his prospects, as he defines them. With other major media, the advertiser must necessarily accept waste circulation, along with his prospect group. Any medium may reach a high percentage of a prospect group; direct mail, however, is the one medium with the capability of providing 100 per cent coverage.

Additionally, direct mail offers the advertiser an opportunity to personalize his message. Since the mailing list is comprised of preselected individuals who are all prospects, they have some characteristics in common. The advertiser could address his message to "station-wagon owner," or even more personally, "Dear Mr. Smith."

Typical Facilities Perhaps the single most important consideration in direct-mail advertising is the choice of names to be included in the mailing. There are two general sources for lists of names to be mailed, *internal* and *external.*   Internal sources include company sales records, credit records, shipping records, trade show registrants, general correspondence, and salesmen's records.   From these sources, the advertiser can extract names that have been his best customers, or those that are likely prospects for new products.

Externally, the sources are unlimited.   Specialized list houses, list brokers, and original list compilers supply lists of virtually every demographic breakdown.   Specialized list houses offer the most sophisticated lists, in terms of conforming to the marketing objectives of an individual advertiser.   These houses, through the use of computer data cards, make it possible to combine demographic factors, such as age, sex, income, and geographic locale, to build the ideal prospect list.

List brokers serve as agents between list owners and list users.   By maintaining files of available lists, brokers are able to rent lists tailored to individual client marketing needs.   More sophisticated list brokers, because of their wide experience with direct mail, often counsel their clients in use of the medium.

The list compiler, on the other hand, develops lists which are useful in general product categories, and then attempts to sell them to the various companies with products in those categories.   Auto registration lists—an excellent example of the compiled list—are available for sale to automotive-industry manufacturers.

Basic Units of Sale   The unit of sale in direct mail is the list of names.   The list can range in size from ten of the best customers of a small manufacturer as determined from his sales records, to approximately 45 million car-owning households.   There is no limit to the number of different lists that can be purchased from the more than 700 classifications in the *Direct Mail List Rates and Data Catalog* of Standard Rate & Data Service.

Lists can be verified for both accuracy and currency through processes commonly called *purification.*   Purification of lists entails checking to make sure an advertiser is getting exactly what he orders.   In other words, an advertiser may check whether a list is up to date by mailing first class, return requested, to make sure the prospect is still at the address.   If he is not, the piece will be returned.   Additionally, prospects can be checked by randomly mailing, to a small sample of a total list, questions relative to their prospect classification.   Purification mailings are usually available to advertisers at no cost by direct-mail houses.   Currently, a purification mailing is the only method of auditing a list.

Creative Units   The creative unit to be mailed—known as the *direct-mail piece*—can be as simple or as elaborate as the advertiser desires.   He is limited solely by budget and postal regulations.   Unlike the other major media, which handicap the imagination by space or time requirements, direct mail has no form limitations.   There are seven common types of direct-mail pieces.

The *letter* is the most common type, because it is the simplest and most personal form.   Because it appears to be a personal communication, it is likely to be opened and read completely.   More important than the production technique is the approach used in the letter.   A straightforward, friendly approach is most appropriate.

Enclosures are another common form of direct mail.   The enclosure is least expensive, since the advertising rides free with a bill, letter, or other correspondence.   A common example of an enclosure is the advertising carried with telephone bills.   Enclosures are limited in format to the requirements dictated by the original mail piece.

Self-mailers are direct-mail pieces which do not require envelopes.   They can be as simple as a postcard or as complex as a catalog.   The self-mailer is usually folded, with one side free for postage and addressing.

Catalogs and *booklets* offer a wide variety of opportunities for the advertiser to list his product or services.   The catalog or booklet is usually not less than eight pages, and features descriptive listings of the products being offered, their specifications, and prices.   A widely recognized example of the catalog is the annual publication of Sears, Roebuck and Company.

Distributing *product samples* is a highly effective form of direct mail.   Product samples can be either mailed or hand-delivered, as dictated by the market situation.   Product sampling is most common where new products, which can be economically packaged in small quantities, are being introduced.   One obvious advantage with product sampling is that consumers are given the opportunity to try the product.

Many advertisers make use of their *internal publications* as mailing pieces, e.g., employee publications.   Newsletters, bulletins, annual and special reports and statements, and company magazines are often used as direct-mail pieces.   This type of mailing serves an indirect function such as creating goodwill or owner loyalty, as opposed to regular sales-oriented advertising.

Coupons and *contests* are other direct-mail approaches. Coupons are discount offers used to stimulate sales. They are most commonly utilized for the promotion of grocery and package-good items. Contests and sweepstakes offer customers a chance to win valuable prizes. They draw attention to the advertiser's product by generating customer enthusiasm and interest. Coupons and contests are often found in a cooperative mailing in which other advertisers jointly participate. An obvious advantage of the co-op mailing is that various participants in a mailing share the cost of the carrying envelope, addressing, and postage.

Spectacular mailings are elaborate. They generally consist of three-dimensional objects, which are meant to be retained by the recipient. These direct-mail pieces, such as rulers, calendars, paperweights, and pens, usually carry a brief advertising message. They serve as reminders, keeping the advertiser's name in front of the customer.

Finally, there is the general area of printed matter which includes broadsides, circulars, stuffers, and reprints. These units are basically alike; however, they differ as a result of the size and printing process used.

Cost of Purchase

There are four basic cost areas in direct-mail advertising: (1) list, (2) production, (3) mailing operations and handling, and (4) postage. Each of these areas must be treated separately in arriving at an overall cost.

List costs vary by the quantity, quality, and availability of the desired list. An average list cost is $20 to $25 per 1,000 names.

Production costs will vary depending on the size, shape, quality, and quantity of the direct-mail piece. Material costs are included in production costs; therefore, the most expensive direct-mail pieces are likely to be spectaculars, product samples, catalogs, and booklets. At the other end of the spectrum are simple postcards and letters which usually are the least expensive. There are no "average" production costs, since there are so many variables which come into play in determining a final cost. Mailing operations and handling costs include folding, envelope stuffing, addressing, and posting of the direct-mail piece. Large list houses often include this cost in the purchase price of the list. While list compilers and brokers primarily rent or sell lists, they often offer, as an additional service and expense, mailing operations and handling. As with production, these costs depend upon the piece being mailed. The more complex the mailing operations, the higher the cost.

Postage costs are determined by the number of pieces being mailed, the weight of each piece, and the class of mail being used. Third-class bulk rate is most commonly used for direct mail. In January, 1968, the minimum rate per piece became 3.6 cents. Books and catalogs cost 16 cents per pound to mail; all other direct-mail pieces, 22 cents per pound. First-class and airmail postage offer the advertiser greater control over timing, and tend to lend an added touch of personal quality to the direct-mail piece. First class and airmail are guaranteed to be delivered, forwarded, or returned to sender, thereby permitting an advertiser to keep his list up to date. The first-class letter rate in 1968 was 6 cents per ounce or 5 cents per ounce for a drop letter, where the envelope is not sealed. Air-mail postage was 10 cents per ounce.

Because of the multiplicity of cost items associated with direct mail, there are no typical costs. The advertiser's budget—as it relates to his objectives—is the most important factor in determining the cost of a direct-mail campaign.

Example to Illustrate Cost Areas   Despite the fact that there are no typical costs in direct mail, a specific example may be useful in illustrating various cost areas. Assume we are marketing a new product in the dental hygiene field. Our objective with this mailing is to familiarize dentists with our product and its advantages so that they may recommend it to their patients. To meet this objective we will mail a one-page personalized letter to approximately 100,000 dentists in the United States. We will use a specialized list house which will provide all the direct-mail services required to complete this mailing. The costs are as follows: [1]

List (100,000 dentists)	$21.00/thousand	$2,100
Production (printing and stationery)	5.00/thousand	500
Mailing operations	50.00/thousand	5,000
Postage (bulk rate)	36.00/thousand	3,600
Total		$11,200

[1] R. L. Polk & Company supplied list, production, and mailing operations cost.

Cost Efficiency Direct-mail cost efficiency must always be equated with other media on a prospects basis only, never on *raw* cost per thousand, since direct-mail circulation involves very little waste, if any.

Direct-mail cost efficiency introduces the additional problem of distinguishing space or time cost from other costs. For example, a radio or television cost per thousand (CPM) is based solely on the time cost. When the cost of a direct-mail campaign is computed, production, mailing operations, and postage are more than likely included in deriving a CPM. Thus, with direct mail, the per-thousand cost is more of a selling cost than an efficiency measurement.

The direct-mail advertiser may more easily evaluate the cost of a campaign in terms of the number of responses the campaign stimulated. Depending upon the objectives of the campaign, these responses may simply be replies, leads, or even sales.

Research Information

Direct mail is not supported by the extensive research characteristic of the other major media such as those by Simmons, Starch, and Brand Rating Index in the magazine area, or Nielsen and the American Research Bureau in the television area. However, there is a wealth of direct-mail research. These studies are useful insofar as they apply to a specific direct-mail problem. Studies on coupon redemption are an excellent example of this type of specialized research. The pulling power of direct mail in coupon redemption is higher than in any of the other media. The Nielsen Clearing House found that 14.9 per cent of direct-mail coupons are redeemed, compared with 5.9 per cent for magazine coupons.

Tests on Single Campaigns The most important area of research in the direct-mail field is the individual research the advertiser does on his own campaign. Through response control an advertiser is able to test the effectiveness of various copy approaches, price structures, or packaging designs. He can also determine demographic characteristics of his product's market. This type of testing can be done inexpensively with small, random samples of the population. Results can then be used in formulating a strategy for a major campaign.

An advertiser is also able to test cost factors relative to direct mail, to determine cost per inquiry or sale of the item advertised. An individual advertiser can measure the efficiency of the medium with respect to his own marketing objectives.   This type of information could be more valuable to an advertiser than all the extensive research studies of the other major media.

Uses of the Medium

Direct mail, like any medium, must fit specific advertising objectives.   In designing a meaningful direct campaign, all uses of the medium must be carefully examined.   With the presence of these objectives, direct mail can be advantageous in the following cases:

1. *When an advertiser has to reach a specific, preselected market, and no other medium can efficiently provide this audience.*   Selectivity is the major advantage offered by direct mail.   An advertiser can reach all his prospects, assuming the list is available or can be compiled.   A key point in taking advantage of the selective nature of this medium is the precise definition of a prospect group.   If the prospect group is unknown, direct mail is likely to prove to be misdirected and inefficient as a result.

2. *When an advertiser wishes to personalize his message.*   Direct mail is the form of advertising closest to direct personal selling.   The advertising message is being sent to one individual and is meant only for him.   This is likely to enhance a message's impact on the consumer.   Moreover, it is able to reach him in a climate (e.g., his home) in which his attention may be sustained for a longer period.

3. *When it is important to an advertiser to avoid direct competition with the messages of other advertisers.*   Direct mail offers the opportunity to reach prospects with a single sales message, with no editorial or other thought competing for the individual's attention.

4. *When specific timing or strict geographical control is necessary to a marketing plan.*   Direct mail permits an advertiser to control the message as it is received across the country. For example, direct mail can be made to fit distribution patterns so that prospects receive the advertising along with product availability in their location.   Direct-mail messages can usually be changed at the last moment, thereby eliminating the burden of early closing dates.

5. *When an advertising message is too complex to fit the time or space requirements of the other major media.*   Direct mail offers the necessary latitude to satisfy complex sales messages with the various

formats available.   The communication can be so contructed as to fit the requirements of the advertiser rather than the medium.

6. *When sampling or couponing is desirable.*

7. *When it is the objective of the advertiser to test a facet of his advertising,* direct mail can be used to implement necessary controls.

8. *Mail-order direct-mail advertising* serves an important function in doing the complete sales job for an advertiser who does not have the distribution or sales force to service widespread customers.

Major Users of Direct Mail

Direct mail is the third largest medium in dollar volume, behind newspapers and television, with approximately $2.5 billion in billings per year.   The eight largest users of direct mail in 1967 [2] fell into three general categories:

1. The magazine publishers, Time Inc., Reader's Digest, and Cowles, who use direct mail extensively for subscription solicitation

2. The soap companies, Procter & Gamble, Colgate-Palmolive, and Lever Bros., who use direct mail for coupon offers, sweepstakes, and new-product samples

3. The automobile manufacturers, Ford and Chevrolet, who use direct mail to contact owners of competitive makes at model year introduction and for continuing owner loyalty campaigns to maintain present owners

Future of the Medium   Direct-mail advertising distinguishes itself from the other media by its ability to pinpoint prospects.   With the advent of Zip coding, new opportunities in both the areas of economy and selectivity of mailing have become available.   As advertisers learn how to use this valuable tool, direct mail will become more of a science.   Zip Code areas will be defined by their own demographic characteristics, allowing advertisers to mail to individuals in diverse preselected areas.   Assuming there is a degree of homogeneity within any Zip Code, generalizations could be made which would eliminate the necessity for more costly demographic breakouts.   Thus direct mail is keeping in stride with technological advances of other major media.

Summary

In summary, direct mail provides an advertiser with the opportunity to communicate with a preselected prospect group.   Additionally, it

[2] Direct Mail Advertising Association.

provides the capabilities of a personalized communication without competition from other advertisers.

The direct-mail medium offers numerous opportunities creatively and provides controls for testing and product analysis.

Since direct-mail cost evaluation includes all aspects of the medium—list, production, handling, and postage—some caution should be exercised when comparing its performance against another media approach.

OUTDOOR

Description of the Medium

Outdoor advertising is an organized medium of mass communication (constructed out of doors) between advertisers and the public, established to provide coverage of entire markets.   In this, it is analogous to radio, television, newspapers, and magazines.   It is also similar in terms of standardization of operating practices and structures which make it available to advertisers on a uniform basis.[3]

Values of the outdoor medium are its size and dominance, market-by-market flexibility, and according to available research, a relatively low cost-per-thousand factor (based on total potential exposure).   In addition, the medium affords a continuity of exposure and the opportunity strategically to position advertising close to the point of sale.

Advertisers and their agencies have tended to regard outdoor advertising as a supplementary medium.   This is caused partly by the fact that creatively the medium is restricted by its ability to communicate only a short selling message.

Typical Facilities   Many persons believe that any sign with a commercial message which appears out of doors is outdoor advertising. Actually, only some 300,000, less than 5 per cent, of all signs seen belong to the standardized medium of outdoor advertising.

These signs can be divided into three basic types—*posters* displaying 24-sheet, 30-sheet, and bleed posters; *painted bulletins,* and *spectaculars.*

1. POSTERS.   Throughout the United States, there are approximately 275,000 illuminated and nonilluminated poster panels in 9,471 markets.   A *market* is defined as towns individually or groups of towns sold as units.   These poster panels are owned and maintained by 700 outdoor advertising companies—generally known as

[3] "This Is Outdoor Advertising," Institute of Outdoor Advertising, New York.

plant operators—and are built on private land the plants either own or lease.   In turn, the plant operators sell advertising space on these structures for a specified period of time.[4]

Standardized poster structures measure 25 feet long and 12 feet high overall.   The copy area of the 24-sheet poster measures 8 feet 8 inches by 19 feet 6 inches.   The 30-sheet poster measures 9 feet 7 inches by 21 feet 7 inches, and affords the advertiser 25 per cent more display area.

A recent development is the "bleed" poster, which extends the artwork right to the frame of the panel by printing on the blanking paper as well as on the poster (Figure 1).   The copy area of the bleed poster averages 40 per cent larger than the 24-sheet poster.   There is no additional space charge for the larger sizes.   As a point of reference, the terms "24-sheet" and "30-sheet" do not mean that posters are made up of that many individual pieces of paper, although they were many years ago.   Today presses are larger, and posters are usually printed in ten to fourteen sections (Figure 1).

In addition to the conventional 24- and 30-sheet poster units, it is also possible to purchase:

3-SHEET POSTERS.   A small poster which provides a copy area measuring 6 feet 8 inches high by 3 feet 3 inches wide.   Usually located on outside walls of retail stores.

6-SHEET OR JUNIOR POSTERS.   A poster which provides copy area measuring 4 feet 4 inches by 9 feet 10 inches wide.   Usually located on outside walls of retail stores.

7-SHEET POSTERS.   A poster which provides a copy area measuring 8 feet high by 7 feet wide.   Usually located in the vicinity of retail stores.

2. PAINTED BULLETINS.   Painted bulletins represent less than 10 per cent of all standardized outdoor structures although they account for about 30 per cent of outdoor billing.   Their greater cost is because of their dominant size and maximum traffic locations.

There are two basic forms of painted bulletins available to the advertiser.   The first type offered are *rotating bulletins*.   These units are physically moved periodically (usually thirty or sixty days) to new locations.   Their overall size can range up to 1,200 square feet or more.

[4] National Outdoor Advertising Bureau (NOAB).

Permanent bulletins are the other basic painted-bulletin form. These vary in size since they are designed to fit the unique requirements of each available location.   The display remains in a fixed location.

For dominant effect, painted bulletins are frequently embellished with cut-out letters or dimensional effects.   They extend beyond the frame, but are limited to a maximum of 5 feet 6 inches at the top and 2 feet at either side.   Advertisers can use bleed face or standard bulletins (Figure 2).

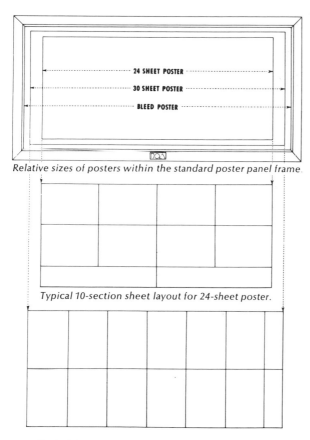

Relative sizes of posters within the standard poster panel frame.

Typical 10-section sheet layout for 24-sheet poster.

Typical 14-section sheet layout for 30-sheet poster.

Figure 1

Figure 2

The painted-bulletin message is hand-painted directly on the face of the bulletin, often in sections in the plant's paint shop.   The sections are then assembled on the site.

3. SPECTACULARS.   The third type of outdoor unit consists of spectaculars.   These fixed-location units, which are almost always situated on a market's prime arterials, command a high monthly space charge.   In addition to this basic cost, there is a fabrication cost which is usually amortized over the life of the contract (usually three to five years).   This fabrication cost can range widely, depending on the unit's complexity.   Good examples of spectaculars can be found in New York City's Times Square.

Basic Units of Sale   The total display of poster panels is called a *showing,* and thirty days is the normal display period.   The usual contract period is also one month.

Poster showings are normally sold in No. 50 and No. 100 showings.   The number of panels in a showing varies market by market depending upon population, area size, and extent of the major traffic arterial patterns.

The basic outdoor unit, a No. 100 showing, includes supposedly the number of panels required to provide daily exposure equal to the population of the market.[5]   Showings of sizes smaller than No. 100 provide proportionately less intensity and coverage.

Fixed-location or rotary painted bulletins are usually sold with contractual commitments ranging from one to three years.   The basic cost of the unit includes three paints per year, but does not include the cost of cut-outs, embellishments, extensions, or bleed.

Creative Units   The creative variations available within the outdoor medium are numerous.

For example, an advertiser can use a black-and-white or color poster in 24-sheet, 30-sheet, or bleed size.   It is even possible to use embellishments on poster panels in several of the larger markets. There is, however, an additional cost for embellishments.   Painted bulletins offer more creative flexibility.   Bulletins can be standard (with molding) or bleed (without molding) units.   In addition, newly mastered techniques—plastic-faced, backlighted units; moving messages; unusual treatments of light and color, etc.—offer even more flexibility when coupled with cut-outs or extensions.

Spectaculars are fabricated from the bottom up in accordance with the advertiser's blueprints.   There is virtually no limit, except local ordinances, to what can be constructed for a spectacular.

Cost of Purchase

Posters are, of course, the least costly, and spectaculars the most expensive.

Table 1 illustrates the range in cost in Chicago for spectaculars, painted bulletins (fixed and rotary), and posters.   The cost of one spectacular in a top location in Chicago will finance almost 9 fixed painted bulletins, almost 20 rotary painted bulletins, and about 116 poster units for a one-year period.

[5] "This Is Outdoor Advertising," Institute of Outdoor Advertising, New York.

TABLE 1   Range in Cost for Spectaculars, Painted Bulletins, and Posters

Unit	Space cost per unit Month	· Year	Production cost per year *	Total annual cost	Unit index
Spectacular:					
Top location	$9,000	$108,000	$50,000	$158,000	1.0
Avg. location	4,000	48,000	30,000	78,000	2.0
Painted bulletins:					
Top location					
(fixed)	1,500	18,000	. . . .	18,000	8.8
Avg. location					
(fixed)	500	6,000	. . . .	6,000	26.3
Rotary plan	675	8,100	. . . .	8,100	19.5
Posters	110	1,320	48 †	1,368	115.5

* Three-year amortization.

† Assumes volume production of paper.

SOURCE: National Outdoor Advertising Bureau

Typical Costs   As discussed earlier, the number of a showing (sometimes referred to as *intensity*) does not refer to the number of posters, but simply indicates a relative measure of coverage.   Obviously, the number of posters in a No. 100 showing in a large city will be much greater than in a smaller city.   In either case, the degree of coverage is supposed to be the same.   A No. 50 showing generally will include approximately half as many posters as a No. 100 (Table 2).

TABLE 2   Number of Posters in a Showing and Costs in Some Large Cities

City	Population in thousands	No. 50 showing No. of panels Unill.	Ill.	Monthly cost	No. 100 showing No. of panels Unill.	Ill.	Monthly cost
New York · · ·	8,011	74	224	$32,540	37	112	$16,270
Detroit · · · ·	2,510	10	132	15,312	5	66	7,656
San Diego · · ·	1,215	36	34	6,406	18	17	3,203
Minneapolis ·	1,083	18	57	6,450	9	29	3,268
Wichita · · · ·	281	16	16	1,920	10	10	1,200
Lincoln, Neb.	145	7	12	1,310	4	7	760

SOURCE: National Outdoor Advertising Bureau (1968 rates).

Showings are normally made of both regular (nonilluminated) and illuminated panels. Cities with heavy after-dark traffic have a higher ratio of illuminated panels in a showing.

National Costs   The cost of implementing a No. 100 showing on a complete national basis is prohibitive. Most advertisers purchase the medium on a more selective basis—top 100 markets, etc. (Table 3).

TABLE 3   Costs of a No. 100 Showing on a Selective Basis

	Population in thousands	No. of panels		Monthly cost
		Unill.	Ill.	
All markets	165,714	20,844	7,376	$1,523,546
Top 100 cities . . .	85,323	2,040	3,838	485,889
Top 50 cities . . .	67,028	1,419	2,871	368,786
Top 10 cities . . .	29,800	469	1,041	144,404

SOURCE: National Outdoor Advertising Bureau (1968 rates).

Cost Efficiencies   Posters are the most efficient, from the point of view of cost, and spectaculars the least efficient. This situation is analogous, however, to the efficiency of a 200-line newspaper advertisement versus a full-page advertisement; a significant difference in impact exists between the two techniques.

The poster medium follows the pattern of local media in general, becoming more expensive in the smaller market group (Table 4).

TABLE 4   Posters More Expensive in Smaller Markets

City size	CPM population (No. 100 showing)	Index
Top 10	$ 4.85	100
11–20	5.99	124
21–50	6.05	125
51–70	6.20	128
71–100	6.55	135
Remainder United States	12.90	266
Total United States	9.19	189

SOURCE: National Outdoor Advertising Bureau.

The TAB (Traffic Audit Bureau), a tripartite trade association, is the only official outdoor body that validates circulation for individual outdoor companies (plants).

To date, outdoor plants customarily report their circulation to TAB on the basis of averages—in the form of average daily exposure opportunities for all panels in a typical showing.

Each panel in a given market is afforded a basic circulation value based on effective (usually 50 per cent) traffic via auto and pedestrian. Mass-transportation passengers are also included, usually at a lesser value (25 per cent).

Cost-per-thousand data can be compared, market by market, utilizing these TAB circulation figures.

Table 5 indicates that *costs per thousand* range from $0.11 to $0.26

TABLE 5 Cost per Thousand in Some Typical Markets

| City | Population, in thousands | No. 100 Showing | | | |
		Daily circ., in thousands *	Circ.-pop. ratio	Monthly circ., in thousands	CPM
Boston	2,662	3,512	132	105,360	$0.20
Baltimore . .	1,969	1,356	69	40,680	0.25
Miami	1,571	1,547	99	46,410	0.26
Houston . . .	1,092	1,490	136	44,700	0.11
Buffalo	924	923	100	27,690	0.20
Norfolk	679	1,068	157	32,040	0.17
Nashville . . .	518	842	163	25,260	0.13
Mobile	284	215	76	6,450	0.20
South Bend	252	209	83	6,270	0.23
Evansville	167	197	118	5,910	0.26

* Traffic Audit Bureau audits.
SOURCE: National Outdoor Advertising Bureau.

based on a sampling of typical markets. It is also significant to note that the intensity of a No. 100 showing does not necessarily match the goal of daily circulation equaling the market's population.

Hopefully, for the advertiser, TAB will be successful in its goal to get plant operators to guarantee circulation for poster showings. The guarantee will probably be about 90 per cent of today's circulation figures. If a guarantee should not be met for some reason, such as a loss of location, then there would be an adjustment. Guarantees for each plant will be supported by affidavits.

TAB also intends to audit painted bulletins, which has not previously been done.   This is why media planners are less likely to compare and analyze painted bulletins or spectacular locations on an efficiency basis even though many plant operators provide traffic audits for these locations.   The CPMs for rotary paint range from $0.31 (New Orleans) to $1.06 (Twin Cities) based on plant-supplied traffic counts in the top fifty markets (Table 6).

TABLE 6   Rotary Paint, 1968, Cost per Thousand Circulation (Top 15 Markets)

Market (No. of Plants Reporting)	CPM
1. New York	$0.86
2. Los Angeles (3)	0.76–0.88
3. Chicago (2)	0.61–0.84
4. Philadelphia	0.47
5. Detroit (2)	0.46–0.68
6. Boston (2)	0.55–0.59
7. San Francisco-Oakland	0.73–0.79
8. Washington	1.00
9. Pittsburgh	0.61
10. St. Louis	0.44
11. Cleveland	0.66
12. Baltimore	NR
13. Newark	0.83
14. Houston (2)	0.31–0.34
15. Minneapolis-St. Paul	1.06

SOURCE: National Outdoor Advertising Bureau.

Research Information

The outdoor medium is the oldest form of advertising with the exception of word of mouth.   Yet it remains with a limited amount of acceptable audience data both from qualitative and quantitative standpoints.   From 1950 to 1967, there were only twenty-nine major, published local-market studies of the outdoor medium, i.e., painted bulletins and posters.   These studies did not include the TAB traffic audits.

Standard Measures   In addition to circulation data, TAB also provides a measure of the efficiency with which a poster panel dominates the effective circulation to which it is exposed.   This measure, called *space position value* (SPV), is based on four factors—length of approach, speed in travel, angle of the panel to its circulation, and its relationship to adjacent panels. SPV is based on a 10-point scale, and most major market plants average between 9 and 10 for their average showings.

Special Studies Among the advertising studies performed, Foster and Kleiser has sponsored several designed to measure awareness of specific campaigns in outdoor and their potential audience reach. The awareness studies have limitations, and many media research persons consider them only as good attempts toward providing a means to study this medium further. The limitations stem primarily from the lack of data control on copy in the study and not from the technique of measuring awareness.

A continuing problem, besides the awareness issue, is to determine how many posters are needed adequately to cover different markets. As mentioned earlier, it is difficult to use the intensity (showing) measure supplied by the plant operator because of the variance market to market. For example, a No. 100 showing in Nashville will reach a daily circulation 63 per cent *greater* than the population of that city; whereas a No. 100 showing in Baltimore will produce a daily circulation equivalent to only 69 per cent of that city's population.

While there are a number of ways to solve this problem, reach and frequency estimates on a market-by-market basis appear to be the most logical solution.

A number of four-week reach and frequency studies by the A. C. Nielsen Company reveal that reach of posters is relatively high, even for a No. 25 showing (Table 7).

Need for Data on Frequency These studies emphasize that the crucial need for the media planner is accurate data on how many posters are required in each market to reach a predetermined frequency level. The National Outdoor Advertising Bureau has completed experimental work in the area of reach and frequency for individual markets. Specifically, it has developed data on how many panels are required to achieve monthly frequency levels (12, 24, and 36) against car-owning households in the top fifty markets.

For example, to achieve a 24 frequency in Detroit, approximately 149 panels are required. The nearest published showing is a No. 75 with 153 panels.

NOAB's data were based on analysis of traffic flow and license plates (of passing cars) in twenty-four markets (published by OAAA in 1961).

TABLE 7 Reach of Posters

	No. 100		No. 75		No. 50		No. 25	
	Reach	Freq.	Reach	Freq.	Reach	Freq.	Reach	Freq.
Los Angeles-Orange	92	29	91	22	88	14	77	7
Seattle	93	33	91	26	87	18	77	10
San Francisco-Oakland	94	23	92	18	89	11	72	7
San Francisco	94	21	93	16	89	10	72	6
Los Angeles	98	38	97	29	95	19	90	11
Northeast New Jersey	97	31	93	24	91	19	73	10
New York City. . . .	86	32	83	26	79	18	66	10

SOURCE: A. C. Nielsen Company, based on individuals.

Nielsen has also compiled a study of reach and frequency in San Francisco, combining these data for painted bulletins and posters. Nielsen concludes from this study that a combination of paint and posters will deliver a high frequency of impact (reach) within a single month (Table 8).

TABLE 8 Combination of Paint and Posters Delivers High Frequency of Impact

Painted bulletins			Paint and posters		
No. of units	Reach	Frequency	Number showing	Reach	Frequency
4	42	5	100	95	25
			50	91	13
			25	80	9
8	58	7	100	95	27
			50	91	15
			25	84	11
12	69	8	100	95	28
			50	92	17
			25	86	12
24	78	12	100	95	32
			50	94	21
			25	89	16

SOURCE: Nielsen, San Francisco, 1961. Data for posters alone are not reported in this study.

In a more recent study in New York, Nielsen concluded that:
1. The reach of the poster medium tends to be higher against the

older (over thirty) and more affluent people—that segment of the population representing the heaviest drivers.

2. As would be expected, reach and frequency levels for the poster medium are highest among men.

3. The initial reach of the first month of a bulletin campaign is considerably lower than that of posters because of the smaller number of locations used. However, after rotation to six or twelve different locations over the course of a year, painted bulletins can achieve a reach as high as posters.

4. The large number of locations used for posters, as compared to painted bulletins, yields a substantial reach for posters at the end of the first day. A No. 75 showing in New York City can reach nearly one-third of all men in one day. It takes a No. 25 showing one week to match the single-day reach of a No. 75 showing against men.

Uses of the Medium

Advertisers who use the outdoor medium generally use it to support specific objectives.

These objectives usually are:

Broad and rapid frequency of exposure for a simple copy theme. The preceding data reveal that a No. 100 showing will achieve almost maximum reach within one week and that frequency is the principal additive for the remainder of the poster schedule.

Low cost per thousand circulation. An examination of TAB circulation and monthly cost data shows that this medium is the least expensive one available to the advertiser. CPMs for outdoor range from $0.11 to $0.26, compared with spot television, for example, at $3 to $3.50 for a fringe 60-second commercial.

Flexibility in terms of seasonality, copy treatment, and market-by-market levels of exposure. Posters are one of the most flexible media available to the advertiser. For example, automotive advertisers can vary the featured model in accordance with regional preferences.

For regional advertisers, a lack of waste circulation. Outdoor can be placed in an advertiser's exact marketing area. For example, a local bank could place posters or paint in its trading area, whereas other local media cover the entire market.

Availability of color at no extra cost and on a local basis. Most other media charge for color and have limited availabilities on a local basis.

Package identification. Package-goods advertisers can achieve rapid and strong brand and package identification for impulse items.

There are limitations to this medium. The most severe is probably the short copy message. It is impossible to present more than one strong selling argument for a product in this medium. Another limitation is the inability to control the frequency of exposure with standardized showings.

Major Users

The automotive advertiser is the major consumer of this medium. Other major users are advertisers of soft drinks and beers.

Automotive advertisers spend heavily in outdoor because of its proximity to the motoring public—their prime prospect. They also use the medium because it allows them to achieve rapid identification of their new models.

The brewers are heavy users of the medium because there are more local than national breweries. This medium also permits the brewery to support strong distributors within a single trading area with a minimum of waste circulation.

Organizations Serving the Outdoor Industry

IOA The Institute of Outdoor Advertising is a new organization closely affiliated with the OAAA, whose purpose is the development of research, creative ideas, promotion, and effective uses of the medium of outdoor. It is a central source of information on outdoor at the service of advertisers, agencies, member plants, sales organizations, and the public.

The institute publishes the *Outdoor Buyers' Guide,* a quarterly publication containing rates and panels per showing in over 11,000 markets, and the quarterly reports of outdoor advertising expenditures. It distributes a monthly news letter to 10,000 advertiser, agency, and plant executives. It sponsors the annual outdoor advertising art competitions. It maintains liaison with agencies and advertisers on creative and research aspects of outdoor. Headquarters are in New York.

OAAA The Outdoor Advertising Association of America, Inc., is the trade association of the standardized outdoor medium whose plant members operate more than 90 per cent of the medium's facilities in this country.   Incorporated in 1925, its origin goes back to 1872.

The association advises and assists the members of the industry in matters pertaining to public, press, and governmental relations.   It recommends standards for the construction, illumination, and placement of outdoor advertising panels and for acceptability of copy.   It established the Outdoor Advertising Foundation at the University of Notre Dame for studies on the advancement of the medium.   Offices are in Washington and New York.

NOAB   The National Outdoor Advertising Bureau, Inc., is a service organization cooperatively owned by approximately two hundred advertising agencies and their branches.   It gathers cost data and prepares estimates for any combination of markets; does the contracting, billing, and paying of individual outdoor plants; performs field inspections; sends posting and paint instructions to all plants on a schedule; and in short, performs all except the creative functions of an agency in connection with outdoor advertising.

TAB   The Traffic Audit Bureau, Inc., is a tripartite corporation sponsored jointly by advertisers, agencies, and the outdoor industry.   It audits circulation of outdoor panels by actual counts of traffic.   It also evaluates their visibility on factors such as length of approach, speed of travel, angle of the panel, and the relation of the panel to adjacent panels, and assigns space position value ratings. The combination of circulation and visibility determines the effectiveness of a panel or a complete showing.

Sales Organizations   Many individual plants are represented by sales organizations, which maintain sales offices in major cities such as New York, Chicago, Detroit, and Los Angeles.

TRANSIT

Description of the Medium

In spite of its origin and the fact that until only a few years ago interior car cards were the only transit media available in standard sizes, transit advertising is by no means confined to this form.   Today it covers broader media types, although until the beginning of the 1960s as a *national* medium car cards were the predominant form.   The variety of transit forms covers three areas.   The first is *car cards,* which generally appear on the inside of buses, streetcars, subways, and suburban trains.   A second form is the *station poster,* which is displayed on station platforms of transit properties.   The third is *exterior posters,* which are carried on the outside of public vehicles.

Car Cards   Car cards differ from other formats in that they are generally presented in a standard "siderack" above the reader's head, often on a curved surface.   They are also displayed on a flat surface at the standing level of the passenger at the side or ends of transportation vehicles.   Since car cards are limited in size, and in consideration of the conditions under which they are displayed, copy must be relatively short.   Although the average transit ride is 23 minutes, the conditions of the ride, in most cases, are usually not conducive to detailed perusal of car cards, especially those which appear overhead. The overhead card, therefore, generally attempts to focus the passenger's attention on the bottom of the ad, rather than the "headline."   Apart from this copy anomaly, good car advertising is usually similar in design to advertisements which appear in other forms of print media (e.g., magazines, outdoor, etc.).

Since car cards reach a relatively unselected group (40 million riders per month), they are most suitable for advertising products of wide appeal and low unit cost.   They are not well suited to the advertising of industrial goods, luxury goods of high unit cost, or goods that require a good deal of explanatory copy.   Product categories best suited to car-card advertising are such items as headache remedies, soaps, chewing gum, breakfast foods, banks, finance companies, cigarettes, beer, and liquor.   Dependent upon need, other types of advertisers will use car cards to supplement their other media and to aid in facilitating brand identification.

The availability of car cards as media vehicles is generally restricted to urban areas, in communities of 25,000 or more population where transportation vehicles are readily available to accommodate the form.

Sizes of Cards   The standard car card in most of the major markets throughout the country is 11 by 28 inches.   Originally the traditional form was 11 by 21 inches, which is still used in smaller markets.   Other commonly used sizes are the "jumbo," 11 by 42 inches, and the "large indoor bus" size, 11 by 56 inches.   A junior-size card of 11 by 14 inches is also available, but is infrequently used.   There is also an "over-door top end" 16- by 44-inch card.   In addition to the overhead cards there are the 22- by 21-inch "square" end cards usually positioned at the end of the cars, and the 22- by 21-inch "square side-space" cards at the sides of the door of the vehicle.   Most of these sizes are available inside subway cars; however, buses are generally restricted to the card sizes of 11 by 21 inches, 11 by 28 inches, and 11 by 42 inches.

Production Processes   Almost any type of production process can be used for making car cards; however, for best results they should be printed on four- or five-ply horizontal-grain stock.   Often where 700 units or less are produced, advertisers employ a silk-screen process to produce displays in two or more colors; where magazine-style illustrations of food or beverage products require color separations, or when more than 1,000 units are to be produced, advertisers often use lithography.   Where thousands of units are required (such as with leaflets to be taken by the passengers), letterpress or offset printing will generally be used.

Since the cards are held in a rack, a bleed effect can be achieved with the advertisement if desired.   However, important material should be kept at least 2½ inches from the top or bottom and ¾ inch from either side of the card.

How Sold   Car cards are sold on a monthly basis generally in one of four ways:

Double run—two cards in each car

Full run—one card in each car, or two cards in half of the cars

Half run—one card in every other car

Quarter run—one card in every fourth car

In the larger cities the advertiser can buy certain routes.   For example, in New York the various subway lines can be bought individually.   Typical costs for the standard 11- by 28-inch car card, full run, on a monthly basis, are:

$14,148 for 3,834 car cards in New York ($3.69 per card per month)

$3,618 for 1,652 car cards in Los Angeles ($2.19 per card per month)

$4,960 for 1,566 car cards in Boston ($3.17 per card per month)

$13,568 for 4,240 car cards in Chicago ($3.20 per card per month)

$7,403 for 2,388 car cards in Philadelphia ($3.10 per card per month)

Station Posters   The main advantage the station poster has over the car card is the ability to generate a high frequency of exposure. It is usually seen by many people who wait on the same station platform every day and thus have ample time to read the complete poster. For this reason more detailed copy as compared to that for car cards can be used.

Like car cards, station posters reach a relatively unselective group, but their location on the station platform is such that readers can easily stop by those posters which most attract them. Thus, the products they advertise can be more specialized than in car cards. This type of poster is not confined exclusively to the station platform; they are also found at airport and railroad terminals.

Station posters should be printed on 70-pound stock suitable for outdoor use; preferably the paper should be uncoated. One-inch margins should be allowed on all four sides of the poster. Station posters generally come in one of three different sizes:

1-sheet posters (30 inches wide by 46 inches high)
2-sheet posters (60 inches wide by 46 inches high)
3-sheet posters (42 inches wide by 84 inches high)

As with car cards they are generally bought on a monthly basis in one of three ways:

Intensive—which is considered a full showing
Representative—half the intensive showing
Minimum—half the representative showing

In many of the larger markets the advertiser can buy selective locations in addition to the full-market coverage. Typical costs for a 2-sheet poster, representative showing are:

In *New York* a showing of 900 2-sheet posters costs $8,712 a month (an average unit cost of $9.68).

In *Chicago* a showing of 196 2-sheet posters costs $3,675 a month (an average unit cost of $18.75).

In *Philadelphia* a showing of 65 2-sheet posters costs $658 a month (an average unit cost of $10.12).

Unit costs are higher than for car cards ranging from $10 to $20.

Exterior Posters   Exterior posters have one major advantage over the interior car cards and station posters in that they reach persons other than just those using transit facilities, for example, motorists and pedestrians. Their audience is therefore even less selective, and they are especially suitable for advertising products of wide appeal and low unit cost.

Advertising for exterior posters is akin to outdoor advertising. There is virtually no time for detailed perusal of the poster; moreover most posters are read from a distance. Copy must be extremely brief and easily readable. Moreover, owing to the kaleidoscopic street scene, copy must be eye-catching in design and color.

Exterior posters appear on the outsides of buses. They have four main positions: right side, left side, front, and rear end. Unlike car cards, not all exterior-poster sizes are standardized. However, where they are, the standard height of the poster on the side of buses is 21 inches, with three optional widths of 27, 36, and 44 inches. This form of poster is generally known as the traveling display. Sides of buses can also carry the "queen"-size poster (21 by 88 inches) and the "king"-size (30 by 144 inches). The standard size of the front-end poster is 11 by 42 inches; the rear-end poster has two standard sizes, 21 by 72 inches and 7½ by 60 inches. As yet, however, not all these sizes are available in all market areas. The most universal are the traveling display (21 by 44 inches) and the king-size poster (30 by 144 inches).

Because of their exposure to the weather, exterior posters must be sturdy and weatherproof. Traveling displays and front-end and rear-end posters should be produced on at least ten-ply waterproof horizontal grain stock, and varnished after the printing. A 1-inch margin should be allowed on all sides of the display. King-size posters should be produced on 70- or 80-pound waterproof opaque poster paper; these will eventually be bonded onto ⅛-inch Masonite panels supplied by the transit company. For long-term showings the copy may be silk-screened directly onto the Masonite panels themselves for additional durability. A 1½-inch margin should be maintained on all sides of the poster.

Special visual effects can be obtained through the use of three-dimensional posters and photographs. The more effective exterior posters include brief copy, bold headlines, dominant color areas, and strong illustration.

Exterior posters are sold on both a per-unit and a showing basis. Rates are generally quoted on a twelve-month basis; however, the display may be changed monthly at no additional cost. Costs vary widely by market, but typical major markets unit costs for a 21- by 44-inch side card representative showing are:

In *New York* $9,000 per month for a 1,000 showing—average unit cost of $9

In *Boston* $2,000 per month for a 200 showing—average unit cost of $10

In *Chicago* $2,100 per month for a 200 showing—average unit cost of $10.50

In *Philadelphia* $2,000 per month for a 200 showing—average unit cost of $10

Unit costs are therefore similar, in most cities, to those for station posters, ranging from $9 to $11.

Costs of a National Campaign

The previous section dealt with individual costs in several major markets. Thus at this stage, a review of costs for various sizes of national campaigns is appropriate. Although most transit advertisers use the transit medium on a selective-market basis, several do make intensive use of the medium on a national basis by advertising in the top 25, top 50, or even the top 100 markets. While the monthly cost of such a national campaign would not be considered prohibitive, for most advertisers extensive use of transit advertising in, for example, the top 100 markets, would represent a substantial investment, particularly on an annual basis. Tables 9 and 10 document the national costs of a full showing campaign in car cards and king-size posters.

TABLE 9   Cost of a National Campaign in 11- by 28-inch Car Cards

No. of metro. markets, rank order of size	Population		No. of car cards, full showing	Monthly cost, in thousands of dollars	Annual cost, in thousands of dollars
	In thousands	Per cent United States			
10	48,100	24.1	19,715	57.1	685.7
25	69,423	34.9	27,018	71.2	854.5
50	91,181	45.8	32,292	79.8	958.2
100	113,164	56.8	36,530	86.8	1,041.8

SOURCE: Mutual Transit Advertising.

TABLE 10   Cost of a National Campaign in 30- by 144-inch Exterior Posters

No. of metro. markets, rank order of size	Population		No. of exterior posters, full showing	Monthly cost, in thousands of dollars	Annual cost, in thousands of dollars
	In thousands	Per cent United States			
10	48,100	24.1	2,720	112.8	1,354.0
25	69,423	34.9	4,240	173.0	2,075.9
50	91,181	45.8	5,612	229.8	2,758.2
100	113,164	56.8	6,868	280.9	3,370.3

SOURCE: Mutual Transit Advertising.

For many advertisers such costs for an intensive national campaign in a "supplementary" medium are prohibitive.   Consequently transit advertisers tend to use the medium on a local (selected markets) rather than national basis.

Substantial increases in rates in the major metropolitan markets have occurred for both car cards and station posters since 1951, the year in which Standard Rate & Data Service first issued a rate book for transit advertising.   Rates for traveling displays (exterior posters) have shown a lesser rate of increase (Table 11).

The real increase in all rates occurred in 1967 when several big

TABLE 11   Index of Trends in Monthly Transit Advertising Rates, Major Metropolitan Markets, 1951–1968

Year	Car cards, 11 by 28 inches, full run	Exterior posters, 21-by 44-inch traveling display, representative showing	Station posters, 2-sheet poster, 46 by 60 inches, representative showing
1968	241	158	274
1967	243	180	253
1966	158	96	140
1965	142	97	140
1960	157	103	127
1955	122	97	92
1951	100	100	100

SOURCE: Indexes based on SRDS average rates.

changes in ownership of transit media occurred. Until as late as 1966, car-card and station-poster rates were only 50 per cent over their 1951 rates, and the exterior-poster rate for traveling displays had remained relatively the same as in 1951. The 1967 and 1968 rates for both car cards and station posters were approximately 2½ times their 1951 levels, and the traveling display rates showed more than a 50 per cent increase.

Research Information

This concerns measurement of audience and expenditures.

Measurement of the Audience Each form of transit advertising has its own system of circulation count. Car-card circulation is defined as the sum of all unit trips taken by persons riding vehicles with car cards. Zone riders passing through more than one zone count as only one trip. Trips taken by paying passengers, paid and nonpaid transfers, nonpaying passengers, and school children are all included in the count. The sum of all such trips is the potential audience of interior advertising. The Transit Advertising Association reports members' estimated car-card circulation to SRDS with notarized affidavits. Nonmembers supply sworn circulation statements directly to SRDS. Available research studies such as "The Transit Millions" by Sindlinger & Co., contain valuable data on transit riders—the numbers of rides in the average day, the average month, the time spent riding, and demographic characteristics of riders.

Circulation of the station poster is determined by a count of the number of daily fares paid at each station. This estimated station-poster circulation is certified on a semiannual basis by the Transit Advertising Association.

The circulation of the exterior poster is naturally much more difficult to determine than that for car cards and station posters. Several research organizations have undertaken to measure exterior bus-poster circulation in individual cities. This has generally been accomplished by sampling the population of the city and tracing the day-to-day routes of these people throughout the city. Some surveys have also attempted to measure the reach of the outside bus poster by devising methods by which the individual sample members can report on actual or potential exposure to the poster. Other surveys have used actual identification of the poster by the sample population to measure reach, and others such as Alfred Politz Media Studies have used electronically controlled cameras to determine who actually sees the poster.

One of the more comprehensive of these surveys has been that carried out by R. H. Bruskin and A. C. Nielsen for Metro Transit Advertising, a division of Metromedia. This series of surveys, commencing in 1966, attempted to measure the reach and frequency of exposure of all three forms of transit advertising in several major cities: Los Angeles (A. C. Nielsen), New York, Boston, Chicago, and Philadelphia (R. H. Bruskin).

Each of these studies has shown the two-week potential reach of an average campaign in any one of the three transit media to be high: from 40 to 60 per cent for car cards; from 70 to 99 per cent for traveling displays; and from 20 to 30 per cent for station posters. It should be emphasized that these are estimates of the potential reach of an average showing *over a two-week period only*. Any extension of this to one month or longer would naturally build reach, and particularly frequency, to even higher levels. (All frequency of exposure levels tend to be high also, owing to the way in which transit users tend to duplicate their transit usage from day to day.)

Measurement of Expenditures   Another form of transit advertising research is carried out by the Transit Advertising Measurement Bureau, which compiles statistics of dollar expenditures in the transit advertising medium by major advertisers and by product category.

In 1967 total transit advertising dollar expenditures, both national and local, were $33 million, which represented a 13 per cent increase over the previous year. The proportion of nationally placed to locally placed advertising was almost identical—$16 million national versus $17 million local advertising. However, an examination of the breakdown between the types of transit advertising, as inside (car cards) versus outside (exterior bus posters and station posters), shows the latter to be more than twice the size of the former—$10 million inside volume and $23 million outside volume.

Total transit advertising volume has grown considerably over the past ten years, especially since 1961—$21.5 million was expended in 1957; thus 1967 represented a 54 per cent increase over this figure. (Table 12.)

Reasons for Using Transit Media

At the start of the discussion on transit advertising, several features of this form of advertising were mentioned. These features are examined below, and provide the reasons for choice on the part of those advertisers who include transit advertising as part of their media mix.

Mass Audience   Of the 123 million adults in the Continental United States, 70 million, or 57 per cent, ride 70,000 public transit vehicles each year (this figure is probably closer to 80 per cent of adults in the major metropolitan areas).   Of these 70 million transit-riding adults, 40 million use transit facilities each month and 12 million each day.   Each person rides transit an average of twenty-four times each month and spends an average of 23 minutes on each ride.

TABLE 12   Total Transit Advertising Volume

$ million

SOURCE: TAA estimates based on reports from approximately 75 per cent of transit advertising business, compiled by the Transit Advertising Measurement Bureau.

Of the remaining 53 million non-transit-riding adults, most, although not using public transportation, help constitute the pedestrian and motorist audience to the exterior bus poster.   Thus, in an average year, nearly every adult in the United States is in the potential audience of transit advertising.

Low Unit Cost   Overall the costs of all three forms of transit advertising provide a low per-individual unit cost.   Car cards enjoy a particularly low unit cost ($2 to $4 per month) but are possibly less effective per unit than station posters ($10 to $20 per month) or exterior posters ($9 to $11 per month) because of the quantity and proximity of competing car cards.

One of the reasons for transit advertising's low unit cost relative to other media is that the advertiser does not have to pay for the support of the advertising plant to quite the same extent as does the television advertiser, who has to pay indirectly for program production.   In general, the transit advertising plant is paid from passenger fares, thus reducing costs to the transit advertiser.

Low Cost Efficiencies   The cost of reaching a thousand persons with transit advertising is low relative to other media.   For example, in the five-county Philadelphia metropolitan area over a four-week period, 39,912,000 [6] rides are made by adults in 2,600 buses, trolleys, and subways.   The monthly cost of an 11- by 28-inch car card (2,388 showing) in Philadelphia is $7,403; the CPM for adults is therefore approximately 20 cents.   Using Philadelphia as an example, 4,989,000 [6] adults wait on 75 station platforms over a four-week period.   The cost of a two-sheet station poster (65 showing) in Philadelphia is approximately $658; the CPM is therefore approximately 15 cents.   Still, in Philadelphia 19,208,000 [6] adults are exposed to advertising on 200 sides of buses in an average four-week period.   The cost of a 21- by 44-inch travel display (200 showing) is $2,000; that is a CPM of 10 cents.

For all types of transit advertising cost efficiencies are extremely low, ranging from 10 to 20 cents on a monthly basis.

Flexibility   In car cards, station posters, and exterior posters the advertiser has a wide range of sizes to choose from, ranging from the junior car card (11 by 14 inches) to the 3-sheet station poster (42 by 84 inches) and the king-size poster (30 by 144 inches).   He also enjoys considerable flexibility as to showing size (number of units used and position) and the duration of his advertising.   The medium is suited to both the large and the small advertising budget.

Geographic Selectivity   Not only can the transit advertiser select any combination of major metropolitan markets for his advertising, but he can also, within many of the individual markets, select a particular coverage plan.   Furnished with maps of the transit lines in a market, he can select those specific areas which he feels constitute the best location for reaching the bulk of his target audience; for example, the Fifth Avenue bus route in New York.

High Potential Reach   The reach of transit advertising is a more complex dimension than circulation and is thus open to a wide range of interpretation as to its size.   Nevertheless, all the studies of the measurement of reach have concurred on one point: the potential reach of all three forms of transit advertising is high.

[6] Metro Transit Advertising Research, October–November, 1968.

A series of well-conducted, highly regarded studies [7] still in progress has, to date, measured the reach of transit advertising in four major cities: Los Angeles, New York, Chicago, and Philadelphia. In, for example, the Philadelphia five-county metropolitan area, it was found that over the average two-week period 41 per cent of adult men and 50 per cent of adult women are the potential reach of a 2,600 car-card showing. Sides of buses do even better; over a two-week period 80 per cent of adult men and 73 per cent of adult women are the potential reach of a 200 showing on the sides of buses (left sides generally obtain a slightly higher reach than right sides, but the above represents an average for both sides). Station posters do not achieve quite so high a level: a 75 poster showing reaches 29 per cent of adult men and 22 per cent of adult women over an average two-week period.

Thus sides of buses, owing to their high potential audience, achieve the highest reach over a two-week period. Car cards achieve approximately only two-thirds, and station posters only one-third, of the exterior-poster reach levels in the same two-week period.

A comparison of the reach of advertising on the sides of buses in Philadelphia with that in Los Angeles, New York, and Chicago shows similar high reach levels in these three latter cities. Whereas 80 per cent of adults are reached by a 100 showing on the sides of buses in the five-county Philadelphia metropolitan area, 76 per cent are reached in Los Angeles (Los Angeles County), 93 per cent in New York, and 81 per cent in Chicago (six-county metropolitan area).

High Potential Frequency Since the average transit riders make twenty-four trips per month, frequency levels corresponding to the reach measurements shown above are similarly high. The same series of studies [8] showed that in the five-county Philadelphia metropolitan area the average adult reached by a 2,600 car-card showing is exposed to that showing eighteen times over a two-week period. An exterior poster with a 200 showing on sides of buses has an average frequency of five against adults over a two-week period; a station-poster showing of 75 has an average frequency of four against adults over a two-week period.

Frequency levels in the Los Angeles, New York, and Chicago areas

[7] Studies by R. H. Bruskin and A. C. Nielsen for Metro Transit Advertising, a Division of Metromedia.
[8] *Ibid.*

tend to duplicate those for Philadelphia. Two-week frequency levels for sides of buses (100 showing) against adults are seven in Philadelphia, five in Los Angeles, six in New York, and six in Chicago.

Thus over a two-week period car cards enjoy the highest frequency of exposure levels (along with relatively low reach). Traveling displays and station posters do only one-fourth as well, although the exterior poster does compensate for this with its higher reach levels.

Unlimited Use of Color   There are no printing restrictions inherent in preparing copy for transit advertising, except in relation to the paper stock on which it is printed.   Thus the transit advertiser can display the copy he feels best suits the product advertised, making use of the most appealing color combinations and textures.

Point-of-sale Value   Transit advertising is essentially a supplementary medium.   It reminds the consumer of the particular merits of a product; it reminds him of the name of the product and usually also of the appearance of the package; and it does all these things at a time when he can shortly be at a convenient outlet selling the product. This point-of-sale value is of particular importance in relation to the advertising of foods, cigarettes, beverages, and other household products on transit routes used by shoppers about to make purchases.

The major product categories advertised in transit media are alcoholic beverages (liquor taking precedence over beer and wines), finance companies, media, food, and entertainment.

Transit Advertising Expenditures

	1967, in millions of dollars	*1966, in millions of dollars*
Alcoholic beverages	4.2	4.4
Finance companies	4.0	3.2
Media	3.4	2.9
Food	3.1	2.6
Entertainment	2.5	2.1

SOURCE: Transit Advertising Measurement Bureau.

Other important users are manufacturers of tobacco products, cars, pharmaceuticals, and soft drinks, and companies offering transportation services.

By far the largest transit media representative is Mutual Transit Advertising, which is active in national transit advertising in forty states; other large national representatives are Nation-wide Bus Advertising and Philbin & Coine.

The largest transit advertising users in 1967 were Schenley Industries and P. Lorillard, both at more than $500,000, and Wm. Wrigley, General Motors, and American Home Products, each at more than $400,000. Since transit advertising tends to be a supplementary medium, its major users will fluctuate from one year to the next as to the amount they spend in transit advertising.

One important influence on the dollars spent in transit advertising in 1967 and 1968 was the various transit strikes in 1966 and 1967 in many of the major cities. This seems to have had an important effect on the dollar advertising volume of such companies as Schieffelin, which ranked first in 1966 at $558,100, but dropped to seventeenth place in 1967 with only $165,700, and was not even among the top 100 advertisers in the first half of 1968. Other companies that have drastically cut back their expenditures in transit advertising are Pepsi-Co. (nearly $500,000 in 1965) and Whitehall Laboratories (nearly $500,000 in 1964). In 1966 Wm. Wrigley cut its transit advertising expenditures from more than $1 million to less than half this, and is currently maintaining this new level.

The top twelve transit advertisers, all national advertisers, account for a sizable portion of total national transit advertising volume: 27 per cent in 1967 and 32 per cent in 1966.

Transit advertising has played a significant and efficient role in the advertising of a variety of different industries and probably nowhere more efficaciously than in the soft-drink industry. The advantages inherent in the use of transit advertising, such as mass audience, high repetition of exposure, point-of-sale value, and geographic and placement flexibility, have resulted in soft-drink bottlers and franchise companies placing more and more emphasis on the selling power of the transit advertising medium. In 1963 just over $500,000 was expended on soft-drink advertising for transit placement; in 1966 this figure was $875,000, and in 1967 it was more than $1 million.

Other industries placing increasing emphasis on transit advertising are transportation (particularly passenger airlines and tours) and automobile manufacturers. Many of these transit advertisers, such as Pan American, Trans World Airlines, and General Motors, expended little or nothing in transit advertising five or more years ago, whereas they are now among the largest transit advertisers.

Companies such as Wm. Wrigley, and those in the tobacco and

alcoholic-beverage industries, were always big investors in transit advertising and continue to be so.

POINT-OF-PURCHASE

Description of the Medium

The actual development of point-of-purchase (POP) display materials began in some period lost in antiquity when the barber's pole and the pawnbroker's three golden balls began to emerge as symbols of those rather basic professions. The cobbler's giant shoe and the optician's outsized spectacles are other, less stylized examples of displays that were developed and handed down from a time when few could read and write. As communities grew, the emerging entrepreneur began to recognize the necessity of informing a larger circle of the public than that which could be reached by word of mouth that his was the place to find some needed product or service. Before the comparatively sophisticated representations mentioned evolved, we can be sure that other sellers displayed their blankets or pottery, their clothing, or food, or tools in a way calculated to inform and attract the buyer.

All this was, of course, advertising; the only advertising that existed when man was without the benefit of movable type and the coaxial cable. It is, in essence, the same advertising that is found today at the place where the goods are sold and where their manufacturer makes one last attempt to sway that prospective buyer away from his competitor's product and to his own. Now, this first of all advertising is called, variously, *point-of-purchase* or *point-of-sale*. Choice of which of the two terms is more acceptable is up to the user. Point-of-purchase appears to be the current favorite of those who consider the term point-of-sale too commercial and too much oriented to the seller's frame of reference.

By the mid-1800s point-of-purchase had begun to take on very much of the form, shape, and general usage that we know today but it was not until after World War I that point-of-purchase became a $1.5 billion business.[9]

[9] For those who are interested in a more comprehensive study of the historical development of point-of-purchase advertising, a paper prepared by George Kress of Loras College, Dubuque, Iowa, is suggested. It is available through the Point-of-Purchase Advertising Institute, Inc., New York.

Today point-of-purchase has a few limitations as it had the day an enterprising barber-surgeon first wound a cloth red with blood around his gatepost and thereby fathered the barber's pole.   Point-of-purchase, like other mass media advertising, carries an advertising message.   There all similarities between point-of-purchase and other advertising forms cease.

The placing of displays used at the point-of-purchase varies almost as much as the materials with which the displays are made.   General display-placement areas can be counted as window, floor, wall, counter, shelf, and ceiling (or suspended).   Some also count outdoor displays in shopping malls.   It is a matter of choice.

Value of the placement area is in direct ratio to the amount of traffic the area receives.   Counter and check-out area displays are the most favored, not only because of the traffic they enjoy, but also because they provide a then-and-there opportunity for purchase of the items being advertised.   Because of this very desirability, these areas are targets of a very high percentage of POP material.   Because of this heavy competition for the space, a lower proportion of point-of-purchase pieces presented can be used by the merchandiser.

Cost of Purchase

Size and shape of displays vary as widely as methods of their construction.   Anything goes where construction materials are concerned.   Hence, the cost of individual point-of-purchase pieces can vary tremendously.   Some indications of the average percentage of the budgeted expenditure for advertising of a few representative national advertisers might provide a guideline to overall budgeting:

Soft drinks . . . . 40–55 per cent
Cosmetics . . . . 30–50 per cent
Food specialties . . . . . . 26–45 per cent
Liquor . . . . 20–40 per cent
Beer . . . . 25–30 per cent
Drugs . . . . 15–25 per cent
Food staples . . . . 10–20 per cent

SOURCE: "Colonial Study," *Progressive Grocer*, p. C81.

What few rules are followed by those who produce point-of-purchase are generally based on needs and desires of retailers who are the ultimate users.   Even so, clean breaks from established patterns and usage are not unusual, and new variations and adaptations are welcome provided positive or beneficial results can be expected.

To increase their chances of having their POP pieces included among those that are set up, advertisers have adopted a number of stratagems that add to cost of the medium. Foremost among these is the giving of special allowances on goods ordered during the time of the promotion. Advertisers buy the display space through discounting their merchandise at wholesale. Other methods of gaining the same goal include incorporating something of value into the display —a tea cart has often been used as a rack for the display of merchandise. Such self-liquidating items as cameras and dolls are regularly included. They all become the property of the store manager when the displays are dismantled.

Special sweepstakes for the retailers are popular, often with an entry blank packed in with each display kit. The idea is that once the box is opened, the display is much more likely to be put up. Sometimes merchandisers are encouraged to use the display on the promise of receiving duplicates of prizes that customers may win— and competitions are conducted for the best retail displays on the basis of photographic evidence submitted by the merchant. Who knows? The manufacturer may even supply the camera for making the shots, free to the store manager.

Research Information

The typical consumer, it has been estimated at Yale Research, forgets approximately 40 per cent of the commercial messages he receives within twenty minutes of the time he receives them. Within four hours as much as 60 per cent of a given message's content will be lost. This makes a strong argument for the importance of getting a sales message up at the time the customer is in a position to make a purchase, the time he spends in the retail outlet.

In a 1962 survey conducted by the Point-of-Purchase Advertising Institute (POPAI), 5,215 shoppers were interviewed at thirty-six food outlets regarding their buying habits. Their answers showed that 81.9 per cent were aware of displays, 44.9 per cent claimed to use display information in making their purchase decisions, and 33.1 per cent said they made an actual purchase as a result of seeing a display. This survey underscores the high awareness of and dependence on displays by consumers.

A peripheral advantage of point-of-purchase displays is that of cumulative effect. With successive impressions tending to intensify awareness and interest on the part of the consumer, an increasing potential for purchase action is built up.

This cumulative effect becomes more important with the increase in expenditures in other forms of mass media advertising. The eyes and ears of consumers are literally being pounded to insensibility with the weight of advertising messages.

> The volume of advertising in this country has increased some 500 per cent in the past twenty years. America's ability to absorb it has increased only 50 per cent. . . . It can be estimated that the average adult now has a minimum of 560 [10] advertising messages (excluding outdoor advertising, point-of-purchase, transportation advertising and window displays) placed before him every waking day.[11]

A cross section of the opinions of retailers themselves on what they find effective—and not so effective—in display merchandising is enlightening.

Some years ago 237 supermarket managers, 85 headquarter officials, and 87 grocery wholesalers were interviewed by Audits and Surveys Company for a study sponsored by *Family Circle* in cooperation with the U.S. Department of Agriculture. They rated posters, pennants, and streamers first in preference, shelf-talkers second, and animated displays third. Mobiles came in last. Use of color in the displays was felt to be mandatory and the featuring of two, three, or even four products per display was desirable. National media support was considered a requisite if "retail acceptance of POP regardless of its nature" was to be forthcoming. It was perishables first, with meat and produce departments revealed to be those areas for which point-of-purchase was most welcome—with the departments that carried things that would keep coming in last.

Uses of the Medium

How is it that point-of-purchase has become so important a factor in today's marketing mix? How does it speed the flow of products from

[10] Most commonly quoted figure is 1,500 daily advertising exposures, but this would mean more than 100 exposures per hour per individual, which does not seem realistic.

[11] Charles F. Adams, "Common Sense in Advertising," McGraw-Hill Book Company, New York, 1965, p. 5.

manufacturer to user? What marketing objectives can it achieve?

Perhaps the foremost reason is that it "gives the advertiser a last word before purchases are made." [12] The Seventh DuPont Consumer Buying Habits Study (1965) points out that in-store decisions account for almost 70 per cent of all food-store purchases.

The development and spread of self-service retail outlets, first to food, then to drugs and more recently to other wares, was one of the determining factors that led to the tremendous surge in the use of more, better, and more expensive point-of-purchase material. Material varies from a simple shelf-taker or take-one card with a cents-off offer to an elaborate creation that featured lights and motion—and even a pitchman's voice actuated by a treadle or some other device. Displays are disposable and therefore soon to be discarded, as well as solidly built and offered as permanent additions to the fixtures of the stores which agree to accept them.

Second, the fact established by the DuPont Buying Habits Study, that fewer shoppers carry shopping lists, tended to make more important the influence of point-of-purchase material.

Print and broadcast media, though effective, were not considered adequate to do a complete selling job in this new world in which consumers make their own buying decisions and serve themselves, no longer relying on the advice of a favorite grocer or druggist. Quite often, the customer in the marketplace, with a number of buying decisions to be made, is presented with a difficult choice. She is faced with selecting from a number of practically identical detergents at highly competitive prices. Or she feels compelled to choose one of the numerous hair sprays about which she has probably once read or heard something, somewhere. The advantages to be gained by getting the last word at the instant of purchase decision are obvious.

Third, point-of-purchase serves to remind a consumer of a need for a product, or it can remind him of a desire to have the product, which desire might well have been conceived at the time of a previous stimulation by another advertising medium.

William W. Mee, former executive director of the Point-of-Purchase Advertising Institute, Inc., said in a speech before the American Marketing Association on January 4, 1962: "Point-of-purchase

---

[12] Harry Walker Hepner, "Modern Advertising Practices and Principles," McGraw-Hill Book Company, New York, 1956, p. 283.

advertising produces the most significant results when it works in conjunction with mass media advertising. It is designed to tie together all facets of the marketing campaign at the retail store where product can be identified and sold."

This tying-in of mass media advertising can consist of reprinting consumer advertisements on displays and counter cards, reproduction of merchandising ads modified to include such necessaries as contest entry blanks, additional promotion of offers made in print and broadcast, and so on.

Fourth, as a means of helping to prevent brand substitution, point-of-purchase is an effective marketing tool. Consider two competing food brands with only minor differences; one has instituted an in-store display poster campaign, the other has no POP display. Assume a weekly store traffic flow of 7,500 customers, and that the brand having the display is in an average location. Since the average shopper spends twenty-nine minutes in the store and passes 57 per cent of the product locations, the display will receive approximately 4,300 consumer exposures per week. Multiply this by 10,000 outlets —not an unreasonable figure—and the brand with POP will have had 43 million more exposures during a one-week period than will the brand without the in-store displays. In addition to the value of the exposures themselves, consider also the value of these multiple exposures in registering the brand name impressions on the consumer, the "cumulative effect" mentioned earlier.

What are the factors which determine the best possible point-of-purchase program in any given set of circumstances? How can we assure that the very best display will be developed under these circumstances, a display that will complement and reinforce product advertising and at the same time help to sell the product independently of its advertising?

Development of Successful POP   Before going into details of the display itself it is wise to consider first what contribution, if any, outside display organizations are to make in the program. A good creative display service can do everything from analyzing the problem to shipping the finished displays—or merely provide technical knowledge or services in any areas in which need arises. The amount and nature of the display house's contributions will be determined by how much of the job can be effectively handled by the originating organization.

Importance of Sales Ideas   In general, the type of display will be dictated by the sales idea or ideas.   The most popular type of display is one that features the product itself, either actual or reproduced, and either alone or with some or all of the total product line.   Product use and product development displays, also highly product-oriented, are variations of the main theme.   It should be kept in mind that whatever the type of display, the graphics should be bright and striking so as to gain the prospective customer's attention and should be designed so as to ease the selling of the product by the dealer and at the same time simplify the purchase of the product by the customer.

Problems of Distribution   While work on the display piece goes forward, it is none too soon to consider the problems of distribution, for any given display is moving into an area that is increasingly overcrowded and in which many displays are discarded without ever having been unpacked.   Point-of-purchase, a most effective medium when properly circulated, does not have the built-in circulation of a magazine or a television program.

It is most important that the involved sales staff or other distributing organization be kept up to date on all aspects of the promotion that they should know about; that all instructions be followed up on to ensure that they are carried out correctly; and that any government regulations that might apply to the promotion be thoroughly checked.

In a recent comment on retailers' attitudes to POP, W. Robert Lane, president of Food Advertisers Service, Inc., a leading vendor of point-of-purchase support, said:

> Retailers use point-of-purchase as brand managers use TV—that is, to position themselves in the marketplace.   Their No. 1 concern is setting a price image; their No. 2 concern is establishing a general store atmosphere.   POP material that fails to meet these two criteria will be of no interest to the retailers.

For the advertising and sales promotion manager who is responsible for the production of point-of-purchase displays, the use of a comprehensive checklist is strongly recommended.   The one put out by *Media-Scope* magazine, New York, in cooperation with POPAI, is definitive.   Under eight major headings this lists each step as it should be taken toward the successful setting up of POP units in retail outlets.

PART SEVEN
Research

CHAPTER TWENTY-TWO

Measurement of Sales Effectiveness of Advertising*

CHARLES RAMOND *President, Marketing Control, Inc., and Editor,* Journal of Advertising Research

Advertising effectiveness means different things to the groups responsible for its different effects. To the writer or artist effective advertising is that which communicates the desired message. To the media buyer effective advertising is that which reaches prospective buyers a sufficient number of times. To the advertising or marketing manager effective advertising is that which, together with other marketing forces, sells his brand or product. To the general manager, effective advertising produces a return on his firm's expenditure.

In fact, effective advertising must achieve a sufficient combination of all four goals, delivering messages to the right audience, thereby creating sales at a profit. Most advertisers have begun only recently

---

* Parts of this chapter were published originally by the Long Range Planning Service of the Stanford Research Institute as a report that included contributions by Ronald R. Larson, senior industrial economist.

to set goals in all four areas and measure progress toward them. Some advertisers have set communication and audience goals, and measured copy and media effects, but few advertisers have set dollar goals and measured sales and profit effects. The result is that advertising has rarely been a part of corporate planning. "Money is commonly appropriated for advertising with extreme laxity," the National Industrial Conference Board found in a 1962 survey, ". . . most often simply on the basis of a fixed percentage of sales or in conformance with past spending habits." The NICB attributed this laxity to management's failure to insist on specific objectives and to its belief that it is hard or impossible to measure advertising effectiveness.

Changes Since Early 1960s

Both conditions have been changing, particularly since the start of the 1960s. Management's failure to set advertising goals has been diagnosed and prescribed in the study "Defined Advertising Goals for Measured Advertising Results," which was commissioned by the Association of National Advertisers. While emphasizing the goals of message communication and media audiences to the virtual exclusion of sales and profits, this book must be regarded as a milestone in advertising's progress toward control.

A second milestone was published in 1969, Roy Campbell's "Measuring the Sales and Profit Results of Advertising," Association of National Advertisers. It reviews comprehensively the available measures of advertising and makes a good, practical case for the experimental method. Thus, management's belief that advertising measurement is difficult or impossible is also changing, largely as the result of the increasing number of studies which have obtained relatively unambiguous and actionable measures of advertising, not only in terms of audience and communication, but also in terms of sales and profit. These studies are relatively new, and undertaken by larger companies. This chapter will review these analyses to show what effects are being measured, the techniques used, the obstacles and conditions over and under which successful application can be expected, the likelihood that these conditions will become more prevalent, and the possible consequences of all this for various business activities and industries.

WHAT TO MEASURE: COMMUNICATION OR SALES?

Since 1960 the single most debated issue in United States advertising has been whether advertising should be evaluated according to its effect upon communication (awareness of brand, attitude toward the brand, knowledge of the advertising message) or in terms of sales. Communications measures have been defended largely by agencies and agency-oriented advertisers, accustomed as they have been to using these measures to make rapid decisions among alternative forms of copy or media. Sales measures have been advocated by larger advertisers for whom a small per cent increase in advertising sales efficiency would more than pay for the research required. Agencies objected to sales measures because, as they said, sales were the result of many factors over which they had no control: price, distribution, or product quality. They failed to note that communication also results from such factors.

While the argument still simmers, many advertisers and agencies have agreed that measures of both communications and sales are necessary. Without the sales measures no guidance can be had to adjust the budget and its allocations toward demonstrably more profitable combinations. Without communications measures no guidance can be had to improve the advertising itself toward provably motivating copy and media. Many client-agency pairs have agreed to divide the research responsibility in terms of the decisions the research helps to make. Thus agencies measure communications effects in the hope of improving the copy and media decisions, while advertisers measure sales in the hope of improving their budgetary decisions.

TECHNIQUES FOR MEASURING ADVERTISING EFFECTIVENESS

Theme or Platform Research

Selection of the appeal, theme, or platform for the advertising campaign is considered by some authorities to be the most important step in the entire campaign. And yet, all too frequently this step receives only limited testing, much less than copy and media. While almost all firms nominate several themes for consideration, only a few of the larger firms go so far as actually to test the relative merits of each. Most firms use market research inputs to varying degrees, along with suggestions or recommendations from sales or management and the agency, in combination with their experience and judgment. However, few make effort to ferret out systematically the needs and motives of existing and potential customers and to translate them into various possible platforms. In many instances, last-minute pressures allow too little time to do this sort of thing, even where management might be encouraged to do so.

Theme or platform testing is especially important for established products which have few physical characteristics that differentiate them from their competitors. Where there is a product difference that provides a competitive advantage, the general theme or platform selection is less important—it is essentially dictated by the product itself as long as these features are real to the consumer. Theme testing sometimes can be deceptively important when a product difference exists in the mind of the producer, but is not evident to the potential consumer. Seldom does the advertiser or agency spend the time or investment needed to develop coordinated copy or media for fuller testing of alternatives.

In the 1950s various motivation-research techniques came into use to identify unconscious or hard-to-express consumer motives that would identify a good advertising theme. Depth interviews, projective tests, and other paraphernalia of the clinical psychologist became popular tools in advertising research.

More recently, motivation research gradually ceased to be regarded as the search for exploitable unconscious motives. Instead it has been redefined more modestly as the study of those psychological variables which might be related to the consumer's purchase of products or services. It is considered the study of relationships between the psychological attributes of a brand or product (its "image") and the psychological attributes of the consumer (his "personality"). The thesis is that if markets can be segmented according to psychological as well as demographic variables, then it should be possible to fashion advertising appeals which are unusually effective in causing sales among the appropriate population segments. A panel study by J. Walter Thompson Company showed that subgroups selected for their scores on certain traits bought more of a mail-order product than did an unselected control group, in response to a direct-mail advertisement designed specifically to appeal to that particular subgroup's psychological needs.   Neither group bought very much—a result deemed statistically significant but practically unimportant.

So, in fact, have been the relationships found ever since between personality variables and purchases of beer, coffee, tea, and toilet tissue.   Brand loyalty, store loyalty, and amount purchased correlate significantly with certain demographic and personality traits of the 8,900 members of the panel.   These correlations, however, though statistically significant, are too small to give practical guidance.   It seems safe to conclude that until more discriminating personality scales are developed, perhaps for the specific purpose of predicting purchase, psychological market segments will not be significantly more useful to the advertiser than demographic market segments.

Copy Research

Having learned the needs of his prospects and chosen general appeals or themes by which to reach them, the advertiser must then determine how best to execute those themes.   Which copy, headlines, illustrations, or perhaps music will best communicate his message?   Studies answering questions of this sort have traditionally made up the bulk of advertising research, and are still called, even in the age of television, *copy research*.   (See Chapter Twenty-three, Copy Research.)

Media Research

Having decided what to say and how to say it, the advertiser must then decide where, when, and how often to say it.   Surveys and analyses which guide these decisions—media research—should have as their aim the determination of the audiences for advertising placed in media.   Such studies are few and not to be confused with the many studies which are intended to determine the audiences of only the media themselves.   (See Chapter Twenty-four, Media Research.)

Sales Research

Knowledge of motives, copy, or media will not tell the advertiser what, if anything, his advertising has done to influence the sales of his product.   For this information he must conduct sales research, which isolates the contribution his advertising expenditures makes to sales.

Three kinds of evidence are cited to link sales to advertising expenditures. The most frequently practiced is the correlation of expenditures with sales. This method lends itself to both an informal, judgment treatment, as well as to more systematic statistical assessment. For those firms which base sales predominantly on advertising this can be a meaningful measure. For those firms in which other marketing efforts are relatively more important, such measures are not particularly definitive because they do not necessarily reflect cause-and-effect relationships that would better aid managerial judgment. For most business firms, some form of correlation, whether in management's mind or by specific tests and programs, probably represents the key basis for allocating advertising dollars, despite the widespread intellectual recognition of the deficiences of such an approach. (See Table 1.)

Also widely employed are correlations of reports of advertising exposure with reports of purchase. This approach is accepted by most segments of the advertising fraternity, but it is also questionable how well cause and effect are measured. It is unclear to what extent—or even whether—attitude toward, or recall and recognition of, advertising copy cause the sales associated with these scores. For example, car buyers tend to be more aware of car ads after purchase. Whether or not these studies are consistently correct or consistently misleading cannot be adequately demonstrated. Despite a fair number of incorrect conclusions, these approaches are helpful enough to warrant their continued use—as indicated by the present market for them. There is a widespread appreciation of their limitations and a hope that something better can be done. Certainly the fairly high degree of management uncertainty on the part of advertisers reflects this and suggests a fundamental improvement opportunity.

Experimental Method A third approach and one that is currently in limited but growing use in advertising-sales research is the experimental method. It requires, among other things, that extraneous influences on sales be dealt with; that controllable factors be controlled; uncontrollable but measurable factors be measured and accounted for statistically; and enough experimental units be in each treatment to permit accurate estimates of their variability. The object is simply to obtain results which provide more meaningful conclusions, i.e., what causes what. Properly handled, this approach can provide results that make the other techniques relatively ambiguous by comparison.

TABLE 1 Sources of Ambiguity in Methods of Relating Sales to Advertising

Method	Observed result	Possible meaning of result
Correlation of advertising expenditures with sales	The more a company spends for advertising (per year, per city), the higher its sales	Advertising causes sales Advertising is arbitrarily budgeted as a fixed per cent of sales Advertising and sales are similarly affected by other causes, e.g., population Measurement error or chance
Correlation of reports of exposure to advertising with reports of purchases	People who recall relatively more of a brand's advertising buy relatively more of the brand	Advertising causes purchase Purchase of a brand or product makes people more sensitive to that brand's or product's advertising The same people overclaim both exposure to advertising and purchase Measurement error or chance
Comparison of groups (of cities, stores, people) randomly assigned different advertising treatments (copy, media, amounts)	Improbable difference between treatment groups	Advertising causes purchase Measurement error or chance: These two interpretations can be rendered extremely unlikely by using proper experimental design, care in execution and large numbers of cases in each group

Perhaps thirty to fifty experiments have been reported publicly, and an unknown number conducted for private consumption. Most have been by larger firms, but such techniques are not limited to firms with their resources. At a recent meeting of major British advertisers, perhaps a third of the firms in attendance had conducted some type of designed marketing experiment. A limited number of United States companies are known to have done the same. The results have not been uniformly salutary. Unusable results have occurred for many reasons. Despite the many problems encountered, most of the published research has provided good results.

Costs

An important barrier to widespread use of experimental techniques is their cost. While the total cost may range from virtually nothing to substantially over $10,000, or multiples thereof, a frequently encountered range is from $15,000 to $40,000. Data collection is consistently the most expensive requirement, because most firms do not now collect sales data in a manner which is useful for this purpose. The cut-in costs of altering programs can also be inordinately expensive when a firm extensively uses network television. This is less a problem when spot announcements are employed. These constitute the key cost barriers at present, while the manpower costs of actually conducting the experiment are relatively low.

WHEN AND HOW TO ESTIMATE THE SALES EFFECTS OF ADVERTISING

From an analysis of the publicly available studies measuring advertising and sales, it appears that the designed experiment typically works better when certain conditions are present. The sales effects of advertising can be most accurately estimated when:

   The product or brand has no direct substitute now or in the foreseeable future. Competing products or brands are few, and technology is unlikely to make the item obsolete during the period of experimentation.

   The buyers of the product or brand can be unambiguously defined; can be reached easily by advertising and interviewers; are geographically concentrated; and spend little time "in the market."

The lot size of the purchase is constant from purchase to purchase by the same buyer, and the same from buyer to buyer.

Price is constant over time, markets, and amount purchased.

Channels of distribution are many.   The more there are, the less likely the consumer is to be frustrated in an advertising-induced attempt to buy.

Levels of distribution are few.   The more wholesalers, dealers, and distributors stand between producer and consumer, the more individuals must decide before purchase can occur, and the more there are to be influenced by advertising.

The influence of personal selling is constant over time and over markets.

Competitors' technical services do not differ.

The copy platform is constant and unambiguous.   The fewer the copy points, the easier it is to tell if communication has occurred.

Special promotions are not undertaken.

Packaging is distinctive and constant.

The producer is the only advertiser of the brand, i.e., there is no cooperative or local advertising.

Competitors are slow to respond to changes in marketing strategy and maintain more or less the same marketing policies.

Competitors' advertising and marketing policies are relatively constant in all markets.

Potential sales can be accurately estimated for small geographical units, e.g., counties or census tracts, and during short time periods such as weeks or months.

Government controls over product design, price, competition, and advertising are minimal or at least unchanging.

Clearly, not all these conditions are applicable to all advertisers. Meeting them, moreover, does not guarantee a conclusive experiment, but only the avoidance of certain common errors.   Experimentation is increasingly popular, not because it always works, but because in many cases it is the only way to have a chance of getting unambiguous measures.

If enough of the conditions exist to warrant the conduction of a field experiment, then great care should be taken in its design.   The assumptions involved in analyzing data from such a study must be met, but also the more common pitfalls encountered by the early experimenters in advertising measurement must be avoided. If all the precautions listed below are followed, the results of the experiment are much more likely to reflect the true relationships in the marketing system and permit managerial action to be taken. Some of these features may seem rudimentary or self-evident, but nevertheless are vital to successful experimentation and frequently not fully appreciated.

Use random samples of defined populations. This ensures that the results of the experiment will be projectable to that population. A representative sample of a small population will provide more actionable results than an unrepresentative sample of a larger population.

Randomly assign experimental units (people, stores, cities) to different treatments. This ensures that any difference between treatment groups is due only to the treatment or chance—and the chance explanation can be reduced as far as the experimenter wishes by adding more cases to each group. This principle of randomness is the keystone of experimental design, almost eliminating the possibility that the results obtained could be caused by any nonchance factor other than the differential treatment given the groups.

Whenever feasible, administer every treatment to each group, but in a different order so as to control the influence of one treatment on its successors. An advertiser, for example, might give one group of cities high advertising and then low, while an equivalent group of cities receives low advertising and then high. (This is the simplest form of the Latin Square design.) If no order effect is anticipated, a single group should receive every treatment one after the other. The advantage of exposing every person, store, or city to each different treatment is that the effect of the differing treatments can be estimated without regard to the inevitable differences among individual persons, stores, or cities. Instead of comparing one group with one that perhaps is comparable—but possibly is not—the group is matched against itself under a different condition. Thus the precision of the comparison is bettered by eliminating the within-group variance.

Whenever possible, administer different levels of two or three different treatments simultaneously, so as to observe their joint effects.
Often these joint effects are surprisingly different from those that might come from adding their individual effects. Two positive marketing forces may be antagonistic, for example, and cancel each

other; or two relatively neutral marketing forces may combine to produce a surprisingly large positive effect.   These interactions cannot be observed unless two or more variables are investigated simultaneously.

Keep the experiment going long enough to observe delayed effects of marketing forces.   Much advertising takes time to exert its effect on sales or communications.   The study should be conducted long enough to detect these lagged effects.

Great care should be taken to ensure that the desired treatment is in fact administered to the group that should receive it   This is particularly important in media studies where cities or other geographical regions are the experimental units.   Merely to instruct the agency media department to double the level of advertising in markets A, B, and C will not usually guarantee that these instructions can or will be executed.

Equal care should be taken to ensure that the response measured in each treatment area comes only from persons from that region.   Receivers of advertising in Region A may well shop in Region B.   Failure to take account of such crossings of the line between geographically separate groups has been the downfall of more than one marketing experiment.

When powerful extraneous forces can be identified before the experiment, the samples should be stratified by levels of this force.   If previous brand share, for example, is known to exert a continuing influence on current brand share, the sample should be divided into comparable groups of stores or cities wherein brand-share levels are approximately equal.   Then each stratum should be randomly assigned to a different treatment.

When powerful extraneous forces can be identified only during or after the experiment, they should be accounted for statistically, usually by analysis of covariance.   Observable but uncontrollable extraneous factors can be dealt with by adjusting the payoff variable according to its correlation with that force.   Temperature, for example, affects daily sales of soft drinks, but cannot be controlled; any attempts to measure the influence of the soda fountain's in-store advertising on sales of drinks should take into account the daily temperature and adjust for its correlation with sales after the experiment. If "hot" and "cold" regions can be reliably identified beforehand, stratification by region should be used.

TABLE 2 Selected Instances of Advertising-Sales Measurements in Respect to Amount of Advertising Used

Company, product, and brand advertised	Number of levels of each variable studied	Number and kind of measurements and/or statistical techniques	Results	Tentative conclusions of possible value to other firms
Du Pont Nonstick cookware "Teflon"	3 levels of spending 13 cities 2 time periods	1,000 women telephoned each period, asked about purchases	Advertising expanded total market 21%, "Teflon" 100%	Advertising increase may borrow sales from the next period
Du Pont Product not given	5 levels of effect on brand choice	Markov process model; market experiments; over 70,000 contacts	Sales and profit effects predicted within 1%. Advertising budget reallocated among sales territories	Market share for each territory can be predicted. Profit from any budget level can be predicted. Territory profits can be compared
International Latex Corp. Women's undergarments Playtex	4 cities (3 control) 2 levels (TV and non-TV)	Store sales audited 2,500 interviews 1,000 before campaign 1,000 after campaign 500 from first	Sales were 200% better in brassieres, 150% better in girdles, interviews produced no sales increase in TV markets as opposed to control city markets. Results may be somewhat biased by introduction of a new girdle in one control city	Advertising does increase short-term sales. Not clear if benefits equaled or exceeded costs. Telephone interviews not effective in measuring demand changes revealed in store audits

USDA Dairy products No brand given	2 groups (distribution or nondistribution of leaflets on home routes) 1 time period (10 weeks)	Sales audited	Sales increase but not statistically significant	All studies do not provide conclusive results, or specific forms and amounts of promotion are ineffective in increasing sales
USDA Cottage cheese No brand given	7 cities (2 control) 2 test areas (North and South) 1 time period (6 weeks)	Sales compared with previous years	Sales increased during promotion then dropped. Southern cities maintained higher sales than before test	Advertising can maintain its effects to a certain extent. Changes in basic economic factors at time of experiment cloud the results
USDA Oranges No brand given	Not given	Theoretical study with one concrete example; two factors studied quantitatively—demand elasticity and long-run effects	Results of expenditure for ads comparable with those of previous years	Determination of optimum advertising expenditures depends on measures that are very difficult to obtain
Pillsbury Food products No brand given	Not given (Study of two food products: to determine repeat buyers of one, ad expenditures for other)	Repeat-purchase data feedback on first; tabular measurement of various ads and deals on other	Increased advertising expenditure aimed at new buyers of first product. Advertising for other was planned just to maintain distribution and prevent profit loss	Management should be involved in advertising research to control expenditure

TABLE 2 (Continued)

Company, product, and brand advertised	Number of levels of each variable studied	Number and kind of measurements and/or statistical techniques	Results	Tentative conclusions of possible value to other firms
Dryer Pharmaceutical Co. Dryer cold tablet	3 test markets, 3 control markets 1 time period (1 year) 2 budget levels	3 test markets had 50% increase in spending. Store audits taken every 4 weeks. Two telephone surveys taken, 200 interviews in each market, each survey	Audits: Control market up 15%. Experimental markets up 95%. Telephone survey: Results showed nothing. This product had lower recall in summer months	200 seems too small a telephone sample. Beware of the product selling seasonally
Fiesta Barbecue Sauce Sauce Media or amount test. One media amount (TV) varied	2 cities 1 time period (10 weeks) 2 TV media weights	Telephone surveys, 6 months apart, about 1,000 in each city. Store sales	55% increase in sales in test city. No increase in control city, over whole period. Awareness increased 30% in test city, decreased 2% in control	A well-designed experiment gets good results
Baker Corned Beef Hash Hash	2 cities, 1 control city 2 time periods (26 and 13 weeks)	200 housewives interviewed with 7-month interval, on telephone	Spot TV advertising not significantly effective. 13-week advertising appeared to have a greater positive effect than 26-week	Sample should be larger than 200

OUTLOOK

The outlook for the next decade is for major improvements or advancements in the assessment of copy, media, and level of advertising effort, frequently in terms of their sales effects.   Copy and theme research should yield additional communication improvements, but the major step forward is likely to be the direct linking of certain present measures to sales.

In media assessment, development of data on consumer response to various media and configurations thereof is likely to be a key advance; computer-based models will aid in planning schedules.   The latter improvement, however, is dependent on the availability of more valid data.

In general, the measurement of advertising effectiveness may move from its present level, an ability to avoid major errors, to one where the effectiveness of the acceptable campaign can be demonstrably improved.

If the rate of progress of the last decade is maintained, by 1975 most major advertisers will have had the experience of having learned the sales effects of their advertising campaigns.   Many of them will have compared copy platforms' ability to sell the product.   Others will have compared alternative media strategies by the same criterion. Still others will have found, through large-scale experiments, the joint effect of marketing forces which produce more sales than the sum of their individual effects.   The most sophisticated advertisers will have gone beyond the mere identification of influential factors and combinations to estimate the optimum level of expenditure each should receive to obtain maximum profit.

These advances will not be achieved without cost.   Many studies will prove inconclusive, ambiguous, or perhaps merely so unpalatable that their findings will not be used for marketing planning. Other studies will be deliberately scotched by competitors.   Still other analyses will no longer apply by the time the marketing plan is prepared.   Indeed, widespread advertising control awaits the development of faster and more objective data inputs.

Continuous Marketing Experimentation

If on-line, real-time sales feedback can be obtained from the retailer or consumer, or both, the experimental and analytic techniques now used with only occasional success will come into their own. In 1975, continuous marketing experimentation will be commonplace for the few firms that might be developing these data, and some firms may find it expedient (as one does today) to allocate their whole advertising budget according to principles of experimental design, simultaneously testing variations in copy, media strategy, and levels of expenditure. Test marketing, in the sense of one- or two-city comparisons, will be obsolete. Instead, as the marginal costs of data collection will have become virtually zero, multicity studies will be used. Game theory may find application as competitive moves and countermoves are known quickly and analyzed. Marketing plans will be revised quarterly, monthly, or even weekly as feedback becomes faster. A competitive edge will be maintained by that firm whose growth of understanding of its marketing and advertising systems consistently surpasses that of its competitors. But the dynamic, sophisticated mathematical models which express this understanding will become popular only as the data become good enough to warrant the effort of creating them.

IMPLICATIONS FOR MAJOR ADVERTISERS

The availability of feedback where there had been none before will catalyze a reshuffling of the structure and procedures of those firms with considerable commitments to advertising. The larger that commitment, the more numerous and various will be the concomitant changes. Among firms whose advertising budgets consistently require several times as many dollars each year as the company earns, these changes can be expected to permeate the whole organizational structure sooner or later.

Advertising Department

As comparisons of copy and media strategies gradually accumulate, advertising management will begin to tease out principles of copy and media planning uniquely applicable to their product class and competitive situation. Such principles will require constant updating or even rediscovery, but continuous information systems will eventually make this inexpensive. Demonstrably profitable strategies will be favored to the exclusion of the unprofitable, but a more subtle effect will be the neglect of unmeasurable strategies. Those which cannot be justified to an increasingly cost-conscious management will perforce give way to those which can.

Another result of reliable feedback may well be an increasing variety of advertising approaches. The absence of objective measurements in advertising is doubtless responsible for the tendency of otherwise creative advertising men to imitate any apparently successful approach. This bandwagon effect would be reduced by the company's ability to compare alternatives in terms of its individual marketing problems. Fewer media and copy techniques may survive in each product class, but every category and perhaps each advertiser will have its own distinctive group of effective techniques.

Marketing Mix

In some cases knowledge of advertising's sales effect may cause less use of other marketing techniques. Dollars spent on dealer promotion, for example, may be reallocated to advertising when it becomes possible to show the dealer that those dollars move more of his stock than the same amount spent on price cuts.

Market Research Department

Increasing measurement of advertising effectiveness will mean that the market research department will report, if it does not already, to the company's chief marketing officer. If the market research department evaluates the performance of the advertising manager or the sales manager—even indirectly—then the market research manager will have to report to the same person as the other two if his evaluation is to be accepted.

Carrying out major advertising-sales experiments will try the patience of both doers and users of research. Dealing with complex situations involving large advertising budgets and high research costs, some managers will find their careers affected, at least temporarily. Improvement in data systems will frequently be needed to reduce the occurrence of failures and inconclusive results. In some firms advertising research will become anathema.

Sales Department

Research and advertising effectiveness will likely indicate that some products cannot be sold so profitably with the present reliance on advertising. For such products, a larger sales force will probably be employed. Inevitably, however, it will also be determined that other products will be sold more efficiently through mass media than through personal selling. In those product classes salesmen will either be reduced to order takers or elevated to technical ambassadors. The latter would require more and better sales training, as well as higher salaries.

When the sales effectiveness of mass media advertising becomes a demonstrable fact, salesmen will be able to exploit this knowledge in their dealings with distributors, wholesalers, brokers, and other middlemen who may require such evidence of demand before agreeing to stock the product. Thus, salesmen will use the proven effectiveness of advertising as an instrument for getting distribution of the product. This "pull through" effect of advertising, today usually just an argument in the salesman's kit, will in due course become a known fact that he can use to advantage.

Demonstrations of advertising effectiveness will harass as well as aid the salesman. During an advertising experiment, when control and observation are required, salesmen will either remain uninformed about its duration and nature, which will annoy them, or be instructed to keep sales pressure as before—even though advertising has been raised or lowered—and report additional observations in the field for experimental purposes. Neither of these instructions is likely to leave salesmen enthusiastic about marketing experimentation.

Such human factors may be reduced by the installation of computers at the retail level. As retail inventory control increasingly becomes the responsibility of computers, the existing personal relationship between salesman and client will not dwindle, but will be broadened to include the customer's managerial and analytic problems in using his computer effectively. The majority of salesmen will acquire increasing expertise in the political and analytic subtleties of computerized inventory control at the retail level.

IMPACT ON MANUFACTURING INDUSTRIES

New-product Introduction

Product planning cannot help but improve as it becomes possible to pretest a new product's advertising before carrying the item to final development. Such improvement will be most noticeable in those industries in which the cost of advertising dwarfs the cost of product development, and in which brands differ little in the physical characteristics that lead to consumer satisfactions. When variation is relatively difficult to achieve by R&D, brand differentiation by advertising and other marketing means is usually essential if the firm is to capture a stable share of the market. Companies in these circumstances may concentrate their developmental effort on those products for which demonstrably persuasive advertising can be had in advance. For these firms, techniques of testing product concepts in advertising could conceivably become as important as new physical research techniques have been to the chemical and metals industries in recent years. Progress in finding methods will depend largely on the ability of the test to simulate all product attributes which contribute to the satisfactions received by the consumer from the product. Rough television commercials will likely replace dummy print advertisements or other purely verbal representations of product ideas as the most popular means of exposing such ideas to a test panel.

These and other techniques of concept testing will dramatize to the advertiser of 1975 the importance of the joint effects of advertising and product quality. Use tests have shown repeatedly that consumer preferences can change radically when brand names are removed. A certain best-selling brand of coffee was found *least* well liked by consumers in blind product tests. Such consumer "franchises" are specific to product types. In the paper industry, for example, one leading manufacturer's name has been found to indicate quality to the consumer for only one type of paper product and not for others. Yet in blind product tests, the same consumers rank these products much the same. As evidence of this sort accumulates, manufacturers will become increasingly wary of introducing a new and improved product without having tested the ability of advertising to communicate the benefits of the changes to consumers.

Data Collecting Equipment

The primary drawback to more effective advertising measurement is the absence of valid data input. Answers to interviewers' questions in particular have increasingly fallen into disfavor, largely because their biases and inadequacies have become increasingly evident. Growing disenchantment with interviewer-based methods has led to interest in other methods. Management believes it can make more accurate inferences from objective behavioral observations. Opportunities may exist for manufacturers to design and market anything from an inexpensive transmitter for use with home television receivers to a facsimile reproducer which permits questionnaires to be delivered instantaneously.

Unless there is vocal public outrage, television and radio receivers may some day be fitted with a transmitter or some other device which will indicate whether the set is on or off and to which channel or frequency it is tuned. This would settle once and for all the question of broadcast ratings in terms of sets in use; sampling will not be an important issue since there could be a very large number of sets with such an attachment.

If a talk-back capability were incorporated in such receivers, consumers would be able to order products advertised within moments of receiving the advertising message. This would permit the pretest of broadcast advertising quickly and inexpensively. If these cost and time advantages of creating national advertising are not somehow duplicated by print media, television may add still more to its value as an advertising medium.

Perhaps the major contribution of technology to the measurement of advertising effectiveness will be as an instrument which can not only gather data from the respondent, but also reward her for responding. A small computer terminal in the kitchen, for example, on which a shopper records her purchases and through which she can be further interrogated by branching programs, could upon completion of the interview present her with a comparison of her shopping decisions with those of other panel members, or advise her of departures from her own budget. Such computer terminals would not only eliminate the subjectivity and short-cutting of increasingly bored interviewers, but would also improve the data by obtaining a higher proportion of the originally drawn sample to continue participating in the panel. Once the fixed costs of establishing such a panel were incurred, the variable costs of gathering additional data would be so small as to encourage advertising evaluations of all kinds.

IMPACT ON RETAILING

Computer-based stock-control procedures have already brought the retailer new opportunities for measuring advertising. Data used for ordering stock can also compare one food retailer's stock movements with those of similar members of the same store chain.   As more food chains use these methods of inventory control, more retailers will accumulate a realistic knowledge of which promotional tactics sell which products in their stores.

Increasing competition by supermarkets for the same customers has reduced the retailer's profit margin to its lowest level ever.   Among other things, this has led to a reappraisal of distribution costs—product by product, brand by brand, store by store, and even package by package.   Conditions favor the continued importance of such cost analyses, and these probably will be linked to various advertising efforts.   As the effectiveness of in-store promotions becomes measurable, it may be possible for retailers to flatten seasonal and weekly fluctuations in demand, reducing distribution costs still further.

Promotion of a particular product typically brings results in other product lines as well, and assessment of the amount of these sales attributable to advertising is exceedingly difficult.   Yet advertising managers of large retail firms may believe they can devise more effective means for using their budgets, or even for setting the total amount.   Chains will probably develop the strongest programs of this type, as they have the geographical dispersion to give them wider coverage, large advertising budgets, and a form of organization that favors such a program.

IMPACT ON MEDIA

Those media which deliver sales at lowest cost will certainly be favored by objective measures of advertising effects.   Conceivably, one or more classes of media could be eliminated by persistently poor performance against the new measurement standards.   Findings of sales experiments to date, however, would argue against this.   It appears that even when one medium exerts more sales effect than another, the joint effect is such that one medium amplifies the influence of the other.

For example, in 1963 Du Pont advertised Lucite paint by newspaper and television only in nine groups of three markets.   Each three-market group received one of five possible levels of expenditure in each medium.   One group of three cities received no newspaper and moderate television advertising, and each of the other eight groups received a different combination of amounts of both media.

About 10,000 persons were interviewed before and after the campaign, and sales were checked in all twenty-seven markets throughout the experiment.   As expected, the more advertising in either medium, the greater was awareness of Lucite.   However, advertising on TV communicated knowledge about Lucite but did not significantly affect its sales, while advertising in newspapers communicated no knowledge of Lucite, but did significantly increase its sales.   It was concluded that while TV taught the main sales message (dripless paint), potential paint buyers tended to look in the newspapers for their dealer's name.   Each medium contributed a specific part of the total effect and the two media together had more influence on both communication and sales than the sum of their individual influences: newspaper advertising amplified the communication effects of TV, and TV enhanced the sale of newspapers.

Today media spend heavily on research to demonstrate the size and characteristics of their audiences.   As the sales effects of advertising through media become better understood, it will be possible, for the first time, to evaluate some of these audience measures against a different criterion of higher reliability and importance.   Comparisons with these criteria will eliminate many of the measures now paid for by the media merely for fear of not being represented.   The wasteful duplication of media audience measures will thus be reduced, to the primary benefit of the media themselves.

IMPACT ON ADVERTISING AGENCIES

As the advertiser gradually assumes more responsibility for the sales evaluations of his advertising, most agencies will give up the pretense of measuring the same thing.   As today, they will devote the majority of their research efforts to the preparation of advertising copy and to coverage.   Copy and media research will remain the responsibility of the agency, with the knowledge that this effort is being evaluated by the advertiser from time to time.

A more subtle effect within the agency may be its franker recognition of the value of research as an argument-settling device.   When it has been demonstrated several times that slight variations in the copy approach or the media plan do not influence the sales resulting from the campaign, then the copy writer and media planner will be encouraged to try more extreme variations.

The expanding requests by advertisers for more and better copy testing will cause a drain on agency profits. The sharp rise in such pressure in the past few years has already started to do so. Requests for additional services may do more than any other single factor to bring the demise of the commission system.

The measurement of advertising will increase the variety of services rendered by agencies to their clients; successful agencies will be invited to perform more services, whereas unsuccessful agencies will not. Among the former, the fee system will be necessary to cover the additional services and allow the agency to make a profit. Among the unsuccessful agencies, the fee system will become essential, because the client will be unwilling to allow a 15 per cent commission when he receives no services to speak of. By 1975 the commission system will appeal chiefly to those clients whose advertising has been paying off in this fashion for so many years that they hesitate to break up a winning combination.

Agencies will be charged with developing copy that sells more effectively to market segments than to broad areas. This will put pressure on research and on pretested copy for these segments. Campaigns will have to be coordinated to persuade some groups without alienating others.

IMPACT ON RESEARCH AND CONSULTING ORGANIZATIONS

Potential government activity may drastically affect research-supplying organizations. In 1966, Representative Oren Harris withdrew his threat to put the Census Bureau into the broadcast ratings business if companies supplying such information improved their techniques. In disbanding his committee, Representative Harris noted that it would be up to the buyers of ratings to register any protest. So far they have not acted, probably because nothing preferable is available. Coming administrations may encourage the government to set up something better. If the Census Bureau begins to measure broadcast ratings in its Current Population Sample of 36,000 per month, many other periodic advertising research measurements will suffer so by comparison that they will have to be improved or dropped.

Advertising research efforts will bring both benefits and strains to market research firms providing consumer panel or retail stores sales data.   For example, in one $1 million-plus study of the effectiveness of advertising weight, approximately one-third of the total is being spent for various data costs.   For most studies, information is needed about a specific geographic region, and panels which can provide appropriate broad regional or national data coverage have inadequate representation in specific communities.   Advertisers are not apt to disrupt many major markets for tests.   There appears to be an opportunity for firms to develop more detailed coverage in a number of communities, thereby providing an easily available data base for advertising research studies.

Accounting firms may provide marketing service departments which include the service of auditing the client's advertising effectiveness.   Their privileged access to the client's financial history may help them to enter the field of advertising measurement.   Consultants will flourish as smaller companies require interpretation and translation of the new techniques to fit their more limited needs.

THE LARGEST ADVERTISERS

Major United States advertisers vary widely in the proportion of their sales spent on advertising.   They vary equally widely in the earnings they realize on these sales.   There is apparently no relationship between average industry expenditures on advertising and the overall profit margin of companies in that industry.

The high-margin industries include those which spend much on advertising (drugs and cosmetics, gum and candy) as well as those that spend a relatively small proportion of their sales on advertising (chemicals, oil).   The low-margin industries also include those with a high advertising-sales ratio (soaps) as well as those with a relatively low ratio (tires, appliances, automotive).   This being the case, the anticipated better measurement of advertising effectiveness is unlikely to have any general influence on the level of advertising expenditure in all industries.   Some industries will find they have been spending too much, others that they have been spending too little. Within each industry, too, some companies will discover they have been overspending, others that they have been underspending.   Perhaps the only overall prediction that can be defended is that, as advertising becomes evaluated with great accuracy, the individual ad-

TABLE 3A Industries Grouped by Their Average Advertising Expenditures and Profit Margins, 125 Largest Advertisers, 1968

Advertising as a percentage of sales	Profit as a percentage of sales		
	Low (under 6%)	Medium (6%–8%)	High (over 8%)
Low (under 3%)	Tires (4)* Automotive (4) Appliances (3)	Metals (4) Airlines (6)	Oil (6) Chemicals (4)
Medium (3%–10%)	Food (20) Beer (4)	Liquor (3)	Tobacco (6) Paper (2)
High (over 10%)	Soaps (4)	Softdrinks (3)	Gum and candy (3) Toiletries and cosmetics (10) Pharmaceuticals (4)

* Number in parentheses indicates number of firms in this industry which were among the 25 largest advertisers in 1968 and also were listed in the *Fortune* 500.   Companies with high advertising/earnings ratios that year are shown in Table 3B.

TABLE 3B Advertising/Earnings Ratios of Major U.S. Advertisers, 1968

Ratio	No. of cos.	Drugs and toiletries	Food and soft drinks	Beer and liquors	Soaps, autos, airlines, tobacco, etc.
Over 3.0	4	Miles Laboratories			Colgate-Palmolive Lever Brothers Rapid American Mattel Inc.
2.0 –3.00	3	Sterling Drug	Pillsbury		
1.50–1.99	6	Bristol-Myers Chesebrough-Pond's Richardson & Merrill	General Foods Standard Brands Armour		
1.0 –1.49	12	Warner-Lambert	National Biscuit Norton Simon Quaker Oats General Mills Wm. Wrigley Kellogg	Jos. Schlitz	American Motors P&G Liggett & Myers Loews Theaters
0.75–0.99	11	Revlon	Beatrice Foods Campbell Soup Borden Carnation H.J. Heinz Pepsico	Seagrams Heublein	TWA Gillette
0.5 –0.749	13	Johnson & Johnson Pfizer Smith, Kline & French American Home Products	Coca-Cola Ralston Purina	Anheuser-Busch Pabst	W.R. Grace Purex Phillip-Morris United Airlines American Airlines
Totals		11	18	5	15

vertiser will learn to use his advertising dollar with greater skill, hence will reduce what he spends to achieve a given turnover.

This will be true only if other causes of sales are reasonably equivalent; one which is certain not to remain equivalent among competitors in each industry is the rate at which they introduce new products. Thus, even though advertising efficiency improves, each advertiser will find himself competing with more and more brands for an only slightly larger market.   Meanwhile, inexorably rising costs of mass-media advertising and other marketing forces will limit the number of companies which can compete effectively in any market for any product.   This rising "entrance fee" will turn most mass markets into the kind of oligopolistic competition currently observable in cigarettes—where six major firms proliferate brands for lower and lower profit margins—or in cake mixes—where three companies proliferate flavors in an attempt to change the relatively stable shares of this market.

Such oligopolies are the kind of steady state that can be expected in most highly competitive, highly advertised product classes.   An ex-

TABLE 4   Suggestions for Evaluative Market Research

Industry or product	Marketing force worth testing	Major obstacle to conclusive text
Soaps and toiletries	Copy, especially TV spot commercials	Little brand differentiation
Pharmaceuticals	Media (detail men vs. mail vs. journals)	Cost of interviewing doctors
Food	New-product concepts	Changing tastes
Beer	Packaging; amount of advertising	Cost of finding heavy users
Soft drinks	Market expansion themes	Bottlers' independence
Liquor	Trade-up themes	Consumption data often inaccurate
Cigarettes	Amount of advertising	Importance of new types
Automotive	Direct mail	Infrequent purchase
Candy	Trade deals	Large number of retail outlets
Paper consumer products	Sampling of potential customers	Product not uniformly distributed
Gas and oil	Copy effects on dealers; amount of advertising	Outlet location swamps other variables

amination of specific industries shows what additional implications the measurement of advertising effectiveness may have.

Soaps and Toiletries

For many product classes in this group, the oligopolistic situation already exists; Procter & Gamble often leads Lever Bros. and Colgate-Palmolive in market shares.   This, plus the crucial importance of advertising, may imply that the measurement of advertising effectiveness will become relatively more important for Lever and Colgate than for P&G.   All three use advertising research extensively, and have conducted marketing experiments comparing copy approaches, media plans, or levels of spending.   Each has its own preferred methods of pretesting television commercials, and has explored the exotic as well as the straightforward applications of operations research to marketing problems.   Together they spend at least $10 million annually on marketing research for all products.   It is probable that an increasing slice of these expenditures has gone for methodological research intended to improve existing measurement techniques and develop new ones.   If and when the rigid security which prevails in this highly competitive industry is ever relaxed, companies in other industries may benefit widely from these methodological studies.   For example, if principles of game theory have ever been tested in a realistic business situation, it may well have been in this product group where it is not unheard of for one competitor to foil another's experiments by increasing his advertising or distributing free samples in the test areas.

A Madison Avenue anecdote of ten years ago told of the manufacturer who tested a TV commercial for a hypothetical product, found that it worked, and then invented the product.   First associated with Alberto-Culver, this method of new-product introduction is now by no means hypothetical for several manufacturers of drugs and toiletries.   By 1975 the gains and risks of new-product introduction will have become so great that this technique will be used by many competitors, especially those whose R&D has been unable to develop a real performance advantage.

Pharmaceuticals

In no product class, perhaps, is the opportunity greater for the accurate measurement of the payoff in brand-share changes due to advertising. The target of 180,000 doctors is small (if not always cooperative), the marketing forces are few (usually just detail men, journal advertising, and direct mail), and the product categories are well defined so it is relatively clear what competes with what. Most importantly, the brand chooser (the doctor) is required by law to record his choice by prescription—a means that is open to later surveillance.

Services now tabulate prescriptions and furnish drug advertisers with almost ideal feedback: their own and their competitors' shares. Each sale is identified by its individual brand choosers (not even by household), by specific class, by short-time periods (months or weeks if necessary), by stores, by price paid. All this is continuously furnished for the same doctors without worry about how they might be conditioned by the measurement; they are unaware of it. If the doctor elects to specify no brand, but uses the drug's generic name, this too is recorded.

In this product class the data inputs and market conditions are close to those required by brand-switching analyses now inappropriately performed on the inadequate data of mail panels of consumers. If these analyses provide the kinds of insights some have promised, then individual doctors' purchasing habits and susceptibilities to the few available media will become so predictable as to make feasible market segmentation of the finest grain possible: person by person. Even if this rather fanciful possibility is not accomplished, it may be approached by pharmaceutical advertisers who grow to know their customers better than most businessmen might think possible.

Food

In many product classes the major food processors make frequent introductions of new products and flavors with short life cycles, perhaps in an attempt to include as many different market segments as possible within the ranks of their customers. As advertising measurement permits the identification of copy and media strategies uniquely suited to such segments, the lives of new products should be extended; this in turn should render the food market more stable.

Improved research techniques will also be applied to the forthcoming generations of new-product ideas. At least one major food manufacturer has placed a new brand favorably in a highly competitive product class by giving the brand those physical attributes most preferred by uncommitted consumers of this product class. It should be possible to measure the effectiveness of advertising for such consumer-positioned brands with more efficiency than heretofore if only because the particular market segment to whom the product appeals has already been isolated. Thus not only do improved advertising measurement techniques lead to improved product design, but improved product design in turn leads to more efficient advertising measurement.

Food processors of many seasonal items have difficulty in controlling the availability and price of their raw materials. These gluts and shortages are among the major planning contingencies of food processors, thereby placing a premium on the efficiency of the marketing effort to adapt to them. As the measurement of advertising effectiveness begins to improve marketing efficiency, the greatest profits may be shared by those firms whose marketing effort can be most responsive to oversupplies and undersupplies of raw material.

Beer

'Brewers have perhaps the narrowest product line and that in which physical product innovation is least likely. Innovation will probably continue to come in the convenience and availability of a product in its containers, in their opening, and in the variety of quantities which can be purchased. Repeat purchase and brand loyalty will still be determined more by the taste of the product, and different brands will probably continue to have perceptibly different tastes. Thus advertising which emphasizes the convenience and availability of a brand should be expected to be more effective in attracting new experimenters than in reinforcing present customers in their preferences.

Since a high proportion of all beer sold is consumed by a relatively small proportion of the population, studies of market segmentation and brand switching will become unusually important. If convenience messages can be efficiently aimed at heavy users of brands from which a company's customers have been found most likely to come, that company will be relatively better able to couple its convenience innovations with its advertising to gain additional market share. As in the case of highly segmented food markets, advertising measurement itself will become easier and more accurate under these conditions and should in turn suggest future combinations of innovation and market.

Soft Drinks

Mergers with other food companies have by now diversified the Coca-Cola and Pepsi-Cola companies and their smaller rivals to such an extent that many comments about food companies also apply to these companies.   Unlike the market for food, beer, and distilled spirits, however, the market for soft drinks is expanding rapidly.   Per capita consumption in 1965 was 40 per cent higher than in 1955, while per capita consumption of distilled spirits has risen only 16 per cent and that of beer has actually declined 4 per cent.   These trends underscore the unusual competitive advantage soft drink manufacturers hold over brewers and distillers: a market which is expanding, not just with growing population, but also with greater per capita consumption.   Since soft drink advertising has expanded the market as well as increased per capita consumption, the measurement of advertising effectiveness will be of greater importance to it than in other product classes where advertising has not performed both these functions so well.   On the other hand, the many outlets for soft drinks will complicate the development of accurate measurement techniques.

Liquor

The four major North American distillers vary in profitability partly because some of them have mastered the marketing of their premium-priced brands better than others.   Since it costs little more to make and promote an expensive whiskey than an inexpensive one, and since per capita consumption cannot be expected to rise significantly, profitability in this product class lies mainly in the capacity of the distillers' advertising to persuade existing consumers to buy more expensive brands.   Another limitation on the role of liquor advertising is its enforced absence from television.   This restriction could possibly be lifted by concerted action by distillers; they may feel, however, that competitive TV advertising would only raise the costs of liquor marketing without increasing the total market, and thereby lower each competitor's earnings.   Unless new roles are learned for liquor advertising, and unless the ban against liquor advertising on television is broken, improved advertising measurement will be less crucial to the earnings of distillers than to other manufacturers.

Cigarettes

While cigarettes are a mature and stable industry, their brand structure becomes increasingly fragmented, partly because an unadvertised brand can be profitable with 0.1 per cent of the market, and partly because of the proliferation of types. After regulars came kings, then filters, menthols, and combinations, and currently the charcoal and water filters. By 1975 cigarette brands will be flavored and differentiated in ways not yet imagined by the consumer. Experience shows that a brand often maintains dominance in its type, e.g., Pall Mall in kings and Winston in filters. In hopes of dominating the newest type, cigarette manufacturers are currently spending more on product tests than ever before. As preestablishing the acceptance of a new type becomes more feasible, the evaluation of advertising effectiveness may well become less important.

Automotive

Among the leaders in the use of experimentation to evaluate advertising, Detroit's Big Two nevertheless have given few signs of having obtained useful guidance from their research. GM's continuing $800,000 advertising evaluation obtained both communications effects and sales effects but reports have not shown a linkage of the two. Ford's multimedia experiments have been announced but never reported, although it is understood that the company learned a great deal about direct-mail advertising effectiveness via the experimental method.

CHAPTER TWENTY-THREE

Copy Research

ALLAN GREENBERG *Vice President and Research Director, Doyle Dane Bernbach, Inc.*

SCOPE OF COPY RESEARCH

Copy research in this chapter will concern practices designed to assess advertising effectiveness before large-scale advertising funds are committed. There are two other conceptions. One is the search and screening for advertising ideas, and the other probes actual effects after the advertising has been run.

The search or screening for advertising ideas is not a rigorous procedure and does not lend itself to formalized research techniques. Psychological evaluations are used chiefly in the early stages of formulating advertising strategy. Procedures associated with psychological evaluations represent individual performances rather than a set of prescribed techniques. Strategy, of course, can stem from the product itself, market conditions, hunch, intuition, or a combination of these. These are generally considered outside the sphere of copy research.

23-1

While research can explore some of the implications of creative concepts, it cannot tell which creative concept is right or best. A creative concept becomes meaningful only when it is executed. In research terminology, tests of creative concepts are stimuli to response situations which represent a gestalt that is quite different when an execution of the concept is the stimulus. It is the executed concept that is the content area of copy testing.

Posttesting and Pretesting

Posttesting an advertisement or campaign after it has run is not nearly so important or controversial as pretesting. Many so-called posttests are actually pretests. The consumer in such tests is exposed in natural conditions and is not aware that he or she is part of a test. Many of the pretest measures covered in this discussion are readily adaptable to true posttests of advertising effects. The major effort in advertising testing, however, is that of evaluation of advertising before it is run. The emphasis here will be in this area.

Measurements of Effectiveness

Effectiveness, whether pre- or post-, is measured either directly or indirectly: by means of actual consumer behavior (sales or purchases), or by simulated consumer behavior (attitude and preference measures). Everything, however, is not quite so simple. Even the conception of effectiveness is replete with controversy. For instance, some researchers use *recall* as an effectiveness measure by obtaining levels of recall. As a side product, nature of recall is used for diagnostic evaluation, which would then imply knowledge of ways of making the advertising more effective. Nature of recall is regarded by many practitioners more as a measure of communication than as a measure of effectiveness.

Proponents of communication measures maintain that to be effective an advertisement has to communicate in some fashion. However, the correlation between communication and effectiveness is rather tenuous. Most researchers would agree that communication is a necessary component of effectiveness, but not the only one. Differences of opinion in this area create basic problems in copy testing. These differences relate not only to the function of advertising, but also to whether effectiveness can be measured in advance.

Unfortunately, semantics plays a role. To avoid getting enmeshed in a semantic jungle, this discussion will proceed on the assumption that the concept of copy testing concerns attempts to measure varying degrees of effectiveness.

PERFECT TECHNIQUES LACKING

Despite the progress made in copy testing over the past years, most will agree that the perfect copy-testing technique has not yet been found.   The principal reason for this is the disagreement over which criteria to use in providing the basic guidelines.   There are any number of reasons for this disagreement.   First is the lack of consensus on how advertising works.   Another area of disagreement concerns the major criterion to use in evaluating effectiveness.   Some regard recall as a principal criterion to assess advertising effectiveness, whereas others depend on tests measuring some form of attitudinal or behavioral changes.   Finally, there is widespread disagreement over which technique to use for any selected criterion.

To understand the rationale of copy testing, it will be necessary to touch on various models of how advertising communication is thought to work.   This chapter will cover a very short review of current copy-testing practices and a discussion of some of the continuing problems.

Advertising is a form of persuasive communication.   To measure its effectiveness, it is important to know how psychologists define *persuasive communication*.   Most are agreed that a sequence of mental processes takes place.   However, they disagree as to the order and definition of sequences.   It may well be that the time between the steps in the sequence is so short as to be practically nonexistent.

How Advertising Works

To illustrate, here are six conceptual models in common use, each of which purports to describe how advertising should function: [1]

Model A	*Model B*
Be *seen*	Catch *attention*
Be *read/absorbed*	*Arouse* desire
Be *believed*	*Induce*
Be *remembered*	*Satisfy*

[1] See also Chapter 8, "How Advertising Works," by Paul E. J. Gerhold.

Model C	*Model D*
Attract *attention*	Bring *awareness*
Create *interest*	Bring *comprehension*
Stimulate *desire*	Bring *conviction*
Lead to *action*	Bring *action*

Model E	*Model F*
Produce *attention*	Make the unaware *aware*
Produce *interest*	Make the aware *know*
Produce *comprehension*	Make the knower *like*
Produce *impact*	Make the liker *prefer*
Produce *attitude*	Make the preferer *convinced*
Produce *action*	Make the convinced *purchase*

These models clearly display the great amount of variation among the formulators of these models as to how advertising does work. The reason for this disagreement is that no one has yet proved conclusively that any of these conceptual frameworks is operative. Much research has been done in the area. Findings have been very contradictory and controversial. Studies show that there are examples of sales increases not accompanied by increases in brand knowledge, and vice versa. Studies have also shown that there are examples of sales increases not accompanied by measurable favorable changes in attitudes, and vice versa.

Hierarchy of Effects?

The idea of advertising's effect seen as a step-by-step succession of mental states through which the individual must pass is not consistently borne out by available research evidence. This suggests strongly that no one really knows exactly how advertising does work in stimulating action on the part of the consumer. One cannot assume that advertising works the same way every time. Researchers will keep searching for the connecting links between initial awareness and the actual purchase. Until the keys to the proper measurement of persuasive communication are found, advertisers should seriously question any copy-testing technique which is being proposed as the long-awaited solution to advertising preevaluation problems.

What Is Being Measured?

The question of what these techniques are measuring is vital. If doubts are being expressed about the conceptual framework of these techniques—that is, How important is comprehension? How important is attitude change?—no copy-testing technique should be accepted until one is convinced not only that the technique is valid and measures what it purports to measure, but also that the measurement represents an important influence in the ultimate buying decision. This leads to another important consideration, the place of copy testing in one's total advertising program.

No Substitute for Judgment

Many advertising persons use research results to replace judgment. Since no one technique has yet been conceived that measures all effective characteristics of an advertisement, overdependence on copy testing would appear to be rather dangerous. Often advertising is evaluated on the basis of a single score. There often is a difference in opinion between creative and research persons. Some creative persons say that a single score cannot evaluate all aspects of a commercial or advertisement, and are thus led to reject almost all figures from a copy-testing study. On the other hand, researchers, in their attempt to develop a system, tend to place great faith in the figures developed. There is room for a more intelligent interpretation and use of research findings. Copy-test results should be an aid rather than a replacement for creative judgment. While much lipservice is given to this principle, practice often negates it.

SINGLE OR MULTIPLE EXPOSURES?

The general approach to copy testing is to measure consumer desire or knowledge of the brand in terms of specific objectives set for the advertised brand. Whether measurements are taken on the basis of single exposure or on the basis of multiple exposure,[2] the final objective is essentially the same: to measure whether the advertising succeeded in improving desire for the brand (either as the sole purpose of the advertising or as an index of sales effect) or to measure the actual sales effect.

Ideally, the most valid pretest would be a measurement of sales effect of advertising (or share of the mind if the advertising campaign dictates it) under conditions simulating the real thing, that is, multi-

[2] Multiple exposure can range anywhere up to a full-scale advertising campaign.

ple advertising exposures, under natural exposure conditions. Some researchers try to measure behavior, or set up experiments in which an attempt is made to simulate realistic behavior by studying advertising effect on a cumulative exposure basis.

The preference for such a design is supported by the belief that testing of individual advertisements for effectiveness on a one-time exposure basis does not give a realistic evaluation of a campaign's effectiveness over time.   One advertisement exposure is only a part of a campaign, and needs the additional support of other exposures and cumulative impact.

Economy in Design

While researchers recognize the validity of the arguments of the proponents of cumulative-exposure testing, they are hampered by the complexity of workable economical design, and by necessity have turned to single-exposure testing.   The overwhelming efforts in pretesting of copy are made on a single-exposure basis.   The proponents of multiple-exposure testing argue that the users of single-exposure techniques are making the assumption that results of tests utilizing only one exposure to an advertisement are in a one-to-one relationship with results from multiple exposure.   However, since this assumption may not hold, the risk of discounting a potentially good campaign still remains.

1. The proponents of *single-exposure testing* argue that relative differences between advertisements (individual advertisements as entities or as representative of campaigns) are meaningful and hold up over cumulative exposure.   There is also less expense involved, less time required to obtain data, and experimental procedures can be more tightly controlled.

2. Proponents of *multiple-exposure testing* are making determined efforts to develop more economically feasible ways of testing advertising on a cumulative basis.   From a research point of view in-the-market tests, while realistic, present a major problem in the ability to control the experiment.

At the same time, continuing efforts are being made to improve and validate even more sophisticated methods for testing advertising on a single-exposure basis, mainly because these are the methods which have been developed and are in use today, and because of the cost of multiple-exposure testing.   Many of the measuring techniques used for single-exposure tests can be applied to multiple-exposure tests once a feasible method for exposure has been developed. For the most part, however, the discussion to follow centers around current testing methods—and these are single-exposure measurements.

CLASSES OF MEASUREMENTS

Measurements used in copy testing can be put into three basic classes: perception, communication, and influence.

Perception can be defined as the degree to which people are aware they have seen the advertisement.

Communication can be defined as the degree to which people receive some impression of the advertisement—or knowledge of its content.

Influence can be defined as the degree to which people are affected or influenced by the advertisement. The steps in the models of how advertising is thought to work and all copy-testing techniques fall into one of these three classes.

Criteria of Validity

Regardless of the technique there are certain necessary qualifications for a valid measurement.

Over the years literally hundreds of copy-testing approaches have been advanced. The number for which there is evidence of meeting any of the traditional criteria for gaining acceptance for a measure is pitifully small.

The traditional criteria are four: sensitivity, stability, reproducibility, and predictability.

Sensitivity. Should reflect meaningful change in consumer's response as a function of exposure to stimulus.

Stability. Similarity of results should be obtained from test to test.

Reproducibility. Similar response should be obtained between two matched groups when exposed to same conditions.

Predictability. Should have a high probability of predicting some subsequent behavior, within limits.

METHODOLOGICAL ISSUES

More efforts have been expended in gathering evidence for major methodological decisions than in meeting the criteria of validity. While this may be disturbing to some, in practice it has not hampered the development of more refined measurements. The major methodological issues still arousing some disagreement refer to:

Form of the advertisement

Types of measuring tools

Experimental design

Method of exposure

Moment of measuring

It will not be possible to explore all these in as much detail as they deserve. Highlights of some of the considerations going into decisions in each of the areas will be touched on, however. In the process the most frequently used copy-pretesting approaches will be covered.

Form of Advertisement

The most desirable form for testing advertising effectiveness is the finished commercial or print advertisement. The more the stimulus moves away from final finish, the more reasons there are to question the validity of the test results. This is particularly critical for mood-and-effect commercials. The other side of the coin is that the rougher the form of the advertisement, the less expensive it would be to produce it and the greater the number of advertisements which could be tested. Which is the best form of the advertisement for testing purposes is still an open question. Most experiments which have been conducted have been attempts to determine whether rough advertisements would give the same result as finished ones within the framework of a particular technique. Thus, few experiments have been conducted using rough commercials in tests where a commercial has been put on the air. The general feeling is that the closer to the finished advertisement, the better the test. Many researchers insist on testing only finished advertisements. The only consensus is that for certain specific problems such as comprehension, a less than finished advertisement might be adequate.

Types of Measuring Tools

There are two broad types of measuring tools, and each type can be split into two. There are advertising-oriented measures, divided into nonverbal and verbal measures, and brand-oriented measures, divided into mental and action measures. The various response measures used in copy testing can be allocated within each of these four groups. One typology is the following:

Advertising-oriented	*Brand-oriented*
Nonverbal measures:	Mental measures:
Physiological devices	Awareness
	Attitude
	Preference
	Purchase disposition
Verbal measures:	Action measures:
Recall	Simulated purchase
Comprehension	Coupon redemption
Recognition	Normal purchase
Interest	
Persuasion	
Favorableness	
Believability	

Advertising-oriented Measures

The nonverbal-response measures employ the use of mechanical devices in laboratory-type situations. The devices are direct response measures in that they do not require any verbalization on the part of the respondent and reflect responses to stimuli on an involuntary, subconscious level. The principal devices are the psychogalvanometer (for skin-reaction measurements), the eye camera (for eye-movement measurements), and the perceptoscope (for measurement of pupil dilations).

The major problem in the use of these mechanical devices is the difficulty of interpreting the results in terms of the effectiveness of the advertisement, even though they do give an objective measure of its ability to stimulate, excite, or hold the eye. The translation of mechanical-device results into more commonly accepted measures of effectiveness has so far been a rather formidable task.

Recall Measures The most frequently used verbal-response measure is that of *recall*. Recall measures are generally acknowledged as valuable techniques for measuring what the reader or viewer gets out of an advertisement. Comprehension, interest, persuasion, favorableness, and believability are secondary measures, and as they are commonly used, many tend to be by-products of a recall measure. Recognition measures are somewhat different.

There are two major components in recall measures. One is commercial or advertisement recall—unaided or spontaneous recall of advertisement for brand advertised; or aided, via a product-type cue, product-type and brand cue, or product-type and brand and advertisement cue. These simply refer to the amount of aid given to the respondent to determine the level at which the advertisement can be recalled. The second component is content recall, again either on an unaided or aided basis. In the latter case, advertisement-content cues are used to aid recall.

To many researchers recall measures present problems in their meaning and relationship to effectiveness. The fact that people can play back the message does not necessarily seem to result in a more favorable attitude or proportionate increase in sales. Easy-to-recall phrases may carry only little conviction, moderately recalled points may implant selling points strongly. Recall measures have been criticized for a variety of reasons—as not measuring the importance of an advertisement's selling point to the consumer; as not being able to give any information on the mood elements of a commercial; as not being able to measure the extent to which an advertisement is provocative; as not being able to measure negative reactions. Despite these reservations, recall measures are very widely used.

Comprehension Comprehension is basically a measure of the understanding of the advertising message. Thus it has a very important diagnostic value. However, this value is dependent upon an unequivocal statement of what the advertising is intended to communicate. In practice, comprehension measures are sometimes indistinguishable from recall measures. It is, of course, possible to obtain a comprehension measure that is not dependent on memory.

Interest, Persuasion, Favorableness, and Believability In the context used here these are infrequently utilized in today's armament of copytesting techniques. Asking consumers for their opinions of the effects of advertising on them is too subjective. Much doubt has been thrown on the validity and reliability of such subjective answers. The trend has been to what are considered more objective measures. Recognition ratings are believed to be of minor value as a criterion for judging advertising impact. This technique is rarely used as a pretest measure.

Brand-oriented Techniques

In the last few years there has been a shift to techniques that are brand-oriented. Awareness measures such as *total brand awareness* (all brands mentioned on an unaided or aided basis)—actually a knowledge measure—have shifted to top-of-mind awareness or first brand mentioned. This has been extensively utilized as a measure of the effect of exposure to the stimulus of an advertisement. Top-of-the-mind awareness does not appear to be a complete measure. The meaning of awareness, and change in awareness, can be determined only by other measures such as attitude change or recall or both. There is some evidence that a shift in top-of-the-mind awareness is related to subsequent shifts in brand purchase.

Attitude Measurements The most important brand-oriented measure currently in use is that of attitude. *Attitudes* may be defined as mental sets which direct an individual's response to a stimulus. They are psychic summations of knowledge, emotions, motivations, and intentions. Because most researchers seem to agree that the formation of a favorable attitude toward a product brings a person a step closer to making a purchase, attitude-change measures have been widely accepted.

But much work is still being done to prove that if a change in attitude occurs, then a change in behavior will be more likely to occur. The basic assumption is that an effective advertisement should increase the degree to which individuals are favorably disposed toward buying the advertised brand. Therefore the respondents are called upon to indicate their perceived rating of the brand in question. This involves the use of various devices by which the respondents indicate how they feel about a given brand by selecting one of the graded series of specific attitudinal statements or scale descriptions. The variety of rating devices which have been utilized to measure attitudes and the ways of developing attitude scales are the sole subjects of scores of books and technical papers.

Preference and Purchase Dispositions Measures of brand preference or purchase disposition are attempts to determine consumers' nearness—directly or indirectly—to the purchase of an advertised brand. A variety of measuring devices has been developed for determining brand preference. Just a few are direct brand preference; constant sum scale (asking a respondent to divide a set sum of points or money among two or more brands); paired comparisons (preference between two brands); and brand lottery (gift choice). Similarly, new response measures intended to express purchase intent are being devised constantly. A few of the more common in use are intention to buy next; playing a buying game (by setting up the conditions); and forced switching (brand respondent would buy under preset conditions).

Action-response Measures Some researchers have criticized brand-preference and purchase-disposition measures as just another form of attitude measurement. Others have criticized them (and attitude measures as well) for not being true behavioral measures. Those who criticize them for this reason obviously prefer action-response measures. These concern either coupon returns, in the case of print advertisements, or simulated coupon returns in a studio setting or at point-of-sale.

There are numbers of ways in which such action measures have been conducted. Split runs with coupons have been conducted for years. Advertisements have been sent by mail with coupons included. Coupons have been given out in laboratory settings and in trailers parked in shopping centers with cents off for purchase, with and without competitive product coupons. The major advantage of these action measures is their rapidity of response. They have been criticized because not all readers or viewers respond to the offer. Those who do represent a self-selected sample and may be atypical. The offer could be too attractive, creating artificial results.

And finally, there are the advocates of actual sales as the sole criterion of an effectiveness measure. Their difficulty is in finding a realistic sales measure under the impact of one exposure in a pretest situation.

Experimental Design

While there have been dozens of experimental designs which have been used in copy tests, the bulk of the testing is conducted with a few standard designs. The paradigm at top of page 23-13 gives those most frequently used.

Some measures fall naturally into one of the categories. Comprehension measures, of necessity, are postexposure design studies. On the other hand, attitude measures can be obtained by either a pre-post design or a post-only design. In this latter case an unexposed group

Incremental Measures	*Nonincremental Measures*
Pre-post design	Post design
(Same sample)	(Exposed group only)
(Matched samples)	
Post design	
(Matched samples)	

would have to be used so that the incremental value could be ascertained.

To make this concrete it might be of value to visualize the measurement given by each design.

Incremental Measures

Pre-post design: same sample
  Premeasurement exposure to advertisement postmeasurement
  (Difference between pre-post scores is the increment)
Pre-post design: matched samples
  Premeasurement exposure to advertisement postmeasurement
  Premeasurement no exposure to postmeasurement
  (Difference between the two pre-post increment scores is the overall increment)
Post design: matched samples
  Exposure to advertisement postmeasurement
  No exposure to postmeasurement
  (Difference between the two postmeasurement scores is the increment)

Nonincremental Measure

Exposure to advertisement postmeasurement

These are only the major designs. Many factors dictate the choice of research design. One of the major determinants is that of the standard used for determining whether the results are good or bad. This question is just as likely to be asked of recall or comprehension as it is of attitude-change measures. The answer is that all such results are relative. Results are generally compared to one or more of several benchmarks. One might ask how an advertisement compares relative to the norm of the product category, or relative to the last advertisement tested for the brand, or relative to the brand's average. A *norm* is defined as a standard of achievement derived from experience of previous tests. It is a measure of average performance from a series of testings. The benchmarks or norms one uses can create many statistical and interpretive problems. Ideally a norm should be a decision-guiding measure to be of any real value.

But statistical problems arise because in many cases norms are based on different populations. Pure statistical variations present another problem. In many cases more than one type of measurement is taken. The results may not *all* lead to a similar conclusion, creating problems in a decision.

The same dimensions hold whether one advertisement or more than one are being tested. However, if more than one advertisement are being tested, then one can compare one set of results with results from the test of a second advertisement. In multiple-advertisement testing norms can be dispensed with.

METHODS OF EXPOSURE

The exposure of the advertisement stimulus in a copy test can be either a natural exposure or an artificial exposure. Much can be said for both methods. Natural exposure is preferred primarily because it represents the way the advertisement will actually be seen. It allows a viewer to ignore the advertisement, half see it, or see it all. It is a realistic setting. Artificial exposure conditions allow for more control. They are especially favored when many advertisements, over time, will be tested and similar conditions for each test will be required. They also allow for much more flexibility. For instance, commercials can be tested in a theater, in the home with a standard projector or a rearview projector, or in a trailer facility. The sample to be interviewed can be chosen with care.

The distinction between natural and artificial exposure conditions does not exhaust what has been done in copy tests. For instance, respondents have been recruited to watch a specific program on their own television sets. The area of specific interest is concealed by having the respondents believe they will evaluate the program carrying the commercial. The same technique has been used with a dummy magazine. The exposure mechanism is natural, but the viewing or reading situation is not.

In some instances the nature of the problem will dictate the method of exposure. When advertisements for a new product not yet on the market are being tested, one is forced to use an artificial viewing or reading situation.

Natural or Artificial Exposure?

Which exposure mechanism—natural or artificial—is the better one? No definitive answer can be given. Research practitioners designing a copy-test format look for both purity of design and realism of exposure. Unfortunately, the properties are not compatible. In other words, to attain one, the other must be sacrificed. For example, proponents of controlled exposure tests, (e.g., van test, in-theater tests) seek to control the exposure by excluding external variables. However, by this procedure, the realism of the exposure situation is given up. On the other hand, practitioners seeking a more realistic exposure situation (e.g., on-air tests) must sacrifice purity, in that they cannot control many external variables affecting the test conditions. If one accepts effectiveness of an advertisement to be a function of attention, persuasion and other less determinable criteria (that is, familarity of brand, program environment, testing situation) then in controlled-exposure experiments, one sacrifices measurement of attention, while in natural-exposure tests one reduces the precision of measurement of persuasion.

Moment of Measuring

Another area of disagreement among copy researchers is that of the moment of measuring after exposure to the stimuli. The problem can be stated simply: Should measurements be taken immediately after exposure or should there be a delay after exposure before taking a measurement? The delay can be anywhere from a few hours to two or three days.

The advantages of the immediate measurement are numerous. The exposed person's reaction is taken at its zenith. Testing immediately after exposure makes it possible to obtain more extensive information with no loss due to memory. It also provides a clean measure in that the respondent has virtually no chance to be exposed to supporting or competitive advertising, and this results in less confusion, thus giving full credit to the advertisement.

The delayed measurement also has advantages. The technique indicates the more lasting effect, which may simulate better how advertising works. It gives a better idea of how the main ideas of the advertisement are retained. It takes into account normal competitive advertising activity, thus providing a measure of the advertisement's competitiveness.   While it may provide a less sensitive measure than an immediate one, the leveling and sharpening effect of the time delay may give a more realistic measure.

The time interval used for a delayed measure also has supporting arguments at each time point.   Again, no definitive answer has been forthcoming from practitioners, although practice has standardized what has been called the 24-hour delay.   This delay actually varies from 16 to 24 hours.   Some researchers utilize two measures, one immediate and one delayed.   However, this does not resolve the difficulty, since the two measures are generally not the same.

SUMMARY

Much has been left out of this discussion of copy testing—split-cable developments, the Milwaukee Advertising Laboratory, test-market studies, and so on.   The major reason is that while they can be used for copy-testing purposes, they tend to be considered measurements of the total marketing mix rather than an evaluation of copy per se.   Besides, justice cannot be done to all the ways of copy testing within the framework of a single chapter.   Instead, this discussion has been centered on those aspects of copy testing which are most volatile and controversial.

As practiced, copy pretesting has a variety of techniques from which to choose.   None of the techniques is wholly satisfactory.   Some find them unsatisfactory because they relate primarily to one-time exposure measurements.   However, advocates of a cumulative measure have not been able to come up with an economic, controllable multiple-exposure measurement technique.   Proponents of single-exposure measurements feel there is a serious question as to the value of a multiple-measurement technique.

What to Measure?

Still others find many of the current measurements unsatisfactory because of disagreement as to what to measure.   There are proponents of recall as well as proponents of attitude-change measures.   Much debate still revolves around natural-conditions testing versus non-natural or laboratory-type measures.   Some try to get around some of the difficulties by using more than one type of measure.   This does not appear to be a complete panacea though it does avoid some difficulties.

Are there answers to these problems?   While experiments are constantly being conducted, it would appear that until there is some consensus as to how advertising is supposed to work, no definitive judgment can be made on which technique is the *best* technique for copy pretesting.   And this judgment rests on the assumption that there is a single way that advertising does work.

Until consensus is achieved on the more basic questions, the copy-pretesting techniques used will probably remain a matter of choice, subject to some experimentally derived data on specific criteria having some face validity.

BIBLIOGRAPHY

ADLER, L., ALLAN GREENBERG, and D. B. LUCAS: What Big Agency Men Think of Copy Testing Methods, *Journal of Marketing Research*, November, 1965.

AXELROD, JOEL, Attitude Measures That Predict Purchase, *Journal of Advertising Research*, March, 1968.

HOVLAND, C. I., A. A. LUNISDAINE, and F. D. SHEFFIELD: "Experiments on Mass Communication," Princeton University Press, Princeton, N.J., 1950.

HYMAN, H. H.: "Survey Design and Analysis: Principles, Cases and Procedures," The Free Press, Glencove, Ill., 1955.

LUCAS, D. B., and S. H. BRITT: "Advertising Psychology and Research," McGraw Hill Book Company, New York, 1950.

MARKETING SCIENCE INSTITUTE: "Advertising Measurement and Decision Making," Allyn and Bacon, Inc., Boston, 1968.

"Pretesting Advertising," *Studies in Business Policy*, no. 109, National Industrial Conference Board, New York, 1963.

"Proceedings," Annual Conferences of the Advertising Research Foundation, New York.

STOUFFER, SAMUEL A., *et al.*: "Measurement and Prediction," Princeton University Press, Princeton, N.J., 1950.

"Yale Studies in Attitude and Communication," Yale University Press, New Haven, Conn. C. I. HOVLAND, I. L. JANIS, and H. H. KELLEY: Communication and Persuasion: Psychological Studies of Opinion Change, 1957; C. I. HOVLAND (ed.): The Order of Presentation in Persuasion, 1957; I. L. JANIS, *et al.*: Personality and Persuasibility, 1959; M. ROSENBERG, *et al.*: Attitude Organization and Change: An Analysis of Consistency among Attitude Components, 1960.

CHAPTER TWENTY-FOUR

Media Research

EDWARD PAPAZIAN *Vice President, Media Director, Batten, Barton, Durstine & Osborn, Inc.*

ADVENT OF THE COMPUTER

In 1961 BBDO publicized a revolutionary concept—the application of computerized mathematical models to assist its media department in making better recommendations for its clients. The design was ambitious. Audience estimates for all media, with demographic breakdowns, cost structures, and marketing objectives, were assembled and fed into a system that examined every possible combination to determine the one mixture that exposed the largest number of primary prospects at the lowest cost per contact.

Competitive agencies rushed to create and unveil their own machines, while critics sprang forth to defend the rights of the individual and attack the menace of the computer. They raised the specter of advertising decisions made by an insensitive and totally automated system, that relied solely on statistics to arrive at its recommendations.

How could a computer factor in that vital human contribution, judgment? Some made speeches deploring the trend, while others coined phrases like GIGO (garbage in, garbage out) or experimented with various fruit-and-vegetable combinations before reluctantly settling on the traditional protest to comparisons of any kind: "It's like comparing apples and oranges," anyone knows you can't do that.

Value of Alternatives

Viewed from perspective, the breakthrough was more significant than anyone suspected. Advertising's "new math" quickly uncovered the fact that most of our media strategies were developed without considering alternatives and were dominated by bias. Integrated media reviews were a rarity in advertising. Network television was advocated, evaluated, and purchased by TV programing departments, assisted by small, elite staffs of so-called experts, who specialized in forecasting and interpreting Nielsen ratings. The agency's media department formed a distinctly separate and lower echelon that concerned itself with magazine or newspaper recommendations, local broadcast buying, network servicing (station-clearance problems), and peripheral matters no one else would bother with. Media research groups consisted of a few veteran "analysts" who supervised trainees in a number of clerical operations and familiarized them with the complexities of desk calculators and multicolored coverage maps before forwarding them to buying or "planning" duties. Media research had the primary responsibility of guarding the media department's much-prized supply of green visors, and additional duties included the compilation of competitive advertising expenditure reports (that no one ever read), county-by-county analysis of television station signal areas, and calculating the duplication rates between subscription audiences of various magazines (based on a formula by Dr. Daniel Starch and his associates in Mamaroneck, New York).

Three-network Competition

By 1960, the climate was changing. ABC's ascendancy and the ensuing three-network contest had a deep and lasting effect on television. Exceptionally high ratings became a thing of the past, as audience splitting grouped more and more programs around the average level. Mortality rates rose to alarming proportions, and advertiser involvement was replaced by numbers-oriented "scatter plan" buying. Television had become a much riskier business, and rising costs were no longer justified by constantly increasing audiences.   Adding to the crisis, Nielsen's new media service was turning out data on the leading dual-audience publications among women's magazines that indicated a sizable quantitative edge over the average nighttime television show, and the belated decision to examine demographic data was producing other surprises.   Questions were being raised and answers were needed.

Computers in Media Research

BBDO and its computer signaled a new role for media research. The agency had devoted the better part of two years to developing a massive data bank, containing audience and demographic breakdowns on all the major media vehicles in print or broadcast.   Its media analysis department uncovered everything of value from published sources and found unpublished, but very incriminating, surveys.   In addition, the agency went so far as to sponsor two total-audience projects of its own, dealing with some forty magazines. Though its initial efforts seem primitive by today's standards, BBDO was one of several agencies seeking a businesslike approach to media selection, and its first print-outs were provocative.   On a purely statistical basis, nighttime television was *not* the way to reach the largest number of consumers at the lowest cost.   Radio and magazines won over most prime evening programs, by margins high enough to raise eyebrows.   Many of the combinations that came out of the computer offered new and valuable insights and the promise of more to come.

Demand for Data

Like most infants, the mechanical monsters had insatiable appetites, and their masters quickly discovered the need for expanded and more detailed inputs.   The stakes were high and documentation was necessary.   A new breakthrough occurred in late 1962 when W. R. Simmons responded to the call and launched what became his annual media-marketing service.   Norton Garfinkle added his ingenious Brand Rating Index, and other entrepreneurs joined in a vast, unprecedented numbers race.   The advertising community abruptly found itself inundated by total-audience estimates for a large number of so-called selective magazines, which for years had not defined the full dimensions of their readership. Now the advertiser and his agency had access to data that came in regularly every year, regardless of the sponsorship or cooperation of the publications under investigation.

New Syndicated Services

The new syndicated services included an impressive array of questions on product usage and brand preferences and provided a complete description of television's adult audience, with program-by-program breakdowns, time-period dimensions, and duplication patterns. Now, for the first time, the inquisitive media planner or analyst could peruse these findings and become a valued expert on television as well as on print audiences. His outlook was broadened and his sources offered an infinitely superior demographic picture. While Nielsen produced his meterized set-usage data, and an occasional viewer-per-set estimate with broad age and sex distributions, the media department could examine television's performance on a more objective, detailed basis—its life cycle, socioeconomic, and geographic breakdowns—and base its observations on viewer, not household, behavior patterns. It had the additional option to move directly to product-usage definitions, and could examine programs or program types based on their ability to expose heavy, moderate, or light users. If the advertiser was unable to supply a description of his primary marketing prospects, the media executive had his own sources, and these provided data that frequently proved more valuable than the information emanating from standard marketing sources.

Influence on Media Planners

The ensuing upheaval has completely transformed the media department and its functions. Armed with a vast array of statistics on nearly every quantitative facet of media performance, a new breed of planners and analysts emerged. Facts and figures are replacing guesswork, and a new lexicon dominates our discussions. We are engrossed by great debates on the relative merits of reach-and-frequency mixes and contending formulas that are used in such computations. This is the age of Metheringham equations and beta functions, of simplex algorithms and exotically titled mathematical systems such as linear programing, Midas, high assay, Telmar, Compass, Cousin, and so on.

No Time for Complacency

While all this is good, there is nothing to be complacent about. Media research has made great strides in describing the physical characteristics of broadcast and print audiences, but its efforts to explore their communication functions have been limited to a few inconclusive forays. To a great extent, our data revolution has overwhelmed us, and our self-preservation instincts are compelling us to seek the security of accepted procedures. We operate under a protective mantle of systems and gadgetry, and standardization is becoming a substitute for inquisitive analysis. The system is paramount, and adherence to its rules is more important than effective problem solving or the quest for relevancy.

Reach and Frequency Estimates

One of our favorite pastimes is the preparation of estimates indicating a proposed schedule's reach and frequency patterns. These are intended to tell us how many people in a target group will be exposed to one or more issues, or broadcast segments carrying the client's message, and how often this will occur. Thus, a monthly television schedule with a "60 reach and a 4 frequency" is assumed to have contacted 60 per cent of the people involved, an average of four times each. In some obscure way, such computations are assumed to have vast significance, and a recommendation that raises reach without sacrificing frequency (or shows gains in both) is greeted with considerable enthusiasm.

How valid are these comparisons? In a statistical sense, they are projections of *media* audiences, nothing more. While the surveys they are drawn from are reasonably accurate, they have no relation to the commercials themselves. Let us consider the question of television viewing more closely.

TELEVISION RESEARCH

A number of studies have approached this question, using secret observation methods or subtly detailed questioning to establish what actually happens when people are exposed to commercials in their own homes, under real life conditions.

TVAR and Chicago Studies

One of the more interesting so-called observational studies was commissioned by Television Advertising Representatives, Inc. (TVAR) in three major markets during the spring of 1964. The approach was unusual. The Eugene Gilbert Company recruited a group of 307 teen-agers who agreed to spy on the viewing activities of their parents for one evening. Each spy received special training, along with a form that was used to record the minute-by-minute behavior of every adult viewer while the set was on. TVAR's teen-agers reported that the typical viewer distributed his nightly "viewing" time as follows:

Approximately 60 to 65 per cent of all "viewing minutes" were devoted to *fully attentive* viewing.

About 20 or 25 per cent of the time, audiences were *completely or partially distracted,* but still in the room.

From 10 to 15 per cent of the time, the viewer was *out of the room, or just leaving.*

A contemporary spy study conducted in Chicago by several hundred college students produced similar findings. This project, described by the late Gary A. Steiner in a paper entitled "The People Look at Commercials," [1] reported that 70 per cent of nighttime network program viewers were fully attentive, while 30 per cent were partially attentive or totally uninvolved during the minute immediately preceding a typical nighttime network commercial.

In both cases, the design permitted investigators to report on commercials as well as program content. What happens when the advertiser's announcement is aired? The answer is both plausible and sobering, for the proportion of viewers at full attention dipped below 50 per cent, while partial attention or complete distraction rose to 35 or 40 per cent and absentee viewing (people leaving the room) increased significantly.

Research into Exposure

What happens when a viewer is exposed? Thousands of surveys have sought to explore the viewer's ability to remember television

[1] *Journal of Business,* University of Chicago, April, 1966.

commercials and play back their contents.   The most common procedure employs a telephone interview to establish whether the respondent saw the program in question.   This is followed by specific inquiries about his recall of the commercial (or commercials) being investigated.   Interviews are conducted during the course of the telecast, shortly afterwards, or a maximum of 24 hours later.

Print Media Studies Print media have sponsored a number of studies, using the unaided recall method to measure television commercial impact.   As a rule, these produce a very low level of spontaneous commercial recall, indicating that most viewers require prompting to be able to play back brand names and copy points, even when exposure occurred only a few minutes before the interview. Typical of these is a project completed between January and March, 1963, in Wichita, Kansas, for the local newspaper (*The Wichita Eagle-Beacon*).   Approximately 2,800 telephone interviews were conducted with adults during the prime evening hours and each respondent was asked these questions:

Is your television set on at this time?

Are *you* watching television?

What program are you watching?

What was the product advertised on the last commercial?

On the average, only 23 per cent of the adult viewers could name the last advertised product or brand.

Study by Bureau of Advertising A more recent study, conducted in May, 1965 for the Bureau of Advertising (ANPA) provided another analysis of unaided viewer recall levels.   Telephone interviews were completed with 1,000 adults who had just been exposed to prime evening programing in three large markets.   Once their viewing was ascertained, respondents were asked a number of questions to establish the degree of attention they had just been giving to the show. Tabulated results revealed that 72 per cent of those who reported being in the room claimed that they were doing nothing but just watching.   The remaining viewers admitted a variety of distracting activities, ranging from reading (7 per cent), eating (4 per cent), and housework (3 per cent), to typing, entertaining, sewing (all 1 per cent).

At this point, the interview turned to commercials with the following question:

Thinking about the very last commercial that was on before I called, can you tell me what brand or product or company it was for? Tell me everything you can remember about it.

When confronted with this type of questioning, 60 per cent of the audience was unable to offer any kind of answer, and many who did reply produced hazy or inaccurate descriptions. Only 18 per cent correctly identified the last commercial, while 14 per cent cited a message that actually appeared *earlier* in the telecast.

C. E. Hooper Study Though much of this research is sponsored by competitive media, a number of broadcast surveys have ventured into this area and obtained similar results. A fall, 1968, effort was undertaken by C. E. Hooper as part of its network television rating studies. Each prime-time viewer was asked special questions dealing with his attentiveness and commercial recall. He was called upon to name the last brand he had seen advertised, and produced an average response rate of 17 per cent. Thus, 17 per cent of the people who had just been exposed to television could name any brand that was advertised—but 83 per cent could not.

Combination of Aided and Unaided Recall

Though many researchers regard immediate recall as the most desirable method of measuring viewer response, the cost of obtaining a significant number of interviews right after each commercial is usually prohibitive. The customary solution is a combination of aided and unaided recall, coupled with a longer time lag between exposure and interview. Methods used to aid respondents generally take two forms:

Clues describe the general nature or action sequences in the commercial (without identifying the product or the brand).

Product class and brand names are provided (without a description of the commercial).

Batten, Barton, Durstine & Osborn's continuing series of "Channel One" studies demonstrate the outcome of most aided-recall studies. The agency purchases a half-hour nighttime dramatic or action program in a small or medium-sized market and inserts client commercials in each telecast, just as any normal sponsor would. After the telecast, staffs of experienced interviewers make random telephone calls in search of adult viewers. Each respondent is told the program's name, broadcast time, channel number, and star, and asked if he happened to see that evening's episode.   Those who qualify as program viewers are read descriptions of portions of the show that preceded the commercials and asked if they recall seeing each of these segments (on the average, only 65 to 75 per cent of the answers are affirmative).   Then the focus shifts to commercials and viewers are asked questions that go something like these:

What products do you recall seeing advertised on (program) tonight?

What brand was that?

What did the commercial for (brand) lead you to expect?   What did it tell you about the product, etc.?

Many viewers are unable to respond without further prompting, so additional clues are offered.   These identify the product class, and if necessary, the brand itself, but a significant proportion are beyond help.   With all the prompting, only 30 to 40 per cent of the audience is able to remember its exposure to an average announcement, and just under 25 per cent can offer a reasonably acceptable description of the advertisement's content or its basic claims.

Are Consumers Convinced?

Our brief excursion into attentiveness and commercial impact studies is not intended as a definitive discussion of this fascinating, but very complex subject.   The surveys reviewed form a very small part of the evidence on these questions, and their primary function in this discussion is the illustration of a very fundamental point.   Our standard media comparisons dealing with reach or frequency data purport to describe a campaign's coverage, but have little to do with its performance in reaching or convincing consumers.   A hypothetical television schedule that reaches 60 per cent of a brand's target group (based on telecast audience patterns) may actually expose less than 50 per cent to its commercials (depending on definition of exposure), and the estimate that an average viewer will see four messages per month is certainly an illusion.

Seller-dominated Research

Ever since its inception, television's research has been *seller-dominated*.   Its leading audience source is devoted to the principle of measuring *every telecast*, and its fixation with meters and the precise minute-by-minute data rests on the underlying assumption that people cannot really be trusted to report their exposure.   Thus, the industry is saddled with a system that churns out great volumes of information on set-tuning patterns and offers the security of seemingly definitive, but produces conspicuously irrelevant reach and frequency tabulations, household demographics, and other analyses. Most of these data are used by the networks, who sell their wares on the basis of rating points or cost-per-thousand comparisons.   Their analysis makes no effort to explore the complexities of viewer-response patterns.   There are occasional improvements.   Nielsen is offering viewer estimates, so the networks now present their offerings with tables indicating "young adult" and "old adult" breakdowns (the former includes anyone under fifty, the latter anyone over fifty), and purchases are negotiated on these simplistic yardsticks, as well as on household ratings.

Advertisers and Agencies at Fault   How do they get away with it? The answer is discouragingly simple.   Television's leading advertisers and agencies have permitted the sellers to determine the basic makeup of the medium's primary rating service, and much of its output is geared to the seller's interests.   The networks are not stupid. They know that finer demographics could be offered in Nielsen's reports and viewer data emphasized over tuning statistics.   They realize that audiences are too fickle to be universally interested, and that attentiveness is *not* constant, but varies from telecast to telecast, and in many cases, within the telecast itself.   A number of interesting studies have been performed by the networks and other broadcast organizations in an honest effort to isolate and examine some of the elements that govern television's impact and its ability to generate a response, but these are carefully hidden away and will never see the light of day.   They are "private investigations."   Airing them might cause trouble.   Let's keep things nice and simple.   Let's use numbers that everyone is familiar with.   Let's play it safe.

Refusal to Accept "People Data"   Incredible though it may seem, a number of our giant television advertisers still refuse to accept people data in making their network and spot-buying decisions.   The reasoning is a classic example of Orwellian double-think.   The advertisers hold the view that information obtained from individuals (by diaries or interviews) will never match a meter's accuracy.   Thus, program-by-program comparisons, based on viewer projections, are less reliable and should not be used, even when Nielsen provides them.   In other words, an assumed superiority in technique obviates the question of relevancy.   Are household statistics meaningful?   Is it more important to establish *who* is in front of the set?   How many younger households are tuned in with children as the *only* viewers, and so on?   Questions like these are ignored on the theoretical grounds that meters are a better way to record *set tuning,* while diaries are less accurate as indications of *viewing.*   No one seems to realize that these are *different* dimensions, and accuracy is a relative function that has meaning *within a specific context,* but does not necessarily apply between contexts.

Meters versus Diaries   Some of these are pace-setting advertisers, whose expenditures in television are staggering, yet an intellectually debilitating assumption, using 1950 logic, dominates their media research thinking. No one, including their sophisticated New York ad agencies, has succeeded in rectifying the situation.   Consider the matter logically.   Diary studies are "less accurate" than meters. That is the basic premise.   If that is really so, why do allegedly inaccurate people surveys produce *set-tuning* estimates that parallel the meter results so closely that their findings are almost interchangeable?   They are so close that Neilsen, itself, has conceded the similarity and used diary surveys to support the validity of its meter data in the 1963 Congressional hearings on broadcast ratings.   If diary-keepers are incapable of describing their own viewing, what explains their "precision" and "accuracy" when listing set usage and channel selections in the same diaries?

Misleading Research   When it finally comes, the realization that much of our statistical media research documentation is, at best, woefully misleading is sure to be followed by an outraged protest and a demand for a new system, one that develops a standard adjustment factor and allows us to resume our activities.   Once again, media research will have the responsibility to come up with an answer.   If it wishes, it can establish, with a reasonable degree of confidence, the "average level" of television commercial exposure and make similar adjustments for print media, but the averages it generates will take precedence and obscure real opportunities unless finer direction is offered.

Who Pays Full Attention?

As I have indicated, there is impressive evidence that only two-thirds
of the television audience is paying full attention to the program just
before an average commercial appears. The remaining viewers are
divided roughly as follows: 10 to 20 per cent are present in the room
but *partially* distracted (by eating, knitting, sewing, talking with
others), and 5 to 10 per cent are present in the room but *fully* distracted (by activities ranging from passive reading to passionate love-
making). An additional 5 to 10 per cent are absent from the room and
an equal number are not tuned in at that specific moment (but watch
enough of the telecast to count as members of its audience). Thus, a
seeker of averages might arbitrarily count all the fully attentives, and
half of the partially distracteds, and the outcome would be an all-
encompassing "correction factor" that lowers all the published audience estimates (by 25 per cent) to conform to a predetermined definition of commercial exposure. Why bother? There is no point to it,
they say. No gain. No broadening of our knowledge. No appreciation of television's ability to "reach" people's minds as well as their
bodies.

Continuing Program of Research Though most of the surveys in
this area have been small-scale probing actions or specific copy-testing
investigations with limited objectives, the industry now has access to
a continuing program of research, with fully projectable national
samples, that offers detailed breakdowns for every time period, every
network program, and demographic distinctions to boot. The data
are a standard part of the annual Simmons surveys and had their
origin in 1966, when Simmons was approached by BBDO and asked
to modify his viewer diaries to include a scaling device to rate attentiveness.

The customary procedure had involved a conventional personal-
placement system, and each respondent was induced to keep a written
record of his viewing for a two-week period. A small booklet (diary)
was provided (with spaces for every quarter hour on a day-by-day
basis), and viewers were instructed to list the name of the show and its
channel number every time they watched television. At BBDO's
suggestion, three additional columns were included to permit viewers to rate the intensity of their exposure. One signified that the
respondent was fully attentive during most of the quarter-hour

viewing period. The second indicated a state of partial attention, while the third accommodated those who were absent from the room most of the time, but viewed enough to qualify themselves as members of the audience.

The experiment proved successful. Though the diary design had obvious limitations, its authors hoped that the "full attention" scale would turn up a reasonable *and* sensitive measurement, even if the "out-of-room" levels were understated by diarykeepers who were reluctant to admit such indiscretions. This is exactly what happened. On the average, two-thirds of all viewing entries were made by respondents who indicated that they were in complete attention while watching the program. Approximately 20 to 25 per cent reported some degree of distraction, but less than one-tenth cited themselves as predominantly "absent" viewers during a typical quarter-hour interval.

Vast Differences in Response and Exposure The important contribution is not the "average pattern." This is a useful statistic, because it offers a confidence-building comparison with other studies on the subject, but that is the extent of its value. The Simmons study presents a full range of analysis possibilities, and his findings, even on a relative scale, define vast differences in viewer responsiveness and the possibility for commercial exposure.

To illustrate, these are some of the most important observations we can draw from the 1967 and 1968 Simmons diary entries:

Men consistently claim to be more attentive than women.

Older adults (especially those living in smaller households) and people with low incomes or educational attainment are very attentive viewers. Young persons (particularly the under-twenty-five group) and upscale elements are comparatively inattentive.

Viewer interest levels vary perceptibly at different times of day. Attentiveness is very low in the morning, but peaks in the middle of the afternoon (when women watch network serials and quizzes on weekdays and men view sports telecasts on weekends). Early evening offers many distractions, and attention levels dip sharply between 5 and 6 P.M., but this is followed by a steady buildup, as viewers relax with prime-time network entertainment features. The highest attentiveness scores are recorded during the quiet, solitary-viewing periods after 11:30 P.M.

Individual programs generate different levels of attentiveness because of their time period, the characteristics of their viewers, and most important, because of their content and execution. Daytime serials top quizzes by a substantial margin, and their lead over morning comedies is more impressive. Nighttime features vary from very low scoring "family adventures" and general varieties to highs attained by emotional "involvement" programs like "Peyton Place" and suspense dramas, mysteries, or Westerns.

While I have refrained from citing specific numerical values, the distinctions reviewed are sharply delineated and of considerable consequence. "Peyton Place" generated a full attention rate of almost 90 per cent for women viewers, but masculine shows like "Rat Patrol" or "Combat" drew in the low or mid-60s. Serials averaged between 70 and 80 per cent, but most of the daytime comedies placed in the 50s. Early evening time periods fell as low as 45 or 50 per cent (for women), but the same viewers reported themselves as 80 or 85 per cent attentive when watching late movies at midnight.

Mood of the Viewer   While the Simmons' measurements will never match a meter's precision (or accuracy) and are a poor substitute for the perfect method—an invisible, undetected camera—they offer the media researcher an unprecedented opportunity to draw inferences about the *mood* of the viewer as he watches and the medium's ability to create attitudes that might be related to commercial content.

MAGAZINE RESEARCH

Thus far, our focus has been on television, because its vast importance and potential for effective communication is clouded by an infuriatingly parochial outlook on media research. Though television is infinitely more complicated than most of its primary users realize, our analysis of other media is equally muddled, and magazine research, in particular, merits some attention.

The Recognition Technique

The standard magazine "total audience" survey uses a recognition technique to arrive at its answers. The interviewer asks certain screening questions and establishes, through these, whether the respondent may have seen any issue of the magazine in question at some time during the last six months. At this point, those who might have read the magazine are asked to examine a stripped-down copy (regular editorial features and ads excluded), ostensibly to determine their opinion of its editorial content. The purpose of this procedure is to provide the respondent with a recognition aid, without his knowledge that the real object is to establish whether or not he has read the issue under study.

The Critical Question Once the editorial contents of the skeleton-ized issue have been examined and the comments of the respondent noted, the interviewer asks the critical question. Usually, it goes like this:

> As you know, articles and features in different magazines often look very much alike. Now that you have been through this magazine, could you tell me whether this is the first time you happened to see this particular issue, or have you looked into it before?

Only those who are sure they have seen a copy of that issue before the interview took place are counted as part of the magazine's total audience.

From the advertiser's point of view, such surveys produce an estimate of the number of readers who claim to have read a copy of the issue carrying his ad, and that is all. Like television ratings, they have nothing to do with the reader's probability of opening to the page carrying the ad, and even less to do with the possibility that he will see it. As with television, the assumption has been made that proper research techniques are lacking to measure less conventional questions, so the subject of advertising exposure is largely ignored and most magazine buys are evaluated on simple cost-to-audience relationships. While readership data are described by finer demographic distinctions than television is accustomed to, the decision-making yardstick is the same and is equally irrelevant.

Value of Pass-along Readers

In some quarters, the problem is recognized, but proposed solutions have gravitated toward a formula answer and effective analysis is minimized. Several agencies handle the question of reader intensity by ascribing a general lack of value to the pass-along (readers whose households did not buy the copy) or out-of-home audience, and discount them by margins that are quite substantial, usually 50 per cent. The premise is logical. Pass-along readers tend to be reached away from their homes, and are less interested in the magazine. This leads them to spend less time with it and read it less carefully.   Thus, a number of broad investigations have yielded average pass-along recall scores that are lower than those attained by primary readers, and other data on repeat exposure, reading time, etc. indicate less thorough readership.   This sort of evidence is used to support a policy that reduces pass-alongs' weight when making cost-per-thousand comparisons.

Danger in a Discount Formula   The danger is clear.   An average discount procedure confines its impact to the relative distribution of primary and pass-along readers within a magazine's audience. Thus, publications with high reader-per-copy ratios lose more heavily than those with lower incremental audiences, and the planner or analyst is relieved of the obligation to consider the *kind* of ad he plans to insert in the magazine, its *compatability* to editorial environment, and the reading situation it engenders.   The formula is convenient. It saves him the trouble of worrying about advertising subtleties and the ad's role in his communication scheme.   That is someone else's job.   From a media standpoint, the magazine is just a number, one little number.

Writing for BBDO's media department, I disagreed with this practice in an April, 1967, "Point of View" bulletin and commented as follows:

> We object to a formula approach that treats all products, all copy executions, all elements of timing, demographics, etc., as if one simple rule applied.   Certainly the pass-along reader *is less thorough* about his advertising exposure, but this limitation applies primarily to *less visual* ads, particularly text-laden copy, black and white and small space units.   These are the kinds of ads that the pass-along reader is most likely to miss, not the full-page, four-color message, the spread or back cover.
>
> BBDO's media data bank has a unique assembly of facts.   It contains *separate* breakdowns for each magazine on a primary, pass-along and total-audience basis.   This allows our planners the option to discount pass-along by any factor they feel appropriate, or not at all, if they choose.   All we require is a specific reason for the adjustment, one which relates directly to their planned copy approach, their marketing strategy and their media objectives.   We have no average clients, nor do we write average ads; and few of our problems seem to be average.   In consequence, BBDO does not believe in an average approach to the pass-along reader.   When he is likely to have little value we discount him.   If not, we let the poor fellow alone.

Issue Audiences and Advertising-page Exposure

The problem of distinguishing between issue audiences and advertising-page exposure is not very difficult to handle, provided the media researcher is willing to use some speculative judgment and take modest liberties with data available to him.   In 1964, Politz produced a conventional total-audience survey for a number of general editorial and women's magazines, including repeat exposure (reading days) and ad-page opening measurements.   I used these findings to estimate *Life*'s average page audience for women as follows (from a BBDO media department report):

> According to Politz, *Life* magazine reached 14.8 million women per issue.   Of this total, 8.8 million are exposed in their own home and 6.0 million exclusively away-from-home.   The average in-home reader reads her copy on 1.5 different days and opens about 75 per cent of the issue's ad pages per day.   In contrast, the average out-of-home reader reads her copy 1.2 different days and opens 69 per cent of its pages per day.   Let us explore the significance of these statistics.
>
> First we must recognize that the 1.5 reading days per in-home *Life* reader is only an average.   Most of these people read *Life* only once, but some read it two, three, or even four times.   The same point applies to the out-of-home readers, only here, the once-only reader represents nearly all of the audience.
>
> Using standard mathematical probability methods, and the findings from other Politz studies, we estimate that the distribution of repeat exposures for in and out-of-home readers looks something like this [see Table 1].

TABLE 1   Estimated Distribution of *Life*'s Women Readers by Location and Extent of Issue Exposure (Base: Average Issue)

No. of reading days:	In-home readers	Out-of-home readers	All readers
Saw copy only once	66%	85%	74%
Saw copy twice	18	10	15
Saw copy three times	12	3	8
Saw copy four+ times	4	2	3
Total audience	100%	100%	100%
Average no. of reading days per reader	1.5	1.2	1.4

All told, three fourth's of *Life*'s total issue audience (last column) sees their copy once, 15 per cent see it twice, and the remainder are exposed three or more times. In whole numbers these can be projected as follows [see Table 2].

TABLE 2   **Estimated Distribution of *Life's* Women Readers by Location and Extent of Issue Exposure, 1964**

No. of reading days	In-home readers, in millions	Out-of-home readers, in millions	All readers, in millions
Saw copy only once	5.8	5.1	10.9
Saw copy twice	1.6	.6	2.2
Saw copy three times	1.1	.2	1.3
Saw copy 4+ times	.3	.1	.4
Total audience	8.8	6.0	14.8
Average no. of reading days per reader	1.5	1.2	1.4

Politz also tells us that the average in-home reader opens 75 per cent of the pages in her issue per reading day. Therefore, she misses 25 per cent of the pages per day. This, too, is an average. Some readers open all of the pages while others open half of them or less. For the purpose of this example, let us assume that the 75 per cent in-home page-opening factor is relatively constant for all in-home readers.

If we make this assumption, it is possible, using statistical probability, to estimate the per cent of *different Life* in-home readers exposed one or more times per ad page. For those who read the issue only once, the unduplicated ad page exposure factor is, of course, 75 per cent. For those who saw the issue twice (with 75 per cent ad page exposure each time) the net page-opening factor would be computed by assuming that 75 per cent of the first day's audience was also part of the second day's audience. Thus, 56 per cent of the issue's two-time readers (75 per cent multiplied by 75 per cent) saw the average page twice, and subtraction tells us that 19 per cent must have seen it on the first day but missed it on the second, while another 19 per cent reversed this process. All told, the formula produces the estimate that 94 per cent of the readers who saw their copy twice probably opened an average page in the issue at least once. The following table completes these computations for the remaining in-home readers [see Table 3].

TABLE 3   Probability of Eventual Ad-page Exposure for *Life's* In-home Women Readers by Number of Times They Read Their Copy

No. of reading days	Per cent of pages opened per day	Unduplicated per cent of pages opened for all readings
Saw copy only once	75	75
Saw copy twice	75	94
Saw copy three times	75	99
Saw copy four+ times	75	99+

Out-of-home readers were less likely to open a page in their copy. The average page-opening factor was 69 per cent, and the following table projects these in the same way as the in-home reader table [Table 4].

TABLE 4   Probability of Eventual Ad-page Exposure for *Life's* Out-of-home Women Readers by Number of Times They Read Their Copy

No. of reading days	Per cent of pages opened per day	Unduplicated per cent of pages opened (for all readings)
Saw copy once	69	69
Saw copy twice	69	90
Saw copy three times	69	97
Saw copy four+ times	69	99

Now we are ready for our final set of projections. We have estimated the number of issue readers who will see their copy once, twice, three, or four times and each group's chance of eventually seeing an average ad page (at least once). Let us multiply these and see how many of *Life's* 14.8 million women readers probably get a glance at a typical page in their issue [see Table 5].

If our assumptions are correct, 83 per cent of *Life's* in-home readers will open the average advertiser's page, but only 72 per cent of the out-of-home readers will be reached. Thus, *Life* reaches 14.8 million women *per issue* (without regard to thoroughness) and delivers 11.6 million women openers per page, and this means that only 22 per cent of *Life's* total issue audience does not come into physical contact with a typical advertiser's message.

TABLE 5   Estimated Number of *Life* Women Readers Reached by the
Average Ad Page (Based on 1964 Politiz Study)

Reading days	In-home readers			Out-of-home readers		
	Reached per issue, in millions	Eventual page openers	Reached per page, in millions	Reached per issue, in millions	Eventual page openers	Reached per page, in millions
1	5.8 X	75%	= 4.4	5.1 X	69%	= 3.5
2	1.6 X	94	= 1.5	.6 X	90	= .5
3	1.1 X	99	= 1.1	.2 X	97	= .2
4	.3 X	99+	= .3	.1 X	99	= .1
Total	8.8 X	83%	= 7.3	6.0 X	72%	= 4.3

BBDO duplicated this particular analysis for a sizable number of magazines and noted significant differences between them. Women's monthlies, like *McCall's,* tend to reach more of their readers per page at some time during their three-month measurement cycle (generally about 85 per cent), but take much *longer* (than *Life*) to generate this exposure.   Exceptionally high pass-along publications, like *Business Week, The New Yorker,* and others, expose their subscriber and newsstand readers at comparable levels, but an average page misses a substantial number of out-of-home pass-along readers and total page-opening factors, for all readers, often dip below 60 per cent.   Similar computations by *demographics* produce more interesting variations, for primary readers invariably get more weight and they tend to be the most affluent and better-educated segment of the audience.   Thus, the average page's audience profile is different from the issue's pattern and the distinction has distinctly favorable implications for print, in general.

Competition with Television

Some of the larger magazines have concluded that the primary obstacle to increased advertising revenues is not the competition from other publications, but the less obvious, though devastating impact of television.   The typical package-goods advertiser spends two-thirds of his budget in television, and the largest ones average closer to 90 per cent.   Publishers have tried many ways to counteract this unprofitable distribution, but few have proved successful.

Inter-Media Reach and Frequency Game   One of the commonest approaches is the inter-media reach and frequency game.   Here's how it goes.   First you take a TV-only schedule.   Perhaps it consists of six daytime, three fringe, and two prime-time network announcements per week.   Then you have Simmons or Garfinkle plot its four-week reach and frequency pattern.   The results are conventional. In TV jargon, 70 per cent of our housewives will be reached and the average woman will see six commercials.

So far, so good.   Now we break these tabulations down into demographic groupings.   The TV-only schedule skews away from the upper income categories and concentrates rather heavily in the middle and lower brackets.   Good, but not good enough.   Now we refine our view.   This calls for a quintile analysis.   More jargon. This time, we've cut up our total monthly audience into equal fifths, ranking them by frequency of exposure.

Now we've found a real television weakness!   One *fifth* of the audience does half of the viewing.   How terrible!   How unbalanced!   Quickly we draw a chart.   The key figure is a pyramid.   Its apex is at the 70 per cent mark (that's our four-week reach), the top is narrow.   Those are the light viewers.   They only see one or two commercials.   But the bar widens and down at the bottom are the heavy viewers.   They see fifteen or sixteen commercials.

Next, we delete some of the prime-time TV announcements and substitute ads in our magazine.   If we're lucky, its a one-for-one exchange.   If not, we may include some of our friendly compatriots in the mix.   In any event, the new schedule has magazines in it, and the triangle has changed.

The new tabulation shows that the advertiser's four-week coverage has spurted to 76 per cent.   Six points higher!   That's almost 4 million women added by print.   Even better, the bar is a little thinner at the bottom and plumper in the middle.   Remember those light viewers who only saw one or two commercials?   We've lost a few of them, but the survivors now see 1.7 TV commercials and read 1.8 magazine ads.   That's a big gain.   Much bigger (on a relative basis) than the change at the old heavy-viewing end.   Here, print's contribution is minimal—only 1.5 ads read and TV is down to only 13.8 commercials exposed.   Order has been restored.   Our new configuration has the right shape.   It is more balanced.   Its heavy quintile does only 43.4 per cent of the viewing or reading.   The old TV-only heavy quintile did 50 per cent of the viewing. This demonstrates that the new plan is better.

Real Issue Ignored   Why are these efforts unsuccessful? The answer is obvious. They ignore the real issue. Television dominates the thinking of food and soap advertisers because they regard it as the most powerful form of communication and consider an average TV commercial to be infinitely more effective than a magazine ad. Quintiles, demographics, and cost per thousands have little to do with their attitude, for such considerations are applied at a much lower level, *after* the basic choice is made. Once the advertiser reaffirms his dedication to television, they are used at the buying level, to discriminate between programs or program types, and the relative mixture of daytime, fringe evening, and prime-time units. Thus, the standard magazine media-mix presentation is irrelevant. It tells a story that any media expert is already aware of, but even if he is not up on his statistical comparisons, it offers no tangible reason for a change in strategy.

Trend to 30-second TV Spots   The recent trend to 30-second television commercials as a basic unit for package-goods brands has lowered the morale of the reach and frequency gamesters. Their games are not fun anymore. When 60 seconds was the standard prime-time unit, television's average cost per thousand for women was $4.50 or $5, and this was substantially higher than the magazine range of $2.50 to $3.50 for a four-color page. When you eliminated prime-time minutes and replaced them with magazine ads, the tabulations always came out in your favor. But network 30-second units cost half as much and deliver the same audience. Now the reach and frequency bars favor television, or at best, show only a minor edge for a media-mix plan. Why? That's easy. The print comparisons are still based on four-color, full-page units, not correspondingly smaller ads, and they just don't have a chance.

Test-marketing Give-away Technique

A number of publishers have recognized this difficulty and approached the matter differently. One method is the test-marketing give-away technique. A large television-oriented advertiser is induced to try magazine ads in a test-market situation (either in a media mix or alone), and this is compared to his normal TV-only plan in another area. The magazine pays many of the costs, including sales auditing, and in some cases, commercial cut-in charges, and everyone waits expectantly for the results.

In many cases, the design is incredibly naïve and the *only* barometer of performance is a store audit or some other indicator of sales trends. Advertising awareness, copy-claim registration, and the related measurements are excluded, and specific studies designed to identify the particular contribution of the individual magazine ads or television commercials are not even contemplated. In short, the focus of the venture is a simple-minded fix on cause-and-effect relationships. There is no concern for strategic subtleties or knowledge building, and the sponsors do not seem to understand that independent variables are almost certain to be involved. The omission of media-oriented data prevents them from analyzing their results and determining the contribution of print or broadcast segments. When the tests prove inconclusive, as they often do, magazines are saddled with the blame, because no one has bothered to establish which elements played the critical role in determining the final outcome. Print is always suspect, so the advertiser goes back to his original thinking: TV is the only medium that can sell our product.

Two Direct Approaches

Occasionally, a more direct approach is used. Two publications have attempted to measure TV commercials and compare their findings with similar observations on magazine ads. Six years ago, *Look* duplicated the standard TV commercial-testing method (described earlier), and found that an average 60-second commercial in nighttime television generated about the same degree of memorability as a typical page four-color ad in *Look*. Nighttime viewers had been contacted the day after exposure and cued about the commercial (by citing its product class), to see how many could play back at least some of its content, while *Look* subscribers were contacted 24 hours after reading their copies and asked similar questions about ads in their issue.

In 1965, *Life* magazine commissioned Simmons to produce an "advertising retention" study that contrasted the ability of nighttime viewers and *Life* readers to identify correctly ads they had seen 24 hours earlier. Respondents were shown the actual ads or commercials, but these were interspersed with an equal number they could not have seen. Each was asked to identify those he remembered watching or reading "yesterday." Again, the average result was parity. Television and print advertising were equally memorable.

Suggested Questions

For much the same reasons, these projects have joined the test-market and media-mix ventures, as interesting but inconclusive experiments. In each case, the essential reason is the same. They offer no specific guidelines on media values. They tell us nothing about media communication. The average recall scores between television and print in the *Look* and *Life* studies are the same. Fine! But assuming the technique and definitions were meaningful, shouldn't these projects have been a little more specific? How about these questions?

Do certain *types* of ads function best in *any* medium, print *or* TV?

What kinds are strong in only *one* medium? Is there a generic pattern? Do soap or detergent commercials always prove more effective than corresponding print executions? Do cigarette ads draw consistently higher scores in print than TV?

What is the relative influence of color and motion on television compared to the static, but detailed pictorial image in print? How do the media convey their messages? What elements are retained?

What is the interaction between the two media? How many readers can be stimulated to visualize a TV commercial by seeing the same campaign in a magazine ad?

What kind of person is most susceptible to television advertising? What kind of reader pays more attention to print ads? Are there differences by product class or style of execution that can be isolated and used as a guide in future copy designs?

What is the impact (if any) of editorial or program environment? Are certain messages more effective in women's magazines or mass dual-audience publications? Are some commercials stronger in daytime serials and others better for prime evening action or suspense features?

What is the relative advertising impact of one exposure in TV plus one in print, contrasted with two exposures in TV, or two in print? Does the copy mix produce better results?

Admittedly, these are tough questions to answer, but they are the ones that really interest advertisers and agency media strategists. If answers could be found, by well-controlled probes of copy awareness, using large samples and carefully tested questionnaires, our attitudes might be altered, but research that relies on average answers, without explanations or the postulation of specific applications for nonaverage conditions, is next to worthless.

WHAT KINDS OF SURVEYS ARE NEEDED?

We have devoted the bulk of our discussion to a review of existing media research practices and the penchant for overgeneralized wheel-spinning.   Before closing, let us look at the future.   What kinds of surveys must be developed to meet the needs of an enlightened advertising industry, one that has stopped talking to itself and seeks the view of the consumer?   What will replace the artificial security of the flow chart, the quintile study, and the reach and frequency table?

There are a number of subjects that should be explored by the syndicated research services and offered as part of their basic packages or separate, but continuing, endeavors.   These are:

An advertising-campaign rating service

An audience-responsiveness and attitude study

A commercial and ad recall service

Advertising-campaign Rating Service

Most of the larger agencies (or advertisers) undertake periodic advertising-awareness surveys.   Though other variations are used, the standard procedure involves a low-cost telephone interview that asks respondents about their product usage rates and brand familiarity, and ends with a series of questions designed to establish how many persons can correctly identify the brand's basic advertising claims.   While other methods might provide more data, the telephone approach has the vast advantages of speed and relative economy.   In short, it is a reasonably effective device and affordable.

Let us consider the applications of this type of research in media analysis and media planning.   Suppose one of the leading research houses undertook to offer a monthly measurement, involving approximately 1,500 men and 1,500 women respondents per product class. Suppose each person was questioned on the following subjects:

General product usage rates distinguishing between *personal* consumption and *family* purchasing, as necessary

Brand preferences, with first and second choices
Brand satisfaction and attitudes (pro or con)
Advertising awareness for each competitive brand, including:
    Brand claim recognition
    Claim acceptability
    Recency of exposure
    Amount of exposure
Media exposure patterns:
    Time spent with TV and radio by dayparts
    Number of magazines read and exposure to specific publications
Demographic characteristics

While many of these subjects have obvious marketing and copy applications, the primary opportunity in the design is the integration of the media planning function with other advertising activities. Every month the planner receives a fix on how many people are able to recall his message and how his campaign stacks up with his competitors'. The survey tells him how these patterns are developing by age, socioeconomic status, and other demographics, and enables him to judge whether the right kind of person is responding, again in comparison with competitive brands. Finally, he can plot his awareness and relate these findings to the way his schedule is laid out.

The latter is an important point. Suppose you are a TV-only advertiser, with particularly heavy daytime serial exposure. Suppose your average awareness level is 30 per cent but is not increasing as anticipated. Suppose your score among very heavy daytime viewers is 50 per cent and building, but light and nonviewers are way below average and holding steady, or dropping. The inference is clear. The commercials are working, but the media plan is too limited and is missing a lot of people by emphasizing daytime. More nighttime exposure (or other media) is needed to broaden reach and stimulate awareness gains.

That is one interpretation. Let us take another view. Suppose the average awareness is 30 per cent, as before, and our schedule is mostly in daytime serials, as before, but awareness is equally high in *all* population groups, regardless of media exposure. Thus, light viewers are just as familiar with our claims as very frequent viewers, and all segments are holding steady. Again, there is a clear inference, but this time our copy is suspect. It is not achieving the desired results among people who are heavily exposed, and a new approach may be called for.

An Essential Form of Intelligence This kind of survey is an essential form of intelligence to the planner who visualizes himself as a competitor whose opponents are the other brands in his field. It gives him an admittedly imperfect, but running check on his status in the marketplace and permits him to *react* whenever this seems appropriate. He can use it to spot opportunities or his own mistakes, and get away from a style of thinking that calls for one plan a year, regardless of its performance. Consumers have no interest in annual budgets, fiscal or crop years, and the rest of our systems. Their sole frame of reference is their own needs and problems, and their experience with a product is an important element. You can change your strategy once a year, but it isn't a new ball game.

Audience-responsiveness and Attitude Surveys

A second and less explored area concerns the mental attitude of the audience and the way it is reached. While the Simmons attention studies are an important new contribution in media research, they highlight the need for a more definitive qualitative approach for each medium.

Psychographic Studies Several investigators have attempted to incorporate so-called psychological measures in media studies, but their efforts have not been specific enough to be useful. Emmanuel Demby coined the term *psychographics,* and purports to measure a magazine reader's creative spirit by tracking his behavior. Thus, upscale readers of approximately equal age, and the same income or education, are categorized as creative or passive, depending upon their venturesomeness and willingness to buy unusual (or modern) appliances or engage in creative pastimes. The implication is an association with the magazine itself. If *Time* magazine has a higher proportion of so-called creative readers than *U.S. News*, this is presumed to reflect its value as an advertising medium, and serve as a useful description of its audience, one that offers finer insights and helps us to make better planning distinctions.

In fact, the study offers no support for this hypothesis, because it makes no inquiries about the magazine, and the definition of creative and passive consumers is not very helpful because we are told nothing about the *kinds* of advertising claims that might influence such people.

Susceptibility to Advertising   Another researcher, Herbert Kay, has produced intriguing studies that seek to establish whether a consumer is susceptible to advertising as a means of inducing brand switching.   This is a unique distinction, for only some brand switchers are influenced by advertising, while others take advantage of price-offs, promotions, deal packs, and so on.   If these groups can be isolated, with their media habits, some important changes could occur in conventional advertising practices.   For all we know, our standard product-usage and brand-user profiles do not identify the kinds of people who are most likely to be influenced by our media and copy strategy.

Unfortunately, Kay's research, like Demby's, is too generalized, and offers no information on the nature of the attitudes he purports to measure.   Thus, we are unable to determine why a respondent is susceptible to advertising in a particular product class, what made him brand-switchable, and what we can do about it.

Questions for Attitude Studies   The attitude study of the future would try to answer these questions.   Each of its respondents would answer standard demographic, marketing, and media audience questions, and then the critical stage would begin.   The object would be the exploration of questions like these:

What kind of person are we dealing with?   Is he conservative or liberal, extroverted or introverted, aggressively decisive or emotionally insecure?

What is his attitude toward each medium?   What feelings do they convey?   How attentively or thoroughly do they expose their audiences?

What is his attitude toward each product class and brand?   What are the specific attributes he responds to?   What appeals might motivate him to react to the advertising?   Which ones are unbelievable or offensive?

While this study would be difficult to execute, its merits are obvious.   The object is specific attitudinal data and an opportunity to study the interaction (if any) of copy appeals to consumer interests. Some interesting and unsuspected relationships might emerge.

Commercial and Ad Recall Studies

The third of our new media research services would focus directly on advertising. Its objective would be a periodic measurement of a large cross section of ads or commercials, with sufficient sampling to isolate the influence (if any) of media environment. Several hundred viewers would be interviewed on each television show and an equal number on each of the larger magazines.

As in conventional copy tests, audiences would be given certain cues and asked about their recall of the advertiser's message. Unlike the *Life* and *Look* studies, its scope would be large enough to permit discrimination between common campaigns in different media. Thus, we could track ads wherever they appear (in network TV or the larger magazines) and plot differences in recall that might be traceable to media environment. Does a certain commercial always do better in the same TV setting? Does a certain kind of ad develop more impact in specific magazine context?

Once again, the premise is integration. The media planner's job does not end after the plan is approved and the buy is made. It never ends. He must associate himself with the success or failure of his campaign, and seek new ways to improve its performance.

A Modern, Inquisitive Approach In some circles, there is a strong feeling that the media department has lost its function and that most advertisers will eventually assume these duties or automation will take over. If media decisions continue to be made on a purely statistical basis, with cost per thousands as the only indicator of effectiveness, this will probably happen. In fact, it *deserves* to happen. In this chapter, I have sought to demonstrate that many of our media research activities are essentially clerical and have no bearing on advertising. But what if the media planner assumes a new role? The role of a strategist, a marketing expert who relates his activities to the advertising plan and capitalizes on every opportunity to outthink the opposition. A modern and inquisitive approach in media research could help to make this possible. It's worth a try.

CHAPTER TWENTY-FIVE

Uses of the Computer and Other Technological Developments in Advertising

ARTHUR S. PEARSON *Director of Market Planning and Research,*
Bristol-Myers Company

PROGRESS TO DATE

The computer came into most businesses as an accountant and as a labor-saving device. To some extent both uses have tended to mask the true potential of the machine and slow its development in other areas. Until recently, the computer has been seen by most managements as a labor-saving device among white-collar clerical help with the potential to replace executive personnel in time. The idea that the computer will in effect redefine work and working relationships in altogether new ways is a fairly recent one. (See Simon [1] for a discussion of the computer as an extension of man.) It is not surprising, therefore, that at this point in our history the impact of the com-

---

[1] Herbert A. Simon, "The Shape of Automation for Men and Management," Harper & Row, Publishers, Incorporated, New York, 1965.

puter in marketing has been scant.   In an ANA report of August, 1967,[2] A. E. Miller reported that 76 per cent of the surveyed companies were conducting sales analysis on their computers, but less than 10 per cent had a continuing program to monitor and evaluate advertising effectiveness.

Computers in Their Infancy

In reality the computer revolution is still in its infancy.   We are in the early stages of a learning process.   The computer has been fairly broadly applied to most of the well-known and widely used analyses of the precomputer era.   Advances into more sophisticated areas have been more tentative and not particularly successful.   However, from these unsuccessful ventures and sometimes expensive mistakes, considerable progress has been made in defining the nature of the coming impact of the computer in marketing.   The nature of that impact, the ways that it will affect marketing, and the developmental steps necessary to implement those computer programs now seem fairly clear.   The somewhat simple but overriding idea is that the process is necessarily an evolutionary one.   The impact tomorrow will be the result of what is done and learned today.   We cannot get there from here without going through specific steps which in effect will train a new generation of marketing people, systems analysts, and programers.   Tomorrow's systems will evolve from today's systems.   One perceptive analyst has noted, "If we only had the system today we would be able to design a better system now."   See John Diebold's book, "Beyond Automation," for a discussion of the evolutionary nature of computer and systems developments.[3]

Progress Is Slow

In 1963 Robert Buzzell thought that 1970 would be an optimistic estimate of the time when top management people would be working generally with mathematical models in the conduct of their business.[4]

[2] A. Edward Miller, "Application of the Computer in Marketing and Advertising Decision Making," Association of National Advertisers, New York, August, 1967.

[3] John Diebold, "Beyond Automation," McGraw-Hill Book Company, New York, 1964.

[4] Robert D. Buzzell, "Mathematical Models and Marketing Management," Division of Research, Harvard Graduate School of Business Administration, Boston, 1963.

It appears quite clear that 1970 was in fact an extremely optimistic estimate. We have not trained that generation of marketing and management people in the fifteen years since computers came significantly into the business world. There are companies today which are reasonable stand-ins for the Buzzell statement, that is, companies where managements are thoroughly quantitative and reasonably conversant with the use of computers in the solving of business problems. If you were to examine the development of the capability in these companies you would discover that it has taken time because time is a necessary ingredient in training an organization to new ways. But time alone is not enough. Otherwise, many more companies would have trained their organizations in the effective use of computers by early 1969. Later we will examine some of the problems of developing effective computer applications and cover ways to overcome them effectively.

Figure 1 shows the evolution of computer applications for marketing and management in terms of the sophistication of use and the

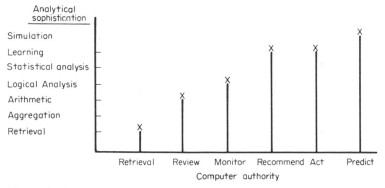

Figure 1 Evolution of computer analytic sophistication and authority in business. (*Courtesy of Arnold E. Amstutz, MIT, Cambridge, Mass.*)

level of authority given to the equipment. Based on the ANA report prepared by Miller, it would seem that most current applications are at "arithmetic" on the analytic sophistication scale and at "review" on the level of authority granted to the computer application. Although there have been moves in the past into higher levels of development by occasional innovators, the author knows of no marketing or management system in the full sense where the computer authority is beyond the "recommend" level, and although there are a number of simulations in use, mostly in the media area, none known to the author is part of a full operating marketing system. Those simulations which are in use in marketing are usually representative of a part of the environment and used only on an intermittent or job basis. Also, most exist as data apart from the basic data operating people are using in the conduct of the business, which is perhaps one reason why they have not been more successful.

On the vertical scale in Figure 1 are shown the different levels of analytic sophistication related to computer usage. The higher one goes on the scale, the greater the sophistication of the usage. On the horizontal scale is shown the level of computer authority delegated by management to the computer system. The farther the movement to the right, the greater the level of authority granted to the computer. Although greater computer authority and greater analytic sophistication imply senior systems, it is possible that a well-developed system at one level of authority or sophistication is more complex than higher systems. For example, most existing systems have a long way to go before they have fully developed the potential for really effective retrieval or monitoring systems.

PROBLEMS IN ACHIEVING SUCCESSFUL APPLICATIONS

In the light of the findings by Miller on how little impact the computer has had on marketing at this time, it would seem best to examine that history of the computer to understand from it some of the problems in achieving its full potential rather than making a detailed review of that history. If the reader is interested in a detailed description of some of the more significant developments in the computer's history in marketing, this may be found in "Models, Measurements and Marketing," edited by Peter Langhoff [5] and "Mathematical Models and Marketing Management," by Robert Buzzell.[6] The Langhoff book describes some of the principles and analytical techniques applicable to the solution of marketing problems, and the Buzzell book describes in some detail several of the specific computer

---

[5] Peter Langhoff (ed.), "Models, Measurements and Marketing," Prentice-Hall, Inc., Englewood Cliffs, N.J., 1965.

[6] Robert D. Buzzell, *op. cit.*

projects conducted in marketing up until a few years ago.   For our purposes, we will examine that history briefly to understand better its possible effect on future developments.

Communication between Planners and Users

The fundamental problem so far in the early history of the computer in marketing is communication between the planners and the users. It is the characteristic problem of innovation in business.   The problem solvers, generally the technicians, have not reached the level of knowledge of the problems comparable to those who work with them daily and whose responsibility it is to solve them.   The result of this poor communication has been that many systems are incomplete or are designed to solve problems that are slightly different from the real problems.   Aside from the obvious need for formal systems in the planning and development of each project and the need for close involvement of prospective users in the design of systems, the solution to the communication problem is probably time and experience.

Adjustment by Operating Personnel   Very few organizations have clearly recognized the basically evolutionary process required for the effective use of the computer in business.   There have been very few areas where a computer system has been developed in the broader context of the total system.   There has been little recognition of the need for specific steps to get the involvement and use of the system by operating personnel.   It is usually assumed that they will simply adjust a lifetime of habits and training to the new ways.   The facts are that they cannot.   System design must recognize this gradual process in two ways: by not asking too much of users in the early stages, and by building systems that reflect their business style and their concept of how the world is.   The IMPACT [7] system which is being used by many wholesalers and retailers to control inventories is a system of this type.   First, its broad application has high payoff initially, even though the system is not theoretically perfect or complete.   And second, IMPACT will change over time as its users change and get more sophisticated and comfortable with it.

The Bristol-Myers STAR system for the management of the media-buying function is a similarly well-conceived system.   It has not tried

[7] IMPACT, Inventory Management Program and Control Techniques, IBM, Technical Publications Department, White Plains, N.Y., 1966.

to tackle some of the tough theoretical problems which have blocked the use of so much of the work in media planning, but at the same time it makes a major contribution to a difficult and complex administrative process.   It also has the capability for development toward a more sophisticated system whenever the users are trained and ready.

Complexity of Marketing Problems

The complexity of marketing problems is certainly a fundamental reason for the lack of greater advances.   In the preface to his book "Marketing Management," Philip Kotler has aptly described the complexity of the marketing process:

> Marketing decisions are among the most difficult of business decisions to make.   The variables are not likely to exhibit the neat quantitative properties of many of the variables found in production and finance.   Attitudinal variables play a larger role in marketing: marketing expenditures affect demand and costs simultaneously. . . . Marketing decisions must be made in the context of insufficient information about processes that are dynamic, lagged, stochastic, interactive, and downright difficult.[8]

The simplification of the marketing process which we sometimes observe in models can mislead us perhaps more than if we had no model at all.   The only way to deal with this problem adequately is to work with sophisticated systems people, keep them in close touch with the using marketing group, set realistic goals that do not have overwhelming theoretical problems, and test the output of the models with historical data if possible and then in the real world.

Complexity of the Systems

Perhaps the most underrated problem by management personnel is the size and complexity of the systems work to develop useful computer applications.   The amount of resources needed in many of these applications is greater than most companies seem willing or able to commit.   There has also been a lack of adequate numbers of persons trained properly in a field of rapidly changing technology. And the new technology is often essential for the efficient systems application to many marketing problems.   A good systems man can

[8] Philip Kotler, "Marketing Management," Prentice-Hall, Inc., Englewood Cliffs, N.J., 1965.

have an efficiency factor on the ultimate operating system of many hundredfold over the average performer.   There are similar potential differences in efficiency throughout all aspects of the computer development process, from securing the proper equipment to programing the system.   It is not surprising that many are discovering that the costs of software are running in excess of the costs of hardware.

SOME GUIDING PRINCIPLES

What should you do about the computer in your marketing?   Many managements today are disappointed by the lack of progress so far, and they are psychologically resigned to the idea of limited progress and are not providing the necessary leadership for systems development.   The computer can make major contributions to marketing —not in the print-outs from the machine but in its effect on the organization.   It can affect the character of administration and decision making throughout.   More important, it can build better managers.   The manager who knows how to use the computer is a better manager because it has extended his capacity to plan, administer, and control.   It is, therefore, important to train an organization for effective computer usage, for the longer the delay in moving in that direction, the longer it will take to accomplish it.   There is no collapsing the leadtime to take an organization through the necessary experience to achieve ease and effectiveness with computers.

Principles for Development of Systems

Below are some principles that should be useful in the development of computer-based marketing systems.
   1. Develop an internal systems capability, but do not be reluctant to use outside consultants to accomplish this most effectively.
   2. Keep the systems group organizationally in close working relationship with marketing.
   3. Set reasonable goals that are achievable in the relatively short-term, but that relate to a broader, longer-range systems plan.   If you have adequate resources, it may be worthwhile to work on longer-range projects with significant theoretical problems.   However, such efforts should be fully recognized ahead of time in terms of time commitments and management's expectations.

4. Develop systems that relate to current operations and to current styles of management but are capable of more sophisticated development over time.   It is absolutely essential to get significant involvement of the marketing personnel who are using the system.

5. Develop systems which are not print-out oriented, although naturally they should have such capabilities as might be needed. Develop analytical systems with monitoring and exception-reporting capabilities.

6. Select marketing problems for potential applications that have significant financial leverage or those that will have a fundamental effect on the activities and capabilities of key personnel.

7. Do not ask marketing people what they need.   Design systems from an intimate knowledge of marketing activities and computer capabilities.   Do get marketing involvement in the early developmental stages.

WHAT IS AVAILABLE NOW FOR YOUR USE?

What programs under development and perhaps not yet proved have the greatest promise of successful payoff in the future?   Obviously a sensible answer to these questions would depend on many factors, such as the amount of marketing leverage in the organization, the number of persons and varied activities represented, the nature of the business, and of course, the level of systems and computer skills in the organization.   However, under most circumstances the general principles outlined above would apply.

Emphasis on Evolutionary Nature   Greatest emphasis perhaps should be on the evolutionary nature of computer development and the need for programs that will effectively involve personnel and train them for future computer methods.   It is possible that these principles could be applied effectively in different ways in different areas of marketing activity.   In the early stages it might be best to pursue separate programs in the different areas of new products, market research, established brand market, media analysis, etc.   The appeal of the total-systems concept is very strong to many managements, but it seems likely that the way to a total system is not by attempting to build such a system from the outset, but rather by separate developments aimed at specific activity areas for different groups of people.   This may lead to individually inefficient systems, but it should lead to systems that are used and are valuable to the organization.   Later the separate systems can be integrated to achieve maximum systems efficiency.   Such an approach also encourages short-term payoffs which may be the best insurance for long-term practicality.

In every area of marketing, computer programs can be developed for each step in the process: planning, execution, control, and evaluation.   In the ultimate system each phase of activity is interrelated to every other phase, and they operate continuously so that the last evaluation provides the framework for the next plan.   Even the most elementary system should be oriented to this mode.   Further advances will simply contribute to the efficiency and the quality of work done at each of the separate phases.

Sales Planning and Control

The account-oriented system (AOS), which is the name given to the sales planning and control system of Bristol-Myers Products, is just such a system.   The basic data of the system are in the sales invoice covering the billing of the company's customers.   In this respect it is like the sales reporting and analysis system of other companies.   But this system has been designed to do much more.   The data file has been organized in such a way that in conjunction with an efficient retrieval system and generalized programs almost any question on sales performance can be efficiently answered.   The underlying principle of AOS is that the purchasing behavior of an account over time and across brands will follow a discernible and meaningful pattern.   The analysis and detection of these patterns should provide valuable information to sales and marketing personnel.

The systems solution, however, is to be able to do this efficiently and with great flexibility to handle most of the kinds of questions that will arise.   In most systems today, aside from standard routine reports, new programing is required to generate these types of analyses if it is possible at all.   It is easy to see that in the early stages of use, sales and marketing people will be learning much from the system, and that learning will affect the direction of the system.   For example, sales and promotional quotas in the future will be developed in terms of distribution objectives by types of accounts.   Goals for new products will translate the new brand's national objectives down to individual account objectives by months by relating the overall sales patterns of earlier new brands.   As AOS develops usage by marketing and sales, new data such as retail sales and media data will flow into the system.   The subroutines will get more sophisticated, and the sales and marketing activities will be much more goal-oriented with the goals functionally related to the steps necessary for them to be accomplished.

Sales Forecasting

Sales forecasting is an activity that is coming of age as a result of the computer.   The basic models and forecasting concepts have been around before, but the computer has made many of these techniques feasible by its ability to do the arithmetic quickly and at low cost.   For example, regression techniques have been used in forecasting for many years, but the computer can generate regressions so fast that separate ones can be developed for individual brands and the regression equation can be updated efficiently as new data become available.   Other techniques which give differential weights to the various pieces of data, such as the exponential-smoothing techniques, are clearly products of the computer era.

New Forecasting Methods   New forecasting methods such as those based on simulation models have been appearing, but are not in broad usage.   In the future it would seem likely that significant improvements in forecasting approaches will grow out of simulation techniques.   The value of computer forecasts is their objectivity and their timely availability.   In many respects they are no better than precomputer forecasts.   Forecasting still requires hypotheses about future events—the computer, at least today, does not do that.   But what it does do, it does relentlessly and objectively.   Perhaps the most important thing it does is to provide mathematically accurate estimates of the future in terms of factors now operating and discernible in the marketplace.   This has added another dimension to forecast analysis.   The trends of the forecasts over time are probably more meaningful than a given forecast at a particular point in time.

A number of companies are combining computer-based sales forecasting systems with programs for financial analysis.   These programs in combination will provide the expected quarterly profit-and-loss and balance-sheet information for financial planning.

Media Planning, Execution, Control, and Analysis

Each area of media activity has been the subject of extensive and varied computer developments over the past few years. An examination of the proceedings of the Advertising Research Foundation over the last few years will reveal presentations on the media models of at least three advertising agencies. A number of large advertisers have also developed computer-based media-buying guides. In addition, commercial research companies have also been active, and today one can purchase media-planning and analysis programs from a number of private research companies. In addition, a large-scale media model was developed under the COMPASS project through the joint efforts of a number of advertising agencies. Alongside this activity stands the fact that most media planning and analysis is not very different today from what it was ten years ago. All the activity reflects the belief of many people that media information will lend itself to computer-based management.

Unreasonably Optimistic Objectives It has probably been unsuccessful in the past for two principal reasons which we have discussed earlier. Objectives have been unreasonably optimistic, and model builders have not recognized the need to work with existing people and structures. Of course, there are many unresolved theoretical questions, and the quality and kind of data are not all that are needed, but the need for administrative systems simply to keep track of the many decisions which need to be made should have led to more progress by this time.

It would seem likely that we will see the development of more and more administrative systems to report availabilities and match these with advertisers' needs. Such systems will recognize the need for decisions by many of the persons presently operating in the field. If theory advances, and it is most likely to advance through the use of systems which provide planning data to users who must make decisions and then provide performance data for them to evaluate those decisions, we will be able to move to more advanced media models. Media and advertising in general should lend themselves to the systems approach. Later we will discuss adaptive systems which we expect in the future will be the mode of many of these activities.

New-product Planning and Development

Five years ago many people were talking about conducting test markets on a computer.   Batten, Barton, Durstine & Osborn developed a program called DEMON which reportedly did this.[9] Arnold Amstutz of MIT has reported the development of simulation models which enable the user to determine the expected level and pattern of sales for a new brand depending on the promotional and advertising programs.[10] Both DEMON and the Amstutz model require extensive amounts of time and money for development, and it is not clear how general the models are and how applicable they are over time.   They are, however, indications of what is in store for the future and signposts on our progress toward scientific marketing.

There are, however, some valuable programs in use today.   The natural sales projection model of Young & Rubicam is a simple simulation model which does not require new theory and which does provide useful data in planning new products.   In using this model the user makes assumptions about the new brand's consumer trial rate, repeat purchase patterns, and repurchase interval.   These are usually based on knowledge from other products which can be related in some manner to the product being forecast.   These data are then used by the model to do the necessary arithmetic and to predict monthly sales volume figures over the first year or two for the new brand.   As with many models its major value is in forcing the new product planner to consider all of the possibilities, to be specific about his assumptions, and to translate those assumptions into sales estimates.   These figures contribute to the plan, but more importantly they provide the framework for evaluating the new product.

New-product Concept Development   In the area of new product concept development a number of analytic programs have been developed over the past few years which examine consumer perception of the various product characteristics available in products currently on the market.   In covering the area of existing product characteristics the program identifies those characteristics which consumers desire

[9] DEMON, name of a marketing model developed by Batten, Barton, Durstine & Osborn, Inc., New York.

[10] Arnold E. Amstutz "Computer Simulation of Competitive Response," The MIT Press, Massachusetts Institute of Technology, Cambridge, Mass., 1967.

but which have not yet been supplied from existing products. The process is called *Perceptual mapping* and was first developed by Volney Stefflre, who did the original work in this area. Computer programs have been developed by others, including the Marketing Science Institute.

The management of total new-product development programs is a challenging task with many critical factors present in the development of each product. The administrative control of large-scale programs with many products and the many diverse tasks associated with development can be handled by a computer. PERT programs, originally developed in the military for control of complex R&D work, have been developed which identify the critical path of a product's development and monitor the product over time to be sure that it continues on its schedule. Since many activities have long lead times and the completion of subsequent tasks is dependent on prior tasks, a well-organized PERT program can contribute much to programs with many complex, interrelated development steps. On the other hand, the development and management of a PERT system require a substantial effort, so its needs should be clearly identified and its value anticipated before it is considered for use.

Perhaps the most promising new programs for use in new-product development are those designed to analyze consumer-purchase panel data from test markets. Brand-switching programs, such as Markov chain analysis, have been valuable in analyzing trends on existing brands. Similar programs have been developed to analyze new-product purchase data in the early months. Such programs yield prediction of the first year to eighteen months in sales based on sales over the first four to six months depending on the repurchase cycle. Again, the further development of such programs will continue as use is broadened and experience with more new brands is built into the new models.

Analytic Programs

Basically, research analysis is concerned with determining the relationship of variables in order to gain understanding of a marketing process or to predict the future. Understanding of the contribution of different variables to a marketing result is fundamental to the development of advertising and marketing strategy. Many of the statistical techniques used to analyze data today have been in use for many years in social sciences, but have only recently been widely used in marketing. It would seem that a number of these techniques will find broader use in marketing in the future as more people become familiar with them. Also, the availability of packaged computer programs from service bureaus or through time-shared computer systems will contribute to their broader use. The need for these techniques in marketing is clear. Much of the data from market research is sample data, and thus its proper use requires an analysis of its reliability. Also, techniques such as factor analysis which reduce large quantities of data to manageable and meaningful form are needed to match our current ability to produce data. Below is a list of some of the statistical techniques available, with a brief comment on their meaning and use. Computer programs have been developed for all of them and most are available through the service bureaus.

Factor analysis is a technique to reduce redundancy in data. The computer program identifies those variables which are associated together and thus enables the researcher to find a limited number of them that explain most of the variation in data. It is widely used with survey data to reduce the number of factors to the most important ones. Although it is a fairly sophisticated technique, the naming of the factors themselves is a subjective process that depends largely on the judgment of the analyst.

Chi square analysis is a technique to determine whether the differences observed in sample data from the theoretical expectations are "real" or whether it is likely the differences are due to chance. It is a useful technique to determine whether the observed frequencies in a distribution, such as usage of product by age, are statistically significant.

Regression and correlation refer to techniques which measure the association of variables. These are perhaps the most widely used currently in marketing. For example, correlation analysis would be used to determine whether or not a relationship existed between changes in advertising and changes in sales by various sales areas. Regression techniques are widely used in forecasting or predicting.

Analysis of variance is a statistical technique essential for the analysis of marketing experiments. It enables the experimenter to analyze the contribution from the different variables to the experimental result. Since we can anticipate much greater use of controlled marketing experiments in the future, there will be much broader use of these techniques.

THE FUTURE

The evolutionary aspect of computer applications has been emphasized in all the preceding discussion. The experience gained in each new advance is essential to the next advance. Eventually this will lead to making the computer a true extension of man rather than something that helps out on the side with data which require extensive study and analysis. Computers in the future will provide the basic administrative system for many of the diverse and complex aspects of marketing planning, execution, and evaluation. In that distant day in the future the computer will not only conduct the analysis, but also make the decision based on the rules and logic developed by sophisticated marketing personnel. These persons will spend much of their time in building the models and simulations, developing inputs and testing them on computers, as well as in the marketplace. Some of the concepts which will undoubtedly contribute to that state have recently been emerging. It would seem that further advances in computer utilization will depend on the ability to develop effectively these new emerging concepts.

Monitoring and Control

A shift from data generation to data monitoring and control will probably be the first main step in future advances. This will require extensive work by operating and systems people to develop standards and criteria against which to compare performance data. The advancing computer technology and software developments will make it efficient to monitor continuously many detailed aspects of the marketing system and to conduct this monitoring with sophisticated criteria. Not only will sales performance be monitored, but the buying behavior of customers also will be monitored. It is clear from the monitoring concept that it will not come to pass until management involvement with the computer has been achieved. The monitoring criteria must be developed out of management's plans and policies for the firm.

Adaptive Systems

Adaptive systems is a term coined by John Little of MIT.[11]   It refers to a technique of systematic market planning and monitoring. In a fully operating adaptive system the marketing plan is executed so that measures of the relative productivity of the various important marketing inputs are developed.

For example, in a given plan one-third of the markets receive advertising levels of 100 gross rating points, with another group at 75 gross rating points and the remaining third at 125 gross rating points.   Each separate portion of the test is matched with the other two parts to ensure comparability.   The sales results of such an adaptive system, if properly executed, would provide a relative measure of the sales elasticity of the advertising dollar between 75 and 125 gross rating points.

The important element of the concept is that adaptive systems are a marketing way of life, where each plan is executed to obtain maximum information.   It is a continuing process which yields new and current information about the relationship of the various important marketing variables.   Each aspect of adaptive systems including the planning, execution, and evaluation requires extensive monitoring and control: for example, the statistical process to select the areas, the selection of the media, the controls to ensure that the gross rating points are meeting the experimental requirements, and the analytical programs for evaluating the results.   If the complexity of one adaptive experiment on one brand is multiplied by many brands continuously over time, the need for a systems solution is quite clear.   Adaptive systems are certainly the wave of the future in marketing, but it will take computer and sophisticated support systems to make them feasible.

Time Sharing

Time sharing is the name of the system where a large central computer is used by many separate users who have access to the computer from remote terminals.   Time sharing is efficient because the programing includes a queuing procedure which ensures efficient equipment utilization.   The separate users pay only for the computer time

[11] John Little, Adaptive Marketing Systems: A Working Paper, Sloan School of Business, Massachusetts Institute of Technology, Cambridge, Mass.

actually used and a nominal monthly rental for the remote terminal. Time-sharing systems are available through several large service companies which have canned programs available for use by their clients.

Generally speaking, it is not efficient at the present time to use time-sharing computer services where large retrieval files are necessary for the procedures. The most useful current applications are the statistical techniques discussed earlier and other canned programs which require some simple data inputs from the operators. Time-sharing programs are essentially computationally oriented rather than data processing oriented. As the technology develops and costs of the large-scale computers decline, the time-sharing concept will probably be the mode of large corporate computer installations in marketing as well as other areas. In this case, sophisticated retrieval systems and large files will come into use. The important aspect of time sharing is the direct interaction of the individual with the problem and the computer, and the ability to search for a solution on demand. Also, the ability for successive interrogation will be an important part of these future developments.

Decision Analysis

One of the more successful time-sharing programs being used in marketing is decision analysis. Decision analysis enables the decision maker systematically and mathematically to measure the pros and cons of a particular decision. Essentially, the decision-analysis program calculates the expected value of a particular course of action. This expected value can be calculated for the various levels involved in the decision. Although the system depends heavily on the judgment and experience of the decision maker, increasingly in the future he will be able to call on history files which will help him to relate the corporation's previous experience to his current problem. In an area which depends so heavily on judgment and experience, it would seem likely that decision analysis will be an increasingly important area of computer usage in marketing. In fact, the systematic rigor which it requires and the relative ease with which marketing people can understand the concepts make it an ideal area in which to commence computer training among marketing people.

PART EIGHT

Special Kinds of Advertising

CHAPTER TWENTY-SIX

Advertising Management's Sales Promotion Responsibilities and Activities

DONALD M. LEWIS, JR. *Manager of Advertising and Customer Services, Consumer Markets Division, Eastman Kodak Company*

WHAT IS SALES PROMOTION?

Sales promotion, like middle age, is one of those specialized terms that lends itself to different definitions.

Some say, for example, that sales promotion is *anything* that promotes the sales of a product. If we accept this broad concept, then we find that sales promotion must include everything from the initial design of the product to the way it is displayed on the dealer's shelves. This definition is too generalized to be of much help in our attempt to focus on one of the most important functions in today's advertising-sales effort.

If we narrow our scope a bit, however, we can arrive at a workable definition. Sales promotion is almost any organized means by which a company, working through its sales and advertising personnel, can increase the sale of its products.

26-1

Because definition of sales promotion is so hard, many managements allow individual marketing divisions within their companies to decide their own needs for sales promotion and the relation of sales promotion to the advertising program.

What has happened in the corporate structure is the development of both advertising and sales promotion departments.   It is of paramount importance that these two groups work closely and well with each other, whether as independent units or as interrelated groups under the same supervision.   Only by such cooperation and support will either achieve its maximum potential in contributing to the company's growth.

If the advertising manager does have responsibility for sales promotion—as is often the case—then he must decide how deeply it will be imbedded in his advertising program.   He must also assess the relation of sales promotion efforts to the program of the sales department, making certain that his plans do not encroach on any of sales' functions.

In the past, the sales force has been a go-it-alone group.   It has often looked on advertising or any other kind of help as unnecessary.   But there has been great progress in recent years.   As the complexity of markets has increased, sales people have come to accept sales promotion as a valuable tool, and some—notably the salesmen themselves—have expressed a desire for *more* promotional assistance.

The Functions of Sales Promotion

A number of years ago, the Association of National Advertisers surveyed member companies on the sales promotion functions handled by their advertising departments.   One or more of the following activities were listed by the respondents: [1]

1. Handles sales contests
2. Does sales analysis work
3. Builds sales kits
4. Prepares educational trade literature
5. Provides window and counter displays for branch offices and dealers
6. Provides exhibits for branch offices and conventions
7. Prepares sales bulletins

[1] Study of 202 ANA member companies in 1946.

8. Assists in sales training
9. Supervises trade-association activities
10. Prepares trade-paper advertising
11. Maintains close relationships with branches, dealers, and sales agents
12. Promotes packaging and packaging improvements
13. Promotes cooperation with sales department
14. Prepares direct mail to the trade
15. Organizes trade meetings
16. Handles merchandising of advertising
17. Promotes personal contacts among the trade
18. Arranges special meetings for retail executives
19. Assists in sales-training meetings for sales personnel
20. Assembles and sends out samples as requested by branch offices
21. Provides advertising materials to dealers
22. Maintains sales schools for the trade
23. Reports on new merchandising trends

By today's standards, some of these items would be eliminated from this list because they have become accepted functions for the advertising department. On the other hand, a similar survey made today would result in a considerably longer list of sales promotion activities. Chief among these are the many special events, both on the local and national level, that many advertisers sponsor: selection of beauty queens; promotions to special groups; parades; and sponsorship of other activities that range from Little League teams to Indianapolis race cars.

Close Relationship Needed   In all these areas, there is the need for a close relationship between the activities of advertising and sales promotion.

A consumer promotion of a product, for example, must have the support of advertising at all levels—in trade and consumer publications and broadcast media—to give it strength. A special promotion that is related to the theme of the advertising program and capitalizes on this theme has a far better chance for success than a promotion that is expected to stand alone.

In the same way, media selection, whether made by the advertising or promotion group, must support the theme of the campaign and be geared to reach the greatest number of persons in the potential market.

A coupon promotion to introduce a new food product, for instance, would probably go through the following media stages:

Trade-paper advertising to grocers

Direct mail to dealers and distributors

National magazine advertising to women

Local newspaper advertising

Cooperative advertising for dealers

Direct mail to housewives, or house-to-house distribution of samples with coupons (Caution here: mailing costs are increasing.)

Window and counter displays

Radio and television spots

Mention in the company's other advertising programs

The theme of any promotion should be carried out through all the advertisements developed for print and broadcast media as well as in displays, exhibits, and point-of-purchase materials. Obviously, company salesmen must have up-to-date information on promotion plans as well as adequate supplies of materials they will need for their part in the campaign.

Planning a Promotion

Promotion ideas do not, as a rule, spring full-blown from the brow of the advertising manager. The process that brings them into being might be called *sales-minded creativity,* and like any creative effort, it may be time-consuming, frustrating, and even mildly painful.

Here are ten questions that form a preliminary checklist for those involved with the birth and nurture of a special promotion:

1. Is a promotion needed at all? Why?
2. What products or services will be promoted?
3. To whom should the campaign be directed?
4. What will be its objective(s)?
5. What theme should it be built around?
6. What form will the promotion take?
7. How much trade and consumer advertising support should it have?
8. How much money should be budgeted?
9. How long should the promotion continue?
10. What will be the starting date?

Frequently, the answers to most of these questions will be dictated by circumstance or by a worried call from the product manager, suggesting that something be done to push Product A or B, or Products A, B, *and* C.

One of the most successful promotions for a complete product line in recent years has been Kodak's "Open Me First" Christmas campaign.

Cameras have always been good sellers during the holiday season. One year, the company decided to promote inexpensive camera outfits that would contain everything the novice photographer needed to start shooting pictures as soon as he opened the package.

During the planning meeting, a staff member suggested that the recipient of one of these camera outfits should use his gift to take pictures of the family's Christmas festivities.   After all, family Christmas photos have always been a favorite subject for snapshooters.

At this point, someone else suggested that the package containing the camera outfit should be the first to be opened.   This, in turn, led to the special Christmas gift-wrapped package and the tag stating boldly, "Open Me First."

National magazine, newspaper, and television advertising played up the idea.   Dealers were advised of it through trade-paper advertising and publicity stories.   Special window and counter displays were created to promote the idea at the point of sale.   Salesmen pushed the concept with enthusiasm.   The result was a tremendous rise in the sale of camera outfits.   Incidentally, this same idea, with variations, has been promoted every Christmas since.   This example suggests that a successful promotional idea must have a strong element of appeal both to the consumer and the dealer, and must lend itself to publicity.

In this case, the costs of the camera campaign were minimal, involving only the gift wrap and the "Open Me First" tags.   All the other advertising and creation costs for window and counter displays were budgeted as part of normal Christmas promotional expenses.

PLANNING

The Kodak camera promotion came about because first someone had a good idea.   Most promotions, however, must be created to meet a special need or to solve a problem, without the benefit of a ready-made theme.

At the preplanning stage, and as the campaign takes shape, the sales field force is a vital factor in developing a promotion and making it work.

While the headquarters staff—sales, advertising, product planning, marketing—can see the *need* for a promotion and can plan accordingly, it is the men in the field who have firsthand contact with the consumers.

They know their dealers, and through them, the customers. They know the prejudices, fears, and the potential for enthusiasm far better than anyone at headquarters who may view the ultimate consumers only as pins on a map or holes in a punch card.

While a promotion is still in the planning stage, it pays to present it to the field forces. Their reaction, however, should be carefully analyzed for salesmen, even the best, tend to steer away from any changes in techniques that they have found to be successful.

In looking for new ideas, the promotion staged by a small-town dealer in some remote community may provide the germ of an idea for a campaign of national proportions. Sometimes, a salesman himself may pinpoint a widespread sales or product problem in his report, and a successful promotion may be created as a result.

Use of Outside Idea Sources

Use of outside firms, advertising agencies, for example, is sometimes profitable in developing promotion ideas. The agencies maintain large creative staffs that may be tapped for new approaches. However, this type of assistance is not usually a major part of their services. In some instances, sales promotion people have even found good promotion possibilities in rejected advertising campaigns. Detection of such ideas calls for constant alertness.

Sales Promotion Agencies Sales promotion agencies, on the other hand, can be a prolific source of ideas. They are in constant contact with campaigns conducted by all types of businesses. Frequently, a successful promotion staged by one company can be adapted for another, noncompetitive firm.

An excellent example is the offer of recipes that feature a company's food products. This approach may seem commonplace—at one time or another, recipes have been part of the promotional package for everything from soup to nuts—but the sales promotion man who coined the original idea obviously made a rich profit for his client.

When faced with the task of choosing an outside promotion agency, look for a group with a solid record of success, and check with some of the agency's other clients before making a final decision.

Ideas can come from many other sources.   A secretary might suggest a new method of packaging or a container that has special appeal for feminine customers.   Former sales personnel who have moved up the executive ladder are often the source of useful ideas.   Possibilities are endless.   What is most important is that others in the company recognize that the headquarters promotion staff welcomes suggestions and follows through on profitable ideas.   In this kind of atmosphere, the promotion staff is certain to receive a steady stream of ideas from other employees within the company.

Coordination with Other Advertising and Merchandising Efforts

Coordination of all advertising, merchandising, special sales promotions, and long-range marketing programs is essential at the earliest planning stage.   This kind of cooperation is vital not only to avoid any interference with long-range plans but also to take advantage of them.

Strong lines of communication with other departments and with the sales field force must be established from the start.

A valuable aid in a sales promotion operation is a chart of *all* scheduled events sponsored by the company within the next year. This memorandum, for distribution to department heads, should include the starting dates, duration, and extent of the company's advertising campaigns, the products to be advertised, and the themes. Special sales promotions should be listed, with incentives, dates, participating personnel, and other details, as announcement dates for new products and policy changes, sales meetings, sales-training sessions, dealer meetings, and convention dates.

If even one department does not have a full picture of the company's promotion and advertising plans, it is easy to see how conflicting and even competing events can be scheduled by groups which should be working for and not against one another.

Early Planning Essential

The time it takes to develop the germ of a promotional idea into a profitable venture is always longer than anticipated.   Legal clearances, budget and other approvals, printing schedules, product production forecasts, advertising closing dates, availability of television and radio time spots, and even vacation schedules can delay the start of a promotional program.

The best way to maintain the original enthusiasm for the plan is to anticipate these delays and allow ample time for each.   Copies of the proposed promotion and schedule, forwarded to all who will later be involved, can stimulate quicker action in all departments.   A positive starting date may draw protests at the outset, but it will surely lead to redoubled efforts to meet it.

Budgets and Financial Control

Potential costs are never as clear-cut in a proposed sales promotion as they are in an advertising campaign, but estimating them and getting them down on paper are vital.

Many of the best promotions are relatively inexpensive in terms of products sold or results achieved.

In one case, a manufacturer made a simple change in his promotional program and turned a loss into a bright success.   The company made baby lotion and powder.   For years, they sent discount coupons and free samples of the products to new mothers, whose names they easily gleaned from the birth announcements in local newspapers.   The response was slow, and the sales picture for the products was only fair.   Remember, also, that each coupon or free sample cut further into the final profit picture.

After consulting with a sales promotion firm, the manufacturer changed his approach.   To his product samples, he added hand lotion (another company product) to keep mother's skin soft as she touched the baby; a diaper; and two booklets—one on infant care and another on baby names—and offered women a "baby bundle" at a low cost.   Results were astonishing.   The manufacturer not only got women to try his products but also reaped a profit on the promotional item itself!

Regardless of the kind of promotion, however, it is important to arrive at a budget that reflects careful assessment of *all* the potential costs.   Here is a list of some of the activities that are frequently a part of the promotional package:

Direct mail to salesmen, dealers, and other participants

Advertising, above and beyond normal expenditures

Special packaging of featured products
Point-of-purchase displays
Publicity materials and press kits
Press-conference facilities
Sales kits
Travel expenses by company personnel
Entertainment of dealers, the press, and selected consumers
Cooperative advertising
Reprints of advertisements and articles
Coupons and premiums
Sales bulletins
Salesmen's and dealers' prizes
Exhibits
Photography and model charges
Preparation of case-history reports
Clipping services
Research to ascertain the effectiveness of the promotion

Obviously, all these items would not be included in every promotional effort.

Legality

Today, more than ever before, it is vital that the company's legal department review each promotion plan, particularly if any form of cooperative advertising is involved or if the promotion is apt to appeal to one group of dealers more than another. A promotion that favors one group—even though no favoritism was intended—may lead to charges of discrimination and eventual legal action against the company.

Incentives

Every promotion should have built-in incentives for three groups: the customer, the dealer, and the company salesmen. These incentives may be cash, merchandise, premiums, or even less tangible rewards such as increased prestige or personal recognition.

Of course, the most important incentive involves the consumer. He must be motivated to look, to buy, or to do whatever is necessary to make the promotion meet its objectives—even if the company only wants its customers to think more kindly of its products or policies (and promotions can be built to do just that).

In recent years especially, large corporations associated in the public mind with causing air or water pollution have gone to great trouble and expense to run full-page advertisements that detail their efforts at conservation.   The headline for such an ad might read: "Do you know another company that spends $2 million on pollution control each year?"

Companies also develop advertisements that promote their public service activities.   A typical example is a picture of five tough-looking young men, with the tag line: "Unemployable? Don't be so sure.   At one of our plants, we hardly hire anyone else."

There must also be an incentive for the dealer so that he is willing to invest the time and energy to promote the product.   This incentive may take the form of cash, a trip for him and his family, bonus merchandise, or greatly increased store traffic.   This last incentive—or any other benefit that enhances the dealer's business—is the most significant for the promoting manufacturer, for it assures him a better and stronger dealership for his other products as well.

The salesman who calls on the retailer must also have an incentive.   After all, he must take the time to imbue the dealer with enthusiasm for the promotion and the extra work it involves, and also use the promotion to bring in more participating dealers.

Unless everyone along the way shares in the incentive, there is certain to be a weak link in the promotional chain.

The trickiest problems occur when the manufacturer must work through a wholesaler in order to reach the individual dealer.   Under this system, the manufacturer, in essence, loses control over the distribution of the incentive.   The wholesaler will often retain the incentive, particularly if it is cash or merchandise or added discounts.   From then on, he will run the promotion in any way he sees fit.   The great difficulty here is that the manufacturer may not even know the names or locations of the dealers because many wholesalers keep their customer lists confidential.

Clear Communication

Many of the activities connected with a special promotion must be carried out through the written word: letters of explanation to the sales force, interoffice memos, printed material for dealers, and advertising copy for the ultimate consumer.

Naturally, the sales promotion staff seeks to make this written material as clear as possible.   However, a variety of pitfalls awaits the copy writer who is "overfamiliar" with the setup and goals of the campaign.

One way to make sure that the copy is understandable *and* complete is to test the letter or memo or set of instructions on a group of employees who have had nothing to do with the promotion or who know nothing about sales methods or advertising.   Ask them to read the material and play back the message.

This method works especially well in testing the instructions that accompany display pieces.   Ask someone to read the instructions and then set up the display item *without* assistance.   This may lead to drastic revisions in the copy.

Responsibilities

Assignment of individual responsibilities for a promotion involves great care and planning.   Everyone involved must know his duties, the progressive phases in the campaign, and the completion dates.

Personnel assignments should be made and discussed in detail during the initial stages of the campaign.   This arrangement assures the full benefit of everyone's ideas early enough to permit changes if better ways are found to handle any phase of the program.   Last-minute changes are costly.

The responsibilities of the sales force as well as other employees concerned in the final thrust of the promotion should also be delineated as early as possible.

Implementing the Plan

If the budget can be stretched to meet the costs, the manufacturer should plan on national advertising to support a major promotion. A company-sponsored television show, for example, is the perfect spot for commercials that highlight the promotion.   Advertisements should also be scheduled in national magazines that reach the proper audiences and in selected newspapers around the country.

Dealers who plan a tie-in advertising campaign of their own should be supplied with copy and pictures by the company.   Complete advertisements that carry out the promotional theme should also be available.   Dealers should know the national advertising schedules so they can buy local space to run their tie-in ads at the proper time. If special packaging or new products are featured in the promotion, the sales force should make certain that dealers have ample stocks on hand. Orders should be placed far enough in advance so they can be filled in time—an arrangement that often calls for close coordination with plant production schedules.

One of the collateral advantages of such a national advertising campaign is that it compels everyone involved with the promotion to meet the target deadlines. When a campaign is keyed to the issuance dates of national magazines or broadcast slots for national television, there is no temptation or opportunity to alter the schedule, because these media have early closing dates.

It is almost imperative today that a company launch any major promotion with general advertising backup. If a manufacturer relies solely on window displays, window banners, and hit-and-miss dealer support, he is courting almost certain failure.

Even a small-scale promotion within a region or county should be reinforced by advertising in the local papers, dealer-sponsored tie-in advertising, and radio and television spots—even a brass band, if it will help!

Television and radio are fast becoming a vital link in the promotional chain. Radio reaches a vast audience, especially in the daytime hours. Millions of car radios are in use at any one time by commuters, salesmen, delivery people, and women on the way to shopping centers. In addition, countless housewives do their work to the tune of the radio and the talk of a disc jockey. And don't forget the teen audience with their ubiquitous transistor models.

In some areas, and for some markets, FM radio is a relatively low-cost medium for reaching selected groups of consumers. Many chain stores and supermarkets, for example, use piped-in FM or taped programs as background music for shoppers, and arrangements can usually be made for promotional announcements on these broadcasts.

The diversity of radio audiences and the clear-cut definition of certain listening groups for certain stations offer promotional possibilities that are just now being explored.

Cooperative Advertising

Cooperative advertising can make the difference between success and failure for a promotion. Certainly, dealers must be encouraged to buy space and time in their local newspapers and on local stations.

Whether or not the manufacturer pays for a part of this localized advertising is a matter of company policy.

Even when a company does not contribute financially to its dealer advertising, there may be a temptation to make some form of compensation available.   Any arrangements here may be fraught with hazard and should be carefully checked with the legal department.

In some instances, window displays and other point-of-purchase materials, if supplied by the company, may come under cooperative advertising regulations.

There is little doubt that the added advertising support from local dealers can be invaluable for a promotion, and it is natural for a manufacturer to foster this support through incentives.   However, unless *all* dealers participate in such a program, it is probably better to let the company sales force *sell* the individual dealer on the advantages of buying his own advertisements in his own locality for the benefit of his own business.

Cooperative Promotional Ventures

Another form of cooperative promotion is the joint venture between two or more manufacturers of noncompeting products.

A well-known example of such a project is the "America's Junior Miss" pageant, promoted jointly by Eastman Kodak Company; John H. Breck, Inc., which manufactures hair-care products; Chevrolet Division of General Motors Corporation; and Kraft Foods.   All share in the sponsorship of the television program, the prizes, and the scholarships.

Products that are generally used together or that complement one another lend themselves to joint promotions.   Examples are numerous: an aluminum foil wrap with food products, a hair brush with shampoo, a measuring cup with detergent.   In a department store promotion, it is possible to link an even wider variety of products, as Kodak has done, for instance, with cameras and bathing suits.

Admittedly, there are problems in the joint sponsorship of such programs.   Company policies and rules may differ; equitable cost sharing must be planned; and such a project usually involves two different advertising agencies with individualized approaches to merchandising techniques.   But the opportunities are there for the companies that are willing to accept the possible disadvantages.

Customer Relations

One of the most important functions of the advertising department during a sales promotion is the establishment of effective communications between the company and its customers.   Every communication—however minor—should be reviewed not only for its content, but also for its tone.   Too much of the incidental correspondence from a company tends to be stiff and formal.

Letter writers for the company should constantly strive for a closer, warmer relationship with the customer.   The tone of a letter can be an effective selling tool if it is designed, for example, to interest a dealer in an upcoming promotion or to alert him to a call by a company salesman.   A letter that is friendly, warm, and intriguing will be read and remembered.   It may have that special competitive edge over the other correspondence that crosses the dealer's desk each day.

Direct Mail

Direct mail is becoming increasingly costly, and many companies are dropping it as a part of their promotional efforts.   It does play a part, however, in maintaining the lines of communication between the company and its dealers.

In a prolonged promotion, weekly newsletters with reports on the progress of the promotion as well as articles on activities of other dealers can be effective in maintaining and stimulating interest. Use of direct mail *by* the dealer himself is not usually recommended unless he is aiming at a very limited clientele in his area.   On the other hand, participating dealers generally appreciate and use envelope stuffers prepared by the company that can be sent out with bills or even statement envelopes that bear the company message promoting the campaign.

The Conclusion and Follow-up

The follow-up to a special campaign is just as important as the carefully planned opening.   The promotional staff should maintain accurate records of sales throughout the campaign.   Some research may be necessary here, because dealers do not always place their orders to coincide with the dates of the promotion.   In many cases, reports from salesmen provide valuable backup information.

If the company's products are sold through wholesalers and jobbers and a complete list of dealers is not available, a clipping service may be employed to scan newspapers in the areas involved to keep trace of any dealer advertising in support of the promotion.   Finally, the promotion staff should try to survey dealers, salesmen, and customers themselves for reactions to the campaign.

The final step is the assembling of all these details as a report to management *and* as a guide to those preparing future promotions.

WORKING WITH OTHER DEPARTMENTS

The role of the advertising department in implementing a sales promotion program ranges from development of the initial plan and preparation of the advertising and display materials, to supervision of the final program.   In fact, as indicated earlier, many companies organize the advertising and sales promotion staffs into one department.

In addition, there are a number of other groups in most companies that play key roles in the sales promotion area.

Product Design

When new products are under development, it is often advisable for members of the sales promotion and advertising team to sit in on the meetings of the product planners.   Their knowledge of consumer likes and dislikes in the company's markets can be helpful.   Sometimes, a minor design change will result in a more marketable product.   These initial discussions may also spark a promotion idea that can be developed and ready to go as soon as the product itself.   Because most new products need strong promotional efforts, it is advantageous to initiate special sales campaigns as soon as possible.

Package Design

In addition to the product itself, the package it comes in should have promotable elements.   A good package designer recognizes this fact, and he will often welcome the views of the promotion department.

The first and primary function of the package is to protect the product in shipment from the manufacturer to the dealer.   This protection must be maintained, moreover, in the dealer's warehouse and on his shelves; and frequently, it must continue for the lifetime of the product in the consumer's hands.

Some manufacturers of children's bubble bath, for example, now promote their product in plastic packages shaped like jolly cartoon characters.   These containers must stand up to the nightly bath activities of a spirited child, be convenient to use so that the mother does not break a fingernail getting the container open, and remain waterproof to protect the bubble bath that remains inside.

The package has another and very valuable function, too, while on the dealer's shelf: it serves as a selling tool.   The package must be attractive and easy to handle.   It must stand out from products of other manufacturers.   And it must carry the salient selling points of the product inside.

Self-display Pieces   In recent years, product packages have also functioned as self-display pieces.   Next time you are at a supermarket, look at the boxes that hold the washday detergents and see how they "scream" at the buyer.   Or notice the eye-catching hang-tags that now come with the clothing on department store racks—tags that instruct one to "Look for my match mate" or "Wash me in your machine.   I'll love it!"

In some high-volume products, such as laundry detergents, where the production of packages is a continuous operation, notices of special promotions are often incorporated into the design of the package itself.   The promotion may be a special premium offer, a two-for-one deal, a discount, or perhaps a combination offer with another company's product.   A manufacturer of spaghetti, for instance, might feature a discount coupon for tomato paste.

The length of time that a package is retained in the home or in the hands of the consumer is also an important factor in its design. Throughout its life, the package is creating an image in the user's mind.   That image, if it is good, may be a powerful factor in creating the impetus for a repeat sale.

General Management

It may seem a bit presumptuous to list the officers of a company as a "tool" for sales promotion, but the presence of these executives at the sales meetings that launch a major promotion can lend considerable importance to the event.

In many cases, the advertising department may draw the assignment of preparing the executive speeches for these occasions.   The writer should make every effort to be sure not only that the speech reflects management approval and interest in the promotion, but also that it is cordial and sincere.

If the president or vice president is the first to address the meeting, his speech should cover the general background and need for the promotion. Thus, he will set the stage for the vice president in charge of sales to announce the actual promotion and provide a broad outline for the campaign.

Of course, management should also be kept informed of all promotion plans and should receive brief but informative reports on the progress of current campaigns.

The Sales Department

Obviously, the sales department is the most important group that the advertising department will work with in its promotional efforts. Cooperation and coordination between the two departments are essential.

In addition to special promotions, moreover, there are a number of other areas where the advertising staff will be called on to work with sales.

For example, the advertising department that incorporates sales promotion functions will be expected to assist at sales meetings, sales training classes, conventions, and exhibits. All these activities really *are* sales promotions, for the objective of each is to increase the sale of the company's products.

Sales Training   In most cases, the only role of advertising and promotion personnel in sales training sessions is to speak to the group of trainees on the functions of their department, explaining their part in developing sales. This is also an excellent opportunity, however, for the promotional staff to indoctrinate the new sales force with the need for promotion, to tell them how to recognize specific problems, and to provide them with guidelines so they will be able to develop ideas of their own once they are in the field. Moreover, the salesmen should be impressed with the fact that the promotion staff always welcomes their ideas.

Sales Meetings   A general sales meeting can be a major event, depending upon the number of salesmen the company employs and the importance of the news to be announced. Although the overall plan of the meeting will probably be handled by the sales department itself, advertising and sales promotion personnel may be called to assist.

Obviously, the meeting must be both interesting and inspiring. There are outside organizations that will handle all the details, such as hotel accommodations, meeting rooms, entertainment, and the dramatic skits that are utilized to feature company products at most sales meetings today.

Someone from within the company must be assigned to work with this outside agency to make certain that the message is handled properly in the dramatic skits and that the information for collateral material—charts, sales, portfolios, graphs—is prepared correctly.

Some manufacturers, on the other hand, prefer to use only company personnel for sales skits. In this case, the responsibility for writing the skit, selecting actors, and rehearsing them is usually the duty of the advertising and promotion staff.

The program for a sales meeting should alternate technical discussions and executive speeches with lighter talks or film showings. Audiovisual materials play a major role in most sales meetings these days. If a color-slide show is planned, a script should be prepared and rehearsed, perhaps with the remarks taped in advance and the appearance of a company executive at the end of the program to answer questions and thus provide a change of pace.

Product literature should be ready in ample quantities for distribution during the presentation.

Conventions

A convention is itself a special promotion. It is significant because it brings together in one place and at one time many of the customers, dealers, and other individuals who are important to the company. If a major showing of products is to be a part of the convention along with regular meetings, plans should be made to handle these two functions separately.

It is possible that no one from the advertising or promotion department will need to be on hand for a convention where only technical papers are presented. The only promotional interest in such a meeting might be to gather background technical material or information on other manufacturers' products and developments. If your company is sponsoring one or more technical papers at such a convention, however, copies of your presentation should be reproduced cleanly and bound in attractive covers bearing the company insignia.   The reports should be distributed widely to convention delegates and the trade press.

If the convention is attended by dealers, there will probably be numerous sessions on the promotion and advertising campaigns planned by individual companies.   These meetings afford an excellent opportunity to learn what other manufacturers are doing, and more importantly, to assess the coming trends in overall trade policy.

Sometimes a company will use these advertising meetings to launch a teaser campaign suggesting momentous events to come.   The company does not provide any positive clues, however, beyond a key word or phrase that will be used during the actual promotion.   Two or three days after the close of the convention, details of the promotion are finally presented by mail or by company salesmen to the individual dealers.

Trade Shows

Trade shows are vitally important to both the large and small manufacturer.   Plans should be under way well in advance for a major show, and a year's lead time is not unusual.

Such advance planning and early budget commitments are essential if the company is to ensure adequate and desirable booth space at the most prestigious shows.   The best locations—opposite the entrance and at the front corners—are often reserved from year to year by the same manufacturers.

The measure of success at any trade show is not only the amount of traffic passing the exhibit, but the number of people who actually turn aside to visit the display.   It is clear that the design of the booth is a matter of paramount importance here, and if the company does not have its own exhibit coordinator, or exhibits group, it is wise to contract for the services of professionals who specialize in this type of work.

Devices to Attract Visitors   Numerous devices are employed to attract visitors to trade-show exhibits:

Pretty girls to pass out literature or product samples

Product or process demonstrations

Continuous motion pictures or slide shows

Working models of the product or oversize models of small products

Moving exhibits that visitors can operate by pressing buttons

Electronic quiz shows with illuminated questions and answers actuated by the visitors

A pretty girl who makes souvenir photos of visitors

Attractive rest areas

Free soft drinks

One exhibitor at a recent trade show incorporated a slowly moving platform into his display space. When visitors paused to watch an intriguing dramatic sketch, they found themselves being transported *into* the exhibit.

In preparing the display, allow ample time to check all the details before construction begins. Although the promoters of the show will furnish blueprints, someone involved in the exhibit planning should inspect the actual floor area. Sometimes, blueprints omit supporting posts or the location of a window that might force reorientation of an entire display.

Costs and Staffing Effective exhibits cost money, and careful attention must be given to the budget. Moreover, the estimates of expenses should include transportation costs and the employment of extra help required by local union regulations even though the company can furnish its own setup crew.

Another important consideration is the staffing of the exhibit. In many instances, salesmen are brought in from the field and assigned to exhibit duty. Some resent this time away from their selling and potential commissions. Others view it as a vacation.

Actually, such an assignment can represent a worthwhile sales opportunity. This point should be emphasized when the exhibit staff is brought together before the show for a thorough indoctrination on the background, objectives, and history of the company display. This is also the time to explain working models of the exhibit, review the literature to be given away, and brief the salesmen on *all* the products to be shown. The salesmen's familiarity with the total product line will enable them to refer inquiries to the proper individual or to provide appropriate literature. Staffing the exhibit is a cooperative venture, and salesmen should be warned that the little old lady in tennis shoes who comes to inspect the display may be one of the company's best customers.

Company Literature The company literature that is distributed at the show can also be an effective sales tool. If the manufacturer has an elaborate and expensive catalog, it makes sense to prepare a condensed version for the show and provide visitors with postcards for ordering a copy of the complete catalog.   This approach is also useful in developing a mailing list for future use.

Other notes on trade-show exhibits: If there are working models of the product or equipment on display, someone who understands the operation of the machinery should be on hand *at all times*.   Another helpful item is the guest book for visitors to sign.   An inexpensive souvenir might be offered as subtle inducement for these valuable signatures, which enable the salesmen to check each visitor's name, add prospects to the company's mailing list, and keep a partial tally of the number of people who actually visit the booth.

Evaluation   The *postmortem* discussion is one of the most important facets of an exhibit.   The company management and staff should be asking themselves: What seemed to interest visitors most?   What part of the exhibit did they seem least interested in?   Were any sales made?   Was the groundwork laid for future sales?   What pieces of literature were most popular?   Why?   How long did visitors linger in the booth?   What sort of questions did they ask?   What changes should be made in the next exhibit?

In addition, the show management, or an independent survey organization, will often provide trade-show participants with attendance figures not only on how many people actually came through the doors but also on the types of business and commercial interests represented.

Contests

Many promotions are built around a contest as an incentive for company salesmen, for distributor's salesmen, and for dealers.   Prizes can be merchandise, cash, trips, or almost anything that has sufficient appeal to stir enthusiasm among the participants.

Sales Contests   Awards for the company's own salesmen are given for signing up new business, selling special combination deals, pushing slow-moving articles, or for interesting dealers in some new promotion.

The prizes—cash, merchandise, a trip—are usually awarded on the basis of points credited for each accomplishment.   This allows time for confirmation of the sale, enables the salesman to save his points toward a larger goal, and simplifies the company bookkeeping.   During such contests, many companies send an announcement of the prizes to the salesman's wife on the theory that she will spur him on to greater achievement and will be less critical of his longer hours in the field.   There are agencies that handle such contests, providing a fairly complete catalog of merchandise from which each winning salesman can select the items he desires.   Cost of the prizes is billed to the company.

Dealer Contests   Contests in which dealers participate are handled in much the same way.   Trips for the dealer and his family to Hawaii, Mexico City, Nassau, or Bermuda are very popular. Awards are usually determined on the basis of points, with the minimum number entitling the dealer to go alone as a guest of the company, and additional totals enabling him to take his family.

These trips are also popular with the manufacturer sponsoring them, because company salesmen usually participate in them too. What results is an enjoyable, informal sales convention.

The tax status of the incentive and its relation to any form of co-operative advertising should be considered carefully before a company settles on any prizes or premiums.

Special Events Promotions

Special events on the national level are suitable only for the larger companies that can profit from the broad-scale goodwill.   These events also require a wealthy budget to underwrite the substantial costs involved.   Some company-inspired promotions have become national events in their own right: The General Motors Soap Box Derby, Macy's Thanksgiving Day Parade, the Buick Golf Classic.

A listing of other national events might include beauty pageants, auto races, speedboat contests, and the big area festivals such as the Tournament of Roses in Pasadena, California; the Portland, Oregon, Rose Festival; and the Holland, Michigan, Tulip Festival.

As pointed out earlier, some events, such as America's Junior Miss Pageant, can be sponsored jointly by a number of manufacturers who share in the costs.

Most national special events are run by full-time staffs that will work with any manufacturer wishing to participate.   The biggest decision that a company must make is the extent of its participation. Of course, the company bears the responsibility for capitalizing on its sponsorship with localized promotions that will tie-in with the national event, as well as window displays and other special advertising pieces.

Eastman Kodak Company has sponsored the telecast of the Academy Awards for a number of years because of the close relationship of Kodak with the movie industry.   In one recent year, the company offered its Business System dealers, as a tie-in premium, a high fidelity recording of Academy Award winning songs.

Local Promotions

Company participation in special *local* events can be a problem.   As previously indicated, whatever is done for one dealer must be done for all.

One answer to this problem is to prepare a packaged tie-in promotion for a product that will furnish all local dealers with the banners, window cards, and displays they can easily adapt to their own Snow Carnival, Fall Foliage Festival, or Old Timers' Rodeo.   The kit should also contain suggested advertisements and publicity stories.

The importance of the event can best be determined by the salesman working in that territory who is familiar with local customs and knows how deeply his dealers are involved.

Sales Kits

Often, it is the job of the advertising department to prepare kits for the salesmen's use.   The best approach here is to meet with a group of salesmen and discuss their needs.   Some men will refuse to carry kits of any kind; others will welcome them.   In this case, a compromise is the best solution.   The promotional staff, for instance, might furnish materials such as slides, working models of the product, and literature to be used by the individual as he sees fit, with a second, complete kit for the other salesmen.

Flip charts are often a part of the kits.   If the salesman customarily talks to one or two individuals, the charts can be small and compact. Copy should be short and amply illustrated, preferably with cartoons or simple figures if the product lends itself to such treatment.   Naturally, if the salesman meets more persons at one time, he should be given bigger charts so that the message can be read by everyone present.

For larger groups, slides or motion pictures are more effective than charts.   Sound motion pictures are being used more and more today

to show huge pieces of equipment as well as manufacturing and testing features.   Movies may be produced commercially or by the company's own personnel when budgets are limited.

If a salesman calls on dealers who do not have projection facilities,
he should arrange a showing at a local motel or hotel in the afternoon
or early evening.   This method, of course, entails some entertainment expense, so it is wise to make certain that the show is worth the
expenditure.

Sales Kits for Dealers   Sales kits for dealer use might better be
termed point-of-purchase material.   These will include counter
catalogs, demonstration units, special literature and dispensers, displays, and in some cases, working models of the product.   The more
costly items, such as the working models, should be included only
with large orders.

Sales Promotion Representatives

If the company is large enough and has sufficient interest in promotional ventures, traveling sales promotion representatives are a wise
investment.   In most cases, these men cover a larger territory than
the salesmen, and their prime interest is the development of the company's own promotions.   They also help participating dealers with
special problems and act as a clearing house for reports on promotions by other manufacturers.   The sales promotion representative
frees the salesman from this type of work and offers specialized
knowledge that the salesman may not have.

PUBLIC RELATIONS AND PUBLICITY

Public relations and publicity are two of the most valuable aids in
conducting a promotional program.   The two terms are not used
interchangeably.   Publicity, for the most part, is concerned with the
actual number of column inches or the total number of broadcast
minutes that are carried by the media about the company's products
or promotion.

Public relations, on the other hand, is usually concerned with the
long-term cultivation of editors' trust and confidence, and the overall image of the company held by the public, the press, and the
employees.

The organizational setup of the public relations department will vary from company to company. In some, public relations (PR) involves only that phase of the business that includes the company's relations with its stockholders, the public, and the community. Publicity will cover product news and promotion of the company's products or services. In other companies, the two activities are combined as a joint operation. At Eastman Kodak the public relations department is responsible for corporate relations, while product publicity and promotion of photography are handled by the editorial service bureau. Much of the assistance in promotional programs is also provided by the editorial service bureau.

Using Publicity Effectively

If the publicity staff is to work most effectively for a promotion, they should be invited to all the planning meetings. Often, they will be able to develop and place stories in the trade press or newspapers that will create a favorable climate for the campaign before it starts.

Advance information will also permit the PR staff to explore all possible areas of publicity and develop their own parallel campaign that will dovetail with each step in the sales promotion.

While it is not always possible to publicize every phase of a campaign, trade papers that reach dealers will always run stories on a promotion that will interest or benefit their readers. On the other hand, newspaper stories that will stimulate consumer interest are harder to come by. In the hands of experienced writers, however, even routine promotional material can sometimes be transformed into stories that will interest a newspaper editor.

Canned foods have been around for a long time, yet one company recently came up with a series of new recipes for glamorous dishes that could be made complete from canned goods on the shelf. Food editors around the country liked the idea and used the story. While the manufacturer himself did not get a mention, he got his share of the increased sales as women flocked to supermarkets to stock up on the ingredients for the recipes.

In a similar vein, a company that makes wrought iron railings developed an appealing story on ways to improve the appearance of a house or garden with the addition of selected plants—and railings. The story, with illustrations, was syndicated nationally in Sunday garden columns and led to a significant increase in sales.

Remember that the publicity personnel have been hired because of their expertise.   Take advantage of their services.   Take their advice.

Press Conferences

Press conferences are arranged to announce new products or major changes in company policy.   *The first requirement for a press conference is that the announcement be newsworthy enough to justify the attendance of the editors and reporters.*   If the news turns out to be of marginal importance, it will most certainly jeopardize your company's chances for editorial consideration at future press conferences you may plan.

The conference should be planned well in advance to assure the best possible location for the event (usually a hotel ballroom or meeting room) and adequate time for preparation of necessary exhibits, charts, films, or slides.   Although such conferences are usually held in the home city of most of the publications involved, it is sometimes advantageous to arrange a press meeting at the *company's* home office or at one of the manufacturing plants.   In such cases, particularly if distances are great, the announcement of a new product might not be a sufficient inducement for most editors.   But they are likely to give your invitation favorable attention if you can also arrange for a VIP tour of a major new facility of interest to them or their readers.

The actual announcement at the press conference should be made by a prominent company official.   The product manager might follow, then, with a more detailed presentation.   Technical people should also be on hand to answer any questions.

Press kits, containing photographs, stories, and fact sheets, should be distributed during the session.   Responsibility for preparation of this material rests with the publicity staff.

Groups invited to such meetings include newspaper people, with invitations going to the proper department editors: financial, sports, society, food, photo, general assignment reporters.   The same policy holds true for department editors on general interest magazines, network radio and television personnel, and trade-paper editors.

When the manufacturer makes an announcement that might affect the market value of the company's stock, care must be taken so that all groups are informed at one time.   Restrictions are tightening in this area; it is no longer possible to give one publication or trade paper "advance" notice on a new development.

Press contact may also be handled through smaller meetings between company representatives and three or four editors at a time who get together for an hour or so. This approach allows for more individualized attention to editors' questions and story needs. In some instances, it is even possible to set up meetings between company officials and the editorial staff at the magazine or newspaper offices. This is time-consuming, granted, but it is also the ultimate consideration for the editors involved, and may lead to special attention for your material.

Product Publicity

Product publicity is not limited solely to new products, but also covers improvements, changes in design, and new sales policies. However, when a new product is included in a special promotion, the publicity staff should prepare stories not only on the product itself but also on its uses, new manufacturing processes connected with it, and even prominent persons who have endorsed it.

Case Histories   A case history is a specialized type of magazine article that details the successful use or application of the company's product by a consumer or a dealer. The objective, of course, is to stimulate the reader to use the product himself in the same way or to help him see how he could adapt the product for his own needs.

In most cases, these stories are initiated by the sales department from their field experiences, with the final article researched and written by the publicity staff. Case histories are usually placed in an appropriate trade publication or specialized journal. If the story has sufficient merit, it will be reprinted for distribution to dealers or to any audience the company wants to reach.

Publicity for Dealers

A company's dealers are its most important asset. If you can provide them with useful promotional help for their own undertakings, they will not only appreciate your efforts but also be more inclined to support company-inspired campaigns.

The publicity staff should develop kits of suggestions and materials for new store openings, anniversaries, remodelings, and special sales—events of importance to local dealers. Companies get frequent requests from dealers for such help, and experience has proved that it is easier and more profitable to take the time at the outset to develop complete kits that will answer the majority of these requests. Such kits usually contain an outline of procedures and a timetable, plus suggested newspaper stories, invitations, advertisements, and even proclamations for the mayor to issue.

Complete kits of similar materials can also be made up for dealers who are interested in local sponsorship of little league teams, soap box derby entrants, junior miss contests, fishing derbies, and similar events.

If the company receives numerous requests for such help, the publicity department can prepare the material in looseleaf form and assemble individualized kits to meet individual problems.

Special Events

The role of the publicity department is particularly important in any special events. On the local level, prepared kits, as outlined above, are useful, unless the local event is of sufficient importance to justify individualized effort. There are a number of local events that warrant such time. The El Paso Sun Carnival and the Portland Rose Festival are examples.

On the national level, special events will be handled by the promotion manager, who will either recruit his own staff or ask that publicity people be assigned to work with him during the promotion. Events in this category might include the soap box derby or a national baking contest.

In this case, the publicity group would prepare all news stories and press kits, arrange for press interviews, staff press rooms, arrange press conferences, handle radio and television coverage, coordinate local and national publicity, schedule appearances of celebrities and company officials, and supervise all contacts with the news media. The publicity department would also handle press stories and case histories that emphasize the importance of the promotion to the dealer.

SUMMARY

A successful sales campaign, as has been seen, depends upon the creative promotion of the product's advantages, the company's sales policies, advertising and merchandising techniques, and—most important—the desires of the ultimate consumer.

CHAPTER TWENTY-SEVEN
Public Relations Advertising

CHARLES R. CORCORAN *Vice President, The Equitable Life Assurance Society of the United States*

WHAT IS PUBLIC RELATIONS ADVERTISING?

Public relations advertising as a single phrase seems almost a contradiction, certainly a paradox, and to some, pure heresy. Not too many years ago, and less severely even today, public relations activities were widely separated from advertising. The debate about whether to build image or to sell product through advertising persists in many quarters. Building of image generally is termed *institutional* advertising; rarely, *public relations* advertising. The notion is held by many, and with ample justification, that the opinion of an advertising program held by the audiences it captures reflects the sponsor whether or not the messages are of the selling or of the public relations variety. More than anything else in communications— apart from face-to-face selling and a catastrophic, scandalous, or other newsworthy occurrence—advertising forms the opinion most people retain of the company responsible for it.   Everyone is aware that commercials are drafted by persons imbued with company philosophies.   The overwhelming task is to generate recall of the company in a favorable light.

If one goes the public relations advertising route, perhaps the precept to put high on the list is that it is a mistake to look upon paid time and space solely as paid editorial material.   It is far better to seize upon a cause, launch a genuine public service—if one is not inherent in the nature of the business—publicize it through fitting media, seek readership through creativity, and as the chief aim, get credit for what you are doing—credit in the form of tacit acceptance of your product or service and good name.

Public relations advertising is not designed to incite the public to rush out to trade with you.   It may invite the mailing of a coupon for more complete information, or direct its audience to locations where its members may be served, or help serve in the cause the campaign is espousing.   Any action suggested must be transmitted with the utmost grace.

Advertising Council Campaigns

Of all public relations campaigns extant, those promoted by the Advertising Council [1] deserve prominent notice.   Each campaign is wedded to a purpose definitely tied into the country's and its citizens' well-being.   Since 1942 the council has backed 115 causes.   Most of these are familiar to the advertising business.   It is known, too, that all media contribute by running or airing the stories without charge.   In a single year these contributions can amount to $275 million or more, and since 1942 it is estimated that more than $4 billion in space and time has been contributed.   Moreover, campaigns are added to the list as national problems become urgent.   Most recently, these included "Retraining for New Jobs," stimulated by the expected impact of automation on the job market; "Continue Your Education," and "Youth Fitness," recognizing the thesis first advanced by President Eisenhower and strongly supported by Presidents Kennedy and Johnson that this country must be both Athens and Sparta.   "Equal Employment Opportunity," "Crises in Our Cities," and "Help Prevent Crime" are of overwhelming contemporary interest.   These are just a few examples.   All that would be re-

[1] Material supplied and reprinted by permission of the Advertising Council.

quired, in effect, for a corporation to indulge in pure public relations advertising would be to affix its logotype to messages such as those of the Advertising Council.

There is no suggestion in presenting the following partial list of topics pursued by the council that management be merely ovine in its approach to a theme.   It is inserted as an idea stimulant or as a catalyst.   The final subject, "JOBS," standing for "Job Opportunities in the Business Sector," is being supported with enthusiasm.

Partial List of Advertising Council Campaigns, 1942–1968

War Bonds
Women for War Jobs
Loose Talk Sinks Ships
Forest Fire Prevention (Smokey Bear)
American National Red Cross
Cadet Nurses
Join the WACS
Join the WAVES
Join the CROP CORPS
V-Mail
Victory Gardens
Traffic Safety
CARE
Better Schools
Our American Heritage (Freedom Train)
United Community Funds
United States Savings Bonds
United Nations
Radio Free Europe
Ground Observer Corps
United Service Organizations
Aid to Higher Education
Mental Health
Stamp Out Polio
American Economic System
Mental Retardation
Keep America Beautiful
Peace Corps Volunteers
Youth Fitness
Retraining for New Jobs
Equal Employment Opportunity
Continue Your Education
Zip Code
Help Prevent Crime
Youth Opportunity
Crises in our Cities
JOBS (National Alliance of Businessmen)

The first reaction to this emphasis on the Advertising Council's work must be, "Who has the means to do what they do?"   That is not the point.   The precepts employed can be utilized by anyone, and are a guide to management and the technicians in advertising and public relations.

There is no profound analysis required to note that every campaign is coupled with a forceful public interest.   These campaigns enjoy the creative services of fine agencies (also voluntary, but the emphasis is on creativeness), some of them call for action ("write for" or "visit"), they persist in their principal themes, and they do not attempt to educate per se.

Education Through Advertising

This last point is one of rather robust debate: whether or not one can educate through public relations advertising. It is a question the advertising manager must decide for himself after the selection of a theme and before action.   If he attempts to educate in the sense of training, disciplining, or forming his audience, he is apt to become too wordy or preachy, and will enjoy little if any readership.   This is true even in the sense of developing and cultivating mentally or morally.   On the other side of the coin, should he first attempt to alert, excite, interest, and convey a succinct message, and having imparted it to his audience, enjoy the result of retention and acceptance of his company as one of good character?   Unquestionably, there is no formality in attempting to educate through advertising, but it can be said that properly executed, exposed, persevered in, and supported by all the other arms of public relations, advertising can develop and cultivate over a period of time.   The best approach would seem to be that of regular advertising practice.   Do not strive to educate.   Execute an advertising campaign well and as usual, and the lines of communication will become unblocked; it is not stretching the point to say that there can be a rather subtle form of education accomplished in the process.

Friendly Image Sought

The question was raised earlier, and is another that management must solve in its search for the nature of its paid messages and for many practical reasons must review periodically: whether to sell product or service, purely and simply, or to promote the corporate personality through a public relations avenue. Rather glibly, the selling advertisement says, "Buy my product." The public relations advertisement says, "Like me." There is an overlapping if the message says, "Like the merchant or wholesaler who handles our product," or "Like our salesmen or brokers, or bankers; they are friendly and good men to know." Again, it might be, "Like me enough to vote for me," or "Like me so much you will be on my side in an argument," or as is so true today, "Like me enough to the extent you will invest in or hold my stock."

This indicates that there exists a corollary issue: If public relations notices are elected, should the campaign be simply the "Like me" type, or should it allow the intrusion of dependent messages? The pure public relations campaign divests itself of all selfish interests, and other than its logotype and perhaps a subdued line or two describing its business, seeks nothing but a friendly association with its name.

THE SATURDAY REVIEW AWARDS

This is asking a great deal, but not a sacrifice. Many fine companies have gone this route. Each year since 1953, the *Saturday Review* has granted awards to advertisers considered to be doing best in corporate advertising in the public interest. The awards are voted by twenty judges, including eminent educators, advertising and public relations executives, public opinion analysts, and publishers. Here are the recipients of the Sixteenth Annual *Saturday Review* Awards— first, the entire list, followed by an explanation for a division into special categories, then the separate listings, of which the public relations classification is of most interest. These and future award winners are recommended for study and analysis.[2]

Company	*Agency*
Alean Aluminum Limited	J. Walter Thompson Company
Avco Corporation	McCann/ITSM
Borg-Warner Corporation	LaRoche, McCaffrey and McCall, Inc.
Caterpillar Tractor Co.	N. W. Ayer & Son, Inc.
Commonwealth of Puerto Rico	Ogilvy & Mather, Inc.
Container Corporation of America	N. W. Ayer & Son, Inc.

[2] Saturday Review, Inc., Apr. 13, 1968.

Company	Agency
The Garrett Corporation	J. Walter Thompson Company
General Electric Co.	Batten, Barton, Durstine & Osborn, Inc.
Institute of Life Insurance	J. Walter Thompson Company
International Business Machines Corporation	Ogilvy & Mather, Inc.
International Paper Co.	Ogilvy & Mather, Inc.
International Telephone and Telegraph Corp.	Needham, Harper & Steers, Inc.
McGraw-Hill Book Company (Corporate)	Fladell, Winston, Pennette, Inc.
McGraw-Hill Book Company (Educational)	Olshan, Smith & Gould, Inc.
McGraw-Hill Publications	Ketchum, MacLeod & Grove, Inc.
Metropolitan Life Insurance Company	Young & Rubicam, Inc.
Mobil Oil Corporation	Doyle Dane Bernbach Inc.
New York Life Insurance Company	Compton Advertising, Inc.
Newsweek	Richard Kerr
Olin Mathieson Chemical Corporation	Doyle Dane Bernbach Inc.
REA Express (Air Express)	Ketchum, MacLeod & Grove, Inc.
Republic Steel Corporation	Meldrum and Fewsmith, Inc.
Seagram Distillers Company	Warwick & Legler, Inc.
Standard Oil Company (New Jersey)	LaRoche, McCaffrey and McCall, Inc.
Union Carbide Corporation	Young & Rubicam, Inc.
Westinghouse Broadcasting Company, Inc.	Delehanty, Kurnit & Geller, Inc.
Westinghouse Electric Corp.	Ketchum, MacLeod & Grove, Inc.

Special Mention

The American Cancer Society	The Marschalk Company, Inc.
Camp Harriman, The Boy's Club, of New York	Olshan, Smith & Gould, Inc.
The President's Council on Physical Fitness	Papert, Koenig, Lois, Inc.

Because of the closeness of voting in the committee of judges, six runners-up for awards are also listed:

Company	Agency
ABC-owned Television Stations	deGarmo, McCaffrey Inc.
American Telephone and Telegraph Co. (Corporate)	N. W. Ayer & Son, Inc.

Company	Agency
Better Vision Institute, Inc.	Doyle Dane Bernbach Inc.
British Travel Association	Ogilvy & Mather, Inc.
International Business Machines Corp. (Office Products Division)	Carl Ally, Inc.
St. Regis Paper Company	Cunningham & Walsh, Inc.

Public Service Campaigns

In the balloting for the overall awards for public interest advertising, the judges also voted for the various campaigns in three special categories to add precision to their votes.   Here are the winners in the public service category, corporate campaigns, and public relations.

Company	Agency
ABC-owned Television Stations	deGarmo, McCaffrey Inc.
Better Vision Institute Inc.	Doyle Dane Bernbach Inc.
McGraw-Hill Book Company (Educational)	Olshan, Smith & Gould, Inc.
McGraw-Hill Publications	Ketchum, MacLeod & Grove, Inc.
Metropolitan Life Insurance Company	Young & Rubicam Inc.
Mobil Oil Corporation	Doyle Dane Bernbach Inc.
New York Life Insurance Company	Compton Advertising, Inc.
Newsweek	Richard Kerr

Corporate Campaigns

An alphabetical list of the winners follows:

Company	Agency
Avco Corporation	McCann/ITSM
Borg-Warner Corporation	LaRoche, McCaffrey and McCall, Inc.
The Garrett Corporation	J. Walter Thompson Company
General Electric Company	Batten, Barton, Durstine & Osborn, Inc.
International Paper Co.	Ogilvy & Mather, Inc.
Olin Mathieson Chemical Corporation	Doyle Dane Bernbach Inc.
REA Express (Air Express)	Ketchum, MacLeod & Grove, Inc.
Union Carbide Corporation	Young & Rubicam, Inc.

Public Relations

An alphabetical list of the winners follows:

Company	Agency
Commonwealth of Puerto Rico	Ogilvy & Mather, Inc.
International Telephone and Telegraph Corporation	Needham, Harper & Steers, Inc.
McGraw-Hill Publications	Ketchum, MacLeod & Grove, Inc.
Olin Mathieson Chemical Corporation	Doyle Dane Bernbach Inc.
Seagram Distillers Company	Warwick & Legler, Inc.
Westinghouse Broadcasting Company, Inc.	Delehanty, Kurnit & Geller Inc.

Special Mentions

Three distinguished campaigns were among the winners of this special category of public service advertising: (1) for the detection of cancer, (2) for public support for summer holidays in the country for underprivileged city children, and (3) for individual citizen cooperation in helping urban school officials keep congested-area recreation grounds open after hours.   These campaigns of the American Cancer Society, the Boys' Club of New York, and the President's Council on Physical Fitness are only three among the many fine public service campaigns created voluntarily by public-spirited advertising agencies and then carried to the public without charge by national magazines, newspapers, and radio and television stations.   During 1967, United States advertising agencies and media contributed more than $275 million in services, space, and time for such messages.

WHAT ROLE FOR BUSINESS?

It may be asked: Why public relations advertising at all when the prime reason for paid public messages is to move goods or services or obtain some kind of positive action?   That character must be built and maintained by the average business institution in this country—and particularly in these inflationary times—is only too true if business, especially big business, means to preserve its stature. Without a plethora of detail, it can be stated quickly and simply that the high cost of living, many past centuries of *caveat emptor,* the oppression of workers, the building of fortunes by the few, bossism, and countless and complex other human factors—such as today's ethnic enigma—have given rise to suspicions, antagonisms, muscular union growth, and action, and in many quarters, genuine hostility toward business.   The term *big business* has become part of our language more as anathema than praise.

Two Areas of Concern

There are two areas of concern for the businessman.   If there are to be social advancement, economic security, public enlightenment, equal opportunity, and all the other contributions to a progressive society, he must be mindful of moving his goods or services, of course, but above that he must retain his position in the overall society.   It is the essence of a democratic society that business provides food, clothing, shelter, and the requisites of a well-rounded life to the population.   As we seem to move somewhat in the direction where the value of the dollar is based upon some type of productivity and consumption theory, the businessman basically must supply that productivity —the public, the consumption.   Business must keep money in circulation.   It must foster inventiveness, provide the tools of peace, and when necessary provide the instruments of war.

For all this and more, business requires the cooperation, the skills, the labor, and the respect of its own employees and of the public. Public relations advertising seeks to gain a measure of these demands.   That is its case.

There is a correlation in the major decision as to the theme of a public relations campaign between selection of it and the audience which the sponsoring organization finds affordable to reach.   Of course, "affordable" means budget, but good planning attacks theme and audience first, and subsequently suffers through the nuts-and-bolts work of budgeting, allocation of money, media selection, production costs, art, and copy.   Later on, when the policy has been definitely decided upon, it is put in the hands of the experts who must present it to the company's publics.

FORMULATION OF POLICY

Formulation of the policy is the most pressing of all problems that will beset both the advertising manager and the director of public relations.   In some instances one man will serve in both capacities;

in others, there will be one or the other.   In any event the decision must be shared with the chief executive officer of the organization, and with its outside public relations counselor and its advertising agency, if either or both are retained.

These outside points of view are invaluable primarily because of the varied experience the counselor and top advertising agency personnel bring to the conference table.   They have seen some campaigns succeed and others fail.   Generally, they are acquainted with the reasons for both success and failure.   The expert in these fields avoids assiduously the situation of Mark Twain's cat: she sat down on a hot stove-lid.   She never again sat on another of such temperature; but she would never sit on a cold stove-lid either.

There is a wisdom that lies in experience that equals or surpasses theorizing in the early planning stages of a public relations venture and its subsequent conduct.   What has proved good for one type of business may be bad for another and vice versa.   No idea, unless blatantly harebrained, should be passed over lightly.

The Chief Executive's Posture

In these formulative stages much depends on the posture of the chief executive.   He may know precisely what he wants, and good or bad, that is what it is going to be.   He may lean entirely on his internal and external advisors, or he may share in the give and take of meetings on the subject.   No manager in this area should be unprepared for such meetings, in ideas, extent of the campaigns, company audiences, duration, personnel required for execution, and subordinate merchandising of the campaign through promotional devices, external publicity, house organs, annual statements, and so on.   If the organization enjoys a specialist in the merchandising of all its advertising efforts, he should be included in the conferences also.   It is assumed that the prime decision to put money into public relations advertising already has had, if not final, at least a tentative agreement of sales and marketing executives who will be concerned particularly when final budgets are prepared.

Of no small concern to the retained counselors and the internal experts, aside from the posture of the chief executive, is his observed, abiding philosophy.   Does he pursue the teachings of Heraclitus or that of Parmenides?   The one who taught that the only reality is change and that permanence is an illusion vis-à-vis the one who held that being is an eternal reality and that change is an illusion? Worlds apart, yet they are encountered, and there are many stops on this precipitous journey.

HOW LONG THE CAMPAIGN?

It must be clearly understood that once engaged in a rewarding endeavor, the company pursues it, if not forever, at least until it shows positive signs of erosion; a change in top management takes place with the newcomer's own and conflicting ideas; there is a merger or other vast development within the company that would alter its character; or there is obsolescence probably due to opportunism or to taking advantage of a public situation that diminishes and finally vanishes.

Durable Campaigns

There are examples of campaigns that have continued for many years and with the greatest success. They appear sufficiently substantial and broad-based to last forever. To stay with principles, however, rather than single out individual company efforts, there can be cited the Advertising Council's persevering, highly imaginative, and most effective "Forest Fire Prevention" campaign featuring Smokey Bear. It is now beyond the quarter-century mark and shows no more signs of waning popularity than Santa Claus or Peter Rabbit, or most recently, Peanuts. It has all the ingredients of creativeness, expertise in execution, exposure, and persistence. On the other hand "Retraining for New Jobs" had a relatively brief run. Whether or not it made a contribution can only be conjectured. But the fact seems to be that automation created many new jobs and many people did train for them or newcomers were inducted into them, and companies prepared their personnel for the changeovers. New jobs ranged from the unskilled, such as packaging and shipping of tapes and other requisites, to the highly skilled programing operations. Elevator operators in the many new buildings, no longer needed because of the automatics, were trained for maintenance work. In one known instance with plazas now common around new buildings and with flowers and trees to tend, the operators were trained as gardeners. The campaign no longer was needed.

Other Advertising Council crusades—and that word seems to describe pure public relations advertising the best—that have the basic element of long-term continuance and yet have an immediacy are those listed previously: "Equal Employment Opportunity," "Help Prevent Crime," "Crises in our Cities," "JOBS." The "Continue Your Education" essay has gained strength and participation consistently.   Secretary of Labor W. Willard Wirtz believed that the advertising could have had a great deal to do with the fact that in one year, 1966, one million more students enrolled in colleges and universities than could be accounted for by the increase in population. That crusade seems here to stay also.   While time and space are donated by media, production costs are borne by industry, government agencies, and other sources, termed by the Council their *clients*. Predictions as to longevity must bear this fact in mind.   If production money were to be withdrawn, the crusade would come to an end regardless of its merit, unless a new sponsor provided the bankroll.

ALL CORPORATE ACTS MUST SUPPORT

Assuming that the theme has been agreed upon by all concerned, we are yet to face the budgeting problem in a commercial operation. That follows the task of selecting the theme, a process that is complicated by the need to know specifically the audiences to which we wish to exhibit our personality, to which we want to communicate our ideas and to exert our influence on their values.   It should go without saying that public messages designed specifically to project the corporate body as one of good character will serve that end only so long as all other corporate acts support it.

Public relations advertising is of little or no merit, or may even arouse resentment, if it reflects only what the company would like to have its audiences believe it is.   It must mirror its actual policies, procedures, processes, and products, as genuinely concerned with the interests of its audiences.   In this there are credit and credence. That is another reason for consultation with executives of all major divisions.   The reaction of the public to shoddy goods, poor workmanship, and desultory service is immediate and vitriolic.   The best of crusades will be ignored under such conditions.

CONSIDERATION OF AUDIENCE

If a firm operates nationally and markets a product to the public at large, a first inclination is to paste its message on every wall where it enjoys exposure, and some of it may stick.   On analysis however, and looking ahead to the cost factor, and most likely, media selection, it will be ascertained that the firm's audiences consist of not only the general public, but also its dealers, wholesalers, or retailers; its own salesmen or manufacturer's representatives, whoever moves the goods in the field; its employees in the main office and all its branches; former purchasers of large items, such as automobiles, appliances, home furnishings, securities, insurance; the community immediate to its headquarters' location and perhaps its branch offices; the unions with which it may be involved, and even the families of all those categorized.   Other audiences might include stockholders, governments, and financial and investment interests.

It would be laudable to exert an influence on all these publics. There is a slim possibility of doing so, but it takes a lot of doing and seems scarcely conceivable.   The specific interests of the vast number of publics are so varied that a message appealing to one group or several may leave others cold.   This presents more evidence for the close correlation of the selection of theme and the analysis of audience.   It would seem that the ideal contribution sought for business success involves a theme, planning, and execution of the crusade which is of common interest to the firm's publics, and is an obvious social or economic contribution to them, even though it may be recognized that the story will not filter through to all.   If that is accomplished, one can look to increased tacit acceptance of name, reputation, and products; betterment of employee relationships; pride of ownership on the part of purchasers and their favorable recommendations to others; being looked upon as a good neighbor in the community; high morale and stepped-up activity among those who move the goods in the field—all accomplishments to be applauded.

Analysis of Audiences

The analysis of audiences is simplified in the case of a firm that is capsulated geographically, by specialized product such as hospital, medical, or dental supplies, mining equipment and heavy machinery, or by other highly specialized products designed for a single market.

If it can afford it, it can, in effect, donate to the general public a *bona fide* service by promoting a cause within its geographical bounds if so confined, or nationally if its specialized product is so distributed. This action borders on the eleemosynary in some respects. There are the very practical matters of exerting an influence on those with whom the firm may deal, however few, and on its tax position. It is assumed that in these situations the organization's crusades would be superimposed on its customary selling campaigns in regularly employed media.

Regardless of the limitations imposed by geography or other factors, the principles and routines previously explored for firms marketing a product nationwide still apply, careful consideration of theme being the predominant preoccupation.

Although it would be possible to cover public relations advertising at every level of commercial or noncommercial enterprise, including fund raising and on down to the local storekeeper, not much of it is affordable. Public relations activities are largely in the area of what has been noted as promotion or merchandising. There is no good reason why prosperous and large fund-raising operations, service clubs, and associations should not participate in efforts aimed at the betterment of the social and economic welfare of the nation. If they so chose, precepts and procedures would remain much the same.

THE HOW AND WHEN OF BUDGETS

The prime decisions having been made as to topic and audiences, the knotty fact must be faced: How much should be spent to accomplish the goal or goals determined upon, and what will be the source of the money? It is quite obvious that one problem is leading to another and that there is an imbrication of all. It would have been entirely possible at the earlier conferences for some participant to have said, "Sounds great, but we can't afford it." If cost is permitted to enter the conversations at too early a stage it can be deadly, probably take everyone's mind off the development of the theme, and may even stifle future consideration. Each conscientious executive involved will have cost in the back of his mind along with the question of how much public relations advertising will help the company and his responsibilities in particular. There is the possibility of an executive or committee decision to turn the entire matter over to its advertising agency, after basic goals and audiences have been discussed, with the admonition to "Build us a campaign and come back with your ideas," or quite likely, the instruction to deliver the whole package consisting of ideas, roughs, media, extent, and cost.

THE PROBLEM OF DECENTRALIZATION

Public relations advertising in the community immediately adjacent to a firm's headquarters or in the neighborhood of its branch offices was passed over rather quickly in a prior paragraph. There is another situation that must enter all considerations: the case of the business completely decentralized, and through its marketing operations covering the nation or a large part of it through decentralized selling arms of one sort or another—direct sales, distributors, wholesalers, retailers, traveling salesmen. To the audiences of its many communities the company may be virtually anonymous. Its character and personality are reflected solely by its representatives and its product or service. There is a strong case for public relations advertising in these situations but particularly in the case of the absentee merchant.

Community Citizenship

Good community citizenship can be built on becoming a part of a neighborhood and on fostering genuine respect, admiration, and friendship with those living in it. Communities have varying needs, and these can be understood and incorporated in tailor-made programs by a variety of means. That is the expensive circuit. More conservative would be a crusade encompassing a problem common to all the company's neighborhoods. Many of these exist today.

Media Problem

"How to do it" is mainly a media problem. Some successful methods in use are radio and television messages and public relations copy in the local press. These are easily adaptable to specific communities. In areas where the company has representatives, live or taped interviews with them about the cause the company espouses, while not strictly advertising if donated by the media, are very close to it if billed. Much of the sting so far as cost is concerned can be soothed if the company negotiates a cooperative, share-the-cost arrangement with its people on the goods-moving end who also will profit by increased goodwill and bettered community confidence.   There is a *quid pro quo* in most business affairs.   In the case of community action it is the close-at-hand expression by a business of its genuine interest in the welfare of the community without intrusion, in exchange for goodwill and an eventual share of the benefits to be derived from the community.   Public relations advertising is considered a particularly effective means to this end.

The fact that this exposition of the subject of public relations advertising must of its nature consider all sizes of companies, all manners of marketing, and all types of business or service must lead to considerable generalization.   For example, if the advertising agency was given the entire assignment as a package, it would follow much the same procedure as the do-it-yourself company.   Or if public relations counsel were to share the assignment with the agency, it might return to the sponsor with ideas which if acceptable would be turned over to the agency for execution.   But step by step, each of the bases must be covered by whomever and all steps lead inevitably to "costing out."

HOW MUCH TO SPEND

If there is any truism in the area of budgeting for public relations advertising, it is that there are no hard-and-fast rules to follow.   The company's own experience or that of others in different areas of advertising will not apply, but if available, advice of counsel will serve as a guide.   It will help greatly if the company has had a previous taste of advertising in the public interest.

Naturally, the budget must fit the company's resources, and one of the first considerations is whether all the advertising money will be spent yearly, part of it, or whether it will be superimposed on the current budget.   Sales and advertising executives can have no real quarrel with the latter, but in the first two instances there can be considerable discussion.   The sales executive possibly will argue that there is not enough sales support in a nonselling-type crusade, therefore the advertising will be worthless to his field of endeavor.   The advertising executive and even the company's agency may feel reluctant to the transfer or segmenting of a budget for an endeavor the results of which are difficult to appraise.   These arguments are indigenous to the business of advertising, and in one form or another, have been encountered by most experienced executives. Generally, it is the chief executive's role to act as arbiter or to make the final determination.

None of the arguments expressed should come up in the case where there is no fixed purpose to sell a product or a service, or in the example of firms such as listed previously under the winners of the *Saturday Review's* Public Relations Awards.

The Responsible Executive

If the decision is made to go ahead with a public relations approach, the advertising or public relations executive most likely will be charged with reporting on his plans including media and their costs to his chief executive and possibly to his board of directors. However his plans have been developed, internally, with the help of outside counsel, or solely by his agency, he must fit them to his company's resources and his directives.

The executive who sets the figure is not in an enviable position. "Is there a reliable, if not scientific, method of setting an advertising budget? Can a marketing manager determine when the company is spending too much or too little? Can he even tell after the fact whether he had spent too much or too little for advertising?"[3] Those questions were aimed at product advertising, and it was concluded that the answers were "apparently negative."

Wide Range of Answers

To set an advertising budget, an executive can hope only to raise the relevant questions and answer them as conscientiously as possible. Even if he does this, he will always end with a wide range of possibly correct answers. Even after the event, he will not know whether he spent the right amount. Although this is distressing, it is not by any means unique to advertising. It applies about as much to public relations and also to research and development. Moreover, the executive, even as head of his own household, also has no reliable basis for determining how to allocate his income among food, clothing, entertainment, vacations, education. The problem, thus, is not unique to ad-

[3] Alfred R. Oxenfeldt and Carroll Swan, "Management of the Advertising Function," Wadsworth Publishing Company, Belmont, Calif., 1964, p. 35.

vertising; and interestingly enough, the basic rules to follow probably are similar for advertising and for a family budget.[4]

These rather lengthy quotations serve two purposes: as a compact exposition of the burden placed on the corporate executive in budgeting for a general advertising program, and more important to this treatment of the subject, the additional loads the budgeter for public relations advertising must bear.   He has little if anything to guide him.   The standard methods employed in general advertising seem far out of his reach, such as the percentage of sales method, the task method, the allocation of a set amount of dollars for each unit of sales (a slight variation of the percentage of sales method), the average expenditures of his competitors, an amount in keeping with expected sales, or the same amount as in the previous year which looks to increased sales and subsequent increased net profits.

The man who sets the budget for public relations advertising must review his theme and his audiences and set his objectives in terms of how many people he wants to influence for the good.   Unless he does some precampaign research, he only can guess at current public response and feeling, an argument in favor of this sort of research.   His guesstimate, however, may be very close to correct, ranging the full gamut from excellent and enthusiastic down to negative or resentful.

Chart as a Guide   Based on guesswork then, or if you will, on "educated" guesswork, and regardless of where his company is positioned on the scale of appreciation of its character and personality, he must set his objective on improving or maintaining, if at the top of the scale, its status and stature.   He can visualize this objective by drafting a chart based on his judgment or on research, which graphically indicates where he is today in the pertinent areas and where he wants to arrive in a given time.   Such a chart can be most effective in his presentations to his peers and superiors in his organization.

Positive Dividends   There is a side issue which relates to the basic attitude of his company.   It has been expressed as follows:

> Public service follows *publicity* and *communications* as a type of corporate activity that has been characterized as being central to public relations.   To explain its role the corporation has been interpreted by some to be not only a profit-seeking entity but also an enterprise with a *conscience,* sensitive to its place in society, its responsibility to

[4] *Ibid.,* pp. 35-36.

others and its burden as a citizen in the industrial community. . . . Few managements are willing to spend money in the public interest unless a practical dividend can be expected. Contributing to the social good is not considered an end in itself. It is a means by which the corporation attempts to prosper and grow.[5]

The budgeting action must take into account the corporate posture on the relative weight placed on prosperity and growth and on the pure contribution desired to be made to society.

Selection of Media

Somewhere along the line of his considerations, and vital to his final figures, the budgeting executive must take into account the selection of media. That point probably will be reached when he knows his current situation and when he has resolved his objectives. If he is expert in media, he may make his own selections. He may have a media expert on his staff or he can turn to his advertising agency. If the agency is doing the entire job, it will be keeping the corporation's man appraised of each of the budgeting decisions as they are made.

IMPORTANCE OF OBJECTIVES

If the responsible executive has abided by the precepts enunciated to this point, he will have his theme, audiences, objectives, roughs, media, and costs ready to present for final approval. In the case of the executive who may have overshot the mark in his objectives and was forced to make changes in both objectives and budgets, there may be a profound lesson in the following paragraphs which speak of the importance of objectives:

> The indispensable first step to successful institutional advertising is the establishment of a formal *objective*.
> Such an objective should be carefully arrived at. It should be possible of achievement. It should be clearly understood and clearly stated in written words. Every effort should be made by the advertising to achieve it.
> The objective is the means by which institutional advertising is made *purposeful*. It is the hard backbone of the advertising. In the

[5] David Finn, "Public Relations and Management," Reinhold Publishing Corporation, New York, 1960, pp. 117-118.

production of this advertising, no other element is nearly so important. Without it success is impossible.[6]

Earlier it was emphasized that the selection of theme should come first.   There is no quarrel with giving priority to objectives in the context in which the author of the previous quotation was writing. It would seem to include all the factors enumerated earlier and which are so closely interrelated as to be mutually dependent.

The budget must be adequate to reach the objectives, it must have a reasonable degree of flexibility, the objectives must be within reach, there must be kept in mind the unremitting necessity for continuity, and the budget should be carefully administered and reviewed periodically.

RESEARCH AND ITS PRICE

Research in all advertising has its proponents and opponents.   In public relations advertising it seems a necessity, as mentioned before, in predetermining the atmosphere in which the company is operating in advance of the crusade.   The research does not end with the precampaign effort; it must be continuous in order to measure progress periodically toward the attainment of objectives.   Such a program runs into money—sometimes big money—and must be carefully considered from that standpoint also.

In respect to the financial outlay, whose responsibility it is, and ways and means of accomplishment, a fairly recent article in favor of research advanced this argument:

> The corporation is an endlessly complex structure, with a long history of activity.   Which of the myriad parts or action are the *cues* which touch off the inference that leads to the end-product, image? To take a simple, perhaps apocryphal example, how would anyone know what in the mystique of the American woman led some Europeans to the image that she was immoral?   As the story goes, the cue was that she smoked in the street.   [Author's note: But the full solution is still not at hand.   What is the process of inference?   Why the equation of smoking in the street and immorality?]   The complexity, the mystique, of the American corporation may be even greater, and

[6] George A. Flanagan, "Modern Institutional Advertising," McGraw-Hill Book Company, New York, 1967, p. 15.

unless we know which cues touch off the process of inference, we shall remain in the dark on the formation and change of such images. The second suggestion, then, is that we begin to explore this missing link in the image process. We know the avenues through which the public learns about corporations; we know the end-products, the images; but our respondents must be made to identify in the complex configuration that is the corporation the significant cues or combinations of events, and ideally the processes of inference they employ. What we shall unearth is uncertain, and it will not be an easy problem to explore, but perhaps this will be the frontier of future research on the corporate image.[7]

There are several things in this statement to comment about. It is an excerpt from a very sophisticated treatise on the subject and it assumes or has built up to a knowledge on the part of the company of the "end-products, the images." The situations we have been exploring do not make this assumption except in the case of the companies with previous experience or research.

Success an Uncertain Absolute

Quite a different picture is presented by this lecturer:

Success is an absolute that we shall probably never know. But so is failure. By doing the best we know how, we can guarantee that there is some progress, that momentum is not lost. Actually, it is not possible to appraise events as to whether they have succeeded or failed until we have the benefit of the perspective that time alone can give us. I am sure that many times what appeared contemporaneously to be failure was clearly seen in retrospect to be success, or at the least part of a developing successful pattern. And *vice versa*. Perhaps it is best that we not try to keep score, that we concern ourselves with doing the best we can, and not with trying to assess the results of our efforts, leaving that to time.[8]

In all fairness it must be said that this quotation is taken completely out of the context of the talk. The speaker was addressing himself to the problems of the "open society" and the role of public

[7] John W. Riley, Jr. (ed.), "The Corporation and Its Publics," John Wiley & Sons, Inc., New York, 1963, pp. 75-76.

[8] Glen Perry, Public Relations and the Open Society, Foundation for Public Relations and Research, 1968 (address delivered Nov. 15, 1967, at the Annual Conference of the Public Relations Society of America, Philadelphia).

relations in it.   It is inserted because it represents so well and so concisely the feelings of many regarding research.   Those with a negative view prefer a time and intuition method.   They express a preference for close observation of results, with doing the best they can and for long-term continuance of the crusade they have determined is good for their audiences and for their companies.   Playback may come to them from the public, from their own people in the field, or from their headquarters and its personnel.   Their judgment as to effectiveness can be swayed one way or the other by comments of customers, members of their boards, and other influentials, by awards, by publicity, and by countless other voices.   Given astute management this empiricism can operate.   Given equally astute management and the means to follow it through, research may be decided upon.   In either event the decision whether to indulge in research or not will be shared or recommended by the advertising or the public relations executive.   Again it should be said that both positions may be held by one man and all references to these responsibilities should be considered from that view.

Courses for the Executive

The executive charged with a research program has several roads to follow.   He may call in a research consultant if he does not have any expert in that subject on his staff.   In the latter case in all probability he would rely on captive resources.   He may turn over the assignment lock, stock, and barrel to a research organization after conferring with it on what he wants to accomplish and giving it free access to his office and to his confreres for purposes of gaining a more complete knowledge of his company and its operations.   In this day, when many companies have their own computer systems and the programers to set up the hardware for this job, he may decide to keep the research in the house, employing outside agencies to do the interviewing, or he may make an arrangement with his advertising agency to perform this function, and many are staffed to do so.   All these methods are employed today singly or in various combinations.

Supervision of Research

The executive must engage himself in an iteration of his objectives, the supervising of the drafting of questionnaires, the number of respondents in the sample and their demographics and geographic dispersion.   If he is to do the job within his organization, the same tasks will require closer supervision, expertise equal to or better than that of outside sources, the machinery and the hiring of the legwork.

There is a *caveat* to be observed in doing the research oneself.   It is a sensitive area and can invite the charge of bias, right or wrong. Great care must be exerted in all preparations to make certain nothing done can invite this criticism.   Since the findings eventually must be interpreted, it is well to turn them over to an outside agency for this final step.

All the procedures enumerated go equally well for pretesting as for posttesting.   Except in the latter case there will be benchmarks established as guides for drafting questionnaires and specifying the size and character of samples.

Budget for Research

The money for research must be provided, and if possible it should be in a separate budget each year.   The executive in charge can arrive at a quite accurate cost figure.   Outside agencies will present on request an exact amount, but they may require some leeway for unforeseen contingencies.   The budgeting for the work done within the house depends entirely on the accounting system of the company. The cost may be billed to advertising or as institutional.   In either event those called upon for contributing services will have to estimate their time and charges for the executive.   Of the methods examined, the most expensive in all likelihood would be the retaining of a research organization for the entire package, the least expensive, the house job.   Various combinations fit in between.   You might say "bids for the job" from internal and external sources can be entertained when all data are assembled.

Excessive Research

Excessive research must be guarded against.   Sometimes the zeal to test everything leads to a disproportionate expenditure for the research compared to the cost of the advertising.   Then again, there are those who may conduct research for the sake of research alone. Too often weighty research reports are submitted, never properly interpreted, at best digested for management, and then gather dust on library shelves.   On occasion the intuition and experience of experts within a company are discounted entirely.   The research then may do nothing but what these experts have been saying all along. It is confirmation, of course, and from a statistical and presumably unbiased source. But the question must be answered before engaging in research: Are the results going to be worth the time, effort, and money that must be invested in it?

ULTIMATE RESPONSIBILITY

A great many jobs to be done in the establishment and continuance of a public relations advertising program have been discussed. All these jobs require personnel for their accomplishment, experts in a number of fields, and facilities. Indicated quite often was whether the program should be the responsibility of the advertising executive or that of the public relations head or that of one man responsible for both functions. It seems that there are few companies organized exactly the same in either of these departments. They vary according to the size of the company, the nature of the business or service, general policies, means, talents, and organization charts that reflect human factors. One of the latter may be keeping lines of promotion and opportunity open for valuable people—more roads to travel. Its converse is building up one man for possible future promotion. The variables are numerous, and in the human relations area, unless one knows the inside story, quite intangible and imponderable to the outside observer.

Emphasis can be placed, statistically, on combining public relations with advertising or separating it from advertising. In a study published in 1968, it was shown that about half the companies reporting, 115, utilized the combination, and 127 separated them.[9]

The same study in examining advertising functions pointed out that they might be controlled at either of two levels, corporate or divisional. The study quoted a director of marketing services as saying:

> If the advertising were totally at the corporate level, the divisions would lose an important degree of control over how the monies are spent. On the other hand, if the functions were solely at the division level, with no guidance from corporate, there would be no opportunity for the important "synergistic" effect.

[9] Advertising, Sales Promotion, and Public Relations: Organizational Alternatives, National Industrial Conference Board, Inc., New York, 1968.

Corporate Level

The very few references to public relations advertising in the study place it at the corporate level. That is where it seems to belong and where it is considered in this chapter. Strong emphasis is placed on the point that a synergistic effect can be attained by frequent contact with all those who will be involved, open lines of communication, and a sharing of major decisions.

The study referred to could be quoted at some length. That does not seem necessary since it is of fairly recent date and should be readily available to anyone interested in organizational structures. It is recommended reading.

SUMMARY

This review of public relations advertising leads to the conclusion that a fair amount is being done and with success. Most campaigns currently employed are serving as a useful tool of communications in a highly specialized and different area. Despite the fact that a company must move its products, substantial gains are reported in public respect, recognition of character, and all the sought-for objectives previously covered. Most obvious in this review is its manifest orientation to the newcomer to the field. That is partly by design, mainly in order to set down the task that is involved, the philosophies, and the range of responsibilities. It should prove of interest also to the initiated as a review.

It should be apparent also that the planning and execution of a public relations advertising campaign places the responsibility largely on the shoulders of the executive to whom it is delegated. His response to the challenge could well be the key to its attainments.

CHAPTER TWENTY-EIGHT

Advertising to Business

WILLIAM A. MARSTELLER *Chairman, Marsteller Inc.*

WHAT IS ADVERTISING TO BUSINESS?

Advertising to business is, in itself, a business.   While it uses many of the methods and rests on some of the same psychological premises, it has its own body of media, frequently employs logic instead of emotion, relies heavily on a cataloging of facts, and has its own special problems in effectiveness evaluation.

Advertising to business is often called *industrial* advertising, but this is far too limiting.   This chapter is devoted to advertising of industry to industry, to advertising of scientific or technical products and services, advertising aimed at distribution and merchandising channels, and advertising to the professions.

While a number of local and national associations concern themselves with subdivisions of business advertising, the two broadest are the American Business Press and the Association of Industrial Advertisers, from both of which much specific information is obtainable (as it is, of course, from the publishers of individual business publications within specific business categories).

The American Business Press is composed of most of the leading business and professional publications (sometimes called *trade papers*). Its purpose is to promote the usefulness and function of business publications. The Association of Industrial Advertisers is dominated by business advertisers and advertising agencies with a major stake in advertising to business. Its purpose, essentially, is to raise the standards and effectiveness of business-oriented advertising.

How Is Business Advertising Different?

There are striking differences between advertising consumer products such as gum, cigarettes, even automobiles, and advertising industrial, technical, or professional products, such as machine tools, computers, or prescription drugs.

Some of the variation is inherent in the different channels of distribution, selling costs, pricing, buying practices, and legal restrictions. All these affect what can and should be said in advertising and in the efficiency of available media.

Specifically, business advertising differs from consumer advertising in at least five ways:

1. The audience, while composed of individuals who react as individuals in myriad ways to both rational and irrational appeals, also react in a corporate sense (as representatives of their firm) as buying and specifying agents.

2. Most business buying decisions are plural, and most consumer buying decisions are singular.

3. For many industrial and professional products, need or want cannot be stimulated.

4. The cause-and-effect relationship between business advertising and product sales is usually difficult to trace.

5. For most business-to-business or business-to-profession sales, application engineering, demonstration, and negotiation are necessary.

Each of these differences has profound effect on the decisions that shape the character, content, and aim of business advertising.

1. *The audience reacts both as individuals and as corporate agents.* Early industrial advertising seemed to assume that only faceless corporatons made up the audience. Examination of trade publica-

tions published before the 1950s shows a heavy emphasis on listings of facts, an almost deliberately dull writing style, and an emphasis on detail. Such sales appeals as were used were likely to be brag and boast on the part of the seller. In fact, the forerunner of the American Business Press heavily promoted the use of "tell all" advertising in business papers.

After World War II, business advertising began to loosen up and become less ponderous, helped along by a considerable body of research into buying habits of corporations. Several of these studies, such as one done by *Steel* magazine,[1] probed psychological and emotional influences, as well as the well-accepted theory of the logical, studied approach to purchasing.

Most of the research found, not surprisingly, that buyers of capital equipment, professional supplies, etc., while depending heavily on both scientific and logical appraisals of products, also react as individuals. All things being equal, the research shows consistently that the purchaser has favorites among suppliers.

One specific somewhat emotional factor present in corporate buying is fear of making a mistake. A bad purchase is visible to many persons in the business. So, the safe-buy attitude tends to push purchases toward the companies known to be thoroughly reliable, known to be service- and warranty-minded, and in general, known to be leaders. This has narrowed the gap between product advertising and institutional advertising to a marked degree. A great deal of advertising to business is now *corporate reliability* advertising.

2. *Most business buying decisions are group decisions.* The decision to buy a pack of cigarettes is personal and often impulsive. The decision to buy a new computer is virtually always a group decision and the result of long consideration.

Further, the group will nearly always be composed of men of different disciplines who will approach the problem from differing points of view.

A typical group might include a purchasing agent, an engineer, a research technician, a controller, perhaps a marketing executive and a representative of top management. The engineer's evaluation, for example, may be mostly on performance; the controller's on financ-

---

[1] F. Robert Shoaf, "Emotional Factors Underlying Industrial Purchases: A Motivational Study," *Steel* magazine, Cleveland, Ohio.

ing; the purchasing agent on delivery, terms of sale, and so on.   In no two group buying decisions will the influences of the individuals likely be the same.

Since different men or women will look at the same buying decision through different eyes, with different interests and different standards, the business advertiser who is thorough must reach them all, usually with different messages and different media.   This is at the root of the growth of the business-paper press both in the United States and abroad.   It abounds in specialized magazines for the special interests and disciplines of the corporate and professional market.

3. *For many business or industry products, need cannot be stimulated.*   Styling, color, flavoring, and a host of other somewhat insubstantial factors may be enough to cause a consumer to buy a new car, change to a new nail polish, switch soft drinks, and so on.   By contrast, it is almost always true of industrial and professional products that new demand depends almost entirely upon one or both of two factors: (*a*) an expanded market; or (*b*) a technological product breakthrough of demonstrable importance.

The expanding market opportunity takes many forms.   A power company, to meet the needs of a growing population, erects a new central station.   Millions of dollars of industrial equipment is bought, not particularly because advanced technology has made the old plant archaic, but because need has exceeded capacity.   For all the companies that become suppliers to the central station, no amount of advertising would have created a demand if the central station were not to be built in the first place.   A great deal of advertising, however, is successfully directed against the utility companies, consulting engineers, contractors, financing sources, and so on, year in and year out, so that when the sales opportunity does occur, the company and its products will be well known and well regarded.

In general, established products are dependent upon growing need for growing sales.   Well-established prescription drugs, for instance, are prescribed by doctors according to need, and weather and epidemics have far more influence than advertising and promotion on the total sale of the generic product.   The primary purpose of the advertising then is competitive and corporate-image building.

On the other hand, a true technological breakthrough will stimulate demand, and then the use of advertising is essentially informative and use-oriented.   This period of introduction and instruction may, in fact, be a very extended one.   Introducing a truly new drug, for instance, is a massive and time-consuming communications job.   To reach, convince, and instruct the market may take years.

Likewise, if the new product is something in the order of a new petroleum-refining process, successful introduction of it may also take years.   The problem is to convince corporate buyers that the efficiency of the new process justifies scrapping an enormous capital investment in favor of an even greater one.

4. *The cause-and-effect relationship of sales and advertising is often difficult to prove.*   This is a special problem of business and professional advertising and differs markedly for much consumer advertising.

A simplified example of how a consumer advertiser establishes the impact of his advertising is the case of a manufacturer of adhesive powder for dentures.   He maps out a section of the country, fills the distribution pipelines in the region, and begins buying television commercials.   He increases his budget as long as sales increase.   If they level off, so does his advertising expenditure.   If they drop, he cuts back to the level at which sales results and advertising costs are in balance.

The business advertiser has few such comforting opportunities for measurement of his judgment and strategy.   The advertiser of central station equipment will not see the results of his advertising until much later, when the central station is built.   Even then, the evaluation will be fogged by the complicated nature of the corporate buying decision which involves so much in addition to advertising and promotion.   This introduces another special problem of the business advertiser.

5. *For most business-to-business or business-to-profession sales, face-to-face selling, application, and negotiation are necessary.*   In the example of the denture powder, the contribution of the retail salesman—if indeed the whole transaction is not self-service—will be minimal.   In the example of the central station, whole teams of salesmen, application and specification engineers, and contract negotiators will be involved over an extended time period before the sale is completed.   How much of a role in the ultimate decision did advertising and promotion play?

Often it is very difficult to tell.   Advertisers and business paper publishers have produced reams of research intended to get at this problem.   Most of it shows that the best advertised companies and products consistently outsell underadvertised competition, when price and delivery are relatively equal.   Considerable data on this problem are available in the McGraw-Hill Library of Industrial Research.

Yet the business advertiser finds great difficulty in apportioning his total selling costs among advertising and promotion, direct salesmen, and terms and conditions of sale.

MEDIA OF BUSINESS AND PROFESSIONAL ADVERTISING

Business Papers

The section of Standard Rate & Data Service devoted to business and professional publications is the largest volume in the service, easily exceeding television, radio, newspapers, farm papers, etc.   It lists more than 2,600 specialized publications, classified according to 139 primary industry or disciplinary categories.

In pages of advertising the business press stands at the very top of print media, too.   Year after year one or another of the leading business and professional publications, such as *The Journal of the American Medical Association, Oil and Gas Journal, Iron Age, Steel,* and others, dominate the listing of leading magazines of all types in pages of advertising.

Because the publications are edited for special-interest groups, circulations are relatively small and advertising rates are relatively low.

Of the same 2,600 publications listed in the volume *Business Publication Rates and Data* of Standard Rate & Data Service, approximately 640 are members of Business Publications Audit of Circulation, Inc., and about 260 are members of the Audit Bureau of Circulations.   With the exception of some publications published by and circulated to professional associations, these are the leading business and technical publications.   The remainder tend to be regional publications with very small circulations, directories and yearbooks, and other peripheral publications.   The Verified Audit Company provides an audit of approximately 60 business publications, with an emphasis on regionals, as a part of its general media auditing service.

Business publications are either sold on a subscription basis or distributed free to lists compiled by the publisher. The Audit Bureau of Circulations (ABC) confirms the distribution of paid circulation publications only, while the Business Publications Audit (BPA) verifies the distribution of both paid and free controlled circulation. Both associations are nonprofit organizations managed by tripartite boards composed of advertiser, agency, and publisher representatives. The Verified Audit Company, which is privately owned, also will audit both paid and free circulation, but its efforts have been largely for free publications.

The ABC and BPA audits are similar in many respects. From them, the buyer gets much audience data. The main categories of information in each are:

BPA Audit	*ABC Audit*

1. Average qualified circulation breakdown for the period	1. *a.* Average paid circulation
	   b. Average nonpaid distribution claimed
	   c. Average other nonpaid distribution

2. Qualified circulation by issues with removals and additions for period	2. Paid circulation by issues

3. *a.* Business and occupational breakdown of qualified circulation for issue of (date)
   b. Qualification source breakdown for issue of (date)
   c. Mailing address breakdown of qualified circulation for issue of (date)
	3. Business analysis of total paid subscription circulation for the (date) issue

4. Geographical breakdown of qualified circulation for issue of (date)	4. Geographical analysis of total paid circulation for (date) issue
5. Prices (if paid)	5. Authorized prices and total subscriptions sold
6. Sources (of any paid)	6. Channels of subscription sales
7. Premiums (on any paid)	7. Use of premiums
8. Length of subscriptions (of any paid)	8. Duration of subscriptions sold
9. Status of subscription payments (of any paid)	9. Paid subscriptions serviced pending renewal and extensions

BPA Audit	*ABC Audit*
10. Renewal percentage of qualified paid circulation (if any paid)	10. Renewals of paid subscriptions
11. Additional data	11. Explanatory—paid
	12. Explanatory—nonpaid (if any)
	13. Collection stimulants

From many publications, supplementary information is available on a form developed by the Association of Industrial Advertisers. It covers such additional points as:

Total number of units (plants, stores, or other establishments) in the markets served by your publication's circulation and what per cent of the total is reached by your publication's circulation

Total number of recipients (both primary and pass-along) of an average issue

Number of pages of paid advertising for past five years and major products advertised

Statement of editorial content and publisher's concept of editorial responsibility

Number of editorial pages for last five years; also by types of editorial material

Background of editors

Editorial research and evaluation services utilized

Editorial awards won

Available readership preference studies

Reader service cards and coupons

Editorial reprints sold

In appraising business papers, raw circulation data are only one of a number of considerations, however. Since the audience is specialized, total numbers are of limited significance. Quality factors, some of which cannot be expressed numerically, play a major role in business publication media selection. A valuable checklist of considerations in media buying is published by *Media-scope,* and suggests criteria for examining editorials, reader groups, market potential, advertiser acceptance, space cost, reproduction and mechanical details, and services available to the advertiser.

Much attention is now given to the evaluation of editorial content in selecting business publications, since in many fields circulations are controlled by the publisher and standing alone often offers little choice among available magazines. Starting in 1955 and over a period of several years an extensive study of editorial evaluation methods was conducted by Marsteller Inc., assisted by the University of Illinois and New York University. It suggests evaluation of editorial objectives, editorial recall, and editorial image as valuable media buying measurements.

General Magazines, News Magazines, Newspapers

While the bulk of business and professional advertising goes into the specialized business paper press, an increasing share is going to certain publications for which circulation is not controlled and which are readily available to the general public as well as to carefully defined special groups.

In this category are *The Wall Street Journal,* financial publications like *Forbes* and *Barrons, Fortune, Time, Newsweek, U.S. News & World Report,* and others. Their use is often suggested when the purpose of the advertising is corporate-image building or when there are secondary objectives such as reaching the investment community, stimulating mergers, and so on. So it is that some companies with no products on the market for general consumer sale will use some broadly distributed media.

There are, of course, some products which need explaining to the general business community or to people at large in order to gain acceptance. The computer was one of these.

Direct Mail

At the other extreme so far as tight control of the audience is direct mail. It has always been a favorite communications tool of the business advertiser because it is usually possible to build mailing lists around job functions, titles, and types of companies.

Compared with most other forms of communication, direct-mail advertising can be conducted with minimal waste. There are two disadvantages. Unless it is well done it may not make it through the secretarial screen and arrive on the desk of the intended recipient. (Much medical advertising, in fact, is direct mail, but hand-delivered by the pharmaceutical salesman or *detail man* in order to penetrate this screen.) The second disadvantage, as compared with business publication advertising, is that direct mail is aimed at known prospects and customers, and may miss entirely many hidden buying influences in the corporate committee purchasing structure.

Against these disadvantages are its relatively low cost, geographic and numerical controllability, the ease with which the message can be tailored to individual companies or even people, and its flexibility with respect to timing.   It can also carry a much more detailed message than most magazine advertising.

Some of the most successful and most elaborate direct mail produced comes from business and professional advertisers, who win many of the awards in the annual competition of the Direct Mail Advertisers Association, from which much specific information on direct-mail advertising may be obtained.

Trade Shows

Many, if not most, industries and professions sponsor trade shows and exhibits.   They may be regional or national and held annually or at longer periods.

Because they represent an opportunity to demonstrate products live, to have face-to-face contact with prospects, and to distribute catalogs and literature, they are heavily patronized by the advertiser. For many business or professional advertisers, trade shows may take up to 25 per cent of the advertising budget.

Some trade show participation is either political or "keeping up with the Joneses."   Some trade associations are heavily supported from profits derived from sponsored trade shows, and members are therefore under considerable pressure to participate.   Some advertisers routinely exhibit in some shows simply because competitors do.

Undeniably the best shows are useful.   Because show and exhibit costs are high, unit costs of prospects reached are high.   However, the chance for in-depth selling, and perhaps for order taking on the spot, makes it all worthwhile if the audience is a good one.   A few exhibit managers now provide acceptable audit data on attendance taken from registration cards.   Mere numerical totals are of little value because of multiple visits to the show and the inclusion of personnel from competitors and service organizations.

Information on trade shows is incomplete at any one source.   It is best to determine interest by type of industry or profession and contact the principal association involved.

Consumer Media

Business advertisers are sometimes tempted by the truly consumer media—radio, television, local newspapers, outdoor, and mass magazines. For most business communications jobs, the waste is simply too great to justify the cost. There are, however, significant exceptions, and these relate to unusual marketing opportunities.

For example, facing the Detroit Athletic Club is an outdoor board on which the Clark Equipment Company has long advertised its axles, transmissions, and automotive parts. Virtually all the key contract-buying influences in the automotive world are constant visitors to this club, and the media selection is not really much different from advertising in an automotive trade paper.

A major manufacturer of power tools buys seatback advertising in taxi cabs during the mammoth Machine Tool Show to direct visitors to his booth.

Some of the large industrials reach out to publications like *Harper's* and *The Atlantic,* especially if they have a new technology to explain or if their size or organizational structure may be under attack by some groups.

In cities like Los Angeles and Detroit, to which a very high percentage of the business population commutes by car and faces extended periods driving, the use of drive-time radio advertising is far from uncommon. Radio, as well as newspapers, gets a lot of employee-recruiting advertising from purely industrial companies.

Finally, there are some programs running in consumer media, including network television, by companies with almost nothing to sell the individual consumer other than the good citizenship and business reputation of the sponsor. Usually, these are large companies, with a very large group of stockholders, an involvement with many communities, and a great need to be understood and respected. In most such cases even with expensive mass advertising, the total expenditure for advertising as a per cent of sales will be very small compared to the consumer advertiser.

MESSAGE OF BUSINESS AND PROFESSIONAL ADVERTISING

Industrial advertising is hard to do well. While keeping in mind that the audience is composed of individual human beings, it must be remembered that they cluster in interest groups and that their reasons for buying, as we have seen, are both logical and emotional.

Professor Philip Burton of Syracuse University has concluded that advertising directed to the purchasing agent should emphasize costs, advertising to engineers should stress performance, and advertising to management is most successful if it is built on opportunities for profits.

Such rules are good guides. The best industrial and professional advertising definitely starts from the point of view of the prospect and works backward toward the product. As a consequence, successful advertisers to business will not use the same campaign in appealing to purchasing agents, dealers, distributors, and research engineers.

The basic creative platform on which a promotion can be built may be fashioned from many things. Here is one checklist of elements from which creative ideas come:

From the product. What features does the product have that are unique or can be dramatized?

From the company image. Every company has a preexisting image or look which can, through research, be delineated. What people say about a company—how they describe it—is source material.

From the sales proposition. What does the successful salesman say about the product? What advantages does he emphasize, what uses does he stress, and what resistances does he encounter?

From the application. Are the customers finding unique uses? This is sometimes called *case history* or *reference* advertising.

From the audience or the market. What kinds of people or companies use the product? Why?

From accomplishments or achievements. Is the company first in sales? Does it have the longest product line? What has it done that others have not?

From media use. Where will the message run? What opportunities are there for unique size, shape, color, or juxtaposition?

From an event. Did the company participate in a space shoot, a ship launching, the fast restoration after a flood or fire?

From the communications objectives themselves. Sometimes a simple restatement of the basic objectives of the program can become the creative platform.

From the company's philosophies. Does it have deeply felt and interesting feelings about business management, sociological problems, research, industry standards, community relations, acquisitions, and so on?

From people. Are there especially interesting individuals in management, sales service, or other parts of the corporate structure?

From facilities. Are there new or unique plants, research properties, equipment?

From price. Is either a special or the regular price unusual?

From demonstration. What happens when the product is demonstrated?

From services. Is user servicing out of the ordinary? Are special use helps provided?

From the trademark. Is the trademark omnipresent and can it be dramatized or brought to life?

From fads, fashions, and the contemporary scene. Is there a relationship between the product or the company and that which is new and current?

While at one time it was considered sound to pack business and professional advertising with detail, there is much less of this now. Sophisticated advertisers have concluded that periodical advertising can arouse interest, inform, and develop a valuable base of respect and goodwill, but that it cannot do those things while at the same time trying to substitute for a catalog.

Superficially, there is less difference between business advertising and consumer advertising. Visually, the best business advertising is indistinguishable from outstanding consumer advertising. The remaining differences, which seem likely to persist, are in the thrust of the copy. There is far more "how to" and "reason why" copy in industrial advertising. The best industrial advertising is never superficial. More often than in the case of consumer products, there are real points of difference between technical and scientific products, and good business and professional advertising is aimed at finding and exploiting these differences.

How to Evaluate Results

Because the marketing of business and professional products is affected by so many influences, the appraisal of promotional effectiveness is not easy.

Since budget making is rightly related to the success of the advertising program, the study of effectiveness should be built into any promotional scheme from the start.

The start is in setting up communication objectives. Here are a few typical ones, taken from different communications plans:

To develop inquiries from qualified prospects not now customers.

To communicate the fact that having the broadest product line in the industry, our salesmen are free to recommend only what is best for the customer.

To introduce Model___so that within eighteen months, in its capacity range, it has the highest identification in the industry.

To increase by 15 per cent in twenty-four months the number of bank trust officers who identify us with the pharmaceutical, rather than chemical, industry.

Note that these are all communications objectives, not sales goals. Sales objectives are only practical to the extent that the product is an impulse-purchase item, readily available, which needs virtually no other sales effort than promotion.

Testing

Communications objectives should be measurable through research. Today, most sophisticated business and professional advertisers include a figure in the promotion budget for both pretesting and post-evaluation.

Pretesting is usually message testing. It can be done in many ways. The easiest is simply to expose two or more optional proposed advertisements, direct-mail pieces, or whatever to a group of qualified prospects, asking their opinion. The test becomes more useful as it is refined. In one of its best, but somewhat more expensive forms, optional advertisements are reproduced in a test magazine which is exposed to a prospect who is asked to go through it and is then questioned on the advertisements he remembered. The ads under study, having been thus positioned among all ads, are then exposed again, and the prospect is questioned specifically about what he got from his scanning or reading of the message.

Sometimes the purpose of pretesting is to find out whether the message being received is the one the sponsor intended. For instance, if the objective is to communicate the fact that the company has a full line and no axe to grind, by exposing proposed advertisements to prospects and asking what dominant idea they got out of the ad, some measure of message accomplishment is possible.

Other kinds of pretesting come out of split runs of magazines and use of one or two publications for test before a media schedule involving long lists of magazines is started. These do not differ markedly in principle from consumer advertising techniques except in that having relatively narrow industry and job classifications in the audience, research must be very carefully controlled to match those audience targets.

Posttesting of business and professional advertising is somewhat specialized, too. While all kinds of advertisers may set communications objectives which primarily aim at implanting ideas rather than obtaining immediate sales, for business advertising it is often the only way. A thorough discussion of this subject will be found in "Defining Advertising Goals for Measured Advertising Results" (1961), published by the Association of National Advertisers.

Business-paper advertisers must also handle inquiry records with caution. Many publications bind "bingo" cards into the magazines. These list by number the literature offerings of advertisers as well as those reviewed in editorial columns. Unless great care is taken there will be no measure of the effectiveness of advertising, for the respondent may not have observed the advertisement at all, but instead is either reacting to the editorial mention or may simply be a compulsive card returner.

Nevertheless, careful inquiry analysis is always possible and well worth while. To be useful, however, it needs to be more than mere totals. All inquiries should be keyed to such things as the responsible publication; the specific advertisement or editorial that produced it; customer or noncustomer; sales assignment for follow-up; home office follow-up and results. A few company advertising departments are now putting inquiries on the computer for periodic tracing against new sales orders months and even years into the future.

In the business and professional paper field there are now broad opportunities for message research through the various readership ratings usually provided by the publications, but sometimes sold only directly to the contracting advertiser. These readership studies vary in sample size, to some extent in technique, and to a somewhat greater extent in thoroughness and noncontrol by the sponsor publication, but they are all more similar than different.

In essence they attempt to indicate what per cent of a projectable sample of the readers of the publication has seen the various advertisements and how much of the message it has read.

The pioneer among these readership services is the reports published by Daniel Starch and Staff, which measure approximately thirty-five business publications. A complete list of the applicable research reports and an annual listing of the publications to be studied, by issue dates, are obtainable from the magazine *Industrial Marketing*. In 1969, for instance, 262 business publications offered 1,023 separate-issue readership reports prepared by twenty-four different research organizations.

BUDGETING BUSINESS ADVERTISING

While there is no chart of accounts common to all business advertisers, practice has led to fairly general standardization on what is and what is not in the promotion budget and to some rules of thumb on proportional expenditures.

The most common subdivisions of the budget, by title, are:

Space (and time)
Production of space advertising
Direct mail
Catalogs and sales literature
Trade shows and exhibits
Dealer and distributor materials

On other categories, company practices differ widely. Some include publicity and public relations in the same promotion budget; in other companies they are totally separate. Many companies now allocate the administrative costs of the promotion department (direct salaries and fringes, and in some cases proportionate rental and building services) to the advertising budget.

The best budgets are those that are most free of miscellaneous and unallocated categories and have the fewest subdivisions. Either nonspecific classifications or too many classifications encourage loading the budget with debatable charges, so the promotion budget becomes a catch-all and the money available for prospect and customer development is obscured and diluted.

The methods for setting the business advertising budget are similar to consumer budgeting, except that a direct relationship to sales is rarely useful. Nevertheless, all budgets are ultimately translatable to a percentage of sales. With few exceptions, the percentage of sales for advertising an industrial or professional commodity will be much less than a consumer commodity, generally because the other elements which make up the total cost of sales are so much higher.

Percentage of Sales

There is wide variation by industrial industries in the percentage of sales spent for advertising. Materials such as steel, for instance, will usually spend less than one-half of 1 per cent on advertising, while end products will range from 1 to as high as 5 per cent. Within an industry there can be considerable variation depending upon what is done with promotional administrative charges, publicity, and other functions. Tables which have been prepared on the basis of voluntary surveys of sales percentage have had so many inconsistencies as to be relatively useless. However, general averages, from Internal Revenue Service sources, are published annually by *Advertising Age*.

Task Method

The preferred method of determining the advertising budget is the *task* method, or a modification of it. The task method starts with the setting up of marketing objectives. From these are derived communications and advertising objectives. These should suggest what kind of publications are best suited for the advertising program, whether direct mail is to have a role, and the weight of the role, what catalogs are required, what trade shows seem necessary, and so on. While decisions are subjective as to dollar weighting, the range of disagreement is sharply narrowed if the objectives are relevant and specific.

It is important to keep the budget as *pure* as possible. The logic and relationships in the task method break down quickly as improper expenditures creep into the budget. For instance, it is proper to charge the costs of space rental and booth design and building to the trade show category of the budget, but improper to charge salesmen's time or expenses while tending the booth.

It is wise to reclassify the budget, once a trial total has been arrived at, into the total amount spent reaching prospects who may or may not be reached by the sales force, and that which is spent servicing or reselling present customers. Catalogs and much direct mail, for instance, do not build new and unknown buying influences.   At a bare minimum, half the budget should be addressed to doing exploratory and behind-the-scenes cultivation that the sales force cannot do.

In consumer advertising, space production is usually a small proportion of space costs.   In business and professional advertising, because space costs are low and at the same time separate messages are often prepared for many markets or job titles, production is usually around 20 per cent of space expenditures and for many sound advertisers will exceed 50 per cent.

Another relationship to be watched closely is that between administrative costs and the remainder of the budget.   This is particularly true of the smaller advertiser where it is easy to dissipate available promotion budgets on internal services rather than on the real purpose for which the budget was established—to communicate to customers and prospects. Whenever administrative costs exceed 10 per cent of budget, a close examination of alternative methods of getting the work done is indicated.

CHOOSING THE ADVERTISING AGENCY

A favorite subject of the advertising trade press is the technique of choosing an advertising agency.   Most professionals who have been through the process several times, either as advertisers or agencies, have little patience with involved questionnaires with largely quantitative measurements.

Guidelines

There are some guidelines for choosing an agency for business and professional advertising.   The advertiser should satisfy himself that:

1. The agency is familiar with the problems of business and professional advertising and is currently handling such advertising successfully.

2. The agency has other accounts of the same size which are being handled successfully.

3. The agency pays its creative and account people who handle trade advertising sufficiently so that they are not assumed to be incapable of getting jobs in a consumer agency.

4. The top management of the agency, if it has a mixed clientele, is

just as interested in the business advertiser as the consumer advertiser.

There are, of course, other points individual advertisers may want to pursue. Important is to be sure that business and professional advertising is part of the agency's mainstream effort, not merely a training ground, a supplemental service, or a source of peripheral income.

CHAPTER TWENTY-NINE

Advertising to the Farm Market

CECIL E. BARGER *Vice President, Sander Allen Advertising, Inc.*

BIGGEST SINGLE MARKET

Farming is America's largest single industry. It is three times larger than automobile manufacturing, bigger than steel, bigger than aerospace.

It represents the largest single market for a broad range of production goods and services, as well as consumer items. America's farmers spend more than $33 billion a year to produce crops and livestock. They spend another $12 billion a year for food, clothing, drugs, furniture, appliances, recreation, automobiles, and personal items. These amounts are growing almost every year.

Farm Income

Since the 1940s, farm income has nearly doubled. But income from farm operations is not the whole story. Investments and employment off the farm are increasing also—boosting the farmer's spending power as much as 25 per cent.

Farm Investment

Average valuation of a modern farm has grown tremendously, about ten times in the last three decades.   The farmer's assets, as a whole, are equal to three-fourths of the assets of all corporations in the United States.   The investment in farming is equal to three-fifths of the market value of all stocks on the New York Stock Exchange.

Roughly 5 million workers are employed in farming.   This is more than the combined employment in transportation, public utilities, the steel industry, and the automobile industry.

Productivity

Productivity of the American farmer has become almost phenomenal.   In 1938, one farmer produced enough food and fiber for ten persons.   By 1968, this figure had climbed to forty.

With advanced farm technology, greater use of chemicals, more mechanization, genetic advances, there is every indication this productivity will continue to keep pace with America's growing population.

A DYNAMICALLY CHANGING MARKET

Coincident with its growth, farming has been America's fastest-changing business.   Small, inefficient farms have dropped out at a rapid rate.   Those remaining are larger and more productive, with higher yields from every acre.

Change has become part of the regular and continuous pattern in the farm market.   Some of the major trends include:

1. *Fewer farms.*   The number of farms has been declining since World War II.   From more than 5 million farms in the 1940s, the total has been reduced to around 3 million.   This rate will probably continue, with about 100,000 fewer farms each year.

This does not mean any less farm purchasing power.   It simply means many small-acreage, inefficient farms are being added to a larger, more productive unit, thus achieving greater efficiency, greater productivity, and greater total income.

2. *Larger farms.*   In 1950, the average farm in the United States

consisted of 212 acres.   Eighteen years later the average was 369.   At this rate, farm size will double by 1975.

With modern tractors and farm equipment, weed killers, and other technological developments, one man can work more land.   He needs more land, both to carry higher investment in machinery and livestock and to provide for the constantly rising standard of living that farm families are enjoying.

3. *More specialization.*   Caught between rising costs of production and lowering prices for produce, the farmer's profit margins have been squeezed smaller and smaller.   His answer to this dilemma has been greater volume.

He has cut back or eliminated the less profitable enterprises and expanded the more profitable lines.   Thus farming has become a low-profit-per-unit business; but the farmer has more than made up for small margins by going to greater volume and a larger operation.

4. *More livestock—in larger herds.*   Total numbers of hogs, beef cattle, turkeys, and chickens increase every year to meet the growing demands of the American consumer.   This livestock is being produced on fewer farms than ever before, resulting in larger herds and flocks.

Practically the only livestock decreasing in numbers is dairy cows.   As these fewer cows move into bigger, better-fed, better-bred, and better-cared-for herds, the milk production per cow mounts yearly.

5. *More integrated operations.*   As livestock enterprises grew larger, with emphasis on volume and mass production, the size of the farmer's investment grew also, resulting in the need for greater capital resources.   This has led to greater vertical integration in the farm industry.

There has been a growing tendency, for example, for feed manufacturers or feed dealers to finance the producer, providing feed on credit until market time and then sharing the profits.   In some cases, the company may actually own the livestock, provide the feed, and process and market the end product.   The farmer may contribute labor and housing, and receive compensation by sharing profits, or by being paid a fee for his services.   Broiler, turkey, and laying-hen operations have become integrated to a high degree, and a considerable number of cattle-feeding operations are integrated also.

YOUR "NEW" CUSTOMER

The modern American farmer is a new breed.   Compared with only a few years ago, he thinks differently, he acts differently, and he buys differently.

He is more of a businessman.

He is more progressive.

He is a more knowledgeable buyer.

As a larger and more specialized operator, he has come to appreciate the value of extra efficiency in every step of his operation. Therefore, he applies a tough yardstick to everything he buys for his farm production: *"Can I definitely depend on your product to help step up my efficiency and raise my net income?"*

As a big businessman, the farmer is sharp.   He has to be to survive. But the bigger he gets, the more he likes to do business with reputable companies on whom he can depend.   He places great value on quality and performance, because he has found these essential to the high efficiency he needs to stay in business.

He Is Tougher To Sell

You do not gain his confidence easily.   As a hardheaded businessman, he wants and demands facts, figures, and results, backed by hardcore proof.

Some of the changed thinking and psychology of the modern farmer is indicated in studies made by J. M. Bohlen and George M. Beal of Iowa State University:

1. *He is more profit-minded.*   Farming is no longer considered just a way of life.   The modern farmer looks upon his efforts as a business venture.   He recognizes land, labor, and capital as his resources, to be managed for greatest profit.

2. *He is science-guided.*   In the past, the farmer relied heavily on his own personal experiences or that of his neighbors in planning or managing his operation.   But no longer.   Today he insists on technically valid information, relying heavily on the farm press, commercial and college research reports, and advice of technical experts. The adoption of new technological advances has reached a highly accelerated rate.

3. *He is risk-conditioned.*   He no longer leans over backward to

avoid risks, or play it safe.   He knows calculated risks are an inherent part of his business, and he has developed a degree of self-confidence in his own judgment and business acumen.   Under prevailing conditions, he is less worried about debt and more concerned about obtaining maximum credit.

4. *He is management-oriented.*   Hard work and long hours used to be the basis of his whole philosophy.   Now he considers brain-power one of his most important assets.   He thinks of labor as another input that must be managed wisely.   He knows time spent behind his desk can mean as much to his net profit as time spent on the tractor seat.

This, then, is your new customer.   He depends more on his brains, less on his brawn.   He depends on scientific research and the diagnostic laboratory for guidance, less on his own observations.   He seeks greater land control to make his operation more efficient, but is less concerned about actual ownership of the land.   He uses credit and borrowed capital as operating tools, but worries less about keeping out of debt.   He is more of a manager, less of a laborer.

Besides being head of a business, the farmer is also a consumer. And while his farming operation has become more specialized— with greater differences among types of farming and among various parts of the country—almost the opposite is true of his home life.

Higher Standard of Living

Farm living has become more homogeneous, with smaller regional differences.   Farm homes have become much more like suburban homes.   The farm wife in Missouri and the rancher's wife in Arizona both read the same home magazines and watch the same television programs as the suburban wife in Scarsdale.

The farm wife wants and buys the same kitchen appliances, the same rugs and furniture, the same food items, and the same cleaning agents as the city homemaker.   The farm family wants and buys the same automobiles, the same television sets, and the same recreational equipment as families everywhere.

The new approach to farming has given the farmer and his family more leisure, with time to enjoy sports, hunting, traveling, and hobbies.   It has given them the means to upgrade their standard of living, both inside and outside the home, thus creating a bigger market for consumer goods.

VICE PRESIDENT IN THE APRON

Traditionally the farm woman took care of her household, planted the family garden, spent long hours canning fruits and vegetables, and managed the backyard poultry flock. In addition, she helped with farm chores and even did a stint in the fields during rush seasons.

Her role on the modern farm is entirely different. She is much more involved in the business as an integral part of its management. She may pursue her own activities entirely apart from the farm, taking a more active part in the community or working off the farm in business or the professions.

Sharing Management Decisions

A farm wife has always been involved in the family business to some degree, simply because she has been so close to it. Living on the farm, home life and business life were closely integrated. There was more opportunity for her to discuss day-to-day operational problems with her husband.

As the farm grew in size and complexity of operation, she became increasingly involved. Generally, she took over the responsibility for the records and books, vital for tax purposes, but also increasingly important as guides to management. This brought her into even more active participation in farm management decisions.

A study at the University of Wisconsin shows that in a majority of cases, decisions to borrow money, purchase land, or buy heavy equipment are made by the husband and wife together.

Being close to the books, the farm wife knows what is being purchased; but more importantly, she is apt to know why. She is intimately familiar with costs and has a broad knowledge of the efficiency of many products used on the farm. Her opinion can, and does, carry much weight in deciding on type, kind, and brand of items to be purchased.

From her role as secretary, receptionist, bookkeeper, and purchasing agent, she has gradually evolved into the managerial assistant on many farms. In fact, she might properly be considered the vice president of the business.

At the same time, she is also apt to discuss with her husband any major purchase for the home. It is a matter of allocating available family funds to the business and home sectors of the living-farming setup.   Being close to the farm business, the wife has an appreciation of the need to invest in the farm enterprise for greater profits, which can mean more home improvements later.

In advertising farm production items—tractors, fertilizer, insecticides, herbicides, hybrid seed, animal health products—you cannot overlook the wife's influence.   In advertising major products for the home and family—appliances, rugs, furniture—you cannot overlook the husband.   The purchase of a new clothes dryer could mean the postponement of buying a new automatic waterer needed in the feedlot.

Outside Careers

Labor-saving equipment, both on the farm and in the farm home, coupled with specialization, has served to free the farm wife to follow her own inclinations.   Today she is not bound to the farm and homestead.

Many farm women prefer to pursue an outside career.   Working part-time or even full-time, the farm wife may take a job as secretary in an office, cashier in a bank, or other business position.   Depending on her previous training, she may go into professional work as a nurse, teacher, or home economics specialist.

Her reason may be economic, adding extra money to the family income, so the family may enjoy a higher standard of living.   It may also be related to her sense of usefulness in today's world and her sense of personal fulfillment.

In any event, whether she works on the farm or off the farm, she is an activist.   She is no stay-at-home.   She has a strong feeling for her community, and she is deeply involved in church, school, and club activities.

The farm woman is not parochial.   She is as greatly concerned with state and national affairs as with those of her immediate community.

She is informed and up to date, but practical-minded.   When she reads your advertisements she wants good, sound reasons why your product is the one that fits her household needs.   She wants good, sound reasons, to give her husband, why the product will contribute more vital benefits to the family than a new piece of farm equipment.

CHANGES IN DISTRIBUTION PATTERNS

Big changes in the farmer, linked with big changes in farming, are necessitating many changes in distributional patterns of products sold in the farm market.

Modern farming is a growing market for all kinds of production goods—fertilizer, chemicals, petroleum products, tires, formula feed, animal health products, and building materials. In some cases, such as tractors and farm machinery, unit sales may not be so high as formerly; but dollar volume has increased as farmers step up to more advanced engineering or more horsepower.

Market Different from Usual Growth Market

The situation is much different from the usual growth market. While total sales climb higher each year, the number of farm customers grows smaller. This has the effect of shifting the market from a growth stage to a more mature, more competitive stage for many basic production items.

While the U.S. Census lists about 3 million farms, there are only some 1 million commercial farms with gross incomes of $10,000 or more. Yet these farms account for nearly 85 per cent of expenditures for farm production. They are the major market for such items as crop driers, larger tractors, forage harvesters, automatic feeding systems, and environment-controlled buildings.

The other 2 million farms, in the aggregate, still account for a sizable portion of total sales of items needed on every farm, including fencing, fertilizer, seed, petroleum products, and paint.

Bigger Farmers in Driver's Seat

More and more the big customer is in the driver's seat. He demands more services along with the product, more complete programs, more quality, and more convenience, all at highly competitive prices.

He demands more information. As products become more technical, he often finds the farm dealer is not fully familiar with the many technicalities of advanced products, and the knowledgeable customer may know more about them than the dealer does. This creates the problem of informing and training the dealer, so that he is better equipped to serve today's bigger businessman-farmer.

Dealers to Keep Up with Needs

Many farm dealers are not fully equipped to service complicated machinery, or to apply precision chemicals to specific tolerances necessary to the efficiency of the farmer's operation. Today's mobile farmer can and does drive many miles to another town to patronize a dealer who has essential modern service facilities.

More and more the farmer is asking the manufacturer to send out a nutritionist, or a design engineer, or an agronomist. Standard patterns of distribution are being short-circuited as manufacturers explore ways of narrowing the communication gap between themselves and their farm customers.

Some firms, for example, are leaning to company-owned and employee-operated stores. This allows direct communication between buyer and supplier. It allows greater flexibility in pricing products and better control over quality of service.

Manufacturers Must Upgrade Dealers

Other firms are selling direct to bigger farmers, while also selling through independent dealers in the same community. Some, particularly the feed companies, have joined bigger customers in integrated broiler, turkey, or cattle-feeding operations, which puts them into direct competition with their own customers.

All these changes are having the effect of scrambling the lines of distribution, and the trend will probably continue as companies seek ways to effect marketing efficiencies and meet farmer demands.

The farmer has taken off like a rocket, and many inefficient dealers are being left behind on the launching pad. Marketing plans of the manufacturer must include provision for improved dealer facilities and better-informed and better-trained dealers, or his products may very well be left behind.

"Tomorrow's farmer will be a specialist with endless technical requirements and field service," said one sales manager. "He will be a demanding customer who will insist on accuracy and precision from everyone who supplies him."

PLANNING THE FARM ADVERTISING PROGRAM

Defining the Market

Farming is a diverse business.   It runs the gamut from a small plot of flue-cured tobacco in North Carolina, or a confined laying-hen house in Alabama, to a 5,000-cow dairy herd in California or a 5,000-acre corn-and-soybean farm in Illinois.

The market may involve a few thousand turkey growers, scattered from Minnesota to Texas, or it may be 3 million who grow cultivated crops.   It may be general farming, livestock production, grain farming, or specialty farming.

If the product fits into livestock farming, is the prime market in beef cattle, dairy cattle, swine, sheep, or poultry?   What particular type of operation, cattle feeding or raising the cow-calf herd?   Producing eggs or growing meat birds?   Maintaining the swine breeding herd or feeding hogs for market?

The next step is deciding on the penetration of a given market. For example, in selling to the hog producer, will one shoot for those who feed 50 head a year, 100 head, 300 head, or 500 head and more?   In the dairy field, will he aim advertising to dairymen with herds of 20 or more cows, 30 or more, or 50 or more?   Or will he include those with even fewer than 10 cows?

For general consumer products, will the product yield best returns by his aiming at farmers with gross incomes of $40,000 or more, or by including those with incomes as low as $2,500?

Answers to these questions will depend, of course, on the potential for product, distribution, budget, and other similar factors.

U.S. Census figures offer a tremendous amount of demographic data on the farm market, even to the county level.   More current data can also be obtained from the USDA Statistical Reporting Service in Washington.

Strategy for Farm Advertising

Since the farmer is a knowledgeable buyer and businessman, he places high emphasis on quality and performance of the products he buys.   He places great value on the reputation of the suppliers on whom he depends.   He values the services that go along with the products.

To sell him, you have to make your brand name meaningful as a dependable and trustworthy supplier. You have to assure him over and over again that your product merits his serious consideration—proving that it will help increase his efficiency, reduce his risks, and widen his profit margins. You have to show by example after example that your product is *the* buy in terms of what he gets for his money. You have to reassure him beyond doubt that the retail dealer is fully capable of serving his specialized needs.

The farm advertising program, then, usually involves this four-step strategy:

1. *Building brand acceptance*
    a. Build a brand image of quality and reliability in the farmer's mind.
    b. Associate the brand name with advanced, modern farming, and with other bigger and more efficient farmers.
    c. Build a reputation as an aggressive, forward-looking company, attuned to modern farm needs, worthy of consideration in any efficient farming operation.
2. *Building acceptance of the dealer who sells the product*
    a. Show how he is backed by research and by technical authorities in the field.
    b. Make prospects aware of his special training and knowledge in helping them with their problems.
    c. Promote the dealer as a dependable source of supply for products and services that step up the farmer's efficiency.
3. *Building preference for the products*
    a. Show how the product meets the specialized needs of the modern producer.
    b. Be specific, present facts, figures, and details.
    c. Back up sales proposition with results, proof of performance, solid evidence.
4. *Stimulating dealers and distributors to greater action*
    a. Provide the dealer and distributor with special incentives to spur sales action.
    b. Give them the sales tools and merchandising aids to help them do their job.
    c. Cultivate the dealer's pride in being associated with an aggressive, live-wire organization—and in selling the effective and efficient products you offer.

The relative importance of these four steps will vary among different products and different advertisers, depending on how well the company, the brand, or the product is known in the farm market. But all four are important to a marketing program, and none should be overlooked.

EFFECTIVE FARM ADVERTISEMENTS

The strong farm advertisement contains a promise of vital aid to the farmer in helping him solve his problems. It gives him a compelling, believable impression that "here is some straight dope that will be of big help to me in my farm operation."

In farm advertising, the specific, concrete selling idea—the basic appeal to the farmer's business needs—is the most powerful force in making the advertisement effective. The headline, layout, and illustration all combine to put this idea across to the reader, quickly and easily, and heighten the farmer's desire to read more definite facts about how he can attain the stated or implied benefits.

Characteristics of Good Farm Advertisements

An analysis of the readership of 820 farm advertisements—including 647 farm equipment ads which appeared over a six-year period, and 173 livestock feed ads in a three-year period—provides some valuable clues as to the characteristics of effective farm advertisements. It delineates important guidelines for making farm advertisements more dynamic and harder-working in selling farm production items.

The highest-noted and best-read advertisements included in the study displayed these six characteristics:

1. Every ad was keyed to helpful or important factual information.

2. Practically every ad offered important benefits, and either directly or indirectly offered the farmer solutions to his most pressing problems.

3. Many of the top-read ads offered vital news—all offered a new concept or fresh approach.

4. Most of the ads were specific and concrete in the headlines—all were specific and factual in the copy.

5. All were well within the limits of believability, and the superlatives were backed by proof.

6. All the ads were impressive, tended to upgrade the prospect, and built pleasant associations for the company.

Conversely, the low-noted, low-read advertisements never quite came to grips in helping the farmer with his down-to-earth livestock and crop production problems. These weaker, ineffectual advertisements showed a predominance of generalities, with little that the farmer could put to immediate use. He was not excited by vague promises like "Save time, labor, and money" or "Make quality hay." He has heard these a hundred times before.

The farmer will not buy a pig in a poke. He will not read the advertisement just to see whether what you have to say is worthwhile. He is not playing games. When he reads an advertisement he is all business.

The farmer wants the facts of your message—straight from the shoulder and strictly to the point. Wishy-washy words, braggadocio, flim-flam, irrelevance, or vagaries have no place in good farm advertising.

Types of Illustrations   Illustrations in top-scoring advertisements were mainly authentic, on-the-farm scenes into which the farmer could easily place himself. They were action scenes which showed the product in use, preferably demonstrating an outstanding benefit or advantage.

Further, they were working illustrations that tied in closely with the headline, giving the farmer the gist of the message, clearly and succinctly, at a 10-second glance. While field or feedlot views were preferable to studio shots of the product, good art renditions were readily accepted.

Farm Advertising Checklist

Based on these studies, and others of a similar nature, as well as many years of experience in preparing farm advertising, here is a suggested checklist for use in preparing farm advertisements that will communicate a vital message and leave a lasting, selling impression.

1. Does the ad offer a basic message of vital importance—a powerful benefit, big news, the promise of helpful information, the solution to a burning problem?

2. Does the ad talk the language of today's businessman farmer, get down to brass tacks, strike at the very heart of the problem, talk straight from the shoulder?

3. Is the ad keyed to what the farmer wants to know, not to what the manufacturer wants to tell him?

4. Is the sales proposition presented in fresh, up-to-date business-like terms, or does it consist of dull, flat, overworked phrases?

5. Are the illustrations dynamic, story-telling, in a relevant farm setting, or are they static and uninspired, with their purpose obscured?

6. Is the headline clear, concise, to the point, or is it general, vague, and wordy?

7. Do the headline, illustration, and tone of the ad all work together to tell the farmer that here is something vital to him and his business, not just horn tooting?

8. Is the ad believable and persuasive, supported with sound proof, or is it dubious, blatant, and superlative with unsupported claims?

9. Is every statement technically accurate in both fact and concept, logically put together to make sound common sense to today's technically minded farmer?

THE DYNAMIC FARM MEDIA

Farm media have gone through some dynamic and drastic changes in keeping pace with the fast-running farmer.   The traditional homey, folksy farm paper, edited for the fireside, is long gone.   Today's farm magazines are professional, colorful, exciting business papers. There is plenty of evidence that modern farm magazines are well read, that their prestige is high, and that they fill a vital role in modern farming.

Progressiveness of Farm Media

In adjusting to the needs of today's bigger and better farm business-men, many bold changes have been made in content, emphasis, and method of editing.   Perhaps the three most outstanding changes include:

1. *More technical information.*   Today's scientific-minded farmers are on familiar terms with many complicated technological principles and procedures.   Besides the "how," they want to know "why"—why the idea works, why it produces results, and why it fits into their operations.

2. *More management help.*   The farmer is acutely aware of his

tremendous capital investment, bigger than ever before. He wants to know how to manage his assets and resources, how to apply economic laws to his enterprise, and how to reduce his risks and increase his net profits.

3. *More professional editing.* As the farmer became more businesslike and stepped up his own operational standards, he became more critical of the media that served him. The editors have responded with more quality presentations—crisp, clear-cut visuals, and concise, to-the-point editorial features—that convey ideas more directly and clearly.

Four Main Groups of Print Media

From the standpoint of market coverage, we can classify print media into four main groups:

National and Regional Horizontals Dominant leaders in the farm field are the broad-coverage national and regionals, *Farm Journal, Successful Farming,* and *Progressive Farmer.* They offer thoughtful, authoritative material which forward-thinking farmers are seeking. To many national advertisers, in both farm and consumer fields, they provide efficient means of reaching the broad, rich farm market.

These publications also offer state and regional editions, making them flexible and efficient in tailoring advertising coverage to the distribution area. *Farm Journal* and *Successful Farming* publish regular special editions that go to top hog, beef, and dairy producers, providing specialized coverage under the masthead of a high-prestige national or regional magazine.

State Farm Papers Most of these are old-established papers—particularly those in northern and western states, and some southern states—with a loyal following of readers who want local news and information on local problems. Many of these magazines run striking four-color covers and editorial presentations (as well as four-color advertisements). Many still have a folksy touch, but with a more professional insight into the modern farmer's needs. Circulated in one or more states, they generally saturate their coverage area. With two editions a month in many cases, they offer wide flexibility in scheduling.

Class Magazines As more production moved into fewer hands representing a larger share of farm income, a new type of farm magazine emerged. This is the class publication, reaching a select list of big-acreage, high-volume, high-income farmers.

Pioneer was *The Farm Quarterly* (which retained the name when it went to six times a year). Another was management-oriented *Doane's Agricultural Report,* offshoot of Doane's agricultural newsletter service. A later entry was *Big Farmer,* designed for the big-scale executive farmer.

Vertical Farm Papers As the trend to specialization developed, a number of new specialty magazines began publication. In some cases, this served to fractionate an already reduced number of producers. Small circulation made it difficult to put out an aggressive publication with vital, in-depth reporting. However, this was counterbalanced by the growing size and need of the specialty fields.

Gradually many of these vertical books have built a strong reputation with producers, and there is reason to believe they will continue to grow in importance and stature. Selected carefully, they can add much strength to farm media schedules, and may even be a prime medium for highly specialized products.

Broadcast Media

Weather reports, livestock and grain markets, and spot farm news have an enduring place in the farming picture. So the continuing importance of radio and television seems assured. Television also has the advantage of being able to provide details through demonstrations or visuals, contributing greatly to the farmer's understanding and knowledge.

However, the farmer's radio and television listening habits are changing. Outside of several strong farm stations with well-known farm directors, the farmer's listening and viewing often go to the nearby local station. Except during seasonal farm activity, the traditional 5 A.M. farm broadcast may find him still "in the hay." But he keeps up by listening to programs later in the morning or during the noon hour.

The wide range and diversity of farm media, broadcast and print, offers many possibilities for tailoring the farm media program to meet the precise needs of a product, its distribution, its market—and its budget.

A LOOK AHEAD: MORE GROWTH

Each additional million people in the United States will require 172,000 more beef cattle, 433,000 more hogs, and 1,300,000 more laying hens.

Population growth continues at an unprecedented rate—more than 2 million a year. Standards of living are rising, also, with greater consumption per capita of meat and other nutritious foods. In addition, evidence points to a growing demand from abroad for food.

In the years ahead, the farm market will benefit from the fastest-growing demand for food in the history of the world.

The American farmer will move boldly to accept this challenge. He will adapt his business and farming practices to meet the need. He will invest in more efficient machinery, buildings, and equipment; adopt new technology; buy advanced new products; and experiment with bold new ideas to step up production.

Increasing productivity, higher operational efficiency, greater income per farm, all add to an advancing, active, growing market. They add up to a dynamic marketing opportunity for manufacturers of all kinds of modern farm production tools and supplies, as well as all kinds of modern consumer goods to meet the farmer's higher standard of living.

CHAPTER THIRTY

Retail Advertising

BUDD GORE *Vice President, National Retail Merchants Association, Publisher,* Stores *Magazine*

The cart, the computer, and costs have caused what any history of retailing in this third quarter of the century will call a revolution.

Nature of the Retailing Revolution

Like all revolutions, the initial phase possessed the shock waves. It was the period of the 1950s and early 1960s when discounters (later described as *mass merchandisers*) appeared on the retailing scene. Initially, old and abandoned mills in New England were filled with what was largely distress and odd-lot merchandise, and consumers were noisily invited to come in, help themselves, and save money. The supermarket cart became the symbol of the actuality. The quick success of discounting soon shocked so-called traditional retailers.

Spread of the Discounters Lines broadened rapidly, and by one or another of ingenious means, the discounters acquired considerable quantities of nationally advertised and branded merchandise, often employing "wanted" items as loss leaders or "footballs" to attract customers. Discount food and drugs and cosmetics appeared on the shelves and in island displays. Above the frost line, antifreeze in winter and fertilizer in the grass-growing season attracted bargain hunters. The wearers of mink mingled with those capped by babushkas. It became smart to boast about acquiring bargains in a battered, run-down building.

The tax-and-spend economic philosophy of World War II and postwar governments resulted in driving high-income families to search for savings, the better to offset spiraling tax bills. "I can get it for you wholesale," whenever expressed, would prick up the ears of the wealthy just as quickly as those of others. With store payroll reduced, thanks to the customer pushing the shopping cart, lower prices could be achieved in many instances in the shop-for-yourself, self-selection stores.

Response of Traditional Retailers Traditional retailers responded. L. S. Ayres & Co. of Indiana, headquartered in Indianapolis, Dayton's in Minneapolis, and Hudson's in Detroit broke out with mass-merchandising units. Ayres created Ayr-Way Stores, Dayton's its Target Stores, and Hudson's came up with Budget Stores. Kresge's with K-Mart stores, Woolworth with Woolco units, and Penney's with Treasure Island stores followed largely in the 1960s and continue to do extremely well.

One result of research made the traditional retailers happy. They found that the customers of their mass-merchandising units were overwhelmingly new customers. There was no drain from the ranks of customers of the old, established downtown and suburban branches. Bulk of those shopping in the mass-merchandising units were found to be relatively young married persons who apparently believed that higher prices were charged in the same store organization's traditional units. Thus, entirely new and large clusters of customers were added when mass-merchandising units were opened.

Most but not all traditional stores have a policy of prohibiting the sale of identical brands in their mass-merchandising and traditional units. At least, any overlap of identical brands and certainly of identical models occurs in a minimum of cases.

How Computers Have Helped

In addition to the cart making for lower overhead and lower retail prices, the computer is at work on the same assignment.

Costs have skyrocketed in retailing. Traditionally, retailing has been based upon personal service, meaning people on the payroll, much investment in sales training, the expense of supervisory personnel. In addition, there are the sharply increased costs of maintenance, materials, and advertising media.

Hence, the computer comes as a welcome guest. Not only does it contribute to the automation of payroll and inventory and accounts receivable, but it also presents the very real opportunity to increase efficiency in marketing.

In many retail organizations, the computer is identifying customers and what they buy, the income and rental and land values they enjoy, the characteristics of their households in respect to working members, the age and sex of children.

Retailers can now pinpoint their promotional targets. Buyers of books can be identified. So can the purchasers of particular brands of cosmetics. So can the buyers of particular sizes of wearing apparel. This almost endless opportunity to characterize groups of customers and prospects makes it possible to approach them with pointed, individualized sales promotional messages, be the messages in print or in broadcast. Luxury items can be offered to the dwellers in luxury-living areas. Infant items can be described to the mothers who have the very young.

Branch Stores and Their Problems

Retailers have been described as geniuses in the selection of sites for their stores. In the days of heavy downtown foot traffic, store proprietors were found clustered about the main stream of buyers. The stores themselves generated additional traffic by the attraction of their wide offerings in merchandise and services. Success in attracting people was enhanced by a location near public transportation depots or stops.

When the move to the suburbs became definite, retailers were quick to follow with branch stores. In the late 1920s, when many of the initial branches were established, the rate of growth of suburan living and the increase in incomes were underestimated. Early branches were too small, but the retailer either enlarged his units or built new and larger ones still farther from the central city.   He still is as expert in identifying automobile traffic patterns as he was when his first store location was selected downtown and traffic was largely pedestrian.

In respect to marketing, the new branches or units, some as much as 200 or 300 miles away from the flagship or original store, pose problems.   How many newspapers are necessary to reach the potential of prospects and customers?   Is radio advertising an answer?   Can television advertising play an important role?   Much research is being done to find the answers, and out of it is coming the *media mix*, the allocation of funds to several media, as newspapers, radio, television, direct mail, and special events.

The Marketing Vice President

The advent of the marketing vice president is another new and significant development for department, chain, and variety stores and major specialty-shop organizations.   Common for almost a decade among manufacturers, the position of marketing vice president or manager has just begun to be noted in retailing, although less than half a dozen retail organizations now have such a man.

The trend is certain to grow.   The first and most critical reason is the factor of conflict.   A general merchandise manager and a sales promotion manager are organizational equals, both reporting to the store president or general manager.   Through the years, and perhaps because of overspecialization, all too often they are two very different personalities.   The merchandise manager is what might be described as "tangible-oriented" and the sales promotion manager is "intangible-oriented."   One may like to think of himself as a realist, dealing daily in hard, cold merchandise that can be felt, seen, smelled, counted, displayed, sometimes demonstrated, and sold. The other may like to think of himself as creative, courageous, and imaginative.   Types of such extremes, if and when they exist, are not too likely to be objective about each other.   All too often the store general manager or president spends considerable time in attempting to solve the organizational, functional problem of such persons, and how to get such types to cooperate enthusiastically has been an immense challenge.

Now comes the marketing vice president, who in the instances to date is a happy mixture of merchandiser and promoter. Two who are now functioning started in the retail store advertising department and became advertising managers. They then went into merchandising and did buying. One had five years experience, also, as sales promotion manager of a resource that sells its manufactured goods to retail stores.

Trend to Generalists Overspecialization has been costly to retail store organizations. Now the trend is toward generalists who have had as much experience in the merchandising arena as in sales promotion. They can direct skilfully the buying as well as the selling of goods and services. They program from start to finish. They supervise what, when, why, where, how, and from whom to buy, and when, why, and how to sell.

This trend is likely to reduce sharply wasted effort and money. No longer should a buyer be able to enter the market, purchase a carload of unspecified goods, and then pounce upon the advertising manager of the store, saying, "I've got a carload of stuff. Now I have to advertise it to sell it." It is good to have merchandise for sale, but it is not good to try to promote and sell it without first knowing whether it fits into a carefully developed master plan, and whether the customer wants to buy that merchandise at this time and at the settled price. A manager in charge of both buying and selling can solve this problem.

The basic in retail advertising is to determine the rate of sale of merchandise *without* advertising. As soon as one discovers the price level, style, the color, or model of an item that walks off the counter or floor without advertising, *then* and *only then* is the item ready to be advertised.

Almost every pioneer merchant of note has been quoted as saying, "We waste half of our advertising, but we don't know which half." It is high time the expert marketing man in retailing finds out. If an item will not sell by itself, it will not sell with advertising. But if it *does* sell by itself, then mount the promotional guns and sell in great volume. This is not only possible, it is probable.

are not very precise, the growth in international billings of United States agencies is instructive.   From 1953 to 1968 the international billings of United States agencies grew from an annual rate of about $100 million to over $1 billion, approximately doubling every five years.

As late as the middle 1950s six "domestic" agencies and a handful of "export" agencies accounted for over 90 per cent of all known international billings of United States agencies.   Since then the internationalization of United States business increasingly has required international service from United States agencies.   As a result more than 70 United States agencies and several dozens of European and Japanese agencies now have the capability of serving clients in multiple countries.   Other agencies are scrambling to develop such capabilities.

In addition there are hundreds of foreign agencies in local markets which can serve international clients on the same basis as they serve local clients.   (See 616 Agencies Outside U.S. Bill $3.67 Billion, *Advertising Age,* Mar. 25, 1968, pp. 1ff.)

Estimates of the volume of world advertising show a heavy concentration in a few countries.

TABLE 1   Volume of World Advertising (1964)

	Millions of U.S. dollars	Per cent
In 14 industrial countries	21,109.0	90.9
In 20 other high-income countries	1,528.4	6.6
In 18 still-developing countries	593.9	2.5
Total in 52 countries	23,231.3	100.0

SOURCE: "Advertising Investments around the World," International Advertising Association, New York, 1965.

Probably the total volume of world advertising (in noncommunist countries) now exceeds $25 billion, and is increasing at an average annual rate of 6 to 7 per cent.   Over 60 per cent of the total is spent in just one country—the United States.

Annual per capita advertising expenditures range from more than $75 in the United States to just a few dollars in low-income countries.   Advertising as a percentage of national income ranges from

CHAPTER THIRTY-ONE
International Advertising

GORDON E. MIRACLE *Associate Professor, Department of Advertising, Michigan State University*

THE NATURE AND VOLUME OF INTERNATIONAL ADVERTISING

International advertising includes not only export advertising, but also advertising that is placed by local foreign distributors, offices, or subsidiaries when such advertising is planned, coordinated, or influenced from outside the country.

International advertising usually is cross-cultural communication. This fact, along with the fact that international political boundaries are crossed, explains why special knowledge and skills are required. The international advertiser must be as professional and as technically competent as his domestic counterpart; and he needs additional knowledge of foreign economic, social, psychological, political, and legal conditions.

Although estimates of the total volume of international advertising

31-1

more than 2.5 per cent for the United States and Switzerland to less than one-half of 1 per cent in such countries as Costa Rica, Iran, and Norway; in most European countries it ranges between 1 and 1.5 per cent.

THE CLIMATE FOR INTERNATIONAL ADVERTISING

Social, Economic, and Business Climate

Public criticism of advertising seems to be more or less universal, although it is often even more severe outside the United States than within. For example, one authority describing the situation in England has said:

> Selling and advertising have never been accepted by the English as they have by the Americans. The attitude has always been partly hostile, partly derisive. Selling and advertising have never been constituted a really respectable activity. Socially they grade lower than business in the abstract, much lower than the professions. *A salesman projects his ideas to other people and there is something ungentlemanly about this invasion of privacy.*[1]

The role of, or need for, advertising is different from country to country. The economic need for advertising usually is greater in a society of abundance than in an economy of scarcity. However, economic factors alone certainly do not explain adequately the climate for advertising. Traditions, customs, social organization, and other social and cultural factors play an important role in the development of attitudes toward advertising. For example, religious leaders in Chile denounce advertising as morally upsetting to the values held by Chilians. Thus, since television in Chile is under the control of the universities, and since the universities are under the control of the Catholic Church, television commercials are discouraged. Nevertheless in 1966 advertisers in Chile reportedly spent about 11 per cent of their budgets (on the average) on television.

It is common for business firms in the United States to view adver-

---

[1] A. Charles Buck, "The Climate of Advertising in England and the Work of the Advertising Standards Authority," a paper presented at a meeting of the American Association of Advertising Agencies, White Sulphur Springs, W.V., Apr. 25–27, 1963. (Italics added.)

tising as a component of the marketing mix.   This positioning of advertising is in part due to the customer orientation of United States firms and their advanced understanding of the interrelated marketing activities which go to make up a marketing program.   However, businessmen in many countries do not hold this view of advertising's functions; they often depend less upon preselling through advertising, and more upon personal selling and working with middlemen; or, they may regard advertising primarily as a public relations activity.   Because of differing views of the functions of advertising, we find wide differences in the volume of expenditures, the caliber of personnel assigned to handle advertising, and the nature of advertising decisions with regard to messages and media.

Legal and Political Climate

In many countries a basic tenet of political philosophy is that the government exists to serve the needs of citizens, individually and collectively.   It is from this broad mandate of government to look after the interests of its citizens that we derive certain ideas about the need for regulating, taxing, or exerting governmental influence over advertising activities or over those persons who are concerned with such activities.

Since societies differ in their outlook on advertising, there are bound to be differences of opinion as to whether or not advertising should be regulated, and if so, how.   In view of the controversy over the nature and proper role of advertising in society, in the economy, and in the business world, and in view of the widely differing economic and industrial circumstances found in nations around the world, it is not surprising to find virtually no governmental control of advertising (and even favorable legislation) in some countries and "oppressive" controls in others.

Brand and Trademark Protection   Brand protection is one of the essentials which makes much advertising and selling not only desirable, but feasible.   Without brand protection manufacturers would find far fewer opportunities to advertise profitably, and consumers would find it more difficult and time-consuming to buy intelligently.

Brand protection is offered, first, at the national level, and second at the international level.   Virtually all countries have some system for registering and protecting trademarks.   The nature of the protection afforded brands depends on the national legislation of each country.   Most countries are code-law countries and follow the *priority-in-registration* doctrine.   In such countries the date of registration, rather than prior use (with certain exceptions) determines who shall have the rights to use the brand.

Some countries, however, protect brands even though they are not registered as a trademark.   These countries, even though they may have codified their trademark law, have retained the *priority-in-use* doctrine of the English common-law tradition.   Thus the rights to a trademark (with certain exceptions) depend upon priority in use.

There are a number of international agreements which amplify and extend national legislation so as to provide protection for foreigners.   By virtue of these international agreements United States businessmen can expect in about ninety countries to receive national treatment, that is, treatment equal to that afforded local citizens in the protection of their trademark.   The Bureau of International Commerce (within the U.S. Department of Commerce) has information on international agreements and on most of the trademark laws of the world.   However, the many complexities in international trademark protection suggest that marketers should consult legal counsel at an early stage when they plan to sell products abroad.   In fact, it has become routine among many large United States concerns to register trademarks abroad at the same time they are registered in the United States.

Taxation of Advertising   At least a dozen countries place direct taxes on advertising billings or on the institutions that handle advertising—agencies and media.   Italy, for example, has a 4 per cent tax on newspaper advertising, 15 per cent on radio and television commercials, 10 per cent on cinema and prizes, and 10 to 12 per cent on outdoor; Chile places a uniform 6 per cent on all radio and press advertising; other countries such as Angola, Austria, Brazil, Colombia, Greece, India, Iraq, Peru, the Philippines, Portugal, and the United Arab Republic (Egypt) place a variety of types of taxes and at varying rates from 1 per cent of billings to more than 10 per cent, depending on the media in which the advertising is run.[2]

A few countries place a tax on *imported* advertising materials. For example, Aruba and Curacao place a 4.5 per cent tax on imported

---

[2] "The Advertising Agency Business around the World," American Association of Advertising Agencies, New York, 1967, various pages.

print advertising and promotional materials and on film commercials for television and cinema; it has been reported, however, that the tax on print materials often is waived, and the duty on films sometimes can be avoided by using airmail instead of freight and by shipping the films directly to the television station instead of to the advertiser or agency.[3]

In November, 1966, as reported in *Advertising Age,* a Canadian economist D. H. Fullerton told the Canadian government that it could fight inflation by imposing a tax on advertising. Fullerton made his suggestion to the joint House of Commons Senate Committee, which was investigating Canada's rising cost of living. Shortly thereafter the parliamentary committee also heard a second request for an advertising tax from Consumers' Association of Canada. Reaction from Canadian advertisers, advertising agencies, and other economists was quick with regard to the effects of such a tax on the economy, employment, broadcast media, future advertiser budgets, and so forth. The Canadian government took no immediate action on the tax proposal.

While it is difficult to forecast the actions of governments with respect to future taxation of advertising, it has been reported that a number of nations have been giving the matter increasing attention. Thus, it seems likely that we will see more and heavier taxation of advertising before we see less.

Control of Advertising Messages Many countries have laws that in one way or another restrict the nature, content, or style of advertising messages. For example, Germany does not permit the use of the comparative form, or comparisons with competing products. Thus in Germany a company cannot say its product is "better," or "better than another product." Likewise, unless it can be proved correct, a company in Germany cannot use superlatives, saying its product is "best," "fastest," "most effective," and so forth.

Certain product or industry categories are also the target of regulatory action. For example, cigarettes cannot be advertised on television in Great Britain, or at all in Italy.

Other product classifications in which advertising is widely regulated are pharmaceuticals, food and beverage products, and cosmetics and beauty aids. In beverage advertising, for example, the use of the

[3] *Ibid.,* pp. 13 and 57.

word "orange" sometimes is restricted to products with certain percentages of orange juice.   Or, in the case of medical products, many countries require packages, labels, brochures, and literature on "prescription" items to contain the statement: "To be taken only on a doctor's recommendation."

It seems likely that future regulation and control of the content and nature of advertising messages will be concerned primarily with those products which are important to the health and welfare of nations.   Broad restrictions on advertising are difficult and complex to enforce.   Moreover, the experience in Germany with the prohibition of comparative advertising has led some to the conclusion that freedom of entry to new manufacturers with superior products is being restricted.   As understanding grows that freedom of communication facilitates optimum allocation of resources to meet the needs of society, it seems reasonable that sooner or later nations should limit their actions primarily to fostering truth in advertising and punishing those who engage in false or misleading advertising.

Control of Advertising Media   Control of media can be exercised in a number of ways, ranging from prohibition of commercial radio or television to monitoring specific practices or policies.

With the exceptions of Belgium, Denmark, France, the Netherlands, Norway, and Sweden, commercial radio and television are available to advertisers in most of the major countries of the world. A few countries permit only spot announcements on television, rather than permitting program sponsorship, and sometimes "spots" are available for only limited periods during the day—for example, Western Germany permits only 20 minutes per day, all during four 5-minute blocks at half-hour intervals between 6:15 P.M. and 8:00 P.M.

The issue of whether or not to allow commercial television was important in many countries during the 1950s and early 1960s. Commercial television was first permitted in Great Britain in 1954.   More recently, in 1963 and 1964, respectively, Germany and Switzerland established commercial networks.

The most recent (1967) movement into commercial radio has been in India; advertising is now also permitted on television in India, but is not significant since the country's only television station in New Delhi serves only about five thousand sets.   Commercial television in France and Holland also seems likely in the next few years.

In some countries permission must be obtained in order to utilize certain media.   In Aruba, for example, it has been reported that "there are strong government restrictions on outdoor advertising. Permission to put up billboards is required, and this permission is usually not granted.   There are perhaps 25 billboards in existence on the entire island." [4]

Control of the Size of Advertising Expenditures   In 1965 India initiated a regulation limiting advertising expense deductions to 4 per cent of annual sales volume.   The effect of such a tax is to limit the number of dollars which companies spend on advertising.

The approach to limiting advertising expenditures in Great Britain has been more selective.   In 1966 it was reported:

> The British Monopolies Commission charged Unilever, Ltd., and Procter and Gamble, Ltd., have pursued advertising and promotion policies that have resulted in excessive prices for their household detergent products.   The commission recommended substantial cuts in wholesale prices which it suggested might begin on the basis of an average price reduction of 20 per cent . . . the Monopolies Commission made a similar report criticizing Kodak, Ltd., for excessive color-film prices, and recommending a price reduction of 20 per cent at retail levels.
>
> The report contended that nearly 25 per cent of the final retail price paid by the consumer was a result of manufacturers' selling expenses, mainly advertising, sales promotion and market research.   It asserted that promotional campaigns involving the use of "gifts" distracted the customer's attention from the merits of the detergent and were therefore open to objection. [5]

The companies did not agree with the commission's conclusions or recommendations, pointing out that advertising may result in savings greater than their cost because they generate economies of scale in their operations and in those of their suppliers and distributors, making lower prices possible.   Unilever and Procter and Gamble agreed, however, to cooperate in talks with the Board of Trade, using the findings of the Monopolies Commission as the basis for discussions leading to a determination as to what action the companies should take on the commission's recommendations.

In April, 1967, it was reported that "the two companies have

[4] *Ibid.*, p. 13.

[5] Unilever, Procter and Gamble Unit Accused of Excessive Detergent Prices in Britain, *Wall Street Journal*, Aug. 11, 1966, p. 5.

agreed to freeze prices on their leading brands for two years and to widely distribute alternate brands of soap and detergent products of comparable quality at prices 20 per cent below those of advertised products." [6] The outcome of the British attempt to reduce advertising may have interesting repercussions.   If the low-price brands succeed, there will be an incentive for other nations to act in a similar fashion; if they do not succeed, they will serve as evidence of the impact of advertising on sales volume, per-unit costs, and prices.

Social Responsibility and Self-regulation

Sometimes "organized" self-regulation occurs as a result of adherence to standards of conduct and ethical concepts which businessmen for one reason or another have come to follow—for example, the concept of *enlightened self-interest*.   Certain industries and trade associations, as well as individual businessmen, have long recognized that long-run success depends in part on continued consumer acceptance of their products and service, which in turn depends upon adherence by members of the industry to generally accepted behavior and standards.   Such standards differ from country to country, in accordance with the local environment.   Standards may be rigid in certain countries, based perhaps on well-developed sets of intellectual or religious beliefs; standards may be loose or nonexistent in other countries in which different social and cultural circumstances prevail.

National organizations of advertising agencies exist in many countries—organizations which correspond in some degree to the American Association of Advertising Agencies.   Some of these associations have adopted codes of professional conduct which are binding on their members.   For example, it has been reported that the Hellenic Advertising Agency Association (Greece) has adopted a code of professional conduct for its members which relates to policies on commissions, soliciting of accounts, and proselyting of personnel.   It had also been reported that Sweden's recognized advertising agencies and the Swedish Newspaper Publishers Association have an agreement on standards for newspaper advertising.   The agreement also deals with amounts of commissions, terms of payment, and periods of credit.

---

[6] Britain, Procter and Gamble Unit, Unilever Agree on Prices to Avoid Stringent Curbs, *Wall Street Journal*, Apr. 27, 1967, p. 7.

In some countries fairly sophisticated arrangements to enforce compliance with codes exist. For example, in England the Advertising Standards Authority (ASA) serves as the industry watchdog.[7] The origin of the ASA came about as a result of responsible action by British advertisers and agencies. The Incorporated Society of British Advertisers (ISBA—similar to the Association of National Advertisers, in the United States) and the Institute of Practitioners in Advertising (IPA—similar to the American Association of Advertising Agencies, in the United States) jointly commissioned research to ascertain the public image of advertising in England, especially the attitude of government. Subsequently discussions between officials of the government and representatives of the advertising industry were held. The result was governmental blessing for self-regulation, for an indefinite number of years.

On a worldwide basis there are also organizations of businessmen which are concerned with self-regulation of advertising. In 1955 the International Chamber of Commerce (ICC), with headquarters in Paris, published a Code of Standards of Advertising Practice. The code placed responsibility for international observance of certain rules on the shoulders of advertisers, agencies, and media. The code dealt with rules of advertising ethics vis-à-vis the consumer, rules of ethics among advertisers, and rules of ethics governing advertising agencies and media.

In 1963 the ICC published rules of conduct for television advertising. The ICC recognized the existing International Code of Principles for Advertising on Television which was produced by the International Union of Advertisers' Associations (an organization composed of members from ten European countries) and adopted by them in June, 1962. The ICC recognized that while the code is helpful in stating broad principles upon which commercials should be made, more detailed rules are needed.

The ICC's basic rules stated general principles:

> . . . All television advertising should be truthful, honest and clean. It should be presented in good taste and conform to all the legal requirements or professional regulations of the country. Because of the collective family viewing of television, special care must be taken to

---

[7] The following information on the ASA is adapted from the paper by A. Charles Buck, *op cit*.

ensure that advertising is of a high moral standard and not likely to disturb, offend or embarrass viewers in any way.[8]

The ICC then went on to lay down specific details on methods of advertising, with special reference to advertising in programs intended for children, false or misleading advertising, unfair comparisons or references, guarantees, and testimonials. Special references were also made to certain categories of products such as alcoholic beverages, cigarettes, personal products, and medical products, to restrict the appeals to be used and the manner in which they are to be presented.

In order to promote adherence to the code the ICC has established an ICC International Council on Advertising Practice. The council stands ready to examine cases of unfair advertising, submitted by the parties concerned. Any person or body affected in a case of unfair advertising may seek the intervention of the council. If the council decides that a violation has occurred, the council will endeavor to dissuade the offending party from continuing the unfair practices.

PLANNING INTERNATIONAL PROMOTIONAL PROGRAMS

Planning international promotional strategy involves essentially the same matters as planning domestic promotional strategy, namely: (1) setting promotional objectives, (2) deciding on the types of advertising and promotional messages, (3) selecting media, and (4) determining how much time, effort, and money to spend.

Communication Objectives

Decisions on the elements to be included in the promotional mix depend on a company's communication or promotional objectives. The possible objectives of international promotional efforts are indeed large in number. For example, they might include not only creating an awareness and interest in a company's products, but also creating a favorable name and reputation in the minds of customers, distributors, suppliers, or even foreign governmental officials or reg-

---

[8] *Code of Standards of Advertising Practice* (1955) and *International Rules of Conduct for Television Advertising* (1963), International Chamber of Commerce, Paris, p. 10.

ulatory agencies.   Usually it is best to establish specific goals, such as (1) to convince buyers of the durability of a product, or (2) to illustrate the effectiveness of the product in satisfying a particular want. Although objectives of international advertising are both numerous and complex, it is helpful sometimes to divide them into two categories, *local* and *international*.   For example, the communication of specific product information to a target audience may be primarily a local objective, that is, it is part of the mix of local promotional activities to meet the information needs of local customers.

Also, since a company's image may have an effect on the general acceptance of the company and its products in a market, most companies use promotional activities to improve their corporate reputation or image.   Because modern transportation and communication media have fostered increased mobility of men and ideas, it often is important for companies to have a uniform, or at least a compatible, image from market to market.   Massey-Ferguson, for example, a large producer of farm equipment, has attempted to establish a worldwide corporate identity.

Planning Promotional Strategy

Preliminary steps in the planning of a promotional program include an assessment of the size and extent of markets, customer behavior and buying habits, and competitive circumstances.   Consideration must be given to the channel(s) of distribution that a company uses, both among nations and within each foreign market.   The nature of the product line, brand policies, the price of the product, and other aspects of the overall marketing effort also must be considered.

With the appropriate information at hand on markets, competition, channels, product characteristics, and price, a company can formulate its general promotional strategy, decide on the advertising platform and the timing of the several stages of the campaign, and make decisions on specific advertisements and media.   Finally, the company can add up probable costs to arrive at the total cost of the program—a proposed budget.   Then, the company can reexamine the budget to be sure that it is within general company guidelines.

The planning of a promotional program can be accomplished by headquarters personnel, by joint efforts of headquarters' and local personnel, or by local personnel.

Since local promotional activities as well as corporate reputation-building activities influence a company's total sales and the success of a company's operations in multiple markets, a central staff may serve to assure that local and corporate communication objectives, and the methods by which they are achieved, are in harmony with the interests of the company as a whole, both in the short and in the long run.

Local management often is in the best position to judge local market and competitive conditions and to make the final decisions as to *how* the company's communications objectives are to be achieved, that is, the specific messages and media to be employed.   But, even in the planning and preparation of local campaigns, local management often needs help.   The advancement of knowledge in the field of marketing and communication is rapid.   The marketing concept, new developments in communication theory, the application of new techniques in assessing media effectiveness, and the many other new concepts and ideas which are constantly being developed, domestically and in other areas of the world, suggest that the corporate or international division staff should perform a clearinghouse or information-transferral function.   While all new ideas may not be immediately and totally applicable in all countries, local management needs to be kept informed.

Generally, centralized planning of promotional strategy seems to be most appropriate for those products that are sold on the basis of the same selling propositions worldwide (e.g., health, beauty, safety, durability), i.e., when buyer motivations and the usage of the product are similar in all markets.   On the other hand, for products that must be adapted from market to market to meet varying tastes or esthetic requirements (e.g., food tastes, personal dress, or household furnishing customs), i.e., when buyer motivations for purchase vary, promotional programs ordinarily are planned locally.   Among companies with subsidiaries the trend is toward greater centralized guidance and joint planning among headquarters, subsidiaries, and their advertising agencies.   But among companies using licensees to manufacture abroad, or distributors to sell abroad, the policy ordinarily is still to depend on the licensees or distributors to plan and formulate the program; such manufacturers usually confine their efforts to providing information, guidance, and support.   Joint planning of promotional programs varies from mail and telephone communication to frequent travel by specialists from company headquarters to work locally.   In some companies, the international division advertising manager (or members of his staff) and representatives of their advertising agency participate in discussions at the planning sessions of subsidiaries. The local advertising agency persons also may play a significant role at these sessions.

The trend among many companies seems to be toward greater headquarters participation in planning promotional programs, not only programs of subsidiaries, but also those of distributors and dealers. The participation of headquarters personnel frequently is limited primarily to the generalized portions of promotional mix planning. For example, companies often find that assistance in identifying market targets and assistance in identifying and evaluating systematically the relevant factors which influence promotional mix decisions are the principal contributions of headquarters' personnel. The majority of companies leave to local advertising personnel the task of planning the details of promotional campaigns.

Planning Creative Strategy [9]

The advertising task is essentially the same at home or abroad—namely, to communicate information and persuasive appeals effectively. The requirements of effective communication are fixed, and cannot vary with time, place, or form of communication; therefore, the same approach to communication, that is, the same approach to the preparation of messages and selection of media, can be used in every country. It is only specific advertising messages and media strategy that sometimes must be changed from country to country. In international marketing and advertising as well as in domestic advertising, the communicator must learn about his audience, define market segments as precisely as possible, and study backgrounds and motivational influences in detail before he begins preparing an advertising campaign. In recent years advertising men in the United States and in other countries have discussed widely the degree to which ideas and advertising materials created in one country can be used in another. Erik Elinder, head of a Swedish advertising agency, has said: "Why should three artists in three different countries sit drawing the same electric iron and three copy writers write

[9] This section consists of materials excerpted, by permission, from Gordon E. Miracle, International Advertising Principles and Strategies, MSU Business Topics, Autumn, 1968, vol. 16, 4, pp. 29–36.

about what after all is largely the same copy for the same iron?" [10]
Mr. Elinder believes consumer differences are diminishing from
nation to nation, and he would prefer to put top specialists to work
devising a strong international campaign, which could then be presented "with insignificant national modifications rendered necessary
by changes in language." [11]

Mr. Elinder and those who hold his point of view argue that sometimes the appeals, illustrations, or other features of advertisements
need not be changed from market to market.   They have rightly observed that in many respects, consumers in diverse markets are similar
and that human nature is basically the same in most societies.   Men
everywhere require satisfaction of physiological and psychological
needs.

However, on the other side it can be argued that a communicator
should rightly take cognizance of the differences between consumers
in his own country and those in other countries.   They not only
speak another tongue, but they adhere to other religions, philosophies, and traditions; they differ with regard to family patterns,
childhood training, and the role of members in the family.   The occupational hierarchy varies among nations; climate and geography
and other aspects of consumers' physical environments are diverse;
consumers engage in a wide variety of sports, hobbies, and other
forms of amusement and entertainment.   These environmental differences play an important part in shaping the demand for specific
types of goods and services and in determining what promotional appeals are best.   Thus it may be argued that products, or the appeals,
illustrations, and other advertising features used to sell them, often
must differ from market to market.

Appeals   Appeals must be in accordance with consumer tastes,
wants, and attitudes—in short, in harmony with the prevailing
mentality of the market.   In some countries, the use of a certain
brand of lipstick or toothpaste by a well-known fashion model will

[10] Erik Elinder, International Advertisers Must Devise Universal Ads, Dump
Separate National Ones, Swedish Adman Avers, *Advertising Age*, Nov. 27, 1961, p.
91. See also Erik Elinder, How International Can European Advertising Be?
Journal of Marketing, April, 1965, pp. 7–11; and Erik Elinder, How International Can Advertising Be? in S. Watson Dunn, "International Handbook of Advertising," McGraw-Hill Book Company, New York, 1964, pp. 59–71.
[11] *Ibid.*

enhance the product's appeal in the eyes of a working girl. But, "in Belgium [for example] it doesn't. Models are scarce and their trade is hardly considered honorable." [12]

The health appeal varies in effectiveness from country to country. In France, the suggestion that the use of a certain toothpaste will help prevent dental caries is likely to be less effective than the same appeal in the United States, since Frenchmen are not so inclined as Americans to be concerned about the numbers of cavities in their teeth. In nearby Holland, health attitudes are quite different from those in France. The Dutch show greater concern about their health. To the Dutch, the vitamin content and energy value of some foods are more important than taste.

For products that are identical physically but which are used differently from one market to the next—for example, cornstarch, cake mixes, instant coffee, margarine, and many other food products—the advertising message often has to be adapted for each market segment.

The list of companies that are trying to locate universal appeals for their products, which can serve as the basis for preparing prototype campaigns, is increasing. Revlon, a large manufacturer of cosmetics, is one of the best examples. "Revlon is particularly concerned that their international advertising . . . contribute to the overall Revlon image. Latitude is granted field managers in revising individual ads or budgets; but even these must be cleared first with headquarters." [13]

One of the most widely heralded international themes is Esso's "Put a tiger in your tank." After considerable success in the United States, the company decided to test the slogan in Europe and Asia. Minor modifications in wording had to be made; for example, in France the word "tank" is *reservoir,* which in the context of the phrase could be risqué, so the word *moteur* was substituted. Consumer research showed the campaign was highly successful in European countries. The theme was also appropriate in some countries in southeast Asia where the tiger is a symbol of power and luck.[14]

---

[12] Dan E. G. Rosseels, Consumer Habits and Consumer Advertising in the Benelux Countries, *Export Trade and Shipper,* Jan. 28, 1957, p. 17.

[13] *Grey Matter,* January, 1966, p. 4.

[14] Put a Tiger in Your Tank, *Marketing Insights,* Nov. 28, 1966, p. 11.

However, in Thailand, the tiger is not a symbol of strength, and the campaign was not understood.[15]

Illustrations and Layout Illustrations and layout are perhaps more likely to be universal than other features of advertisements. Certain types of illustrations are being used with increasing frequency in several nations. For example, advertisements for Canadian Pacific Airlines which were created in Mexico City have appeared not only in United States and Canadian publications but also in newspapers in such faraway places as Tokyo and Hong Kong. The advertisements originally were planned for people in cities along the company's Latin American routes, but the airline found much of the work suitable for worldwide use as well. A company spokesman said: "It's one of the best campaigns we've got going. It's too good to limit it to Latin America. A slight change in copy, and we find it does the job as well for us in Vancouver or Hong Kong." [16]

The campaign to which the Canadian Pacific Airline spokesman referred had several features which may account, at least in part, for its wide suitability. The advertisements displayed large attention-getting photographs, usually with no more than 20 per cent of the space used for copy. For example, a picture of a Canada goose, a symbol of the airline, is captioned, "He knows the best routes south, so does Canadian Pacific." [17] Short and simple copy with the same message, of course, can be written for other routes.

Perhaps some forms of artwork are understood universally, and hence the same illustrations sometimes may be appropriate in different markets. On the other hand, cultural influences may dictate that illustrations for the same product must differ from country to country. In German magazines an advertisement for cheese might show a large foaming glass of beer with the cheese, which would whet the appetite of a Bavarian. But in France an advertisement for cheese would more appropriately substitute a glass of red wine for the beer.

Copy There is considerable diversity of opinion with regard to the translation of copy from one language to another. On the one side are those who warn against translations. They point out that while

[15] Margaret Carson, Admen in Thailand, Singapore Find Unusual Problems, Novel Solutions, *Advertising Age*, Nov. 27, 1967, p. 50.

[16] *Advertising Age*, Aug. 6, 1962, p. 70.

[17] *Ibid.*

mistakes can be made in any language, even by local copy writers, it is more likely that they will be made if advertisements are prepared in one country, translated, and inserted in international or foreign media without review by competent local linguists.

On the other hand, a spokesman for a company selling in South America says that English copy can be translated into Spanish if it is done by a person who has (1) good literary knowledge and command of the technical terminology of both languages, (2) a good understanding of the technical aspects of the products, and (3) copy-writing ability which can re-create the persuasive tone of English copy.[18] Therefore, it appears that there is a need for a creative, not just a routine word-for-word, translation.

The effects of dubbing and adapting television commercials have been studied by a commercial research organization, the Schwerin Research Corporation.[19]   In one study, Schwerin tested thirty-one commercials shown in Canada.   English versions were tested in Toronto and French-dubbed versions were tested in Montreal.   The report concluded that it is possible for television commercials originally designed for one particular market to obtain comparable results in a market where a different language is spoken.

Complete Advertisements   Professor S. Watson Dunn of the University of Illinois has reported [20] on the results of a series of field tests to find out under what conditions an entire American advertisement would be successful in a foreign market.   Five products, all low-priced convenience items which were widely used internationally, were chosen.   They had all been advertised in at least one American magazine, and the appeals featured in the advertisements violated no cultural or other taboos in France and Egypt, the countries in which the test was run.   The results showed surprisingly little difference in the effectiveness of the various versions.   There was little evidence to support the idea that it is necessary to show a local model in the ad-

[18] Emmet P. Langen, How to Write Spanish Copy—without a Yankee Accent, *Industrial Marketing,* July, 1959, p. 49.

[19] The Effects of Dubbing and Adapting Television Commercials for Foreign Markets, *Schwerin Research Corporation Technical and Analytical Review,* no. 9, Summer, 1961.

[20] S. Watson Dunn, "The International Language of Advertising," a talk presented at the East Central Region Annual Meeting of the American Association of Advertising Agencies, Detroit, Nov. 16–17, 1966.

vertisement, or that one must attribute the message to a local (as compared with a foreign) source.   There was only limited evidence that the message which is started from scratch in a foreign country is any more effective than a good, refined translation from the United States original.

Some Generalizations   Generally speaking, most advertising men would agree that it is unlikely that Elinder's recommendations for "uniform advertising" can be successful for all products, for all companies, in all markets.   Thus the critical questions are *when* will Elinder's approach be successful and *when not?*   And, *what criteria* can be used to make a selective judgment?

The factors which influence the appropriateness of uniform advertising for various market segments (whether national or international) are:

1. *The type of product.*   When there are certain universal selling points for some products—for example, razor blades, electric irons, automobile tires, ball-point pens—products are sold primarily on the basis of objective physical characteristics.   These objective characteristics are likely to be considered by consumers to be identical, regardless of market differences, suggesting that the same appeals will be effective in all markets.

2. *The homogeneity or heterogeneity of markets.*   When aggregate characteristics such as income, education, and occupation are alike, individual consumer characteristics such as needs, attitudes, and customs may also be alike, thus suggesting that the advertiser use the same selling points.

3. *The characteristics and availability of media.*   If certain media are available in one country but not in another, certain messages and materials may not be usable.

4. *The types of advertising agency service available in each market segment.*   If in some markets only poor agency service is available, a firm may be forced to rely on centralized control of advertising with necessary uniformities in messages and media strategy.

5. *Government restrictions on the nature of advertising.*   Some governments prohibit certain types of messages, thereby making certain appeals or copy unlawful.

6. *Government tariffs on artwork or printed matter.*   Such expenses may offset a cost advantage achieved by centralization of the art and production functions.

7. *Trade codes, ethical practices, and industry agreements.* In some countries there may be a "gentlemen's agreement" among competitors: they will refrain from using certain media, such as television, an expensive medium, which in a limited market might only increase "competitive advertising."

8. *Corporate organization of the advertiser.* If a company is organized to conduct business on a multinational basis, and if personnel are available, uniform advertising may be feasible—for example, if a company has "controlled" subsidiaries, it can often control advertising better than companies that use independent licensees to produce and market their brands abroad.

People the world over have the same needs, such as food, safety, and love. But people sometimes differ in the ways in which they satisfy their needs. Just as it is important to provide physical variations in products to meet the varying demands of diverse market segments, so it is also important to tailor advertisements to meet the requirements of each market segment. But it is the demands of the market segments which are diverse, not the approach to planning and preparing marketing programs. The principles underlying communication by advertising are the same in all nations. It is only the specific methods, techniques, and symbols which sometimes must be varied to take account of diverse environmental conditions.

Campaigns in International Media

A majority of large United States companies with foreign operations advertise in international magazines or trade journals. Typically, creative materials for campaigns in international media are planned and prepared by the international division advertising manager and his staff and their advertising agency. Most United States companies employ either a domestic or "export" agency to prepare and produce such advertisements. Ideas and materials, such as suggested layouts or artwork, may be solicited by the advertiser from selling locations abroad. More frequently, however, the advertising agency has full responsibility for the creative work, subject to the advertising manager's approval. Only rarely does a subsidiary or branch of a United States company exercise any direct influence on advertisements in international media placed by headquarters except to provide ideas and materials when asked.

Campaigns in Foreign Media

United States company policies on the preparation and placement of advertisements in foreign media range from virtually complete control by headquarters personnel to virtually complete autonomy by local personnel.   To some extent policies on control of advertising vary according to company organization and method of doing business abroad, but not nearly so much as might be expected.   Manufacturers with similar products, selling in similar markets, often follow decidedly different policies.

Centralized Preparation of Advertisements   Since the late 1950s a number of major companies have prepared prototype campaigns and miscellaneous materials for use by their overseas offices.   Most such companies based their campaigns initially on marketing research done in a small number of selected, and hopefully representative, overseas countries.   Often they found that it was necessary to increase the number of countries in which they did research, and increased costs sometimes counterbalanced the claimed advantages.   A major benefit to such companies has been increasingly professional advertising from those in the foreign offices—as a result of working more closely with those from headquarters.

Centralized control of the preparation of advertisements does not imply centralized control over the nature of the promotional mix. In fact, among companies that prepare advertisements centrally, subsidiaries ordinarily decide how much emphasis to place on print media, direct mail, salesmen's aids, and so forth.   Likewise, although they prepare advertisements at headquarters, some companies *produce* the final promotional pieces or advertisements abroad.   Promotional mix and production decisions tend to be made somewhat independently of the decision as to where advertisements are created or produced.

Local Preparation of Advertisements   Companies leaving creative responsibility to subsidiaries and their local advertising agencies may provide central support, advice, and assistance, or they may establish only broad policy guidelines.   A few companies that provide central guidance and assistance also require that locally prepared advertisements be submitted to headquarters for approval.   However, most companies do not pass final judgment on creative work of their subsidiaries.

Logically one might expect that certain types of products which can be differentiated by advertising and which would gain most from a uniform, well-known image would be given relatively greater support and guidance from headquarters. However, a recent survey by this writer of more than twenty companies failed to indicate a clear pattern. Some producers of inexpensive consumer items such as cosmetics, pens and pencils, and packaged goods try to establish a uniform product image, while others do not. Similarly, some manufacturers of household appliances give considerable central support to their local distributors, while others give little.

Planning Media Strategy

Media Structure, Usage, and Costs Although the number, types, and characteristics of media vary considerably from country to country, there are two broad categories of media that are useful to distinguish: (1) *international media*—those print and broadcast media that circulate, or are heard or seen, in more than one nation, and (2) *foreign media*—local, domestic media. International media attract a relatively minor share of the money spent by international advertisers; the great bulk of international advertising budgets is spent in local, foreign media. The availability and suitability of advertising media vary considerably from country to country. With the exception of broadcast media, major types of media are in existence in virtually all local foreign markets. The estimated advertising investments in the various media as shown in Table 2 gave an indication of the relative importance of media in a wide variety of countries.

The costs of media, as well as media discounts to agencies, cash discounts, and volume discounts, vary widely from country to country. Table 3 seems to indicate that the 15 per cent agency commission is fairly widespread, which is essentially correct. However, considerable variations in fees and volume discounts partially obscure this apparent sameness. A local representative, thoroughly conversant with local costs, conditions, and practices, is essential to buy media intelligently in local foreign markets.

Basic Considerations for Media Planning The general approach to formulate media strategy is as follows:

1. Define the market targets, in the aggregate and according to the behavioral characteristics of buyers.

TABLE 2   Estimated Advertising Investments in Media in Selected Countries (1966) in Per Cent

	News- papers	Maga- zines	Outdoor and trans- portation	Direct mail	Radio	Tele- vision	Cinema	Misc.*
Argentina	22	10	11	6	11	18	2	18
Australia	40	15	8	—	9	25	2	—
Belgium	25	15	15	18	3 †	—	2	19
Brazil	12	21	3	—	35	29	—	—
Canada	31	7	6	17	9	11	—	29
Chile	—33—		19	—		11	5	2
Colombia	33	2	2	—	26	14	2	22
Costa Rica	—34—		2	—	41	21	2	—
Denmark	32	11	1	14	—	—	2	40
Ecuador	40	1	—	4	20	4	—	31
France	22	28	8	12	9	—	7	12
W. Germany	32	25	3	30	2	8	—	—
Israel	61	5	5	6	6	—	6	11
Italy	21	17	6	6	5	8	6	34
Japan	35	6	9	4	4	33	1	7
Mexico	25	5	5	3	20	35	5	2
The Netherlands	41	13	5	39	2	—	1	—
Sweden	37	13	3	22	—	—	—	24
Switzerland	22	16	7	15	—	3	1	36
Turkey	36	9	18	15	5	—	4	11
United Kingdom	31	17	5	8	1	18	1	19
United States	34	8	1	15	6	17	—	19

SOURCE: "The Advertising Agency Business around the World," 5th ed., American Association of Advertising Agencies, New York. 1967; and "International Advertising Expenditures," The International Advertising Association, New York, 1963, and *The International Advertiser,* December 1967.

* Sometimes includes direct mail, outdoor, and cinema, when those categories are not stated separately. Other examples of miscellaneous are catalogs, leaflets, calendars, window and interior displays, exhibitions, counter and aisle point-of-purchase items, and miscellaneous sales promotion such as free samples and gift schemes.

† In Luxembourg only.

2. Define other environmental factors, such as the availability of media, conditions of competition, legal restrictions, and so forth.

3. Define the communication objectives—the impact which is to be made on buyers or buying influences in the market target(s).

4. Assess the media available in relation to their suitability to accomplish the stated objectives.   Typically this involves careful study of such characteristics of media as circulation, audience, credibility, cost per thousand, and so forth.

It is necessary to develop carefully and in great detail an under-

TABLE 3   Advertising   Agency   Compensation   as   a   Percentage   of   Media
         Billings *

	News-papers	Maga-zines	Radio	Tele-vision	Cinema	Outdoors
Argentina	15–20	15	20	15	15	15–20
Australia	15	15	15	15	15	15
Brazil	20	20	20	20	20	20
Canada	15	15	15	15	15	15
Chile	15	15	15	15	15	15
Colombia	15	15	15	15	15	15
Costa Rica	15	15	15	15	15	15
Finland	15–30	15	—	15	15	15
France	15	15	15 *	15 †	15	15
Italy	15	15	15	15	15	15
Greece	20	20	20	—	20	20
Iraq	20–25	NA	NA	10	25	NA
Ireland	12½–17½	15	15	15	15	15
Israel	25	NA	20	NA	NA	NA
Japan	15–20	15–20	15–20	15–20	15–20	15–20
Mexico	15	15	15	15	15	15
Sweden	15–20	15–20	—	—	15–20	15
Switzerland	5	5–15	—	0	5–10	NA
Thailand	0–10	0–10	0–10	0–10	0–10	0–10
United Kingdom	10–15	15	15 ‡	15	15	15
United States	15	15	15	15	15	16⅔
Venezuela	15	20	20	20	20	15
West Germany	15	10–15	15	15	15	15

SOURCE: "An Analysis of Advertising Billing and Payment Procedures in Thirteen Countries," The International Advertising Association, New York, April, 1963; and "The Advertising Agency Business around the World," 5th ed., American Association of Advertising Agencies, New York, 1967.

* Percentages in this table usually represent an agency's minimum media commission or compensation. Cash discounts, additional fees for services of widely varying amounts, and additional volume discounts ranging from 2 to over 30 per cent are common.

† On commercials prepared for use in markets that permit broadcast advertising.

‡ Off-shore radio stations.

standing of the basic considerations that are part of this general approach. *Media-scope* has published an extensive list of such considerations (Table 4). This list can serve the international advertiser well as a guide to structuring his thinking in making media decisions.

TABLE 4   Media Buyer's Checklist

*Basic Considerations for the United States–based Advertiser or Agency
Contemplating the Use of Overseas Media*

I. *Organizational Considerations for Method of Placement*
   A. What is the client's policy with respect to supervision of advertising? (May vary by product and by territory.)
      1. Predetermined use of specific media.
      2. Preselected method of placement through specific agencies (local).
      3. Placement through selected affiliates.
      4. Placement through established international agency, United States–based.
   B. What advertising facilities and personnel does the advertiser have overseas? Can they help in media analysis, planning, and buying?
   C. Who will do what?
II. *Advertising Budgets*
   A. Established by client.
   B. Based on refined media recommendations of agency.
   C. Based on local brand or distributor recommendations.
   D. Relationship to sales.
      1. Budget to be set for market exploration purposes.
      2. Budget to be set as a percentage of expected sales.
      3. Budget to be organized on a long-term development payout plan.
   E. Period for which budget is set (as for calendar year).
   F. Breakdown of budget for media, promotion, production, research costs.
   G. Extent to which current budget is part of a program extending over several budget periods.
   H. Tie-ins with local distributor.
III. *The Market*
   A. What are the market areas?
      1. Europe.
      2. Latin America (South America, Central America, and the West Indies).
      3. Africa and Middle East.
      4. India–Pakistan and Southeast Asia.
      5. Far East (Japan, Philippines, etc.).
      6. Oceania (Australia–New Zealand).
   B. What is the market to be reached?
      1. Consumer—luxury goods.
      2. Consumer—mass market goods.

TABLE 4   Media Buyer's Checklist (*Continued*)

3. Industrial—light industry.
4. Industrial—heavy industry.
5. Agricultural.
6. Manufacturing.
7. Military and government.
C. Who are the people within each market to reach?
   1. What levels of management may influence purchases of industrial goods?
   2. Who in the household (wife, husband, children, servants) influence purchases of consumer goods?
   3. Availability of audited information.
   4. Comparability of media data.
D. Market size.
   1. Group markets.
   2. Common markets.
   3. Population.
   4. Annual per capita income.
   5. Per cent illiteracy.
   6. Distribution channels.
      a. General wholesalers.
      b. Franchised outlets.
      c. Owned subsidiaries.
      d. Types of retail outlets.
E. Market factors.
   1. Language.
   2. Economic factors.
      a. General considerations of market growth. Specific consideration of income level at which product is bought in each country.
   3. Unusual geography.
   4. Social customs.
   5. Local competition.
   6. Local manufacture versus imports.
   7. Tariffs and their effect on landed costs.
   8. Effect of local codes and standards.
   9. Transportation, utilities, or other elements significant to sales of the product.
   10. Political considerations.
   11. Government bureaus and officials.
IV. *The Media*
A. Selection of proper media.
   1. Audiences reached.
      a. Size of audience.
      b. Type of audience.
      c. Where reached (international or local).

TABLE 4 Media Buyer's Checklist (*Continued*)

---

    2. Cost factors.
       a. Standard rates.
       b. Volume and frequency discounts.
       c. Variations from published rates.
       d. Can inter-media cost comparisons be drawn?
       e. Cost of color.
       f. Cost of special positions or premium time.
       g. What is trend of rate changes?
       h. What media do not offer agency commissions? How much are commissions?
    3. To use or not to use special issues.
    4. Competitive advertiser activity by specific media.
    5. International consumer media.
       a. United States–based.
       b. Based in other countries.
    6. International trade media.
       a. United States–based.
       b. Based in other countries.
    7. Local consumer media.
    8. Local trade media.
  B. Media characteristics.
    1. Suitability of media to fit product or services advertised.
    2. Class of audience.
    3. Print media distribution (paid, controlled, etc.).
    4. Print color facilities.
    5. Nature of publication editorial content.
    6. Television coverage areas.
    7. Radio coverage areas.
    8. Nature of broadcast programing.
    9. Noncancelable contracts.
    10. Space or time purchase in local currency versus U.S. dollars.
    11. Merchandising services.

V. *Helpful References*
  A. Standard Rate & Data Service and British Rate & Data jointly sponsored editions covering France (*Tarif Media*), West Germany (*Media Daten*), Italy (*Dati e Tariffe Publicitarie*), and Mexico and Central America (*Medios Publicitarios Mexicanos*).
  B. "Advertisers Annual" (United Kingdom and Common Market), Admark Publishing Co., Ltd., London.
  C. "The Advertising Agency Business around the World," American Association of Advertising Agencies, New York.
  D. *The International Advertiser,* International Advertising Association monthly publication.

TABLE 4   Media Buyer's Checklist *(Continued)*

E. *Media/scope* reports, including What Is Happening among International Media, February, 1962; How U.S. Business Press Is Expanding Overseas, March, 1962; AAAA Cites Opportunities and Pitfalls as Agency Services Expand Overseas, November, 1962; International Media: Efficient Road to Foreign Markets, February, 1964; and International Media Buying at McCann-Erickson, November, 1965.

F. World Radio and TV Handbook, published by *Television Age.*

G. "Rome Report of Expenditures in International Media."

H. *International Commerce Weekly*, publication of U.S. Department of Commerce.

I. World Trade Data Annual, published yearly by *Business Abroad.*

J. Office of Certified Circulation Audits, International and Local Media (mostly Latin America).

K. See also publications of the Advertising Committee, U.S. Council of International Chamber of Commerce.

SOURCE: *Media/scope*, April, 1966.

Many of the factors to be taken into consideration, when formulating multinational media strategy and when selecting specific foreign and international media, are identical to the considerations which are important when making "domestic" media decisions. On the other hand, there are additional considerations which make international decisions more complex. Of particular importance to keep in mind is that *specific knowledge of foreign markets and foreign audiences* is essential to good media selection. Such knowledge is not usually so readily available, and executives do not often have so much relevant experience and knowledge on foreign markets as they do on the domestic markets with which they are familiar. Likewise in planning an international program the decision maker may have comparatively little specific information on foreign media. Thus, an important step in media selection must be a careful enumeration and analysis of the characteristics of various media which are available in the relevant markets.

Media Objectives After a thorough analysis of the relevant environmental factors, the media strategist may finally be ready to specify his objectives realistically. Media often are evaluated in terms of (1) *reach* (the number of individuals or households reached), (2) *frequency* (the number of times a message is delivered to target audiences), (3) *continuity* (the pattern of message delivery), and (4) *size* (the space or time unit employed). It is also desirable to evaluate the qualitative characteristics of media, e.g., the credibility and reputation of the medium, and general impact of messages that it carries. For example, some media are better suited to demonstration of the use of a product while others are better suited to portray the color or other physical characteristics of a product.

In terms of general effectiveness in accomplishing promotional objectives, the capabilities of media in various countries are similar. Newspapers are a good medium to indicate where and at what price a product is available; magazines are suitable for reaching specialized audiences or for promoting products that require considerable explanation or perhaps display in color; outdoor or transportation advertising is good for brief visual messages; television and cinema are appropriate to demonstrate the use of a product.

However, the specific effectiveness of media in terms of reach and continuity differs greatly from one country to the next.

Newspapers There is a great deal of variety in the types of newspapers and the reading habits of people from country to country. In some countries, such as Canada, the United States, and the developed countries of Europe, the great majority of the population reads a daily newspaper. In other countries, characterized by low educational levels, a low rate of literacy, and low consumer incomes, coverage by the press is very poor indeed. In Italy, for example, the number of copies of newspapers per thousand inhabitants is 104; in Great Britain it is 573.[21] Only 24 per cent of Italian housewives read a daily newspaper.[22]

In some countries the relationship between newspapers and political parties, or the relationship between newspapers and religious groups, can have a profound effect on the size and nature of the newspaper's audience and the impact of the newspaper on its audience. Most people—regardless of country—will read those papers that are of the same political persuasion as their own, or that adhere to the same religious position.

In some countries there are national daily newspapers which pro-

---

[21] R. M. S. Beatson, Dateline: Italy: How Effective Are Italian Advertising Media? *Broadcasting*, Nov. 29, 1965, p. 74.

[22] *Ibid*.

vide good national coverage—at least among the more educated population. This is true in Turkey, for example, and to some degree in England, where the *London Times,* the *Manchester Guardian,* and a few other papers have wide national readership.[23]   In Italy, in contrast, the press is best suited for localized advertising because all newspapers are local or regional, and no newspaper has a circulation above 500,000.[24]

In some countries, such as Spain, cities with populations as low as 25,000 typically have three and four newspapers, with none dominant.[25]   Under these circumstances it is very difficult to put together a newspaper advertising campaign which will reach a substantial proportion of Spanish housewives.

Magazines   Foreign magazines often are a difficult medium for international advertisers to utilize.   In Europe, for example, there are hundreds of consumer magazines, most with limited circulation compared to national magazines in the United States.   In Spain there are more than 400 magazines (in a country of 32 million population) with the largest circulation by *Hola,* with 315,000 gossip- and news-hungry female buyers.[26] But even though circulation of individual magazines may not be large, the audiences reached by magazines often are important.   In Italy, for example, about 50 per cent of all women buy a women's magazine.[27]

Technical and business magazines, which often are considered an important part of the media mix for industrial advertising in such countries as Canada, England, Germany, and the United States, do not exist in many markets.   Often either the lack of periodicals, or the excessive number of small-circulation periodicals, forces international advertisers to rely less heavily on these media.

Outdoor and Transportation   Posters, signs, and car cards seem to be used relatively frequently in low-income countries, sometimes accounting for as high as 20 per cent of total advertising.   Much out-

[23] John Fayerweather, *International Marketing,* Prentice-Hall, Inc., Englewood Cliffs, N.J., 1965, p. 91.

[24] Beatson, *op. cit.*

[25] See Marketing around the World: Spain's Media Mix: Broad and Developing, *Printers' Ink,* May 12, 1967, p. 27.

[26] *Ibid.*

[27] C. Laury Botthof, One Common Market or Six Markets?, *Journal of Marketing,* April, 1966, p. 18.

door advertising is designed for viewing by pedestrians or those who use public transportation.   Buses and streetcars are major means of transportation and reach large, important audiences.   Since posters, painted signs, metal signs, and electric signs require local installation and regular maintenance, it is desirable to administer such advertising locally—through a local advertising agency, or perhaps the local retailers who sell the product.   Centralized ownership of outdoor advertising facilities is rare; rates fluctuate widely and municipal ordinances differ greatly.   Therefore purchase of such facilities must be handled by someone who is intimately familiar with local conditions.

Cinema   Cinema is an important advertising medium in many countries, especially in countries without top-quality press or broadcast advertising facilities.   Since cinema attendance often is very high, even in poor countries, cinema can be used to reach a high percentage of urban audiences.   In Spain, for example, cinema is a major entertainment vehicle.   In Scandinavia 74 per cent of the urban population in the fifteen to twenty-four age group reportedly can be reached with a four-week schedule in selected cinema houses.[28]

Radio   Radio can be an important advertising medium for products with a broad market.   Radio tends to be used more widely in Latin America than in Europe, in part because of European restrictions on (or prohibition of) radio advertising.   The medium is of special value to sell consumer products when the literacy rate is low.   It penetrates to the lowest socioeconomic levels, reaching potential market segments which are otherwise inaccessible at reasonable cost.   In India, for example, with a majority of the population illiterate, radio advertising can reach more people than any other medium.

Television   Television is well developed as an advertising medium in only a few countries of the world.   The greatest progress in this regard has been in the relatively affluent countries that permit commercial television to operate with a minimum of restriction.   Some countries in which television is government-owned permit television advertising, but restrictions usually are severe.

In countries with limited television time available to advertisers, there have been occasional or even regular periods during which it

[28] *Screen Advertising in Scandinavia,* Scandinavia Screen Contractors, Copenhagen, undated brochure distributed September, 1965, p. 5.

has been extremely difficult to buy time. In Spain the fact that network buys are made only once a year causes an incredible scramble among advertisers and agencies. In Switzerland the entire year of television advertising time was sold out eighteen months in advance of the launching of Swiss commercial television; [29] reportedly, time is still difficult to obtain. In Germany time must also be booked well in advance—allegedly it requires influence in order to obtain time when it is wanted. Overbooking is common, and time buying takes on some of the aspects of a game.

Cost per thousand still seems excessive in many markets, but has been declining steadily, even dramatically, in many countries. In Germany, for example, cost per thousand (based on number of sets) declined approximately 50 per cent from 1960 to 1966. As technical problems of compatibility are resolved—between the major European and United States systems—so that worldwide transmission by satellite is feasible, from a cost as well as a technical standpoint, the possibilities for the growth and expansion of television advertising are numerous.

Direct Mail Direct mail can be useful as a direct-action vehicle or in a supporting capacity; it can be useful to stimulate dealers or to reach ultimate consumers. Direct mail can take many forms—letters, catalogs, technical literature, or as a vehicle for the distribution of samples or premiums.

One of the major problems in the effective use of direct mail is the preparation of a suitable mailing list. The U.S. Department of Commerce, and its governmental counterparts in other countries, often can be helpful, especially as a guide to the sources of lists, e.g., various directories, trade associations, and so forth.

Ordinarily direct mail can be handled best by local foreign subsidiaries, distributors, or licensees. The objectives of direct-mail campaigns are usually local objectives, e.g. to provide samples, to tell customers where they can get the product, or to announce a special sale.

Trade Fairs Trade fairs are another medium that is extremely important for some industries. They are of two general types: (1) the broad, general type, well-established annual affairs, and (2) the spe-

---

[29] Commercial TV in Switzerland Is Sellout 18 Months before Debut, Schweizer Reports, *Advertising Age*, July 23, 1962, p. 54.

cialized type, for products in specialized groups or industries. Trade fairs can be valuable not only to well-established firms—for purposes of prestige, public image, introducing new products—but also to new firms that might have no other readily available way of getting their products displayed before the right audience, at low cost.

House Organs   House organs can serve as an effective means to provide company, distributor, or licensee personnel with knowledge of the success of other distributors or licensees.   House organs may be a vehicle for promotional ideas, company news, the results of contests, employee commendation, and so forth, and therefore may be an important device to stimulate enthusiasm and effective sales performance abroad.   Most companies prepare, edit, and produce house organs in the home country, but a few companies with well-established international operations have separate foreign editions, prepared and produced locally, with only a minimum of central direction and control of content.   Of these, probably the most successful are those in which there is a systematic or planned sharing of information and interchange of ideas among the various international or foreign editions.

Point-of-Purchase Materials   Manufacturers of consumer packaged goods such as cosmetics, paper-tissue products, or proprietary pharmaceuticals sometimes find it desirable to provide point-of-purchase (POP) literature and displays to subsidiaries, licensees, distributors, and retail dealers.   Local POP materials sometimes can also be tied in with advertisements run in local media.   Such materials may also contribute to, and be in harmony with, the uniform worldwide image which the manufacturer may desire to achieve.   Some companies prepare POP materials domestically in rough form for shipment abroad.   Local foreign representatives usually handle production and printing.

Public Relations   Public relations activities should be considered to be an integral part of the international marketing effort, designed to accomplish marketing objectives.   In general, the purpose of public relations activities is to achieve objectives which cannot be achieved by other means or which cannot be achieved as cheaply by other means.   For example, if a company desires to gain recognition as a company that is aware of its social responsibilities in foreign locations, this objective often may be accomplished much more effectively by a carefully planned campaign to receive favorable editorial mention than by using paid advertisements.

Among the most widely used tools of the public relations staff are press releases and prepared editorial material. Such materials often are prepared on new products, the opening of new plants, the accomplishments of the company, the activities of company personnel in community or governmental activities of locally recognized merit, the favorable impact of the company on the local economy, or the role of the company as a local employer.

In many companies public relations materials for international use originate from the domestic operation. A few, however, attempt to solicit ideas and materials from foreign operations. For example, a clipping service may be maintained to demonstrate the success of local public relations activities. Or a story may be written on the successful application by a foreign customer of the company's product, for submission to an appropriate trade journal as editorial content. Reprints of such material may then be utilized by salesmen or the public relations staff in another country.

Basic Media Data Except for the developed countries of Europe, Japan, and North America, adequate information on media is rarely available. Publications which are essentially similar to Standard Rate & Data Service (SRDS) in the United States are available in such countries as Australia (*Australian Rate and Data Service*), France (*Tarif Media*), Germany (*Media Daten*), Italy (*Dati e Tariffe Publicitarie*), Mexico (*Medios Publicitarios Mexicanos*), and the United Kingdom (*British Rate & Data*). Modest amounts of information on media and media representatives are available also from a variety of trade publications such as *Business Abroad* and *Editor and Publisher* (*International Yearbook*). Generally, however, local sources must be exploited by personnel situated in the market who are intimately familiar with local conditions, in order to obtain the best information available. Nevertheless, in the last few years some progress has been made in making media information more readily available.

Over the past several decades a number of circulation audit services have been established in many countries of the world. In 1963, nineteen of these auditing organizations established the International Federation of Audit Bureaus of Circulation (IFABC). The IFABC serves as a vehicle to encourage and facilitate the exchange of information and experience between member organizations, to work toward greater standardization and uniformity in reporting circulations, to encourage the establishment of audit bureaus of circulation in countries where such bureaus do not exist, and to facilitate cooperation with national and international advertising associations.[30]

Audience Measurement Services   In 1961 the first major report on the availability of audience measurement services around the world was published by the International Advertising Association.[31]   The report was limited primarily to continuing services, although a few intermittent surveys which appeared to be of exceptional value were included.   The report included information by country on the media audiences measured, and several details on the nature of the study methodology and frequency of reports.   Another source of information is Intam Limited, the international advertising and marketing division of the London Press Exchange in the United Kingdom, which has published a number of volumes of information on mass media audience surveys in European countries.

It is noteworthy that mechanical measurements of broadcast media audiences (e.g., by Nielsen Audimeters) are in use in a few countries such as Germany, Japan, the United Kingdom, and the United States.   In addition, audience surveys of print media,[32] as well as broadcast media,[33] employing a variety of methods, are available in most European countries and in a few countries in Africa, Asia, and Latin America.

Control   Control over planning media strategy and selecting media for inclusion in a campaign depends on such considerations as (1) the objectives of the campaign, (2) the availability of information on the relevant possible media selections, (3) the knowledge and experience of media specialists, and (4) the degree to which media must be super-

[30] For additional details, and for information on members, see *Circulation Auditing around the World: 1965*, a memorandum report by the Secretary General, International Bureaus of Circulations, 123 N. Wacker Drive, Chicago, 1965.

[31] Edwin F. Wigglesworth, Audience Measurement Services, *The International Advertiser II*, November, 1961, p. 9.   Reproduced in Dunn, "International Handbook of Advertising," *op. cit.*, p. 701.

[32] See, for example, *Research in the Service of Press Advertising*, Institut de Recherches et D'Etudes Publicitaires, Paris, 1961.

[33] See, for example, *Revised Survey of Research into Radio and Television Advertising in Various Countries*, Document no. 250-1/11, International Chamber of Commerce, Paris, October, 1960.

vised locally to ensure proper performance. For example, if objectives are primarily corporate in nature, rather than local, control is likely to rest at the corporate level. Or if relevant detailed information on certain media is available on an adequate basis only at the local level, decisions are more likely to be made at that level. Or if personnel with adequate background and experience are not available at the corporate level, decisions are not likely to be made at this level. Or if local media must be monitored closely to ensure performance, company representatives at the local level are more likely to be involved in both planning and control of media strategy. Thus the question of centralized versus decentralized control has no universally applicable solution.

Campaigns in international media often are planned at the international division or corporate level, rather than locally. But selection of foreign media ordinarily is left to local personnel. Since media conditions differ substantially from country to country, the centralized direction of most companies consists largely of policy guidelines on the use of media and criteria for evaluating media. The criteria vary somewhat from company to company but generally include: (1) circulation and readership of print media—or set ownership, listenership, and viewership of broadcast media; (2) the character, reputation, and image of the media; (3) media rates and cost per prospect; and (4) mechanical requirements, especially as they may affect the costs of producing advertisements.

The basic reasons that those on the local level can do the media selection job better are (1) they know the market better and which media will influence it effectively, (2) they know the true costs, fee structures available to local advertisers, and local taxes that apply, (3) they know at once whether an advertisement is running at the right time and place, and can make necessary corrections without costly delay, and (4) they can get an advertisement into media with limited time or space—which can be exceedingly important in the case of television time which is severely restricted in some countries.

Cooperative Advertising

Cooperative advertising often plays an integral part in a multinational company's media strategy at the local level. From the manufacturer's standpoint the basic decision is whether or not a cooperative advertising program should be established. This decision rests on such fundamental considerations as the nature of the product, the role which local dealer advertising plays in influencing customers, and the types of marketing channels which the company uses—and their interest in having a cooperative program available to them. The decision must be made not only on the basis of whether or not cooperative advertising is desirable from the standpoint of influencing customers, but also on the basis of whether or not it can be implemented and controlled successfully among the marketing intermediaries.

Those companies selling products for which the end use is similar in many countries (e.g., farm equipment, industrial machinery, automobile tires) ordinarily desire to control the nature and features of cooperative advertisements. Artwork, mats, photographic materials, appeals, themes, sample copy, sample layouts, and even complete advertisements or commercials which have been employed successfully in the United States or elsewhere are provided free or at nominal cost. Although some companies require that local merchants participating in the cooperative program use only materials they supply, many do not, or cannot. But, even when manufacturers do not require the use of the materials they supply, such materials are used frequently.

Selection of media is ordinarily left in the hands of the local dealer or distributor. In the typical cooperative program the manufacturer will establish policies for the use of each medium, leaving it up to the dealer to take advantage of funds for the media he feels are appropriate.

The primary features of a successful cooperative advertising program are that it meet the needs of the market for information, the needs of the dealer for assistance, and that it be tightly controlled by the manufacturer to avoid abuses. Thus, a cooperative program requires careful planning and a detailed statement of conditions under which the dealer can avail himself of the program—clearly understood by both the dealer and the manufacturer.

Budgeting

Budgeting can refer to the allocation of a fixed money expenditure among alternative media, message strategies, or campaigns, or it can refer to the method of determining the total amount to be spent. Although both questions are interrelated, decisions on allocation of a fixed budget can be made largely on the basis of the kinds of analysis suggested in previous sections of this chapter.

The second question, however, requires further elaboration. Ideally, one might argue that companies should make use of the objective and task method, coupled with profit planning. However, the difficulty of specifying international advertising objectives precisely and determining exactly what must be done to accomplish them limits the value of this approach. Thus, as a practical matter, most companies must take a far more arbitrary approach.

When a company's overseas subsidiaries or branches are charged with profit responsibility, they virtually always have the final authority to set the size of their advertising appropriation. A few companies place either maximum or minimum percentage-of-sales guidelines for or restrictions on foreign subsidiaries, but they will allow exceptions for a good reason.

A fairly common procedure is for branches or subsidiaries to prepare their budgets and submit them to the international division advertising manager for consolidation into an overall budget, which then is given general approval by international division management if it is within percentage limitations. Some companies require detailed accounts of how money is spent—breakdowns by media and by products.

Probably the most effective budget control is exercised in those companies in which (1) the international advertising manager at headquarters participates with local personnel in planning and preparing promotional campaigns, (2) the corporate and subsidiary objectives of the proposed expenditures are clearly understood by all concerned, and (3) care is exercised at each step to ensure that the proposed expenditures are reasonable with respect to accomplishing the objectives.

ADVERTISING AGENCIES

Advertising Industry Structure

For many years prior to the 1950s a small number of agencies, primarily in Europe and the United States, stood ready to meet the international advertising needs of some of the relatively few major international advertisers in the world. But today more than seventy United States agencies and several dozens of European and Japanese agencies have the capability of serving clients in multiple countries. Although the majority of international billings is still concentrated in a few agencies, latecomers are expanding rapidly.

Advertising Agency Policies

In general most United States advertising agencies feel that 100 per cent ownership of foreign offices is best. However, there are numerous arguments and adherents for other points of view.[34] Agencies with wholly owned foreign offices point out that they have greater control and freedom to bring in their own people and to select and train local people; in short, to develop their own type of operation.

Some go so far as to argue that ideally branches should be started from scratch. They argue that when acquiring a foreign agency one may purchase bad habits as well as local expertise, or incompetent as well as capable personnel. On the other hand, it is often argued that existing agencies which have developed to the point where a merger becomes attractive have demonstrated that they have a capable management, competent personnel, and a knowledge of local markets, advertising media, commercial customs, laws, and governmental regulations. American know-how, added to an aggressive local going concern, produces an organization which is ideally suited to serve United States clients abroad.

Advocates of a majority-interest holding (rather than 100 per cent) point out that such an interest is sufficient to control techniques, standards, and quality of service. However, the minority voice is strong enough so that the agency maintains its local knowledge and skills. Thus, it is argued, it is possible to achieve a blend of United States and local know-how. Also, a minority interest by key foreign personnel gives them identification with the fortunes of the agency and encourages their continued best efforts.

Those who prefer a minority interest believe that it is important to retain the members of the original management who successfully developed the agency, so as to make use of their accumulated knowledge and to continue to reward them by keeping them involved with ownership and profits.

[34] For a detailed discussion, see Gordon E. Miracle, "Management of International Advertising," Bureau of Business Research, Graduate School of Business Administration, University of Michigan, Ann Arbor, 1966, chap. 6.

A joint venture, sometimes called a *joint agency,* is a third corporation formed by two or more agencies.   In the typical situation each partner will own an equal percentage, although complex variations in the degree of ownership and the arrangements for ownership are common.   The third corporation makes use of the personnel and services of the local partner to serve the foreign partner's clients. The costs of creative work, media selection, and marketing, as well as other costs, are charged to the joint agency, as are client commissions.   Some agencies feel that joint ventures tend to break up, and because the primary devotion of both partners is toward their own agencies, joint ventures do not receive strong direction and consequently do not serve clients well.

The preceding discussion suggests how agencies with differing policies on how to expand internationally also differ with respect to the type and quality of service they can provide to the clients.   And, since the needs of clients dictate (ultimately) the service that agencies must supply, we may be able to predict future trends in agency policies by examining trends in the needs of clients for service.

Some clients, of course, require an integrated and coordinated program in many countries; others require only service on a local basis in each foreign market.   Generally speaking, multinational corporations with a worldwide outlook require a multinational advertising agency.   If the advertiser is organized according to geographic areas, an advertising agency with regional coordinating offices, suitably staffed, may be required.   If the advertiser is organized by product lines, advertising responsibilities may be assigned on a worldwide basis, and the company's advertising agency must be capable of providing the same type and quality of service in all relevant markets, suitably controlled from headquarters.   If a multinational advertiser has counterpart staffs at the corporate staff and subsidiary or divisional levels, the company may require an advertising agency with a similar structure.

Companies with virtually autonomous foreign operations—and there are still many of these—may require only the services of a local agency in each foreign market.   However, with the trend toward multinational business, the trend among advertising agencies seems to be toward agencies with wholly owned branches, properly coordinated, with open lines of communication among all levels, and organized so as to facilitate meeting the varying needs of multinational advertisers.[35]

Selecting an Agency

Selecting an advertising agency requires not only a knowledge of the structure and policies of the international advertising agency business but also a careful assessment of the advertiser's specific needs for service.   In some cases the nature of the products, and the nature of the markets in which they are sold, are the prime considerations.   In other cases the advertiser's organization and policies on centralization or decentralization of control are paramount.   Also the characteristics, qualifications, and personalities of corporate officers are a critical factor.

The process of selecting an agency to provide international service is essentially the same as the process of selecting one to provide domestic service.   However, the relative importance of certain considerations is different.   Far greater attention must be given to the agency's organizational structure, location of offices, and relationships with other agencies or suppliers in countries where service will be required.   Also, because the service required may differ somewhat from country to country, it is often advisable to prepare a more detailed statement of what is expected of the agency and the methods of compensation for various kinds of agency services.   Often a written agreement is preferable to an oral arrangement.

Frequently an advertiser will find it desirable to employ the same agency for international service as for domestic service.   The agency and client already are familiar with the company and its products; the experience gained in the domestic market is likely to be helpful in the preparation of advertising for international or foreign media. On the other hand, since many foreign operations of large international firms are responsible for profits, they must have a voice in selecting their advertising agencies.   In some instances the local branch office or associate of the agency used domestically is not the best available local agency.   Moreover, there simply are not enough agencies

---

[35] For details on the relationship between the needs of advertisers and the characteristics of advertising agencies, and the policies of United States advertisers in selecting agencies to serve them abroad, see Miracle, "Management of International Advertising," *op. cit.,* especially chaps. 2, 3, and 4.

capable of providing both domestic and international services for the great number of clients seeking this arrangement. A reasonable policy—followed by many United States–based companies—is to encourage but not attempt to require the use of the same agency by subsidiaries, licensees, and distributors.

Those advertisers who do prefer to use the same agency throughout the world give the following reasons: (1) The agency can coordinate the planning and preparation of advertising and promotional programs; (2) the agency can transfer creative materials from one location to another; (3) small accounts in some countries receive services that, on an individual basis, might not be profitable for the agency [36]—that is, the advertiser receives service that he could not get from another agency; and (4) the agency can furnish periodic reports on the services it has performed for subsidiaries.

In spite of the trend toward greater coordination and cooperation in planning, preparing, and running advertising campaigns in a number of foreign locations, only a minority of United States–based advertisers utilize a United States–based agency with branches or associates abroad. Most allow their foreign operations to select and utilize local agencies as they deem appropriate.

[36] This does not necessarily imply that such small accounts are unprofitable for the agency, since services performed or advertisements prepared in one location may be utilized in another. For example, in some locations the advertiser's annual budget may be only a few thousand dollars; 15 per cent of $5,000 may not be enough to cover the agency's costs in planning and preparing a campaign, but it may be enough to cover the cost of modifying a successful campaign run elsewhere.

PART NINE

Legal Matters

CHAPTER THIRTY-TWO

Managing the Legal Aspects of Advertising*

GILBERT H. WEIL *General Counsel, Association of National Advertisers and Advertising Research Foundation*

PERSPECTIVES

Legal ramifications are implicit in every facet of the advertising process. They generate in the relationships and activities which develop among advertisers, agencies, and media; and they extend to the interfaces of that complex with further parties, including members of the public and arms of government. Coping with this catalog of complexity is best accomplished prophylactically, cure being ordinarily more expensive and less satisfactory.

In the final analysis, responsibility for anticipating and dealing

* The author gratefully acknowledges the outstanding contributions to this chapter of his associate, James A. Kirkman III, who gathered the necessary materials and prepared its initial draft, and of his partner, Alfred T. Lee, who meticulously reviewed and substantially improved the penultimate writing, most especially with respect to the sections on trademarks and unfair competition.

with legal problems must rest with the lawyer.   However, he cannot act until he has been alerted; nor can he perform to his most constructive potentiality without thoroughly understanding his client's business policies, objectives, and operations.   Neither can the client utilize a lawyer's services to their full benefit without sensing when the company's proposed activities approach perilous legal domain.

In short, a constant "in harness" working relationship between client and lawyer is needed for the former to develop and sharpen his instincts against incipient legal dangers, and the latter to imbibe sufficient knowledge of his client's functioning to evolve legal solutions which are commercially as attractive as the law will allow.

Finally, the partners in that process of cross-education must take care to avoid an inherent pitfall.   Knowledgeable as he may have been made of a client's operations, the lawyer ought not undertake —nor be expected—to make business decisions.   Conversely, the client, astute though he may have become under his attorney's tutelage, should not allow himself to feel he can act the lawyer.   The pace of change is too rapid, and the influence of subtle differences between one situation and another upon the ultimate event are too potent for either the lawyer or the client to assume such high degree of self-confidence in the other's field of primary expertise.

One of the most difficult occasions for preserving this distinction between responsibilities, and also one of the most important in which to do so, is that of deciding whether to take a *calculated legal risk*.   It is an unfortunate characteristic of advertising that many of the legal questions its process raises cannot be answered with impressive certainty.   As will appear in later discussion of specific problem areas, the legality of a particular advertisement or activity may turn upon economic considerations or be critically affected by subjective philosophical, psychological—even emotional—reactions, or political orientations of government regulators and judges.   There probably is no business activity which can be undertaken with a complete absence of risk.   Forecasting the ultimate legal outcome of operations related to advertising seems to possess an inordinately low degree of confident predictability.   Only by abandoning the field can one forego all advertising activity which could possibly be held invalid.

Hence it is often unavoidable to choose between the detriments that may follow if contemplated conduct turns out to be unlawful against those attendant upon rejecting the program.

The factors to be taken into account in such judgments are, for the lawyer, as close an approximation as possible of the likelihood that the act will eventually be held improper, and the potential magnitude of penalties in that event.   Involved here are not only the monetary liabilities attendant upon governmental prosecutions or resulting from private damage actions, but also (here the client's point of view enters into the mix) the effects upon the image of the company with the public, or within professional circles of importance to the company (e.g., medical, engineering, security analysts), or in the eyes of governmental administrators with whom the company must live, not overlooking congressional committees.

The client, of course, must also evaluate the importance of the proposed undertaking from the business point of view.   And, most important of all, it is the client who must finally judge whether the potential commercial benefit does or does not outweigh the lawyer's evaluation of legal risk.

This process is neither immoral nor unethical; nor is it avoidable. The laws which govern advertising are largely technical, economic, and amoral.   Even issues over misleading advertising turn not upon the moral honesty of an advertiser or agency but upon the technical exactitude of the representation when measured against the subjective impression of Federal Trade Commissioners (at times only two in number) as to what the advertisement may mean to members of the public whom the Commission rates as being notably ignorant, credulous, and literately inept.

Even utmost honesty cannot assure legality when such are the criteria.   Thus, the most honorable of advertisers and agencies must still deal with the possibility that their advertising may nonetheless be proclaimed unlawful.   They cannot escape the task of deciding when to and when not to accept that business risk.

The prime purpose of this chapter, in short, is to assist those concerned with the operational aspects of advertising to sense areas which are likely to involve legal complications, so that they may be communicated to counsel for his earliest and most creative attention, and his advice understood and utilized most fruitfully. The thrust will be problem identification and control rather than solution.

ADVERTISER–AGENCY–THIRD-PARTY RELATIONSHIPS

A. Advertiser-Agency

1. Respective Functions   In simplest terms, it is the function of the agency to render services and of the advertiser to pay for them.   The duties of advertiser and agency, each to the other, are keyed essentially to those concepts.   There is a broad spectrum of choices to be made in each area, and the selection is a matter of business, not legal, judgment.   The agency's service obligation may range, for example, from mere preparation of copy and artwork to copy or market testing and research, furnishing of computer bank data, media planning and administration, designing, conducting, or addressing sales or trade meetings.   Advertisers who engage several agencies may wish to centralize in one of them the performance for all of certain services, such as media or broadcast program purchasing.

Modes of compensation keyed to the particular agency services involved may include virtually limitless variants and combinations of media commissions, special fees, time charges, cost-plus arrangements, or straight fees somewhat in the nature of legal retainers or accountants' charges.

2. The Written Contract   Thus, when an advertiser and an advertising agency enter into working relationships with each other, the fundamental legal question they must face is the extent to which they desire to have a comprehensive catalog of their respective obligations reduced to a formal, written contract.   This is essentially a matter of individual preference, and arrangements have been recorded in documents running the gamut from multipage, fine-print instruments attempting to specify the correlative rights and duties in every detailed contingency, to a simple interchange of letters of appointment and acceptance to act as agency for the client.   The Association of National Advertisers and the American Association of Advertising Agencies maintain files of illustrative agreements and contractual provisions for their members' reference.   These can be helpful, and should be consulted.

a. DETAILED OR GENERAL?   The arguments in favor of extensive detailing are that possible areas of controversy arising out of unanticipated future events will be obviated (1) by the mere process of stretching minds to forecast all possible eventualities in the attempt to provide for them in the contract, and (2) by negotiating the resolutions of such situations before they become active issues. If so, greater amicability will certainly be preserved in the subsequent relationship between advertiser and agency.

The contrary school of thought is that such details impose too much rigidity upon a relational process which is best for both parties when left flexible to cope with developments as rapidly changeable and constantly fluid as those with which the advertiser and agency are concerned.

The author's view is that most instances are best served by an intermediate approach. Realistically, if sufficient rapport and goodwill do not exist between an advertiser and its agency to stimulate every effort to accommodate to new situations, a long contract will not keep their association intact. When their disposition to continue working together is strong enough, they will find their way through new or controversial situations as they occur. If the underlying relationship has become stale, however, it will not be improved by one party or the other standing on its technical rights under a legal document, and such resolutions will, therefore, probably be temporary at best. Indeed, they might even be sources of additional provocation.

b. TERMINATION PROVISION. It is important, however, under this concept that there be a carefully formulated record of agreement between the advertiser and the agency as to their particular rights upon termination of their relationship, for when that stage is reached the climate is less conducive to rational and cooperative accord as to who is entitled to what.

A predetermined specification for termination, made when a will to compromise is present, can reduce this area of abrasion and make the severance more orderly and efficient. Fortunately, the issues which are most likely to create strife at this stage can be anticipated. Generally, they involve the time of termination, final compensation arrangements, and ownership of property, including plans and creative ideas.

(1) TIME. The contract should ordinarily be made terminable at the will of either party and specify the length of the notice period, e.g., "sixty days' written notice." Since the relationship will usually prove fruitless for both when either of the parties becomes basically and unresolvably dissatisfied with the relationship, the termination

period should be made as short as possible so that the advertiser and agency can be free to seek out other pastures. A good yardstick for determining the length of the notice period will relate to the amount of time both parties reasonably need to put their houses in order once notice has been given.

An agency which must undertake costly training of personnel or other major adjustments in order to take on the account may want the contract for a minimum period, or a provision calling for reimbursement of these expenses if the advertiser terminates before a specified period has run.

(2) COMPENSATION. Because of its nature, the agency's work cannot be turned off like a faucet. Undoubtedly some of its product will spill over into a period following the notice of termination, or even after the cessation of the relationship. It is fair that the agency should receive remuneration for this work if it inures to the benefit of the advertiser. Conversely, it is also appropriate that the advertiser's duty to compensate cease within a reasonable time after the notice, and that it be modified to the extent that past fees and payments may be allocable to such items.

There is no pat formula for balancing these equities. The agreement may provide for regular compensation up to the notice date or to the actual termination date. Reimbursement based upon agency commitments to media and suppliers can be predicated upon their cancelability and whether they were made before or after the notice to terminate. Or the advertiser and agency may want to simplify the compensation procedures by providing for a lump-sum settlement based on an average monthly compensation figure or some other equation.

(3) PROPERTY. At termination, rights to the agency's creative work product and materials can become a knotty issue. The advertiser and agency can each produce cogent arguments why it should be entitled to the property. As in the case of compensation, it is best that such debate be deliberated and resolved while the relationship is being established. Once again, many options are open to the parties. For example, ownership may be keyed to compensation, so that the advertiser retains all work for which the agency has received its normal compensation, and conversely, the agency retains all materials for which, because of the termination, it will not receive payment. Or the advertiser may inherit only such work product as it

has approved, but not that which it has rejected. Alternatively, the advertiser may be given an option to purchase—at cost plus, or hourly, or other formula—such materials (concrete or abstract) as the agency has created in the course of serving it to which the advertiser would not otherwise be entitled.

A most simple solution, and one that will eliminate a prime source of controversy, is to grant the advertiser full freedom to use anything which has been submitted or suggested to it by the agency. This is not so extreme as it might first seem. Rationally, it may be considered that the agency's overall compensation entitles the advertiser to own whatever the agency has conceived for it during the time of its paid service. And the concept parallels the practice familiar to many agencies and advertisers of refusing to accept suggestions from outside sources without an unqualified waiver of rights by the submitter. Less than that leaves the advertiser unreasonably vulnerable to lapses of memory or gaps in records as to suggestions casually made years earlier, or even to fraudulent or grossly mistaken claims. An intermediate approach might be to grant the advertiser full rights as to any proposals made longer ago than a stipulated number of years prior to their use; the particular period of time being chosen to reflect that during which the advertiser may reasonably be expected to maintain and search records of such submissions, or to remember them, if oral.

Provision should be included that upon termination the agency will assign and transfer to the advertiser (and take all steps in aid thereof) all media contracts, and all other materials or agreements which may be outstanding in the agency's name, or in its possession, but in fact in the client's interest.

c. THIRD-PARTY LIABILITY PROVISION. The activities of an agency or advertiser may under certain circumstances subject the other to legal liabilities to third persons. These areas will be dealt with more specifically in later sections of this chapter. In general, however, they fall into the two broad classifications, referred to in law as *contract* and *tort*. The first includes those obligations which are created by voluntary agreement between specific persons and made legally enforceable under the law of contracts. Typical of these would be liabilities to pay for services or goods furnished by media, suppliers of materials, and employees, artists, performers, or others engaged to render personal services.

Torts embrace violations of those rights which the law recognizes as belonging to members of the public generally, as a matter of public policy and independent of contractual agreements. Libel and slander, invasion of privacy, infringement of copyrights, and trademarks are examples of tortious conduct.

Since, as will be discussed later, the contract liabilities of an advertiser and an agency will turn largely upon the extent to which the latter has been authorized to enter into agreements as agent of the advertiser, it is advisable that the scope of such authority be recorded, if not in the original written contract, then at least in supplements to it.

Where torts, or even criminal exposure, are concerned, it is possible for the conduct of either the advertiser or the agency to impose responsibility on the other. An advertiser, for example, may—albeit in good faith—furnish its agency with inaccurate information which can leave the agency vulnerable to government enforcement or penalty proceedings. An agency, on the other hand, might fail to obtain proper clearance, thereby subjecting the advertiser to liability for right-of-privacy violations or copyright-infringement claims. Provision in their contract might, therefore, be desired governing the extent and conditions of indemnification by each of the other as related to the degree of underlying fault.

3. Status of Matters Not Covered by Express Agreement   With rare exceptions that do not warrant discussion here, rights and duties as between advertiser and agency can be determined by agreement and will be given effect by a court in accordance with their mutually specified arrangement. No contract or set of contracts, however, can be prepared with the foresight to encompass every conceivable future development; nor can such instruments be written with a clarity that can preclude later dissension in some respect or other as to their intended meaning.

Where such gaps or ambiguities become the area of controversy, a court's first effort will be to ascertain what the parties had actually and conjointly intended the answer to be before the conflict arose, even though they did not express it definitively in writing. The court will search for clues to such intention in the past conduct of the parties in similar or rationally analogous situations, in the custom of the trade as to how such matters are ordinarily treated (if such a pattern in fact exists), and in such shreds of expression as may be found in correspondence, memoranda, or oral interchanges. In other words, anything which relevantly casts light upon a mutually entertained, although not articulated, understanding between the parties might sway the court's decision as to what standard shall govern them.   If such search proves fruitless, some independent principle of law (e.g., a general duty to observe ordinary standards of reasonable care and competency, or of honest and faithful dealing) may, in a relatively few instances, be available to serve as a guide to the court's ruling.   Failing all that, the court will be compelled to hold that the party who makes claim against the other (ordinarily the plaintiff, but in some instances a defendant who has asserted a counterclaim) has not succeeded in proving his right to a judgment.

All the uncertainty which such a legal process entails is, of course, the greatest argument in favor of as faithful a written record as possible of precisely how the advertiser and agency wish their relationship to be governed in each important respect.   Nonetheless, the practicalities of the situation, earlier mentioned, make this goal more ideal than attainable. ·

In the main, however, it will ordinarily suffice for the initial written agreement to provide in detail for matters which involve liabilities between advertiser, the agency, or both to third parties or to the government (such as are discussed later), or for those as to which it is foreseen that controversy will have to be resolved in circumstances when harmony between the advertiser and agency cannot be anticipated as a motivating factor to produce a reasonable and mutually acceptable contemporaneous accommodation (e.g., severance of the relationship, or matters which will involve large sums of money or highly valuable property).

Different advertisers and agencies have various views as to what is proper with respect to an agency's representing conflicting accounts. They disagree even over what constitutes such a conflict.   Since this is a debate that can develop a high emotional charge once it arises, the criteria should be agreed upon and reduced to writing as early as possible in the relationship.

Agreements that the agency's books of account relating to its transactions for the advertiser will be open to its inspection, and that the agency will take all reasonably possible measures to protect the secrecy of confidential client information (both before and after termination), usually can, and should be detailed in writing.

Matters relating to the daily rendition of and compensation for the agency's services can be broadly described at the outset, with more detailed provisions added from time to time to cover specific situations on a current basis as they arise. A coincident desire of advertiser and agency to keep working together will in most instances facilitate a meeting of their minds. If not, then the termination provisions will come into play before long.

B. Third Parties

Aside from the rights and duties between advertisers and agencies, there is the area of their respective liabilities to third persons. Generally, this group breaks down into four major categories, although with considerable overlapping: suppliers, the public, competitors, and the government.

1. Suppliers These include the various media, printers, photographers, models, performers, program producers, and others who provide personal services or materials. Whether the advertiser, the advertising agency, or both jointly will be liable to a particular supplier depends on the combined effect of the agreements or understandings among all the parties. For example, if the advertiser authorizes the agency to contract with a broadcaster for facilities, the advertiser, under the law of agency, would be solely liable on the contract if the advertising agency acts properly within its authority and discloses the identity of its principal (the advertiser) to the media at the time the contract is made.

Yet the agency and the third-party supplier are free to agree amongst themselves that the latter will look only to the former for payment, thus absolving the advertiser-principal of responsibility to the supplier and making the advertising agency solely liable. This, presently, would invariably be the case in the broadcaster situation since the current "Standard Order Blank" contains such a provision. If the parties do not wish the agency to be thus liable on such standard order forms, the agency should be authorized to amend them by striking or modifying that provision on their faces. Conversely, where the advertiser does not wish to stand liable directly to the broadcaster, it should be stipulated that the agency will *not* alter that clause.

A certain amount of confusion is created by the fact that the word "agency" does not necessarily carry into the term "advertising agency" the connotations which it possesses in legal parlance. The juridical concept of an agent is one who possesses the power to enter into a contract on behalf of another (his "principal") which then is binding upon the other and not upon the agent. Usually such authorization must be expressly given by the principal to the agent but it can, in certain special circumstances, be implied as a matter of law. The mere engagement by an advertiser of an advertising agency does not, in and of itself, give rise to an agency relationship of the legal sort. This, then, becomes a consideration of importance when the advertising agency, in the fulfillment of its functions, enters into contracts with suppliers, media, or personnel for the benefit of the advertiser. Unless authorized to do so—by contract or operation of circumstances—as a legal agent, it is the advertising agency rather than the advertiser who will stand primarily responsible.

Generally speaking, then, the advertiser will be solely liable on contracts to suppliers made by the advertising agency if: (1) the advertiser has given authority for the agency so to contract, or has acted in such a manner as to lead the supplier reasonably to believe that the advertising agency has such authority; (2) the advertising agency properly acts within the authority given to it expressly or by implication from the conduct of its principal; (3) the advertising agency discloses the identity of its principal to the supplier; and (4) there is no agreement, express or to be implied, between the advertising agency and supplier to fix the liability solely upon the agency. Conversely, the advertising agent may be held liable to the supplier on the contract if both agree to that effect, or if the agent fails to disclose his principal, or if the agent acts beyond the authority conferred upon him by the advertiser (expressly or implicitly) or by trade custom.

Moreover, liability may be affected by union arrangements which are applicable to suppliers such as actors, musicians, directors, and others who provide such specialized services. Union contract rules should also be perused for their effect on such matters as employee rights and method of compensation. This is especially important in television commercials, where the particular manner of using a performer (e.g., featured, background, part of choral group, voice off camera) can change costs by many thousands of dollars. Customarily, advertising agencies will have experts in this area on their staffs. Their detailed knowledge of the provisions of contracts with such unions as Screen Actors Guild (SAG) and American Federation of Television and Radio Artists (AFTRA) should be drawn upon constantly in planning commercials so that wasteful or uneconomical use of talent or production personnel may be avoided.

Where the advertiser stands liable for payment to a third party, delivery to the agency of funds to cover the obligation does not exonerate the advertiser until the creditor has actually been paid. Where the advertiser has any concern over the financial status of the agency, he should, therefore, consider special means to see to it that the monies are transmitted directly to the supplier or otherwise handled in a manner that they cannot be seized upon by general creditors of the agency, or that the suppliers agree to look only to the agency for payment.

2. Competitors   Potential liabilities to this group arise from the dissemination of advertising which infringes upon a competitor's trademark or copyright, improperly disparages or defames his goods or business practices, or is untruthful in a way injurious to the competitor.

In these areas the major risk falls upon the advertiser. Having the final voice over the advertisement's content and publication, he must bear primary responsibility for its consequences. Moreover, the advertiser is more likely than the agency to be aware when an advertisement is unfairly competitive vis-à-vis business rivals. Thus, in practice, competitors have usually sued the advertiser alone. In theory, however, there is no reason why an agency, under some circumstances, could not be held legally accountable. If, for example, it negligently conducted product performance tests or research which caused the advertiser, reasonably relying upon them, to authorize the publication of a false comparative advertising claim, the agency might be liable to its client for his losses suffered as the result of an action against him by the competitor. The agency would be liable, of course, for any recovery against its client by a competitor—or a member of the general public—for any wrongs, such as those mentioned in the preceding and following paragraphs, if, as suggested earlier, it falls within the scope of an indemnification clause.

3. The Public   Defamation, invasion of privacy, copyright infringement, and piracy of another's creative ideas are types of conduct which precipitate problems with individual members of the public. The availability and widespread use of insurance to cover these potential risks has obviated the practical importance of fixing responsibility between advertiser and agency.   Care should be exercised, however, to make certain that insurance policies adequately covering the parties are actually in existence.

Breach of a warranty found in an advertisement is an expanding source of liabilities which, unless they fall within a product liability policy, are not usually covered by insurance.

Each of these subjects will be covered in greater detail in a separate later section of this chapter.

4. Government   While there is a plethora of federal, state, and local laws and regulations directly affecting advertising, and a host of governmental agencies charged with enforcing them (to be discussed), the primary concern of most advertisers and agencies is with the Federal Trade Commission, the Federal Food and Drug Administration, and the Post Office Department in their policing of advertising.

Just when an advertising agency will be held jointly liable along with the advertiser is not certain, although there is no doubt, as a legal proposition, that it can be so charged.   In recent years, the Federal Trade Commission (FTC), at least, has shown an increased tendency to attack the agency.   The famous Colgate case (the sandpaper mock-up) is representative.   Addressing itself to the advertising agency's culpability the Commission stated:

> While [the advertiser], as principal, is unquestionably responsible for the advertisements broadcast on its behalf, it would be strange indeed if [the agency], as the moving party in originating, preparing and publishing the commercials, and having full knowledge not only that the claim was false but that the "proof" offered to the public to support it was a sham, should be relieved from responsibility.

The United States Court of Appeals affirmed the Commission, noting that it could "see no reason why advertising agencies, which are now big business, should be able to shirk from at least prima facie responsibility for conduct in which they participate." Colgate-Palmolive Co. *v.* FTC, 326 F.2d 517, 523–524 (1st Cir. 1963) reversed on other grounds, 380 U.S. 374 (1965).

Thus, an agency which actively participates in the formulation of the advertisement and knows or has reason to know that it is false is vulnerable to Federal Trade Commission attack. The ramifications, expensive and aggravating, of such a procedure will be outlined later.

C. Agency-Employee Relations

The chief legal problems associated with employees are pirating of accounts or personnel and disclosure of confidential information. These raise essentially two questions: (1) What legal rights does the agency have when such abuses occur and (2) what can it do to prevent them?

1. Agency's Legal Rights in Piracy Situations   Generally speaking, the agency probably has no legal remedy against an employee who does not formulate and implement the piracy scheme until *after* he has left the agency's employ.   Absent contractual provision, cessation of the employment relationship terminates his duty of loyalty to the employer and places him on an equal footing with the rest of the agency's competitors.   One of the hallmarks of the competitive process is the right of business rivals to vie for each other's customers and talent, and courts will not intervene against that.   Promises of better service, offers of a better salary, and all such similar overtures normally used to attract another's clients or employees are not unfair methods of competition.

While the law does deem it a wrong for one person knowingly to induce the breach of a contract between others, many courts will not invoke this doctrine where, as is usually the case with the agency, the customers and employees are under no contractual obligation to remain for a lengthy, definite term.   However, some states have held to the contrary.   For example, a New Jersey court, in Wear-Ever Aluminum, Inc. *v.* Towncraft Industries Inc., 182 A.2d 387 (1962), held that defendant by hiring thirty-five of plaintiff's salesmen, had induced the breach of their employment contracts; even though, under those agreements, the salesmen were free to leave the plaintiff's employ at any time.   Thus, in some jurisdictions, the inducing-breach theory may provide the agency with a remedy, especially where, as was the case in Wear-Ever, there is a substantial loss of employees or customers which severely cripples or threatens the viability of the business.

If the employee plots his piracy *before* he leaves the agency, he may be held liable, because of the conflict of his own interests with the duty of loyalty he owes to a present employer.   In Duane Jones Co., Inc. *v.* Burke, 306 N.Y. 172 (1954), a group of the plaintiff agency's directors and employees agreed while in its employ to leave en masse, set up their own shop, and stock it with plaintiff's accounts and staff. Their venture proved quite successful and within a short time the new agency had acquired nine of the plaintiff's accounts and about half of its personnel.   In sustaining a $300,000 verdict for the plaintiff, the New York Court of Appeals cited four facts which it felt mandated approval of the jury award: (1) Defendants occupied positions of trust and confidence with plaintiff; (2) they conspired to injure plaintiff while in such positions and thus were false to the fundamental duties of loyalty and fair dealing owed an employer; (3) they profited by such conspiracy, and (4) plaintiff was substantially damaged.

It is clear from the opinion that the absence of any one of these facts would have been fatal to the plaintiff's action.   Thus an agency which would rely upon the rule of this case must be prepared to prove each of the four elements.

One final point must be stressed.   The law governing business conduct undergoes constant and significant reevaluation.   The courts demand and enforce increasingly high standards of ethics in the commercial world.   As a result, decisions are likely to crop up which defy rationalization under precedent cases and doctrines.

In short, the future may see increased legal protection for the agency in piracy situations.

2. Trade Secrets   It is usually when a key employee changes jobs that problems arise in this area.   As a general rule, he is free to take with him his own skills, experience, and general knowledge, but not his past employer's business secrets.   A business or trade secret is usually considered to be any type of information "which is used in one's business, and which gives an opportunity to obtain an advantage over competitors who do not know or use it."   [Restatement of Torts, §757, comment *b* (1939).]   Whether the information is "secret" will usually depend upon the extent to which it is known to outsiders and the degree of difficulty a competitor would have in properly acquiring it.   For example, a business's sales figures, advertising expenditures, and organizational structure will not be considered secrets if a rival can secure or construct the information from trade publications or sources other than the complaining company's private records.   However, information that an agency's client is about to launch a vigorous campaign for a new product may constitute a trade secret, or at least protectable confidential information, if the client and agency have taken steps to keep the nature of the campaign and product a secret, and if the secrecy is important to the commercial success of the venture.   In such a situation, the agency or indeed the client, since it is his interests which are primarily at stake, may be able to enjoin the defecting employee from revealing this information or prohibit his new employer from using it.   In deciding whether to grant such an injunction the court will weigh the extent of the possible injury that exposure of the information would cause the agency or client against the effect such an injunction would have on the employee's ability to find new employment, or upon his new employer's capacity to conduct business in a properly vigorous competitive manner.

The outcome of these cases can be quite unpredictable and will depend on such factors as the nature of the particular industry, the extent to which the employee's job responsibilities encompassed the activities involved in formulating the "secret," and whether he knew that the employer guarded the information as confidential.   The results in such cases turn immeasurably upon the ethical aura which attaches to the defendants' conduct, and the degree of moral aversion or commercial callousness that characterizes the subjective orientation toward it of the particular courts that decide them.

Certainly the agency has a strong case where its employee has no claim of ownership to the information and simply uses it to tantalize a competitor into giving him a better position.   Also, many states make it a misdemeanor to bribe employees in order to obtain a rival's secrets.   [See, for example, N.Y. Penal Law §180.00.]   However, short of these intentional and flagrant types of trade-secret infringement, the agency's right to block disclosure of confidential information in the hands of a former employee cannot be flatly stated in terms of a pat rule, and will ultimately depend on the facts and atmosphere of each particular case.

3. Preventive Measures   Agencies can expand, strengthen, and clarify their rights in these situations by incorporating post-employment restraints into the employee's contract.   Such provisions prohibit the ex-employee from engaging in specified activities for a prescribed period of time.   They must be drafted with extreme care.   The law generally abhors restrictions upon the freedom of an individual to work in a position or for an employer of his own choosing, and—especially—to engage in those pursuits for which his experience particularly equips him.   Contracts which purport to limit such rights are disfavored as a matter of public policy, and are, therefore, enforced cautiously and narrowly at most.

Thus, to be valid, such restraints must meet certain rigorously applied criteria.   First, they must be "reasonable" (i.e., not excessive) as to the time and area of their restrictions.   A contract which bars an employee from competing with his former employer for "six months in Illinois" might be reasonable, whereas "six years throughout the United States" would ordinarily be held unreasonable.

Second, the restraint must reflect a real need on the part of the agency to protect a legitimate and substantial business interest.   In this regard, the agency's customers and secrets would appear in the eyes of the law to be worthy objects of protection, but the limitations upon the employee must not exceed what is necessary to serve those ends.

Third, the agency's need for the restraint must be greater than the hardships it causes the departing employee.

A post-employment restraint which meets these tests will probably be upheld, with one caveat.   Some states have specific statutes which limit such restrictive contracts.   California, for example, prohibits them entirely, except in connection with the sale of a business.   New York allows them only with respect to employees possessed of company trade secrets, or having unique talents.   In short, the applicability and content of particular state laws must be studied.   Also, there are two important procedural rules which the agency should consider with regard to restrictive agreements.   First, it is preferable to settle the agreement with the employee *before* he is engaged. This prevents him from later claiming that he was coerced into signing it in order to keep his job.   Second, the agency should adapt the agreement to fit the particular circumstances of each employee. Boiler-plate contracts can lead to trouble, because restraints valid as against one employee may not be so for another.   Stock-option agreements are often utilized to effectuate arrangements which cannot be implemented via an employment contract alone.

LEGAL ASPECTS OF THE ADVERTISEMENT

Thus far the discussion has dealt with the legal implications arising from the formation and operation of relationships between parties brought together in the course of the advertising process. The following sections will explore the legal problems which may spring from the end product of those relationships—the advertising itself.

A. Deceptive Claims

Although the question of whether a representation is deceptive will ultimately depend on the circumstances of each case, the nature of the product or service involved, and the applicable standards of the particular forum in which its truthfulness is tested, there are certain general rules to guide in the preparation of copy claims.

1. Understanding by the Public Generally, to invalidate an advertisement it is not necessary for the complainant to prove that deception has actually taken place. Usually all that need be shown is that the representations have a capacity to deceive a significant portion of the public.

The courts, and such administrative bodies as the Federal Trade Commission, have made it clear that the "public" includes not only the educated and skeptical but also the ignorant and credulous. Thus the advertiser always runs the risk that his claims will be measured against the standard of the meaning they are thought to convey to people of that character, which may turn out much differently from the way he intended it to be understood by normally intelligent purchasers.

Take, for example, the case of the hair-dye manufacturer who advertised that his product was a permanent hair color. What he meant and thought the average woman would comprehend was that the dye would not wash out. The Federal Trade Commission held, however, that the permanency claim would be interpreted by a substantial number of women to mean that the dye would color hair yet to be grown—in other words, that one application would last a lifetime. [Gelb v. FTC, 144 F.2d 580 (2d Cir. 1944).]

The case reflects the fact that the touchstone of consumer intelligence against which a claim will be evaluated is generally a low one, and advertisers must prepare their copy to ensure that even the stupid and gullible cannot be misled. The case also illustrates the commission's almost carte blanche power to declare ex cathedra what is the public's understanding of an advertisement, even in the face of contrary evidence, for every one of the many consumer witnesses who had testified stated that she did *not* interpret the claim in the manner held by the commission.

The advertiser must also take into consideration the aspirations and characteristics of the particular audience to which the advertisement is directed.   An advertisement addressed to children, for example, may be prohibited if it misleads them, even though adults would not be deceived by it.   Similarly, persons in their eagerness to find relief from pain, obesity, pimples, or some other unpleasant condition may be inclined to read promises (which the advertiser never intended) into claims beamed in their direction.   Conversely, however, an advertisement which is selectively aimed at an audience of particular sophistications (e.g., engineers, purchasing agents for specialized equipment) will be construed in light of their refined perceptions in reading.   This is significant for trade, industrial, and professional advertising.

2. Total-impression Test   In determining the meaning of the advertisement, courts and administrative agencies look to its entirety, judging it by the overall impression.   Each of its individual assertions may be true and nondeceptive standing alone; yet they may combine or juxtapose to give a composite impression that is misleading.

For example, an advertisement which prominently headlines a broad claim may be deceptive if any necessary qualifications or conditions are put in the body in a way that a casual reader would not perceive them.

3. Meaning of the Words Used   The advertiser should strive for words that are precise and unequivocal in their meaning and implications.   Ambiguous or vague terms will almost inevitably lead to trouble.   For example, if a claim is susceptible to two interpretations—one deceptive and the other nondeceptive—it will be measured against the misleading construction, and it is no defense that the advertisement could be, or even by most readers would be, construed nondeceptively.

Vague or generalized claims will be interpreted in their broadest sense.   A representation that XYZ's medication is "for colds" can mean that it will cure all colds regardless of their causes.   Even the narrower claim that the remedy will "relieve colds" may be too general.   Such a representation may still be interpreted that the product will completely relieve all symptoms in all cold cases.   Another example of the vagueness problem arises from use of the word "guaranteed."   By itself, the word implies that the advertiser will unconditionally indemnify the purchaser for all damage arising from any shortcoming of the product.

Generally speaking, all guarantees should "clearly and conspicuously" disclose the parts of the product covered; the duration of the guarantee; the duties imposed upon the person who seeks to use it (e.g., return the product at his own expense, pay a service charge); what the guarantor will do under the guarantee; and the identity of the guarantor.   Aside from the fact that the guarantor must reveal all the conditions of the guarantee, he is also responsible for the truth of any material representations implicit therein concerning the product itself.   For example, an advertiser who guarantees his batteries for two years has made a claim that they will normally last for that period.

Use of the word "free" is another source of confusion.   As in the case of guarantees, all conditions which the purchaser must meet in order to obtain the "free" commodity must be fully and clearly set forth in immediate conjunction with the term.   Moreover, if the purchaser must buy a certain article to get the free one, the advertiser cannot increase the usual price of that article or reduce its quality or quantity.

A recapitulation of the Federal Trade Commission's views as to the requirements relevant to advertising guarantees and "free" offers (as part of the larger subject of deceptive price claims) has been prepared by it in the form of "Guides."   While these guides are merely advisory, they should be seriously considered.   They are, at the least, a solemn warning that the Commission will not brook disrespect for them; and their major principles have been upheld in court rulings. Since space limitations preclude a full exposition herein of all the material contained in these guides, it is recommended that they be consulted where a more detailed analysis is desirable.   Copies of the guides can be obtained from any office of the Federal Trade Commission.[1]

---

[1] The Commission has issued additional guides which pertain to the special areas of advertising adhesive compositions, cigarettes, fallout shelters, radiation-monitoring instruments, shell homes, chemicals used to melt snow and ice, watches, leakproof batteries, and automobile tires.

Even if the words in an advertisement are specific and unequivocal, they may still be capable of conveying a misleading impression. Terminology can develop meanings and associations in the public's mind which do not accord with strict dictionary definitions. Moreover, the context in which words appear can often produce subtle but significant variations in their meaning. Artwork and visuals, especially, can greatly affect understanding, as can headlines, sequence, and typographic emphasis.

4. Silence as Misrepresentation   A statement which is itself truthful may yet be deceptive if the omission of facts bearing upon it creates a false impression. The case of P. Lorillard Co. *v.* FTC, 186 F.2d 52 (4th Cir. 1950) is illustrative. There a leading magazine published a laboratory study which concluded that all the major cigarette brands were equally harmful because their respective differences in tar and nicotine content were so small as to be insignificant from a health standpoint. The table used in the article to demonstrate these minute variations in content did show that Lorillard's brand had the least amount. Fastening on this table, the manufacturer advertised that a leading study showed its cigarettes to be the lowest in tar and nicotine of all those tested. This was held to be deceptive on the ground that by disclosing only a portion of the article Lorillard had created an entirely misleading impression that the differences in content were significant to health, when in fact the true outcome of the study had been to show the opposite.

This principle has been extended most recently to cover over-the-counter iron and vitamin preparations offered for relief of such symptoms as tiredness, loss of strength, run-down feeling, nervousness, or irritability. Although recognizing that those products will relieve such symptoms when they have been caused by a deficiency in the vitamins or iron which the medicines contain, the Commission also decided that the vast majority of cases presenting those symptoms are due to other causes which cannot be satisfactorily treated by self-medication with them. It held, therefore, that it would not be sufficient in advertising the remedies to limit the promise of relief expressly to such symptoms only if they are due to the simple nutri-

---

Views attributed throughout this chapter to the Commission must be rechecked from time to time. Changes in personnel, and in prevailing economic, social, or political concepts, are apt to be reflected in shifting attitudes of the Commission in related areas.

tional deficiencies.   That, according to the Commission, would not take care of the further implicit misimpression that such causation is more common—and the products thus beneficial to more people—than is true.   To correct that silent misrepresentation the Commission ordered that the advertisements affirmatively disclose:

> ... clearly and conspicuously that: (1) in the great majority of persons who experience such symptoms, these symptoms are not caused by a deficiency of one or more of the vitamins contained in the preparation or by iron deficiency or iron deficiency anemia; and (2) for such persons the preparation will be of no benefit.

5. Objective and Subjective (Puffery) Claims   There is a distinction made between representations which attribute objective qualities to a product ("This car gets 20 miles to the gallon") and those which merely state the advertiser's personal and subjective opinion of his product ("This car is fabulous").   The advertiser is held strictly accountable for the truth of the objective claims, whereas the law is generally permissive for the purely subjective ones, primarily because they are readily understood by the viewer for what they are: nothing more than a self-serving boast, and devoid of any concrete meaning so far as tangible performance is concerned.

Sometimes, however, the line between objective and subjective claims is not clear.   For example, use of the word "perfect" to describe a lubricant for cars was considered to be puffing [Kidder Oil Co. v. FTC, 117 F.2d 892 (7th Cir. 1941)] whereas the claim that yogurt is nature's "perfect" food was held to be a representation of an objective fact, i.e., that the product contained a complete complement of all necessary nutritional elements.   [Dannon Milk Products Inc., 61 FTC 840 (1962).]   In disallowing the puffing defense, the Commission noted:

> With the present day emphasis on dieting and the importance of nutritional values, to make a claim that a food is perfect (a claim which concerns nutrition), is more than mere puffing or an exaggeration of qualities; it is a misrepresentation as to a material fact.

Presumably, "nature's food with the perfect taste" would have brought a different result, although in those instances (tea, for example) where quality of taste connotes some objectivity of standard, such a representation might not be exempt from legal control.

6. Materiality Not all misrepresentations, even objective ones, are illegal. Those which, as a practical matter, do not induce or influence any substantial segment of the public to purchase a product or service cause no injury to either consumer or competitor and thus are not legally actionable. For example, if an automobile manufacturer's advertisement should overstate the number of miles of roads in the United States, it is doubtful that such an inaccuracy would affect a purchaser's decision.

Claims which are capable of having such an effect, however, are deemed "material." Practically speaking, most representations will fall into this category as they are ordinarily offered for that very purpose.

It is no defense that a misrepresented product is equally as good as the one which the public was led to believe it would get. For example, offering used oil as new is materially deceptive even though the re-refined oil is identical to new in composition and performance capability. The consumer is entitled to get what he has been told he will have, if that is what he wants, even though there is no rational basis for his preference. [Kerran *v.* FTC, 265 F.2d 246 (10th Cir. 1959), *cert. denied* 361 U.S. 818 (1959).]

Such consumer predilections need not relate to intrinsic qualities of a product. A number of people may prefer goods which are imported, or domestic, government approved, recommended by a well-known institution, or endorsed and used by a famous personality. Claims relating to such matters would be material. This is true, as well, of representations concerning the status of the advertiser. Whether he is a wholesaler or retailer, a profit or nonprofit organization, affiliated with government or private, or actually operates a mill, a laboratory, or the like, or merely distributes the goods of others who do so, is likely to bear materially upon purchase decisions.

Similarly, it is a materially deceptive practice to exaggerate the usual price of an article so that the normal price may be held forth as a sales price, even though it is the fair value of the product and the purchaser receives his money's worth.

Likewise, it is unlawful for a national manufacturer to advertise a list or preticketed price that appreciably exceeds the highest price at which substantial sales in the product are made. (The Federal Trade Commission "Guides against Deceptive Pricing" contain a detailed analysis of these and related problems.)

Notwithstanding that a commodity measures up to intrinsic qualities attributed to it, an advertiser can still be guilty of material deception if he uses misrepresentation as a means to induce the public to purchase it.

This was dramatized by a Supreme Court decision in Colgate-Palmolive Co. v. FTC, 380 U.S. 374 (1965).   There a television demonstration depicted a razor cutting a clean swath down sandpaper to which the advertiser's shaving cream had just been applied.   A Plexiglas acrylic plastic mock-up had been substituted for actual sandpaper which, for technical reasons, did not reproduce well through the television system.   The Commission contended that even if real sandpaper could have been shaved exactly as shown, the demonstration was, nevertheless, materially deceptive because viewers had been mislead into believing that they had actually seen proof made of the claim (with Rapid Shave one can shave sandpaper) before their own eyes when in fact they had seen only an illusion. The high court agreed.

While its decision raises more questions than it answers, its essence seems to be that where visual demonstrations are used to prove and verify independently a claim an advertiser makes for his product, everything used in producing such graphic material must be authentic, unless affirmative disclosure to the contrary is made.

Whether misrepresentation of this type (undisclosed use of artifice) is unlawful is dependent upon its materiality to the buying decision. Where, for example, a commercial shows persons in the background supposedly eating ice cream, which actually is mashed potatoes so that it will not melt, and the audio proclaims how delicious it is, there probably would be no problem.   But if the picture zooms in to a product close-up while color or texture of the "ice cream" is extolled, the legal situation would be quite different—notwithstanding that the true color and texture of the ice cream, when purchased, will be precisely what the televised mashed potatoes make it seem to be.

There are further situations where misrepresentations will be prohibited even though they do not affect the ultimate purchase decision.   For example, advertising a well-known product at a very low price in order to lure customers into a store for the purpose of selling them something else is deceptive if the store has no intention of honoring its offer.   This "bait advertising" is unlawful.   (FTC has issued "Guides against Bait Advertising" on this subject.)

Similarly, deception designed to gain initial contact with a potential customer may be unlawful even though the misrepresentation is corrected before any purchase is made and hence cannot affect that decision. For example, misstatements in advertisements designed only to solicit inquiries from the public which then will be pursued in a completely truthful manner can nonetheless be illegal, as may be falsehoods calculated to get a house-to-house solicitor's foot in the door.

Perhaps one of the most extreme illustrations of holding misrepresentations unlawful even though they do not relate materially to any buying decision is found in the line of cases the Federal Trade Commission has prosecuted against "many and varied ruses [which] are often employed in obtaining information relative to debts and debtors that would not otherwise have been furnished had the true purpose for the requests for such information been disclosed." While these practices do not, as such, involve the use of advertising, the conceptual orientation of the Commission in taking legal action against them illuminates how panoramically it views the factor of materiality in misrepresentations. The Commission's "Guides against Debt Collection Deception" were effective September 20, 1965.

7. Affirmative Disclosures There exists for every product or service a vast amount of material facts which, because of its nature and limitations of time or space, will not be set forth in the advertisement. Generally, if those claims which are made are truthful and do not create a false impression, affirmative disclosure of additional facts is not required even though they might be expected to have a material bearing upon a substantial number of purchase decisions. For example, whether a manufacturer maintains a union or an open shop would have considerable influence upon many prospective customers. Yet, if his advertisement does not gratuitously open up that subject, he is under no legal compulsion to do so.

As earlier discussed, silence can sometimes generate misrepresentation where the omission of facts material to what has been claimed in an advertisement leaves a false impression. In such situations the law requires disclosure of the absent data to supply the missing half of the half-truth.

Beyond that, however, disclosure of information may also be compelled where its concealment would cause the public to assume that a product possesses a preferred characteristic which it does not in fact have, although the advertisement makes no allusion to the subject either way. For example, it has been held that consumers automatically assume, unless told otherwise, that a book is unabridged. Hence, if it is not, that fact must be revealed even though the advertiser has said nothing to abet the preconception that the book is complete. Revelation of the true composition of a product can also be required where it simulates the appearance of something else—e.g., a base metal which looks like gold. These, in short, are the situations where, for one reason or another, there is an existing presumption by a substantial segment of the public that absent anything said to the contrary a certain condition prevails. Where in fact it does not, the advertisement cannot take advantage of that presumption, but is bound to say to the contrary.

Recent developments indicate that the Federal Trade Commission will push the misrepresentation-by-silence theory as far as possible to force affirmative disclosures, especially in areas related to public health or safety.

8. Trigger Words These are words, such as "guarantee" and "free" discussed earlier, that automatically trigger certain requirements which the Federal Trade Commission, through its guides, advisory opinions, or case decisions has proclaimed must be met by the advertiser to avoid deception. We shall not cover all such expressions, but will focus on those which are the most important.

a. "NEW." The Commission has decided that "new" should be used only to describe a product which is either entirely new or has been altered in a functional and substantial manner. Further, even assuming such a product, the Commission has announced as a general proposition, subject to modification if special circumstances warrant it, that the term must be discontinued six months after the goods have been on the general market since, in the Commission's view, by that time a product ceases to be "new." It should be noted that a bona-fide test-marketing program lasting less than half a year and involving less than 15 per cent of the population will not, according to the Commission, be included in the computation of the six-month period.

b. "PROOF." "Proof" has also evoked strict Commission codes. Generally, it views any term containing that suffix—e.g., "waterproof," "rustproof," "mothproof," etc.—as an unqualified representation that the product will perform the indicated function infallibly under all possible use conditions.   Since such a high standard of performance is rarely attainable, most advertising would do best to use "proof" claims sparingly and with caution.

Trade Practice Rules, which essentially are guides issued by the Commission on an industry-by-industry basis, often contain specific reference to particular "proof" representations.   For example, guidelines for the use of the word "waterproof" are found in Trade Practice Rules for the watch, bedding, masonry waterproofing, and waterproof paper industries.   Trade Regulation Rules cover "leakproof" for dry cell batteries.

c. STATUS WORDS.   Terms connoting business status are also an object of interest.   For instance, a Commission guide states that any firm which handles textiles may not use "mill" as part of its corporate name or in any other self-characterizing manner unless it "actually owns and operates or directly and absolutely controls the manufacturing facility in which all textile materials which are sold under that name are produced."

In similar vein, the Commission has consistently held that using the terms "manufacturer" and "factory" as part of a trade name, or implying such status by use of phrases like "factory prices," "buy direct," and "no middleman," is proper only if the seller owns and operates a manufacturing plant wherein his goods are produced.

"Wholesale" and "wholesale prices" are two related expressions in which the Commission has evidenced a similar concern.   The hallmark of the wholesale function is generally held to be the sale of goods to those who intend either to resell them or use them in a manufacturing process.   Similarly, "wholesale price" is usually defined as that which retailers pay when buying for resale to the ultimate consumer, much as "factory price" is deemed to be a price prevailing to wholesalers or retailers, and hence substantially lower than retail price.   Thus, a business which sells exclusively to the general public cannot denominate itself as a wholesaler.

A less clear-cut question is whether "wholesale" is proper to describe the status and prices of a vendor who sells the identical goods at the same prices to both retailers and consumers.   The Commission has held that if such a retailer-wholesaler sells primarily to consumers and charges them prices higher than those usually paid by retailers, it cannot represent itself to the public as a wholesaler or its prices as wholesale.

According to the Commission, the "usual" prices paid by retailers are "the prices paid by the group of retailers whose purchases constitute the largest percentage of the manufacturer's total dollar volume of sales." Thus, if a manufacturer sells most of its products directly to retailers at a price lower than that charged by a small number of jobbers, the latter cannot represent, either to the public or to retailers, that their prices are "wholesale," since they are higher than the usual price most retailers pay.

"Laboratory" cannot, in the Commission's view, be used unless the firm does own or control a suitably equipped laboratory where its products are made or research directly related to its business is conducted.

The Commission has also made clear that the term "foundation" is a misleading description of any organization which is not substantially supported by charitable or disinterested funds. Similarly, a business may not call itself an "institute" unless one of its primary purposes is to promote education, art, science, or research.

d. WORDS DESIGNATING ORIGIN.   Express statements—e.g., "Made in U.S.A."—while the most obvious, are not the only manner by which one can represent the origin of a product to the public. For example, giving a French name to perfume, or dressing it in a package with labeling completely in French, would be considered by the Commission to depict the perfume as made in France. Similarly, the use of symbols such as a country's flag or national insignia would probably be deemed an implication of origin, as would be trademarks or product descriptions employing the name of a particular country, state, or city, or of a well-known landmark of a country in connection with products which are associated with that nation (such as the Eiffel Tower for cosmetics or London Bridge in connection with woolens).

Conversely, a seller of foreign goods may be in violation of the law if he fails to reveal affirmatively such fact, since the Commission takes the position that generally the public prefers domestic goods, assumes goods are domestic unless told otherwise, and hence, is deceived if their foreign origin is not disclosed. Thus, unless the advertiser can persuade the Commission that there is no domestic inference or preference for his particular type of product, he is required to disclose its foreign origin in a manner sufficient to advise the consumer of that fact.

Domestic products containing foreign parts present a more difficult problem. Unfortunately, no general rules can be drafted concerning their disclosure requirements, as that ultimately will depend upon the particular facts of each case and such questions as whether the part retains its identity when incorporated into the product, and the relative importance of the part to the whole.

B. Cooperative Advertising

When a seller in interstate commerce either (directly or indirectly) pays for services or facilities furnished by his customers in connection with the resale of his products or supplies his customers with such services or facilities, he is required, under the provisions of the Robinson-Patman Act [15 U.S.C. §13(d) and (e)] to make the payments or services available on proportionately equal terms to all his customers who compete with those receiving them.

This act is the most artificial and perhaps the murkiest of the statutes that govern marketing. In many areas it would be but foolhardy to predict the reach of its requirements as the Federal Trade Commission hypertechnically administers them. For example, the Commission will not, when it chooses not to, excuse a discrimination because it is minuscule. On some occasions it has held guilty advertisers with sales annually in the hundreds of millions and advertising in the tens, for a single in-store promotional contribution of a few hundred dollars. One such case was the fault of a regional manager who had acted contrary to company instructions and without its knowledge!

The best that can be done at this time, and all that I shall undertake, is to flag those spots and discuss briefly the problems they entail. Their status should then be checked as they become relevant to a contemplated program.

1. Services or Facilities Generally speaking, "services or facilities" includes any form of advertising or promotional arrangements made in connection with the buyer's resale of the supplier's product. Cooperative advertising, window and floor displays, handbills, catalogs, demonstrators, push money (or other incentive payments to salesmen and clerks), direct-mail pieces, promotional contests, special packaging, would all fall within this category.

2. Pays or Provides The act contemplates the rendering of such promotional services or facilities in two ways. The supplier can himself do so, as by furnishing his customer countercards, or he can pay the customer for performing a service—e.g., setting up an in-store or window display of the product, or running newspaper advertising in which it is featured.

It is not necessary that the supplier make such payments or furnish such facilities directly to the customer in order for the act to apply. For example, a tripartite arrangement instigated by a broadcast network wherein it agreed to grant certain retailers free air time in return for their promise to provide in-store promotions for the products of the suppliers whom the network could get to pay for that time was held to be within the act. Even though the payments went to the network, the fact remained that promotional aids had been conferred upon some of the suppliers' customers, and payments for promotional services had been made for their benefit, which the law required the sellers to make proportionately available to all competing customers.

Competing customers have been interpreted to mean those who compete on the same functional level. Thus allowances given a wholesaler customer need not be offered to retailers and vice versa. It should be remembered, however, that the functional classification of the customer depends not on the particular name he uses to describe himself but rather on the nature of the trade to which he resells. Reliance on mere commercial functional labels can open the supplier to an unintended, but nevertheless actionable, violation of the act. To illustrate, a large chain of food stores which does central buying, warehousing, and assumes other functions ordinarily performed by a wholesaler is nonetheless treated under the Robinson-Patman Act as a retailer, solely because its customers are consumers rather than further resellers of the product. Conversely, a purchaser who supplies retail outlets is a wholesaler even though he maintains no inventory or sales staff and does no more than solicit orders by telephone and relay them to manufacturers for drop shipment. In short, then, the true requirement is that promotional payments or facilities extended to a customer must be made available to all other customers who compete with him for resale to the same potential trade. It does not matter what name the industry assigns to them or what their other functional characteristics may be.

In a landmark decision of vast implications to the whole area of co-op advertising, the Supreme Court has ruled that a supplier who gives an advertising allowance to a direct-buying retailer customer must offer it to competing retailers who buy the supplier's products through wholesalers. [FTC *v.* Fred Meyer Inc., 390 U.S. 341 (1968).]

In effect, the court held that retailers who purchase through wholesalers are "customers" of the supplier, and since they do compete in the distribution of the supplier's products with his direct-buying customers, they are entitled to receive the promotional allowance given to the direct buyers.

The Federal Trade Commission guides, promulgated in March, 1969, to implement the principle of Meyer, expand the concept of "customer" even further to include "any buyer of the seller's product for resale who purchases from or through a wholesaler or *other intermediate reseller*" (italics added). Thus, for example, a "customer" would include a retailer who buys the supplier's products from a jobber who had purchased them from one of the supplier's wholesaler customers.

However, the guides do specifically exempt from the broad definition of "customers" purchasers of distress merchandise and retailers who purchase from other retailers, make only sporadic purchases, do not sell the supplier's product regularly, or do not usually sell the supplier's type of products. These exceptions do not apply, however, where the supplier "has been put on notice that such retailers are selling his product."

3. Customers Who Compete   The supplier must make the allowance available to only the customers who compete with those receiving the allowance. Thus, a manufacturer who distributes nationally can offer a promotional plan to his West Coast customers without having to make it available to East Coast customers, since the two do not compete.

If, however, one of the Western buyers is itself a national distributor, then the supplier may have to grant the allowance to its Eastern customers, as in such a situation there is competition between the two, unless the original allowance is limited to only those goods which the Western customers resells in the Western market area.

Moreover, the supplier must concern himself with customers on the fringes of the cooperative promotion area who compete with those within it, for the benefits must be made available to them as well.

One final point. Ordinarily, the supplier need grant proportional equality only to customers who purchase the promoted products contemporaneously, or nearly so. For example, if a promotional allowance is based upon a percentage of the customer's purchases between June 1 and July 1, a customer who buys from the supplier on October 1 would probably not be entitled to the allowance.

4. Available on Proportionately Equal Terms The staggering, if not intolerable, burden the Supreme Court's expansive interpretation of "customers" thrusts upon the supplier is compounded by this availability requirement.

The supplier must devise a plan that is proportionately equal among all customers eligible for it. While there is no single way to proportionalize, as a general rule plans which base the allowance paid or services furnished on a fixed price ratio to the volume of goods purchased during a given period (which is logically related to the term of the promotional activity) will probably be acceptable.

While this may, at first blush, seem relatively easy, in reality it can, because of a "functional availability" criterion, be quite difficult. This rule is that an allowance is not truly available to a retailer if it is not within his practical business capacity to do what is required in order to earn it. For example, allowances for television advertising only will be held to be illegally discriminating against those retailers who are too small to engage in it. Some alternative performance, such as displays, handbills, or mailing pieces, which do lend themselves to use by those customers, must be incorporated into the plan.

Thus, while it is no small task to devise an "available" and equally proportionalized promotion plan which ranges from large direct-buying retail chains down to "mom and pop" stores, it must be done.

Adding to the supplier's woes is the fact that he must notify all eligible customers that the plan exists, for it has also been ruled that a benefit is not "available" to one who is unaware of its existence. Since retailers who purchase through wholesalers are now, under the Meyer doctrine, deemed customers of the initial supplier, this duty is indeed an onerous one.

Under the Commission's guides, the supplier "must take reasonable action, in good faith" to notify eligible customers of the promotion program and to design into it the necessary alternatives which will ensure its functional "availability" to all competing customers.

While direct notice is preferred under the guides, indirect methods—e.g., putting notification in or on the product, on its shipping container, or in an appropriate trade journal—are acceptable as long as the notice contains the terms of the promotional plan, or a summary thereof with a source indicating where more information can be obtained, and the particular method chosen is reasonably calculated to reach all the eligible customers.   The guides also indicate that the supplier may demonstrate his "good faith" by testing the adequacy of his notification procedures through periodic spot checks on a representative cross section of his indirect-buying customers.

With regard to the availability requirement, the guides point out three basic requirements.   The plan must (1) have a sufficient range of alternatives which will allow all competing customers to participate; (2) be made in "good faith"; and (3) ensure that it or an alternative thereof does not prevent participation by any eligible customer. The guides specifically state that if these duties are met the failure of one or more customers to take part in the program does not place the supplier in violation of the act.   Similarly, although not expressly stated, it would appear that the failure of a few eligible customers out of a large class to receive notification would not subject the supplier to prosecution so long as he has complied with the guides' reasonableness standard.

The supplier can, under the guides, delegate a wholesaler or other third party to handle all the administrative duties of the promotion program.   However, by so doing the supplier does not necessarily relieve himself of legal responsibility under the act.   The maladministration of the promotion by a third party can render the supplier liable.   One final point about the guides.   Their core concept— "reasonableness"—is an extremely plastic and subjective one. Hence, only until the Commission, by applying the guides to actual cases, begins to reveal what it considers specifically reasonable or unreasonable, will the legal climate for cooperative advertising in the post-Meyer era become reliably predictable.

5. Products   A supplier who inaugurates a cooperative promotional program with respect to a given product (e.g., ham) is under no legal compulsion to extend it beyond that article (e.g., to bacon).   A largely unanswered question exists, however, as to what is or is not the same product within the meaning of the applicable sections of the Robinson-Patman Act.

Under another portion of that Statute—section 2(*a*), dealing with price discrimination—the Supreme Court has recently held that products having the same intrinsic qualities are products of "like grade and quality" notwithstanding that one is a nationally advertised brand commanding impressive consumer goodwill and the other may be a little-known, private-label version.   The cooperative promotion provisions of the act, however, do not describe the products to which it applies as those of "like grade and quality."   Rather, they require that the benefits accorded to one person dealing in a product be extended on a proportionately equal basis to all others who compete with him in the resale of "such commodity."   While it seems apparent that commodities which are not of "like grade and quality" would also not be "such" products, it does not necessarily follow that, conversely, merely being of like grade and quality must make them the same product.   Where the Supreme Court refused to take consumer acceptance into account as a "quality" of a product, it might do so in analyzing whether two commodities are the same product, where the relevant context is promotional activity, to which customer goodwill is so directly related.

This, at the present time, however, is an open question, and should be checked specifically whenever its answer might be pertinent to a proposed program.

6. Performance   The price discrimination section of the Robinson-Patman Act makes it illegal (assuming certain facts) for a manufacturer to sell the same goods at different prices to different buyers. Hence, payments by a supplier made pursuant to a promotion program may constitute an illegal price discrimination if the customer does not perform the services for which the payment is made.

Going beyond that, however, the Commission maintains by its guides that the supplier must take "reasonable precautions" to ensure that all his customers provide the promotional activities for which payments have been given and that the monies have been completely used up in rendering these services.   According to the guides, a supplier in good faith who "takes reasonable and prudent measures to verify the performance of his competing customers" has satisfied this requirement.   What is "reasonable and prudent" will, of course, depend upon particular circumstances.   As the guides indicate, when proof of performance is "readily available"—e.g., tear sheets or invoices from the media—the manufacturer should require such evidence when payment is made.   Where such verification is not easily available, a random spot check by the supplier should be sufficient.

7. In Connection with Resale   The mere giving of money or services to a customer is not enough to put the supplier within the cooperative promotions provisions of the act (although, as pointed out above, it might violate the price discrimination section).   The payment or service must be connected with promoting the customer's *resale* (not its purchase) of the supplier's goods.

It appears that the requisite connection is present even though the recipient of the allowance uses it solely to advertise and promote his own name.   In R. H. Macy & Co., Inc. *v.* FTC, 326 F.2d 445 (2d Cir. 1964), for example, merchandise suppliers had made contributions to Macy's centennial anniversary promotion.   The resultant advertising was to create in-store traffic with the expectation that purchases would ultimately result, including products of the participating manufacturers.   Thus, the payments were made in connection with the resale of such commodities.

The Commission has adopted a broad definition of "resale," recently holding that a hair-dye manufacturer's promotional payments to beauty salons came within the act although the salons did not resell the dye intact, as received from the supplier, but rather used it themselves in the process of coloring their patrons' hair.   [Clairol Incorporated *v.* FTC, 410 F.2d 647 (9th Cir. 1969).]   The act also applies when the supplier's product is in fact resold by the customer in its integral chemical form, although no longer recognizable, as an ingredient in a larger product.   In Corn Products Refining Co. *v.* FTC, 324 U.S. 726 (1945), the commodity for which advertising allowances were paid was dextrose, which the favored customer incorporated into its candy bars and resold in that form.   These candy bars were advertised to be "rich in dextrose."   The Supreme Court held the dextrose manufacturer's allowances for that advertising to be within the act, as the dextrose was in fact resold, albeit as part of another product.

8. Meeting Competition   Some leeway is allowed a supplier to discriminate in favor of a particular customer in order to meet a competitor's offer.   This is a highly complex area of the law, however, made infinitely more difficult by the Commission's innate dislike of its permissiveness.   There are, for example, such narrowing concepts which the Commission has evolved as that the discriminatory program can only "meet" but cannot "beat" the competing offer, that it must be extended only on an individual customer-by-customer basis as needed to meet specific offers by the competitor to each such customer, and that the supplier must be prepared to prove that the competitive offer actually was outstanding at the time he purported to meet it.   There are others, and the legalities of all are so intricate that it would be a disservice to attempt to expound them all here. Suffice it to say, where there is bona-fide reason to believe that a competitive offer is extant and should be countered, the supplier should consult his attorney to ascertain the extent to which the given facts may permit him to do something about it.

9. Miscellaneous Points Suppliers should also be aware that by paying a retailer for his advertising, the supplier may be held liable if it is deceptive.   Thus, it is always good practice to require that all cooperative advertising be checked and cleared by the manufacturer before publication by the retailer.   This is automatically controlled if the manufacturer supplies the newspaper mats, radio scripts, and similar source materials.

Also, a supplier cannot use a promotion plan to further an illegal purpose.   To illustrate, if the supplier's plan requires the retailer's advertising to state the "regular price" of the product at a certain amount, the plan may be deemed to be an unlawful attempt to fix resale price maintenance.   Whether that would be the result where the requirement goes no further than to disqualify retailer advertising if it affirmatively carries a price below a certain amount (while leaving the retailer free to sell at any price he wishes) is a different question.   At the present time, the Commission, however, has expressed itself adversely to that condition as well, except where the limitation is operative for only limited, sporadic periods.

Finally, the recipients of a promotional allowance may be subject to liability under section 5 of the Federal Trade Commission Act if they know or have reason to know that the payments or services they receive from the supplier are not available on proportionately equal terms to their competitors, within all the refinements that have been alluded to above.

C. Lotteries, Contests, Games, and Premiums

Lotteries are illegal, while contests, games, and premiums are, with some exceptions due to state regulations, lawful.   Thus it is important to distinguish among these promotional devices.

A lottery comprises three elements: (1) the distribution of prizes, (2) according to chance, (3) for a consideration. If any one of these features is missing, there is no lottery. Since all lottery, contest, game, and premium schemes offer a "prize" in some form or another, the key elements which will be crucial in determining whether a particular plan is a lottery are consideration and chance.

Generally speaking, a consideration is deemed to be anything of value which must be rendered in order to qualify for the prize. If, for example, purchase of a product is required to participate, consideration is thereby present. Even if a purchase is not technically required essential to qualify, consideration will still exist if the promoter leads the consumer to believe that a purchase is necessary or may be helpful to winning. Thus it is advisable to state clearly and conspicuously in the promotional literature and advertising that no purchase is needed or advantageous in the contest.

Unfortunately, a semantic coincidence has complicated the law in this field. The aspect of consideration which makes lotteries objectionable as a matter of public policy is that it causes people to part with money (or property) which they may not be able to afford in the hope that fortune will smile upon them. In short, it is the gambling feature that makes it bad. In the law of contracts "consideration" has a different purport. It is the rendition or performance of anything of value which has been bargained for in return for a reciprocal promise or action. Thus, mowing a lawn is consideration to hold the other party liable on his promise to pay for that service; and the promise to pay is consideration adequate to bind the other person to his agreement to mow the lawn in return. Since it is the basic orientation of contract law to give effect to what the parties mutually intended their bargain to be, a court will not evaluate the economic sufficiency of the consideration they have agreed upon, leaving that to their judgment and desire. Thus, contractual "consideration" can be quite minimal.

Borrowing from that, really irrelevant, branch of the law, the courts have held in lottery cases that the consideration necessary to illegalize a scheme can be found in rather minor activity by the participant if it benefits the operator of the lottery and is bargained for by him—i.e., if such performance is a prerequisite to participation. Confusion abounds because courts are not consistent in applying this principle. Thus, in a series of "Bank Night" cases many years ago, some courts held that the necessity of one whose name has been picked by chance at a motion picture house to be present in the lobby in order to qualify as a winner was consideration—and hence made the program unlawful. Others held that it was not. Clearly, if the requirement had been that the participant must buy a ticket and be in the theater before his name was chosen all courts would reach the lottery conclusion.[2]

A fine distinction in the law of contract carries over to that of lotteries. Every condition that a person must fulfill in order to receive reciprocal payment is not necessarily consideration. For example, seeing a poor man in the street on a cold day, one may offer to give him an old overcoat if he will come home with the donor to get it. The recipient's doing so is not a consideration that would convert the promise into a binding contract. On the other hand, if it is plain to both parties that the person offering the overcoat is afraid to travel home unaccompanied, and is actually bargaining to obtain an escort, the rendition of that service would then bind the agreement as consideration.

In the lottery context, troublesome questions therefore arise over whether action required of the entrant is merely a condition which must be met in order to facilitate the operation (e.g., sending in his name and address so that it might be picked as a winner and he be notified) or as genuine consideration (e.g., sending in his name and address so that it can be incorporated into a mailing list of commercial value to the sponsor).

Thus, the expenditure of substantial effort or time by contestants to the benefit of the sponsor, if such is necessary for participation, may be decreed a consideration. Generally, the time and effort involved in going to a store to pick up an entry blank is not deemed substantial enough to amount to a consideration. However, the statutes of some states and their attorney generals' interpretations of them indicate that going to the store would in those jurisdictions constitute consideration on the theory that the promoter obtains benefits through increased exposure to his goods displayed in the store irrespective of

---

[2] Having to buy a ticket in order to collect a prize after one's name had been chosen would, of course, also be consideration; but in that instance, chance would be lacking since the payer would know before making the purchase that he had won. His payment would be for collecting the prize, not for buying a gamble at winning it.

whether anything is in fact purchased during the visit in question. It has been held, however, that the commercial benefits of increased radio audiences and advertising exposure flowing to a promoter as a result of his sponsorship of a giveaway program do not constitute a "consideration," and thus such shows are not lotteries. [FCC *v.* American Broadcasting Co., 347 U.S. 284 (1954).]

It is also generally held that the purchase of a newspaper or magazine to obtain an entry form is not a consideration so long as the promotion is not for the benefit of the publisher. By contrast, having to send in a box top would clearly be such consideration. Hence, the customary "reasonably accurate facsimile" alternative, which defeats itself if the performance standard is of sufficient difficulty to discourage its use, and as a practical matter, call for purchase of the product.

"Chance" is present where the winner or the value of the prize is determined in whole or in part fortuitously. Contests and premiums usually have prize and consideration elements, but escape the lottery label because of the elimination of chance (whereas games and sweepstakes accept chance, but attempt to avoid the element of consideration). For example, a premium promotion wherein coupons of equal value are inserted into all packages of a particular product may offer a prize (the coupon) for a consideration (purchase of the product), but it will lack chance, as every purchaser is certain to be a winner. It is otherwise, however, if the coupons are of differing values, unless, of course, the external package clearly states the value of the particular coupon inside.

Contests, in which the winners are selected on the basis of skill and merit, are another means of avoiding chance. However, the contest must be legitimate and the winner, in fact, selected on merit. This would include competent judging, and setting forth in the contest rules definitive, objective criteria upon which the submissions will be evaluated. For example, a contest which awards the prize to the "cutest name" for a baby whose picture is shown would probably be deemed a game of chance because it is so vague and subjective that there is no genuine basis for selecting a winner wholly on merit.

Even if the contest is properly administered and contains sufficiently precise standards for the winner to be judged on merit, it may still be a lottery if the size of the prize is dependent on chance; as where, for example, prize values are based on the number of entrants. Chance frequently creeps into a contest in the course of tie-breaking procedures.   To illustrate, the Post Office maintains that such a criterion as the earlier postmark cannot be used, inasmuch as that is a fortuitous event not entirely dependent upon the contestant's own skill or merit.   This is a debatable conclusion, of course; but it exemplifies how subtle the pitfalls may be.

There are a host of federal and state laws under which lotteries are illegal.   The Federal Trade Commission condemns them as an unfair practice under the Federal Trade Commission Act, and both the Federal Communications Commission and the Post Office Department have authority under the Criminal Code of the United States to prohibit the broadcast and mailing of lottery schemes.   [18 U.S.C. §§ 1302 and 1304.]   It appears that each of these agencies interprets the elements of prize, chance, and consideration in similar fashion, so that a promotion which would not constitute a lottery under the Federal Trade Commission's standards would probably pass muster at the Federal Communication Commission and the Post Office Department.   It is often helpful, therefore, to seek advance advice from one of these agencies (preferably the Post Office) in doubtful instances.

However, such is not the case under the numerous state statutes. As pointed out earlier, some states have adopted a much broader definition of "consideration."   Moreover, a few states prohibit or regulate games of chance, contests, and premiums such as trading stamps.   Obviously, then, the advertiser should always check the laws of the states touched by his contest or premium offer.   The familiar nullification clauses—"void in the states of [etc.]", or "void where prohibited by law"—are generally sufficient to avoid legal complications in these states.   However, they do not eliminate the need to identify such states so as to avoid distributing a prize or otherwise actually conducting the program within them despite the disclaimer.

In 1969 the FTC promulgated a rule dealing with games of chance in the food retailing and gasoline industries.   The rule declares it a deceptive practice to misrepresent the chances of winning, to fail to mix game pieces on a random basis throughout the contest area, to use a game capable of being broken, to provide a new game in an establishment which promoted a prior game without an interval between them equal to the length of the prior game, and to terminate the game or add winning pieces prior to its completion.

The rule also requires that on all game advertising mentioning prizes there be conspicuously disclosed: the number of prizes in each category, the odds of winning, the geographic area of the game, the number of participating retail outlets, and the termination date.

D. Trademarks and Unfair Competition

1. The Nature of a Trademark [3]   In legal essence, a trademark is a symbol of source.   While it need not, like a proper name, specify who is the maker of the goods, it does assure that they continue to originate from or under the auspices of the same sponsor, retaining essentially the same product qualities (unless otherwise noted) as long as they carry the same mark.   It is that function which the law protects.

Thus, a trademark is radically different in legal concept from a copyright or a patent.   The latter are independent, self-embracing items of property (albeit abstract) which derive from statutory grants extended by the government as rewards for creativity in the arts or in the innovative development of new products, processes, or even product designs.   Those grants confer upon their owners the exclusive right to reproduce the artistic work or to utilize the substance of the invention.   They exist for the specified statutory period (generally fifty-six years for a copyright and seventeen years for a patent) and then expire totally.

A trademark, however, is a signal, a communicative device.   It says to the observer, "This product comes from the same source as the others upon which I appear."   That function conditions the applicable legal principles in a number of respects which have special significance to advertising.   So long as it continues to serve in that capacity, it will be protected by the law, whether it be for one or a hundred years.   At the point where it no longer identifies the source of a product, either because it is no longer used or because it has come to mean something else (e.g., if it comes to designate a kind of product, rather than a given producer's version of it—a fate which befell aspirin, cellophane, and thermos), the mark's legal existence terminates even despite the fact that it is covered by an official registration.   As will be seen, trademark registration—although extremely

---

[3] Trademark principles apply as well to services as to products.   For the sake of brevity, I shall refer herein only to product marks, but the discussion may be taken as covering service marks also, unless patently inappropriate in some specific respect.

important—does not possess any independent, legal vitality, except as it relates to a viable symbol of a product's source. Rather, registration serves to confirm and facilitate protection of whatever source identification function the mark in fact performs.

2. The Development of Trademark Rights Trademark rights come into existence immediately upon use of the mark in the sale of goods or services. No governmental grant is involved. Theoretically, one might use a trademark for years, without seeking its registration, and still have full legal protection of it as a so-called common-law trademark.

However, federal or state registration, or both, is most advisable. This is primarily for the reason that common-law rights exist only in the areas where the mark has been used, whereas federal registration confers full national priority applicable even in places where the mark has yet to appear. Thus, a company which test-markets a product in the Northeast with an unregistered mark may find that, in the interim, before it expands to the West Coast, another company has begun to use the identical mark there for the same or a similar kind of product. Presuming the latter acted innocently and without awareness of the test-marketed article, he may not only have the right to continue to use the mark in his area of priority, but also actually be entitled to stop the original user's expansion into that market.

Some companies attempt to ameliorate the risk of an intervening user by obtaining federal registration well in advance of actually marketing the new product. Some small quantities of a product similar in kind to that which is to be marketed are packaged with labels showing the mark and the products are then sold across state lines, usually to an existing customer. This allows an application to be filed asserting, as it must, that the mark has been used in interstate commerce. Once the company receives registration, it may proceed with its test-marketing plans, reasonably safe that it will not thereafter be preempted in other areas. The problem with this approach is that it may take up to a year or even more before the Patent Office indicates its approval, and that may be too long to wait.

The concept of rights flowing from use presents another serious danger which cannot be wholly avoided in the adoption of a new mark. The most painstaking sort of searching cannot, with 100 per cent certainty, turn up every prior use of a similar mark for goods of the same general nature. There are many small manufacturers, distributors, and even retailers who have adopted trademarks which they use in a limited geographic area, but without any effort to obtain registration.   Their rights survive, however, even if another, without knowledge of that use, later obtains a federal registration of the same mark.   The result is that the local firm can bar the registrant from the area and, if it happens to be a large enough territory or even a small one in a major city (making it impossible to keep television, newspaper, or magazine advertising out of that community and thus precluding any effective advertising of the new product in the entire city), force him either to drop the mark for a new one or buy peace with a generous payment to the local firm.   Either way, the result can be quite expensive.

3. Trademark Selection   A trademark may consist of a word, name, symbol, device, or any combination of them.   A great variety of things can qualify as symbols or devices; for example, included are numbers, letters, insignia, and even artistic renderings of animals or people, i.e., a horse, a dog, or a fanciful character.   A package label may qualify under certain circumstances (e.g., McIlhenny's Tabasco Sauce) and so, too, may a unique package configuration (e.g., the Coca-Cola and Haig & Haig Pinch bottles).

While selection of a mark is essentially a marketing and creative decision involving such factors as the mark's uniqueness, memorability, adaptability to advertising in different media, and appropriateness to the product, there are legal considerations and limitations to be taken into account.

a. GENERIC AND DESCRIPTIVE TERMS.   "Automobile" is the generic name for an automobile; "economical," "speedy," and "beautiful" would be descriptive terms applicable to it.   A person wishing to use any of such designations as a trademark for an automobile would not succeed for two reasons.   First, as a matter of public policy the law will not permit him to foreclose his competitors from describing their products by such appropriate vocabulary that is part of the public heritage.   Second, and more closely interlinked to the essential legal concept of a trademark, words which are commonly deemed applicable to a class of commodities, regardless of the origin of particular units thereof, do not serve the trademark function of designating a single source for certain of them.

Because of the second of these considerations, it is possible for an appellation which was a true trademark when initially adopted to lose its validity if public use converts it into a generic or descriptive word, even though it did not originally have that characteristic.

"Aspirin" is an outstanding example of this principle. It was originally a coined mark—i.e., a term newly created by its originator and having no generic or descriptive connotation in the lexicon of the day. However, the general public, with no other familiar name to use when referring to the drug generically, came to employ the term in that undiscriminating sense. Consequently, when the originator's patents expired and other producers entered the market, the public at large called their products "aspirin" as well, and that public preemption of the word removed it from the private ownership, as a trademark, of its original user, and cast it into the public domain.

In illuminating contrast, doctors and chemists referred to the drug quite handily as "acetylsalicylic acid," and the court therefore held that this, rather than "aspirin," was their generic terminology for it. "Aspirin" consequently remained a valid trademark within their particular circles, indicating to them a particular brand or source of acetylsalicylic acid. (The situation changed thereafter. The trademark owner, having little interest in protecting the mark solely within that restricted area, simply allowed it to fall into use as an additional generic synonym even among the technicians.)

b. FAMILY NAMES AND GEOGRAPHIC TERMS. For somewhat similar reasons, trademark rights are extremely difficult, although not impossible, to acquire in family names or geographic terms. Other persons who can use them in an equally truthful appellative sense are entitled to do so.

In the case of surnames, it is generally the rule that no one may be barred from using his own name to identify his business, even though the name has come to be an important trademark of another. The most that the courts usually will do in such situations is to require the second comer to use his first name or initials as a means of differentiation or to employ a legend such as "Not connected with the X company." It is, accordingly, most inadvisable to use a surname as a trademark, or even as part of a corporate name which is likely to become popularized.

Geographic terms, as with descriptive words, are also inappropriate as trademarks since all producers in a given area are entitled to use such a term to indicate their location.

c. SECONDARY MEANING. Since it is the public understanding and usage of a term which dictates whether it means integrity of source (and hence stands as a trademark) or is nomenclature not connotative of commercial origin (and is, therefore, generic, descriptive, or geographic and not a trademark), it follows that there will be instances, albeit rare, where constant, intensive, and effective linkage of an initially common name with a product emanating from one particular source can move the public to superimpose a brand significance secondarily upon the primarily ordinary meaning of the word, when it is used in connection with that particular product line.   For example, "Cadillac" is a geographic name, but its use on automobiles has come to mean those produced only by General Motors.

It will thus be seen that the manner in which the public actually uses a term will determine its legal vitality.   A mark originally good when adopted (e.g., "aspirin") can fall into the public domain, and one originally in the public domain can be converted into an indication of source.   The recurrent question for every trademark is, therefore, how is it used?

Difficulties with respect to secondary-meaning marks arise when rights of truthful generic or descriptive use by competitors come into conflict with exclusionary proprietary rights of a trademark owner who has successfully built up the requisite public understanding of his mark.   For example, suppose a competitor of General Motors should actually manufacture in Cadillac, Michigan.   Usually the courts will strive for a solution which permits the truthful use, but only in a nontrademark fashion.   Thus the rival automobile manufacturer might be permitted to state, in a prosaic and factual manner, that its plant is located in Cadillac, Michigan, but it would not be allowed to give undue emphasis or trademark appearance to the word "Cadillac."

d. SUGGESTIVE TERMS.   "Suggestive" trademarks are to be distinguished from those which are "descriptive."   The difference may often seem one of degree rather than of kind, but its legal consequences are substantial.   A descriptive mark is one that tells what a product will do, or what its various characteristics may be.   "Fast Dry" paint, "Satin" dresses, "No-Wind" watches might be examples. Here again, such characterizations are customary usages of ordinary terminology which the law usually will not permit to be made the exclusive property of any individual.   However, other words may be used which, although having associative overtones relevant to the nature or function of a product, are not commonly used to denote it. These are called "suggestive" rather than "descriptive." "Coppertone" for a suntan lotion, or "Halo" for a shampoo, are representative. Suggestive names make valid trademarks, for the unusual nature of their use—depending upon how bizarre it is—places them somewhere on the scale above descriptive terms, although still below a completely fanciful mark such as "Dacron."

e. FANCIFUL OR ARBITRARY TERMS.   The fact that a word is taken from common language in no way impairs its legal character as a trademark where its meaning is totally unrelated to the product. For example, "Admiral" for radio and television sets, "Camel" for cigarettes, and "Arrow" for shirts suffer no impairment because they are found in the dictionary.

f. RANGE OF PROTECTION.   As stated, trademark rights may be obtained in coined (e.g., "Kodak"), suggestive, or arbitrary words. However, the scope of protection the courts will accord a mark against use by others depends upon which of these categories it is in. A coined term will receive the broadest area of preemption. That is to say, it will not be allowed to be used even for products quite unrelated to those of the originator. Thus, the uniqueness of the term can be preserved from impairment by its use for other kinds of goods. Arbitrary terms receive somewhat narrower protection, though use of them will not be allowed in case of similar or related products. Suggestive terms will be protected to a lesser extent, but, minimally, their use by others will not be permitted upon goods so like those of the originator as to make confusion likely to occur.

g. MULTIPLE MARKS.   A multiplicity of marks may be used for a single product. Usually, this involves a house mark which extends to all of a company's products (e.g., "General Motors"), a product mark which pertains to the particular item in the company's line of product (e.g., "Pontiac"), and a subsidiary mark which indicates a special style or grade ("LeMans") or even a special ingredient or component. All may serve a valid trademark function if they tend to indicate the source of the goods.

Grade, style, shade, or ingredient marks may, however, entail special legal problems. The problem associated with them is that they serve dual functions. For example, a cosmetic manufacturer's denomination "luscious peach" for a lipstick might be interpreted as indicating origin (the trademark function); as designating only a particular color (a nontrademark function), or both.   If it performs the former function, though to a degree it may also perform the latter, then there is a legitimate trademark.   This determination will usually depend on how the mark is promoted and used and whether the public understands the manufacturer to be using the mark to identify origin or merely color, style, or grade as the case may be.   Ultimately, the decision rests upon the particular facts of each case.   Thus advertisers who seek to use such marks should be aware that they present special problems which call for strong supportive measures, such as will be discussed below, to fortify them as protectable trademarks.

h. MISDESCRIPTIVE TERMS.   Even legally strong marks may be vulnerable if they misdescribe a product.   There are numerous cases where the Federal Trade Commission has ordered a trademark stricken because it deceptively connoted an ingredient or characteristic which the product did not possess.   For example, the Commission compelled discontinuance of the mark "Lite Diet" for bread, because it believed that the mark falsely presented the bread as a dietary, weight-reducing product [Bakers Franchise Corp. *v.* FTC, 302 F.2d 258 (3d Cir. 1962)].   The devastating effect of such an order is readily apparent.   In Bakers Franchise, for instance, the manufacturer was forced to abandon a mark which it had spent millions of dollars promoting and advertising over a long period of time.   Thus, the selection of a mark which is free of possibly deceptive constructions should be high on the advertiser's list of priorities.

The intricacies of conducting a trademark search, of determining whether to apply for federal or state registrations or both, and of processing such applications if they seem desirable, unquestionably should be left in the hands of competent counsel, and need not be discussed here.   Indeed, such counsel can fruitfully be used early in the selection stage to save the time and money that might otherwise be wasted in considering a mark that is commercially attractive but legally defective.

4. Trademark Maintenance   The care of trademarks does not end with proper selection, or even with registration.   Having chosen and undertaken to use a mark, the owner must remain vigilant to see to it not only that the right is not lost, but that it is also constantly reinforced and enhanced (especially where, although valid, it was a relatively weak mark to start with).

The gravest danger to the advertiser is, as has already been mentioned, that his mark will become "generic."   When that happens, it is usually because he has used it to describe the nature or characteristics, rather than to signify integrity of the source, of his goods, or because he has allowed others to do so.

The danger of genericalness is particularly acute for new product entities having no preexisting term of identification, or having an identification so complex as to fall into disuse in favor of the simpler, more memorable words used as the trademark for the product.   The danger increases if that brand happens to be the only one available. In this context, the marketer's objective may be the very antithesis of prudent legal practice, for if he succeeds in his aim to convert the public into thinking of his brand automatically when thinking of the product category, he may succeed, as was the case with "thermos," in having the mark commonly used for all products of that nature and thereby lose the right to its exclusive use.   Granted that this is primarily of concern only to market leaders, it is a consequence well worth remembering when the warning signs are flashed by counsel.

Protection against the generic eventuality must emanate from the owner and be unremitting.   Its success turns not upon the actions of the owner as such, but upon the response of the public thereto. Hence, no pat prescription can be offered which, if obeyed, will with certainty fulfill the legal requirements of keeping a trademark valid. Any program which results in the public considering the mark as a description of a general class of products, or as an adjectival characterization of some property possessed by a product, will work toward destruction of the mark.   Anything which succeeds in creating a public image of it as a flag symbolizing that the products which bear it emanate from a continuative, particular source will preserve it.

There are, however, some measures which can be used constructively, and certain traps which should be avoided, as experience has shown they have important influence upon the ultimate result. They are all built, however, upon a common base of making it as obvious to the public as possible that the mark is not being used in the manner of a common component of the English language.

Thus, the mark should always be used in a typographical form distinct from that of its context.   This may range from the minimum of initial capitalization, through consistent embracement within quotation marks, solid capitalization, boldface, or italicized type.

Express labeling of the mark as a trademark, such as by use of the statutory symbol ® or the legends "Registered in U.S. Patent Office" or "Reg. U.S. Pat. Off.", is obviously most helpful. Where a mark is not registered, a notation that it is the mark of the advertiser should nevertheless be included—e.g., "T.M. of A.B.C. Co.," or "Trademark."

It is always wise, but particularly so where the public does not have a ready generic name for the type of product involved, to supply one and give it frequent exposure in contiguous contrast to the trademark's usage, in the hope that the public will use it rather than the mark as the generic terminology. The familiar legend "SCOTCH brand cellophane tape" is an excellent example. "Brand" tells us that "SCOTCH" is used not as a geographic or national descriptive, but as a designation of commercial source, while "cellophane tape" offers the public a name by which to call that general *type* of product, rather than having to resort—generically—to "scotch tape" for that purpose due to lack of a familiar alternative.

There are a wide variety of similar and supplementary devices for guarding against such misuse of a trademark as will erode its integrity, and for policing abuses by others when they occur. Competent trademark counsel will be well schooled in all these, and should be consulted for their optimal adaptation to the particular needs and circumstances of a given advertiser. "Trademark Management: A Guide for Businessmen" and other materials published by the U.S. Trademark Association are highly valuable aids to the layman's understanding of the general nature of the problems for which, with the aid of his lawyer, specific solutions will need to be designed. Reference to them is strongly recommended to supplement this section.

5. Unfair Competition   "Unfair competition" is an "all others" category of commercial conduct which does not fall within traditional doctrinal concepts of illegality (breach of contract, trespass, libel, negligence) but is so grievously at odds with business morality, and potentially so injurious to its trade victims, that courts will not tolerate that it continue. It is a question-begging process, to be sure: practices which the law will thus enjoin constitute unfair competition, and a practice that constitutes unfair competition will be enjoined. Necessarily, then, it is an amorphous, plastic, and unpredictable area, molded by changing business conditions and mores, as well as by subjective judicial factors. Nonetheless, the precedental process yields substantial, though not conclusive, guidelines, and of these we shall focus on those which are particularly relevant to advertising.

a. USE OF ANOTHER'S TRADEMARK.   It is an unlawful infringement to use the mark of another, or one similar to it if that use causes or is likely to cause consumers to purchase the infringer's goods under the impression they are made or sponsored by the rightful owner of the mark.   Such a situation usually, but not necessarily, involves similar or related goods.   The closer their relationship, the greater the likelihood of confusion, and hence of illegality.   Whether goods are related is primarily a factual question, and in addition to such obvious factors as their generic nature, physical appearance, and intended use, will take into account elements such as their respective price levels, how they are distributed, and who buys them.   Thus, if nonidentical products are sold to different types of purchasers at substantially disparate prices and through different distributional outlets, the possibility of confusion is correspondingly lessened.

Where the prior mark owner can show, however, that he is likely in the course of normal expansion to start dealing in goods similar to those of the other, he may be granted protection even though there is no current overlap.

Because the applicable criteria leave much to the subjective judgment of the courts, the results in individual cases sometimes seem to reflect more a sense of judicial outrage than a dispassionate application of the relevant tests.   For example, the brewer of Budweiser beer (Bud) was granted an injunction against an insecticide manufacturer preventing further use of a parody, "Where there's life—there's bugs," of the well-known slogan, "Where there's life—there's Bud." Ordinarily, the respective products would be thought of as so different from one another as to rule out any likelihood of consumer confusion.   It would not appear likely that the public should think the beer company to be connected with the defendant merely because the latter used a perversion of the other's slogan.   Yet, the court held that confusion was likely, a conclusion which seemingly was heavily influenced by a feeling that the mere association—though not in the sense of deception—of an insecticide with a product ingested by the public was too odious to permit.   [Chemical Corp. of America *v.* Anheuser-Busch Inc., 306 F.2d 433 (5th Cir. 1962).]

Closely allied to these situations is that in which a competitor, while clearly identifying his goods with his own mark, uses another's solely for comparative or promotional purposes: e.g., "My car X gets better mileage than car Z." Assuming that the statement is true, can the manufacturer of car Z enjoin the use of his mark by the maker of X? Probably not.

The Supreme Court long ago announced, "When a mark is used in a way that does not deceive the public we see no such sanctity in the word as to prevent it being used to tell the truth." This concept has been generally followed. For example, a court refused to enjoin a manufacturer from advertising that sponges for its Crown 400 mops would also fit plaintiff's O-Cedar mops, on the ground that there was nothing unfair about defendant's reference to the interchangeability with plaintiff's products. [American-Marietta Co. *v.* Krigsman, 275 F.2d 287 (2d Cir. 1960).]

Similarly, a plaintiff was denied an injunction against use of his mark "Christian Dior" on tags reading "Original by Christian Dior —Alexander's Exclusive Paris Adaptation" attached by the defendant to its copies of the plaintiff's original dress designs. [Societe Comptoir De L'Industrie Cotonniere, Establissements Boussac *v.* Alexander's Department Stores, Inc., 299 F.2d 33 (2d Cir. 1962).]

Perhaps the clearest exposition of this doctrine is by the Ninth Circuit Court of Appeals in R. G. Smith *v.* Chanel Inc., 402 F.2d 562 9th Cir. 1968). There a manufacturer had advertised that his cheaply priced perfumes, Second Chance, exactly duplicated the scents of the world's finest and most expensive fragrances. One of these specifically mentioned was Chanel No. 5. Chanel sought an injunction, claiming (1) that defendant should not be allowed to "take a free ride" on the goodwill and reputation of the plaintiff which it had achieved at great effort and expense, and (2) that such use threatened the mark's distinctiveness and could, if continued, cause the mark to become descriptive or generic and thus lost. It was conceded by Chanel that the defendant had a right to copy the unpatented formula for Chanel No. 5, and that defendant's packaging and labeling of Second Chance and its use of Chanel's mark did not create any confusion as to source. It was also assumed for purposes of the proceeding that the defendant's exact duplication claim was true.

The court rejected both of Chanel's contentions and reversed the prior district court decision in its favor, holding that "such advertising may not be enjoined under . . . the common law of unfair competition, so long as it does not contain misrepresentations or create a reasonable likelihood that purchasers will be confused as to the source, identity or sponsorship of the advertiser's product."

Answering Chanel's first proposition, the court stated that a "large expenditure of money does not in itself create legally protectable rights." Moreover, in the court's view, the public interest that is served by allowing competitors to state honestly that they offer comparable products at lower prices far outweighs the interests of the trademark owner. The court opined that unless a vendor is allowed to use the mark of another in this way, he will have no effective means of communicating such facts to the consumer. Further, by allowing such use, the court went on to point out, barriers to entry created by consumer allegiances to well-established brand names are reduced and competition is stimulated.

Chanel's second argument was dismissed on the basis that the defendant had not used plaintiff's mark as a descriptive or generic term. Some states have statutes which prohibit, per se, the unauthorized use of another's mark on goods and labels. While a few successful civil actions have been brought under these laws, the decisions have not been generally favorable to plaintiffs.

One principle is clear, however: the courts will not brook falsity or deception. If the claim of equivalence or superiority is untrue or misleading, or if the mark is used in a way to produce confusion, an injunction will issue.

b. COPYING ANOTHER'S TRADE DRESS. Distinctive trade dress is protectable upon principles quite similar to those applicable to trademarks. As pointed out earlier, even a package configuration may be registered as a trademark if it is distinctive enough to represent the source of the product.

The familiar Haig & Haig Pinch bottle is an example of trade dress. However, inasmuch as trademark principles apply, rather than those applicable to patents or copyrights, the registration does not prevent any and all use by others of a similar bottle configuration, but only those selling a product in such a bottle where the result is to produce a likelihood of confusion. Registration is not necessary to enable a manufacturer to enjoin simulations of it. Generally, where there is a substantial duplication of design, style, and color of a carton or label by a competitor, an injunction will be granted. Ultimately, as in trademark infringement, the trade dress case will be decided on such facts as the degree of similarity between the labels, cartons, etc., the relationship of the goods, and the resulting degree of likelihood of confusion.

There is a vital distinction between copying the configuration or graphics of a package and simulating the appearance of the product itself. The latter cannot be enjoined under general principles of unfair competition. Only design patents or copyrights can protect product appearance, as differentiated from distinctive package configuration or trade dress. The Christian Dior and the Chanel situations described earlier are indicative of the freedom to imitate uncopyrighted and unpatented product appearances and characteristics. More definitively, the United States Supreme Court, in Sears, Roebuck & Co. v. Stiffel Co., 376 U.S. 225 (1964) and Compco Corp. v. Day-Brite Lighting, Inc., 376 U.S. 234 (1964), declared that states cannot, even by explicit legislation, extend exclusive proprietary rights in product design beyond those given by the federal Congress in its patent and copyright statutes. The reason is that the United States Constitution assigns Congress national jurisdiction over those subjects, thus preempting the powers of the states in those fields.[4]

c. DISPARAGEMENT AND FALSE ADVERTISING. These, from the legal viewpoint, are essentially two sides of the same coin. (The status of disparagement in private regulation will be discussed in a later section.) Disparagement arises when one makes false derogatory statements about another's business or products. The law does not bar deprecatory observations when they are true. Nondisparaging false advertising concerns untrue statements about one's own business or goods.

Legally actionable disparagement has three elements when damages, rather than merely an injunction, are sought: falsity; malice; and special damages. Generally, statements of subjective opinions, or those which are mere puffing, are not unlawful since the plaintiff has no way of proving either objective falsity or substantial concrete damage. For example, if a competitor advertises that his product "tastes" better than Brand X, or that his wares are "fabulous" com-

---

[4] There is no such equivalent constitutional empowerment of Congress with respect to trademarks. Whatever regulation of them Congress undertakes must look for its validity to the commerce clause.

pared to Brand X, the manufacturer of X has little hope of demonstrating that these subjective evaluations are untrue.

The malice requirement is less clear-cut than that of falsity. Where the disparaging comment is made by a competitor, improper intent or malice can usually be shown by demonstrating that the statement was made in order to injure the plaintiff or divert his customers away, and that the utterer knew or reasonably should have known that the statement was false and would likely cause injury.

By far the most onerous burden for a plaintiff is proof of special damages. This usually requires showing either loss of sales to specific potential buyers or a loss in general sales proximately caused by the disparaging statements. Obviously it is quite difficult for a manufacturer of widely distributed consumer goods to show that particular prospects were lost as a result of the disparagement. Moreover, even proof of general sales loss may not suffice where it could equally have been caused by economic or market conditions rather than the false statements.

While some courts have mitigated the requirement by allowing less specific proof, the majority still demand more rigorously detailed substantiation of special damages.

There are, however, two instances in which the special damage requirement is avoided. The first is when the statements do more than merely disparage a product, but also impeach the general integrity, competency, or business methods of the manufacturer himself. This may qualify as a defamation per se, in which case the court can award damages without plaintiff having to prove specific monetary losses. Two New York Court of Appeals cases illustrate the differences between disparagement and defamation per se.

In Drug Research Corp. *v.* Curtis Publishing Co., 7 N.Y.2d 435 (1960), defendant's publication on mail frauds mentioned that a distributor of plaintiff's weight-reducing product had agreed with postal authorities not to solicit orders for the product through the mails and that the product was under investigation by the Federal Trade Commission. The plaintiff alleged that these statements not only disparaged its product but also defamed the corporation. The court disagreed with the latter claim, stating, "the article in its entirety [was] at variance with the construction that it was written of and concerning the plaintiff," and held that since no special damages were pleaded, the complaint was deficient with respect to the disparagement allegation.

In Harwood Pharmacy Co. *v.* NBC, 9 N.Y.2d 460 (1961), a television performer said that plaintiff's sleep drug was full of habit-forming drugs, that "nothing short of a hospital care will make you stop taking [them]," and that they will make you "feel like a run-down hound dog and lose weight."

In holding that such statements amounted to defamation of the plaintiff corporation itself, the court commented that here, as was not true in Drug Research, the "language could readily be understood by the television audience as charging the manufacturer of 'Snooze' with fraud and deceit in putting on the market an unwholesome and dangerous product."

A request for injunctive rather than monetary relief may provide a second means of avoiding the special damage requirement. However, some courts flatly refuse to enjoin any type of libel (including that of a product) on the ground that to do so would amount to an unconstitutional prior restraint on free speech. Nevertheless, other courts, by pigeonholing disparagement as essentially an action for unfair competition rather than libel, have circumvented this rule and awarded injunctions. On these occasions the courts have stressed such things as the fact that the disparager was a competitor of plaintiff, the maliciousness of the disparager, the virulence of the particular disparagement, and the clear likelihood of irreparable injury to plaintiff resulting from it.

In short, the question of whether injunctive relief is a feasible alternative for a disparagement victim cannot be answered in absolute terms, but rather will depend on the facts of each case and their careful evaluation by legal counsel.

False advertising, without disparagement, usually occurs when a manufacturer claims that his product is better than it really is. Historically, the law has been opposed to giving a private remedy to firms which are victims of a rival's false advertising. However, while such relief may not have been available under the old common law, a party aggrieved by a rival's false representations may now find statutory help. Section 43(*a*) of the Lanham Act (the federal trademark law) provides:

> ... any person who shall use ... any false description or representation, including words or other symbols tending falsely to describe or represent [his goods or services] ... shall be liable to a civil action ... by any person who believes that he is or is likely to be damaged by the use of any such false description or representation. [15 U.S.C. §1125 (*a*).]

The full ramifications of this Statute are still quite unsettled. However, certain observations can be made. First, it appears fairly well established that monetary recovery (as distinct from an injunction), even under the Statute, requires some showing of special damages.

Second, a plaintiff who seeks either injunctive or monetary relief under the Statute must be prepared to make a strong factual showing that the advertisement is false; it has the capacity of deceiving a significant portion of the audience; the misrepresentations are likely to have an effect on the purchase decision; and the plaintiff is likely to suffer injury as a result.

Failure of proof in either of these areas will probably spell defeat. For example, a wax manufacturer who sought to enjoin another's use of the mark "Glass Wax" on the ground that it falsely described the product (it in fact contained no wax) was denied relief because it had not been clearly demonstrated that the misdescription was material. In other words, there was no showing that consumers would have been likely to purchase another product had they known Glass Wax contained no true wax. Hence, plaintiff could not demonstrate a likelihood of injury causally related to the misrepresentation.

Apart from its own direct legal remedies, a commercially maligned company may turn to the Federal Trade Commission for help, where the disparagement is materially false. If that agency directs an inquiry to the offending advertiser, such evidence of interest alone may cause him seriously to reevaluate his conduct without awaiting its potential, formal action.

Finally, the self-regulating machinery of radio and television broadcasters (which will be later discussed in the section on governmental regulation of advertising) may offer the most expeditious and effective protection (limited, of course, to those particular media) since their codes prohibit "unfair" disparagement, even though it may not be untrue.   Also, their refusal to air a commercial is ultimate in its preventive effects.

E. Copyrights and Ideas

1. Copyrights   A statutory copyright is a legal right conferred on the owner which enables him to control reproduction of his artistic creation once it has been disclosed to the public.

Copyrights do not protect abstract ideas or concepts as such, but only the physical form and manner in which the author expresses them.   A writing or graphic (reduced to concrete form), which is original (in the sense that it results from the author's own intellectual or artistic effort) and contains some degree of creativity, is copyrightable.   Advertisements, despite their commercial purpose, can possess these qualities and be copyrighted.   Illustrations, labels, jingles, texts of the advertisements, instruction pamphlets, catalogs, brochures, photographs, and contest materials are all protectable.

The arguments in favor of copyrighting advertising are persuasive. First, obtaining statutory copyright protection is simple.   Essentially it requires only putting a copyright notice on every copy of the advertisement published (such notice consists of © or "Copyright" or "Copr." along with the name of the owner and year of first publication).   The filing of copies of the advertisement with the copyright office along with submission of an application and payment of a nominal fee is required before an action for copyright infringement can be maintained.

Second, the certification of registration confers important legal benefits and rights upon the owner thereof, such as the right to statutory damages where actual damages cannot be proved against an infringer; and the right to recover attorney's fees incurred in bringing a successful infringement action.

Third, and most important, the copyright is the only meaningful way the advertiser has of protecting his advertising from being copied.   The minute an advertisement is published without the appropriate copyright notice, it falls into the public domain and others may copy its important, artistically valuable, or attractive features. The copyright which a newspaper or periodical publisher obtains for the issue itself does not embrace the advertisements in it or redound to the benefit of their sponsors. The advertiser must seek his own copyright if he wants one.

It is essential to the validity of a copyright that the copyright notice appear on every copy of the material, commencing with the first publication. It is not only proper but an absolute requisite to utilize that notice even though a formal copyright certificate has not yet been obtained. The procedure is to publish first, *with the notice,* and then to apply for the official copyright. If the samples of the previously published advertisement (which must be submitted to the Copyright Office as part of the application) do not display the notice, copyright will be denied.

Advertisers may be held accountable if the material used on broadcasts which they sponsor infringes upon another's copyright. It has been held, for example, that where an advertiser and its agency had control over the content and general production of a television program, they were also legally responsible when the play used therein violated another's copyright.

The right to secure a copyright vests initially with the author of the work. Of course, he is free to assign his rights in the creation to others, who may then, all other conditions being satisfied, obtain the copyright.

It is well established, both under the common law and the copyright statutes, that the rights in a work produced by an employee in the course of his employment belong to the employer. This is called the "work made for hire" rule, and under the statute an employer is deemed to be the "author" of all such materials.

Similarly, the advertiser would, absent agreement to the contrary, own the rights to the work produced at its expense and on its behalf by the agency.

2. Ideas As pointed out earlier, mere ideas are not copyrightable. The question arises, then, whether an idea can be legally protected. One of the most troublesome situations in which this issue arises is where an advertiser receives an unsolicited idea from another and later (sometimes a great many years afterward) uses it, or is alleged to have used it, in an advertisement or promotion. The courts have not been consistent in deciding the question of whether the submitter of the idea is entitled to compensation in damages. Generally they have looked to whether the idea was new, original, and in concrete form when submitted.   However, there has been disagreement as to how these elements are defined.   Two examples are illustrative.

In Liggett & Myers Tobacco Co. *v.* Myers, 101 Ind. App. 420, 194 N.E. 206 (1935), the tobacco company had received an unsolicited plan which suggested that a picture showing one man refusing a cigarette from another and saying, "No thanks, I smoke Chesterfield," would make a good billboard advertisement.   The letter also stated that the plaintiff expected to be compensated if the idea was used. The defendant never replied, and some two years later used a similar format for one of its advertisements.   Plaintiff won a $9,000 verdict. The appellate court affirmed, finding that the idea was new and novel, had been reduced to concrete form by the plaintiff, and as such, constituted salable property which defendant, by its beneficial use thereof, was obliged to pay for.

In a later, similar case, Thomas *v.* R. J. Reynolds Tobacco Co., 350 Pa. 262, 38 A.2d 61 (1944), defendant received a gratuitous suggestion that it should advertise that Camels are more economical because they burn longer than competing brands.   The defendant never answered the submitter, and five years later instituted such a campaign.   The court refused plaintiff's claim for compensation on the ground that his idea was neither novel nor reduced to a concrete form of expression, so that there was no obligation upon defendant to pay for it.

In a later case, Official Airlines Schedule Information Service Inc. *v.* Eastern Airlines, Inc., 333 F.2d 672 (5th Cir. 1964), the plaintiff approached defendant and other airlines with a proposal that they jointly broadcast their flight information on a program to be called "Plane Facts."   The defendant rejected the idea, but later did sponsor a program of its own called "Flite Facts" which, unlike the "Plane Facts" broadcasts, dealt solely with its own flight information.   The court dismissed the plaintiff's claim of misappropriation on three grounds: (1) the idea was not novel; (2) it had not been disclosed to Eastern in confidence but rather was revealed to the entire airlines industry; and (3) Eastern had not used plaintiff's idea since its broadcasts concerned only its own flight information and were not made jointly with other companies as had been suggested by the plaintiff.

There are certain steps which an advertiser or agency can take to minimize the uncertainty and risk in this area.   A specific policy should be followed with regard to all submissions.   It is best that they be reviewed initially only by persons outside the advertising department.   That way, if the submitter later claims that his idea has been used, the advertiser may be able to show that the persons responsible for its advertising never received the submission and hence developed the idea independently of it.

The sole duty of the persons to whom the submissions are thus first routed should be to return them immediately with a form letter stating that no suggestions from outside the company are considered, or even seen by those engaged in the relevant department unless accompanied by a release.   A form of such release should be enclosed.   It should waive any right to payment beyond a minimal stated amount in the event the suggestion is adopted, and should grant full right and title therein to the company.

While this will undoubtedly discourage submissions, that may be one of its chief virtues, since most companies find that the number of worthwhile ideas or materials which come in "over the transom" is far from worth the legal ramifications they engender.

There is a difference in opinions as to whether the company should keep copies of the submissions they have returned.   Pro: It helps disprove a fraudulent claim by one who did not in fact send in the proposal he claims to have proffered.   Con: It arms a plaintiff's claim that his idea was in fact utilized, and that the gesture of returning it to him was a dishonest pretense.

The same policies should be followed both where a submission comes from outside the company and where it originates inside the organization.   Of course, a proposal by an employee whose job includes developing such ideas poses no problem, as the employer, by paying him for such work, is deemed the owner thereof.   Such is not the case, however, when the idea comes from an employee—e.g., a secretary—whose duties do not relate to the nature of the submission.   The employer should treat that suggestion as he would if it had come from outside the company.

F. Libel and Right of Privacy

Although these two subjects are conceptually distinct in their legal principles, they tend to intermingle with respect to advertising.   A libelous publication is one which holds a person up to public ridicule, scorn, hatred, or contempt, or otherwise lowers him in the esteem of those to whom it is addressed.   The right of privacy, being essentially the highly personal right of an individual to remain out of the public limelight if he so desires,[5] is violated when another uses his name or picture without his consent for purposes of trade or advertising.   (One loses his right of privacy for noncommercial purposes when he becomes involved—albeit involuntarily—in a newsworthy event, i.e., one of public interest.   As will later be illustrated, however, this does not similarly dissipate his right of privacy, even respecting the same news or current interest item, for purposes of commercial exploitation of his name or picture.)

Thus a person whose visual image or name is used in advertising without his consent has a cause of action in most states against the advertiser, the agency, perhaps the medium, and other persons collaterally involved in the production and presentation of the advertisement, even if the depiction is highly flattering.   In New York the consent must be in writing and signed, and if the person so used is a minor, such consent must be by his parent or guardian.   If, instead of being complimentary, the individual is portrayed in an unfavorable light he may have a case for libel as well as privacy violation, which accounts for the frequent joinder of these two legally different causes in one complaint based upon the same advertisement.

For example, several years ago a famous gentleman rider, winner of many nationally famous horse races, was shown in riding garb holding his saddle in front of him.   From this saddle there fell from slightly below waist height a white girth, which in the resultant photograph, as described by the court, appeared "to be attached to the plaintiff and not to the saddle."   Although the plaintiff had consented that his picture be taken and used for advertising purposes, he asserted that the consent did not apply to one showing him so ludicrously, if not shamefully; and that he did not consent, and never would have, to the use of the particular picture that was employed. He alleged, as well, a cause of action for libel because of the public ridicule to which the advertisement exposed him.   His suit was

---

[5] In one case, at least [Haelan Laboratories *v.* Topps Chewing Gum, Inc., 202 F.2d 866 (2d Cir. 1953), *cert denied* 346 U.S. 816 (1953)], a court recognized a parallel "right of publicity" for persons (professional athletes, in that case) who had created valuable commercial rights in their names and images by very virtue of having been the focus of much public attention.   The court held that such "property" could not be misappropriated without its "owners'" permission.

highly successful.   [Burton *v.* Crowell Pub. Co., 82 F.2d 154 (2d Cir. 1936).]

As earlier intimated, public figures or persons involved in newsworthy events lose their right of privacy to the extent that their names and pictures may be editorially used without their consent.   Indeed, the Supreme Court in a series of recent decisions has concluded that the free speech guarantees of the First Amendment mandate that even untrue statements about public figures are not actionable unless made with actual knowledge or reckless disregard of their falsity.

However, such public personages do not forfeit their right of privacy against advertisers who use their names or pictures to sell products.   For example, a company which reprinted a newspaper story as part of its advertisement was held to have invaded the privacy of the person whose name appeared in the news article.   The court felt it was immaterial that the plaintiff's name was reproduced solely as part of a news item which had, at the time of its original publication, been a matter of public interest.   It was also irrelevant to the court that plaintiff's name was not mentioned in the advertising copy itself or that its use might be of no particular benefit to the advertiser's business.   The fact was, according to the court, that the news item was used "for advertising purposes" and thus came within the statute.   [Flores *v.* Mosler Safe Co., 7 N.Y.2d 276 (1959).]

In essence, where the advertiser uses a person's name or picture as part of or in direct connection with the advertisement, written consent must be obtained.   Where, for example, an advertiser uses a candid photograph of a crowd as part of his advertisement, written consent should be obtained from any persons who are recognizable in it.   On the other hand, television shots of spectators at a football game offer the sponsor no problem since such onlookers at public events are generally deemed by the law to expect and hence assume the risk of being televised.   If, however, the television camera were to focus on an attractive co-ed in the crowd and the announcer were to chime in: "I'll bet she prefers men who use brand X," the advertiser would have used the picture directly as part of an advertisement and thus should have obtained written consent.

As a practical matter, the approach to protecting advertising against libel and right of privacy complaints is to obtain adequately broad written consent.   It should give permission to use the person's name and picture in any manner whatsoever for purposes of trade and advertising without further approval, and to assign such rights to still others, they, in turn, having similar rights of reassignment. The latter feature is particularly important where stock photographs are concerned which pass from hand to hand. Preferably the signature to the consent should be notarized, and photographs which have been obtained by assignment should be checked to make certain that the consents have actually been executed.

Even such precautions may not be sufficient in particular cases. For example, models often are minors without appearing to be so. In New York, at least, their signed consent is not enough; that of their parent or guardian must be obtained. Further, as exemplified by the Crawford Burton case described above, signatories may claim that the consent they gave was vitiated by placing the picture in a different context with defamatory overtones, or by retouching, or other alteration that substantially changes its nature or import. Wherever there is a possibility of such a claim, it is important that a new consent be executed with the specific advertisement attached thereto and incorporated into it.

Insurance policies of the nature earlier referred to will ordinarily cover libel and right-of-privacy situations. That, however, is no excuse for carelessness, for the premium rates can be severely affected by an incidence of successful claims.

Corporations may not maintain an action for invasion of privacy, since the right applies only to the use of a natural person's name or picture. Under the same rationale, it also appears that the unauthorized use of pictures of a person's house or other property would not come within the statute, provided there is no identification of the owner. Corporations can, however, be libeled, and may recover at law for that injury.

Last, as pointed out in the sections dealing with advertiser-agency contracts, there should be a clear understanding between the parties as to which is responsible for obtaining the releases, and also, who will bear any losses resulting from failure to do so.

G. Advertising as a Warranty

For many years the courts had almost uniformly rejected any direct liability of a manufacturer to those who purchased his products from intermediate distributors. If there was to be any recovery for defects in the goods, the party injured had to proceed against the person from whom he purchased them. Subsequently, this rule was relaxed to permit a direct action against the manufacturer of an inherently dangerous product, e.g., an automobile, which had been negligently produced. Next in the chain of development was the allowance of direct suit in the case of foods and drugs. With respect to these actions, negligence then became an unnecessary element in an increasing number of states, for the manufacturer was held responsible as a warrantor of a defective product, no matter that the imperfection was not the result of a lack of due care.

More recently, the courts, in cases involving food, drugs, or cosmetics, are beginning to hold that advertising representations constitute direct promises, hence express warranties, to the public, and if not true, form a basis for public liability, even if negligence is not shown.

For example, a manufacturer's advertising claim that its cosmetic was "safe" and "gentle" was held to be in the nature of an express warranty rendering the advertiser potentially liable without proof of negligence or bad faith to a purchaser who had lost most of her hair from using the product.

Under this rationale, the manufacturer becomes, in effect, an insurer of the product promises made in his advertising, since no excuse by way of diligent care, good faith, or lack of knowledge of any dangerous potentiality constitutes a defense against the express-warranty theory.

The teaching of this line of cases is that one must be wary of making broad, unqualified claims where substantial injury might be expected to flow from failure to fulfill them. (The substantiality may result either from the large volume of such instances, or from extreme damage—such as death or permanent disability—in a smaller number of cases.) This principle accounts for such examples of qualifications as "Safe for normal skin" (to avoid liability for allergic reactions), or "Safe when used as directed."

GOVERNMENTAL REGULATION OF ADVERTISING

This section will profile briefly the most important of the governmental agencies which regulate one phase or another of advertising. "Briefly," because any businessman who has become sufficiently enmeshed in such an agency's operation will of necessity be in the hands of a lawyer to complete his relevant education.

A. Federal

1. Federal Trade Commission The Federal Trade Commission is empowered to prohibit deceptive advertising. Substantive standards for determining such deceptiveness have already been discussed. So, too, has the Commission's regulatory power over cooperative advertising.

The basic enforcement tool of the Commission is the cease-and-desist order. It is, in form and effect, much like the final injunction that a court issues after trial of a case. Indeed, the entire underlying administrative procedure before the Commission is patterned—so far as procedural form is concerned—after judicial litigation.

It starts with a complaint issued by the Commission and designating summarily the charges of illegality against the defendant (called a *respondent*). The respondent files an answer indicating its defenses to such charges, and after certain pretrial procedures, the case comes on for trial in front of a hearing examiner. Witnesses are examined and cross-examined under oath; evidence is introduced; both sides (i.e., counsel for the Commission and for the respondent) exchange briefs and make oral arguments before the hearing examiner, who then issues an initial decision.

This is ordinarily appealed by the losing party to the full Commission, which then reviews the initial decision in the light of the record of testimony and evidence which was presented to the hearing examiner. The Commission, after reviewing briefs and hearing oral arguments by both sides, renders its decision either affirming, reversing, or modifying the initial decision. If the respondent is dissatisfied with this result, it may then appeal to a federal court of appeals.

While all this takes on the formal appearances of a court case, it seriously lacks much of the substance thereof, primarily for two reasons. First, the Commission—which ultimately decides the case—is the complainant, and has one of its staff attorneys act as the prosecutor therein. Often its own personnel serve as witnesses to furnish the evidence upon which the Commission then passes judgment. Thus, judicial impartiality is lacking. Second, because of the broad discretion which is assigned to the Commission by statute and by court decisions, the scope of judicial review by the federal court of appeals of Federal Trade Commission cease-and-desist orders is much more limited and less effective than for corresponding judgments of federal district courts.

Unlike a court, however, the Commission cannot command the payment of any monetary sum or inflict any other penalty. Its cease-and-desist order merely enjoins further engagement in practices of the kind found to be unlawful. If the respondent later disobeys that order, he then subjects himself to the possibility of substantial penalties, which can run as high as $5,000 per day as long as the transgression continues. Violation of an order, and the penalty therefor, are determined by a court on charges brought by the Commission.

In the case of advertisements for foods, drugs, cosmetics, and devices, the Commission can, prior to its final administrative decision, seek a temporary injunction from a court if such an injunction would be in the public interest. Also, false advertising of such products may be a criminal misdemeanor where they are injurious to health under the conditions of use for which they are advertised or customarily used, or if the advertiser intended to mislead.

The Commission, aside from the cease-and-desist order or case-by-case method of enforcement, has, in some statutorily specified instances, the power to enact certain substantive regulations which have the effect of law. This is true under the Fair Packaging and Labeling Act, as well as under statutes dealing with wool and fur products, flammable fabrics, and textile fiber products. The question of whether the Commission has such rule-making authority dealing with deceptive advertising generally under Section 5 of the Federal Trade Commission Act has not been decided, although the Commission has taken the position, now under challenge in the courts, that it does have such power.

Substantive regulations should not be confused with "guides," "enforcement policies," or other styles of informational pronouncements commonly issued by the Commission to alert the public as to its views regarding the legality of particular commercial practices. These are advisory only and disregard of them does not, of itself, constitute a violation of the law. Thus, if the Commission brings an action against an advertiser because he has transgressed one of its guides as to deceptive advertising, the Commission must still establish that the alleged misconduct breaches the underlying statute which the guide has purported to interpret. Where the Commission has been given statutory power to promulgate a substantive regulation, however, it need only show that such *rule* has been violated.

2. Secretary of Agriculture The advertising of meat, dairy, and poultry products (including eggs) is not within the regulatory jurisdiction of the Federal Trade Commission, but under that of the Secretary of Agriculture, by virtue of the Federal Packers and Stockyards Act.

The enforcement procedure, however, is of the same nature as the Federal Trade Commission's, the administrative proceedings culminating in a final injunctive order, after hearings conducted within the Department.

3. Food and Drug Administration This agency has jurisdiction over the advertising of prescription drugs (i.e., those which by law can be purchased only with a medical prescription), but—theoretically at least—it does not have regulatory power over advertising of over-the-counter drugs.   Its scope is statutorily directed only toward *labeling* of foods, over-the-counter drugs, cosmetics, and devices; such labeling being described as "all written, printed, or graphic matter (1) upon any article or any of its containers or wrappers or (2) accompanying such article."

Nevertheless, Food and Drug, by ingenious extension of its statutory powers over labeling, has, with judicial confirmation, managed to bring within its grasp much that would ordinarily be thought of as advertising rather than product labeling.   It has done this via two main routes.   First, it has persuaded the courts that promotional material accompanies the product where it is intended ultimately to be utilized at the point of sale, even though its transmittal and that of the product are widely separated, both by carriers and by time.   Thus, a regularly published book extolling the virtue of certain foods and drugs was deemed to be labeling of them where it was separately distributed to drug outlets, but with intent of being used there to promote the sale of such items.

Next, the Food and Drug Administration conceived a strategy that has commonly come to be called the "squeeze play." Under its statute, Food and Drug does have power to require that drug labeling include adequate instructions for using the product.   Assume, then, that a manufacturer wishes to advertise a drug item for use in a condition or manner in which he knows the Food and Drug Administration believes it to be ineffectual.   If he attempts to skirt the powers of

Food and Drug by promoting such use only in advertising, and omitting it from labeling, that agency may attack his labeling directly, upon the ground that it does *not* contain adequate instructions for using the article so as to achieve the results claimed for it in its advertising. Then, if the advertiser attempts to meet that criticism by adding such directions to his labels he will subject himself to the jurisdiction of the Food and Drug Administration to proceed against him on the basis that such labeling has itself been made deceptive, in violation of the Food, Drug and Cosmetic Act, by implicitly representing that if the product is used in accordance with such instructions it will accomplish the cited results.

In short, it cannot be automatically assumed that advertising of foods, drugs, cosmetics, or devices, as distinguished from what would ordinarily be thought of as their labeling, is beyond the reach of the Food and Drug Administration's regulatory powers.

The intricacies and complexities of the regulation of labeling, as such, under the Food, Drug and Cosmetic Act is a subject separate from advertising and will not be embarked upon here. It may, however, be pointed out, since this is appropriate to advertising as well, that the Food and Drug Administration, unlike the Federal Trade Commission and the Secretary of Agriculture, must prosecute its enforcement proceedings in court. It does not have the power to issue its own cease-and-desist orders.

4. Post Office Department It is criminally unlawful to use the mails in furtherance of a fraudulent scheme [18 U.S.C. §1341]. However, as is not the case with the Federal Trade Commission and the Food and Drug Administration, to make out a violation under this statute, *intent to defraud* must be proved beyond a reasonable doubt. These requirements have been a major barrier in maintaining many criminal actions against false advertisers.

However, a new law [Public Law 90–590, October 17, 1968, amending 39 U.S.C. §4005] substantially broadens the effective range of the Post Office's powers over deceptive advertising by enabling it to issue, on its own authority, a stop-mail order (a procedure in which the Postal Department intercepts all mail sent in response to the deceptive advertising and returns it to the senders) against any person seeking money or property through the mail by means of false representations. The Department does not have to prove, as under the predecessor stop-mail statute, that the misrepresenter intended to deceive. Moreover, since this statute imposes no criminal sanctions, the Postal Department need not meet the onerous "beyond a reasonable doubt" standard, but rather must show only that "substantial evidence" of a violation exists.   A party aggrieved by a stop-mail order may appeal to a federal district court.   However, he has the burden of convincing it that there is no substantial evidence to support the Department's findings.

Although the tests used by the Postmaster to determine falsity generally conform to those followed by the Federal Trade Commission, the Department is free to develop its own criteria.

5. Federal Communications Commission   This Commission's power over advertising is indirect, through its control over broadcasters. The ultimate weapon in the Commission's arsenal is its licensing power.   It can, in the "public interest," revoke, suspend, or refuse to renew a broadcaster's license.   It can also impose fines upon licensees.   Thus, it would be within the Commission's power to use these sanctions against one who has allowed his stations to convey deceptive or indecent advertising (or even to schedule too many advertisements per broadcast hour).   The Commission has said on occasions that a broadcaster has an affirmative duty to check on the truthfulness of all advertising aired on his facilities.

However, despite these pronouncements, the Commission, at present, has shown little inclination to use its powers to regulate advertising.   On February 5, 1969, the Commission announced a proposed rule which would ban the broadcasting of all cigarette advertising.   This represented its first significant foray into a major area of advertising regulation.   It is, as yet, too early to reach any conclusion on whether this sudden flex of muscle heralds the beginning of a new activist role for the Commission.

6. Securities and Exchange Commission   The advertising of securities, be it in the form of a registration statement, sales literature, or prospectus, falls under the aegis of this Commission.   It has power to move against advertising that contains a material misrepresentation, or omits a material fact when, in light of what is stated, that creates a false impression.

There are a variety of sanctions which the Securities and Exchange Commission may impose.   It may enjoin the dissemination of the false advertising; and in the case of a deceptive registration statement it may impose a stop order on the sale of the misrepresented securities.

Moreover, statutes also provide for civil relief to persons damaged as a result of the false representations, and for criminal prosecution of the advertiser.

7. Alcohol and Tobacco Tax Division of the Internal Revenue Service While the broad jurisdictions of the Federal Trade Commission and the Food and Drug Administration encompass alcoholic-beverage advertising, they have deferred to the Division on this matter.

As a result of its extensive rule-making powers, there are myriad regulations with which liquor advertisers must comply. A wide variety of affirmative disclosures is required in all such advertising and on the labeling of alcoholic beverages. Indeed, all labels must be submitted to the Division for its approval before they can be used.

Violation of any of these regulations can result in a fine or worse, suspension or revocation of the manufacturer's license to distil or distribute his products.

8. Miscellaneous Federal Controls There are other federal agencies, such as the Interstate Commerce Commission and the Federal Power Commission, which have some limited measure of control over advertising in the industries with which they are concerned. Even the Coast Guard is involved, it being empowered to supervise the advertising of ship cruisers. As a general precaution, therefore, advertisers in any of the "regulated industries" should check the statutes, rules, and regulations pertaining to the administrating authority for provisions applicable to their advertising.

B. State and Local Regulation

Regulation at this level consists of a hodgepodge of civil and criminal statutes covering a wide variety of subjects and advertising practices. Perhaps the single most notable development has been the almost unanimous adoption in the states of the so-called Printers' Ink Statute which makes it a misdemeanor to disseminate a false or misleading advertisement. While not all state versions are identical—for example, some require proof of intent to deceive while others do not—generally speaking, if an advertisement would pass muster under the Federal Trade Commission's standards it would do so under these statutes.

While such statutes might appear to be a potent weapon in state arsenals, in practice they have been used very sparingly. This lack of enforcement is probably due to their criminal aspect and the feeling among overburdened prosecutors that they have more important duties to perform.   Only in those cities where local consumer fraud bureaus have been set up to deal specifically with advertising offenses has state enforcement been vigorous.   Current efforts to enact more modern state laws to regulate deceptive advertising will undoubtedly produce new legislation patterned after one or more of a set of "model" acts sponsored by various groups such as the Federal Trade Commission, the American Advertising Federation, and others.

There is, also, extensive state legislation in the area of food and drug advertising.   Most of these laws are modeled upon the federal statutes.   Thus, advertisers who meet the requirements of the Food and Drug Administration and the Federal Trade Commission usually need not worry that they will offend these state adaptations.

Consumer fraud divisions of the states' attorney general offices are probably the most active area of state control.   These agencies usually possess a wide range of sanctions to bring false advertising into line: threat of public exposure, injunction, and fines are a few. Moreover, some states have granted the attorney general power to bring suit to terminate the business of the offender and place it in the hands of a receiver, who would then allow victims of the deception to recoup their losses by sharing in the distribution of the assets.   In New York, as in some other states, the attorney general has formulated voluntary industry-wide codes, similar to the Trade Practice Rules of the Federal Trade Commission.

Additionally, each state usually has a large number of laws that relate to specific advertising or promotional practices.   Outdoor advertising, coupon and trading stamp promotions, lotteries, securities "Blue Sky" laws, advertising for professional services, insurance, banks, real estate, and various agricultural and dairy products are the most common of the many individual areas for which state laws must be consulted.

PRIVATE REGULATION

Media, trade associations, and better business bureaus are the three principal sources of private censorship.

A. Media

The Radio and Television Codes of the National Association of Broadcasters have the greatest impact in this area.   These codes' provisions are comprehensive and contain general standards concerning deceptive advertising as well as specific ones for particular practices and products (e.g., use of an announcer dressed in white medical garb to advertise health products is prohibited); rules concerning the tastefulness of advertising (e.g., on-camera drinking is prohibited in wine and beer commercials, and advertising some products, such as hard liquor, is completely banned); and provisions regulating the frequency and duration with which advertising may appear during a given time period (e.g., advertisers presently are allowed 10 minutes of nonprogram material in a prime-time hour, with interruptions not to exceed four for any show other than a variety, news, weather, sports, or special-event program, in which case different interruption standards apply).

As may be deduced from these types of restrictions, code regulation goes beyond mere implementation of legal proscriptives. It extends to matters which, if not controlled, would, in the National Association of Broadcasters' opinion, provoke adverse public reaction, or other consequences which the broadcasters fear would redound to their own long-term disadvantage. One example will illustrate the extra-legal reach of the code. Disparagement of a competitor or his product is unlawful only when it is false. The code forbids it, however, even where it is truthful, if it is also derogatory in its overtones. Thus, if one of two competing articles is less expensive than the other, the code authority will permit a plain statement, "Product X costs you less than Product Y." But it will not allow a statement, "It's foolish to buy Product Y when you can get Product X for less." This is considered an "ash canning" of Product Y, which the code authority forbids.

Over 70 per cent of all the licensed television stations subscribe to the code; hence compliance with it is mandatory if the advertiser expects to reach the majority of the nation's television audience.

Each of the major networks maintains a separate department to review all advertising before it is broadcast for code compliance, as well as for adherence to the network's own policy requirements. If a network rejects the advertising, the advertiser has several options. He may, where feasible, amend the commercial to correct the cause of the refusal. Where such revision is impossible, however, and the advertiser believes that the commercial does comply with the code, he may be able to get the network to reverse its decision by obtaining the approval of the code authority itself, which maintains an independent office and reviewing staff.   Or, he may try another network, since it is entirely possible that two networks will disagree as to whether a specific commercial violates the code.   If all these steps fail, the only resort left the advertiser is to seek out independent, non-code-subscribing stations, an alternative which will not be satisfactory where maximum nationwide exposure is desired.   To avoid such eventualities, compliance with the codes should be given a high priority by advertisers in the formulation of all broadcast advertising.

Various magazines and newspapers also attempt to check the honesty and tastefulness of advertising in their publications.   However, these media have no uniform code, and policies vary among the separate publications.

B. Trade Associations

Every major industry has its own trade association, and each, more likely than not, has a code of ethics which touches upon some aspects of advertising.   Despite this plethora of codes, and the high intentions they represent, the legal restrictions of antitrust laws upon concerted activity by competitors severely limit the censorship power of such associations.   Since advertising is a form of competition, attempts by associations to impose confining standards upon it may risk being viewed as a conspiracy in restraint of trade.   For example, a Federal Trade Commission advisory opinion criticizes an association code of ethics provision that forbids members from engaging in below-cost price advertising, opining that "sales below cost can be a legitimate method of competition . . . [and hence] any agreement among competitors to refrain from such advertising to that extent restricts competition" (CCH Trade Reg. Rep. §18,350).   Thus, to the extent that industry codes would impose standards more restrictive than those of independent law (such as the Federal Trade Commission Act, or the Food, Drug and Cosmetic Act), they may operate as anti-competitive devices suspect under the antitrust laws.   Even where an association code merely reiterates governmental standards for advertising, an attempt by the association to enforce ("put teeth into") it against a noncomplying member by penalties or by interfering with his business relations would be viewed by the Federal Trade Commission, at least, as unlawful.   Thus, the Commission has advised that it is improper for an association to send letters to media recommending their rejection of a member's advertising unless it is changed to meet the association's standards. Indeed, there is very little an association can do to enforce its standards. The effectiveness of an association code ultimately depends upon the willingness of individual members to abide voluntarily by its terms.

C. Better Business Bureaus

These are nongovernmental organizations set up and funded locally and nationally by business communities. The bureaus seek through voluntary cooperation of companies to prevent and correct deception in advertising and promotional practices and conduct educational programs designed to enable consumers to achieve satisfaction in the marketplace.

The National Better Business Bureau relies upon its own advertising review procedures as well as competitor, media, or consumer complaints and inquiries to discover infractions. Once found, contacts are made with those responsible and effort exerted to persuade discontinuance of the objectionable practices.

Where this procedure is unsuccessful, the bureau may issue statements privately to its members, or publicly to the press, media, and inquirers, reporting its analysis and conclusions. In addition, the facts may be made available to appropriate law enforcement agencies if a violation of law is involved.

Local better business bureaus deal in a manner parallel to that of the national bureau in their respective market areas.

The National Better Business Bureau also makes broad use of the industry-wide approach to self-regulation in advertising and selling. These programs generally are carried on in cooperation with industry trade associations. They usually involve publications and distribution of consumer information literature, and the adoption and policing of advertising and selling standards. For example, such programs are in operation on central air conditioners, room air conditioners, magazines, and reference books.

Generally, advertising which conforms with ethical standards and applicable laws need not fear involvement with better business bureaus. To the contrary, they and especially the national bureau offer many valuable services in aid of that objective, including advisory consultations and a comprehensive, continuously updated publication, "Do's and Don't's in Advertising Copy."

STRUCTURING THE ADMINISTRATION
OF LEGAL SERVICES

The opening section of this chapter observed that legal counsel must be an integral part of the advertising process.   The multiplicity of problems outlined in the succeeding sections illustrate the necessity. We shall now explore how companies can organize and administer their relationships with counsel to best achieve effective and comprehensive utilization of legal services.

A. Continuity

The procedural objective of the structuring should be to implement continuity of contact between counsel and operational personnel.

The further along in its development an advertising campaign progresses, the more costly and difficult it becomes to change it. Many, if not most, legally troublesome situations can be spotted at early stages, when their correction may most easily and economically be made or when, at worst, if they are not solvable, abandonment will sacrifice least by way of investment.   Counsel should be shown the earliest typescripts, storyboards, and rough artwork which the company seriously considers utilizing as the conceptual basis of a campaign.   Even before that, however, inquiries to him as to the legal feasibility of a given approach or statement may keep further efforts from being expended in wrong directions.

Usually the familiarity counsel develops with the purposes and rationale of a campaign by being kept privy with it virtually from its inception enhances his ability to advise quickly on later—sometimes last-minute—modifications, and to tailor all his recommendations as closely as possible to the commercial goals.   By the same token, continuity of the same counsel not only with the one campaign but extending to others for the same or similar products fosters smoother teamwork and more competent judgmental consistency.

Part of counsel's education and area of scrutiny should be, of course, the factual support for advertising claims, and the economic data which may bear upon Robinson-Patman or antitrust questions. Legal battles often must be fought over opposing contentions as to such matters, and neither the client nor the lawyer can blithely assume that information given to them initially, casually, or in generalized form is unassailable. It will pay them well to probe and test it in the manner that might be expected of an adversary.

B. House Counsel, Outside Counsel, and Both

Generally speaking, but subject to individual exceptions, house counsel is somewhat better situated than independent attorneys to maintain the constant hour-to-hour contact with what goes on within his company; while outside counsel, being more the specialist, and drawing a breadth of experience from his representation of a number of different companies—and especially from his forensic background—is more apt to remain in the forefront of developments in the relevant legal areas and to be gaited to advise with greater detachment, objectivity, and practicality. Many internal legal departments do, however, include lawyers with a high degree of expertise in particular fields; and, on the other hand, there are independent law firms which work in intimate, constant, and immediate contact with the advertising and marketing personnel of major clients.

Some of the governing variables are found in the size of the company's own legal staff as related to the total volume of legal work to be done by it for the entire corporation, which in turn determines how much undistracted time is available for advertising and marketing problems; the particular patterns of a given company as to types and numbers of products involved, and the advertising and merchandising policies pertaining to them; the specialized expertise of its legal staff in the areas previously considered in this chapter; and in innumerable personal factors, intangible though they may be, which make for good rapport, or lack of it, between the business and the legal people.

Each company must, and will, develop its own type of structure, probably more through trial and error than a priori schematization. The subject is not unique to marketing, and companies which have reached a fairly definite organizational philosophy with respect to other legal areas—such as taxes, labor, litigation, securities transactions, patents, and the like—will probably be inclined to start with a similar structure for advertising. Nonetheless, advertising has its own peculiar imperatives which may require special accommodation. Few departments of business activity possess the dynamism and fluidity of advertising. The legal factors are equally turbulent. While new approaches and techniques are taking place on the commercial side, equally novel developments appear in law and in regulatory activity by the host of governmental agencies earlier described, as well as by proposals and promulgation of new statutes at federal, state, and even municipal legislative levels.

In short, no plan of organization is good for a particular company unless it optimally makes available legal service that is adept at maximizing productive use of desirable and innovative advertising programs in the light of the most current, and evolving, applicable law as it is being (and about to be) administered by those individuals in pertinent official agencies, and courts, whose determinations are controlling. To this must be added the concomitant interplay of nongovernmental regulators, of which the Television and Radio Code Authority of the National Association of Broadcasters is an outstanding example.

A company whose advertising remains essentially unchanged over relatively long periods, and entails noncontroversial representations, may find that its already existent house counsel can quite satisfactorily supply what legal supervision is needed, consulting outside counsel only on the separate occasions when he feels it wise to obtain specialized advice as to a particular problem. If such a company does not have a legal staff for general corporate purpose, it would hardly pay to establish one merely to service that sort of advertising. An independent firm could readily handle it.

At the other end of the spectrum, a company engaged in voluminous and constantly changing advertising, for a multiplicity of products, involving several operating groups of people, and utilizing hardhitting copy in contentious areas (especially, for example, drugs), could well need both house counsel and outside attorneys working together as a closely coordinated team. Company counsel would maintain close and constant vigilance over the internal operations to guard that legal contact not be lost with any pertinent aspect in the course of their rapid development. The primary role of outside counsel would be to evaluate the advertising proposals in the light of his specialized knowledge and experience, to suggest alternatives for those elements which may be unduly risky (see preceding pages), and to defend, in negotiations or litigation, against government or private attack the resultant campaigns of the client.

C. Directness

Direct lines of communication to legal counsel by the company personnel who are involved in preparing and administering advertising is closely allied to the purposes discussed above under the subject of continuity.   The more immediately and informally an individual working on a particular phase of a campaign can consult with the responsible lawyer about a possible problem, the more time and money will ultimately be saved.   Beyond that, such direct contact between the two is best suited to ironing out a difficulty, if one actually exists, to the best satisfaction of each.

Multiplying the hands through which communications must pass not only slows down the process, but almost inevitably generates misunderstandings in the course of second- and thirdhand recountings of questions and answers.   Such intervention also breeds insulation that can hamper creative interaction which might otherwise occur between the lawyer and the writer or artist when permitted to work directly with each other.   The author is bound to comment that he has never been disappointed, and has often been highly impressed, with the ability of creative talent to solve legal problems most fruitfully, once their essential nature has been understandably explained.   There is no substitute for the one-to-one relationship in achieving that result.

Obviously, avoidance of intermediates in such channels of intercourse is not tantamount to eliminating supervision and apprisal. All who are concerned with the particular advertising should be kept promptly informed of the consultations, against the event that they might have other thoughts or further questions.   Responsibilities for assuring this should be identified and allocated as part of the structure.

D. Protecting the Attorney-Client Privilege

Communications which are made in confidence between an attorney acting in his legal capacity and a client (including a corporation) who seeks his legal advice are legally privileged.   With the privilege in effect, no one, including the government, a court, or an adversary, can compel disclosure of such communications, except the client himself.   Since absolute candor between attorney and client is essential, this privilege is a precious one indeed.   Unfortunately, however, it can be easily lost if the client does not take scrupulous care to preserve it, especially in situations involving communications between a corporation and its own house counsel.

While the latter is recognized by most courts as an "attorney" within the meaning of the privilege doctrine, the courts are prone to find, where possible, that his advice is of a business rather than legal nature, and hence not privileged. Moreover, many courts have restricted the definition of the corporate "client" to only those employees who have the decision-making power to act on the legal advice counsel gives. Thus, communications to counsel by employees outside this group would not qualify for the privilege. Some cases have further complicated the picture by denying the privilege on the ground that the corporation had itself destroyed the confidentiality by disclosing the communication to employees below that decision-making echelon.

While the following list is by no means exhaustive, it does contain some of the precautions and procedures which the company can take to protect the privileged status of its attorney-client communications:

1. The corporate legal department should maintain a separate and distinct identity vis-à-vis the rest of the company by having its own offices, files, and stationery.

2. All written requests for legal advice (obviously, oral requests are preferable), whether addressed to house or outside counsel, should clearly disclose that a legal opinion is sought and under no circumstances should ask for business advice. They might routinely be stamped "Confidential Communication to Legal Counsel."

3. Response from counsel should be organized and worded to manifest that the attorney is acting in a legal capacity and that a legal opinion is being given. It can be legended "Confidential Communication from Legal Counsel."

4. To the fullest extent possible, all copies of such legal memoranda should be kept in the confidential files of the lawyers, and out of the hands of any personnel not authorized to make decisions upon the basis of such opinions, and not especially and consideratively designated to possess them.

Since the writing of this chapter, just about a year ago, there has been such a crescendo of governmental obeisance to consumerism that some awareness of its dramatic emergence must be noted here.

For the most part it is, so far, manifesting itself in legislation (on city, state, and national levels) which enlarges legal remedies and procedures to expand and enforce consumer interests in marketing activities. Consumer class actions, monetary awards and penalties, injunctive actions, restitutions, consumer departments and offices in governments are becoming common parlance. In the main, they do not bear upon the specific matters written of here other than to electrify the atmosphere surrounding questions of business obligations and liabilities to members of the public, both directly and, through governmental regulation and police work, indirectly.

There is one notable exception. On page 32-25 we have discussed requirements for affirmative disclosure in the context of deception via silence. Now, however, the FTC, in an effort to serve the cause of consumers' "rational purchasing" (as distinct from mere anti-misrepresentation), is vigorously endeavoring to expand the doctrine to encompass any information it thinks might be of interest to a consumer's purchase decision. It has, for example, proposed trade regulation rules compelling labels explicitly setting forth light output and durability of light bulbs, octane content of gasolines, and requiring detailed information for the laundering, dry cleaning and care of textile garments.

This will be a rapidly developing area, and bears close watching. Whether such regulation—in effect, new legislation promulgated by the Commission—is within its lawful powers, remains to be litigated.

PART TEN

Glossary of Advertising Terms

**Advertising terms, including
computer terms, and descriptions
of selected advertising organizations**

Access, random (*Data processing*) (1) Pertaining to the process of obtaining information from or placing it into storage where the time required for such access is independent of the location of the information most recently obtained or placed in storage. (2) Pertaining to a device in which random access can be achieved without effective penalty in time.—BoB.

Access, serial (*Data processing*) Pertaining to the process of obtaining information from or placing information into storage, where the time required for such access is dependent on the necessity for waiting while non-desired storage locations are processed in turn.—BoB.

Access, time (*Data processing*) (1) The time it takes a computer to locate data or an instruction word in its storage section and transfer it to its arithmetic unit where the required computations are performed. (2) The time it takes to transfer information which has been operated on from the arithmetic unit to the location in storage where the information is to be stored.—BoB.

Account executive   In an advertising agency, a person who directs the handling of a client's advertising, representing the agency to the client and the client's wishes to the agency.   In larger agencies this executive may be called an *account supervisor*, or if he handles a group of accounts, an *account group head*.

Accuracy   Extent to which a survey result agrees with some well-defined standard or *true* value.   It reflects the extent to which a result is free from both sampling and nonsampling errors.—NAB.

Across the board   A broadcast program scheduled in the same time period five or more days a week.

Address (*Data processing*)   (1) An identification, represented by a name, label, or number, for a register or location in storage.   Addresses are also a part of an instruction word along with commands, tags, and other symbols.   (2) The part of an instruction which specifies an operand for the instruction.—BoB.

Adjacency   In broadcast, a commercial that immediately precedes or follows a specific program.

Advertiser's copies   Copies of a publication given free to its advertisers so they can see how their advertisements were presented.

Advertising   A paid form of presentation and promotion of goods, services, or ideas by a sponsor who is identified.   In this it differs from propaganda or publicity, where the sponsor is not always identified.

Advertising agency network   A small number of advertising agencies (ten to thirty) associated for mutual assistance.   Characteristically there is lack of competition for accounts among its members.

Advertising Council   Founded and supported by the advertising business, its purpose is to conduct public-service advertising programs.   Media publish, broadcast, or display Advertising Council campaigns at no cost for space or time.

Advertising Hall of Fame   Maintained by the American Advertising Federation, it elects each year a maximum of three persons for "special achievement and service in the upbuilding and advancement of the social and economic values of advertising."   A candidate must be deceased for two years.   Hall of Fame was established in 1949, and elections are by a council chosen annually from persons distinguished in advertising.

Advertising Research Foundation   Membership is composed of advertisers, agencies, advertising media, and research firms, and also universities and professional schools.   Function as a nonprofit organization is to further scientific practices and encourage objective and impartial research in advertising and marketing.

Advertising weight   The amount of advertising applied to the promotion of a brand.   Weight may be judged by the dominance of the advertising in a particular medium, its frequency, and its adjacency to the time or point of purchase.

Affiliate   A broadcast station, usually independently owned, that grants a network use of specific time periods for network programs and advertising.

Agate line   Newspaper space measurement, 1 column wide and $\frac{1}{14}$ inch deep.

Agency commission   A discount of 15 per cent usually allowed by space and time advertising media to accredited advertising agencies on their purchases for clients.

Agricultural Publishers Association   Membership is composed of farm publications that are also members of Audit Bureau of Circulations. Function is to develop usefulness of farm publications.

Aided recall   A research technique that uses prompting questions or materials to aid a respondent's memory of the original exposure situation.

Air check   A tape made at time of airing of a commercial or program.

Allotment   A term used in outdoor advertising to indicate number of panels comprising a showing in a market.

American Advertising Federation   Membership is composed of advertising clubs, advertising associations, and advertiser companies.   A merger of the former Advertising Federation of America and Advertising Association of the West.

American Association of Advertising Agencies ($AAAA$)   Association of advertising agencies elected after demonstrating that they meet the AAAA qualifications for membership.   Function is to foster, strengthen, and improve the advertising agency business; to advance the cause of advertising as a whole; to give service to members.

American Business Press, Inc.   Merger of Associated Business Publications and Business Publications Association.   Composed of business publications which are independently owned, with circulations audited by a nonprofit, tripartite auditing bureau, and which agree to abide by the ABP code of publishing practice.   Function is to improve service of business publications to their readers, and to help advertisers use the business press more effectively.

American Marketing Association   Function is to advance the science of marketing.

American Newspaper Publishers Association   Membership is composed of daily newspapers.   Function is to serve its membership and to advance the interests of daily newspaper publishing business.

American Transit Association   Association of transit operating organizations—companies, municipal departments, regional authorities—which operate urban transit systems.   Not to be confused with Transit Advertising Association.

Amplitude modulation (*AM*)   Radio that is listened to on the normal broadcast band (550 to 1,600 on the AM radio dial).   The strength (amplitude) of a transmitting wave is altered (modulated) to correspond to the original sound.

Analog   The representation of numerical quantities by means of physical variables, e.g., translation, rotation, voltage, or resistance.   Contrasted with *digital*—BoB.

Angled poster panel   In outdoor advertising, a panel that is normally viewed by traffic moving in one direction only.   It must be built so that one end is 6 feet or more back from the other end.

Animation   1. In point-of-purchase advertising, the use of motion in displays.   2. In outdoor advertising, the movement of parts on painted displays and electrical spectaculars or the impression of movement created by the flashing action of light.   3. In television, a cartoon-type technique that gives motion to still artwork.

Announcement   A brief broadcast commercial generally outside of a program.   Sometimes referred to as a *spot* or *spot announcement.*

Appeal, advertising   A motivating force directed by an advertiser toward a prospective customer.

Application   The system or problem to which a computer is applied. Reference is often made to an application as being either of the computational type, wherein arithmetic computations predominate, or of the data processing type, wherein data-handling operations predominate.—BoB.

Appropriation, advertising   The amount of money allocated by a company for advertising.

Apron   Lattice or other decorative work below bottom of a poster panel or painted bulletin.

Area sample   A probability sample from predesignated areas of the population, as city blocks.

Arithmetic unit (*Data processing*) The portion of the hardware of a computer in which arithmetical and logical operations are performed. The arithmetic unit generally consists of an accumulator, some special registers for the storage of operands, and results supplemented by shifting and sequencing circuitry for implementing multiplication, division, and other desired operations.—BoB.

Arrears Subscribers whose names are retained on an active subscription list although the period for which they have paid is expired.

Association of Industrial Advertisers Active members are composed of individuals engaged in buying and placing industrial advertising. Associate members are composed of representatives of publishers and suppliers in the industrial field. Function is to improve industrial advertising and related marketing techniques and their skilful use.

Association of National Advertisers Membership is composed of major corporations which advertise on a national or broad regional basis. Function is to promote effective use of advertising as a selling and management tool.

Audience All those who see some part of the editorial content of a publication, or listen to or see some part of a broadcast program, or have the opportunity to read an outdoor, transit, or point-of-purchase advertising message. Synonymous with *total audience.*

Audience accumulation Addition of new persons to a medium's total reach as the advertiser uses additional publication issues or broadcasts.

Audience breakdown In broadcast, the relative share of total audience credited to each station.

Audience composition Kinds of persons reached by a medium or advertising campaign in terms of sex, age, income, or other demographic characteristics.

Audience duplication Persons reached by one media vehicle who are also reached by another.

Audience flow The household audience inherited by a broadcast program from the preceding program.

Audience measurement Research that determines the numbers and characteristics of members of an audience of a medium or an advertising message.

Audience, pass-along Those who read some part of a publication but are not the primary recipients.

Audience, primary Readers of a publication who receive it first in order of time; or those for whom the publication is edited, as distinguished from those, in a business publication for instance, who serve the advertisers.

Audience survey Study of estimated listening to various broadcast stations in a market or those reached by print, outdoor, or other media. Usually shows demographic information.

Audimeter A mechanical device used by A. C. Nielsen Company to monitor radio and television set usage and station selection in a sample of United States households. This is a registered trade name.

Audio Sound part of a television commercial.

Audit Examination of a publisher's circulation or distribution claims by an independent organization.

Audit Bureau of Circulations Membership is composed of newspapers, periodicals, advertisers, and advertising agencies in United States and Canada. Function is to verify and report data on circulations of member publications and other marketing services.

Audit report A document issued by an auditing bureau that attests to the accuracy and validity of a publisher's circulation claims.

Authentication Certification of circulation produced by audits of newspapers and magazines and studies of traffic in the outdoor and transit advertising media.

Automation (1) The implementation of processes by automatic means. (2) The theory, art, or technique of making a process more automatic. (3) The investigation, design, development, and application of methods of rendering processes automatic, self-moving, or self-controlling. —BoB.

Availability (1) In broadcast, the opportunity to buy a desired segment of time. (2) In outdoor, the units which a plant operator has open for an advertiser on a specified date.

Average Generally an arithmetic mean, computed by adding the values in a group and dividing the total by the number of values. This simple average is called an *unweighted mean,* whereas a *weighted average* is obtained by multiplying each value by an assigned weight, adding the products, and dividing the total by the sum of the weights.

Average audience According to A. C. Nielsen Company, the number of homes tuned in during an average minute of network television broadcasts.

Average audience rating A type of rating computed for some specific segment of radio or television time. Sometimes this is called an *average minute rating.*

Average paid The average circulation qualified as paid circulation of all the issues of a publication. It is derived by dividing total circulation of all paid copies in the period by total number of issues.

Back copies Copies of periodicals prior to that of the current issue.

Back lighting 1. In television, lighting of the performer from behind to give depth to the scene. 2. In transit advertising, a full-color advertisement printed on a translucent sheet and lighted from behind.

Balop Short for Balopticon, a machine that projects objects, photographs, or stills.

Banner In point-of-purchase advertising, a rectangular or triangular piece of plastic, cloth, or paper, suspended in windows, on walls, or overhead, carrying advertising messages.

Baseboard In outdoor advertising, the solid enclosure immediately below the lower edge of a painted bulletin or poster panel.

Basic price Price at which a copy or subscription to a publication may be purchased, as opposed to a special price.

Ben Day An engraving process that allows the production of halftone or color effects without use of halftones.

Bias of nonresponse In research this is caused by differences between respondents and nonrespondents in respect to the data evoked by the survey.

Billboard 1. In outdoor advertising, a term formerly used generally to mean poster. 2. In television advertising the term refers to special commercial positions at the start and close of a telecast to announce the name of the sponsor. The credits may also list talent, producer, director, writer, and so on.

Bin In point-of-purchase advertising, a holder for bulk merchandise.

Binary (*Data processing*) A characteristic, property, or condition in which there are but two possible alternatives; e.g., the binary number system using 2 as its base and using only the digits zero (0) and one (1).—BoB.

Blanket contract In outdoor advertising, a contract for a specified amount of money which covers posting space purchased as authorizations are received.—NOAB.

Blanking In outdoor advertising, the white paper border surrounding the poster copy area.

Boards Term for poster panels and painted bulletins originating in the period when theatrical and circus posters were displayed on board fences. —NOAB.

Boldface type   Typography in which the weight of the strokes comprising each character is heavy when compared with the regular or normal typeface.

Booked   A term meaning acceptance of a contract for outdoor advertising space by a plant operator.   In this sense, a showing has been booked when it is scheduled to appear for a definite period.—NOAB.

Boom   In television, a support for suspending a microphone or camera so that it is mobile.

Boxholder   A person to whom mail is delivered at a post office box.

Brand   A name, term, sign, symbol, or design, or a combination of them which is intended to identify the goods or services of one seller or group of sellers and to differentiate them from those of competitors.—AMA.   Similar to *brand name.*

Brand consciousness   Degree of awareness on the part of consumers of a particular brand.

Brand image   The real or imaginary qualities attributed to a particular brand by consumers.

Brand loyalty   Consumer faithfulness toward a brand, measured by length of time or regularity of use.—POPAI.

Brand Names Foundation   An association of manufacturers, advertising agencies, and media.   Its purpose is to educate consumers and retailers concerning benefits of the brand competitive system.   Advertising media make annual contributions so that the Foundation's consumer and trade advertising may appear.

Brand selection   The customer seeks a particular item but has no brand preference, or has two or more brands in mind.   When selection of the brand is made in the store, it is called *in-store brand selection.*—POPAI.

Brand switching   A purchase wherein a customer buys a brand different from his customary brand.

Breakdown   1. In respect to circulation of business publications, the division of circulation as to types of business or industry reached, the functions or titles of recipients, and their demographic characteristics or geographic location.—AIA.   2. In television advertising, the detailing of costs on script for talent, properties, etc., also script marked for camera shots by director of show or commercial.—TvB.

Broadcasting   As a noun, either of the electronic media, radio or television.   As a verb, sending out a signal on the air waves that is capable of being received by radio or television set.—RAB.

Broadside   A single sheet of advertising literature of comparatively large size, folded at least once.

Brochure   A booklet whose production is generally considered to be more expensive than ordinary in respect to quality of paper, printing, use of color and illustrations.

Budget   An amount allocated to be spent on an advertising campaign or in a given medium or market.   Sometimes used synonymously with *appropriation,* although the appropriation is more properly the total amount to be spent by an advertiser in a stated period, and this total amount is *budgeted* among media, markets, and so on.

Bug   A mistake in the design of a routine or a computer, or a malfunction.—BoB.

Bulk sales   To the Audit Bureau of Circulations this means all copies or subscriptions of five or more which promote the business or professional interests of the purchaser.   To the Business Publications Audit of Circulation it means two or more copies of a publication, whether or not individually wrapped or addressed, sent to a single addressee.

Bureau of Advertising of the American Newspaper Publishers Association   An association whose members are daily newspapers chiefly in the United States and Canada.   Its function is to foster the wide and effective use of newspaper advertising by the dissemination of research and market analysis service to agencies and advertisers and by retail advertising planning for staffs of member newspapers.

Buried offer   An offer made by means of a statement within the text of an advertisement for a booklet, sample, or information, without use of a coupon or typographical emphasis on the offer.   To discover the offer, detailed reading of the advertisement must take place.   Also called *hidden offer.*—Ms.

Business publication   One dealing with management, manufacturing, sales or operation of industry, occupation, or profession, and published to interest persons actively engaged in the field it covers.—ABC.   Sometimes called *business paper.*

Business Publications Audit of Circulation, Inc.   An association of advertisers, advertising agencies, and business publications.   Purpose is to audit the circulation of business publications.

Call-back   The repeat of a call made by an interviewer who was unsuccessful in obtaining information from a respondent on the first attempt.

Call letters A broadcast station's name. With few exceptions, those stations east of the Mississippi River start with W, and those west of the river start with K. The letters are assigned by the Federal Communications Commission. A few existing call signals, such as KDKA in Pittsburgh, are at variance with this system because the stations were licensed before assignments began.

Campaign All advertising and related efforts on behalf of a product or service directed toward the attainment of a predetermined goal.

Campbell's Soup position The righthand page immediately following the main editorial section of a magazine. Traditionally requested by the Campbell Soup Company.

Captive rotary A set of locations used exclusively for one client with several different products to advertise.—NOAB.

Car card Former term for *inside transit advertisement.*

Card rate The cost of advertising time or space quoted on a rate card.

Cash discount A discount of 2 per cent granted by media to advertisers for prompt payment of bills for space, time, or other facility. It is collected by the agency and passed along to the advertiser to encourage the latter's prompt payment of bills. The discount is usually figured on the net amount due the medium after deduction of the 15 per cent agency commission.

Census An enumeration of the individuals or establishments or both in a publication's total market.

Center spread (1) In publications, an advertisement in the center of a publication, appearing on two facing pages printed as a single sheet. (2) In outdoor advertising, two adjacent panels using coordinated copy.

Chain A group of broadcast stations connected by cable or microwave relay for the simultaneous broadcasting of a program.

Chain break Times during or between network programs when a broadcasting station identifies itself and gives one or more commercial announcements. The announcements are also referred to as chain breaks.

Channel (*Data processing*) (1) A path along which information, particularly a series of digits or characters, may flow. (2) One or more parallel tracks created as a unit. (3) In a circulating storage, a channel is one recirculating path containing a fixed number of words stored serially by word. (4) A path of electrical communication. (5) A band of frequencies used for communication.—BoB.

Checking Actual physical inspection of poster showings and painted displays to assure fulfillment of contract specifications.

Checking copy   Copy of a publication sent to advertisers and agencies so they can check manner in which their advertisement was published.

Circulation   (1) To the Audit Bureau of Circulations this means paid copies of a publication.   (2) To the Business Publications Audit of Circulation it means copies distributed to recipients who conform to the publisher's description of their qualification within a field served.   (3) In broadcast it means the number of set-owning families within range of a station signal.   (4) In outdoor advertising, it means the number of people passing an advertisement who have a reasonable chance to see it.

Circulation certification   Transit Advertising Association certifies members' circulation to Standard Rate & Data Service, Inc., in notarized affidavits.

Circulation, controlled   United States postal regulations define it as "Copies of a publication circulated free or mainly free which contain at least 24 pages, contain at least 25 per cent non-advertising, issued four or more times a year, and not owned or controlled by individuals or business concerns, and conducted as an auxiliary to and essentially for the advancement of the main business or calling of those who own or control them." The Audit Bureau of Circulations does not use this term and the Business Publications Audit of Circulation has abandoned it for the term *qualified circulation*.

Circulation, effective   (1) That part of a publication's circulation received by individuals or establishments of interest to an advertiser.   (2) In outdoor advertising, *effective daily circulation* consists of individuals who have a reasonable opportunity to observe the display by approaching the face of the unit.   This is usually half of all persons on foot, in cars and trucks, and 25 per cent of all passengers on bus, streetcars, and elevated mass transportation facilities passing a given point during a twelve-hour daylight period or an eighteen-hour period in the case of illuminated panels.

Circulation, franchise   That part of a publication's circulation which is obtained through contractual agreement with business firms which provide lists of their customers or prospective customers to whom copies of the publication are sent free of charge.

Circulation, nonpaid   The circulation of publications which do not charge the recipients as an initial condition of receipt.

Circulation, paid   That part of a publication's total distribution which is delivered to recipients who pay for their copies.

Circulation, qualified   That circulation, paid or nonpaid, distributed to the field served, for which the mailing address conformance to the field served, recipient qualification, and the correct business or occupational qualifications are verified by auditable documentary evidence within thirty-six months. Qualified recipients must receive every issue of the publication, subject to normal removals and additions.—AIA.

Circulation, request   According to the Audit Bureau of Circulations, it is the number of recipients of a publication who do not pay for it, but receive copies upon request, when in the field served by the publication. According to the Business Publications Audit of Circulation, it is the number of recipients on a publication's circulation list who have completed a questionnaire specifically requesting receipt of the publication, or recipients who received a publication by virtue of their individually paid subscription.—AIA.

City zone circulation   Newspapers sold within corporate city limits or, as in the case of heavily populated adjoining areas, newspapers sold within this wider area as designated by the Audit Bureau of Circulations.

Classification   The systematic division of circulation or distribution according to types of individuals or establishments that are recipients.

Classified advertising   Advertising set in solid lines of small type segregated from other advertising and arranged according to the product or service offered.

Classified advertising, display   Classified advertising which makes use of display headings, illustrations, and larger space than regular classified advertising.

Class magazine   A periodical other than a business publication in which editorial contents are devoted to the interests of a particular group of readers.

Clear channel   A broadcast frequency without interference in its primary areas and with only limited interference in its secondary areas, thus permitting the transmission of programs over wide areas and long distances.

Closed-end question   A question whose limited number of permissible answers are all specified.

Cluster sampling   A random or probability sample that uses as a sampling unit groups of people rather than individuals.

Code (*Data processing*)   (1) A system of symbols for meaningful communication. Related to instruction.   (2) A system of symbols for representing data or instructions in a computer or a tabulating machine.   (3) To translate the program for the solution of a problem on a given computer into a sequence of machine language or pseudo instructions and addresses acceptable to that computer. (4) A machine language program.—BoB.

Code, alphabetic (*Data processing*)　A system of alphabetic abbreviations used in preparing information for input into a machine: Boston, New York, Philadelphia, and Washington may in alphabetical coding be reported as BS, NY, PH, WA.—BoB.

Code, error detecting (*Data processing*)　A code in which errors produce forbidden combinations.—BoB.

Code, numeric (*Data processing*)　A system of numerical abbreviations used in the preparation of information for input into a machine; i.e., all information is reduced to numerical quantities.—BoB.

Coding　The classification of responses on a questionnaire, schedule, or diary, according to specified rules, to facilitate their tabulation and summarization or data processing.　As part of this step, code numbers or letters may be assigned to categories of responses.—NAB.

Coincidental survey　A type of interview in which the respondent is asked to report his listening, viewing, or reading activity at the exact time the interview is being conducted or immediately before the interview began. Sometimes called *telephone coincidental survey*.

Collate　To arrange the pages of a book or other publication in proper numerical order; or, in data processing, to compare and merge two or more similarly ordered sets of items into one ordered set.

Color form　In publications, a group of pages locked in a chase or brace which will be printed with one or more colors as well as black.

Color plate　A printing plate which carries all the elements of an advertisement to be printed in a specific color.

Column inch　Publication space measurement 1 column wide and 1 inch deep.

Combination plate　One engraving that combines line and halftone reproduction.

Combination rate　(1) Among publishers of two or more magazines, a special rate offered to advertisers who use space in two or more magazines.　(2) Among publishers of morning and evening newspapers in one city, a special rate offered to advertisers who use both papers.　(3) Among broadcast media, a reduced rate sometimes offered by stations with the same ownership or with a geographical tie-in, if the stations are bought together.—Ms.

Command (*Data processing*) (1) An electronic pulse, signal, or set of signals to start, stop, or continue some operation. It is incorrect to use *command* as a synonym for *instruction*. (2) The portion of an instruction word which specifies the operation to be performed.—BoB.

Commercial audience Number of households tuned to one or more commercials of a specific broadcast. A commercial impression is considered to have been delivered whenever a home is tuned in at the specific minute when the message is aired.

Commercial, integrated An advertising message delivered as part of the entertainment of a broadcast program.

Commercial program A broadcast program paid for by an advertiser, in contrast to a *sustaining program* that is not sponsored by an advertiser.

Commercial protection Specific amount of time between competitive commercials that is allowed by a station.

Community antenna television (*CATV*) Wire-TV services that take television programs from distant areas and "pipe" or transmit them by cable to subscribing households.

Comparability Relative to business publications, it means the susceptibility of a publication's circulation breakdowns to comparison with those of other publications serving the same field.

Comprehensive In print, a facsimile of a proposed advertisement.

Computer (*Data processing*) A device capable of accepting information, applying prescribed processes to the information, and supplying the results of these processes. It usually consists of input and output devices, storage, arithmetic, and logical units, and a control unit.—BoB.

Computer, analog (*Data processing*) A computer which represents variables by physical analogies. Thus, any computer which solves problems by translating physical conditions such as flow, temperature, pressure, angular position, or voltage into related mechanical or electrical quantities and uses mechanical or electrical equivalent circuits as an analog for the physical phenomenon being investigated. In general it is a computer which uses an analog for each variable and produces analogs as output. Thus an analog computer measures continuously, whereas a digital computer counts discretely.—BoB.

Computer, digital (*Data processing*) A computer which processes information represented by combinations of discrete or discontinuous data as compared with an analog computer for continuous data. More specifically, it is a device for performing sequences of arithmetic and logical operations, not only on data but on its own program. Still more specifically, it is a stored program digital computer capable of performing sequences of internally stored instructions, as opposed to calculators, such as card programed calculators, upon which the sequence is impressed manually.— BoB.

Conditioning bias A bias that results from respondents changing their preferences, activities, and beliefs, and hence, their responses to questions about such things because of the mere fact that they are included in a survey.—NAB.

Console (*Data processing*) A portion of the computer which may be used to control the machine manually, correct errors, determine the status of machine circuits, registers, and counters, determine the contents of storage, and manually revise the contents of storage.

Consumer diary A form on which the member of a sample keeps a record of certain behavior or expenditures.

Consumer panel (*Jury, clinic*) (1) A continuing sample of households or persons from whom information on purchase habits, media activities, and related items is obtained.   (2) A sample of prospective consumers asked to evaluate the effectiveness of advertisements or parts of advertisements before they appear in media.—Ms.

Continuity (1) The principle of providing a person the opportunity to be exposed to advertising for a specific product or service without interruption long enough to reduce or cancel the effectiveness of that advertising. It may exist among media or be confined to one medium.   (2) The advertising of a single theme or selling proposition over a long period of time. (3) The complete contents, in typescript, of a radio or television program or a broadcast commercial.—Ms.

Contract year Stipulated length of a media contract.

Controlled experiment A research study in which the effect of a certain influence is isolated by controlling extraneous variables.

Convenience sample In research a sample selected on the basis of convenience or availability, as persons walking down the street. This is not a sample selected on a probability basis.

Cooperative advertising Advertising of a brand or service when cost is shared by the manufacturer and distributor, dealer, or retailer.

Copy The written or spoken advertising message.

Copy platform The formulation of the basic ideas for an advertising campaign and the designation of the importance of the various selling points in it.

Copy research (*Copy testing*)   Research to determine the effect of an advertisement or campaign, either before it is disseminated (pretesting) or afterwards (posttesting).

Corporate image advertising   Advertising that stresses the virtues of an advertising firm rather than its products or services.

Correlation   Relationship between two or more sets of data.

Cost per thousand (*CPM*)   Cost of reaching 1,000 units of the audience of a particular advertising medium.   It may be presented in terms of costs per thousand households reached, or men, women, listeners, readers, and so on.

Counter card   At the point of purchase, a card with brand name and product information.

Counting station   A location scientifically determined as part of the system for counting or verifying the traffic on streets and highways.   These stations are used by federal, state, and municipal highway departments as well as by plant operators and research organizations.—NOAB.

County size group   These groups refer to the classification by A. C. Nielsen Company of counties by population and relationship to urban centers. A and B counties are the metropolitan areas; C and D counties are the more rural districts.

Cover position   Premium-priced cover space for advertisements: first cover—outside front cover; second cover—inside front cover; third cover —inside back cover; fourth cover—outside back cover.

Coverage   The number of individuals or households exposed to a medium within a specified time period according to a selected audience measurement.

Cumulative audience (*Cume*)   The number of different persons or households reached by a number of advertising messages in one media vehicle or a combination of media vehicles over a period of time.   Also called *net audience* or *unduplicated audience.*

Cut-in   Insertion of a local announcement into a network or transcribed program.

Data processing   (1) Preparation of source media which contain data or basic elements of information, and the handling of such data according to precise rules of procedure to accomplish such operations as classifying, sorting, calculating, summarizing, and recording.   (2) The production of records and reports.   Synonymous with *data handling.*—BoB.

Day-Glo Patented trade name for certain inks and lacquers with fluorescent qualities.

Daytime station A broadcast station whose license from the FCC allows it to be on the air only during daytime.

Deadline An advertising medium's final acceptance date for advertising material necessary for the completion of a particular operation in the publication of an advertisement.

Dealer imprint Dealer's name and address in an advertisement prepared by a national advertiser for local insertion, generally added after the advertisement has been plated.—Ms.

Dealer tie-in A manufacturer's advertisement, paid at national advertising rates, which includes a listing of local dealers. Not to be confused with cooperative advertising which is paid at local advertising rates.—Ms.

Decalcomania A process using a printed design which when moistened slips from backing papers and is transferable to another surface.

Delayed broadcast A program transcribed to be rebroadcast at a later time or on a different station.

Demographic characteristics The vital statistics of a population or sample, such as age, family size, sex, income, education, and residence. As used in media, they refer to these characteristics in descriptions of audiences.

Depth interview Popularly, a research interview conducted without a rigid questionnaire and with limited interference by the interviewer, in which respondents are encouraged to speak fully and freely about a particular subject.—Ms.

Diary A written record kept by a sample of persons who record their listening, viewing, reading activities, or purchases of brands within a specific period of time.

Diorama (1) In point-of-purchase advertising, these are elaborate displays of a scenic nature, almost always three-dimensional and illuminated. —POPAI. (2) In television, a miniature set, usually in perspective, used to simulate an impression of a larger location.

Direct advertising Sales messages disseminated by mail or by person to customers and prospects.

Direct mail Delivery of messages to prospects and customers through the postal services.

Direct Mail Advertising Association Membership is composed of users, creators, producers, and suppliers of direct-mail advertising. An international, nonprofit trade association whose primary objective is more effective direct mail for all users.

Display   A device or an accumulation of devices which, in addition to identifying or advertising a company or product, may also merchandise, either by actually offering a product for sale or indicating its proximity. A display characteristically bears an intimate relationship with the product, whereas a sign is more closely related to the name of the manufacturer, retailer, or product.—POPAI.

Display advertising   Newspaper and magazine advertisements designed to attract attention by layout, variety of type, illustration, and relatively large space, and not grouped according to classifications, as in classified advertising.

Distribution   1. To the advertiser, it means the outlets through which his product is sold.   2. To the economist, it means the use of goods and services by consumers.   The term may be used as synonymous with *marketing*.   3. Among business publications, it means the total number of copies distributed per issue, whether paid or nonpaid.   4. In outdoor advertising, it means the placement of advertising messages on main thoroughfares so that they are exposed to as many people as many times as possible, in keeping with the size of showing bought.

Distribution, nonqualified   Among business publications, the copies which fail to conform to the field served and definition of recipient qualifications.

Distributor   Generally synonymous with *wholesaler.*

Double spotting   In broadcast, two commercials placed within one station break.   Also refers to *Triple spotting,* where a second or third announcement or commercial is placed with the first.

Double spread   Two pages facing each other in a publication and presented as a single advertisement.   Synonymous with *double truck* and *double-page spread.*   The term *center spread* is used if the two pages are in the center of publication issue.

Drive time   The time from 7:00 to 9:00 A.M. and 4:00 to 7:00 P.M. when total radio listening is at its peak because persons are listening while driving to and from work.   Usually larger male audience.   Also called *traffic time.*

Dummy   (1) In direct mail, a model for a direct-mail piece indicating its proposed shape, size, weight, and layout.   (2) In periodical publishing, pages on which proofs or facsimiles of contents are pasted to simulate the proposed issue.—Ms.

Dump (*Data processing*) Removal of all alternating or direct current power intentionally, accidentally, or conditionally from a system or component.

Dumpbin A bin-shaped holder designed to stand on the floor and containing merchandise in random order as the merchandise is dumped in from the case.—POPAI.

Duplicate coverage Extent to which two or more competing publications are received by the same individuals.

Earned rate Continuity rates earned by advertisers utilizing longer-term contracts.

Edit (*Data Processing*) To rearrange data or information. Editing may involve the deletion of unwanted data, the selection of pertinent data, the application of format techniques, the insertion of symbols such as page numbers and typewriter characters, the application of standard processes such as zero suppression, and the testing of data for reasonableness and proper range. Editing may sometimes be distinguished between input edit (rearrangement of source data) and output edit (preparation of table formats).—BoB.

Edition, demographic In publications, that portion of the circulation in which the editorial or advertising content is intended for recipients of a segment of the field served by the publication, as those living in certain geographic areas, or possessing certain incomes, or working in certain occupations or professions.

Electric spectacular An outdoor sign in which lighting forms the words or designs. Not to be confused with illuminated posters or painted bulletins.

Electrical transcription Usually an electrically recorded commercial.

Electrotype A metal plate which is a facsimile of another plate and made by the electrotype process.

Em The square of any type size, derived from the letter M, which is as wide as it is high.

Embossed sign A sign on which all or part of the copy is raised so that it stands out from the flat surface, yet is an integral part of that surface.—POPAI.

End-aisle display A display particularly built for placement at the end of a store aisle which accommodates a large group of product units.—POPAI.

End rate   Lowest rate for commercial time a broadcast advertiser can qualify for after every maximum earned discount has been applied.

Envelope stuffer   Advertising material that is sent with mailings of bills, statements, or correspondence.

Establishment   A single place of business at one address.   A company can have several establishments at several addresses.

Estimating   Process of determining cost of an advertising media schedule.

Execute (*Data processing*)   To interpret a machine instruction and perform the indicated operation(s) on the operand(s) specified.—BoB.

Exposure   The act of laying open.   This occurs in a publication when one or more pages are seen by a recipient of the publication.   In any medium it is the physical confrontation of a prospect with an advertisement, and this is independent of copy approach.   It is the physical opportunity to see the average advertising message.   In point-of-purchase, it is the consumer's sensuous contact with a point-of-purchase unit or other advertising media.

Extrapolation   In statistics, the process which permits the extension of data beyond the range within which the data were collected.

Eye-movement camera   A research device to trace the movement of the eye as it perceives material to which it is exposed, as an advertisement or the elements of an advertisement.

Face   Style of type or the raised portion of type which produces printing.

Facing   In outdoor advertising, one or more panels built on the same location visible to the same approaching traffic.—NOAB.

Facing text matter   In print media, an advertising position opposite reading matter.

Factor analysis   In statistics, a determination of the fewest factors that explain the interrelations among a variety of elements.

Fair trade   Retail resale price maintenance imposed by suppliers of branded goods under authorization of state and federal laws.—AMA.

Farm publication   A national, regional, or local publication directed toward the interests of farmers and farm families.

Federal Communications Commission   A federal agency created in 1934 and charged with the regulation of interstate and foreign communications by means of electrical energy, including radio, television, and wire services. It regulates broadcast media in respect to number of stations, power, broadcast hours.

Federal Trade Commission Created under the Federal Trade Commission Act of 1914 to assist in the operation and perpetuation of free enterprise and the competitive system of economy. The act was passed to prevent and correct unfair methods of competition.

Field intensity map A geographic map produced by a broadcast station to plot those areas in which the station can be heard.

Field served Among business publications, the publisher's description of the markets or occupations to whose interest the publication's editorial content is directed. In auditing, an individual or establishment is considered qualified only if known to belong to the field served.

Field work In research, the gathering of data from a designated population by interview or observation.

Fixed position A commercial announcement delivered at a specific time, promised by the station to the advertiser. These spots may carry a premium price.

Flasher In both outdoor and point-of-purchase advertising, a light that flashes on and off at timed intervals to attract attention.

Flat rate In print media, an advertising rate not subject to frequency or quantity discounts.

Flight The period during which an advertiser runs his campaign; a flighting schedule alternates periods of advertising with periods of inactivity, as a period of six weeks of advertising followed by none.

Floor pyramid In point of purchase, a display of merchandise rising from the floor in which products are stacked in the form of a pyramid to approximate eye level.

Flow chart (1) A schedule that shows how media in an advertising campaign will be used over a period of time. (2) In data processing, it is a graphical representation of the solution of a problem, in which symbols are used to show operations, data, flow, and equipment.

Flush The vertical alignment of printing.

Folio (1) A number as it appears on the page of a book. (2) A booklet in which the pages are formed by folding a single sheet of paper once, and which is bound by stapling or saddle-stitching. (3) A large book approximately 12 by 15 inches.

Font   Type assortment of one size and style.

Form   Assemblage of letterpress printing plates or type matter, or both, locked together and secured in a printing press for inking and printing as a unit.

Format   (1) A publication's makeup.   (2) Structure of a broadcast program.

Four-color process   A color printing process using a combination of four photoengravings, each with a different color ink, to reproduce color artwork which has been reduced to its basic colors by a filtration process.

Frame   (1) One picture in a comic strip.   (2) In television, a picture of transmitted image.   (3) A list or other form that identifies all sampling units to be given some chance of appearing in a statistical survey, as, for instance, a set of telephone directories.   (4) In point-of-purchase, a poster frame which may be provided with means for periodic change of posters.

Frequency   (1) Of media exposure, the number of times an individual or household is exposed to a medium within a given period of time.   Frequency of an advertisement is based upon its opportunity for exposure to an audience; in print, the number of times an individual or household is exposed to the same or successive advertisements for the same product in one or different publications; in broadcast, the sum of audiences per telecast in a given time period (four weeks, for instance) divided by the net cumulative audience for that period.   (2) In broadcasting, the number of times per second a wave appears.   (3) In point-of-purchase, the number of times a sign or display is exposed to individuals within a specified period of time.   (4) In statistics, the number of times each element appears in each step of a distribution table.

Frequency discount   A rate reduction granted by media to advertisers who agree to run a specified number of advertisements within a given period of time.

Frequency distribution   In statistics, the number of times each element appears in each step of a distribution table.   For instance, it shows the number of people or homes reached at each frequency level for a particular media schedule.

Frequency modulation   (*FM*)   (1) Static-free, nonfading radio broadcasting by the adjustment of the frequency of the transmitting wave to sound.   (2) The modulation used to transmit the sound portion of television.—Ms.

Fringe time   In broadcast, those times in which normal-sized audiences are not available, as early and late evening.

Fulfillment Delivery of copies of a publication to subscribers with whom the publication has contracted.

Full position In a newspaper, the space occupied by an advertisement so placed that it appears at the top of a column with editorial matter along one side, or is placed next to or following reading matter such as news stories and articles but not advertisements.

Full run (*Full showing*) (1) In newspapers, the insertion of an advertisement in every edition of a newspaper on any one day. (2) In outdoor advertising, the use of a number of panels recommended by a plant operator for adequate coverage of an area. (3) In transit, an inside transit advertisement placed in every vehicle of a fleet.

Full-time station A station which has a license from the FCC that allows but does not require it to broadcast 24 hours a day.

Function In business publications, the type of work a recipient performs. It may or may not be the same as his title.

Galley A shallow tray to hold type set by machine. Also a galley proof made directly from the type in the galley, 20 to 22 inches long.

Gatefold An insert in a publication consisting of a sheet of paper folded one or more times so that its final folded size matches the other pages.

General magazine A consumer magazine not classified as to specific audience.

General rate (*National rate*) A rate that usually applies to advertisers whose products have general distribution.

Giveaway (1) A free premium. (2) Broadcast program featuring free merchandise to contestants or to the audience.

Gondola Island shelving, open on two sides, found in self-service stores.

Gravure A printing process in which the ink is transferred to the paper from etched flat or cylindrical plates. Roll-fed printing using a cylindrical plate is called *rotogravure.*

Gross rating points A summation of the ratings of the various media vehicles employed by the advertiser. It offers a description of the total impression weight being delivered by a particular vehicle (without regard to audience duplication).—BBDO.

Group subscription Subscriptions purchased in quantities of five or more, paid for by an employer for his employees, and mailed by the publisher in bulk or to individual recipients.—AIA.

Gutter The blank space that forms the inside page margins of a magazine, book, or other publication. Advertising space next to the gutter margin is said to have a gutter position.

Half showing Also called *half run* or *half service,* means transit advertising placed in half the vehicles of a fleet.

Halftone engraving A metal plate used in letterpress printing to reproduce original copy, such as a photograph or wash drawing or oil painting, with tonal values. The original artwork is photographed through a *halftone screen* which separates the design into small varied-sized dots which when printed from the plate produce the tonal variation.

Hand composition Setting type by hand, as is sometimes done in display advertisements.

Hanging sign In point-of-purchase advertising, a sign that hangs from a bracket that usually projects from a wall. It generally has advertising copy on both sides.

Hardware (*Data processing*) The physical equipment or devices forming a computer and peripheral equipment. Contrasted with *software.* —BoB.

Headlight display (*Front-end display*) In transit advertising, a poster placed on the outside front of vehicles.

Hiatus A temporary period when an advertiser may discontinue broadcast advertising, especially in the summer. After the hiatus, the broadcaster may resume advertising in his particular time spot.

Hidden offer (*Buried offer*) A special offer concealed in an advertisement so that it is unlikely to be found unless the copy is read. Typographically it is indistinguishable from the rest of the copy.

Hi-Fi Color advertisements preprinted on newspaper-size rolls and inserted by newspapers in their regular issues.

Hitchhiker (*Hitchhike*) An announcement of one of a sponsor's products that appears at the end of the broadcast show but does not refer to the product featured in the regular program commercials.

Holding power Extent to which a broadcast audience listens to the duration of a program.

Holdover audience The audience a program inherits from persons or households who had been tuned in to the previous broadcast program on the station or network.

Homes using radio (HUR) A research term expressed as a percentage of total homes in an area being surveyed that is constituted by those whose radios are in use at a given time.

Horizontal buy A print media schedule that uses various types of magazines to achieve maximum reach. A *vertical buy* uses only one type of magazine, as women's magazines.

Horizontal publication A business publication whose editorial content interests a variety of businesses or business functions.

House agency An advertising agency controlled in whole or in part by one advertiser.

House organ A publication issued by a business organization or association to serve its own interests.

Household A group of persons who occupy a house, apartment, or other living accommodation that constitutes a housing unit. Not all families are households. A family need not live in a housing unit, and some households may contain more than one family. A family is defined by the Bureau of the Census as two or more persons related by blood, marriage, or adoption, and living together.

Households reached Number of households estimated to be in the audience of a broadcast program during a specific time period.

Housewife times Refers to hours in the radio day, usually between 10 A.M. and 4 P.M., when housewives are presumed to be the major audience.

ID Short for identification. Usually refers to 8- to 10-second commercials during the station identification period. Used generally to promote brand awareness.

Illuminated (*Illumination*) Outdoor advertising structures equipped with electric lights. In point-of-purchase advertising, illuminated signs and displays are those with light in any form.

Impact The extent and degree of consumer awareness of an advertisement in a specific medium. It is the combined value of coverage (reach) and frequency of exposure.

Imprinting Printing added to a piece of printed matter after the original has been accomplished, such as the dealer imprint on the bottom of an advertising folder. In outdoor advertising it is a common practice to place dealer imprints across the bottom 20 inches of the poster just above the blanking. Plant operator imprints in outdoor are plaques placed at the top or bottom of a poster panel to identify the owner of the structure.

Impulse buying Unplanned purchases made by persons who happen to see goods on display at the point-of-purchase. *Impulse items* are those that have a high appeal to consumers, causing them to make unplanned purchases.

Incremental analysis Method to estimate the rate of change of size of a media audience at any given level of advertising expenditure.

Independent station One not affiliated with a network. More than half of radio's AM stations are not affiliated with any network.

Industrial advertising Advertising by manufacturers of products that are used only by manufacturers or producers rather than by the consuming public. Also called *advertising to business.*

Industrial Advertising Research Institute An organization composed of advertiser, agency, and publisher subscribing members whose purpose is to develop and conduct research and to provide research-based information and services to increase the effectiveness of industrial advertising.

Industrial goods Goods sold primarily for use in producing other goods rather than goods destined to be sold primarily to the ultimate consumer.

Inherited audience See *Holdover audience.*

Input In computer language, the data to be processed.

Inquiry A request received by an advertiser, usually elicited by advertising, for information about his merchandise or service.

Inquiry test A check on the numbers of inquiries, especially coupons, sent to an advertiser by readers, viewers, or listeners. This check is most useful in gauging the effectiveness of the advertising when sales are clearly traceable to the advertisement. Per-inquiry (or PI) advertising is that in a relatively small number of publications where the rate is based upon the number of inquiries elicited.

Insert (1) An advertisement inclosed in letters or in merchandise. (2) A special page or device of advertising matter prepared by an advertiser for binding into an issue of a publication in which space has been bought.

Insertion order Specifications sent by an agency to an advertising medium that include data on insertion or run, size, position, rates.

Inside panel In outdoor advertising, any one in a group of poster panels erected at an angle to the line of traffic except the one nearest to it.

Inside transit advertising Inside transit advertisements are those placed in buses, commuter trains, and rail transit vehicles.

Institute of Outdoor Advertising (*IOA*) All members are also members of the Outdoor Advertising Association of America. A research, creative, and information organization serving advertisers, agencies, and plant operators and their selling organizations.

Institutional advertising Advertising designed to promote the advertiser company as a commercial institution, rather than to sell specific goods. Sometimes this may be called *public relations* or *corporate image* advertising.

Instruction (*Data processing*) (1) A set of characters which defines an operation together with one or more addresses, or no address, and which, as a unit, causes the computer to perform the operation on the indicated quantities. The term *instruction* is preferable to the terms *command* and *order*. *Command* is reserved for a specific portion of the instruction word; i.e., the part which specifies the operation which is to be performed. *Order* is reserved for the ordering of the characters, implying sequence, or the order of the interpolation, or the order of the differential equation. Related to *code*. (2) The operation or command to be executed by a computer together with associated addresses, tags, and indices.—BoB.

Intaglio printing Printing from a depressed surface. Lines to be printed are cut below the surface of the engraved plate. When flooded with ink and wiped clean, only the inked design remains. Gravure and photogravure are forms of intaglio printing.

Integrated commercial One designed as an integral part of a television program. Also one where related products made by the same sponsor are presented within a single announcement.

Intensity In outdoor advertising, the strength of combinations of poster locations throughout a city in terms of coverage or repetition. Showings are designed as 100 or 50, so a 100 showing has 100 intensity. This varies from city to city, although in some of the larger cities, both larger and smaller showings are available.

International Advertising Association Composed of advertising agencies, advertisiers, media representatives, public relations, and service organizations concerned with international advertising. Purpose is to advance the general level of advertising and marketing proficiency throughout the world.

International Radio and Television Society Function is to provide an assembly for persons engaged in communication through radio and television, where they can exchange ideas and information affecting their common interest and welfare.

Interview A situation in which one person seeks information from another or from a group.

Interviewer bias   A type of response error attributable to an interviewer because he fails to ask questions according to instructions or fails to record responses properly.

Island display   In point-of-purchase advertising, a display designed to stand alone with merchandise available from all sides and separated from other displays.

Island position   (1) In a publication page, an advertisement surrounded entirely by editorial matter.   (2) In television, *island positioning* refers to a commercial isolated from other advertising by program content.

Issue audience   The aggregate of individuals who look into the editorial content of an issue of a publication.   *Issue life* is the time it takes a publication to reach a maximum measurable audience.

Italic type   Topography distinguished by a slanting of each character to the right.

Jobber   A term synonymous with *wholesaler* or *distributor.*

Jumble display   In point-of-purchase advertising, the loose arrangement in a display container.   A *jumble basket* contains many unrelated items, a *dump bin* only one.

Key   Identification within an advertisement or coupon that permits inquiries or requests to be traced to a specific advertisement.

Key station   The station of a network that originates principal programs.

Kilocycle   In broadcasting, 1,000 complete alternations of current in one second.

Kinescope   Film of a live commercial or program made by photographing the television tube image, usually made in the television studio.

King-size poster   An outside transit advertisement 2½ by 12 feet in size.

Language (*Data processing*)   A system for representing and communicating information or data among persons, or between persons and machines.   Such a system consists of a carefully designed set of characters and rules for combining them into larger units, such as words or expressions, and rules for word arrangement or usage to achieve specific meaning.— BoB.

Layout   The graphic presentation of an advertisement.

Lead   A thin metal strip inserted between lines of type to increase the space between them.   Pronounced *led.*

Lead-in The program preceding an advertiser's program on the same broadcasting station.

Lead time The time between the arrival of signs and displays at their ultimate locations and the date the promotion is due to break.—NOAB.

Leftover matter Copy set in type but not used in the printing of a publication.

Legend Legend or *caption* is textual matter, usually explanatory, placed directly beneath the printed reproduction of a photograph or other illustration. Accurately, *caption* should be used for text placed directly *above* the illustration.

Letterpress printing Printing accomplished by pressing an inked raised surface, as type, halftone engravings, or line plates, to paper.

Letterspace To set individual letters of a word or sentence farther apart than they were set in type originally.

Life Length of time during which response may be measured from an advertisement.

Limited-hours station A station authorized to broadcast a limited number of hours daily, usually because it shares its channel with other stations.

Linage Number of agate lines in a specified advertising space.

Line cut A line engraving which reproduces without tonal variation. Tonal variation is possible with a halftone engraving.—Ms.

Linear programing A mathematical technique for solving problems which are characterized by a large number of solutions which satisfy certain criteria. It is limited to situations in which a numerical change in one factor is in line with a numerical change in another factor, and which when exhibited in a graph result in a straight line of change. Can be used in media planning to specify reach, frequency, seasonal, and demographic objectives.

Linotype A machine that sets and casts type a line at a time by arranging brass matrices to form a line of copy and casting them into type ready for printing.

List Names and addresses of persons to whom direct-mail literature may be sent.

List broker An individual or organization that rents direct-mail lists to advertisers.

Listener diary In research, a method by which respondents maintain a record of their listening or viewing.

Listening   In radio, a measurement obtained by asking a person whether he was listening to radio at a particular time or to what he was listening.

Listening area   Geographic area in which a station's signal may be heard.

Lithography   A printing process in which art is photographed on a sensitized metal plate, and treated so that the plate will accept ink only in the areas from which an imprint is desired.   The design is put on the surface with a greasy material, and water and printing ink are applied successively. Greasy parts absorb the ink, but the wet parts do not.   This type of printing is used in offset lithography, offset printing, photo-offset, photo-lithography.

Live   On-the-spot telecasting of events in contrast to transmission by film.   An instantaneous radio or television broadcast as opposed to one by delayed recording or on film.

Local program   A non-network, station-originated program.

Local rate   A reduced rate offered by newspapers and broadcast stations to merchants and other local advertisers doing business in the area served by the medium and lower than that offered to national advertisers.

Log   A broadcast station's chronological listing of programing activities.

Logotype   An advertiser's stylized trade name or trademark to be used repeatedly in his advertising.   It is often a name plate, cast in one block of type.

Lottery   Generally, a promotional device in which a prize is offered to those who render some consideration as a condition for their competition for prizes; the winners are determined by chance.

Lower case   The small letters of the alphabet.   Term derived from the printer's partitioned box of hand-set type, in which the small letters were placed below the capital letters.

Ludlow   A machine that casts type characters in a single metal slug from brass matrices arranged by hand.

Magazine Advertising Bureau of Magazine Publishers Association, Inc. Composed of consumer and business magazine publishers, its function is to promote magazines as an advertising medium.

Magazine, class   A publication whose editorial content is directed to the interests of a particular group of readers, sometimes those with superior socioeconomic characteristics.

Magazine Publishers Association, Inc.   Association of magazine publishers devoted to promotion of their advertising medium.

Magazine supplement   Sometimes called a *newspaper-distributed Sunday magazine*. It is a supplement in magazine form distributed by newspapers. A *syndicated supplement* is produced by a publishing company which distributes it to noncompeting newspapers throughout the country. *Locally edited* or *individual supplements* are edited and published locally by the newspapers that distribute them.

Magnetic tape   In computerization, a tape with a magnetic surface on which data can be stored by polarization of portions of the surface.

Mail-order advertising   Advertisements that ask the reader to order merchandise or service, or to ask for further information. These advertisements are generally in newspapers, magazines, or direct mail.

Make-good   (1) In print, a free, repeat insertion of an advertisement to compensate for an error in the original insertion. (2) In broadcast, in cases in which a commercial has been unavoidably canceled or has been unwittingly omitted from the station schedule, the credit or a broadcast of the same material in another time slot granted to the advertiser.—Ms.

Makeready   Process of preparing a letterpress printing plate so that its impression on paper will be even. This is done by applying thin pieces of paper beneath certain areas of the printing form.

Makeup   Arrangement of printed material on a page or in an issue.

Mandatory copy   Copy that is required by law to appear on the packages of certain products, as liquor and cigarettes. May also be copy required by the advertiser in every message.

Market   A sufficiently large group of people with purchasing power and an inclination to spend it on a particular commodity.—Ms.

Market analysis   An area of marketing research concerned with measurement of the extent and determination of the characteristics of a market.

Market index   The factor chosen to measure relative sales opportunities in different territorial units.

Market profile   A description of the people or households of a product's market.

Market share   Proportion of a company's sales to the actual or potential volume of the industry.

Marketing   The aggregate of business activities that direct the flow of goods from producer to consumer.

Marketing research   All research activities conducted to reduce marketing and distribution costs, increase sales, and achieve maximum profit.

Masthead   Summary of a publication's identification and ownership. In a newspaper it usually appears on the editorial page; in a magazine alongside the table of contents.

Matched samples   Two or more groups within one research study, each selected to include all characteristics significant to the specific problem.

Mathematical model   Mathematical representation of a concept or process.

Mechanical   A composite of the elements of an advertisement to show their relative size and position.

Media buyer   Usually, the person in an advertising agency who actually purchases advertising space and time for a client.   However, any advertiser or advertising manager who contracts for such purchases may be considered to be a media buyer.

Media coverage   The percentage of a population group reached by an advertising schedule.

Media Records, Inc.   An independent statistical organization that offers daily newspaper linage records and an annual daily newspaper expenditures report.

Media vehicle   The medium that brings the advertising message directly to the attention of the consumer, as the issue of a publication or the program of a broadcast station.

Median   The point in a series of statistical data that divides them into two equal halves.

Medium   A unit used to convey an advertising message, as a newspaper or radio station.   Plural is *media.*

Megacycle   Location of a radio station on the FM dial, from 88 to 108 megacycles.

Memory (*Data processing*)   See *storage.*

Merchandising   (1) The planning and supervision involved in marketing the particular merchandise or service at the places, times, and prices, and in the quantities which will best serve to realize the marketing objectives of the business.—AMA.   (2) In an advertising agency, the functions that are not specifically advertising.   (3) The promotion of a firm's advertising to its sales force, wholesalers, and dealers, and the promotion by media to the consuming public of the product advertised, by means of point-of-purchase materials, in-store retail promotions, and guarantee seals or tags backed by the prestige of the medium.

Milline rate   Among newspapers, the cost of placing one agate line before 1 million readers.   It is derived by multiplying the given line rate by 1 million and dividing by the circulation.

Monitor   To record a station's programing and commercials, done generally by an agency, advertiser, or another station.

Motivation research   A method of studying marketing behavior which uses techniques developed by the behavioral scientists.   Purpose is to discover and evaluate motivation forces which impel human behavior in the marketplace.

Multi-network area   According to A. C. Nielsen Company, a group of major markets where programs from all three networks can be received on a live basis.   The thirty markets included in the MNA represent some 50 per cent of United States television population.

Multiple correlation   In statistics, a process that permits adventitious rather than pertinent correlative factors to be uncovered.

Musical clock   A type of broadcast program in which recorded popular music and the time serve as background for numerous commercials.

National Association of Broadcasters   Membership consists of radio and television stations, radio and television networks, and associate members. Purpose is to foster development of broadcasting and to protect the interests of the industry.

National brand   A manufacturer's or producer's brand, usually enjoying wide geographic distribution.

National Newspaper Promotion Association   Membership is composed of promotion managers and others doing promotion work for daily newspapers; associate memberships for weekly newspapers, advertising agencies, business publications, newspaper representatives, and organizations affiliated with or working in the promotion field.   Function is to help develop better promotion programs for all newspapers.

National Outdoor Advertising Bureau, Inc.   An advertising agency cooperative in that it is owned exclusively by advertising agencies.   It helps agencies with all phases of an outdoor campaign.   It gathers costs and marketing data, makes estimates, makes inspections in the field, compiles billing, and pays plant operators.   More than 200 agencies and their branches use the services of NOAB to handle the details of their outdoor campaigns.

National rate (1) Among newspapers, sometimes called a *general rate,* and offered to advertisers who do not do their principal business in the communities in which the newspaper is circulated. (2) In broadcast, a rate used on stations that also have a local rate, and usually applies to advertisers whose home base is not in the same city as the station and whose distribution is widespread.

National Retail Merchants Association Composed of individuals operating department, variety, and specialty stores. Function is to foster retail trade, improve store operation methods, and increase effectiveness of advertising.

Net The amount of money paid to a medium by an advertising agency after excluding agency commission.

Network (1) A group of broadcast stations affiliated with one another for common programing, as American Broadcasting Co., Columbia Broadcasting System, Mutual Broadcasting System, and National Broadcasting Co. (2) A group of newspapers strategically distributed over a wide area, whose space is sold as a unit under one billing.

Network affiliate Radio or television station that belongs to a network and therefore offers network programs.

Network rating In general, the percentage of television or radio households, or of a group of persons among those in a specified area, which is estimated to be in a network's audience in a specified time.

Newspaper Advertising Executives Association Membership is composed of newspaper advertising executives, business managers, publishers, and newspaper representatives. Function is to further understanding and use of newspaper advertising and to improve efficiency in its production.

Newspaper supplement A syndicated publication, edited and printed by a company which then makes it available in finished form to noncompeting newspapers. The term *magazine supplement* usually means the magazine supplement of a Sunday newspaper.

Next-to-reading matter Advertising space position, sold at preferred rates if specifically requested.

Nonpaid distribution See *Circulation, nonpaid.*

Nonpaid request See *Circulation, request.*

Nonprobability sample A nonrandom sample in which bias may not be determined and which, therefore, does not permit an estimate of sampling error or the projection of its results.

Nonresponse A failure in a survey to obtain information from a person originally selected for the survey. It may be caused by failure of an interviewer to talk with a household or individual selected for the survey, by an outright refusal to give information, or other cause.

Nonstructured interview An interview conducted without a prepared questionnaire in which the respondent is encouraged to talk freely without direction from the interviewer.

Occupation Term especially relevant to business publications. The name of one's occupation may be derived from the type of business in which he is engaged, as food process or mining, or may describe the type of work he does, as design engineer or purchasing.

Occupational classification Among business publications, the division of subscribers into groups according to their professional callings or the positions they occupy in a business organization.

Offset printing A process in which impressions are transferred from the engraving plate to a rubber blanket and then printed on paper. A term used synonymously with *offset lithography*.

Ogive curve In statistics, the graphic presentation of cumulative frequency distribution determined by adding each frequency to the sum of all those above it and then plotting it.

One-time rate The highest advertising rate not subject to discount privileges.

O&O station A station that is owned and operated by a national network.

Open-end A filmed or video-taped program in which the commercial spots are omitted so they can be filled locally.

Open-end diary A diary used in broadcast research that does not list specific time segments, but allows the diary keeper to record the time that a television or radio set is first turned on. He is asked then to write down the channel or station, names of programs, members of household in audience, and time periods when set is tuned and when it is turned off.

Open-end question One in which a respondent is allowed a relatively unlimited choice of answers.

Open-end transcription A recorded program that allows local commercial announcements to be inserted at various points throughout the program.

Operand (*Data processing*) A quantity entering or arising in an instruction. An operand may be an argument, a result, a parameter, or an indication of the location of the next instruction, as opposed to the operation code or symbol itself. It may be the address portion of an instruction.

Operations research A mathematical method of examining various possible alternatives for a given basic problem. Answers come as a set of alternative solutions.

Outdoor advertising An advertising medium which employs printed posters, painted displays, and electric spectaculars for the dissemination of sales messages. These are placed at points of relatively heavy vehicular and pedestrian traffic for exposure to consumers.

Outdoor Advertising Association of America, Inc. The trade association of the outdoor advertising business. Members are standard poster advertising and painted display advertising plant operators. Purpose is to promote and increase the efficiency of outdoor advertising.

Out-of-home media Advertising media that reach consumers when they are not at home, as outdoor, transit, and point-of-purchase. Opposed to in-home media, as print and broadcast.

Out of register A printing imperfection caused when a plate or form of type does not print in precisely the place it was intended.

Output (*Data processing*) (1) The information transferred from the internal storage of a computer to a secondary or external storage, or to any device outside of the computer. (2) The routines which direct 1. (3) The device or collective set of devices necessary for 1. (4) To transfer from internal storage on to external media.—BoB.

Outsert Separate printed matter attached to the outside of a package.

Overlapping circulation Situation that occurs when advertising is placed in two or more publications reaching the same prospects.

Overrun The printing of additional copies of advertising material beyond the number ordered. It is done to compensate for copies that may be spoiled in the various stages of the printing process.

Package (1) A container in which a product is packed. It may take many forms, such as box, bottle, can, bag, and be manufactured of many different materials. (2) In broadcast, a combination of announcements offered by a station at a special price, usually on a weekly or monthly plan. (3) In outdoor advertising, 3- and 6-sheet posters sold as groups and tailored within a market to an advertiser's needs.

Package show A program or commercial series, purchased by an advertiser and having all components ready for broadcasting.

Page proofs   Proofs of typographic material numbered in sequence as they will appear as pages in a book, magazine, or other publication.

Painted bulletins   Outdoor advertising structures on which copy is painted directly on the sections.—NOAB.

Painted wall   An outdoor advertising message painted on the wall of a building.

Paired comparison rating   An opinion test in which two or more items (advertisements, packages, products, etc.) are compared in a manner so that each item is compared with every other item in the series.   Generally specific criteria are used in the comparison.

Pamphlet   A term used interchangeably with *booklet.*

Panel   (1) In research, a group of persons or households that is surveyed repeatedly rather than just once.   (2) An outdoor poster.

Pantry inventory   A survey that determines the brands on pantry shelves by actual inspection.

Paper   A dictionary of paper terms appeared in the January, 1965, issue of *Advertising & Sales Promotion.*   It defines terms relating to various types of printing paper and to a few kinds of papers for packaging.   The definitions were obtained largely from American Paper and Pulp Association's "Dictionary of Paper," "Harper's Dictionary of the Graphic Arts," and the "Paper Yearbook."

Participation program   A radio or television program sponsored by several advertisers, each of whom is allotted a definite amount of time for his announcement.   A disc jockey program is an example.   The announcements are called *participations* and the sponsorship is called *participation* or *participating sponsorship.*

Pass-along reader   One who is exposed to a publication which neither he nor any member of his household received by purchase or by *request,* as in the case of nonpaid publications.   Readers from purchase or request households are called *primary readers.*   The total audience of the publication is the sum of primary and pass-along readers.

Penetration   In broadcasting, the percentage of individuals or households in a market that is reached by a particular station.   Among publications, it is the proportion of readers to the total potential audience in a market; among business publications the market may be termed the individuals or establishments in the field served.   *Penetration* is sometimes used loosely to denote the degree of effectiveness of advertising in its impact upon its public.

Performance index   In marketing, it is the relation between the actual sales of a company and what is estimated it should have sold.

Per-inquiry advertising (*PI advertising*)   Advertising that is not paid for at a medium's card rates, but on the basis of a percentage of all money received from sales or inquiries as the result of the advertising.

Periodical   A publication that appears at fixed intervals of more than one day, as a magazine.

Personal interview   One in which the interviewer asks questions of the respondent in his physical presence.

Photoengraving   Reproduction in letterpress printing of illustrations or textual matter from a metal plate whose printing surface stands out in relief.

Photogelatin (*Collotype*)   A printing process which permits facsimile reproduction of artwork in exact tone and detail without the use of halftone screens.

Photogravure   See *Gravure*.

Photo-offset printing   A term used synonymously with *offset lithography*. See *Lithography*.

Photostat   A photographic copy of something that may be written, printed, drawn, typewritten, or photographed in any color or combination of colors at the same size or enlarged or reduced.   The process is performed by a machine called the *photostat*.

Pica   (1) A unit of print measurement, approximately ⅙-inch.   (2) 12-point type.   It is used by printers to measure width and depth of columns or size of margins.

Pickup   In broadcast, the point from which a program is transmitted, its point of origin.

Piggybacking   The combining within a single television announcement of separate commercials for two different products made by the same advertiser.

Pilot film   A sample film to show what a series will be like.   Generally specially filmed episodes of television shows.   In outdoor advertising a *pilot unit* is a bulletin used as a sample so agencies and artists can plan the best way to display an advertising message.

Plan   In broadcast, generally the same as a *package*.

Plans board   Committee in an advertising agency that plans campaign strategies for clients.

Plant   (1) Outdoor structures in a given area operated by one individual or firm.   (2) In business publications it refers to an establishment engaged in producing or selling a product or service at a single location.

Plant capacity   Number of 100 showings available in a plant.

Plant operator   Manager or management of an outdoor advertising plant.

Plate   A section of metal, plastic, or rubber which can be inked and printed on paper or other surface.   The term is often used loosely, and may refer to an original photoengraving (zinc or copper etching), electrotype, stereotype, plastic plate, rubber plate, gravure cylinder, etching, lithographic plate, or embossing plate.—IG.

Playback   (1) In advertising research, a respondent's *verbatim* report of the content of an advertisement.   (2) Reproduction of a recording, immediately after it has been made.

Point   A unit of type measurement, there being 72 points to an inch.

Point-of-purchase advertising   Those devices or structures located in or at the retail outlet, which identify, advertise, or merchandise the outlet, or a product, as an aid to retail selling.—POPAI.

Point-of-Purchase Advertising Institute, Inc.   Membership is composed of creative producers and suppliers, and associate members among advertisers, agencies, and retailers.   Function is to promote more effective and productive use of point-of-purchase advertising materials by providing advertisers, retailers, and producers, with data on all facets of this medium from design through ultimate use in retail outlets.

Population   In sampling, the individuals, households, or families within a specifically defined group to be studied.

Position   (1) An advertisement's place on a page and the location of the page in the publication.   A *preferred position* is one in a newspaper or magazine which when specifically ordered draws a premium rate.   (2) In broadcast, programs or time spots considered by advertisers to be especially desirable.   (3) In outdoor advertising, the situation in which an outdoor advertising structure is erected on a location taken in relation to the line of travel and to other structures which may be on the same location.—NOAB.

Poster   (1) In outdoor, an advertisement that has a specific space requirement.   Sizes range from the 3-sheet, measuring 6 feet 8 inches high by 3 feet 3 inches wide, through the 6-sheet or junior poster; the 7-sheet, 24-sheet, which provides a copy area 8 feet 8 inches high by 19 feet 6 inches wide; to the 30-sheet, 9 feet 7 inches by 21 feet 7 inches. (2) In transit advertising, the advertisement placed on the outside fronts, sides, and rears of vehicles and on walls of stations or platforms. (3) In point-of-purchase advertising, a printed plastic, paper, or cloth banner or sign for window or interior use.

Poster showing   In outdoor advertising, the unit of sale, which may vary from a single panel in a small community to as many as are needed to cover a large market. Showings are designated as 100 or 50 to indicate the comparative size of the showing or the degree of intensity with which the advertisement is displayed to an audience. In transit advertising, inside advertisements are bought in full, half, or quarter showings, these representing proportions of the vehicles in a fleet. Showings of outside transit advertisements vary with markets, but are usually detailed in Standard Rate & Data Service.

Posttesting   Testing of advertisements after they have appeared in a medium.

Predate   To print and sometimes sell an edition of a daily or Sunday newspaper a day ahead of the day it is dated, in order to reach distant points on or before the stated publication date.   A more precise term would be *postdate*.

Preemption   Replacement of a regularly scheduled program with one of greater interest or importance, sometimes political or sports broadcasts, news bulletins, or documentary specials.

Premium   A special item offered in conjunction with the sale of a product to promote its sale.

Premium price   A higher advertising rate charged for special positions in print media, or for time slots in broadcast that a station considers valuable enough to deserve a higher rate, as drive times.

Preprint   Reproduction of an advertisement before its publication in a medium.

Press proof   A proof taken from a printing press as the job is about to be run off to determine printing quality and to detect late errors.

Press run   Total number of copies printed.

Prestige advertising   Messages in which the advertiser tries to influence the attitude of consumers toward his company, brand, or service without striving for immediate sales.   Similar to *institutional, public relations,* or *corporate image* advertising.

Pretesting   Testing of advertisements or their elements before they have been exposed in media.   In point-of-purchase advertising, the exposure of a few display samples in store locations to test their effectiveness before the entire order is placed.

Primary household   A household into which a publication has been introduced by purchase or request rather than by pass-along.   *Primary readers* reside in primary households.

Prime time   Hours from 7:30 to 11:00 P.M., New York time, when television viewing is greatest.   See *Drive time* and *Housewife times* for radio.

Private brand   A brand sponsored by a merchant or agent as against one sponsored by a manufacturer or producer.

Probability sample   In research, the selection of sampling units that is generally accomplished randomly, so that every unit has the same chance of being selected as any other.   This sample of a population may be expected to conform to the total population.

Processing, data   See *Data processing*.

Production   (1) The physical process of preparing advertising in its final form, as the specification of type, procuring of engravings, buying of paper.   (2) In radio and television this extends beyond the commercials to preparation of the program itself.

Profile   Description of a medium's audience by demographic characteristics.

Program   (1) A feature whether sponsored or not that is broadcast by a station.   (2) In data processing, the complete plan for the solution of a problem, more specifically the complete sequence of machine instructions and routines necessary to solve a problem or to plan the procedure for solving a problem.   This may involve among other things the analysis of the problem, preparation of a flow diagram, preparing details, testing, and developing subroutines, allocation of storage locations, specification of input and output formats, and the incorporation of a computer run into a complete data processing system.—BoB.

Program analyzer   A voting machine which permits broadcast listeners or viewers to record continuously their reactions to an entire program delivered in a test situation.

Program compatability   A sympathetic atmosphere between a program and its advertising.

Program, counter   Technique used by networks to regulate audience flow.   Main concern is to offer a program different in type but equivalent in appeal to that of a strong competitor in the same time period.

Program profile   Graphic presentation of the reactions of a group of listeners or viewers who participate in a test involving some kind of program analyzer.

Program rating   A program popularity rating that in general shows the percentage of television or radio households that is estimated to be in a program's audience over a specified time.

Programing, linear   See *Linear programing.*

Progressive proofs   In process color printing, the printer's guide to the exact color effects desired.   A plate is made for each basic color (red, yellow, blue, black).   While the sequence may vary, red is combined with yellow, both are combined with blue, black is printed separately, and finally all are combined to produce the final color effect.   Proofs from these various stages are called *progressive proofs.*

Projective technique   A term used in motivation research for an unstructured interview, the purpose of which is hidden from the respondent, used to obtain information not readily procured by direct questioning, that is, personality aspects and attitudes toward brands and products.

Proof   A trial impression taken at each stage of the printing process, as galley proof, page proof, stone proof, press proof, and others, pulled before the form goes to press.

Psychographic   A term used in reference to media audiences to indicate not their demographic characteristics but their venturesomeness and other psychological qualities that are related to their disposition to buy certain types of products.   A *psychograph* is a galvanometer used in copy testing to gauge nervous reaction to advertisements or their campaigns.

Public relations   A company's efforts directed toward the creation of a favorable attitude toward it on the part of its various publics.

Public Relations Society of America, Inc.   Composed of executives concerned with public relations in business and industry, public relations counselors for industry, trade associations, government agencies, and education.   It serves as a professional society.

Publicity   Communication developed by a company on its behalf in a form which has some informational or feature value for a medium, which, at its discretion, can make use of it without charge to the company.

Publishers Information Bureau, Inc.   Membership is composed of publishers of magazines and magazine sections of newspapers.   Function is to issue monthly reports, account by account, of volume and character of advertising carried by general and farm magazines, and newspaper sections and supplements.

Publisher's statement The statement of circulation issued by a periodical publisher. It is issued unaudited, but subject to audit. (When it has been audited it is called an *audit report*.) A sworn publisher's statement on circulation and distribution is issued by a publisher who is not affiliated with an audit bureau.

Punched card In computer language, a card punched with a pattern of holes to represent data. A *punched tape* is similar.

Purchasing power The amount of money a consumer or group of consumers has to spend.

Pyramid makeup (1) In publications, makeup in which advertisements are arranged with the largest advertisement at the bottom of the page and others forming steps to the top outside of the page. (2) In outdoor advertising, a method of staggering posting dates of several showings to build up to a period of peak intensity.—NOAB.

Quantity discount A rate reduction granted by media to advertisers who buy a specified amount of space or time during a given period.

Quarter run Inside transit advertisements placed in one-fourth of the vehicles in a fleet.

Queen-size poster An outside transit advertisement measuring 30 by 88 inches and generally placed on the curb side of the vehicle.

Questionnaire A series of questions to be answered by prospective respondents. It is essentially a form to be filled out by the respondent himself. The questions may concern publications reading, broadcast listening and viewing, brand-buying habits, or other information useful to advertisers.

Quintile A form of analysis of frequency of media activity in which listeners and viewers are divided into five equal groups, ranging from heaviest to lightest in their interest in broadcast exposure. *Quintile ranges* are a summary of these statistical measures.

Quota sample A nonprobability sample in which quotas are set for the number of respondents of various types that interviewers are to obtain, as those in various geographic areas and with specified demographic characteristics. This sample is designed to mitigate interviewer bias and differences in the variables being studied.

Rack In point-of-purchase, a combination display and stock bin for merchandise which may carry brand identification copy, but which depends on display of the products for its major appeal.

Rack jobber A contractor who places the racks in the retail outlet and maintains them with merchandise, usually nonfood.—POPAI.

Radio Advertising Bureau, Inc. Membership is composed of radio stations, representatives, and networks. Purpose is to promote use of radio as an advertising medium.

Random sampling The quality that assures every individual unit in the population full and equal chance of being included in the sample. Such a sample avoids bias on the part of the interviewer or investigator.

Rate Stipulated cost of publication space and broadcast time and other media facilities as established by media owners. A *local rate* is one offered by local media to local advertisers.

Rate base The circulation figure used by the publisher of a magazine as the basis for his rate structure. Because of rising circulations in recent years, advertisers have been receiving more circulation for their messages than they have been guaranteed.

Rate card A printed document published by advertising media which lists advertising rates and related information.

Rate differential Among newspapers, the difference between national and local rates.

Rate holder In newspaper advertising, a small advertisement run by an advertiser to comply with the terms of a contract that grants him a discount for minimum linage or insertions over a specific period of time. In broadcast, it is an announcement bought mainly to maintain a continuous purchase pattern that earns the advertiser a discount for continuity. In broadcast, rate holders may be 10-second commercials.

Rating A survey estimate of the size of an audience, expressed as a percentage of the total group sampled. Ratings describe the average minute of broadcast-reach level for television and average-issue audience for print. They can be expressed on a household or person basis.—BBDO.

Rating point One broadcast rating point means that 1 per cent of homes in a measured area are tuned to a particular station at least once in a specific period of time.

Reach Total audience of different individuals a medium can or does cover. *Cumulative reach* is the total number of different individuals or households reached in a specific period of time.

Reader An individual who sees some part of the editorial content of a publication.

Reader traffic Movement from page to page by readers of a publication.

Readership (*Reading*)   A measure of the number of readers of a publication or an advertisement.

Reading time   How much time a publication's audience devotes to reading an issue.

Rebate   (1) Among print media, payment by the medium to an advertiser who earns a lower rate by increasing his space commitments beyond his contract.   (2) Among broadcast media, payment by the medium to the advertiser who earns a lower rate by increasing his frequency, volume, or package plan commitments beyond the stipulations of his contract.   (3) Among magazines offering a circulation guarantee, payment accorded the advertiser in cases in which the magazine does not fulfill its guarantee over a period of time.   (4) Other payments because of failure to fulfill contracts by media, as when an advertisement or commercial is marred in its presentation by mechanical failure of the medium.—Ms.

Rebroadcast   A repeat broadcast to reach a different audience or a different time zone.

Recall interview   An interview in which a respondent is asked to remember behavior for some period of time in the past.   *Aided recall* offers a facsimile or verbal stimulant to the respondent.   *Unaided recall* offers no clues of any type to the respondent.

Recipient   The individual or establishment to which a publication is addressed and whose existence as recipient is reported in the publisher's statement and audit report.

Recognition   (1) Agency recognition is acknowledgment by media owners that an agency is considered qualified to fulfill services for which it receives a commission from the media.   (2) A research technique that involves the identification by a respondent of an advertising message as having been previously seen or heard.

Regional rate   Rate charged by a station to advertisers whose headquarters are outside the station's local area but in some logically restricted geographical area, such as the same state.—OSR.

Register   Exact correspondence in position of pages, columns, lines on two facing pages, or in the position of the separately printed parts of a design or picture.   Usually concerned with the exact positioning of different colors printed from separate plates.—Ms.

Relay station   An automatic installation which receives signals from the original television station or another relay station and transmits them to the next relay station or their final destination.

Reliability   A research term synonymous with *precision*. Used in reference to sampling, it is the degree of stability any measure found within the sample is likely to have in the universe from which the sample was drawn. Measures of reliability (the measures of the stability of the data) are used in marketing research to determine the point at which a sample is of size adequate to assure that a larger sample under the same procedures would not affect appreciably any values.

Reminder   Brief messages in any medium used primarily to present a brand name and continue the impact of previous, more extensive advertising.

Remote broadcast   A radio or television broadcast done from some place other than the station's own studio.

Renewal   (1) Extension of an existing contract.   (2) A subscription which has been renewed prior to or at expiration of within six months thereafter.—AIA.   (3) Extra posters sent to plant operators to replace those that may be damaged during the display period.   The number may be from 10 to 20 per cent of the total order.—NOAB.

Repetition   Repeated exposure of the same advertisement in the same medium.   In outdoor advertising it means the average number of times each person is exposed to a showing during the display period.

Request circulation   Recipients of a publication who do not pay for it, but receive it at their own request when qualified.

Resizing   Production of an advertisement in various sizes to conform to the space units of different publications.

Respondent   A person who responds to a question in a survey, whether by personal interview, telephone inquiry, or mail.

Retail advertising   The dissemination of sales messages by retail stores through local media such as newspapers and radio stations.   Purpose is to induce consumers to visit the store and buy its goods.

Retail trading zone   A term significant in respect to newspaper circulation and indicating the area beyond the city zone (or area of corporate municipality) whose residents trade regularly to an important degree with retail merchants in the city zone.

Reverse plate   A printing plate made in such a fashion that the part which was white on the copy becomes black, and vice versa.

Roll out   A marketing process in which a brand is established in a limited area before an attempt is made to introduce it elsewhere.   Some brands receive national introduction at the very outset.

Roman   A style of typography characterized by serifs, perpendicularity, and greater thickness of the vertical than the horizontal strokes.   Distinguished from *italic*.

Rotogravure printing   A process in which the surface to be printed is etched on a copper cylinder.

Rough   A sketchily drawn layout of an advertisement designed to show relative size and position of elements comprising it.

Run   (1) In printing, total copies printed.   (2) In transit advertising, a showing or service, as in a full run.

Run-of-paper (*ROP*)   Usually refers to newspaper advertising and means placement of an advertisement anywhere in the edition at the paper's discretion.   *Run-of-book* is a magazine equivalent.

Run-of-station (*ROS*)   Announcements purchased on a run-of-station basis give a station the right to place the announcements wherever they please in a given broadcast day.—OSR.

Saddle stitching   A method of binding a booklet or magazine through the center fold.

Sales-area test   Test of sales response attributed to advertising in a particular geographical area to determine the advisability of extending the advertising beyond that area.

Sales forecast   An estimate of sales volume for a specified future period.

Sales manager   The executive who plans, directs, and controls the activities of salesmen.—AMA.

Sales potential   The maximum sales likely to be achieved by a company's brands or by all competitors in a market during a specific period.

Sales promotion   Promotional efforts to increase sales which may not involve the use of advertising time or space, personal selling, or publicity. In retailing the term includes all these.

Sample   (1) A representative selection of a total number of people or things so chosen as to permit conclusions applicable to the total to be drawn from it with a minimum degree of error.   (See *Probability sample, Quota sample, Random sample*.)   (2) A product or portion of it distributed free to prospective consumers to stimulate their interest in it.

Sampling error   The degree or likely degree in which a sample differs from the result that would be obtained by a complete census.

Saturation   In broadcast a schedule measured by the number of stations per market that are required, with adequate frequency, to penetrate the total broadcast audience over a period of time.

Scatter plan   A television schedule in which an advertiser spreads his announcements over a variety of network programs, participating in rather than sponsoring them.

Schedule   (1) The list of media, such as newspapers, magazines, broadcast stations, and networks, that have been selected to be used in an advertising campaign.   (2) The list of a company's advertising to be included in a medium vehicle during a specific time.   (3) Chronological list of programs broadcast by a station.   (4) A question-and-answer form that is filled out by an interviewer or by a respondent in the interviewer's presence.

Screen   In photoengraving, the transparent plate ruled with two sets of parallel lines running at right angles to each other, used in the halftone process.   The more lines per square inch, the finer the reproduction.— POPAI.

Script   (1) The complete written guide for a broadcast show, commercial, or film.   (2) A classification of type distinguished by a resemblance to handwriting.

Secondary coverage   An outlying area surrounding a radio station in which reception is obtained but which is beyond the station's primary coverage.

Segmentation   Generally used as *market segmentation,* refers to the splintering of a market in order to develop new opportunities for products and advertising.

Self-liquidating point-of-purchase unit   A unit for which the retailer pays in whole or in part.

Self-liquidating premium   A premium for which the cost to the advertiser is wholly absorbed by the consumer.

Self-mailer   A piece of direct-mail literature that folds to make its own envelope.

Semi-spectacular   A painted outdoor bulletin with special lighting, electrical attachments, or mechanical devices to increase its nighttime effectiveness.

Set solid   The setting of a body of type so that the lines are as close together as possible.

Sets in use (*SIU*)   The number of radio or television sets turned on at any given time.   *Sets-in-use rating* refers to the percentage of some group of television sets or radios that are being used at a particular time.

Share of audience Percentage of the total audience at a specific time that is tuned to a given broadcast station network or program.

Share of market Ratio of an advertiser's actual or potential sales to total industry sales.

Sheet-fed press A printing press which uses paper cut into separate sheets before printing. To be distinguished from a *web-fed press* in which a roll of paper is printed and then cut into separate sheets.—Ms.

Shelter publication A consumer magazine that is concerned with the development and maintenance of the residence.

Short rate A charge made back by media to an advertiser who fails to fulfill the requirements of a contract that would have earned him a lower rate.

Showing See *Poster showing.*

Side stitching Process of stapling or stitching a magazine or booklet through the side instead of through the fold.

Signature (1) The name of an advertiser, usually at the end of an advertisement (also called *logotype* or *slug*). (2) In broadcasting, a musical number or sound effect which regularly identifies a program. (3) A sheet folded ready for stitching into a book or magazine.—L&B.

Sign-off Time station goes off the air.

Sign-on Time station goes on the air.

Silk-screen A printing method in which ink is forced through a stencil of silk or other material. Best used for small printing runs.

Simulcast Simultaneous broadcast of a program on both radio and television.

Single-rate card Rate card of a station that uses one rate for all kinds of business, both local and national.

Slogan A relatively pithy phrase or sentence used repeatedly by a company or organization to aid in the formulation of its image.

Snapper An extra incentive used to stimulate consumers to buy a special product.

Software Documents associated with a computer as manuals, circuit diagrams, the collection of programs and routines. Contrast with *Hardware.*

Solid matter See *Set solid.*

Sound In radio, the station's image as created by character of programing, personnel, and other effects.

Space The pages, their multiples, and subdivisions, in magazines, newspapers, and other printed publications sold to the public or distributed free, in which advertisements may be placed.—MW.

Space buying The selection and contracting for advertising space in newspapers, periodicals, and out-of-home printed media. In agencies, it is done by a *space buyer*.

Space position value A measure of the efficiency with which a poster panel dominates the effective circulation to which it is exposed. It is based upon four factors: length of approach; speed in travel; angle of the panel to its circulation; relationships to adjacent panels.—NOAB.

Space spots Small newspaper advertisements purchased on a volume basis and generally at a discount. Usually five or six advertisements a week are used over a thirteen-week period with a 30 per cent discount normal.

Specialty Advertising Association A trade association composed of specialty advertising distributors and suppliers.

SpectaColor Full-color, preprinted inserts for newspapers with conventional nonwallpaper layouts.

Spectacular (1) An outdoor advertising display built with structural steel and designed for a particular advertiser on a long-term contract. The advertising copy is presented in a spectacular way through the use of incandescent lamps, flashers, chaser borders, luminous tubing, motographs, or any combination of these electrical devices.—NOAB. (2) A large indoor display used in point-of-purchase advertising designed either to stand free or to be used in free-standing stacks of merchandise, often incorporating elements of light and motion.

Split run A facility available in newspapers and periodicals wherein the advertiser alternates different advertising copy in every other copy of the same issue. This makes it possible to compare coupon returns from two different advertisements published under identical conditions.

Sponsor May refer to any advertiser on a broadcast station.

Spot In broadcast, a commercial or announcement (10, 20, 30, or 60 seconds long) placed between programs, whereas a *participation* is an announcement within a program. Purchase of spots may be done on a market-by-market basis, thus allowing advertising weight to be distributed in accordance with sales or competitive behavior.

Spot radio Also *national spot* A national (non-network) radio buy which allows an advertiser to buy commercials in many markets and stations.—RAB.

Spot television   Similar in concept to *spot radio.*

Stability of sample   The relationship between increases in sample size and resulting decrease in the variability of measured results.—L&B.

Staggered schedule   (1) In publication advertising, a schedule in two or more publications so that the advertisements are inserted in rotating or alternating dates.   (2) In transit advertising, a schedule that does not run consecutively, but runs in waves over a specific period of time.

Standard deviation   A statistical measure of the dispersion of a body of data for the purpose of generalization.

Standard error   A universally accepted measure of the probable extent to which a survey is in error attributable to sampling.

Standard Industrial Classifications   A numerical coding system developed by the Bureau of the Budget used in the classification of business establishments according to the principal end product made or service performed at that location.—AIA.

Standard Metropolitan Statistical Area   As defined by the Bureau of the Budget, it is a county or group of counties that contains at least one city of 50,000 or more population.   The Bureau has defined more than 230 such areas.

Standard Rate & Data Service, Inc.   An organization that publishes periodically volumes of all the media, giving advertising rates, circulation, and many other data of use to the media buyer and planner.   The service now includes volumes on the advertising media of several countries overseas.

Star-route boxholder   A person in a rural area to whom mail is delivered by a private carrier under contract to the government.

Starch rating   A measurement of the degree of reading a publication advertisement obtains, based upon a service supplied by Daniel Starch and Staff.

Station break   That time during a program when a broadcast station identifies itself by announcing its call letters.   An advertising commercial may be delivered in that interval.

Station identification   Announcement of station call letters.

Stereotype   A duplicate printing plate cast from a paper matrix.

Storage   (*Data processing*)   (1) The term preferred to *memory.*   (2) Pertaining to a device in which data can be stored and from which they can be obtained at a later time.   The means of storing data may be chemical, electrical, or mechanical.   (3) A device consisting of electronic, electrostatic, electrical, hardware or other elements into which data may be entered, and from which data may be obtained as desired. (4) The erasable storage in any given computer. Synonymous with *memory*. —BoB.

Storyboard   Artwork which shows the sequence of a television commercial with all its major visual changes.—TvB.

Stratification   In sampling, the division of a universe into groups, as according to geographical location or size of household.   It is a method of probability sampling.

Subscription   Contractural agreement by an individual or firm to purchase one or more copies of a publication for a given period that conforms to established rules.—AIA.   There are many forms of subscriptions, as association, franchise, gift, group, and so on.

Sustaining program   A program on a network or station that does not carry paid advertising.

Tabloid   A newspaper approximately half the size of the standard and usually with five columns across the page.

Take-one   A brochure or coupon attached to an inside transit advertisement.   The rider is encouraged to take one in order to receive more information about an advertiser or his product.   In point-of-purchase, a take-one pad is for tear-off by customers and is part of a sign or display.

Tear sheet   (1) A page containing an advertisement sent to the advertiser for checking.   (2) Unbound pages of a publication are also called *tear sheets*.

Teaser   Curiosity-provoking advertisement, generally preceding main campaign.

Telecast   A broadcast by television.

Telegenic   The property of a person or thing to look well on television.

Telephone interview   In broadcast, any interview conducted by telephone.   There are both telephone coincidental interviews and telephone recall interviews.   In the coincidental, interviews are made while a broadcast program is in progress.

Television Bureau of Advertising, Inc.   Members are television networks, stations, station representatives, and program syndicators.   Function is to sell television to advertisers.

TvQ score   Percentage of people familiar with a network program who also consider it one of their favorites.   This is a commercial service.

Television satellite A station, often found in regions of low population density, that is wholly dependent upon another, carrying both its programs and commercials. Purpose is to expand coverage of the independent station and offer service to remote areas.

Test market A limited but usually complete marketing area where a marketer conducts an exploratory advertising or marketing campaign for a brand in order to gain information as to the advisability of promoting it on a regional or national basis.

Tie-in (1) Cooperative advertising effort among two or more advertisers. (2) Cooperative advertising effort between a manufacturer and dealers.

Till forbid (*TF*) An advertising schedule without fixed termination date.

Time, available (*Data processing*) (1) The number of hours a computer is available for use. (2) The time during which a computer has the power turned on, is not under maintenance, and is known or believed to be operating correctly.—BoB.

Time buyer A person in an advertising agency who plans, selects, and buys advertising time on radio and television.

Time standards for advertising copy National Association of Broadcasters has issued (August, 1966) a Radio Code and a Television Code which state certain standards in relation to amount of time to be used for advertising in any single clock hour and define station breaks and prime time and multiple-product announcements.

Total audience Among magazines, refers to all readers of an issue, both primary and pass-along. In television, it includes all individuals or households who have been in the audience for some consecutive period of time, as five minutes.

Trademark A registered name or device that provides identification and legal protection for a product or service.

Trade name A name which identifies a company and its products to buyers and sellers.

Traffic All the people moving out of doors in a given area, whether by motor car, public transportation, or on foot.—NOAB.

Traffic Audit Bureau, Inc. Members are advertising agencies, advertisers, and operators of outdoor advertising plants. Function is to establish standard procedures for measuring the circulation and space position values of individual poster panels, and to supervise and direct practices in connection with the collection, recording, and authentication of traffic and other data related to outdoor advertising.

Traffic count   Physical tally of pedestrian, automobile, and mass transportation traffic passing a given point.

Traffic department   (1) In an advertising agency, the department that schedules the work of other departments and follows it through to completion.   (2) In broadcast, the department responsible for scheduling programs and announcements.

Traffic flow map   A graphic presentation of the traffic volume upon any system of streets, arteries, or highways, the width of lines shown varying with amount of traffic carried.—NOAB.

Traffic, reader   A measure of the number of readers who look at or are exposed to the different pages of an issue of a publication.   Usually expressed in number of readers per page.—AIA.

Transcribed program   The mechanical reproduction of a program by tape or a recording so that it can be broadcast at a later date.

Transit   Fleets of vehicles (buses, rail transit, commuter trains) available to groups of individual fare-paying passengers moving from point to point within an urban area.   Not to be confused with *transportation*, a general term most often applied to city-to-city travel.—TAA.

Transit advertising   This is divided essentially into *inside* and *outside* advertising on fleets of vehicles.

Transit Advertising Association, Inc.   Members are of organizations selling transit advertising space.   Its function is to serve advertisers and advertising agencies, and through research, standardization, and promotion to foster improvement of the medium's efficiency, encourage wider and more effective use, and to collect and disseminate information.

Traveling display   (1) In point-of-purchase advertising a display designed to be shipped from place to place to be reused in various retail outlets.   (2) In transit advertising, a standard outside advertisement 21 by 44 inches.

Triple spotting   Three separate television commercials in consecutive sequence.   More frequent in daytime and fringe evening time than in prime time, as discouraged by the NAB code.

Tri-vision   A painted display embellishment which, through use of a triangular louver construction, permits the display of three different copy messages in a predetermined sequence.   Also called *multi-vision*.—NOAB.

Tune-in   See *Sets in use.*

Turnover   (1) Ratio of a cumulative audience over several periods of time (as four weeks) to the average audience per period of time (as a week). This ratio serves as an indication of the relative frequency with which the audience of a program or of a station changes over a period of time. The greater the turnover in audience, the higher is the ratio.—NAB. (2) Rate at which a consumer repeats the purchase of a product.

UHF   Ultra high frequency, 300 to 3,000 megacycles; the band added to the VHF band for television transmission, or channels 14 through 84.

Unit count   The number of establishments (rather than individuals) included in a business publication's circulation.

Universe   The total units or individuals under consideration. Usually so referred to when a sample from it is drawn for study.

Validate   To testify, as one in a position to know, to the truthfulness or reliability of evidence.

Vehicle   A particular advertising medium, as magazine or station.

Velox   A trade name for a photographic process print with small black dots in a white field to represent highlight areas, and small white dots in a black field to represent shadow areas; a screened photoprint.—POPAI. Velox is used frequently in making a screened photograph for delivery to a photoengraver, instead of having him screen the original copy preparatory to photoengraving it.

Verify   To prove to be true; to establish the correspondence between evidence and actual fact. A term used frequently in the auditing of circulations of publications.

Vertical buy   A print schedule that uses magazines with similar editorial appeal to achieve maximum reach. A *horizontal buy* is the opposite approach.—BBDO.

Vertical publication   A business publication that appeals to a specific trade, industry, business, or profession.

VHF   Very high frequency, 30 to 300 megacycles.

Visual   A rough layout that indicates sketchily the relative positions of various units to be included in an advertisement. Similar to a *rough.*

Wait order   An order sent to a publication to withhold until a later date the insertion of an advertisement which has been prepared.

Wall banner   In point-of-purchase advertising, a large advertisement on a wall or suspended from wire and stretched across a store.

Waste   That part of a publication's distribution considered to be without value to the individual advertiser because of the absence of any relevance of the advertiser's proposition to the recipient's business interest.

Watts   Refers to the amount of power a station is permitted to use in transmitting its signal.

Web-fed press   A rotary printing press which uses rolls of paper instead of single sheets.   As the roll is printed, it is cut into separate pieces. See *sheet-fed press.*

Weight   (1) In reference to printing papers, the definition of paper thickness in terms of pounds per 500 sheets of a certain size.   (2) To assign a value to each of several related elements as a measure of their relative importance.

Window display   A retail outlet display placed in the windows facing outside to attract the attention of pedestrians passing the establishment.—POPAI.

Xerography   A method of photographing and printing in which copy is reproduced and transferred to a surface such as paper by means of charges of static electricity.

Zinc etching   A photoengraving made on zinc.

SOURCES

Acknowledgment is made to the following sources for some of the terms used in the Glossary:

ABC—Audit Bureau of Circulations, "How to Use ABC Reports," Chicago, various dates.

AIA—Association of Industrial Advertisers, "Glossary of Terms Relating to Business Publication Audits," New York, 1967.

AMA—American Marketing Association, "Marketing Definitions: A Glossary of Marketing Terms," Chicago, 1963.

BBDO—Batten, Barton, Durstine & Osborn, Inc., "One Hundred Basic Media Terms Defined," New York, 1966.

BCG—Broadcast Communications Group, Inc., "bcg communique, No. 2," New York, 1965.

BoB—Executive Office of the President, Bureau of the Budget, "Automatic Data Processing Glossary," Washington, 1962.

IG—Irvin Graham, "Encyclopedia of Advertising," Fairchild Publications, Inc., New York, 1952.

L&B—Darrell B. Lucas and Steuart H. Britt, "Advertising, Psychology and Research," McGraw-Hill Book Company, New York, 1950.

Ms—*Media-scope* magazine, "Dictionary of Terms Useful to Buyers of Advertising," New York, 1959–1960, and "Directory of Associations," 1966.

MW—Mark Wiseman, "Mark Wiseman's Glossary of Advertising Terms," New York, unpublished manuscript, no date.

NAB—National Association of Broadcasters, "Standard Definitions of Broadcast Research Terms," New York, 1967.

NOAB—National Outdoor Advertising Bureau, "Lexicon of Terms, Commonly Used in Outdoor Advertising," New York, 1965.

NW—*Newsweek,* "Words of the Computer Age," New York, 1966.

OSR—Ohio Station Representatives, "How Good Is Your Trade Vocabulary?" *U.S. Radio,* March, 1961.

POPAI—Point-of-Purchase Advertising Institute, Inc., "Glossary of Point-of-Purchase Terms," New York, 1967.

RAB—Radio Advertising Bureau, "Radio Manual," New York, 1967.

TvB—Television Bureau of Advertising, "A Dictionary for Television Users," New York, 1967.

TAA—Transit Advertising Association, "The Transit Advertising Wordbook," New York, 1967.

Index